European Politics in Transition

European Politics in Transition

Mark Kesselman
Columbia University

Joel Krieger
Wellesley College

Christopher S. Allen
University of Georgia

Joan DeBardeleben
McGill University

Stephen Hellman
York University

Jonas Pontusson
Cornell University

D.C. Heath and Company
Lexington, Massachusetts Toronto

Published simultaneously in Canada.

Printed in the United States of America.

International Standard Book Number: 0-669-08901-X

Library of Congress Catalog Card Number: 86-82188

For Amrita and Kris

Preface

We wrote this book because of a growing awareness that it has become difficult to teach courses on European politics or on comparative politics more generally that are comprehensive, comprehensible, and attuned to the dramatic contemporary changes in European society. We confess that we are sometimes envious of colleagues teaching American politics who may have an entire term to study a single branch of one government. In contrast, we must introduce whole societies, draw comparisons among entire political systems, and acquaint students with a range of often unfamiliar institutions, political problems, and intellectual approaches.

Increasingly, we comparativists have had to rely on articles and papers that are often too complex for students and always too scattered for instructors, or we have had to settle for textbooks that reflect a narrow and often out-dated understanding of European politics. Some mainly provide treatments of institutional arrangements. Many are limited to the "big four" — Britain, France, Italy, and West Germany — or treat whole regions of Europe without attention to the specificity of each country. Few are sufficiently up-to-date to explore the political implications of the economic recession and the policy responses that followed the energy crisis of the 1970s. None successfully bridges the gap between Eastern and Western Europe in addressing problems of democracy and economic coordination in complex industrial societies.

European Politics in Transition aims to provide an accessible and comprehensive introduction to European politics by presenting the political systems of Europe in terms of change and adaptation to new economic challenges and the increased social pressures that influence the processes of government. After an introductory essay that develops these themes, each of five Western European polities — Britain, France, West Germany, Italy and Sweden — is explored in a comprehensive and readable manner.

In separate chapters within each country unit, the authors trace the emergence of the modern constitutional order, the rise and fall of the postwar settlement, state institutions, social and political forces, and contemporary developments. These units are tied together thematically by a focus on the growth and decay of political consensus in postwar Western European politics and by attention to the growing tension between market processes and democratic demands. We are confident that, as a result, students will view political institutions and political behavior as integrally related to the lifeblood of political competition and conflict. We provide full coverage of institutions, even as we stress political processes, political economy, and the connections among social movements, party politics, and state policy formation.

The inclusion of a substantial unit on the Soviet Union makes the book particularly useful, as we consider in separate chapters the emergence of the Soviet state, the rise and fall of Stalinism, bureaucratic conservatism in the post-Stalinist era, state and party institutions, and the social forces at play in contemporary Soviet life. We also consider the examples of Poland and the Solidarity experience, the peace and environmental movements of East Germany, and other important East European cases. The Soviet unit concludes with an analysis of the Gorbachev team, highlighting potential economic reforms and new foreign policy directions.

Because of its comprehensive institutional, thematic, and geographical coverage, *European Politics in Transition* is appropriate for Western European politics courses designed with a variety of emphases: historical processes, the evolution of political institutions, political economy, political culture, and contemporary public policy. Due to its scope and approach, this textbook suits the design of many Introduction to Comparative Politics courses as well.

The writing is straightforward, and the chronology of events is clear. Terms and concepts are explicated in the text and concretely presented, since we assume students to have no prior background in European politics. The book is amply illustrated with maps and graphic presentations of important data, and selected bibliographies are provided for each unit and for comparative European politics more generally. The thematic emphasis reveals the continuities and contrasts in European politics, illuminating for students the advantages of a comparative approach. We hope that the consistent incorporation of recent scholarship in the field will catch the interest of teachers and excite students to further study.

* * *

We are grateful to specialists who reviewed sections of the book (and who, in some cases, read the entire draft manuscript) for providing stimulating and useful suggestions both on matters of detail and interpretation: Gerard Braunthal (University of Massachusetts at Amherst); Minton F. Goldman (Northeastern University); John T.S. Keeler (University of Washington); Robert Leonardi (De Paul University); John Logue (Kent State University); Alfred G. Meyer (University of Michigan); K. Robert Nilsson (Dickinson College); Alec Nove (University of Glasgow); Jorgen Rasmussen (Iowa State University); Martin A. Schain (New York University); and Christian Soe (California State University at Long Beach).

We have also been fortunate to benefit from the energy, dedication, and excellence of outstanding professionals at D.C. Heath, including Cathy Brooks, Ann Cavan, Gretje Gurevich, and Karen Potischman. We thank Ed Catania, and especially our editor, Linda Halvorson.

M.K.
J.K.
May 1986

Contents

Maps

European Politics in Transition

PART I

European Politics in Transition

Mark Kesselman

Joel Krieger

European Politics in Transition

Today European politics is in ferment, as it emerges from a period of unusual stability that characterized the first two decades of the postwar era. The last twenty years have also seen changes: fiscal crisis and stagflation; the decline of old parties as the standard-bearers of belief and the introduction of new, untraditional parties; and the resurgence of old Left ideologies and the emergence of new Left and new Right forces. The fragmentation of the international economic order strains domestic political coalitions; regional trading blocs, multinational corporations, and international financial institutions weaken the nation-state. The future direction of European politics can be discerned only by understanding the evolution of European societies and appreciating the diverse problems confronting them today.

This text seeks to go beyond "textbook" understandings. Politics in the narrow sense of governmental institutions and formal political processes (i.e., politics as "how a bill becomes a law") is only part of a far more complex story, which involves not only political parties, voting behavior, and the institutions of government, but also the emergence of powerful forces in society outside the government. European politics involves social movements — from the English Chartists of the 1830s and 1840s, who demanded rights of political participation and democracy (some of which still have not been achieved), to the West German Greens Party today, who struggle for nuclear disarmament and ecological concerns and who reject domination by big government and big business. European politics also involves class conflicts between working people and the financial and business elite, conflicts that force the state to intervene in the economy by regulating market forces, managing industrial conflict through political negotiations, and determining how the wealth of society is divided among competing social groups. European politics today involves regional, ethnic, racial, and gender divisions, and includes a range of governments with divergent policy orientations.

Today, Europe is a laboratory in which few political experiments are succeeding as planned and where no positive results seem easily replicated. The Western European states we cover in this text — Britain, France, West Germany, Italy, and Sweden — are in their third phase of political evolution since World War II. The first and longest phase, lasting from the late 1940s to the late 1960s, was a golden era of sustained economic growth and political stability; the second phase, which began in the late 1960s and lasted until the early 1980s, was marked by economic recession, resurgent class conflict, and anti-statist protest on both the left and right of the political spectrum. The third phase is under way today, as political fragmentation defies traditional lines of opposition: Left vs. Right; working class vs. bourgeoisie; socialism vs. capitalism. In the present period, political cleavages centering around class divisions, which were formed a century ago during the emergence of industrial capitalism, are being joined by new axes of political conflict whose outlines are not yet clear. Key issues include a revolt against the oppressive weight of public and private bureaucracies; growing conflicts and inequalities among generations; and struggles over the character, pace, costs, and benefits of technological change.

The Soviet Union has also undergone major political shifts in the postwar era: 1953 marked a crucial transition from Stalinism to the bureaucratic conservatism of Khrushchev and Brezhnev; and there is considerable speculation that the new generation of leadership represented by the Gorbachev team may bring a new, technocratic approach to problems of economic governance, international security, and the mobilization of political support.

To understand this contemporary period of uncertainty in European politics we need to examine earlier moments of transition, when European countries broke with the past and when political institutions were recast in new forms that have shaped the contemporary experience.

Industrialization, State Formation, and the Great Divide

While it is common now for students, scholars, and policymakers to think of two Europes, East and West, this was not always the case. The

Europe
0
200 Miles
0
200 Kilometers
NORWAY
Oslo
NORTH SEA
IRELAND
Dublin
UNITED KINGDOM
DENMARK
Copenhagen
BALTIC
ATLANTIC OCEAN
London
NETHERLANDS
Amsterdam
Elbe
Berlin
Brussels
BELGIUM
Bonn
WEST GERMANY
EAST GERMANY
Luxembourg
Paris
LUX.
Prague
Loire
Seine
Rhine
FRANCE
Vienna
Bern
SWITZERLAND
AUSTRIA
ALPS
Rhone
Po
PYRENEES
Ebro
PORTUGAL
Lisbon
Tajo
Madrid
SPAIN
ADRIATIC SEA
Corsica
ITALY
Rome
Balearic Is.
Sardinia
MEDITERRANEAN SEA
Rabat
Algiers
Tunis
MOROCCO
ALGERIA
TUNISIA

URAL MOUNTAINS
FINLAND
lsinki
Moscow
SOVIET UNION
Volga
Dnepr
Don
aw
CASPIAN SEA
RUMANIA
Bucharest
Danube
BLACK SEA
BULGARIA
Sofia
Ankara
TURKEY
Tehran
REECE
AEGEAN SEA
thens
IRAN
Baghdad
SYRIA
IRAQ
Nicosia
CYPRUS
Beirut
LEBANON
Damascus
Crete

meanings we attach to the political arrangements for any part of the globe emerge historically, and the words we use have important political and ideological implications. For example, expressions like *First World,* which refers to Western Europe, Japan, and the United States, and *Third World,* which refers to the less economically developed states of Latin America, Africa, and Asia, reflect a Eurocentrism in which the capitalist West is given pride of place. And terms like *Western Europe* and *Eastern Europe* are as much political and ideological as they are geographical.

When we look at the evolution of modern European societies, we see two fundamentally transformative processes at work: the emergence of the modern state, and the advent of the Industrial Revolution. As Perry Anderson, a British sociologist, observes, absolutist states emerged in Europe during the sixteenth century. Monarchies with firm, centralized authority replaced the more localized and personal administration of power that characterized medieval Europe. The introduction of permanent bureaucracies, codified laws, national taxes, and standing armies represented the arrival of the first modern European states.[1]

By the eighteenth century, new economic developments associated with capitalist industrialization began to push the state beyond its increasingly archaic monarchical forms. Although bitter feuds between landowners and monarchs were not uncommon, absolutist regimes were generally linked in economic, military, and political terms to the traditional landholding aristocracy. With the Industrial Revolution, the owners of manufacturing enterprises, the bourgeoisie, increasingly gained economic prominence and political influence. A growing incompatibility between old state forms and new economic demands fostered revolutionary upheavals that ushered in more modern constitutional forms of the state. Industrialization and state formation were closely linked historical phenomena: The European states that we recognize today follow from earlier eruptions associated with the growth of capitalist market forces and the struggle for power between the old, landowning classes and the modern, urban bourgeoisie.

There is another point, however, that is crucial to an understanding of both the history of European societies and the organization of this text. Until the Russian Revolution in 1917 and the subsequent post–World War II division of Europe, there was no natural division in Europe between East and West. It was both possible and appropriate to speak of absolutist states in central or Eastern Europe — Austria, Prussia and Russia — in the same way that one spoke of similar centralized bureaucracies in France, Spain, or England.

With the Russian Revolution of 1917 and the emergence of socialist states in Eastern Europe in the aftermath of World War II, a great divide split Europe into East and West. While this distinction is reinforced by each side as part of a global ideological campaign to win allies and secure geopolitical dominance, there are also crucial differences in political and economic processes that separate the capitalist democracies of Western Europe from the socialist societies of Eastern Europe.

In *European Politics in Transition* we are concerned first and foremost with the complex interplay of capitalist economies and formally democratic political institutions. But we are interested also in an issue that bridges the East-West divide: How can contemporary industrial societies reconcile the aims of economic coordination with the aims of political participation? Both Western and Eastern European societies face inherent dilemmas in their efforts to resolve the tensions between economic performance and democratic governance. In the capitalist democracies, procedural rights of *political democracy,* including voting, free speech, and party competition, take priority over questions of equity, justice, and equality in the allocation of resources or control of the economy. In socialist societies, by contrast, there is far less attention to political rights, but more emphasis on *economic democracy:* the right to employment, the reduction of inequalities in the distribution of economic resources, and control over the economy and control within industrial sectors and units of production.

The organization of this text follows from these observations. Because our first concern is with the interplay between *capitalism* and *democracy,* we focus on five major states of Western Europe: Britain, France, West Germany, Italy, and Sweden. But the broader problem of the tension between economic coordination and political participation requires that we also seriously consider the tenuous connection between *socialism* and *democracy.* Therefore, we study Soviet politics, and also draw important lessons from Czechoslovakia, East Germany, Hungary, and Poland.

Democracy, Capitalism, and the Postwar Settlement

"There is a fact," observes a Canadian political theorist, C. B. Macpherson, "which some people find admirable and some people would prefer not to have mentioned . . . that liberal democracy and capitalism go together. Liberal democracy is found only in countries whose economic system is wholly or predominantly that of capitalist enterprise. And, with few and mostly temporary exceptions, every capitalist country has a liberal-democratic political system."[2] As Macpherson is quick to point out, it would be surprising to discover that this correlation between capitalism and democracy were purely coincidental. Why should liberal democracy (defined as a political system involving an extensive franchise and party oppositions within a parliamentary or presidential form of government) coexist so readily with capitalism (an economic system based primarily on private ownership of property and productive resources and a free market for wage labor)? The question seems particularly intriguing in light of the considerable, and broad-based, opinion (particularly in the last century) that the two do not naturally come together. As German social theorist Claus Offe notes, "Nineteenth-century liberal political theory and classical Marxism were in full agreement on one major point: both Marx and his liberal contemporaries, such as J. S. Mill and de Tocqueville, were convinced that, capitalism and full democracy (based on equal and universal suffrage) could not mix."[3] Offe adds that the mechanisms which have reconciled capitalism and democracy — the political party system and the Welfare State — are currently in crisis.

The emergence in the twentieth century of autocratic regimes such as Nazi Germany indicates that the correlation between liberal democracy and capitalism is by no means absolute. Nevertheless, contemporary Western European societies are defined in a crucial way both by the tension between these two sets of principles and by the historically and nationally specific institutions that evolved to reduce the conflict between them.

If capitalist principles of coordination divide groups of people by their economic situation, how can political arrangements, such as party competition, elections, and interest-group representation, reconcile these abiding conflicts of interest? If the capitalist economy creates inequalities of wealth and labor, how can the state sustain these economic relations and at the same time maintain popular support in accordance with axioms of fairness and the rights of citizenship?

We need to explain why the conclusions of Mill, Marx, and Tocqueville do not always apply to contemporary Western European societies. Even more important, by tracing the historical path of capitalism and democracy, it is possible to come to terms with postwar Western European development. It should become clear that the stability that marked the first twenty years of the postwar world represents a moment of carefully institutionalized compatibility between capitalism and democracy, while an increasingly complex tension between these two principles characterizes the transition to uncertainty that defines the current period in European politics.

The Rise of the Postwar Settlement

The years following World War II represented a period of rapid economic growth sustained by secure and widely popular regimes. In Germany and Italy, the Christian Democrats ruled throughout the period, and in Britain, Labour and Conservative governments shared a mainstream consensus. In contrast to the economic depression and social instability of the interwar period, the years following World War II reflected an unusual degree of social harmony.

Many scholars and political elites of this period believed that sustained social, economic, and political conflicts were a thing of the past. Economic growth seemed to provide the solvent for reducing class antagonisms. The more radical social movements that sought a fundamental change in the organization of society and the control of economic resources appeared outmoded. "[T]he performance of capitalism since the end of the Second World War has been so unexpectedly dazzling," wrote one observer in 1965, "[that] it is hard for us to believe that the bleak and squalid system which we knew could, in so short a time, have adapted itself without some covert process of total destruction and regeneration to achieve so many desired objectives."[4] A significant evolutionary process developed in the postwar period that, at least temporarily, served to reconcile capitalism and democracy: the political regulation of the market economy.

Although class conflicts persisted in Europe, especially in southern Europe (Italy and France among our studies), the general trend was toward mediation through nonmarket political institutions. The most common approach involved direct negotiations over prices or incomes between representatives of capital and labor with the coordination and guidance of the state. The state regulated the market economy by intervening to reduce conflicts of interest between labor and capital. The key shift was that the state persuaded organized labor to moderate its demands in exchange for substantial benefits, including full employment, stable prices, welfare programs, and automatic wage increases. The era of strife associated with the transition to an industrial capitalist order was apparently over, and democracy and capitalism seemed reconciled by what came to be called the postwar settlement.

With the benefit of hindsight, particularly in light of renewed political conflict since the late 1960s, it is now evident that this miracle of harmony derived from an unusual set of circumstances. The absence of severe conflict resulted from the dislocations of war, which exhausted political passions and placed a premium on cooperation within and among the states of Europe. At the same time, the division of global influence between the United States and the Soviet Union reduced the possibility of pan-European unity and placed the states of Western Europe in a situation of economic and military dependence on the United States. *Pax Americana* meant that Western European nations lacked the material means with which to challenge the United States' leadership, even as the perceived threat of a Soviet military invasion quelled potential political conflicts.

U.S. military, political, and economic intervention promoted European recovery and helped prevent the emergence of radical regimes in Western Europe. Nevertheless, despite the aims of some policymakers in the United States, convergence between U.S. and European political systems was limited, because historical differences between the two regions were too strong to be overridden. Two factors are particularly important: the difference in the configuration of class forces in Western Europe and the role of the state. European workers were more conscious of their class affiliations and often defined their lives in terms of their participation in political parties and in party- and class-linked subcultures that provided strong bonds of friendship and community. European workers were apt to organize along class lines in the political sphere and support a range of parties — labor, social democratic, socialist, and communist — that sought a substantial alteration of the private market system. Moreover, large numbers of working people in southern Europe were fundamentally, and quite openly, opposed to the entire capitalist system. Thus, contrary to the American experience, political party cleavages within European politics reflected to a considerable extent the class divisions that remained from the emergence of industrial capitalism in the nineteenth century. The pattern of political opposition in Western Europe was complex. Long-standing differences in religious identity, conflicts over secularization, and regional loyalties motivated political choice in Italy, West Germany, and France. In contrast to the United States, however, a fundamental axiom of political life involved the continued conflict between working people (organized through trade unions and socialist parties of one variety or another) and the propertied classes (manufacturing elites and those linked to the world of finance organized through business associations and bourgeois parties).

The role of the state — the bureaucracy, parliament, and the entire range of national governmental institutions — was far greater in Western Europe than in the United States. In Europe, state action within the economic realm was extensive, including provision of substantial welfare benefits, direction of fiscal and monetary policy, regulation of industrial relations, and vigorous efforts to sponsor industrial growth and restructure failing industries. This difference was even more pronounced in the postwar period, when states throughout Western Europe extended their activities in both the economic and social-welfare spheres.

Therefore, the social harmony of the 1950s and 1960s did not lead to an Americanization of Western European politics. Rather, the two factors that most clearly distinguished Europe from the United States — party mobilization along class lines and activist state institutions — produced a special Western European model of politics. Challenges to the capitalist order were repulsed, and a new class compromise ushered in an era of unprecedented growth and political stability. The years from the end of World War II to the 1973 oil crisis were a period of reconciliation between democracy and capitalism. We call this process the *postwar settlement,* a set of nationally specific arrangements in each of the Western European countries, explicitly or implicitly supported by a wide array of state, business, trade union, and political party elites. During this period, the welfare state was consolidated; high levels of employment achieved; anticapitalist forces marginalized; and an unusual degree of social, industrial, and political consent for mainstream (and reformist) policies secured. Both the nature of political participation and the character of the economic system underwent significant change as the postwar settlement was consolidated.

The Transformation of Political Parties

The structure and the behavior of political parties were transformed, as parties with explicit organizational and ideological links to the working classes and parties linked historically to the interests of economic elites each tried to appeal to broader constituencies. As an alternative to more adversarial ideological appeals, parties of both the Left and the Right often sought to generate broad-based electoral support by representing themselves to the electorate, not as the party of the working class or the economic elite, but as the best modernizing party, the one that could master technological change and guide the national economy in a complex system of international interdependence. This shift in appeal represented a process of modernization of party systems, in which pragmatic claims supplanted ideological appeals and performance replaced interest as the axis of party competition. Parties sought interclass support on election day and were less concerned with mobilizing stable subcultures around contested class-based issues.

As parties lost their class appeal and governments assumed responsibility for economic management and social welfare, the focus of the integrative function tended to shift from the party to the state. The very form of mass participation in politics changed, as interest organizations such as trade unions came to represent the mobilized citizenry and became the means for voicing political and economic demands that could no longer be channeled effectively through political parties. Thus, party competition and parliamentary representation became less significant. If democracy and capitalism were to be reconciled, parties and parliaments could not be the central vehicles to effect this purpose: first, because parties no longer tapped (or controlled) class-based energies; and, second, because the active state made the parliamentary organs of liberal democracy increasingly insignificant when compared to the bureaucratic and executive agencies that conducted foreign policy, managed the economy, and implemented the welfare state.

A New Political Framework

The new political framework involved a tacit alliance between the organized working class and large-scale business, an arrangement that had not existed in the past and that would crumble by the 1970s. Under the tutelage of the state, the two groups cooperated in a manner that stimulated economic growth, political moderation, and social harmony. While states politically regulated the economies to ensure nearly full employment, higher wages, and expanded social-welfare provision, the working class accepted as its part of the bargain an explicit set of limitations in both its industrial and political demands.

Political scientist Adam Przeworski has elaborated a theoretical model that helps illuminate the conditions for emergence of the postwar settlement. The working class must be sufficiently organized, cohesive, and centralized so that it can act in a unified manner, and workers must gain a reasonable assurance from business and the state that they will receive a steady stream of benefits, including high employment levels, regular wage increases, and welfare-state provisions. In return, the organized working class, through its accepted leaders within the trade union and socialist party spheres, is induced to moderate its demands in ways that enable business to carry on profitable activities.[5]

Working-class moderation had several elements. In contrast to the past, workers came to accept the prerogatives of capitalist control, both in the overall organization of the economy and within the production process. Business was given relative freedom to direct the economy in industrial terms and the state in political terms on condition that they succeeded in achieving economic growth. In effect, demands for annual wage increases and welfare state programs became a substitute for the satisfaction of other demands that were more threatening to capitalist production (e.g., workers' control over the pace, content, and conditions of work, as well as investment decisions, industrial policy, and technological innovations).

Employers, workers, and the state must accept certain constraints in order for the new agreement to work. The labor movement must be able to give a binding commitment to moderate its demands. In return, business firms must agree to provide workers with high levels of wages and employment. And the state must safeguard the class accord that has been struck; it must appear to be a neutral arbiter, serving the general interest, rather than siding unduly with either employers or workers. If the state were seen as favoring business interests, workers would engage in protest rather than cooperation; if the state were considered to favor workers' interests, capitalists would register their dissatisfaction through a refusal to invest (a capital strike) and economic stagnation would result. The state played an active role in securing the postwar settlement, by instituting economic measures to reduce the effects of business cycles, by sponsoring political institutions that promoted active class collaboration, and by expanding welfare-state programs.

This postwar settlement pattern of class relations appears to replace traditional zero-sum conflict, in which the gains of one class are achieved at the expense of the other. Class compromise seems to represent a situation of positive-sum cooperation, in which both classes gain from their cooperation and restraint. In fact, however, the appearance of universal benefit was misleading. Not all classes and social forces gained from the creation of the new, rationalized capitalist order. Although industrial workers began to enjoy the benefits of the consumer society, they continued to be subjected to the harsh conditions of industrial labor. Given a shortage of labor, due to rapid economic expansion, millions of immigrant workers were recruited to northern Europe from southern Europe (Portugal, Spain, Italy, Greece, and Turkey) and Eastern Europe (especially Poland and Yugoslavia), as well as from Africa and Asia. Immigrant workers were assigned to the most menial positions and received low wages and meager welfare benefits. They were denied citizenship rights and were subjected to serious discrimination in housing and in educational opportunities. Women also received fewer benefits from the new order, as a result of their unequal position in employment and in the domestic sphere and decidedly unequal treatment in welfare-state provisions.

These economic trends generally were set in place in the 1950s and 1960s; however, there were important political differences within the region. While there are exceptions, these political and economic differences divide Western Europe in two: the nations of northern Europe (represented in this text by Britain, West Germany and Sweden), and those of southern Europe (represented by France and Italy). France, however, is a mixed case: Although it became economically developed after World War II and thus converged with northern Europe in this respect, its political-cultural patterns, notably a high degree of ideological conflict, labor militancy, and political fragmentation, were reminiscent of southern Europe.

Workers in northern Europe were more likely to gain citizenship rights early and to be included within the dominant system. In West Germany and Sweden (but not in Britain), labor unions were more unified and workers gained greater benefits from the system. As a result, they were more likely to be moderate in their political stance. In contrast to southern Europe, working-class elements were not excluded from the decision-making process nor did they remain hostile to the existing economic and political order in significant numbers. In northern Europe (including Britain), trade union leaders conducted national negotiations with top-level associations of business or with government. In Sweden, West Germany, and, to a lesser extent, Britain, they restrained rank-and-file rebelliousness against the deals that were struck.

Labor movements in southern Europe were divided internally by ideological and religious differences and, thus, were less centralized. Rival unions engaged in bidding wars to attract members by pressing radical demands. National union leaders had neither the authority nor the mandate to negotiate with business representatives and the state, and rank-and-file workers often refused to abide by the agreements they struck. Thus, the working class was increasingly excluded from the ongoing economic order.

This comparison between northern and southern European labor-movement dynamics finds an important parallel in workers' political activity as expressed through their party identifications. In each of the northern European nations covered in this text, two-thirds of all workers were unified in a single socialist party and these parties were either the first or second most powerful in the society. The British Labour Party and the West German Social Democratic Party participated in the alternation of government with center-Right parties and played crucial roles in promoting progressive reforms. The Swedish Social Democratic Party was in power throughout the period of the postwar settlement. Each of these social-democratic parties made a vital contribution to forging the class compromise that prevailed in northern Europe and this participation had significant consequences. Within social democracy, the compromise is tilted moderately in favor of working-class interests: the state provided more expansive welfare benefits; tax laws were more progressive so that income inequalities were somewhat narrowed; and state policies placed a higher priority on full employment.

In southern Europe, workers divided their support about equally among communist, socialist, and more conservative Christian democratic parties. Within the Left, the communist and socialist parties were highly antagonistic in France throughout the period and in Italy in the 1960s. As a result, the Right governed in these countries, although sometimes in complex and unstable coalitions. This circumstance reinforced workers' exclusion from the political community and also made for more conservative state policies.

Nonetheless, despite important differences in the way that political conflict was structured in the various Western European nations, there was a broad convergence in the policies sponsored by the major Western European governments. This convergence was partly a result of structural requirements associated with the postwar expansionary phase of capitalist development. Rapid industrialization and urbanization required the expansion of housing, education, old-age pensions, and unemployment insurance. Given the preexisting tradition of activist states in Western Europe, it is not surprising to find that states were involved in meeting the new social and economic needs. Moreover, Western Europe was slowly becoming more integrated, in part due to the impact of the European Economic Community, which was created in the late 1950s and provided for lower tariffs and a harmonization of economic policies among member states. Thus, national governments emulated each other's policy innovations, in what might be thought of as a political learning curve. The country sections in this text will review the kinds of policies adopted by each state. Some of the common elements on the postwar policy agenda of all the Western European states covered in the text are listed below.

Economic Policy and the Development of Planning. Within the economic realm, the state provided central direction in order to achieve the goals of full employment, growth, economic modernization, and assistance to export-based industries. In the first years of the postwar period, priority was given to economic reconstruction, especially in basic industries, mining, and transport. At this time, governments, under pressure from labor, often took over direct control (nationalization) of key industries, including steel, coal, telecommunications, and transport. The state's economic steering capacity was strengthened by the development of planning techniques within specially created planning agencies or in finance and economic ministries. Although what passed for planning was a mixture of hopes, estimates, guesses, and policies, planning did serve to moderate conflict among social forces, reduce bottlenecks in production, and build support for streamlining industry through technological innovation. Planning often aimed at reducing class tensions through the creation of tripartite commissions of representatives from organized labor, capital, and the state.

Social Welfare and an Active Labor Policy. Rapid urbanization and industrialization produced pressure for state measures to prepare workers for the labor market and to cushion workers, pensioners, the infirm, and the unemployed from economic dislocations. These programs attempted to undercut opposition to capitalist expansion and to facilitate that expansion by training workers to business' specifications. Among the many welfare measures sponsored by the state were public construction and ownership of housing, provision of medical services, and funds for unemployment insurance and pensions. Although Western European welfare-state programs were far more successful than those in the United States in reducing the costs of rapid industrial expansion, the welfare state involved relatively little redistribution of power and resources among classes. Instead, it helped facilitate broader acceptance of the new order by redistributing resources across age groups (from adult workers to young children and elderly citizens) and preventing extreme inequalities.

Modernization of Political Institutions. After World War II, there was a shift in power from parliamentary to executive institutions within the state. This shift in the balance of power involved at least two elements: First, with the state increasingly involved in macroeconomic policy activities, the economic ministries gained influence in the day-to-day administration of governmental policy; and secondly, the decline of legislative bodies was justified by the presumed need for speed and cohesion in policy making. Parliamentary institutions may represent diverse interests and ventilate options effectively, but they are quite slow-moving and fragmented.

The desire for increased political efficiency was linked to the decline of class conflict (what sociologist Daniel Bell termed the end of ideology):

Why engage in protracted debate if everyone agrees on the desirability of economic growth within the prevailing capitalist economy? An unusual degree of consensus did not preclude differences among European political parties. Leftist parties were more inclined than rightist parties to favor redistributive measures; however, the entire political balance within Western Europe was substantially more to the left than in the United States.

Western European nations also differed quite substantially in their political-institutional mix. Among the countries studied, southern Europe preserved a central role for parliament in making and toppling governments, possibly as a reflection of the greater political tensions in these states. (The situation changed drastically in France with the advent of the Fifth Republic in 1958.) In northern Europe, government formation reflected electoral-party choice, as opposed to party maneuvering in parliament (the situation in southern Europe); moreover, stronger executives managed more enduring governments. For example, in West Germany, the center-Right was in power without interruption from 1949 to 1966 (and shared government with the Social Democrats in a Grand Coalition for three years thereafter). By contrast, governments changed on the average every six months in France (until the founding of the executive-dominated Fifth Republic in 1958) and throughout the postwar period in Italy, stable and cohesive leadership was prevented by the fragmented, multiparty system.

The Fall of the Postwar Settlement

Through the late 1960s, the postwar settlement endured generally throughout Western Europe, as governments promoted welfare and economic policies in a managerial manner and the major social classes maintained their modernizing alliance with the state. For the most part, the central trade-off of the postwar settlements held: full employment and economic growth through governmental steering mechanisms and increased social and welfare expenditures for relative social harmony and labor peace. The tension between democracy (now meaning participation through interest associations and interclass electorally oriented parties) and capitalism (now meaning politically regulated "modern capitalism" with extensive public holdings) was reduced, so long as economic growth was assured. Suddenly, virtually without warning, this social harmony was shattered and a new era of political uncertainties began. What went wrong?

In a way, the renewal of political conflict was first rooted in the process of economic growth itself, which generated a host of political tensions that had been obscured by the strong grip of organized labor, capital, and the state. Migrants from rural areas jammed into hastily constructed blocks of high-rise flats that began to ring older central cities. "Guest workers," the euphemism for immigrant workers, were also crowded into inadequate housing. Women were drawn into the paid labor force in high numbers as a result of a tight labor market and the increase in clerical and governmental service positions. Labor unions paid little attention to the damaging effects of economic growth on workers and the social and physical environment. Further, they generally failed to represent the interests of social forces outside their traditional constituency of skilled, male, industrial workers.

The rapid expansion of the educated, urban middle class helped spark the early phase of militant protest. As students, many had been radicalized by opposition to the U.S. military action in Vietnam, and opposed authority as represented by the constraints imposed by traditional universities. Many sought non-traditional goals: They wanted production to be democratically organized, resisted the traditional demands of marriage and career paths, and were the first to warn of environmental dangers from corporate abuses.

A final element contributing to the first outbreak of protest in the late 1960s was the rebellion of the industrial core of the working class. As the pace of economic change increased, workers were forced to endure intensified work tempos, increased occupational hazards, and tedious work.

Blue-collar workers, particularly those in unionized sectors linked to social-democratic parties, challenged the centrist slide of socialist and social-democratic parties. Increasingly, however, new social forces — the newly militant white-collar working classes; the urban, educated middle-class elites; women and nonwhites neglected by traditional unions and leftist parties — protested against government action and inaction in the face of economic strains and political retreats. Finally, the growing incapacity of states to provide economic rewards in accordance with the postwar settlement combined with Left critiques — a disregard for ecology, nuclear power, youth and women's movement issues — to spawn a resurgence of old Right and a growth of new Right forces. These responses to the decline of the postwar settlement combined in different ways in each of the Western European states, each with particular force and timing and contemporary significance. We can discern, however, two phases of the political crisis that mark the transition from the stability of the postwar settlement to today's uncertainty.

In the late 1960s and 1970s, there was a massive and unexpected eruption of what one study termed the "resurgence of class conflict in Western Europe." The most dramatic instance occurred in France in May, 1968, when nearly half of all French workers, students, professionals, and civil servants staged the largest general strike in history. In Italy, workers and allied groupings waged widespread grassroots struggles outside established political party or legislative channels for workplace control, political influence, and provision of social necessities like health care and housing in the "hot autumn" of 1969. And in Sweden, a series of wildcat strikes, including a bitter and protracted confrontation in the state-owned mines in Kiruna, shattered the tradition of labor peace in the winter of 1969–70.

In the 1970s, as this phase of the crisis deepened, antistate protest began to break with the nineteenth-century heritage of class-dominated politics. What one observer called "the increased transparence of political power and the state" combined with the state's growing inability to ensure economic prosperity, which a restive and fragmented set of constituencies had long taken for granted. As Suzanne Berger, a political scientist, notes,

> In the seventies, the dominant political response to the new transparence of the state [was] to try to *dismantle* it, not to take it over. While this response is not without precedent in European history (the conservative Right often proposed this in the nineteenth century) never before has this conception of politics shaped new political ideas on both the Left and the Right. What has to be explained is why virtually all new political groups and thought in Western Europe have come to focus, in one way or another, on the issue of the breakup of the state; why virtually all new political organization has taken place outside the orbit of the political parties.[6]

Thus, a "crisis of governability" accompanied the new electoral volatility and the weakening of traditional patterns of party opposition. At the same time, more political energies and increasingly significant political ideas emerged outside and against conventional parties, as both new-Left and new-Right movements — the women's movement; neo-fascist, antiracist/anti-immigrant campaigns; nuclear disarmament agitation; the Greens Party's environmental protest; taxpayers' revolts — emerged with considerable force.

During the 1980s, in the third phase of Western European postwar politics, the failure of transformative visions and the growing organizational power of antiwelfarist and highly nationalist forces suggest that the new political activism of the 1970s is settling into a more clearly defined direction. Now in the last years of the 1980s, the dominant tendency in Western European politics seems to be a powerful backlash against the principles of compromise and the balance of public and private power that were presupposed by the postwar settlement and the welfare state. What brought about this rightward shift in the contemporary policy agenda?

The Structure of Decline

If economic growth had continued unabated, social harmony might have been restored. However, the crisis of the postwar settlement was reinforced by the slowdown of the Western European economies. While there are many causes of the continued erosion of the postwar settlement, each cause represents a new item on an emerging policy agenda that has subsequently focused the energies of all Western European governments and made it increasingly difficult for any government to maintain popular support.

Traditionally in the vanguard of industrial production and technological innovation, Europe increasingly lost its leading position. First, Japan and the United States gained dominance in the high-tech industries, causing a trade imbalance in this sphere. Equally serious, Western Europe began to be displaced in basic industry, including steelmaking, textiles, and shipbuilding, by the newly industrializing nations of the Third World (Korea, Taiwan, Brazil, and others).

Growing structural unemployment occurred, as it did in the United States, ironically because of the development of high-tech innovations that were both capital- and labor-saving. As a result, fewer workers were needed to maintain a constant or even expanding level of output.

Western Europe was affected by the wider recession that began with the sharp increase in oil prices in 1973–74. Exports by the oil-producing developing countries grew at the expense of the industrialized nations of the West in Europe and North America. The institutionalization of the welfare state in Western Europe meant that most governments were unable to reduce welfare-state benefits significantly, trade union power limited labor market adjustments, and the increasingly global scale of production encouraged an outflow of investment from flagging Western European economies. In general, international competitiveness declined in Western Europe.

In Western Europe, as in the United States, trade unions, political parties, and government itself have been increasingly unable to maintain support among their traditional followings.

Although this is hardly a full review of the extent of the crisis in European politics, it indicates the distance traveled since the era of the postwar settlement. By the late 1970s, virtually every incumbent European government had been defeated at the polls and the assumptions that had governed the political regulation of the market economy during the preceding period were under heavy attack. Although, given the strength of the working classes in Europe, welfare-state programs have been curtailed less than in the United States, there has been a vigorous search for new political alternatives. In contrast to the 1950s and 1960s, when a trend toward convergence could be discerned in Western Europe, the present trend is toward political ferment and divergence. Yet, after a decade of experimentation throughout Europe, no government has found a formula to restore economic growth and political stability. Three very different attempts, from France, Sweden, and Britain, can be singled out to suggest the range of new alternatives.

Socialism Without the Workers. In 1981, France elected a Socialist-Communist coalition to power, which, in the words of François Mitterrand in his presidential inaugural address, promised to "unite socialism and liberty." (This was the first time since the 1940s that a Communist Party joined the governing coalition of a major capitalist nation.) The regime embarked on a bold new course, the centerpiece of which was a substantial enlargement of the public sector. A number of basic and high-tech industries were nationalized, as well as most of the banking and finance sector. This represented the first time since the 1950s that a Western European government had engaged in extensive nationalization; it also represented a substantial tipping of the balance from private to public economic control. At the same time, in contrast to the United States and Great Britain, the French government sharply increased social benefits for workers and reduced the work week. If the government had been successful in stimulating economic growth, increasing French exports, and enlarging democratic control of the economy, France might have blazed a new path and altered the entire policy agenda of European politics.

However, the experiment ground to a halt within two years. The newly nationalized firms absorbed enormous state subsidies, the entire French economy declined, and the political balance quickly turned against the government. Centralized and stable political institutions ensured the government's survival until the legislative elections in March, 1986. Thereafter Mitterrand shared power with a National Assembly dominated by a center-Right majority and a prime minister from the oppositional ranks. The Mitterrand experiment not only failed, but the defeat may have served to discredit Socialist politics in France.

Revitalized Social Democracy. After six years out of power, the Swedish Social Democratic Party regained control of the government in 1982 on a platform of refurbishing and widening social democracy. The major innovation that the party proposed was to give workers a direct share in the ownership and management of capital through the build-up of "wage-earner funds," administered by regional boards composed of state and labor representatives, with capital derived from a tax on wages and profits. The boards would invest in Swedish industry and, eventually, gain control of many firms. Thus, by a gradual process, Sweden would emulate the French example of enlarging public control of production. It is doubtful that the Meidner Plan will prove any more successful in revitalizing industry and enlarging democratic control. There are growing indications, indeed, that the constraints imposed by the international economy are reducing the egalitarian impulses and fragmenting the organizational initiatives of the Swedish Social Democratic Party and trade union movement.

Two-Nation Toryism. Under Margaret Thatcher, Britain launched a program of returning some nationalized industries to the private sector, withdrew from arrangements that involve direct consultation with trade unions (e.g., incomes policies), and reduced economic steering to ensure a full-employment economy. An ideological assault on the principles of welfare provision, the erosion of trade union rights, and a new Nationality Act that reduces the rights of Commonwealth citizens, have seriously polarized British politics. Thatcher's "two-nation" Toryism, which has divided Britain on class, racial, and regional lines, represents a signal departure from the cross-party consensus that governed Britain from the end of the World War II until the close of the 1970s.

Although the period 1981–86 has shown signs of economic recovery in Britain, the underlying pattern of declining international competitiveness continues. Riots in British cities in 1981 and 1985, and the emergence in 1981 of a powerful new centrist party demonstrate the tensions of British society and a growing uncertainty in the realm of party politics.

Conclusion

Western European politics is in transition: from a stable postwar past to an uncertain future; from a set of conflicts dominated by class-based politics to a more complex set of struggles; and from a situation of First

World hegemony to a period of declining geopolitical and economic influence in a world context. With citizen trust in parties and governments eroded and economies under considerable stress, no clear institutional reconciliation between capitalism and democracy — like that of the post-war settlement — seems at hand.

Moreover, when we cross the great East-West divide, bring the Soviet Union back into focus, and study the lessons of Czechoslovakia, East Germany, Hungary, and Poland, the issues of political participation and economic performance in Western Europe will be put in a larger perspective. Neither existing socialist nor capitalist institutions permit *both* economic democracy and ample exercise of political rights. The need to explore the new forms of protest, to consider the difficulties of economic management, and to analyze the complex problems in reconciling traditional ideals of government with the practicalities of power becomes all the more urgent.

Notes

1. Perry Anderson, *Lineages of the Absolutist State* (London: New Left Books, 1974), pp. 15–42.
2. C. B. Macpherson, *The Real World of Democracy* (New York: Oxford University Press, 1976), p. 4.
3. Claus Offe, "Competitive Party Democracy and the Keynesian Welfare State," in Claus Offe, *Contradictions of the Welfare State* (Cambridge: MIT Press, 1984), p. 179.
4. Andrew Shonfield, *Modern Capitalism: The Changing Balance of Public and Private Power* (Oxford: Oxford University Press, 1980), p. 3.
5. Adam Przeworski, *Capitalism and Social Democracy* (New York: Cambridge University Press, 1985), passim.
6. Suzanne Berger, "Politics and Antipolitics in Western Europe in the Seventies," *Daedalus,* vol. 108 (Winter 1979), p. 33.

Bibliography

Berger, Suzanne, ed. *Organizing Interests in Western Europe: Pluralism, Corporatism, and the Transformation of Politics.* Cambridge: Cambridge University Press, 1981.

Bornstein, Stephen, David Held, and Joel Krieger, eds. *The State in Capitalist Europe.* London: George Allen & Unwin, 1984.

Botha, Andrea, ed. *The European Economy: Growth and Crisis.* Oxford: Oxford University Press, 1982.

Castles, Francis G., ed. *The Impact of Parties.* Beverly Hills, CA: Sage, 1982.

———, ed. *State and Economy in Contemporary Capitalism.* London: Croom Helm, 1979.

Crouch, Colin, and Alessandro Pizzorno, eds. *The Resurgence of Class Conflict in Western Europe since 1968.* 2 vols. New York: Holmes & Meier, 1978.

Gerschenkron, Alexander. *Economic Development in Historical Perspective.* Cambridge: Harvard University Press, 1962.

Giner, Salvador, and Margaret S. Archer, eds. *Contemporary Europe: Social Structures and Cultural Patterns.* London: Weidenfeld and Nicolson, 1978.

Goldthorpe, John H., ed. *Order and Conflict in Contemporary Capitalism.* Oxford: The Clarendon Press, 1984.

Gough, Ian. *The Political Economy of the Welfare State.* London: Macmillan, 1978.

Hirsch, Fred, and John H. Goldthorpe, eds. *The Political Economy of Inflation.* Oxford: Martin Robertson, 1978.

Katzenstein, Peter, ed. *Between Power and Plenty: Foreign Economic Policies of Advanced Industrial States.* Madison: University of Wisconsin Press, 1978.

Lindberg, Leon N., and Charles S. Maier, eds. *The Politics of Inflation and Economic Stagnation.* Washington, DC: The Brookings Institution, 1985.

Maier, Charles S. *Recasting Bourgeois Europe: Stabilization in France, Germany, and Italy in the Decade after World War I.* Princeton, NJ: Princeton University Press, 1975.

Miliband, Ralph et al., eds. *Social Democracy and Beyond: Socialist Register, 1985/86.* New York: Monthly Review Press, 1986.

Offe, Claus. *Contradictions of the Welfare State.* Cambridge: MIT Press, 1984.

Piore, Michael. *Birds of Passage: Migrant Labor and Industrial Societies.* Cambridge: Cambridge University Press, 1979.

Schmitter, Philippe C., and Gerhard Lehmbruch, eds. *Trends Toward Corporatist Intermediation.* Beverly Hills, CA: Sage, 1979.

Shonfield Andrew. *Modern Capitalism.* Oxford: Oxford University Press, 1965.

Zysman, John. *Politics, Governments and Growth.* Ithaca, NY: Cornell University Press, 1983.

PART

II

Britain

Joel Krieger

The Emergence of the Modern British State

We have argued that the evolution of contemporary politics in Western Europe can best be understood by reference to the rise and fall of the postwar settlement. This is nowhere more true than in the United Kingdom, where the consolidation of the postwar settlement involved an impressive degree of political consensus, but the economic preconditions of growth and international competitiveness have eroded the most since the end of World War II. From being a textbook model of stable democracy as recently as two decades ago, Britain has today become a society that is economically exposed and politically divided.

For more than a quarter-century after the end of World War II, Britain's two major parties (Conservative and Labour) shared a mainstream vision that involved modest regulation of the market economy and acceptance of the principles and policies of the welfare state. Since the recession of the mid-1970s, however, and especially since the election of Margaret Thatcher as prime minister in May, 1979, Britain has departed more radically from the postwar consensus than any of the other countries covered in this text.

The cracks in Britain's postwar consensus run deep. In the summer of 1981 and again in the fall of 1985, riots led by unemployed youths erupted in a host of British cities, with special force in London, Merseyside, and Manchester. In March, 1981, several leaders of the Labour Party broke away to form a powerful new centrist party, the Social Democratic Party (SDP), which now challenges the two-party dominance of government by Labour and Conservatives. British troops remain in Northern Ireland, where they were placed in 1969 to control the violence between Catholic and Protestant communities and to preserve Northern Ireland as part of the United Kingdom. A year-long miners' strike, beginning in March, 1984, became one of the most violent and divisive industrial disputes in modern European history.

From being the premier world power a century ago, Britain has dropped in geopolitical terms to the bottom of the second rank of nations. Today, Britain's reputation for moderation and flexibility mixes with vivid reminders of social fragmentation, resurgent ideological politics, and the human costs of seemingly endless economic crisis. How did it get here from there?

The explanation begins with the very processes of state formation that forged the United Kingdom from a set of divided nations.

The Principles of British State Formation

The processes of state formation are complex and controversial. State formation combines national and international forces, redraws the map of economic and class relations, and creates new social and community connections. It taps often contradictory nationalist impulses and, in the end, forges a set of political and cultural values that help define a new constitutional order.

The process of building the nation-state may seem settled for the United Kingdom (U.K.), but basic issues of state formation have reemerged in recent years with unexpected force. Can the interests of England, Wales, Scotland, and Northern Ireland be accommodated within a single, unified nation-state? How well can a state constructed for empire adjust — economically, politically, and institutionally — to a century-long decline? How effectively can British political institutions and constitutional norms reconcile the contradictory pressures of capitalism and democracy?

Nation and State

The first set of problems, concerning the relationship between nation and state, has proved remarkably resistant to solutions, even though the issues often seem invisible to outsiders, in part because of the casual use of language. In the United States, for example, *nation* and *state* are often used interchangeably. By contrast, these terms must be distinguished carefully with regard to Britain, where a unified political entity (or state) includes more than one nation: a community with common historical and cultural characteristics that inhabits a clearly defined territory.

For the sake of simplicity, we have been using the term *Britain* as shorthand for the United Kingdom of Great Britain and Northern Ireland (U.K.). We will use the term *England* when the focus of discussion is on English industrialization in the eighteenth century, for example, as opposed to Welsh, Scottish, or Irish. In law, the U.K. includes Northern Ireland, but Great Britain means England, Scotland, and Wales. The distinction between England and the U.K. is crucial, for the U.K. as a *state* or *nation-state* — which is ruled by the British Parliament seated in Westminister in London and which conducts a unified foreign policy — is comprised of four historically constituted and culturally distinct *countries* or *nations*.

Of the approximately 56 million persons residing in Britain, nearly 47 million live in England, just under 3 million in Wales, some 5 million in Scotland, and over 1.5 million in Northern Ireland. Wales was politically assimilated to England after the accession of Henry VII of the Welsh House of Tudor to the English throne in 1485 and the signing of the Act of Union of 1535. The unification of the Scottish and English crowns occurred when the Protestant James Stuart (son of Mary, Queen of Scots, whose grandmother was a sister of Henry VIII) was accepted to the English throne as James I when the childless Elizabeth I died in 1603. Thereafter, England, Scotland, and Wales were known as Great Britain. Scotland and England remained divided politically, however, until the Act of Union of 1707. Henceforth, a common Parliament of Great Britain replaced the two separate parliaments of Scotland and of England and Wales.

The decline of the postwar settlement exacerbated long-enduring cultural divisions within Britain, and the discovery of vast oil reserves off the north shore of Scotland increased Scottish demands for more extensive national self-determination. The 1970s witnessed powerful movements for *devolution* — the shifting of specified powers from the British Parliament to national parliaments in Scotland and Wales. The growth of Scottish and Welsh nationalist parties seemed to signal a fundamental weakening of two-party (Conservative and Labour) dominance, and there was much talk of a permanent realignment of British politics.

The situation in Northern Ireland raises far more serious problems. The Irish question remained one of the most unsettling issues in British

Britain
0 100 Miles
0 100 Kilometers
Shetland Islands
Orkney Islands
Outer Hebrides
Inner Hebrides
Aberdeen
SCOTLAND
NORTH SEA
ATLANTIC OCEAN
Glasgow
Edinburgh
Newcastle
Tyne
NORTHERN IRELAND
Belfast
Isle of Man
IRISH SEA
Leeds
Hull
Liverpool
Manchester
Sheffield
Isle of Anglesey
REPUBLIC OF IRELAND
Nottingham
Leicester
WALES
Birmingham
ENGLAND
Cardiff
London
Bristol
Thames
Straits of Dover
Southampton
Isle of Wight
Plymouth
English Channel
Channel Islands
FRANCE

Table 1.1 General Statistics: U.K.

	ENGLAND	WALES	SCOTLAND	NORTHERN IRELAND	UNITED KINGDOM
POPULATION					
(000, mid-1982 estimate)	46,799	2,808	5,166	1,567	56,340
AREA					
(sq. km)	130,440	20,768	78,783	14,120	244,111
(sq. miles)	50,363	8,018	30,418	5,452	94,251
POPULATION DENSITY					
(persons per sq. km)	359	135	66	111	231
(persons per sq. mile)	929	350	170	287	598
GROSS DOMESTIC PRODUCT					
(£ per capita, 1981)	3,674	3,049	3,547	2,723	3,605
EMPLOYEES IN EMPLOYMENT					
(000, mid-1983)	17,415	883	1,881	466	20,645
PERCENTAGE OF EMPLOYEES IN:					
(June, 1983, provisional) Agriculture, forestry and fishing	1.6	2.5	2.3	2.0	1.7
Engineering and allied industries	12.6	9.7	9.6	6.9	12.1
All other manufacturing	14.4	13.8	13.3	15.0	14.3
Construction	4.6	5.8	6.4	5.4	4.8
Mining, quarrying, gas, electricity, and water	2.9	6.0	3.8	2.0	3.1
Service industries	64.0	62.2	64.6	68.5	64.0
UNEMPLOYMENT RATE					
(percent, June 1984)	12.0	15.4	14.3	20.4	12.6
AVERAGE GROSS WEEKLY EARNINGS					
(£, all full-time men. April, 1983)	168.1	156.3	167.5	150.5	167.5[a]
IDENTIFIABLE PUBLIC EXPENDITURE[b]					
(£ per capita, 1982–83)	1,539	1,990	1,726	2,335	1,612

[a]Great Britain only.
[b]Excluding borrowing by nationalized industries and some other public corporations.
SOURCE *Britain 1985: An Official Handbook* (London: HMSO, 1985), p. 7. Reproduced with the permission of the Controller of Her Brittanic Majesty's Stationery Office.

politics throughout the nineteenth century. The Home Rule Bill introduced by the Liberal government in 1886 would have given an Irish parliament some limited control over domestic (but not foreign) affairs, but instead it failed and helped precipitate the split and decline of the Liberal party. Continued Irish resistance to British political and economic control kept the question of home rule alive and spawned deep nationalist sentiments. "A history of forcible sequestration of land, bloody coercion of people, religious persecution of the majority and extreme rural deprivation resulted in a nationalist challenge being mounted on the basis of the popular religion — Catholicism," note British political scientists John Dearlove and Peter Saunders. "Because the domination of the Irish had been organised culturally (through exclusion of Catholics) as well as economically, the reaction was organised in these terms as well. Through the nineteenth century, Irish nationalism thus became intertwined with Catholicism, just as in the north-east, loyalty to the union with Britian became the hallmark of Protestanism."[1]

The resulting schism between a British-settler colonial Protestant minority and a Catholic nationalist majority survived passage of the Government of Ireland Act of 1914, and civil war was averted by the outbreak of World War I. But international hostilities provided only a brief interregnum. In 1916 Sinn Fein, an Irish republican organization with both political party and military potential, led a failing Irish nationalist uprising (the Easter Rebellion) in the aftermath of which fifteen leaders were executed and anti-British sentiment led to a Sinn Fein sweep of Catholic constituencies, a boycott of the British Parliament in Westminster, and the creation of a Dublin-based Irish parliament. In response to political pressure, and to attacks on British forces by the Irish Republican Army (IRA), Westminster partitioned Ireland following the Government of Ireland Act of 1920: The six northern counties of Ireland were divided administratively from the remaining twenty-six counties. The twenty-six counties (the Irish Free State and, later, the Republic of Ireland) became an independent nation-state within the British Commonwealth in 1922 (like Canada or New Zealand) and surrendered all formal ties to the U.K. when it ended Commonwealth affiliation in 1949. The six counties became Northern Ireland, a partitioned fourth nation within the U.K., with considerable home rule administered by a Unionist- and Protestant-dominated local parliament (the Stormont assembly). After a civil rights movement calling for Catholic political and economic equality helped provoke Protestant riots in the summer of 1969, the British government sent troops to Northern Ireland, a development which reinvigorated Irish republicanism. By 1971, the Provisional IRA, a paramilitary republican force, was attacking army patrols and bombing

British targets and, under Unionist pressure, the army acted increasingly to repress the Catholic community. In the same year, the British government introduced the practice of internment, which permitted the arrest and imprisonment of persons suspected of terrorist offenses without trial and other traditional legal protections. On January 30, 1972 (Bloody Sunday), troops fired on Catholics during an anti-British demonstration in Londonderry that had been banned by authorities, killing thirteen and wounding a dozen more. On March 28, 1972, Britain abolished Stormont and introduced direct rule from London. Despite a series of British initiatives in the interim, including most recently formalizing the coordination of some Northern Irish affairs with the Republic of Ireland through a treaty signed in November, 1985, the political deadlock in Northern Ireland remains intractable.

In British as well as in European politics, contemporary political developments are rooted in institutional patterns, cultural attributes, and social forces — and specific problems — inherited from the past. Thus, the Irish question is seldom far from Westminster debate and the violence in Northern Ireland is never out of the headlines as Britons continue to hope that one government or another will break the stalemate. The elemental problems of the formation of the nation-state persist, even as the problems of economic decline bring to the fore new questions about state and class in contemporary Britain.

Class, State, and Empire

British state formation, like that of its continental counterparts, involved a long-term process in which the institutions of political power were gradually democratized in accordance, but not always coterminously, with a shifting balance of economic influence. It was noted in Part One that liberal democracy and capitalism typically coexist in contemporary Western European societies. Nevertheless, a reconciliation between the economic principles of market competition and the political principles of representation is neither easy nor automatic. In Britain, industrialization preceded the development of democratic rights of political participation, so there was a considerable lag in the process of adjusting political-administrative control to economic influence. Britain's industrial priority, and the connection between economy and empire, had a lasting effect on the institutional character of the British state. Thus, until a series of electoral and constitutional reforms consolidated the political control of the commercial and industrial classes in nineteenth-century Britain, the economic influence of these classes was not reflected in state forms and policies. Nevertheless, the changing balance of power in society — and particularly the configuration of class power and economic interests — remains the central point of reference for understanding the modern British state.

Industrial Priority. England was the first country to experience an industrial *revolution,* and as a consequence, England's domestic successes quickly transformed the international order. The Industrial Revolution of the mid-eighteenth century involved not simply rapid expansion of production and technological innovation — although both these factors occurred in good measure — but also social and economic transformation.

Over the course of several generations beginning in the mid-eighteenth century, the typical worker was turned "by degrees . . . from small peasant or craftsman into wage-labourer," as historian Eric Hobsbawm observes. Cash and market-based transactions dominated, as industrialization was inextricably tied to commercialization. Merchants and tradesmen were on average far more prosperous than manufacturers in the early stages of the Industrial Revolution, and even the landed aristocracy became more commercially minded, by continental standards. Traditional landowners became nearly as interested in their royalties on coal ore that lay beneath their lands as in farming, and the acquisition of revenue by leasing parcels of land to tenant farmers introduced a decidedly capitalist element into early English agribusiness.[2]

The transformation of English social and economic life was both fundamental and wide-ranging. With the commercialization of agriculture, the peasantry disappeared. The mechanization of manufacturing, which cut deepest in the cotton industry, upset traditional labor hierarchies and permanently displaced skilled craftworkers. Privileged strata of the prerevolutionary economy, notably the hand-loom weavers, became impoverished and socially marginalized. Despite a gradual improvement in the standard of living in the English population at large, the effects of industrialization were often profound for agricultural laborers and particular types of artisans. The period of early industrialization witnessed "wholesale enclosure, in which, in village after village, common rights [were] lost, and the landless and — in the south — pauperised labourer [was] left to support the tenant-farmer, the landowner, and the tithes of the Church"[3] by succumbing to conditions of highly exploited labor.

The Industrial Revolution has generated considerable scholarly controversy. Some historians stress technological innovation, an unprecedented rise in productivity, and a substantial improvement in per capita income.[4] Others stress the unevenness of industrial development, which mitigated the physical burden of toil and enhanced productivity in some trades and had entirely the opposite effect on others.[5] It is not just that scholars still disagree over causes and consequences; for many, the lived experience of this historic upheaval was itself paradoxical. Historian E.P. Thompson explains that the Industrial Revolution may have improved the standard of living in aggregate terms, even as it fundamentally assaulted the quality of life of many working people.

> [I]t is perfectly possible to maintain two propositions which, on a casual view, appear to be contradictory. Over the period 1790–1840 there was a slight improvement in average material standards. Over the same period there was intensified exploitation, greater insecurity, and increasing human misery. By 1840 most people were "better off" than their forerunners had been fifty years before, but they had suffered and continued to suffer this slight improvement as a catastrophic experience.[6]

The effects of the mid-eighteenth-century boom on the processes of state formation are in many ways easier to see. Cotton manufacture, the driving force behind Britain's growing industrial mastery, not only symbolized the new techniques and changed organization of labor of the Industrial Revolution but also represented the perfect imperial industry. It relied exclusively on imported raw materials and, by the turn of the nineteenth century, already depended on overseas commerce for the vast majority of sales of finished goods. The textile industry could grow faster than the expansion of domestic consumption would ordinarily permit because it depended on the development of foreign markets through war and colonization, rather than on domestic consumption. Britain's export orientation thus made the empire both possible and necessary.

Britain in the International Context. With its leading industrial sector dependent on overseas trade, Britain's foreign policy goals remained aggressive throughout the eighteenth century: securing markets; expanding the empire; and defeating European rivals in a series of military engagements, culminating in the Napoleonic Wars (1793–1815). International commerce, propelled by the formidable and active presence of the British navy, helped England take full advantage of its position as the first industrial power.

The end of the Napoleonic Wars, which confirmed Britain's commercial, military, and geopolitical preeminence, inaugurated a truly anomalous period in European history, termed *Pax Britannica,* or "British

Table 1.2 Cotton Spindlage in Major Countries (in thousands)

	1834	1852	1861	1867	1913
Great Britain	10,000	18,000	31,000	34,000	55,576
United States	1,400	5,500	11,500	8,000	30,579
France	2,500	4,500	5,500	6,800	7,400
Germany	626[a]	900	2,235	2,000	10,920
Switzerland	580	900	1,350	1,000	1,389
Belgium	200	400	612	625	1,469
Austria-Hungary	800	1,400	1,800	1,500	4,864[b]

a. 1836.
b. Areas of postwar Austria and Czechoslovakia only.
SOURCE David Landes, *The Unbound Prometheus* (Cambridge: Cambridge University Press, 1972), p. 215.

peace." Britain had the highest per capita income in the world, and in 1870, at the height of its glory, its trade represented nearly one-quarter of the world total. Britain ruled as the hegemonic power. For a full century, indeed until the outbreak of hostilities in 1914, British dominance secured peace among the primary European nations and encouraged largely unrestricted international commerce (free trade).

By the post-1815 period, international commercial interests were able to enforce their economic dominance both abroad and at home. This process involved, first, the reduction or elimination of tariffs and duties, and legislative relief from internal restrictions on trade and, secondly, the formation of a state that would permit financial and commercial interests to prosper at the expense of manufacturing. By 1830, "Britain was not only the 'workshop of the world,' but also its 'clearing house,' and whilst the former status has long been lost, the latter — despite some recent competition from other countries — has not," notes sociologist Geoffrey Ingham. "The consequences of this enduring activity for the development of the dominant classes, the state system, and the economy of Britain can scarcely be overestimated."[7]

By mid-century it was becoming clear that the City (London's financial district), and not its industrial base, represented the leading sector of the British economy. A trade deficit of nearly £60 million in 1865 reached £134.3 million by the start of World War I. Nevertheless, due to the financially oriented commerce of the City of London, which consisted of revenue from foreign investments, brokerage fees on portfolio and money market accounts, profits from currency exchanges, and insurance, the total balance-of-payments surplus increased almost ninefold during the same period (from £21.8 million in 1865 to £187.9 million in 1913). Already established as a world clearinghouse, the City also was keeping afloat a national economy.[8]

The political and institutional consequences of the City's preeminence over industry were substantial. It has been suggested that state formation involves the development of a set of institutions and practices that permit dominant groups to exercise their influence through the political order. Generally, in Western Europe this process involved a shift in influence from the landowning to the manufacturing interests, and here Britain is no exception save for a brief lag in the timing of its adjustment. The parliamentary reform of 1832, which extended the franchise to a section of the middle classes, confirmed politically the changing balance of power from landowner to modern shopkeeper/entrepreneur that the Industrial Revolution had foreordained.

Unique Features of British State Formation. In other respects, however, British state formation followed a less regular path, owing in large measure to the particular character of its economic development. While late industrializers, like Germany and Italy, relied on powerful government support in their industrial take-off period, England's Industrial Revolution was based on laissez-faire (free market) principles. When the state intervened in powerful ways, it did so to secure free markets: enclosure acts ensured a free market for land; the new Poor Law of 1834 dismantled a system of localized wage supplements and, through the threat of workhouses, encouraged both labor mobility and the ready supply of cheap labor; and money and commodities were guaranteed a free market through the repeal of a set of Navigation Laws and the Corn Laws (1846).[9]

By mid-century the British state had helped create nearly ideal free-trade conditions. Other states invested indirectly in manufacturing, mining, and transport, and directed industrial policy from above, but the British state took a far less active role. A hundred years after the Industrial Revolution, the state did little more than encourage an environment of entrepreneurship by removing constraints on market forces. What are the institutional and political-cultural implications of this laissez-faire tradition enshrined in the nineteenth century?

Industrial organization remained the reserve of private entrepreneurship, not the object of government policy. The state's laissez-faire ethos and market-reinforcing practices have had a lasting effect on Britain's political culture and institutional structure. To this day the British have not fully developed the institutional capacities for state-sponsored economic planning or industrial policy enjoyed by some of their competitors, like France of West Germany. Moreover, despite powerful twentieth-century socialist movements in Britain, Lockean principles of individual liberty — the political correlative to laissez-faire — have remained far more powerful than in the rest of Europe, particularly, but not at all exclusively, in the age of Thatcher.

The internationalization of the economy from the mid-eighteenth century and the unique 250-year history of the City of London as the premier world financial center are crucial elements of another unusual feature of Britain's development: the City's *political* influence in British decision making. Although political scientists generally consider the constitutionally unrestricted power of Parliament to be the core principle of British politics, there is an important sense in which the City's economic preeminence, which dates from the eighteenth century, restricted the power of Parliament as it was modernized in the period after the 1832 reforms.

During the period of military engagements in the eighteenth century leading to the Napoleonic Wars, three institutions — the City, the Bank of England, and the Treasury — acted in concert without significant parliamentary involvement. The bank financed the state's debt (mainly from military adventures) through the institutions of the City, and the Treasury paid back the interest through tariffs and duties.

After 1815, protectionism gave way to free trade and *Pax Britannica* reduced the extraordinary expenses of frequent military engagements. But in peace as in war the closely articulated relationship among the City of London, the Bank of England, and the Treasury formed a crucial institutional nexus for state policy. Fiscal and monetary policies were at the core of governmental action and were controlled not by Parliament or the cabinet but by these three interlocking institutions of Britain's financial empire. By the 1870s and the internationalization of the gold standard, "[t]he Treasury's parsimony and the Bank's monetary prudence were . . . complementary and mutually sustaining," notes Ingham. "In this strategic monetary management, the Bank operated quite independently of Parliament; it was the pivotal institution of the 'fiscal constitution' which comprised the 'Holy Trinity of Free Trade, the Gold Standard and Balanced Budgets.' "[10]

The Evolution of the Constitutional Order

England's industrial priority and the particular international focus of state policy formation meant that in practice there were two constitutions.

Britain's real constitution evolved in accordance with changing principles of representation and democracy, and framed its enviable reputation for stability and political moderation. Britain's other fiscal/commercial constitution (a term meant only metaphorically to describe the institutional relations of economic policy formation) developed in step with the internationalization of England's economy and the budgetary and financial demands, first, of empire building and, then, of *Pax Britannica*.

In both domestic political terms (the real constitution) and global economic terms (the fiscal/commercial constitution), Britain's constitutional order was established by the second half of the nineteenth century. However, the two constitutional orders did not come together automatically to form a politically integrated or smoothly running capitalist democracy in the modern sense. On the contrary, economic forms of power and democratic norms of political participation were not easily harmonized. The evolution of the British constitutional order remains a testament to the durability of the emerging capitalist-democratic compromise and demonstrates how difficult it was to reconcile the quite incompatible aims of market forces and aspirations for political representation.

Indeed, the very continuity and longevity of the British constitution and the commonplace references to its flexibility and evolutionary quality should not obscure the fact that tremendous and sometimes violent struggles were fought to shape the structure of the British state. From the end of the seventeenth century, such conflict has characteristically involved efforts by excluded segments of the citizenry to secure representation in the House of Commons, the elected element of Parliament.

In the late 1820s, the respectable opinion of the propertied classes and increasing popular agitation pressed Parliament to expand the franchise to include men of lesser means and to give new urban manufacturing centers, like Manchester or Birmingham, more substantial representation. The Reform Act of 1832 abolished seats representing areas with virtually no people (the *rotten boroughs*) and increased the electorate by about 50 percent above what it had been in 1830, mainly by extending the franchise to include the £10 householder, a person who occupied or owned a property, for commerical use or as a dwelling, that was worth £10 a year in income or rent. The Industrial Revolution had shifted economic power from the landlords to men of commerce and industry, and in principle, this social transformation was confirmed politically by the 1832 reform. In practice, however, the reform enfranchised only quite prosperous middle-class men. In England and Wales, the electorate numbered roughly 653,000 from a population just over 13 million, and in Ireland only 90,000 out of 7.8 million had voting rights.[11] Moreover, a system of open polling ensured that electoral participation was subject to considerable pressure, by landlords of tenants or by prosperous customers of tradespeople.

The reform made clear that economic situation would be used to check the growing pressures for an extension of democratic participation to the common mass of male citizens. "The great Reform Act of 1832," observes historian Dorothy Thompson, "had defined more clearly than at any time before or since in British history, and more clearly than had been done in any other country, a qualification for the inclusion in the political institutions of the country based on the possession of property and the possession of a regular income."[12]

The reform was, therefore, narrow and also highly significant culturally, for it focused greater pressure on the House of Commons as the core institution of British public opinion and representation. It is a measure of the cultural significance of Parliament that the movement for the People's Charter, often considered "the first authentic mass working-class movement in history,"[13] was focused on parliamentary reform. In the aftermath of the Reform Act, a massive popular movement erupted in the late 1830s to secure the program of the People's Charter, published in May, 1938, including universal male suffrage, equal electoral districts, annual elections, and salaried members of Parliament. Adherents of the Chartist movement, men and women who were drawn mainly from the ranks of working people not enfranchised by the Reform Act of 1832, participated in huge and often tumultuous rallies. They formed dozens of local organizations; organized a vast campaign to petition Parliament to accept the points of the People's Charter; and distributed pamphlets, newspapers, and placards. The Chartist movement was an unprecendented effort to change the fundamental terms of the bargain being struck between capitalism and democracy.

The intensity, size, and increasingly radical character of the Chartist movement should not be lost nor should the naive faith in democratic reform, which motivated the campaign, be forgotten. It is difficult to understand today why acute economic distress, in an age when poverty meant vagabondage and not welfare provision, led the lower strata of laborers and the unemployed to struggle first and foremost for political rights and only secondarily for lower food prices and jobs. Nor should it be forgotten that these popular appeals were denied by the reformed Parliament.

Expansion of the franchise proceeded slowly. The Representation of the People Act of 1867 increased the electorate to some 2.5 million but left cities significantly underrepresented. The Franchise Act of 1884 doubled the size of the electorate, but it was not until the Representation

Table 1.3 Electorate as a Proportion of the Adult* Population

YEAR	%
1831	4.4
1868	16.4
1914	30.0
1921	74.0
1931	96.6

*over 21
SOURCE Gregor McLennon, et al. (eds.), *State and Society in Contemporary Britain: A Critical Introduction* (Cambridge: Polity Press, 1984), p. 246.

of the People Act of 1918 that suffrage included nearly all adult men and women over thirty. All adult women were not enfranchised until 1928, and elements of plural voting privileges that favored elites remained in effect until 1948.

The Implications For Contemporary British Politics

Political scientists commonly have treated Britain as a model of Western democracy. Other, less stable societies might learn from its example, and states with less attractive political arrangements can be judged against its standard. "Britain's political culture has long interested students of history, society, and politics," wrote political scientists Bill Jones and Dennis Kavanagh recently. "Because she was the first country to industralise (for most of the nineteenth century, the foremost industrial power) and has long been regarded as a model stable democracy, students have tried to extract lessons from the British experience."[14]

It would be wise (or so the argument goes) to master the lessons of British democracy, perhaps in order to apply them elsewhere with similar results, as follows: constitutional flexibility; a carefully modulated balance between traditions of deference to authority and respect for individual liberties; effective government that permits and even institutionalizes vigorous political opposition; and, but for Northern Ireland and the problems of decolonization, a history of dispute resolution that values mediation above the exercise of coercive authority by the state.

These common assertions about the workings of British government are treated with a certain reverence in Britain and among many observers elsewhere. As empirical observations they hold much validity, and as normative statements of how political life should be organized, many observers find them extremely appealing. These tenets comprise a centerpiece of British political culture — an export model for stable, representative democracy.

We seek a more balanced and contemporary view of the British political system. No one can reasonably question the stability of the government or the longevity of its institutions, but our review of British state formation leads us to suggest that Britain's problems and prospects today may be explained in part by specific features in its evolution.

First, early economic development, linked to the empire and overseas commerce and finance, encouraged a pattern of industrialization that led to dangerous rigidities in the twentieth century. The continued dominance of the City at the expense of manufacturing enterprises left industry uncompetitive, rates of growth below that of many competitors, and the unemployment picture grim.

Second, to a greater degree than any other Western European state, British industrial development began with a laissez-faire emphasis, and it has continued as such. The virtues of free-market individualism have become a source of considerable controversy today. Has this core ingredient in Britain's political culture made it more difficult to compete with those countries, such as France and West Germany (or Japan), that can more effectively apply the institutions of the state to the problems of economic competiveness? Alternatively, has Margaret Thatcher's support for entrepreneurship, competition, and industriousness in the private sector helped provide the basis for newly efficient growth? One's answers to these questions will say a lot about the success of the Thatcher experiment and about one's evaluation of her approach.

Third, contemporary Britain remains plagued by the problems associated with both the formation of the nation-state and the building of an empire that, by the reign of Queen Victoria (1837–1901), encompassed fully 25 percent of the world's population. The 1970s saw politically significant movements for devolution in Scotland and Wales. Even more dramatic, Northern Ireland remains an intractable problem of governance and a constant reminder of the fragility of constitutionalism in the face of complex nationalist, religious, and economic divisions. Similarly, Britain has adjusted poorly to the realization that decolonization has contributed to the creation of a multiracial society. Black Britons have faced considerable racism, and immigrants from the Commonwealth have found legal barriers increasing as the end of steady growth in Britain's economy has reduced demand for labor. A set of immigration and nationality acts have institutionalized a preference for white immigrants, and in 1979, the Conservative victory that made Margaret Thatcher the prime minister was in part due to the candidate's ability to exploit issues of race. Thus, the problems of racism are another legacy of the history of British state formation.

Finally, contemporary British politics demonstrates forcefully our observations that there is no natural identity between capitalism and democracy and that problems of economic performance exacerbate tensions between the economic principles of marketplace competition and the political principles of justice and equality. Current debates about the welfare state and the unleashing of market forces revive the old controversies left unresolved by parliamentary reforms in the nineteenth and early twentieth centuries. Whose interests should Parliament represent? What is the proper balance between political participation and governmental authority? The questions of mass participation raised by the Chartist movement are at the center of debate today, this time focused on the struggle between the Thatcher government and reform-minded and populist municipal authorities.

The United Kingdom is less a model for stable representative democracy than a symbol of the institutional strains and political divisions that have beset capitalist democracies in the postwar world. The unique features of British state formation, which was linked to the empire and skewed by the influence of financial interests, have made British adjustment to its postwar decline particularly difficult. At the same time, the British postwar experience has, with these qualifications, conformed to a general Western European pattern in which the rise and fall of the postwar settlement also marked a fundamental transformation in each country's political experience.

NOTES

1. John Dearlove and Peter Saunders, *Introduction to British Politics* (Cambridge: Polity Press, 1984), p. 405.
2. E.J. Hobsbawm, *Industry and Empire* (Harmondsworth: Penguin/Pelican, 1983), pp. 29–31.
3. E.P. Thompson, *The Making of the English Working Class* (New York: Vintage, 1966), p. 198.
4. David Landes, *The Unbound Prometheus* (Cambridge: Cambridge University Press, 1969), pp. 41–123.
5. Raphael Samuels, "The Workshop of the World: Steam Power and Hand Technology in Mid-Victorian Britain," *History Workshop,* no. 3 (Spring 1977), pp. 6–72.

6. Thompson, *The Making of the English Working Class,* p. 198.
7. Geoffrey Ingham, *Capitalism Divided? The City and Industry in British Social Development* (London: Macmillan, 1984), p. 40.
8. Ingham, *Capitalism Divided,* pp. 10–41.
9. Barry Supple, "States and Industrialization: Britain and Germany in the Nineteenth Century," in *States and Societies,* ed. David Held et al. (Oxford: Martin Robertson, 1983), p. 173.
10. Ingham, *Capitalism Divided,* pp. 132–33.
11. Dorothy Thompson, *The Chartists* (New York: Pantheon, 1984), p. 11.
12. Dorothy Thompson, *The Chartists,* p. 5.
13. Ralph Miliband, *Capitalist Democracy in Britain* (Oxford: Oxford University Press, 1984), p. 22.
14. Bill Jones and Dennis Kavanagh, *British Politics Today,* 2d ed. (Manchester: Manchester University Press, 1983), p. 1.

2

The Rise and Fall of the Postwar Settlement

Generally, when political scientists refer to the postwar settlement, they are referring to a set of implicit and explicit arrangements, made by representatives of labor and capital under the tutelage of the state, that changed the balance between public and private power in the period after World War II. After 1945, the British state deepened and diversified its responsibilities for the conduct of the economy and the provision of social benefits, as did other Western European states. There were three main reasons for the change.

First, the industrial requirements of reconstruction made greater state intervention necessary to ensure efficient retooling and expansion of the economy to peacetime requirements. Second, the ideological pressures for social change exerted from powerful worker-based parties changed the political mandate that postwar governments faced. Demands to reduce capitalist prerogatives in resource allocation and to expand the working-class share of what society produced were now louder and harder to ignore. Third, a general association between the excesses of free-market capitalism — notably the Great Depression beginning in 1929 — and the causes of World War II led to a nonideological and interclass insistence that governments must act to flatten out the business cycle and ensure that never again would the world suffer a cycle of depression followed by cataclysmic war.

The Rise of the Postwar Settlement

It is noteworthy, however, that state intervention increased in Britain to a significant degree during World War I, although that earlier postwar era cannot be identified as one of political harmony and a negotiated settlement among state, capital, and labor. Even though no coherent industrial policy emerged during World War I, government practices certainly were cast in an interventionist direction; for example, the state took increasing control of a number of industries, including railways, mining, and shipping; it set prices and restricted the flow of capital abroad; and it applied fiscal policy to the task of channeling private resources into production geared to the war effort. "In fact between 1916 and 1918 Britain was forced to evolve a first incomplete and reluctant sketch of the powerful state-economy of the Second World War," notes historian Eric Hobsbawm. "It was dismantled with unseemly haste after 1918 . . . . Nevertheless, nothing could be quite the same again."

The fact of considerable government manipulation of the economy openly contradicted the policy of laissez-faire. When the economic downturn of the 1930s arrived, as Hobsbawm observes, even the most sacred noninterventionist policy had to be sacrificed:

> [T]he most dramatic consequence of the slump was the death of Free Trade. And since Free Trade was the almost religious symbol of the old competitive capitalist society, its end not merely demonstrated . . . publicly that a new era had begun, but encouraged the vast extension of government management. While it lasted, government action was an exception, an individual and regrettable departure from the ideal, which had to be carefully scrutinized and strictly limited. After it had gone, what was the point of measuring it in the homeopathic doses of the past?[1]

Thus, in one crucial way, this wartime experience transformed the British political-economic culture. State intervention would no longer proceed only *negatively*, by the use of legislative enactments and administrative measures to reduce constraints in the operation of a free market. Rather, to a new degree, the British state would conform more closely to the continental practices of *positive* intervention, which involved, among other things, the rationalization of industry through amalgamation of production into large units and regulation of prices, the creation of government cartels, and the application of protectionist duties.

The Politically Regulated Market Economy

With the growing political regulation of the market economy in the interwar years, an underlying theme of the postwar settlement began to take shape in Britain well before World War II. The picture is complicated, however, by consideration of the political repercussions of state involvement in the conduct of World War I. As unemployment skyrocketed at the end of the postwar boom — from 2 percent in 1919–20 to 12.9 percent in 1921[2] — industrial tension erupted in a set of epochal showdowns. A Triple Alliance of powerful unions (railway workers, miners, and transport workers) challenged the government's decision to ignore the recommendation of a royal commission that the coal industry be nationalized. In 1921 the coalition government of Lloyd George invoked emergency powers amid threats of a general strike and won capitulation from the miners. Five years later the general strike of 1926 confirmed both the intensity of class antipathy and the capacity of the state — now deeply enmeshed in industrial management — to wield its power to fragment the trade union movement and resist any trade union agenda for a socialist Britain.

In retrospect, then, the postwar settlement after World War II represents both *continuity* and *discontinuity* with the experiences of the earlier postwar era. After both world wars, the evolutionary trend toward expanded economic governance by the state gathered momentum, but in the second postwar era, the political crisis and class bitterness of the interwar years was averted. What accounts for the change?

In some measure, it seems likely that the severe costs of World War II in material terms were, in part, offset by an unusual social benefit: the sense of common purpose that can be aroused by shared suffering. The end of war brought a period of austerity and outright privation. The winter of 1946–47 brought the worst blizzards and the longest freeze-ups of the century, a condition made all the worse by power cuts (due to coal shortages) during the coldest spells. In a diary entry dated August, 1945, a previously well-to-do journalist barely concealed his irritation and sense of loss at what the war had done to the world he had known.

> The war is over; the conditions of war in some respects continue. You need only make a long railway journey in England to become aware of it. I travelled last Sunday to Newcastle on Tyne. The journey which in peacetime took four hours now took eight and a quarter. No food on the train. No cup of tea to be got at the stops because the queues for this remarkable beverage masquerading as tea were impossibly long. At Newscastle an army artillery captain and I got hold of a truck and wheeled our bags along a platform almost impassable through luggage and merchandise waiting to be shifted. No taxi to be got. My hotel towel is about the size of a pocket handkerchief, the soap tablet is worn to the thinness of paper, my bedsheets are torn.[3]

Under these circumstances of shared victory and common misery, reconstruction may reasonably be expected to take precedence over ideological conflict.

Nevertheless, while this broad culture of reconciliation and determined reconstruction made the postwar settlement possible, economic performance significantly influenced the terms of the compromise and the extent of the social transformation implied by the new institutions of state intervention. It is true that Britain shared with other capitalist democracies during the first two decades of the postwar order a propitious set of economic conditions, which are not likely to be seen again in such a combination: Increasing worker productivity encouraged a solid rate of domestic investment; and at the same time, Britain enjoyed low inflation, virtually full employment, and a steady rate of growth. But how is Britain's economic performance to be judged? What conditions did it set for the evolution of specific ingredients in the postwar settlement?

In comparison with the interwar period, Britain's postwar economic growth rate of 2.8 percent represented a record of solid achievement and provided, if just barely, sufficient expansion to encourage widespread support for increased government expenditure on social welfare. However, lacking the much-vaunted "miracles" of economic growth that occurred elsewhere during the same twenty-year period — 6.7 percent in West Germany, 6.0 percent in Italy, 4.5 percent in France — Britain's room for maneuver was far more circumscribed. Equally significant, the structure of growth reduced trade union influence in the conduct of macroeconomic and social policy, since economic performance followed a now-traditional British pattern: The financial sector bailed out a consistently declining industrial sector.[4] With a short period of Labour government (1945–51) and a far longer stretch of Conservative leadership (1951–64) accompanying an unimpressive record of growth, the political regulation of the market economy in Britain assumed strictly limited proportions. Three crucial sets of policies show the directions and the limits of Britain's postwar settlement: nationalization and the changing balancing of public and private resources; economic management; and the emergence of the welfare state.

The Balance of Public and Private Resources. In Britain, the transition to what economist Andrew Shonfield has termed *modern capitalism* had its most visible expression in the transfer to public ownership of a set of basic industries. During the course of Britain's first postwar (and Labour) government, between 1945 and 1951, coal and steel, gas and electricity supply, and the bulk of the transport sector were reconstituted under public ownership. With approximately one-fifth of productive capacity within the state sector, British experience confirms the general Western European trend of a deepening state intervention into the processes of the market economy. Not only was the state more extensively involved in a tangle of macroeconomic policies to regulate and augment capitalist market forces, but with nationalization, the state also added *market-replacing* functions to its policy instruments. Replacing private entrepreneurs and acting through publicly constituted boards of directors for each industry, the state now hired, bargained with, and fired workers; paid the bills; set pricing policies; and invested, planned, and presided over a vast industrial empire. Capitalist prerogative had been a dealt a stunning blow — or had it?

A closer look at the institutionalization and the operations of the public sector reveals a different picture. In fact, given the woeful condition of many of these basic industries in 1945, some comprehensive state intervention was necessary for reconstruction. Compensation to the displaced stockholders and capitalist owners was high, and the new governing boards were dominated by people who, as a matter of ideology and class position, would work to preserve hierarchies and management prerogative. Many directors were the captains of industry from the days of private ownership. Finally, during the 1970s and especially since Thatcher's government began in 1979, the boards of the nationalized industries have practiced increasingly hard-edged industrial relations strategies to defeat public sector unions in both political and industrial terms. It is clear that nationalization in Britain represents capitalist rationalization far more than it does socialism.

Some militant sections of the working class, buoyed by their contribution to the victory in war and Labour's election at home, demanded a public sector that would democratize industrial life and institutionalize workers' control. The Trades Union Congress (TUC), the association of affiliated trade unions that bargained with government over the terms of the postwar settlement, had more modest, but nevertheless significant, political aims for nationalization: The capitalist structure of authority would remain, but workers' representatives would sit on the governing boards, and workers, more generally, were to be given a voice in the determination of policy.[5] Although a few individuals with significant trade union allegiances were appointed to nationalized industry boards, little in the public sector suggested innovation or change.

Rather, nationalization involved efforts by the state to facilitate the reconstruction of the economy. The state takeover of industries was designed to ensure the cheap and reliable provision of essential fuel supplies and transport, to facilitate a modicum of central coordination and "manpower" and investment planning, and at the same time, to preserve the principles of a capitalist Britain. Nationalization was undertaken, to be sure, as a compromise in response to a triumphant working class demanding change from *its* Labour government, but in its moderate form, nationalization was implemented with the definite acquiesence of business interests and the support of their parliamentary representatives. For one thing, capitalists (who in many cases had been disinvesting since the early interwar period) were quite happy to off-load moribund industries onto the state under extremely favorable terms, and for another, the nationalized industries have operated by principles (for example, "buy dear" from the private sector, and "sell cheap") that give all of the advantages and none of the risk to private capitalists.

It is notable, but not surprising, that in 1946 Winston Churchill, the archetypical establishment figure, endorsed the Coal Industry Nationalization Bill. He observed that a major expression of direct state involvement, through systematic reorganization or outright nationalization, represented the only hope for successful reconstruction of the industry and for provision of the large influx of capital necessary for technological innovation.[6] It seems likely, moreover, that Churchill would not have been displeased with the shifting balance of the compromise that has ensued. Statutory guidelines required publicly owned enterprises to break even on the average of good and bad years until 1967, and stricter targets for profitability were thereafter introduced. The publicly owned enterprises have been "progressively integrated back into the market economy long before the question of their 'privatization' came onto the political agenda" under the Thatcher government.[7]

Nationalization was a visible and highly symbolic expression of the postwar settlement, and the meaning of this ostensibly radical gesture is therefore important to a general understanding of the period. The public ownership and state management of basic industries in Britain represented a consensus process of capitalist rationalization, a market-replacing exercise, which, ironically but deliberately, strengthened private sector capitalism. Responding to the urgent signals of a failing economic base, nationalization arrested more radical movements for democratization and control of the workplace and ensured that the mixed economy would survive fundamentally unaltered.

Economic Management. In contrast to France and West Germany, where central economic ministries have exerted responsibility for overall industrial performance, British Treasury policy during the years of the postwar settlement focused mainly on the control of public expenditure.[8] Whereas the French *Commissariat du Plan* (Planning Commission) could be used as an instrument to shape leading sectors of the economy and enhance competitiveness, the shallow British equivalent, the National Economic Development Council (NEDC), introduced under the Conservatives in 1962, has endured but with little effect on economic performance. From the start, in fact, the NEDC was kept at arm's length by state officials and "planning officials were treated as persons working for an independent institution with which the Government happened to have intimate and friendly relations," observes Shonfield. "They had no right of access to official documents or to the Government's discussions about its own plans. Thus during the early stages of British planning in 1962–63 there was a slightly absurd game of hide-and-seek, with the NEDC trying to make shrewd guesses about the probable trend of public expenditure in different government departments for inclusion in its five-year plan for the economy, and the Treasury for its part refusing to disclose its own detailed calculations of future expenditure figures, but trying to ease the NEDC's problem by dropping helpful hints."[9] The institution was never equipped to influence a program of strategic oversight of the economy, and the scope of NEDC narrowed further after its inception, due to opposing pressures from its business and trade union members, inconsistent government direction, and a general British cultural disinclination for state-sponsored economic planning, which was viewed as an intrusion upon Lockean individualism and the free market.

Instead, state involvement in economic affairs, apart from the role of public enterprises, has been notable mainly in its efforts to fine-tune the economy as a whole by adjusting state revenues and expenditures. Thus, when the economy heated up — production rose, inflation increased, credit expanded, labor markets tightened, and the balance of payments was jeopardized — government would act to cool off the economy by running up a deficit and raising taxation or by triggering a rise in interest rates to tighten credit and attract capital inflows to the country.[10] In this way British economic management focused on state regulation of the market economy through the manipulation of monetary and fiscal policy centered in the Treasury and the Bank of England.

Responding to fluctuations in the business cycle while at the same time enmeshed in a party system that encourages alternation of governments with at least somewhat different policy agendas, state involvement in economic management has been relatively ineffectual: An ongoing stop-go cycle of policies has plagued macroeconomic policy, which has probably reinforced as much as it has reduced the natural fluctuations of the market.

Welfare Policies. The increased cost of social services in Britain, as elsewhere in capitalist Europe, is one of the most dramatic facts of state policy in the twentieth century. Social expenditures for income security, which includes pensions, unemployment, family allowances, and national assistance (or welfare, in American terms); medical care; education; and housing increased from about 4 percent of the gross national product (GNP) in 1910 to some 25 percent of the GNP in 1970. In fact, during the rise of the postwar settlement, welfare provision expanded to a point where it accounted for one-half of all state expenditures.[11]

Table 2.1 The Growth of Social Expenditure in the U.K.

	PERCENTAGE OF GNP AT FACTOR COST							
	1910	1921	1931	1937	1951	1961	1971	1975
All social services	4.2	10.1	12.7	10.9	16.1	17.6	23.8	28.8
Social security		4.7	6.7	5.2	5.3	6.7	8.9	9.5
Welfare } Health		1.1	1.8	1.8	4.5			
Welfare						0.3	0.7	1.1
Health						4.1	5.1	6.0
Education		2.2	2.8	2.6	3.2	4.2	6.5	7.6
Housing		2.1	1.3	1.4	3.1	2.3	2.6	4.6
Infrastructure	0.7	0.6	1.0	1.0	3.6	4.8	6.3	6.8
Industry	1.8	4.5	3.2	2.8	6.9	4.9	6.5	8.3
Justice and law	0.6	0.8	0.8	0.7	0.6	0.8	1.3	1.5
Military	3.5	5.6	2.8	5.0	10.8	7.6	6.6	6.2
Debt interest and other	1.9	7.7	8.2	5.2	6.9	6.3	5.9	6.3
Total state expenditure	12.7	29.4	28.8	25.7	44.9	42.1	50.3	57.9
Total state revenue	11.0	24.4	25.0	23.8	42.7	38.5	48.6	46.6
Borrowing requirement	1.7	5.0	3.8	1.9	2.2	3.6	1.7	11.3

SOURCE Ian Gough, *The Political Economy of the Welfare State* (Macmillan Publishers Ltd. and Humanities Press International, Inc., Atlantic Highlands, N.J.), p. 77.

This growth was modest in comparative terms, however. At the end of the period of the postwar settlement in the early 1970s, the British percentage of its gross domestic product (GDP) devoted to social expenditure was almost exactly average for the nineteen industrialized nations that comprised the Organisation for Economic Cooperation and Development (OECD), and at 18.2 percent, it was below the GDPs of France, West Germany, Italy, and Sweden. Britain's rate of growth in these expenditures was well below the OECD average for education and health, and unexceptional (although above the OECD average) for income maintenance.[12]

Table 2.2 Social Expenditure in the Early 1970s: Major OECD Countries

COUNTRY	INCOME MAINTENANCE		HEALTH		EDUCATION		TOTAL
	% GDP IN EARLY 1970s	ELASTICITY EARLY 1960s–EARLY 1970s	% GDP IN EARLY 1970s	ELASTICITY* EARLY 1960s–EARLY 1970s	%GDP IN EARLY 1970s	ELASTICITY EARLY 1960s–EARLY 1970s	% GDP IN EARLY 1970s
U.K.	7.7	1.68	4.9	1.42	5.6	1.27	18.2
U.S.A.	8.0	1.64	3.1	2.54	6.0	1.30	17.1
Japan	2.8	1.42	3.5	1.86	3.6	0.99	9.9
France	12.4	1.09	5.5	1.72	4.5	1.02	22.4
Germany	12.4	1.09	5.5	2.09	4.2	1.23	22.1
Italy	10.4	1.63	5.3	1.78	4.0	1.31	19.7
Canada	7.3	1.64	5.4	2.03	7.7	1.68	20.4
Sweden	9.3	1.93	7.3	1.85	7.1	1.41	23.7
OECD†	8.7	1.42	4.8	1.75	4.6	1.38	18.1

NOTES *Elasticity* is the ratio of growth rates to growth of GDP between early 1960s and early 1970s.
* Elasticity of current expenditure on health only; all other figures refer to current plus capital expenditure.
† Geometric mean of all OECD countries.
SOURCE Ian Gough, *The Political Economy of the Welfare State* (Macmillan Publishers Ltd. and Humanities Press International, Inc., Atlantic Highlands, NJ), p. 79.

Equally significant, the structure of welfare provision, like that of public ownership, indicates the consistently limited character of British state reforms. The Beveridge Report on Social Insurance and Allied Services, published in 1942, set the tone of the welfare policies to come and included strong patriarchal biases: unemployment and maternity policy encouraged a vision of women as wives and mothers who would enter the labor market only as a consequence of extraordinary circumstances.[13] Moreover, compromises quickly eroded the ideological and transformative potential of the institutions of the welfare state.

A group of public sector employees working in community development projects, state-sponsored efforts to improve services in inner cities, captured the contradictory and limited character of British welfare services:

> As socialists we're always taught that somehow services provided by the state are better than those from the private sector. Better be in the hands of a council than a private landlord; better our NHS [National Health Service] than extortionate private medical insurance schemes — and so on. And this seems to be true, but only up to a point. Somehow what we get is never quite what we asked for. The waiting lists for hospital beds were always too long; gradually charges began to be introduced for this and that. Another example is the promise of the new towns after the war — which made Britain famous for town planning, but were somehow, when it came to it, bleak social deserts to live in. It is not just that state provision is inadequate, under-resourced and on the cheap. The way it is resourced and administered to us doesn't seem to reflect our real needs.

They concluded with a widely shared sentiment: "State provision leaves a bad taste in our mouths."[14]

The Fall of the Postwar Settlement

The weaknesses in welfare provision, like economic management and the nationalization of industries, illustrate the ambiguous character of the postwar settlement in Britain. At the start, with a Labour victory and a postwar social consensus, the postwar settlement involved a fine-tuned compromise among class interests and corresponding political elites; in its denouement, the postwar settlement has involved increasing concessions to a growing number of economic constraints. Two decades of stop-go interventionism sapped the ardor and reduced the influence of the Labour party and labor activists who had hoped for more: A moment of broad consensus and unusual social harmony, viewed in terms of programmatic innovation, was largely squandered. The continued downward spiral of Britain's economic performance would soon, nevertheless, make many look back at this ambiguous period of modest innovation and lost opportunities with increasing wistfulness.

Indeed, Britain's economic decline surely must be one of the longest-playing dramas in the history of modern Western European societies.

But for the brief boom after World War I and Britain's participation in the generalized post–World War II recovery, which began to give way in the late 1960s and which ended with the oil shock of 1973–74, this once-preeminent economic power has followed a fairly continuous trajectory of decline since the 1880s, when *Pax Britannica,* based on free trade and unrivaled naval power, began to lose viability. In the period before World War I, Britain was increasingly challenged in economic and military terms by the United States, Germany, and Japan. By the late 1930s, Britain's productivity was below average, and its share of world trade had declined to 14 percent (still the highest) from an 1870 high of 24 percent.[15] Economists have argued convincingly that by the time two decades of the postwar settlement had passed, Britain had experienced a "structural disequilibrium, whereby the trading position of the manufacturing sector in the world economy continues to deteriorate, in spite of increasing cost and price competitiveness." Deindustrialization, measured in the loss of one million manufacturing jobs between 1968 and 1976, is one sign of the economic scope of this disequilibrium.[16]

Table 2.3 British Proportions of World Trade and Relative Labor Productivity

	PROPORTION OF WORLD TRADE	RELATIVE LABOR PRODUCTIVITY*
1870	24.0	1.63
1890	18.5	1.45
1913	14.1	1.15
1938	14.0	.92

* As compared with the average rate of productivity in the other members of the world economy.

SOURCE Robert O. Keohane, *After Hegemony: Cooperation and Discord in the World Political Economy* (Princeton: Princeton University Press, 1984), p. 36.

From 1973 through 1978, Britain's comparative position weakened as it experienced a meager 1.1 percent annual growth rate, only 45 percent of the OECD average. By 1975, Britain's per capita income exceeded only that of Italy within the OECD. Inflation rose at about twice the OECD average in the mid-1970s and exceeded a 20 percent annual rate for six quarters in a row from the end of 1974 to the beginning of 1976. Unemployment more than doubled, from about 2.6 percent in 1973–74 to 5.7 percent in 1977–78, and manufacturing output in 1978 was still 4 percent below its peak in 1973.[17]

Britain's precipitous decline in virtually every category of macroeconomic performance in the mid-1970s shattered the postwar settlement and had deep, and quite possibly lasting, consequences for British state institutions and a wide range of social forces. In fact, it would be difficult to exaggerate the degree to which the modest achievements of the postwar settlement had required economic growth, or the profound political consequences of the quickened pace of economic deterioration.

Economic decline encouraged the growth of a neofascist movement and resurgence of ethnic nationalism in Scotland and Wales. It forced a growing division between a beleaguered Labour Party and a diminished working-class base, and recast the Conservative Party in uncompromising terms that rejected the assumptions of the welfare state and the mixed economy, which had secured a broad interparty consensus. Decline encouraged a further dealignment of party politics with the arrival of a new centrist Social Democratic Party/Liberal Alliance.

The fall of the postwar settlement had such wide-ranging consequences for British politics because it involved above all a growing incapacity of both Conservative and Labour governments to maintain popular support for core elements in their economic programs. The highly visible failures of the Conservative government of 1970–74 and the Labour government of 1974–79 represent not simply the fall of the postwar settlement nor the rejection of particular policies or leaders. These failures of traditional postwar center-right and center-left alternatives cut much deeper to the core of British politics: They signaled an end of mainstream consensus on the modest social-democratic agenda of full employment, welfare-state policies, and a mixed economy; they further created the opening for Margaret Thatcher and encouraged a quite dramatic and far-reaching shift to the right in Britain's policy agenda.

The Decline of the Postwar Settlement: The Conservative Party Version

Before Thatcher, Conservative leaders in Britain generally had accepted the terms of the postwar settlement. Their traditional belief in a hierarchical society and their traditional concern for the permanent interests of society linked to property made them Conservatives. They were conservatives, too, in their unquestioned "commitment to authoritative leadership as a permanent social necessity"[18] and in their paternalism. But these Conservatives were also modernizers, and they were prepared to apply the new steering capacities of the interventionist state within what may be broadly termed a social-democratic mold.

During the period of political consensus, which ended symbolically with Thatcher's selection as party leader in 1975, the position of these mainstream Conservatives became increasingly difficult. Martin Jacques observed this weakening of the Conservative claim for governance and its implications for the rightward evolution of Conservative Party (or Tory) politics:

> The fifties saw the Conservative Party resume what had been its traditional mantle in post-1918 politics — as the main governing party, inextricably linked with the establishment and the national tradition, albeit on a basis of an acceptance of many of Labour's postwar reforms. Such a role was no longer possible in the same way in the new phase; the old assumptions no longer worked and Labour's modernism to some extent deprived the Tories of the centre ground. In response to this situation the Tory party began to shift to the right.[19]

The Conservatives had a problem associated with the rise of the postwar settlement and exacerbated by its decline: They had been the natural party of government in the age of empire, but, despite their continued frequency in office, they became in a sense politically redundant in the period of the welfare state. Neither the education nor the social perspectives that come with privilege encourage special skills for the negotiation of incomes policies, the management of nationalized industries, and the provision of welfare services. Whatever these Conservative moderates could do in a welfarist mold or in support of public policy in keeping with the postwar settlement, the Labour Party should be able to do better.

Economic decline only made the situation for Conservatives more difficult. As Edward Heath was to find during his premiership between 1970 and 1974, Tory centrism was increasingly incompatible with a political situation that seemed to invite radical responses to increasingly formidable problems. By the 1970s public officials no longer saw the world they understood and could master: It had become a world without economic growth and with growing political discontent. Britain was a fragmenting society, beset by racial antagonisms, the psychological burdens sustained by the erosion of traditional communities, and increasing strains within the multi-nation state as Scotland and Wales pressed for greater national autonomy within the U.K. and violence brought British troops to Northern Ireland. Powerful and new, discontented constituencies, such as youth and racial minorities, and increasingly restive core constituencies struggled to achieve a larger share of fixed social resources. The campaign slogan of the victorious Conservatives in 1959, "Life's better under the Conservatives: don't let Labour ruin it," did not reappear. Economic decline lessened optimism, and besides, the Conservatives' "instrumental appeal to the working class"[20] as the party of prosperity, good government, and sound economic management above class and ideology had dimmed considerably. Heath's failure, therefore, holds special significance, for it signals the decline in fortunes of a preeminent political tradition in Britain.

The failure was all the more noteworthy, given the great hopes for change, Conservative modernization, and new competitiveness that Heath had represented. In 1965 Heath had been elected leader of the party by Conservative members of Parliament only after an energetic campaign. This marked a change in organizational procedure, for previous Conservative leaders had simply emerged, without facing a competitive election. Heath was considered a formidable opponent for his Labour counterpart, Prime Minister Harold Wilson. As one observer noted with approval, "A brand-new candidate, Ted Heath, was now presented as the Tories' answer to Harold Wilson, with the same working-class background and technocratic command."[21] He took leadership of the country after an unprecedented round of consultations with experts from universities, government, and business. The Heath government, in its formation, initiative, and appeal to technocratic acumen, promised no less than "a change so radical, a revolution so quiet and yet so total, that it will go beyond the programme for a parliament."[22] What went wrong?

Heath was the first prime minister to feel the full burden of recession and the force of political opposition from both traditional business allies and resurgent trade union adversaries. Operating in an era marked by the previously unheard-of combination of increased inflation and reduced growth (stagflation), Heath could never transcend the constraints imposed by a closing circle of options. In the end, the economic failures of Heath's program for recovery exacerbated the political tensions that emerged when growth could no longer resolve distributional conflicts.

Upon taking office in 1970, the Heath government immediately reduced taxation in what would now be called a supply-side strategy to enhance savings, increase consumption, and swell entrepreneurial investment. This action manipulated monetary policy in a dash-for-growth strategy, which in the short run meant windfall profits for real estate developers and those involved in banking and finance. The government even allowed Rolls Royce to go under (the policy was subsequently reversed) to underscore the seriousness of its laissez-faire, free-market approach to economic policy.[23] All too soon, however, politics took precedence over political economy.

Conflict and rejection first clouded, and then defeated, the government's plans. Core constituencies (both natural allies and increasingly restive adversaries) rebelled, each in its own characteristic manner: There were strikes by workers and strikes by investors. The new government enjoyed no honeymoon period; it was greeted by a national dock strike, which it met decisively but not effectively. First the government convened a court of inquiry, then it declared a state of emergency and recalled troops from Northern Ireland to ensure order at home. Adding to the growing crisis in authority, 125,000 local authority (municipal) workers went on strike in response to the extremely ill-timed announcement of the government's "N − 1 norm," a policy of paying each group of public sector employees one percent below their previous annual settlement. As would also confound the successive Labour governments in the 1974–79 period, confrontations between government and unions became Heath's undoing.

The Industrial Relations Act, introduced early in the Heath government, represented a strong measure to enhance entrepreneurial efforts by sharply restricting the activities of trade unions. The act required the registration of unions, virtually outlawed the closed shop (a firm that could employ only union members), and held unions liable for compensatory damages that might follow from strike-related breaches of contract. The Trades Union Congress (TUC), the peak association of British trade unions, vehemently opposed the statute. Rather than risk trade union disruption, firms frequently colluded with unions to opt out of the law through the loophole of nonregistration.

With the economic stategy for recovery failing and the Industrial Relations Act rendered largely inoperable, in 1972 Heath inaugurated a widely noted U-turn: The government turned from a free-market and anti-interventionist stance to a more conventional and active approach to political regulation of the market economy. After hiving off (selling to private investors) the chemical and construction engineering divisions of the publicly owned British Steel Corporation, Heath withdrew further plans to privatize parts of the nationalized sector. Reversing the supply-side approach, the government announced a new expansionary phase in fiscal policy in the April, 1972, budget, which called for a £1,200 million increase in public expenditure by 1972. The government reintroduced the National Economic Development Council, the classic British device for tripartite planning among business, labor, and the state. Finally, Heath introduced first voluntary, then statutory, incomes policies (nationally set norms that limited annual wage increases).

In the end, despite Heath's energetic policy innovations and technocratic expertise, neither the confrontations with trade unions nor the fundamental U-turn in policy approach served him well. The government was defeated by a failed economic strategy compounded by poor political judgment. Between July, 1970, and July, 1974, more than 3 million workdays were lost in strikes directed against the Industrial Relations Act, and a further 1.6 million against the incomes policies.[24]

In a confrontation that was to provide a dramatic preview of things to come in Thatcher's Britain, the Heath government and the National Union of Mineworkers (NUM) squared off in a pair of notable clashes. In 1972 the NUM effectively broke the government's N–1 pay policy with a rank-and-file–initiated national strike. Politically determined, emboldened by their recent victory, and angered by the Industrial Relations Act, the mineworkers struck again soon after the Christmas holidays, in January, 1974. Despite the presence of sufficient coal reserves to permit normal industrial and commercial activity, Heath tried to turn the nation against the miners by putting Britain on a three-day work week. Then, using one of the constitutional powers of the prime minister, Heath called an election on a theme of "Who rules the country?" Was it to be the miners or the duly elected Conservative government?

Heath lost the election, but the miners' strike was only the proximate cause. The decline of the postwar settlement and the erosion of the Conservative vision of a mainstream government were the deeper sources of Heath's defeat. The government could not improve Britain's international competitiveness nor solve stagflation. It could not mobilize consent from a restive trade union sector, through either restrictive legislation or incomes policies, nor secure the support of recalcitrant allies.

Perhaps most frustrating for Heath, and most significant with regard to the breakdown of political alliances in the face of economic constraints, was his falling-out with economic elites. As the prime minister told the Institute of Directors in a speech near the end of his government:

> When we came in we were told there weren't sufficient inducements to invest. So we provided the inducements. Then we were told people were scared of balance-of-payments difficulties leading to stop-go. So we floated the pound. Then we were told of fears of inflation, and now we're dealing with that. And still you aren't investing enough![25]

Trapped by a restricted range of economic options, Heath explored the limits of governing strategies within a mainstream Conservative tradition. He experimented with modulated confrontation of the trade unions through the Industrial Relations Act and through statutory incomes agreements. Before the U-turn he emphasized free-market, anti-interventionist approaches, and afterwards, he reverted to traditional British mechanisms for political regulation of market forces. He accepted the terms of the postwar settlement: the welfare state, the mixed economy (of private and public enterprises), and the effort to secure full employment. But recession meant confrontations with trade unions and reduced investment by capitalists. In the end, Heath had little room for successful maneuver, but his failure represented only the first act in a deepening drama of defeat for Britain's tradition of political consensus.

The Decline of the Postwar Settlement: The Labour Party Version

Perhaps no area of public policy has demonstrated the fragility of state power during the period of the postwar settlement more than efforts to introduce political regulation of labor markets. Harold Wilson's Labour government took office in February, 1974, in part because of the Conservative Party's problems with labor — just as Margaret Thatcher would be elected five years later in part because of the strikes that battered the Labour government in the winter of 1978.

The Labour Party planned for a new opportunity for national leadership during the period of often bitter confrontation over Heath's 1972 Industrial Relations Act. Concerning industrial relations policy, Labour hoped to demonstrate to the nation that the contrast between parties was very clear: Conservatives brought industrial strife, while Labour engendered cooperation and harmony. The new Labour strategy, it was hoped, would stabilize the economy by involving the Trades Union Congress in an expanded agenda of shared responsibility for economic and social policy. The Social Contract agreed to by the TUC-Labour Party Liaison Committee in February, 1973, called for wage and price controls "within the context of coherent economic and social strategy — one designed both to overcome the nation's grave economic problems and to provide the basis for co-operation between the trade unions and the Government."[26]

Unfortunately, the pressure of economic exigencies, such as mounting inflation and a substantial run on the pound, quickly removed the more expensive (and, for the TUC, the most attractive) elements of the Social Contract. The promises of expanded social provision were jetisoned, and discussion of industrial and economic democracy (however vague those concepts had been) was shelved indefinitely.[27] After the electoral victory in February, 1974, the new Labour government and the TUC agreed to a formal but voluntary incomes policy. New terms would be bargained for each of four annual phases, with decreasing TUC, trade union, and rank-and-file support. If a Labour government couldn't manage its trade union allies, whom could it govern?

The government's economic and political survival required success in promulgating these incomes policies. As its name implies, the Social

Contract took on considerable normative significance in domestic political debates. Equally important, restraints on incomes and promises of reduced social expenditure had been the government's collatoral to the International Monetary Fund (IMF) in return for a $3.9 billion credit to slow a feverish run on the pound in late 1976. With trade unionists feeling the pinch of two years of wage restraints and the government unable to offer the promised nonwage supplements, by the time of Phase Three the Social Contract had been reduced to an increasingly strained anti-inflationary alliance. The government was severely jeopardized.

Following the sudden resignation of Prime Minister Wilson, James Callaghan was selected as the party's leader by Labour M.P.s and became prime minister in April, 1976. Callaghan was soon facing an open rupture with the trade union movement, and the government was forced to go it alone during Phase Three. Despite a growing number of unofficial work stoppages, there was only one official national strike (by firefighters). The TUC refused to authorize national support for the two-month strike, which was settled within the government's 10 percent norm.

With Phase Four, however, the Social Contract fell apart, and with it, the era of the postwar settlement ended quite abruptly. In a confrontational stance, the government insisted on a 5 percent pay norm for the fourth year of the incomes policy. Affronted, the TUC overwhelmingly rejected any "arbitrary pay limit" at its September, 1978, conference, despite the belief cultivated by Callaghan that the announcement of a general election was only days away. The Labour party itself reconfirmed the labor movement's rejection of Callaghan's policy at its own party conference in October.

Both rank-and-file and official strikes, fueled by a seemingly endless series of sharply escalating pay demands, erupted into a winter of discontent, which battered the government. The catalog of industrial action tells a story in itself. The strike season began with a nine-week shutdown by Ford workers. Thereafter, industrial action was concentrated where it would hurt the government most, in the public sector where the government paid the wages: tanker and lorry (truck) drivers; train drivers; civil servants; local government workers; public utilities workers; ambulance drivers, and health support staff. In its last preelection season, the Labour government failed in its self-proclaimed mission to bring industrial harmony. As David Coates observes, the growing division within the labor movement, between Labour Party and trade union elements, made Thatcher's election possible.

> [I]f the blackcloth [background] to the Labour government's arrival in office in 1974 had been the successful miners' strike against the incomes policies of Edward Heath, the blackcloth to the Government's departure

> in 1979 was a pay revolt of even greater scale. The number of workers involved in strikes in January 1979 was the largest of any month since May 1968, and the number of working days lost the greatest since February 1974, at the height of the three-day week. . . . Four years of wage restraint may have given British capitalism a breathing space in industrial costs, but they gave the Labour Government in the end industrial unrest and electoral defeat.[28]

Throughout the period of the postwar settlement, there was a strange symbiosis between the Labour and Conservative mainstream, a unity of electoral combatants defined by a common acceptance of the terms of Britain's postwar settlement. Ultimately, they were unified also in their defeat; both parties were unable to mobilize support among trade union constituencies at a time when the economic recession substantially reduced the available options. In the end Callaghan did for Labour moderates what Heath did for Tory modernizers: He exhausted the options available within the constraints of consensus government.[29]

The fall of the postwar settlement exposed the growing fragility of the British state in two crucial areas: the mobilization of consent for policies among crucial social groups, such as trade unions or business elites; and the management of the macroeconomy. This process involved an increase in industrial conflict and some fundamental changes in electoral competition. The decline of the postwar settlement moved a more ideological and divisive brand of politics to the fore and, in the end, significantly influenced the institutional basis of British political life.

NOTES

1. E. J. Hobsbawm, *Industry and Empire* (Harmondsworth: Penguin/Pelican, 1983), p. 13.
2. Keith Middlemas, *Politics in Industrial Society: The Experience of the British System Since 1911* (London: Andre Deutsch, 1979), p. 154.
3. Quoted in Arthur Marwick, *British Society Since 1945* (Harmondsworth: Penguin/Pelican, 1982), p. 22.
4. Stephen Bornstein, "States and Unions: From Postwar Settlement to Contemporary Stalemate," in *The State in Capitalist Europe,* ed. Stephen Bornstein et al. (London: George Allen and Unwin, 1984), p. 75.
5. Peter Gourevitch et al., *Unions and Economic Crisis: Britain, West Germany, and Sweden* (London: George Allen and Unwin, 1984), p. 22.
6. Joel Krieger, *Undermining Capitalism: State Ownership and the Di-*

alectic of Control in the British Coal Industry (Princeton: Princeton University Press, 1983), pp. 4, 35–36.

7. Grahame Thompson, "Economic Intervention in the Post-War Economy," in *State and Society in Contemporary Britain,* ed. Gregor McLennon et al. (Cambridge: Polity Press, 1984), p. 91.
8. Peter A. Hall, "Patterns of Economic Policy: An Organizational Approach," in *The State in Capitalist Europe,* ed. Stephen Bornstein et al. (London: George Allen and Unwin, 1984), pp. 34–39.
9. Andrew Shonfield, *Modern Capitalism* (Oxford: Oxford University Press, 1978), p. 152.
10. Thompson, "Economic Intervention," pp. 92–93.
11. Ian Gough, *The Political Economy of the Welfare State* (London: Macmillan, 1979), pp. 76–78.
12. Organisation for Economic Cooperation and Development, *Social Expenditure 1960–1990: Problems of Growth and Control* (Paris: OECD, 1985), pp. 23–29.
13. Elizabeth Wilson, *Women and the Welfare State* (London: Tavistock Publications Limited, 1977), pp. 7–26.
14. Community Development Project, *In and Against the State* (London: CDP, 1979), p. 6.
15. Robert O. Keohane, *After Hegemony: Cooperation and Discord in the World Political Economy* (Princeton: Princeton University Press, 1984), p. 36.
16. Ajit Singh, "U.K. Industry and the World Economy: A Case of De-Industrialization?" in *The Managed Economy: Essays in British Economic Policy and Performance Since 1929,* ed. Charles Feinstein (Oxford: Oxford University Press, 1983), p. 249.
17. Richard E. Caves and Lawrence B. Krause, "Introduction and Summary," in *Britain's Economic Performance,* ed. Richard E. Caves and Lawrence B. Krause (Washington, D.C.: The Brookings Institution, 1980), pp. 2–12.
18. Samuel H. Beer, *Britain Against Itself: The Political Contradictions of Collectivism* (New York: Norton, 1982), p. 175.
19. Martin Jacques, "Thatcherism — The Impasse Broken?" *Marxism Today* (October 1979), pp. 7–8.
20. Andrew Gamble, "The Decline of the Conservative Party," *Marxism Today* (November 1979), p. 7.
21. Anthony Sampson, *The Changing Anatomy of Britain* (New York: Random House, 1982), p. 37.
22. Sampson, *Changing Anatomy,* p. 37.
23. Andrew Glyn and John Harrison, *The British Economic Disaster* (London: Pluto Press, 1980), pp. 72–74.

24. Glyn and Harrison, *British Economic Disaster,* pp. 72–74.
25. Gamble, "Decline," p. 9.
26. TUC-Labour Party Liaison Committee, *Economic Policy and the Cost of Living* [The "Social Contract"] (February, 1973), from Stephen Bornstein, "States and Unions: From Postwar Settlements to Contemporary Stalemate," in *The State in Capitalist Europe,* ed. Bornstein et al. (London: George Allen and Unwin, 1984), p. 88.
27. David Coates, *Labour in Power? A Study of the Labour Government, 1974–1979* (London: Longman, 1980), pp. 11–27, 67–80.
28. Coates, *Labour in Power,* pp. 79–80.
29. This discussion of the transformation of British party politics associated with the decline of the postwar settlement follows from previous work. See: Joel Krieger, *Reagan, Thatcher and the Politics of Decline* (New York: Oxford University Press, 1986), pp. 36–78.

3

British State Institutions

What is most remarkable about Britain's constitutional order is its antiquity and its formal continuity. Much admired for its ability to adapt to dramatically changed circumstances since the Constitutional Settlement of 1688, the British constitution antedates the first written constitution — the U.S. Constitution — by one hundred years. Actually, the commonplace characterization of the British constitution as unwritten is an appealing simplification, since the constitution, in fact, includes four elements: *statutory law,* mainly acts of Parliament; *common law,* judicial decisions and rules of custom (such as parliamentary sovereignty and royal prerogative); *convention,* widely agreed rules that govern conduct by political elites but are not enforceable by law (for example, the notion of the collective responsibility of all cabinet members for any action of the government); and *works of authority,* books that address issues of constitutionality and express generally accepted interpretations of constitutional conventions. Clearly, the British constitution is at least partly written, but it is not codified nor constituted in one document.[1]

⽊ The Principles of British Government

Despite the longevity of its constitutional tradition, Britain remains more open, constitutionally, than any of the other countries we consider. Lacking a constitution or, like West Germany, a basic law, Britain has no fixed set of principles that have special status above ordinary law or that require special procedures for alteration.[2] The structure and principles of government, in many areas, have been taken as authoritative for so long that appeal to the constitution, even the unwritten parts based on rules of custom, has enormous cultural force. Convention, rather than law or American-style checks and balances, typically constrains state officials from overstepping generally agreed boundaries and prevents particular state institutions from achieving an undue concentration of power. For example, after a general election, the queen, whatever her likes or dislikes for the individual or her political preferences, will certainly invite the leader of the victorious party to form a government. Similarly, that leader (now serving as prime minister) will surely ask the queen to dissolve Parliament within five years, thereby introducing a new general election. Neither activity is required by statute nor specified in a written constitutional document, but no one in Britain harbors the least doubt that governments will be formed and parliaments dissolved as required by the constitution, that is, by binding custom.

Nevertheless, the absence of a legally sanctified document of binding authority means that rules of conduct are less clear when a condition lacks sufficient precedent. For example, if no party is quite victorious after a general election — if none can assure a majority in the House of Commons — the queen would have considerable latitude in appointing a prime minister. Must she first ask the leader of the party that won the most votes, or plurality, to try to form a government? Or may she consult others with the aim of constituting a coalition government? The fluid situation invites unusual sovereign discretion, for the queen must act without advice of ministers (since there is no government). It may seem curious that such a venerable constitution is also vulnerable in such a basic matter as the formation of a government. Yet, given the current dealignment of the electorate and the fragmentation of support for political parties, the possibility of a genuine constitutional conundrum at the time of the next general election cannot necessarily be ruled out.

Absolute principles of British government, therefore, are few. First, by contrast to the federal systems of West Germany or the United States, Britain is a unitary state: Parliament dominates all other legislative bodies, including territorial assemblies like Stormont. Second, sovereignty rests with the Queen-in-Parliament (the formal term for Parliament), for even though Britain is a constitutional monarchy in that the executive powers of the head of state pass to the hereditary Crown, nearly all these powers must be exercised through officers selected and bound by convention and law. Third, Britain operates within a system of fusion of powers at the national level: Parliament is the supreme legislative, executive, and judicial authority and is comprised of the monarch as well as the House of Commons and the House of Lords. The fusion of legislature and executive is also expressed in the function and personnel of the cabinet. Particularly with the evolution of the modern interventionist state, the executive has acquired preeminent significance in British politics.

The Executive

In *The English Constitution,* an authoritative treatise written in 1867, Walter Bagehot presented a significant new theory of British government. By distinguishing the *dignified* from the *efficient* parts of the constitution, Bagehot contrasted the symbols of legitimate authority (the King and the House of Lords) with the exercise of power (the cabinet and Parliament). "Identify the efficient parts and you identify who governs," one set of commentators recently observed. "Identify the dignified parts and you identify how they are enabled to do so."[3] Bagehot made an additional crucial observation about the institutional structure of the British state when he argued, "The relation of Parliament, and especially of the House of Commons, to the executive government is the specific peculiarity of our Constitution." Expressed another way, that relationship discloses "the efficient secret of the English constitution . . . the nearly complete fusion of the executive and legislative powers." How well has Bagehot's analysis of the British constitution, particularly his distinction between dignified and efficient parts, stood the test of time and radically altered circumstance? How significant is the fusion of legislature and executive?

The fusion of legislative and executive powers has grown more important as the processes of the interventionist state have reconstituted the efficient and dignified parts of the British government. The cabinet remains the pivot of the system, for it bridges the legislature and executive. Through the cabinet, the fluid constitutional conventions, notably collective responsibility, can restrict the formally almost uncheckable powers of the executive branch. In forming a government after a successful general election, the leader of the party that can control a majority in the House of Commons selects approximately twenty ministers to constitute the cabinet. Constitutional convention requires that members of the cabinet be selected mainly from the House of Commons, although members of the House of Lords are often included. A combination of prudence and convention dictates ordinarily that cabinet members represent diverse political tendencies within the prime minister's party, and in general, national reputation and party balance take precedence over technical expertise in the affairs of a particular ministry.

"The Cabinet, as a collective body, is responsible for formulating the policy to be placed before Parliament and is also the supreme controlling and directing body of the entire executive branch," notes S. E. Finer. "Its decisions bind all Ministers and other officers in the conduct of their departmental business."[4] In contrast to the French Constitution, which prohibits concurrent membership in the cabinet and either legislative house, British constitutional tradition *requires* overlapping membership between Parliament and cabinet. Unlike the informal status of the U.S. cabinet, its British counterpart enjoys considerable constitutional privilege.

The cabinet system is a complex patchwork of conflicting obligations and potential divisions. Each cabinet member has responsibilities to the *ministry* that he or she serves as chief executive officer; and unless he or she is a member of the House of Lords, a cabinet member is also linked to a *constituency* (as an elected M.P.), to the *party* (as a leader and, often, a member of its executive board), to the *prime minister* (as an appointee who shares in the duties of a plural executive), and to a *political tendency* within the party (as a leading proponent of a particular social vision). From the perspective of the prime minister, the cabinet may appear as a collection of ideological opponents, potential challengers for party leadership, and parochial advocates for ministerial advantages that defy the overall programmatic objectives of the government.

The convention of collective responsibility normally assures the continuity of government by unifying the cabinet on matters of policy, thus making the probability of parliamentary support extremely high. At the same time, collective responsibility may serve to check the power of the prime minister, by subjecting policy initiatives to effective review by the cabinet. All ministers are bound to support any action taken by an agency in the name of the government, whether or not the action was discussed in the cabinet or known to the minister in advance; however, the prime minister must gain the majority approval of the cabinet for a range of significant decisions, for the budget, and for the legislative program.

The convention of collective responsibility, which does not involve checks and balances subject to judicial review, must bear considerable weight in any evaluation of the stability and responsiveness of Britain's constitutional tradition. As with other constitutional conventions, the existence of general rules of conduct is widely agreed, but the status of these rules, their substance, and their application is open to considerable interpretation.

The convention of collective responsibility involves, specifically, three sets of sub-rules: First, loss of support for the government in the House of Commons must result in either collective cabinet resignation or dissolution of Parliament; second, ministers must show unanimous support for governmental policy during debate in the House of Commons and discussion elsewhere; and third, all cabinet proceedings and exchanges of information, counsel, and opinion within the government must be kept confidential.[5]

Of these three sets of rules, the first has clearest constitutional status (but little current force) and will be discussed in the context of the issue of parliamentary sovereignty below. There is considerable scepticism among those who study British political and constitutional traditions concerning the constitutional status of the second and third sets of rules. S. E. Finer considers the unanimity convention to be simply a *practice* of cabinets since roughly 1832: The principle was breached in 1931 during a coalition government and was explicitly waived in 1975 by Prime Minister Wilson concerning Britain's entry into the European Economic Community (EEC). Finer argues, in fact, that "the collective responsibility of the Cabinet for policy has been central to the working of the constitution, but it is a central *usage,* not a convention."[6] The third set of rules has probably the weakest constitutional status and the most limited effect. As Geoffrey Marshall wryly observes: "The confidentiality rules reflect the principle that the proceedings of the cabinet and the relationships between ministers and their advisors are confidential (except when publicised by leaks, briefings or ministerial memoirs)."[7]

Collective responsibility is an informal set of constraints subject to fluid and often strategic interpretation. Cabinet ministers may disagree with government policy with apparent impunity when they are speaking in a nongovernmental capacity, for example, as members of the party's executive at the annual conference. At other times perhaps the threat of dismissal, or banishment to a less-favored ministry, will constrain a cabinet member in debate. Moreover, prime ministers can manipulate the membership of powerful subcommittees (which are often secret even to other members of the cabinet) to make genuine collective responsibility in the full cabinet nearly impossible.

Insofar as collective responsibility is a fluid principle whose meaning is shaped by usage, its interpretation is subject to the discretion of the prime minister. In this sense, collective responsibility becomes a political resource: Will a breach of confidentiality or a public lapse in the unanimity principle by a cabinet minister result in dismissal? In 1969 Wilson declined an opportunity to dismiss James Callaghan from his cabinet, despite Callaghan's public denunciation of projected trade union legislation from his seat on the Labour Party's National Executive Committee. Although Callaghan was Wilson's chief rival, a dismissal would have disrupted the party and weakened the government.[8]

By contrast, Prime Minister Thatcher has been accused of intimidating opponents within the cabinet through the shuffling of cabinet posts and threats of dismissal. She has reduced the variety of opinion represented in the cabinet, and with her eighth cabinet reshuffle since 1979, her most prominent ministerial critic, James Prior, left the government in September, 1984.[9] Where Wilson used discretion in applying the principle of collective responsibility to reconcile opponents and balance the cabinet in ideological and programmatic terms, Thatcher applies the principle and the power of dismissal to the more resolute purpose of consolidating her personal leadership. Thatcher's cabinet, observes Donald Shell, "which she had once referred to as her 'political advisors,' was [by 1984] . . . 'regarded with little greater respect than parliament' while ministers appeared to feel their major responsibility lay upwards to Downing Street rather than outwards to parliament and country."[10] Thatcher's style of government and its constitutional implications will be discussed further in Chapter 5. On balance, cabinet government represents a durable, "can do" formula, and the powers of the prime minister to manipulate the vagaries of cabinet responsibility extend the constitutional powers of the office.

Considered collectively, the executive dominates within Britain's constitutional framework. Its power is expressed *institutionally* in the cabinet and *operationally* in control of legislation and the parliamentary agenda. The processes of the interventionist state have expanded the powers of the executive, which, broadly construed, includes not only the cabinet and prime minister but also the whole range of state bureaucratic and para-public administration of economic and social affairs.

The expansion of the executive in the postwar era has had significant constitutional ramifications. First, neither ministers nor the cabinet at large may be involved significantly in the day-to-day affairs of the bureaucratic state that actually implements policies. Second, as the discussion of the legislature below will indicate, the functions of Parliament have been reduced greatly since the days of Bagehot. In the end, it may be right to distinguish the dignified from the efficient parts of the constitution, but the line may have to be drawn differently: The exercise of power now begins in the cabinet room at 10 Downing Street and extends to a vast network of state and para-public agencies that the cabinet only partly administers or controls.

The Legislature

Legislative proceedings are conducted according to time-honored customs and procedures. A law begins in draft form as a parliamentary bill.

There are private bills that concern matters of individual or local interest, but most bills are public bills sponsored by the government and the most important of these have generally passed through an elaborate consultative process before they reach the floor of the house. Bills are circulated to relevant professional and voluntary associations and issue-oriented pressure groups. In the case of highly significant or contentious legislative proposals, the government will set out "white papers," which are subject to parliamentary debate before the formal introduction of a bill. Sometimes consultative documents, called "green papers," are issued in order to facilitate public debate of proposed legislation that is still in a formative stage. For example, the secretary of state for social services issued a green paper in June, 1985, which set out the government's reasons for proposing significant changes in the social security (income maintenance, family support, housing benefit) program.

To become law, bills must be introduced in the House of Commons and the House of Lords, although approval by the latter is not required. The procedure for passing a public bill is quite complex. Normally, in the House of Commons, the bill is formally read upon introduction (the *first reading*), printed, distributed, debated in general terms, and, after an interval (from a single day to several weeks), given a *second reading*. The bill is then sent to a standing committee for detailed review and is then subjected to a report stage during which new amendments may be introduced. The *third reading* follows; the bill is considered in final form without debate, unless there is a motion by six M.P.s (a fairly common occurrence) that the question "be not put forthwith." Alternatively, the House may vote to limit the time for debate by passing a timetable motion (or "guillotine" as it is called).

After the third reading, a bill passed in the House of Commons follows a parallel path in the House of Lords. There the bill is either accepted without change, amended, or rejected. According to custom, the House of Lords passes, without alteration, bills concerning taxation or budgetary matters, and the Lord's amendments to other bills (which must be approved by the House of Commons) are often technical and editorial, intended to add clarity in wording and precision in administration. Bills concerning finance must be enacted within one month of being sent to the House of Lords, and nonfinancial bills that cannot be agreed between the two houses of Parliament but are passed by the House of Commons can be delayed by the House of Lords (with some exceptions) for up to roughly thirteen months. When a bill passes through all these stages, it is sent to the queen for royal assent, after which it becomes a law and is referred to as an act of Parliament. The royal assent was last refused in 1707.

In constitutional terms, the British government is a system based on parliamentary supremacy (often called parliamentary sovereignty), in that no act of Parliament can lawfully be set aside by any act of the executive or judiciary, nor is any Parliament bound by previous enactment or presumed statutory precedent. In practical terms, however, it is necessary to acknowledge that parliamentary sovereignty and the function of Parliament have been curiously adulterated by the processes of the interventionist state. Is the House of Commons still at the core of the efficient part of the constitution? Is it still the ultimate authority in the operation of government, backed by the ultimate sanction: its capacity to unmake cabinets and, thus, remove governments from office?

Certainly, Parliament is no longer treated with the august bearing such an interpretation would imply. The words of a recent evaluation of the weekly magazine *The Economist,* belie any claim of ultimate authority:

> Britain is the mother of parliaments, and has an ill-shaped, mistreated, brawling brat to prove it. The upper house of parliament has a permanent majority for one party and is chosen by noble birth and self-selection, or by prime ministerial favour; the lower house, supposed to represent the opinion of the nation, does so — at best — by accident, thanks to a distorting electoral system. MPs are underpaid, understaffed, underinformed and work absurd hours.[11]

The House of Commons

The House of Commons, the lower house of Parliament, exercises the main legislative power in Britain. In consort with the two less-active elements of Parliament, the queen and the House of Lords, the House of Commons, or Commons, has three main functions: to pass laws, to provide finance for the state by authorizing taxation, and to review and scrutinize public administration and government policy. As the only elected element in the legislature, the Commons includes at present 650 members of Parliament (M.P.s), who are elected by adult suffrage in single-member constituencies (election districts). It is an anomaly of Britain's imperial past that not only British citizens but also citizens of other Commonwealth* countries who reside in the U.K. (all considered British

* The Commonwealth is a voluntary association of forty-nine independent states, which were formerly British colonies or dependent territories. The Commonwealth includes the older former colonies of Australia, Canada, and New Zealand, whose independence was recognized in the Statute of Westminster of 1931, and newer members that joined upon independence in the postwar period. The *New Commonwealth* began with the independence of India and Pakistan in 1947, and grew with the inclusion of Ghana in 1957, the first African dependency to become self-governing. South Africa ceased to be a member of the Commonwealth in 1961, and Pakistan left the Commonwealth in 1972 (and hence is no longer included in the New Commonwealth).

subjects) as well as citizens of the Irish Republic may vote and may be elected as M.P.s. Of the 650 constituencies, 523 represent England, 38 represent Wales, 72 represent Scotland, and 17 are for Northern Ireland. In 1985, twenty-five M.P.s were women, and there were no black M.P.s.

The preeminence of the executive and the power of party loyalties tend to define the Commons as a supreme debating society. The Commons, whose average of "sitting" days numbers 175 annually, comes alive during party-motivated challenges to the government in debates over legislation and in the routine scrutiny of cabinet members during *question time,* the period from 2:35 P.M. to 3:30 P.M. from Monday through Friday when ministers give oral replies to questions submitted in advance by M.P.s. The vituperation and the flash of rhetorical skills bring drama to the historic chambers, but one crucial element of drama is nearly always missing: The outcome in these debates seldom is in doubt. Deeply ingrained traditions of strict party discipline lessen the significance of legislative debates, and the historical evolution of the Commons has greatly reduced the likelihood that its ultimate authority, to defeat a government, will be invoked.

Table 3.1 The Proportion of Government Bills Approved by Parliament

PARLIAMENT (GOVERNMENT)	BILLS INTRODUCED	APPROVED	PERCENTAGE APPROVED
1945–50 (Labour)	310	307	99.0%
1950–51 (Labour)	99	97	98.0
1951–54[a] (Conservative)	167	158	94.6
1955–59 (Conservative)	229	223	97.4
1959–64 (Conservative)	251	244	97.2
1964–65[a] (Labour)	66	65	98.5
1966–69[a] (Labour)	215	210	97.7
1970–73 (Conservative)	192	189	98.4
1974–79[a] (Labour)	260	263	90.8
Totals	1,688	1,638	96.6

[a] Omits final session of Parliament, interrupted by government calling a general election, voiding all pending bills.

SOURCE Richard Rose, *Politics in England,* 4th ed., p. 91. Copyright © 1986 by Richard Rose. Reprinted by permission of Little Brown and Company.

In the period from 1846 to 1860, an independent Parliament administered defeats to eight successive governments. Six of these occasions forced the resignation of a cabinet, and two led to a general election.[12] Only once since the defeat of Ramsay MacDonald's government in 1924, however, has a government been brought down by a defeat in the Commons. James Callaghan's Labour government was defeated by one vote after the desertion of eleven Scottish National Party M.P.s in March, 1979, over the issue of devolution. Even this case could have been avoided, but the government declined an ailing supporter's offer to be wheeled bedridden to the Commons to register his vote.

The constitutional convention that collective responsibility defines the consequences to the government of a loss in the Commons has lost its applicability. It is no longer certain that a defeat results in cabinet resignation or a dissolution of Parliament. "There seems now a consensus (though there was not ten or fifteen years ago) that even serious defeats on matters of policy or legislative measures need not entail loss of confidence," observed a constitutional scholar in 1985. "This seems to have been the result of a period of smaller government majorities and less internal party stability."[13] As with the dismissal of a cabinet member for a breach of the unanimity rules, the application of the sanctions associated with the loss of a vote in the Commons remains subject to the discretion of the prime minister. The executive has expanded its discretion in questions of confidence in the Commons and has reduced the power of Parliament accordingly.

The House of Lords

The House of Lords, the upper house of Parliament, participates in the legislative function of Parliament within strict constitutional limits. The Parliament Act of 1911 curtailed the veto of the House of Lords, or Lords, to a period of two years for bills passed by the Commons in three successive sessions and abolished the veto over bills dealing with taxation or expenditure. These limitations were extended by the Parliament Act of 1949, which reduced the delaying powers of the Lords from two years to one year for bills passed in two successive sessions of the Commons. In addition to its legislative function, the House of Lords serves as the final court of appeal for civil cases in the whole of Britain and also for criminal cases in England, Wales, and Northern Ireland. In theory, all Lords may participate in the affairs of the house when it functions as a court of appeal, but in practice, judicial business is conducted exclusively by the Lords of Appeal, or law lords.

Membership in the House of Lords is divided into two categories: the *lords spiritual* include the archbishops of Canterbury and York, the bishops of London, Durham, and Winchester, and twenty-one other senior bishops in the Church of England; the *lords temporal* include all hereditary peers, life peers (who are appointed by the Crown on the recommendation of the prime minister), and law lords (who are appointed to assist the house in its judicial duties and who become life peers).

In modern times, the House of Lords has served mainly as a chamber of revision, designed to complement the Commons and provide expertise in redrafting legislation. Since the introduction of life peers in 1959, however, the Lords' activities have greatly increased, and government defeats have generated considerable interest and sometimes compromises. In the interwar period and in the 1950s, Conservative peers rebelled over progressive legislation, as one might expect, but during the Labour government of 1964–70, the Lords sometimes took on a more aggressive posture and in 1968 helped to bring about a narrow defeat of the Rhodesia Sanctions Order, which was intended to block trade with the white rebels who were resisting British efforts to negotiate independence and majority rule.

Table 3.2 Government Defeats in the House of Lords

PARLIAMENT	TOTAL NUMBER OF DIVISIONS	NUMBER OF GOVERNMENT DEFEATS	DEFEATS AS % OF DIVISIONS
1959–64	299	11	3.7
1964–70	273	116	42.5
1970–74	459	26	5.7
1974–79	445	355	79.8
1979–83	725	45	6.2

Source Donald Shell, "The House of Lords and the Thatcher Government," *Parliamentary Affairs,* vol. 38, no. 1 (Winter 1985), p. 17, Oxford University Press.

The Heath government (1970–1974) suffered twenty-six defeats in which the upper house often amended legislation in a *progressive* direction: The Lords improved the rights of immigrants in the 1971 Immigration Bill and amended the 1973 National Health Service Bill to provide free contraceptive services. During the Labour government of 1974–79, the House of Lords was extremely active and used its delaying and amending powers aggressively. Due to the government's very thin majority in Commons (after 1976 it was effectively a minority government, relying on the Liberals and support from nationalist parties), the pressure from the Lords often proved significant. Paradoxically, the Conservative government of Margaret Thatcher has experienced rebellion among Conservative peers, and the House of Lords has taken on great importance as a countervailing power to the government.[14] The surprising relationship between the Lords and the Thatcher government will be considered more fully in Chapter 5.

Parliamentary Sovereignty? It is a sign of the contemporary decline of Parliament that constitutional commentators stress the significance of the Lords. Today, the balance of true sovereign power has shifted toward the executive: "Supposedly, parliament, lords no less than commons, checks and controls the executive. In practice it is the other way around."[15] Indeed, the structure and operation of Parliament preserves governmental authority amid a growing dissolution of party discipline. Even disgruntled backbenchers — M.P.s who are not on the payroll as members of the cabinet or as private secretaries — are disinclined to jeopardize their standing in the party by challenging government leadership. For that matter, opposition M.P.s (particularly those in marginal seats) may not wish to risk forcing the dissolution of Parliament and, subsequently, facing the uncertanties of their own reelection. In addition, the government's strict control of the parliamentary agenda reduces risk. Nearly all bills are offered by the government, none by the opposition as such; fewer than two dozen private members' bills are offered by M.P.s chosen by lottery, and the government routinely permits a free vote of conscience, outside party discipline (and not subject to votes of confidence), on highly controversial issues like capital punishment or women's right to abortion.

Paradoxically, in recent years the chance that prospective government bills will be withdrawn because of backbench opposition has increased, as has the possibility of actual defeats of bills. But the likelihood of wholesale cabinet dismissal or the resignation of the government as a consequence of such reversals has very nearly disappeared. Opposition has become more commmon but less consequential: Neither careers nor governments are often jeopardized. Thus both the constitutional and legislative functions of Parliament are circumscribed: Governments, not parliaments, make the laws and decide the timing for the next general election.

The practical sovereignty of Parliament is thus doubly checked: by its tight symbiosis with the executive agency of the state, which controls its affairs through cabinet prerogatives and party discipline; and by its negligible influence on the many issues of crucial import that are articulated through the "fiscal/commercial constitution" discussed in Chapter 1 or the myriad state bureaucratic and para-public agencies. The power of Parliament, therefore, has been considerably diminshed by the growth of the interventionist state, a process that has had quite the opposite effect on the judiciary.

The Judiciary

For criminal cases in England and Wales, the magistrates' courts are the courts of original jurisdiction for offenses that normally carry penalties of fines not exceeding £2,000 or imprisonment of up to six months. Above the 25,000 magistrates (justices of the peace or JPs) sit the High Court judges and circuit judges of the Crown Court, which has both appellate jurisdiction and original jurisdiction for more serious crimes. Appeal may lead from the Crown Court to the Court of Appeal (Criminal Division) and, under very controlled conditions, to the House of Lords. In Scotland, criminal justice is divided between the district court and the sheriff court, and the High Court of Judiciary remains the highest appeals court.

Civil cases in England and Wales are treated primarily by the county courts, above which stand the High Court, the Court of Appeal (Civil Division) and, in extraordinary cases, the House of Lords. In Scotland, civil cases are brought to the Court of Session, and appeal may likewise be made to the Lords.[16]

The study of the judiciary has remained a neglected area within the field of British politics, and not without some justification. The function of the British judiciary has been far more limited than that of significant continental (French, West German) or U.S. counterparts. Indeed, long before the U.S. Supreme Court used the 1803 decision in *Marbury* v. *Madison* to secure its right to determine the constitutionality of actions by the executive and legislative branches of government, British constitutional doctrine had taken its judiciary in a less activist and ostensibly less controversial direction. The Glorious Revolution (1688) had enshrined the principle of parliamentary sovereignty and, in so doing, effectively depoliticized the courts by limiting their role to the interpretation of statute law and the application of common law. How limited has the role of the courts been in Britain? How have the rise and fall of the postwar settlement and the attendant stresses on British social life influenced the conduct of the judiciary?

Traditionally, parliamentary sovereignty has meant that judicial restrictions on the action of state agencies have been "through the back door," and the exercise of such restrictions has been infrequent and of relatively little importance. By convention, British courts were empowered to apply a common law standard that the exercise of power was contrary to a concept of natural justice. Alternatively, the courts could rule that government action was *ultra vires,* beyond the powers authorized by statute or the appropriate act of Parliament. The rule of common law was applied interpretively, not to bind Parliament directly, but to enforce parliamentary sovereignty through principles of common law, a process that indirectly permitted limited review of executive acts. The courts have no power to judge the constitutionality of legislative acts.[17]

In recent decades, however, a more assertive and controversial judiciary has emerged as part of the general dynamic of postwar British politics. First, a more activist bench developed in the 1960s, as the extent and diversity of state intervention pushed the courts to invoke common law precepts in order to determine if the executive had intruded too far on individual liberties. Second, the erosion of the postwar settlement politicized the judiciary, as powerful interests pulled the courts into highly contested battles over the conduct of public policy concerning the rights of local councils, the role of police and trade unions in industrial disputes, and the activities of police in urban riots. Jurists have also participated in the wider political debate outside of court, as when they have headed royal commissions on the conduct of industrial relations, the struggle in Northern Ireland, and riots in Britain's inner cities.[18] Some are concerned that governments have used judges in this way to secure partisan ends, displace criticism, and weaken traditions of parliamentary scrutiny.

Another kind of activism has been forced on British courts by the U.K.'s extranational entanglements. Parliament passed the European Communities Act in 1972, to seal Britain's entry into the EEC, with the provision that existing European Community law be binding on the United Kingdom. The act specifies that British courts must adjudicate any disputes of interpretation that arise from relevant treaties. Also, British acceptance of the enabling treaties of the EEC means that cases that reach the House of Lords must be referred to the Court of Justice of the European Communities for final ruling. As a result, British courts may be forced to involve themselves in what could amount to the conduct of foreign affairs and, moreover, to look to extranational bodies for principles that take precedence over previous parliamentary enactments.[19]

The fact that newly activist and politicized courts are increasingly called into the breach when the normal interplay of party, group, and institutional politics cannot resolve contemporary disputes raises serious questions about British democracy. Should unelected officials, as are all senior judges, be granted such a crucial role in resolving disputes among interests in society and, indirectly, in social and economic policy formation? Moreover, does the strong homogeneity of the judges' social background, economic circumstances, race, gender, generation, and political perspective disqualify them for the task of fine-tuning the balances of power in society or articulating the compromises between capitalism and democracy with fairness and understanding? As John Dearlove and Peter Saunders noted in 1984:

> [J]udges come from a particular class; stay in that class (in 1981, High Court judges were paid £32,000); and by and large have the social and political views characteristic of that class. Inevitably a body of elderly upper-middle-class men who have lived unadventurous lives tend to be old-fashioned and conservative in their views and out of step with social, cultural and ethical change, for they have no firsthand knowledge of how the great majority of people live their lives.[20]

Trained and practiced in a legal profession from another era and with a different sensibility, British judges may not be the best suited to the whole range of extralegal tasks they have been assigned. This problem is becoming increasingly significant as the government's search for politically safe and insulated mechanisms for conflict resolution alters the historical function of the judiciary.

Local Government

Throughout most of the postwar period, local government has received very little attention as a subject for study, as a source of political controversy, or as a nexus of public policy. Historically, with policy-making powers concentrated largely in Parliament and in the state's administrative centers in London, Britain has never developed the "well-defined organizational links to lower-level government" typical of France or West Germany.[21]

In some measure, national politics within a multi-nation state has absorbed the administrative agenda of federal issues. Thus, in the 1970s the question of the devolution of power to Scotland and Wales and, of course, the urgency of the struggle in Northern Ireland tended to monopolize the limited public agenda in Britain for local challenges to central authority.

Local politics is largely contained within national party competition and programmatic debate. Until the 1970s, *urban politics* was not seen as a distinct milieu of social and political forces nor as an academic subdiscipline in political science. While U.S. studies of urban/local politics became the main arena for broad debates over the meaning of power and class with the community power debate of the 1950s and 1960s, the British approach to local politics has been narrower. Political processes in cities and towns, as the subjects for academic study and as the arena of real world politics, have been explained predominantly by reference to the interplay of local elites, who were insulated from citizen pressures by nationally focused political choice, frequent one-party local control, and the professionalism of council staffs.[22]

Since there is no federal structure within the British political framework, no powers devolve to states (as in the United States) or Laender (as in West Germany). Therefore, local council government retains the potential for great importance within the constitutional scheme. From a place of apparent irrelevance in the 1950s and 1960s, local government gained significance in the 1970s. For example, an administrative reorganization of the National Health Service gave local councils greater participation in implementing policies for health care and medical provision. Also, in the early 1980s councils began to pursue experimental and often contrasting policies: Conservative councils introduced the practice of contracting out (and thereby privatizing) services to private enterprise; Labour councils, in contrast, attempted a range of socialist or progressive initiatives, including the promotion of local job opportunities, the creation of nuclear-free zones, the reduction of fares for public transportation, and the funding of community groups.[23]

A growing struggle between left-wing Labour councils and a right-wing national administration that is bent on significant reductions of welfare provision and firm budgetary administration has pushed local councils to the forefront of British political debate. Riots in a host of British cities in 1981 and 1985, and the much-vaunted Battle for London—between Ken Livingstone, leader of the Greater London Council (GLC), and Prime Minister Thatcher—have galvanized some of the most hard-edged debates about class and democracy in recent British history. Today, local government has been politicized as never before, a strong indication of the contemporary transition in British politics. We will return to this theme in Chapter 5.

Para-Public Agencies and the Policy Process

By contrast, public administration at the national level displays considerable continuity with the past, despite the proliferation of new governmental forms and administrative processes. With the development of the interventionist state of the postwar period, British public administration extended beyond the traditional focus on finance, foreign affairs, and problems of law and order. Public administration, which includes both the activity of public servants and the structure of executive government through which their activities are conducted, has increased in scope and complexity during the twentieth century. The number of public servants has increased from 3.6 percent of the employed population in 1891 to some 30 percent in 1980. Similarly, the part of the gross national product consumed by public administration grew from less than 15 percent at the turn of the century to roughly 50 percent in the late 1970s. Of the 7.4 million people employed in the public sector in 1980, only half worked for the civil service (central government) or local authorities; the other half included those employed in public corporations (e.g., the British Broadcasting Corporation, the National Enterprise Board, or the Central Electricity Board), the National Health Service, or nondepartmental public bodies (e.g., the Arts Council).[24] In 1984–85, total public expenditure in the U.K. was £125,503 million, of which £32,127 million was expenditure by local authorities.[25]

With the increased scope of executive decision making came new complexity. New institutional arrangements meant that the processes of public administration might have far-reaching consequences for the political directions of state policy. In Britain, however, the changes wrought by the new institutions of the public sector have been more significant in form than in substance.

"In every democratic state the development of the welfare state poses a difficult choice between sustaining existing political institutions and adapting them to a more complex policy environment," observes political scientist Douglas E. Ashford. "If this choice seems less significant within the British political system, it is because British leaders and society accepted the welfare state without encountering severe political conflict and without being forced to reconsider key political relationships at the pinnacle of the policy-making process."[26] Curiously, as a consequence of the compromises structured into the policy-making processes of the interventionist state, the British have outdone the French in following that old aphorism: "The more things change, the more things stay the same."

Thus, throughout the rise and fall of the postwar settlement, the policy process remained firmly embedded within a two-party tradition of alternating governments and until the age of Thatcher, the range of policy outcomes remained fixed within a broad welfare-state and mixed economy consensus. On the one hand, the processes of state interventionism encouraged the transfer of a growing set of executive functions to a new generation of quasi-nongovernmental organizations (QUAN-

GOs), such as the following regulatory agencies: industrial tribunals, which consider claims of unfair dismissal, and pay discrimination on gender or racial lines; other tribunals, which review rent increases, social welfare benefits appeals, decisions concerning immigration, etc.; single-purpose executive bodies, such as the Hops Marketing Board; and advisory bodies, such as the Advisory Committee on Pesticides.[27] On the other hand, while broad programmatic consensus persisted, there was little firm evidence that QUANGOs operated much differently in substance from first-generation public corporations, the boards of nationalized industries, for example, or from traditional executive bureaucracies staffed by civil servants.

QUANGOs should not be viewed as an element apart from the ongoing evolution of the interventionist state but, rather, as a part of the complex and fluid dynamic of class forces, party politics, and the epochal drama of the rise and fall of the postwar settlement. Like other institutions of public administration, QUANGOs must be viewed within the context of diverse interests pursuing their claims; the pressure of the labor movement and business elites; and the strategies that parties adopt in elections and, thereafter, use to mobilize consent for their legislative and broader political agendas.

We now turn in Chapter 4 to a consideration of these broad social and political forces and their implications for contemporary British politics.

NOTES

1. Philip Norton, *The Constitution in Flux* (Oxford: Basil Blackwell, 1984), pp. 1–39.
2. S.E. Finer, *Five Constitutions* (Atlantic Highlands, NJ: Humanities Press, 1979), p. 34.
3. John Dearlove and Peter Saunders, *Introduction to British Politics* (Cambridge: Polity Press, 1984), p. 21.
4. Finer, *Five Constitutions,* p. 52.
5. Geoffrey Marshall, "What are Constitutional Conventions?" *Parliamentary Affairs,* vol. 38, no. 1 (Winter 1985), p. 34.
6. Finer, *Five Constitutions,* p. 54.
7. Marshall, "Constitutional Conventions," p. 34.
8. R.K. Alderman and J.A. Cross, "The Reluctant Knife: Reflections on the Prime Minister's Power of Dismissal," *Parliamentary Affairs,* vol. 38, no. 4 (Autumn 1985), p. 391.
9. Donald R. Shell, "The British Constitution in 1984," *Parliamentary Affairs,* vol. 38, no. 2 (Spring 1985), p. 131.

10. Shell, "British Constitution," p. 131.
11. *The Economist,* November 5, 1985, p. 64.
12. Samuel H. Beer, *The British Political System* (New York: Random House, 1973), pp. 95–96.
13. Marshall, "Constitutional Conventions," p. 34.
14. Donald R. Shell, "The House of Lords and the Thatcher Government, *Parliamentary Affairs,* vol. 38, no. 1 (Winter 1985), pp. 16–19.
15. *The Economist,* November 5, 1983, p. 64.
16. See: Finer, *Five Constitutions,* pp. 70–71.
17. Norton, *Constitution in Flux,* pp. 134–35.
18. Dearlove and Saunders, *British Politics,* p. 133.
19. Norton, *Constitution in Flux,* p. 143.
20. Dearlove and Saunders, *British Politics,* p. 137.
21. Douglas E. Ashford, *Policy and Politics in Britain: The Limits of Consensus* (Philadelphia: Temple University Press, 1981), p. 167.
22. Patrick Dunleavy, "Analysing British Politics," in *Developments in British Politics,* ed. Henry Drucker et al. (London: Macmillan, 1984), p. 284.
23. John Gyford, *Local Politics in Britain* (London: Croom Helm, 1984), p. 9.
24. John Greenwood and David Wilson, *Public Administration in Britain* (London: George Allen and Unwin, 1984), pp. 4–12.
25. Central Statistical Office, *Social Trends,* ed. Deo Ramprakash (London: HMSO, 1985), p. 101.
26. Ashford, *Policy and Politics,* p. 54.
27. See: Greenwood and Wilson, *Public Administration,* pp. 163–174.

4

Social and Political Forces

Before the age of Thatcher signaled a dramatic rightward shift in Britain's policy agenda, a broad postwar settlement consensus acted to constrain the rush of political forces that, with the economic downturn of the 1970s, would emerge to fragment British political life. Until then, as Samuel H. Beer once observed, "the Conservatives have been regarded as the party that has no ideas but which can govern."[1] One might add that Labour was a party with deeply felt ideas but which nevertheless governed much like the Conservatives.

Although the institutional changes of the welfare state are ideologically associated with social democracy in Western Europe generally and with the 1945–51 Labour government in Britain, both cross-party and interclass consensus were a crucial part of the postwar settlement. The Conservative Party of R.A. Butler in the early 1950s and Harold Macmillan in the early 1960s neither attacked the institutions of welfare provision, which had grown dramatically during the Labour government of Clement Atlee (1945–51), nor abandoned the crucial postwar-settlement principle of full employment, despite the mounting pressures of recession and unemployment. In marked contrast to Thatcher's macroeconomic strategies, which have permitted a rise in unemployment to 13.2 percent in March, 1986, the Macmillan government felt that it had violated a full employment commitment when efforts to lower the inflation rate through monetary policy at the height of the 1958 recession contributed to a 2.8 percent unemployment rate in early 1959. It is important also to note that the National Economic Development Council (NEDC), the classic British institution for the political regulation of market forces and economic planning, was inaugurated by the Conservative party under Macmillan.

Traditional Tories are clearly committed to the terms of the postwar settlement: expanded welfare provision; state intervention to neutralize the consequences of unchecked market forces; and consistent government efforts to secure full employment. In fact, the commitment of consensus-oriented Conservatives (Tory modernizers) and mainstream Labour alike to a common road of mild social democratic reforms is revealed in the proliferation of cross-party labels: *Butskellism,* combining the name of the leading Conservative economic voice R.A. Butler with his Labour counterpart Hugh Gaitskell; and the less common *MacWilsonism,* which likewise combines the names of Harold Macmillan and Harold Wilson. This period, from the late 1940s to the mid-1970s, represents the high-water mark of interparty consensus, the broad acceptance of postwar-settlement goals, and the pervasiveness of a welfarist ethos.[2]

Viewed against this backdrop, the 1970s appear as a crucial turning point, a period in which a long trajectory of economic decline (viewed in comparative international terms) finally led to actual economic reversals in the standard of living of many Britons. As a consequence, economic strain occasioned significant political fragmentation: dealignment in party politics; the intrusion of new social movements that would shake up electoral politics and challenge basic tenets of British political culture; and the reconstruction of traditional group loyalties, which had oriented British party politics for more than half a century and had framed the class-based substratum of politics from the age of the Industrial Revolution. How did the institutions of British politics and society attempt to control these new issues and contain powerful new causes? How did these new social forces, in turn, influence the evolution of British state institutions? The answers to these questions provide the basis for understanding the unexpected rise of a new Tory variant, the conservatism of Margaret Thatcher, which intentionally shatters the Butskellite consensus and redefines the terms of the historic compromise between capitalism and democracy. These questions are crucial not only to an understanding of the evolution of postwar British politics but also to an appreciation of British politics in transition. It is, therefore, to the panorama of social forces in the aftermath of the 1973 recession that we now turn.

The Party System

National party competition in Britain, as elsewhere in Western Europe, changed considerably once parties that were linked directly to the interests of working people began to compete with parties of order and business.

Parties like the prewar German Social Democratic Party and the British Labour Party began to fulfill the function of political integration, by making "groups and their members previously outside the official political fold full-fledged participants in the political process."[3] In this task, acting as what political scientist Otto Kirchheimer calls a "class-mass" party, the Labour party was very successful, integrating working-class voters into the mainstream of party politics and thus stabilizing the political order. By the interwar years the expansion of political representation and the universalization of the adult franchise set in place the conditions for a new balance between capitalism and democracy. In general, citizenship had expanded from an eighteenth-century basis in *civil rights* (individual freedoms and legal protections) and beyond the nineteenth-century norms of *political rights* (participation in the exercise of power, which involved initially the right to vote and subsequently the availability of a party or parties that represented nonelite interests). Twentieth-century citizenship in Britain as elsewhere also included *social rights* (provisions for a modicum of economic welfare and security, which reduced the natural pattern of social inequality in a capitalist society).[4]

The Labour Party

Both the emergence of the Labour Party to advance working class political representation and to further specific trade unionist demands, and its subsequent efforts to gain middle-class respectability as a party of government, have had crucial consequences for the evolution of the British party system. After a period of trade union militancy from 1889 to 1891 was met by a series of legal counterattacks and violent strike-breaking activities, trade unions inaugurated a Labour Representation Committee (LRC) in 1900. Six years later, the LRC, which then consisted of a small number of M.P.s and a group of affiliated organizations (mainly unions), became the Labour Party. In the years preceding World War I, the party expanded its trade union affiliation but progressed only weakly in electoral terms.

In 1912 the German Social Democratic Party polled over 4 million votes, and in 1910 the French socialists gained over one million votes, but in the general election 1910, the British Labour party secured but 372,000 votes (7.1 percent).[5] The radicalizing effects of the war and the expansion of the franchise in 1918, broadened the Labour Party support to 22.2 percent in 1918 and turned its program from the defense of trade union rights to explicitly socialist appeals.

The Labour Party landslide 1945 victory demonstrated at once a modernization of the British party system and a significant democratic challenge to capitalist Britain. The famous Clause Four of its party constitution, introduced in 1918, slightly amended in 1929, and still printed on each membership card, states a classic socialist aim:

> To secure for the workers by hand or by brain the full fruits of their industry and the most equitable distribution thereof that may be possible upon the basis of the common ownership of the means of production, distribution and exchange, and the best obtainable system of popular administration and control of each industry or service.

Representing nonelite interests, and programmatically and financially linked to the trade union movement directly and to a broader range of welfarist and genuinely socialist concerns indirectly, the Labour Party had now taken its place squarely within the competitive party system. Full Labour Party integration into the party system meant a significant measure of nonelite political integration. At the same time, the active presence of the Labour Party ensured that the policy agenda would include claims for redistributive welfare measures, further nationalization of industry, and an educational system geared to the reduction of social inequalities.

Thus, changes in the party system contributed to an important transition in the capitalism-democracy compromise. Britain moved towards what T.H. Marshall calls *class abatement* through welfare provisions designed to reduce the material inequalities and social costs of capitalism and class. Democracy expanded beyond the exchange of political elites to include mass participation in the political system (within narrow representative structures). Changes in party politics encouraged the smooth working of a postwar-settlement capitalism based on postwar economic growth. Put simply, this new postwar-settlement package was superimposed upon a stable, preexisting structure of party competition.

The Liberal Party, the Social Democratic Party, and the Alliance

Since 1945 and until the end of the politics of growth, the British party system has had a set appearance. The Labour Party, which emerged in 1906, and the Conservative Party, with roots going back to the eighteenth century, have alternated governments routinely throughout the postwar period. The Liberal Party, which last formed its own government between 1906 and 1916, foundered as a nonrival third party until its recent alliance with the Social Democratic Party (SDP), which was formed in 1981.

Since the 1920s, the Liberal Party has been the main third force at the center of British politics, serving as a moderating influence to the Labour and Conservative parties. When the two-party Butskellite consensus dominated British politics, the role of the Liberal party as a centrist counterforce became largely redundant. Its electoral fortunes reflected this situation, as it reached its lowest point of popularity with 3 percent of the national vote in 1951 and 1955.

The more confrontational climate of the 1970s enhanced the Liberal appeal, to some degree. When Conservative Prime Minister Heath challenged the miners during the general election of February, 1974, the Liberals received 20 percent of the vote. They also played a significant political role in the 1977–78 period of the Lib/Lab Pact, when they were needed by the Labour government to maintain a majority in the Commons. With support for the party heavily down as a consequence of headlines concerning the involvement of Jeremy Thorpe (party leader until May, 1976) with a male model, the pact inaugurated by Prime Minister Callaghan and the new Liberal leader, David Steel, brought the party new prestige. For the first time since 1931, a government explicitly depended on an outside party for its survival.[6] The Liberals were once again marginalized by a firm Conservative victory in May, 1979, and only returned to a position of some importance as a result of a quite dramatic development: the launching of the Social Democratic Party in 1981.

The polarization of British politics in the late 1970s created a favorable climate for the emergence of a new centrist party from a divided Labour Party. Disillusionment with the rightist slide of the Callaghan government, signified by the 1976 appeal to the International Monetary Fund, the increasingly narrow definition of the Social Contract discussed in Chapter 2, and the reduction of welfare expenditures, resulted in post-1979 attacks on the 1974–79 government. The party was increasingly divided into at least three wings: a right wing, which defended the Callaghan government and saw the party's future in the direction of the electoral center; a left wing, which wanted more rank-and-file and trade unionist (rather than M.P.) dominance, a withdrawal from the EEC, and an alternative economic strategy with a populist and socialist cast; and a center-left wing, which sought to reconcile traditional Labourism with checks on trade union influence within the party and support, broadly speaking, for a postwar-settlement program. In 1980, the Labour Party approved a series of constitutional changes, which failed to resolve the increasingly intense disagreements over the balance of trade union versus M.P. power in party affairs. A May conference at Wembley approved a set of policy statements in sharp contrast to the Callaghan government's policies and made clear that the party was moving toward a nonnuclear defense policy and a call for British withdrawal from the EEC.[7]

Quite a different withdrawal occurred with the formal launching of the Social Democratic Party on March 26, 1981, under the leadership of a set of prominent former Labour ministers (the British "Gang of Four") and, by the end of 1981, a complement of twenty-seven M.P.s. Since its formation, the SDP has become highly significant in political, electoral, and possibly constitutional terms. Politically, particularly after the sound defeat of Labour in the 1983 general election, the SDP has helped foster a centrist realignment in Labour ranks and, more generally, among anti-Thatcher forces. Electorally, the SDP/Liberal Alliance has shown considerable strength. The Alliance, which operates by a 1981 agreement to contest elections together, came in second in five out of six by-elections (elections for vacated seats in the Commons) in 1984, won the sixth, and scored high in opinion polls, which, early in 1986, indicated a 34 percent share, for a close second-place ranking behind Labour.

The Alliance may also prove significant in constitutional terms. "The basic idea of responsible government, with a clearly defined group of ministers drawn from a single party, collectively responsible for all government actions, has depended upon the two-party system," notes Donald R. Shell. "The reasonably regular alternation of those two parties in office has been widely viewed as instrumental in maintaining a consensus about the basic rules according to which politics was carried out and more than this, a degree of consensus about policies pursued."[8] The absence of a binding constitutional document underscores the importance of a stable party system, and the conventions of collective responsibility require governmental support in Commons. The growth of a strong third force in the form of the Alliance raises the spectre of a *hung Parliament* (one in which no party can control a majority) and introduces the possibility of constitutional uncertainty in the formation of a government.

The Conservative Party

There is far less uncertainty about the historical role of the Conservative Party. Its pragmatism and flexibility have made it one of the most successful center-right (or at present right-wing) parties in Western Europe. In contrast to the conservative parties in Italy, France, and West Germany, it has remained free of both religious overtones and association with fascism during World War II. As a result, the Conservative Party entered the postwar period without serious impediments to its role as a modern party that could operate within a political context set by the postwar settlement. Although the associations of the Conservative Party with the economic and social elite are unmistakable, it is also true that Conservatives in Britain are associated historically with the birth of the modern welfare state during the government of Benjamin Disraeli (1874–80). The creation of a "long-lasting alliance between an upper-class leadership and a lower-class following"[9] has made possible Conservative Party dominance in modern British politics and guaranteed for the Conservatives electoral support from about one-third of the working class throughout the postwar period.

Thus, the decline of the Conservative Party version of the postwar settlement discussed in Chapter 2 and the advent of Thatcherism are watershed developments in British political history. During the Conservative government of Edward Heath (1970–74), the Butskellite consensus on mixed-economy welfarism was broken, as stagflation and Heath's inability to mobilize support from business allies or secure consent from trade unions forced him into a celebrated policy U-turn. Heath's failure and vacillation opened the door for a radically new Conservative agenda.

Thatcher's government is the first to explicitly reject the principles of the postwar settlement. Its highly ideological stance on the state's economic management role, its assault on trade union rights, its program to privatize significant parts of the public sector, and its controversial treatment of issues of race and nationality have divided the Conservative Party and made it a far more ideological party than ever before. Today, the party is split between mainstream Conservative modernizers within a Butskellite mold (called "wets") and the right-wing core of Thatcher's support.

Minor Parties

The party competition also includes a set of ethnic/nationalist parties with firm regional ties, notably the Scottish National Party (SNP), which dates from 1934; the Welsh-based nationalist equivalent, the Plaid Cymru, founded in 1925; and a range of parties based in Northern Ireland with denominational and Irish nationalist or pro-English (unionist) appeal—currently, the Ulster Unionist, Democratic Unionist, Ulster Popular Unionist, Social Democratic and Labour, and Sinn Fein parties. In addition, in the 1983 general election, the National Front Party, Ecology Party, and the British National Party each ran more than fifty candidates for Parliament. As we shall see, the decade of dealignment of the 1970s witnessed a marked increase in the electoral significance of a whole range of minor parties.

Electoral Behavior

Until the erosion of the postwar settlement, it was right to stress continuity and stability in an analysis of British electoral behavior. One could expect in Britain's party system and electoral behavior the alternation of Labour and Conservative governments with a Butskellite predisposition and within a highly predictable two-party system. As with other elements of British political life, however, the end of the politics of growth unsettled the placid appearance of party competition. In the 1970s, at least for a time, electoral loyalty to the dominant Labour and Conservative parties declined as a new group of parties (ethnic/nationalist parties, such as the SNP and Plaid Cymru) gained support. Meanwhile, new parties, particularly the National Front, influenced the terms of political debate and, quite possibly, both the electoral strategies of major parties and the behavior of the electorate.

A complex process, which had been underway throughout the evolution of the postwar interventionist state, would lead in the 1970s to a modest shake-up of the party system and to considerable uncertainty in the 1980s. In a sense, the process was a direct offshoot of the political integration of the working class through the Labour Party. This very process of integration through political parties can backfire, however, since constituencies that are brought inside the political and party systems, unionized workers, for example, may become dissatisfied with the performance of their affiliated party. By the mid-1970s, labor movement activists increasingly blamed the Labour Party for the government's inability to deliver the higher wages and expanded welfare provision that they had come to expect during the two decades of postwar growth.

At the same time, modernization of the economy led to the decomposition and occupational segmentation of the working class. A unitary blue-collar, or manual, working class with natural ties to the Labour Party was replaced by a variety of working people, from state and service-sector employees to those employed in traditional manufacturing industries, with diverse occupational aims, levels of compensation, life expectations, and political preferences. In response to the changing political map, with fewer voters who could be relied upon to cast reliable class-loyalty votes, parties accordingly reduced their own class identification. As Kirchheimer put it, "catch-all" parties replaced "class-mass parties." Hard programmatic differentiation and deep party identification declined as the linkage between parties and interest groups (for example, Labour Party and trade unions) weakened. In Britain, therefore, postwar politics involved a decrease in the importance of ideological differences in party electoral strategy during two decades of postwar growth, a process that mirrored the consolidation of a broad Butskellite consensus.

Party Politics in a Period of Economic Decline

By the 1970s, however, it was increasingly clear that the evolution of the party system from a class-based to a catch-all orientation, which followed from the rise of the postwar settlement, had not adequately prepared Britain for politics in an age of economic decline. The end of economic growth caused the tensions within society to emerge with new force. Ideological differences had never really been resolved, and interests outside the Butskellite consensus had been neglected. Damaged by the economic failures they had administered, both the Conservatives and Labour suffered declining support in aggregate terms in the 1970s as the electoral share of the two major parties declined. This loss of support for traditional parties as the standard-bearers of the political process accompanied a growth in what political scientist Suzanne Berger calls "anti-political" parties linked closely to untraditional social movements. In Britain and elsewhere in Western Europe, these movements were often anti-big government, antibureaucratic, or antihierarchical.

There followed a rapid expansion of the influence of a whole range of movement-based parties, which represented new constituencies that could not be easily assimilated into the left/right, working class/middle class, Labour/Conservative binary context of British politics. There were neofascist and anti-immigrant forces in the National Front; resurgent ethnic/nationalist forces of the Plaid Cymru, the Scottish National Party, and Sinn Fein and other *republican* forces (supporting the creation of an independent Irish Republic, including the six counties of Ulster/Northern Ireland, free of English control); feminists in the women's movement; and peace activists in antinuclear and nuclear-freeze campaigns, to name a few. After the economic downturn of the mid-1970s, the active role of the state in managing economic affairs and choosing among constituencies became more obvious to increasingly disgruntled citizens, for tough policy choices were needed once competing interests could no longer be accommodated. As Berger observed, "[i]n the seventies, the dominant political response to the new transparence of the state [was] to try to dismantle it . . . . Never before has this conception of politics shaped new political ideas on both the Left and the Right."[10]

Party and Partisan Dealignment

British politics would perhaps never be the same. By the 1970s at least three crucial features of stability that had characterized the highly predictable two-party system for a quarter-century had eroded. First, from 1950 to 1970 the Conservative and Labour shares of the vote had always fallen within a six-point range (from 43 to 49 percent each) and the average swing between them was a very narrow 2.5 percent. Second, the distribution of voting fluctuations was uniform throughout Britain. In each of the elections at least three-quarters of the swings in constituencies were within two percent of the national median. Third, the two leading parties enjoyed a virtual monopoly of parliamentary representation and a remarkable share of the votes cast. From 1945 to 1970 the two parties won an average of 92 percent of the vote and 98 percent of all seats in Commons.

The three elections of the 1970s — in February, 1974, October, 1974, and May, 1979 — displayed a marked departure from this pattern. In February, 1974, the Conservative share of the vote fell 8.6 percent (the largest slump any party had experienced since 1945) and Labour's share was reduced by 6.0 percent. The Liberal party was the main beneficiary of the decline in major party support, as its share of the vote rose from 7.5 percent to 19.3 percent. Likewise, the Scottish National Party's share of the votes in Scotland rose dramatically, from 11.4 percent to 21.9 percent. In 1979 there was pronounced electoral instability once again. At 5.2 percent, the national swing from Labour to Conservative was the highest two-party swing since the war.[11]

Not only were fluctuations extreme in British terms, but lack of geographical uniformity was very pronounced, as the swing to the SNP in Scotland illustrates. Perhaps most significant was the decline of two-party dominance. In February, 1974, the two major parties shared 74.9 percent of the vote, and in October, 1974, thirty-nine minor party candidates were elected (a postwar record). As Bo Särlvik and Ivor Crewe observe, "The 1970's therefore mark the decade in which the mass foundations of the two-party system were, if not toppled by electoral earthquakes, at least weakened by electoral tremors."[12]

In addition to the growing evidence of volatility, the British electoral system also displayed specific signs of both *class* and *partisan* dealignment.[13] In the 1950s and early 1960s British electoral behavior displayed a strong correlation with class and occupational position: those not engaged in manual labor voted Conservative three times more commonly than Labour; and more than two out of three manual workers, by contrast, voted for Labour. During the 1964 to 1974 period, however, the apparent connection between occupational experience and electoral behavior declined. This *first* period of decline involved a reduced association between nonmanual workers and the Conservative Party. The decline in the Conservative *lead* over Labour among nonmanual workers, i.e., white collar voters, slipped steadily from 50 percentage points in the 1964 general election to 30 percentage points in the second 1974 general election (both narrow Labour victories). (See Table 4.2.)

Table 4.1 Electoral Results, 1945–83

	Electorate and Turnout	Votes Cast	Conservative	Labour	Liberal (1983 Alliance)	Welsh & Scottish Nationalist	Communist	Others (Mainly N. Ireland)
	73.3%	100%	39.8%	48.3%	9.1%	0.2%	0.4%	2.1%
1945[a]	32,836,419	24,082,612	9,577,667	11,632,891	2,197,191	46,612	102,760	525,491
	84.0%	100%	43.5%	46.1%	9.1%	0.1%	0.3%	0.9%
1950	34,269,770	28,772,671	12,502,567	13,266,592	2,621,548	27,288	91,746	262,930
	82.5%	100%	48.0%	48.8%	2.5%	0.1%	0.1%	0.5%
1951	34,645,573	28,595,668	13,717,538	13,948,605	730,556	18,219	21,640	159,110
	76.8%	100%	49.7%	46.4%	2.7%	0.2%	0.1%	0.8%
1955	34,858,263	26,760,493	13,311,936	12,404,970	722,405	57,231	33,144	230,807
	78.7%	100%	49.4%	43.8%	5.9%	0.4%	0.1%	0.5%
1959	35,397,080	27,859,241	13,749,830	12,215,538	1,638,571	99,309	30,897	145,090
	77.1%	100%	43.4%	44.1%	11.2%	0.5%	0.2%	0.6%
1964	35,892,572	27,655,374	12,001,396	12,205,814	3,092,878	133,551	45,932	169,431
	75.8%	100%	41.9%	47.9%	8.5%	0.7%	0.2%	0.7%
1966	35,964,684	27,263,606	11,418,433	13,064,951	2,327,533	189,545	62,112	201,032

	72.0%	100%	46.4%	43.0%	7.5%	1.3%	0.1%	1.7%
1970	39,342,013	28,344,798	13,145,123	12,178,295	2,117,033	381,818	37,970	486,557
February,	78.1%	100%	37.8%	37.1%	19.3%	2.6%	0.1%	3.1%
1974	39,770,724	31,340,162	11,872,180	11,646,391	6,058,744	804,554	32,743	958,293
October,	72.8%	100%	35.8%	39.2%	18.3%	3.5%	0.1%	3.1%
1974	40,072,971	29,189,178	10,464,817	11,457,079	6,346,754	1,005,938	17,426	897,164
	76.0%	100%	43.9%	37.0%	13.8%	2.0%	0.1%	3.2%
1979	41,093,264	31,221,361	13,697,923	11,532,218	4,313,804	636,890	16,858	1,043,755
	72.7%	100%	42.4%	27.6%	25.4%	1.5%	0.04%	3.1%
1983	42,197,344	30,671,136	13,012,315	8,456,934	7,780,949	457,676	11,606	951,656

NOTES

[a] University seats are excluded: other 1945 figures are adjusted to eliminate the distorations introduced by double voting in the fifteen two-member seats then existing.

SOURCE David Butler and Dennis Kavanagh, *The British General Election of 1983* (London: Macmillan, 1984), p. 300.

Table 4.2 Manual and Nonmanual Voting, 1964–74

	PERCENTAGE CONSERVATIVE LEAD OVER LABOUR				
OCCUPATIONAL CLASS	1964	1966	1970	February, 1974	October, 1974
NONMANUAL	50	44	40	36	30
MANUAL	−36	−44	−30	−40	−34

NOTE This table shows the percentage of Conservative support minus the percentage of Labour support in each occupational class among people identifying with the two major parties.
SOURCE *Developments in British Politics,* edited by Henry Drucker, Patrick Dunleavy, Andrew Gamble, and Gillian Peele. © Patrick Dunleavy 1983 and reprinted by permission of St. Martin's Press, Inc.

It is interesting to note, however, that during this period between 1964 and 1974, manual workers' electoral support for Labour indicated no consistent trend. Rather, the decline of working-class electoral support for Labour occurred in the *second* decade of dealignment, beginning with the October, 1974, election. As Table 4–3 indicates, class dealignment has been a major factor in Thatcher's electoral success. As the *Conservative lead over Labour* columns illustrate, the nonmanual/manual divide was still salient in October, 1974, as the Conservative lead dropped by 53 percentage points (from 28 to −25) when the junior nonmanual workers' electoral behavior is compared to that of skilled manual workers. While this shift remained considerable throughout the period, a startling new trend emerged with greater force: By 1979 the Labour lead over Conservatives was down to one percent from 25 percent in 1974, and by the 1983 general election, the Conservatives actually led by one percent among skilled workers. Indeed, by 1983 Labour support was down to 43 percent among manual workers, and remarkably, Labour and Conservatives split the vote of union members evenly (34 percent each, with the SDP/Liberal Alliance trailing narrowly at 32 percent).

Britain may be a model of stable constitutional democracy, but speaking more narrowly, electoral behavior is far less stable than it has been for some time because the continuity of electoral support by individuals and social groups no longer can be assumed. How can these processes of class and partisan dealignment and the greater volatility in electoral behavior be explained? What is the linkage between electoral behavior, the broader evolution of social forces associated with the rise of the postwar settlement, and the political and social fragmentation left in the wake of its decline?

Table 4.3 Class Dealignment: 1974–83

	Occupational Class			
	Managerial (AB)	Junior Nonmanual (C1)	Skilled Manual (C2)	Other Manual (D)
Conservative lead over Labour (Con vote — Lab vote)				
October 1974	53	28	−25	−37
1979	49	37	−1	−33
1983	43	40	1	−10
Swing to Conservatives from Labour (+ = to Con: − = to Lab)				
1974–79	−2.0	+4.5	+12.5	+7.0
1979–83	−3.0	+1.5	+1.0	+6.0
Swing to Liberals/Alliance from other two major parties				
1974–79	−8.0	−1.5	−10.5	−9.0
1979–83	−20.0	+6.0	+16.5	+11.0

SOURCE *Developments in British Politics,* edited by Henry Drucker, Patrick Dunleavy, Andrew Gamble, and Gillian Peele. © Patrick Dunleavy 1983 and reprinted by permission of St. Martin's Press, Inc.

Interest, Class, and Party

The explanation for changed electoral behavior lies in the dissolution of the postwar settlement and the complex process by which fragmenting interests and declining institutional capacities recast the inner balance of party forces. Perhaps no aspect of public policy has shown the potential for growing chaos within Britain's Butskellite consensus more than the area of industrial relations, for it is there that the state must try to contain the traditional workplace and trade unionist core of class-based politics.

As explained in Chapter 2, the collapse of the Social Contract during the 1974–79 Labour government represented profound problems with a governing strategy and a social vision that had inspired both Conservative and Labour governments throughout the postwar period.

The breakdown of the Social Contract is significant for at least three reasons. First, the disruptive power of the trade unions and the failure of the Labour Party's efforts to politically and economically integrate the trade union movement marks the high-water mark and, at the same time, the true end of the postwar settlement. No longer would the Butskellite consensus contain the class conflicts and the new social movements that had emerged.

Second, Margaret Thatcher's election in May, 1979, and the rightward shift in the policy agenda that her victory represented, and that her government would articulate, followed directly from the perceived failures of the center-right government of Edward Heath and the center-left government of James Callaghan. Once Britain's version of pragmatic social-democratic reform, which contained mainstream Tory and Labour party elites, had lost its claim as the program of political stability and economic performance, a new path was opened for political leadership that would take Britain in a different direction.

Finally, the collapse of the Social Contract symbolizes the dissolution of a historic symbiosis between the trade union movement and the Labour Party. Before this final rupture in the postwar settlement, the Labour Party and the trade unions could be said to constitute a reasonably unified, broad-based labor movement. They displayed a pattern of cohesion that helped anchor the two-party system around clear class and partisan affiliations. After the Social Contract unraveled, the breakdown in the alliance between party and union contributed significantly to electoral volatility, dealignment of party politics, and general fragmentation in British political life. To understand this point fully, it is necessary to appreciate the unusual structure of the Labour party (before a set of constitutional changes were implemented in 1980).

Perhaps the traditional British Labour Party can best be understood by reference to its structural divisions: It functioned as a tripartite organization composed mainly of constituency (local) parties; trade unions; and members of Parliament, who constitute the Parliamentary Labour Party (PLP). The Labour Party was governed by its annual conference, where the trade unions in a typical year cast 6,450,000 votes of the 7,206,000 total votes, in blocs proportional to the size of their membership as compared with the total of all party members. As a result, the engineers and the transport and general workers (truckers) between them cast some 30 percent of all conference votes.

The Labour Party is nevertheless also a party of government. Accordingly, the program voted by trade unions and almost incidentally by M.P.s, constituency members, and participants in affiliated cooperative societies, must also be the basis for a claim to govern, which is asserted in a general election. As democratic theory and catch-all party strategy suggest, this claim is made not only to trade unionists turned voters but also to all British electors. Thus, the Labour Party must serve as both a party of the working class and a party of government.

The Labour Party is further divided between the trade union leadership, which negotiates incomes policies and casts the bloc votes at the annual conference (in some unions without polling the membership), and the rank-and-file trade unionists. Further, those party members who are far removed from these negotiations are more likely to seek short-term, practical results, such as improvements in wage levels, secure employment, and economic stability. As a result, multiple divisions are structurally cast within the Labour Party, and between the trade unions and the party within the broader labor movement, as follows: tripartite organizational division within the party; PLP versus trade union domination of party policy; and elite postwar-settlement strategies versus rank-and-file interests.

With these divisions in mind, the paradox of increased labor militancy and the decreased salience of class in the electoral behavior of working people becomes easier to understand. Not only did the diffusion of class position through a range of middle-class and white-collar occupations fragment the class awareness of working people, but the failure of the Labour Party and associated trade union elites to deliver the goods of economic well-being also weakened the historical ties between rank-and-file and party elites. As a result, party partisanship broke down, despite other indications in the industrial sphere that class politics flourished unabated.

Of course, there is another side to class politics: the influence of financial interests, multinational firms, and small-scale British-based industrial enterprises. Chapter 1 discussed the historical dominance of the financial interests of the City over manufacturing and its influence in state formation. Today, City influence over economic policy and Tory politics remains considerable: Senior Treasury officials move in and out of the City freely and are widely believed to implement policy congenial to financial interests; the governor of the Bank of England quite explicitly lobbies for City policies; and, a large number of Conservative M.P.s have interests in finance (rather than manufacturing industry). Multinational firms have often joined financial elites to press the government for stable exchange rates and the unrestricted flow of capital and against excessive state intervention in industrial planning, expanded public ownership, and any reduction of management prerogative in the name of industrial democracy. Finally, small- and medium-scale home industry, which provides much of the constituency-level leadership of the Conservative Party, is organized politically through the Confederation of British Industry (CBI), a body that has not been as influential as one might expect even under Conservative governments. Thus, after a highly publicized round of criticisms of Thatcher's economic management in 1979–80, which hurt manufacturing with high interest rates, Sir Terence Beckett, director-general of the CBI, soon lowered his profile as public critic of the Thatcher government. In general, it seems that government economic policy, under both Labour and Conservative control, tends to follow the interests of the City and multinationals because of common perspectives and social and occupational linkages, more than from explicit pressures. There is certainly no relationship between the Conservative Party and the CBI like that which connects the Labour Party to the Trades Union Congress or affiliated trade unions.[14]

There are also interests that are exerted on government mainly from outside the arena of class-based influences. These vary considerably in aims and in significance. Richard Rose identifies six possible relationships between pressure groups and the broader cultural values in society that condition the response of those who are involved in the policy process: *harmony* (e.g., the Royal Society for the Prevention of Cruelty to Animals); *increasing acceptability* (e.g., women's rights or single parents' organizations); *fluctuating support* (e.g., groups supporting nuclear disarmament); *advocacy in the face of cultural indifference* (e.g., the National Society of Non-Smokers, before the growing awareness of the medical hazards of smoking); *advocacy opposed to cultural trends* (e.g., groups advocating religious observation in an increasingly secular society); and, *conflict with cultural values* (e.g., groups advocating pacificism without qualification).[15] Although some interests are linked to clearly defined and narrowly organized pressure groups, others find expression in broader social movements with deep cultural and political significance.

Race, Gender, and New Social Movements

The reduced cohesion of the labor movement and the underlying crisis of economic performance that troubled both Conservative and Labour governments in the 1970s had profound effects on Britain. This complex process illustrates a deep erosion of the normative basis of British politics and indicates the seriousness of racial, gender, and generational tensions.

The "romantic revolt"[16] of the 1960s became the attack on the nation and social order in the 1970s. Antistate movements and antiestablishment subcultures (anti-Vietnam War; student movements; punk rock; anarchist collectives, such as the Angry Brigade; and the troops out movement, which supported Irish republicanism) contributed to a breakdown of norms and a widening sense of social anomie. The British army remained an occupying force in Northern Ireland while the government lost a set of human rights cases before the International Court of Justice at The Hague for their detention practices there. The economy was out of hand and the trade unions unmanageable. Urban violence against the elderly and against blacks increased.

Table 4.4 Predominantly Female Occupations

	ALL PERSONS (THOUSANDS)	WOMEN (THOUSANDS)
90% OR OVER FEMALE OCCUPATIONS		
Hand and machine sewers, embroiderers	238	230
Nurses	432	394
Maids, valets, etc.	443	428
Canteen assistants	304	293
Typists, secretaries, etc.	770	759
75% AND UNDER 90% FEMALE OCCUPATIONS		
Shop assistants	969	786
Charwomen, sweepers, and cleaners	522	456
Kitchen hands	122	100
Office machine operators	177	153
Hairdressers, etc.	159	124
Telephone operators	107	89
60% AND UNDER 75% FEMALE OCCUPATIONS		
Clerks and cashiers	2475	1546
Waiters and waitresses	113	82
Primary and secondary teachers	496	318
Packers and labelers, etc.	183	121
Bartenders	103	73

SOURCE *Annual Census of Employment* (June 1974). Cited by Hilary Wainwright in P. Abrams, *Work, Urbanism and Inequality* (London, Weidenfeld and Nicolson, 1978), p. 169.

Women remained locked into discriminatory employment patterns. Over half of the employed women remained in three service-sector pockets of employment: professional and secretarial work; distributive trades (such as retail sales); and miscellaneous services (hairdressing, catering, or cleaning, for example). Two million women worked in jobs that were almost totally segregated (over 90 percent female), as nurses, maids, typists, or sewing machinists. In 1977 women in full-time employment earned only 75.5 percent of what men earned.[17]

The women's movement attacked traditional attitudes toward family life and sexual relations and challenged the basic construction of a society that divided men's and women's expectations and experiences in family, social, political, and economic life. In the 1970s a set of highly visible feminist campaigns emerged: for reproductive control (including the defense of abortion rights); for unrestrictive definitions of sexual identity; and against male violence. Other campaigns included efforts to strengthen the provisions of the Equal Pay Act of 1970 and the Sex Discrimination Act of 1975. Women sought to challenge the deeply entrenched patterns of discrimination in job segregation and unequal pay, education, housing, pensions, taxation, immigration and nationality law, and the provision of social services. Women's campaigns were directed also against discrimination and indifference within the Labour Party and the trade union movement.[18]

These often-powerful social and political movements involved fundamental assaults on male privilege; the military; English dominance within the multi-nation state; traditional career paths; and deep-seated cultural values of order, authority, deference, and patriotism. They contributed to a general perception of the breakdown of consensus and an expectation of sharpening conflict. As one study noted, "The categories of crime, sexuality and youth were raw materials from which the image of a violent society was constructed."[19]

Worse still, the economic crisis and the crisis of race were often thoughtlessly, but very significantly, thrown together: "Race is always present whether the issue under discussion is the growth of unemployment, the role of the police in inner-city areas, or the [1981] 'riots' in a number of major cities. . . . The battle lines between 'society' and its 'enemies' were more clearly drawn by the end of the seventies than they had been for decades."[20] This linkage of social forces frames the contemporary moment of uncertainty and transition in British politics.

NOTES

1. Samuel H. Beer, *The British Political System* (New York: Random House, 1973), p. 157.

2. Bob Jessop et al., "Authoritarian Populism, Two Nations and Thatcherism," *New Left Review,* no. 147 (September/October 1984), p. 39.
3. Otto Kirchheimer, "The Transformation of the European Party Systems," in *Political Parties and Development,* ed. Joseph LaPalombara and Myron Weiner (Princeton: Princeton University Press, 1966), p. 182.
4. T.H. Marshall, "Citizenship and Social Class," in *States and Societies,* ed. David Held et al. (Oxford: Martin Robertson, 1983), pp. 248–71.
5. Geoff Hodgson, *Labour at the Crossroads* (Oxford: Martin Robertson, 1981), pp. 14–15.
6. David Butler and Dennis Kavanagh, *The British General Election of 1979* (London: Macmillan, 1980), p. 34.
7. David Butler and Dennis Kavanagh, *British General Election,* pp. 67–72.
8. Donald R. Shell, "The British Constitution in 1981," *Parliamentary Affairs,* vol. 35, no. 2 (Spring 1982), p. 118.
9. Beer, *British Political System,* p. 19.
10. Suzanne Berger, "Politics and Antipolitics in Western Europe in the Seventies," *Daedalus,* vol. 108, no. 1 (Winter 1979), p. 29.
11. Bo Särlvik and Ivor Crewe, *Decade of Dealignment* (Cambridge: Cambridge University Press, 1983), pp. 30–32.
12. Särlvik and Crewe, *Decade of Dealignment,* p. 31.
13. The argument closely follows that of Patrick Dunleavy, "Voting and the Electorate," in *Developments in British Politics,* ed. Henry Drucker et al. (London: Macmillan, 1984), pp. 30–58.
14. David Coates, *The Context of British Politics* (London: Hutchinson, 1984), pp. 63–75.
15. Richard Rose, *Politics in England* (Boston: Little, Brown, 1986), pp. 248–51.
16. Samuel H. Beer, *Britain Against Itself: The Political Contradictions of Collectivism* (New York: Norton Press, 1982), pp. 107–148.
17. Coates, *Context of British Politics,* pp. 63–75.
18. Sarah Perrigo, "The Women's Movement: Patterns of Oppression and Resistance," in *A Socialist Anatomy of Britain,* ed. David Coates et al. (Cambridge: Polity Press, 1985), pp. 132–44.
19. John Solomos et al., "The Organic Crisis of British Capitalism and Race: The Experience of the Seventies," in *The Empire Strikes Back,* ed. Centre for Contemporary Cultural Studies (London: Hutchinson, 1982), p. 23.
20. Solomos et al., "Organic Crisis," pp. 26–27.

5

British Politics In Transition

"What have you changed?" someone asked the new prime minister in 1979, and Margaret Thatcher promptly replied, "I have changed everything."[1] Thatcher has not changed *everything*, although she has attempted with considerable success to recast British political culture in a strongly individualist direction and in so doing has altered the balance of class forces and redrawn relationships between state and society in Britain. Beyond Thatcher's boast lies the undeniable truth that her government represents a new policy regime in the United Kingdom and one of the boldest experiments in postwar Western European governance.

By the end of the 1970s it was clear that the defeats, in turn, of Heath and Callaghan had exhausted the options of party alternation and programmatic continuity within the social-democratic and Butskellite mold. Like the complex symbiosis between sections of the Labour party — constituency, PLP, and trade unions — the set formula of two-party competition between mainstream representatives of the Conservative and Labour parties relied on the vitality of the postwar-settlement vision. The stability of British politics rested on the political perseverance of a growth coalition, which in turn required more growth, high productivity, and an increasing standard of living.

There is no denying, however, that Britain is in profound economic straits. Economist Ajit Singh has argued persuasively that the British economy suffers from a "structural disequilibrium, whereby the trading position of the manufacturing sector in the world economy continues to deteriorate, in spite of increasing cost and price competitiveness." Deindustrialization, measured by the loss of one million jobs in manufacturing between 1968 and 1976, is only one of the more heralded symptoms of this disequilibrium.[2] The record level of unemployment (estimated to be about 3.5 million workers or 13.2 percent in March, 1986) results from structural weakness in British competitiveness and a shrinking of the manufacturing base.

The findings of a recent study by the Organisation for Economic Cooperation and Development (OECD) correspond with Singh's measured pessimism. The 1983 economic survey noted a severe fall in production in the British economy and observed that despite a declining rate of inflation, "the downturn in output and employment has been greater [in the U.K.] than in most other member countries." The report emphasized a sharp fall in manufacturing production to a level roughly 16 percent below Britain's 1979 peak and stated that British international competitiveness, measured in relative unit labour costs, deteriorated by some 55 percent in the course of the 1970s. The OECD study concluded bleakly, "Under these circumstances it is not surprising that the industrial base has contracted and unemployment risen strongly."[3]

Britain also declined in geopolitical terms from the late 1950s through the 1970s. In 1956 a joint Anglo-French effort failed to regain the Suez Canal after it was nationalized by the Egyptian government. In the 1960s, the British withdrew all forces east of Suez. Later, de Gaulle's rejection of British entry into the EEC and Wilson's futile efforts to influence U.S. war policy in Vietnam confirmed Britain's retreat from international dominance.

By the time the International Monetary Fund forced Callaghan's government to accept cuts in domestic spending in return for a $3.9 billion loan in 1976 (the largest ever granted), it was clear that Britain had ceased to be a global or economic power. As one British observer noted recently, "The rational task of modernization in Britain, then, is to make the U.K. a relatively thriving but nonetheless second-rank country."[4] Instead, Britain displays many signs of continued economic deterioration and appears to be a nation beset by harsh industrial and social divisions. Why has Britain so turned against itself?

The Emergence of The Thatcher Government

In some ways Thatcher's victory is easily understood. Her 1979 campaign emphasized the issues of economic decline and trade union power (an understandable strategy in the first spring after the notorious winter of discontent, when, as explained in Chapter 2, trade unions rebelled against the Social Contract in a crescendo of disruptive strikes). The campaign is memorable, however, for other issues such as race and immigration, and the sale of public housing back to tenants. These policies went beyond simply introducing the program of a new prime minister; they inaugurated a transition in British politics to the age of Thatcher.[5]

In the May, 1979, campaign, the Conservative manifesto took the high ground, setting out a new philosophy of government, rather than a set of explicit proposals. Thatcher focused her presentations on a set of antiunion, anti-interventionist-state themes. She insisted that government should reduce public expenditure, lower inflation by tighter control of monetary aggregates, and cut taxes to unleash entrepreneurial energies. Warming to the antiunion theme, Thatcher promised to challenge trade union power by legislatively restricting the rights of those not directly involved in a strike to aid striking workers, requiring postal ballots of *all* union members in advance of a strike, and cutting unemployment benefits previously available to strikers.

Two side issues proved crucial in the campaign and highly significant for the shape of contemporary British politics: housing, and race and immigration. The Conservatives pressed the issue of housing by promising an act of Parliament that would require councils to make residences available for purchase to all tenants of council (public) housing at up to 50 percent below market value. The first statement of Conservative policy written under Thatcher's leadership (titled, appropriately, *The Right Approach*) staked out their ideological turf: "Most people want to become home-owners. Yet we devote the overwhelming majority of our resources to public rented housing. . . . [T]he Labour Government has pursued the traditional vendetta against the private sector."[6] The Conservatives thus recast the housing issue from the problem of availability of good housing to one of individual freedom versus socialist public-sector bias. They thereby justified the genuine personal desires of many Britons by supplying a partisan ideological assault on the consensus traditions of public housing and other welfare-state provisions.

Race and Immigration

The most heated issue in the 1979 campaign concerned immigration, an issue that connects most closely to a powerful racial undercurrent that has pulled at British society with great force throughout the 1970s and 1980s. The postwar period has witnessed the gradual erosion of racial tolerance in Britain as nonwhite, New Commonwealth residents have experienced cultural isolation, employment prejudice, and increased physical harassment. Britain has adjusted slowly and, by most accounts, poorly to the realities of a multiracial society; for example, black citizens, many of whom were born in Britain, are still commonly referred to as immigrants.

Moreover, beginning with the 1962 Commonwealth Immigrants Act, a growing body of law has served to keep many nonwhites out of Britain by increasingly restricting the residence rights associated with citizenship: "Because of the large number of citizens of Commonwealth countries who, prior to independence, were entitled to citizenship of the United Kingdom and its colonies under the British Nationality Act of 1948," observes Tom Rees, "pressure built up to distinguish, in law, between those United Kingdom citizens who in some sense 'belonged' to the United Kingdom itself, and those United Kingdom citizens whose closest ties were in some territory within the Commonwealth." Britain created a new kind of citizen, "stateless in substance, though not in name."[7]

The 1962 act, passed over strong Labour Party opposition, removed from most Commonwealth citizens (and from all colonial citizens not of recent British descent) the right to enter and settle in Britain without restriction. (This was the last significant example of Labour Party resistance to a set of racially suspect exclusionary policies.) After the settlement of several tens of thousands of ethnic Asians, British subjects resident in East Africa who were displaced by the Africanization policies of the Kenyan government, the Labour government rushed the 1968 Commonwealth Immigrants Act through Parliament in three days. Despite previous assurance of protection, the new act eliminated the unqualified entitlement of citizens of Commonwealth countries to residence in Britain. The 1971 Immigration Act made the preference for white immigrants even clearer. The word *patrial* was invented to describe people with one or more British grandparents, or those who had been naturalized or resident in Britain for five years. Only patrials and their immediate families, or families of other Commonwealth citizens legally residing in Britain before 1973, retained full rights to live and work freely in Britain; all other Commonwealth passport holders needed permits. By contrast, EEC citizens could enter freely: Western Europeans, of course, are more likely to be white than are the citizens of the Commonwealth.

The extent of immigration was minimal, never exceeding 38,000 entrants per year from the New Commonwealth and Pakistan in the 1970s. Nevertheless the Conservatives pledged in 1979 to increase restrictions with a new nationality act (they later did with the 1981 British

Nationality Act). Official Conservative policy argued, on the one hand, that "relations between different communities have been remarkably harmonious" and assured any observers that racially motivated violence or discrimination are "wholly abhorrent to our British way of life and must be unequivocally condemned." On the other hand, Conservative policy asserted that "racial harmony requires . . . an immediate reduction in immigration . . . [and] a clearly defined limit to the numbers of those to be allowed into this country."[8]

By implication, therefore, nonwhite residents were, by their very presence, responsible for the racist attitudes and practices by which they were victimized. Thatcher drew the connection between law and order and immigration in a widely noted interview in January, 1978, on the popular television program "World in Action":

> If we went on as we are, then by the end of this century there would be four million people of the New Commonwealth or Pakistan here. Now I think that is an awful lot, and I think it means that people are really rather afraid that this country might be rather swamped by people with a different culture, and you know, the British character has done so much for democracy, for law and order, and so much throughout the world that if there is any fear that it might be swamped, people are going to react and be hostile to those coming in. . . . so if you want good race relations, you have got to allay people's fears on numbers.[9]

The signs of this thinly veiled racist appeal were immediate and unmistakable: Thatcher's support in opinion polls jumped 11 percent after the broadcast; 61 percent approved of Thatcher's remark that Britain was in danger of being "swamped" by people of different cultures; and 70 percent of those sampled in a Gallup poll agreed with the Conservative policy to reduce the flow of immigration.[10]

Thatcher's immigration policy stole the thunder from the National Front (NF). This minor political party emerged in the mid-1970s with a neofacist and racist program that manipulated themes of unemployment, fear of street crime, and anticommunism into an antiblack campaign, which gained some adherents in unions, schools, and church and community groups.[11] The NF elected a number of local town councillors and stood candidates in more than fifty English constituencies in the October, 1974, general election. Its electoral influence declined after a peak in 1976, quite possibly because of the increasingly hard-line program of the Conservative party on immigration, the NF's calling-card issue. Certainly, the May, 1979, election results support such an interpretation. *The Economist* estimated that the issues of immigration and race provided a margin of victory in sixteen seats. Far more significant, the two-party

Table 5.1 Net Migrant Flows: U.K., since 1964, by Citizenship of Migrants

	CITIZENSHIP (000S)							
	ALIEN, EXCLUDING PAKISTAN[a]	OLD COMMON-WEALTH	NEW COMMON-WEALTH & PAKISTAN[a]	UNITED KINGDOM		TOTAL		
				CONTROLLED[b]	OTHER	INFLOW	OUTFLOW	NET[c]
MID-YEAR TO MID-YEAR								
1964–65	+22	+ 1	+55		−136	223	281	−58
1965–66	+24	− 2	+42		−141	210	286	−77
1966–67	+30	+ 5	+45		−175	232	326	−94
1967–68	+23	−10	+55	+15	−128	241	286	−45
1968–69	+21	− 2	+48	+ 8	−144	227	296	−68
1969–70	+24	− 3	+37	+ 6	−146	224	306	−82
1970–71	+21	− 5	+33	+ 9	− 98	227	266	−39
1971–72	+15	+ 6	+16	+16	− 97	196	240	−44
1972–73	+22	+ 3	+13	+34	− 76	225	230	− 5
1973–74	+21	+ 6	+14	+10	−122	183	255	−72
1974–75	+18	−	+20	+13	−116	194	261	−67
1975–76	+12	+ 3	+29	+12	− 79	197	220	−23
1976–77	+ 2	−	+24	+ 9	− 63	181	209	−28
1977–78	+ 3	+ 1	+25	+ 6	− 71	162	198	−36
1978–79	+ 9	+ 4	+38	+ 4	− 49	194	187	+ 6
1979–80	+23	+ 3	+34	+ 3	− 67	205	209	− 4

NOTES

[a] Pakistani citizens are included with New Commonwealth throughout, although Pakistan left the Commonwealth in 1972.

[b] U.K. passport holders subject to immigration control from March, 1968.

[c] Excluding net immigration due to direct traffic with the Irish Republic.

SOURCE Social Trends 12, Table 1.6. Reproduced with the permission of the Controller of Her Brittanic Majesty's Stationery Office.

swings from Labour to Conservative in London constituencies were exceptional, particularly in areas where voters had witnessed the most sustained NF organizing effort and a host of often violent confrontations between NF supporters and antiracist demonstrators. Indeed, six of the ten constituencies with the highest two-party swings were in these constituencies and apart from the importance of race and immigration issues, they were in every other way (employment, demographics, historical partisan loyalties) comparable to constituencies in the north of England that experienced the lowest swings and where race was not an issue. In fact, one NF leader supported this analysis when he explained his party's poor showing (1.4 percent, down from a high of 3.6 percent in 1970) by saying that "Mrs. Thatcher's apparent anti-immigration stance was the central cause of NF's electoral decline."[12]

Housing

Margaret Thatcher's housing platform was also a significant vehicle for her auspicious debut as party leader in the 1979 general election. As one observer noted, housing "was electorally crucial in dividing a working class movement, deeply disillusioned by the apparent inadequacies of the Welfare State and politically embittered by the economic policies pursued by the Labour government after 1976, by its populist appeal to the anti-bureaucratic, individualist and self-sufficient ideology of home ownership."[13] Electoral data supports this observation: In the thirty-seven English constituencies in which council tenancy exceeded 50 percent and where, it might be assumed, the offer to sell public housing to tenants at cut-rate prices held particular interest, the swing to the Conservatives was astonishing. Conservatives gained an average increase in support against all parties of 9.5 percent as compared to their October, 1974, tally (a 39.4 percentage gain in votes cast for Conservative parliamentary candidates).

Interclass Appeal

It was not these issues alone, however, that accounted for Thatcher's victory. Her ideological and programmatic rejection of the Butskellite postwar-settlement accord generated broad interclass appeal. As one observer explained, "Labour lost the election because of an immense shift of working class support to the Conservatives."[14] The Conservatives gained handsomely among both skilled and unskilled workers (the latter category including the underclass recipients of pension and welfare benefits). A fragmented working class, disillusioned with Callaghan's ineptitude and worn out by the failure of social democracy, was divided into small pockets of self-interest: Some wanted tax cuts, while others wanted to buy their council houses at the promised 30 to 50 percent discount from market rates, and many were drawn to Thatcher's appeals to entrepreneurship and individualism. The upper- and professional-class vote held Tory, and Conservatives gained 11 percent, while Labour dropped to 50 percent, among skilled workers. Even among unskilled laborers, the Labour Party lost significant ground (9 percent of its October, 1974, tally) and held a majority of only 51 percent.[15]

In a great many ways, Britons have gotten what they asked for by electing Thatcher, although perhaps a little more of it than they anticipated. We earlier dismissed as a mere boast Thatcher's claim that she had "changed everything." But she has shattered the old Butskellite consensus and in some significant ways changed the terms of the compromise between capitalism and democracy. The Thatcher government has vastly increased the political and managerial power of capitalist elites through privatization policies and restrictions on trade unions, for example. It has also narrowed the meaning of citizenship and reduced the political participation of nonelite groups in society. If a new political accord is to emerge in Britain, it will be very different from the old Butskellite consensus.

Contemporary British Politics: The Search For A New Accord

Political theorists who write about democracy have often assumed that Western societies would evolve in ways that increased the political participation of ordinary citizens and expanded their rights. As noted in Chapter 4, T.H. Marshall argues that in the twentieth century rights of citizenship include the social rights of material well-being and state provision for education, health, and income security. So long as the Butskellite consensus and the postwar settlement endured in Britain, governmental practice reinforced this theoretical design. As a result, for twenty years or more the terms of reconciliation between capitalism and democracy involved substantial political regulation of the market economy, as well as an expansion of democratic participation to integrate the working class, women, minority races, and a variety of ethnic groups. Kirchheimer may have been too optimistic when he expressed the hope that politics might become the "cooperative enterprise of all social classes,"[16] but during the height of the welfare state, British society certainly appeared to be moving in that direction.

Strong signs of potentially divisive and destabilizing undercurrents in British politics began to be visible long before Thatcher's victory in 1979. We have discussed the occurrence of class dealignment in the electoral sphere alongside the strong expression of class and trade unionist sentiments in the industrial sphere during the Heath and Callaghan governments in the 1970s. We have also noted the power of particular issues to change the partisan alignment of parties, for example, ethnic-regionalism expressed in support for the Scottish National Party and the Plaid Cymru (Welsh nationalist) parties or antiblack, anti-immigrant appeals by the NF and the Conservative Party. We have observed that these new developments in electoral and interest-group pressure expressed deeper changes in British society. The 1970s was a decade in which broad youth-movement challenges to values of order and authority and divisions that involved race and gender changed the map of social forces in Britain.

Thatcher did not create the new divisions in British society, which drew a sharp distinction between "society" and its "enemies," but she has exploited them. If a Thatcherite accord is consolidated in Britain, it will be of a new, deintegrative variety, recasting the political community to reduce meaningful participation of blacks and ethnic minorities. This consensus will minimize the political influence of trade unions, expand the prerogatives of capitalists, shrink the public sector, reduce social expenditure, and cut the twentieth-century rights of citizenship associated with welfare provision.

Thatcherism: The Institutional And Policy Implications

Three policy areas indicate most clearly the changed course of British politics during the Thatcher governments: industrial relations (particularly as regards the public sector); economic management; and welfare provision. We will now consider the significance of Thatcher's innovations and assess the consequences that follow for the institutional principles of British government.

Industrial Relations

Throughout the period of the rise and fall of the postwar settlement until Thatcher, British governmental efforts to reduce industrial strife, constrain the political power of trade unions, and increase productivity by limiting wage increases have been mainly of two kinds. On the one hand, governments have sought to implement statutory restrictions on trade union rights (for example, the 1972 Industrial Relations Act of the Heath government); on the other hand, efforts have been made to expand the involvement of the Trades Union Congress (TUC) in the conduct of macroeconomic policy and, by "turning the poacher into the gameskeeper," to involve trade union elites in the enforcement of wage restraints (for example, the series of Social Contracts negotiated by the 1974–79 Labour government with the TUC, initially, and with particular trade unions, as discussed in Chapter 2). In fact, Labour and Conservative governments alike have tried both approaches but have had only fleeting success, and the alternation of the two approaches represents another instance of Britain's notorious stop-go policy upheavals.

There are strong indications that the Thatcher government has altered this pattern, and with dramatic consequences. "From the beginning, Thatcher has been anxious to break the old consensus," observe British political scientists Huw Benyon and Peter McMylor, ". . . the old class compromises were not for her, neither were collective forms of life and relationships. With all *corporate* forms apparently in crisis (such as income policies, etc.), the powerful articulation of individualism was made to seem both fresh and plausible. In this way of thinking, the phrase 'right to work' became deflected from its original social-democratic meaning of a *public* commitment to full employment, towards a citizen's right to sell, unhindered, one's labour as an *individual* in the market-place."[17]

This ideological shift has prefigured a fundamental change in the meaning of labor-management disputes, which under Thatcher have become an opportunity for defeating trade unions and reducing their industrial and political influence. As a result the balance of forces in society is shifting from the public to the private sector and from the trade unions back to the private owners and managers.

Thatcher's industrial relations strategy involves two elements: legislation and direct confrontation. To date three pieces of legislation, the Employment Acts of 1980 and 1982, and the Trade Union Act of 1984, legally individuate trade unions and substantially reduce the rights with which British trade unions have been collectively endowed since 1906. Taken together, these acts hold union officials as individuals financially and legally responsible for a wide range of illegal activities (including large-scale picketing, strikes to protest government activity, and secondary strikes); severely restrict the institution of the closed shop; expand owners' ability to dismiss strikers and union officials; and remove legal immunity from unions (and officials) who authorize otherwise legal industrial action without meeting particular balloting procedures.

Thatcher's second industrial relations strategy began, in a sense, even before the election of her government. The memory of the defeat of her Conservative predecessor, Edward Heath, in 1974 has figured prominently in her policy. Soon after becoming party leader in February, 1975, Thatcher commissioned two internal Conservative Party reports that apparently influenced her thinking considerably. Lord Carrington, Heath's energy minister (and later Thatcher's foreign secretary until his resignation in 1982 for his handling of the Falklands War) was the author of the first report, which dispelled the belief, widely held by senior party officials, that Heath's failed showdown with the miners had been a consequence of weak leadership. Instead, argued Carrington, society was being challenged by strategically powerful and self-interested groups of workers, particularly in the energy sector. Society was at a disadvantage in such industrial disputes due to extreme economic dependence on electricity and the fact that neither miners nor electricity-generating–plant personnel could be replaced by the armed forces during a strike.

The second report, written by Nicholas Ridley, who was to become financial secretary to the Treasury in 1981, laid a blueprint for a political plan to overcome the technological and organizational problems identified by Carrington. Referring to the likelihood of a political threat, Ridley urged a carefully orchestrated set of confrontations with energy sector unions. These challenges would begin with the weak and divided and come to a climax with the National Union of Mineworkers (NUM), who had defeated the last Conservative government.

The miner's strike of 1984–85, it is widely agreed, was triggered by government threats to reduce substantially the size of the NUM workforce and to challenge once and for all the political power and industrial clout of the NUM. Perhaps the most violent strike in several decades in Europe, it has raised significant questions about the political roles forced on the police and the judiciary by the Thatcher government. Police action was coordinated through a national reporting center at Scotland Yard, which made the police look like a national force although, in fact, police

action involved the coordination of forty-two separate forces. Police methods, moreover, were questionable: They set up innumerable road blocks to disrupt the efforts of pickets and operated with considerable menace in mining villages, often in riot gear. The courts, too, played a controversial role, sequestering the entire assets of the NUM and ordering many miners brought before magistrates to refrain from picketing and be subject to exacting curfews and travel restrictions as part of the terms of granting bail.

Beyond these institutional issues, the miner's strike, won by the government after twelve months, recast industrial relations in harsh class-conflict terms and underscored the unprecedented determination of the prime minister even as it furthered concerns that her approach was divisive and too costly in human terms. In her customary annual speech to Conservative backbenchers (M.P.'s with no governmental responsibilities) in July, 1984, Thatcher drew a parallel between the "enemy without" (the Argentinian forces in the Falklands War) and the "enemy within" (striking miners). She reportedly stated that the internal enemy was "just as hard to fight and just as dangerous to liberty" as the external enemy. As one observer notes, "Conservatives as well as others thought such language gratuitously offensive, and many were distressed by the impression of government indifference to the suffering caused by the dispute, and to its social consequences."[18]

It is a very rare postwar European government that would intentionally exacerbate class tension in an effort to restore a political balance in class forces to a pre-postwar-settlement point. This seems to be the intention of the Thatcher government, not only in industrial relations, but also in the general conduct of economic and social welfare policy.

Economic Management and Welfare Provision

The handling of industrial relations illustrates a general pattern of ideological and programmatic change associated with the Thatcher government. It is the first postwar European government to deny any obligation to secure full employment and the first to challenge, not simply the cost, but the principle of public provision of housing or health care. Thatcher's boast that she has "changed everything" is clearly untrue, but she has gone quite far in changing the way people think about a great many things. It is at the juncture where the attitude about and the conduct of public policy come together that Thatcher has effected a serious revision in British social and economic life.

The Thatcher record on public expenditure is mixed. The first five years of the Conservative government show that the commitment to reduced spending could not be sustained, largely because of recession-triggered rises in income support and unemployment benefits. Spending grew overall by more than 6 percent in real terms in the first four years (up to 1982–83) and by about one percent in 1983–84, and official projections of zero growth for the remainder of Thatcher's second government may be unrealistic. Within the total public expenditure, not surprisingly, ideologically linked distinctions appear: by the end of 1984–85, spending on defense and police programs was 40 percent greater in real terms than in 1978–79; education and transport have been held roughly constant; and expenditure on housing had been cut by more than half by 1982–83. Additional cuts in all three areas are planned.[19] Income support and health and social services programs have grown, due in part to the effects of recession and the great difficulty of containing health care costs.

Macroeconomic trends during the Thatcher government are also mixed, though generally consistent with ideological and programmatic preferences. In 1984 the economy continued to expand, but at a slower rate than officially predicted (about two percent): Fixed investments and exports have grown, while consumer demand slumped and inventory reorders declined significantly. Both the government's most impressive success and its most serious economic failure show little sign of changing: the rate of inflation remains fairly steady (at about 5 to 5.5 percent) and unemployment remains extremely high (at about 13 percent).[20] By 1986, the recovery that began in 1981 had lasted longer than any other postwar recovery in Britain, the balance of payments was in surplus, and rates of profitability had improved. Nevertheless, with North Sea oil production peaking, oil prices falling, and the value of the pound appreciating, there was concern that the strong contribution of the oil sectors to growth would ease and soon would be reversed.[21]

There is, of course, divided opinion about the advisability of the government's macroeconomic strategy — how much responsibility it should claim for the modest recovery in output since 1981 and how much blame it deserves for unemployment and competitive weakness in manufacturing. It is not surprising that the government's analysis is linked closely to the "neo-laissez-faire" celebration of market forces. British ministers argue that a free-market economy, operating without prices and incomes control, has accomplished the difficult task of reducing inflation from 18 percent in 1980 to 5 percent in 1984. Unemployment, they believe, could be reduced by free-market means and generalized economic recovery, but for rigidities imposed on the labor market by trade unions. The neo-laissez-faire perspective holds that further wage restraint would benefit the economy by bringing additional downward pressure on the economy and improving competitiveness and that relations between competitive and noncompetitive sectors would be enhanced. Union resistance to technological change, which influences differentials or reduces labor requirements must be ended, and the effects of restrictive work practices must be diminished. This is where the political agenda of trade union legislation, augmented by strategic industrial confrontation, becomes part of the current government's macroeconomic approach.

Despite the controversial character of the Conservative strategy, two observations may be registered. First, it seems clear that governmental management of the economy and conduct of public expenditure shows some important continuities across the Wilson/Callaghan and Thatcher governments. The metamorphosis from a postwar-settlement consensus to a neo-laissez-faire approach began when the Labour government introduced monetary targets, cut social welfare expenditure to meet loan conditions set by the IMF, and began to doubt that its own macroeconomic policy and corporatist stance could control either inflation or unemployment. Second, the change in macroeconomic policy, forced by international exigencies and weakened competitive position, brought no significant change in British ideology until the age of Thatcher. The Labour Party clung, perhaps foolishly, to the vision of the postwar settlement and to the advantages of integrative strategies past the point where resurgent economic performance was likely to resolve growing distributional conflicts. Increasingly monetarist in practice, the last Labour government was still welfarist in sentiment, certain that the battle against inflation would be won by responsible cooperation. Employers and trade unions would serve the higher community need, and when the battle was won, full employment would be restored and the social welfare rights of citizenship expanded.[22]

The ideological meaning of Thatcher's economic and social policies seems quite different from that of preceding postwar governments. Monetarism, market forces, and privatization (a return to private ownership of state-owned enterprises) orient a carefully orchestrated movement away from the postwar-settlement consensus. Just as the right to work has taken on new individualist connotations, so too has the right to decent housing been replaced by a statutory right to buy, resulting in the transfer of half a million units of public housing to private ownership. The denationalization of British Telecom and a host of other operations and the widely noted inducements made to encourage small units of investment herald the popular face of privatization: the creation of a nation of shareholders.

But there are more subtle gestures of privatization and policies that weaken the public sector and powerfully reinforce an individualist ethos. Currently, the National Health Service (NHS) has shifted resources into care for the chronically ill, a move fully justified by both the poor quality of these services and the expanded need arising from demographic changes. At the same time, reduced overall funding has meant weaker service and longer waiting lists in other areas of NHS provision, often in services used by persons who could afford to seek private care or acquire private health insurance. Once the centerpiece of Britain's welfare state, the NHS is experiencing further erosion through budget constraints, the shifting of resources, and government supports for expanded private insurance coverage.

"Implicit privatization"[23] completes a careful, explicit program of privatization, a process that complements budgetary reductions in selected areas of social welfare provision. Alongside revisions of more traditional rights mandated by the Nationality Act of 1981, which introduces new categories of citizenship and further restricts the right of entry of many Commonwealth citizens, these policies significantly reduce widely accepted social rights of citizenship that have been common to Western European societies throughout the postwar period.[24]

British Politics and the Thatcher Experiment

In policy terms, the implications of the anti-integrationist theme of Thatcher's government seem clear: Industrial relations policy encourages class conflict, as social welfare and economic policy more broadly divide society into winners and losers. As a result, Thatcher's government has contributed to some significant institutional transformations.

Local government has gone from a neglected backwater of public administration to the subject of one of Britain's hottest controversies. Through acts of Parliament, the Thatcher government has reduced the local councils' power to set and allocate property taxes for welfare state purposes (transport or housing), and *abolished* a set of metropolitan councils, notably, the leftist Greater London Council, in March, 1986. In a system with no federal tier, such as the states in the U.S. or the Laender in West Germany, these developments have significant constitutional implications, for they represent an unparalleled reduction in checks on the central powers of the executive.

Likewise, the House of Lords has been politically invigorated during the Thatcher government. Thatcher's control of the cabinet and the weakness and fragmentation of the Labour opposition have meant that for relatively long periods "some of the most effective parliamentary opposition to Mrs. Thatcher's government came from the Upper House."[25] In the 1983–84 session the government was defeated twenty times in the House of Lords, often on crucial bills, including the Telecommunications Bill, the Trade Union Bill, and the Housing Bill.

The government also generated powerful opposition in another unlikely quarter: the Church of England. In 1984 the Anglican bishop of Liverpool urged the government to work harder to ameliorate the suffering caused by unemployment. Throughout the miners' strike, church leaders such as the bishop of Durham criticized the government and the National Coal Board. A number of bishops, including the archbishop of York, irritated the government by offering themselves as mediators in the dispute. For many, these highly unusual interventions in public policy by church leaders confirmed a view that things had gotten out of hand and that the Thatcher government had, perhaps, gone too far.

SOURCE *The Star,* London.

The words *continuity, harmony, stability,* traditional descriptions of British politics, no longer identify Britain of the 1980s. Riots in a host of British cities in the spring and summer of 1981 and again in the fall of 1985 indicate the violence and civil disorder that high unemployment and government-sanctioned racial isolation can foster. A new Anglo-Irish agreement between the U.K. and the Irish Republic, inaugurated in November, 1985, led to a Unionist strike in Northern Ireland in 1986 by Protestants who reject any hint of power sharing, but to no increase in the prospects for resolution of "the Irish problem." The occupation of Northern Ireland by British troops continues and its duration will soon exceed the lifespan of most of the soldiers stationed there. The 1984–85 miners' strike demonstrated the persistence of class politics, despite the class and partisan dealignment of electoral behavior. The expansion of support for the SDP/Liberal Alliance shows, by contrast, the yearning for a moderate course once again in British politics. British politics is in transition: Where is it heading?

The growing problems of economic performance, which have placed Britain near the bottom of the OECD nations, have severely strained the traditions of consensus that consolidated the postwar settlement. As slow growth in the 1950s and 1960s gave way to sharply circumscribed competitiveness after the 1973–74 recession (triggered by the rise in oil costs), the symbiosis between Conservative modernizers and mainstream Labourites was broken. Heath's failed industrial strategies, like the dramatic failures of the Social Contract during the 1974–79 Labour government, marked the demise of the postwar settlement. Trade union recalcitrance and unwillingness to accept the costs of decline combined with governmental failure to reverse a failing economic trajectory. Thatcher broke the stalemate and has surprised many by her staying power.

The 1983 Election and Beyond

Some claim that Labour lost the 1983 election, rather than the Conservatives winning it. Either way, there is evidence to suggest that decline in Labour support was linked both to an erosion of sentiment for the social-democratic project of the postwar settlement and to the continued interclass appeal of Thatcher's Tory party. As Ivor Crewe observes:

> Defection from Labour was widespread across the entire social spectrum of the Labour vote. But it was especially heavy on the periphery of its social constituency — 38 percent of 1979 non-manual Labour voters switched in 1983, 36 percent of its white collar union vote switched, and so did 33 percent of its non-union vote. The largest-scale switching occurred among homeowners (44 percent switched from Labour), working-class owners as much as middle-class owners. The Labour vote held up best — although still not very well — among council tenants (21 percent switched), blacks (21 percent), and those over 65 (25 percent). But there is scant comfort for Labour here. Council tenants are a slowly diminishing group; blacks are a tiny minority; and those over 65 will rapidly depart from the electorate.[26]

For Labour the results were devastating, and the party has had difficulty recovering the initiative, despite a change in leadership. In the second term of Thatcher's government, British political life bears the mark of her experiment. Inflation has been reduced to quite manageable terms and unemployment has increased to a level exceeding that of the Great Depression. The political culture is dominated by principles of individualism, and socialism is in considerable disrepute. Management prerogative has expanded enormously, and both union militancy and union power have abated from the level of the 1970s. The Labour Party is divided, and under the leadership of Neil Kinnock, it has set itself on a pragmatic course that reinforces the ideological drift toward the Alliance. But Labour is split over a National Executive Committee decision to expel a number of leading Liverpool members who belong to a hard-left political group banned by the party. At the same time, early in 1986, the Thatcher government was beset by what is widely considered to be her deepest crisis since she became party leader ten years ago: The Westland affair, which involved government improprieties in advancing an American takeover bid to rescue an ailing helicopter company, raised grave concerns about Thatcher's handling of the cabinet and led to a highly dramatic senior cabinet resignation.

Each party has its own expectations for the future, but none seems capable of mobilizing consent for a sustained political agenda. Will there be a return to a Labourite social-democratic vision, an anticlass politics of moderation led by the Alliance, or will a Thatcherite plan set the course for the remainder of the century? The path seems uncertain and not very hopeful. Social fragmentation and poor economic performance make acceptance of a resurgent postwar-settlement accord unlikely, and yet Thatcher's anti-integrationist politics is increasingly seen as too costly in terms of harmony and national unity.

Considered in terms of Western European comparisons, Britain has struck a very unusual compromise between capitalism and democracy. The democratic integration of the working class, women, and ethnic and racial minorities has been considerably narrowed and the social benefits of twentieth-century citizenship limited. Market forces have been unleashed, but apart from a considerable reduction in rates of inflation, the economic record is at best ambiguous, with unemployment causing severe hardship and the manufacturing base narrowed. Contemporary British politics does not offer an attractive export model for representative democracy as did the conventional model of British politics as Thatcher's government has taken Britain further from the postwar-settlement consensus than any other Western European country has thus far dared to go.

Notes

1. Anthony Sampson, *The Changing Anatomy of Britain* (New York: Random House, 1982), p. xi.
2. Ajit Singh, "U.K. Industry and the World Economy: A Case of De-Industrialization?" in *The Managed Economy: Essays in British Economic Policy and Perfomance Since 1929,* ed. Charles Feinstein (Oxford: Oxford University Press, 1983) p. 249.
3. Organisation for Economic Cooperation and Development, *OECD Economic Surveys: United Kingdom* (Paris: OECD, February, 1983), p. 51.
4. Anthony Barnett, "Iron Britannia," *New Left Review,* no. 134 (July/August, 1982), p. 62.
5. This discussion closely follows previous work. See: Joel Krieger, *Reagan, Thatcher and the Politics of Decline* (New York: Oxford University Press, 1986), pp. 59–108.
6. Conservative Central Office, *The Right Approach: A Statement of Conservative Aims* (London: Conservative Central Office, 1976), p. 50.
7. Tom Rees, "Immigration Policies in the United Kingdom," in *'Race' in Britain,* ed. Charles Husband (London: Hutchinson 1982), p. 88.
8. Conservative Central Office, *The Right Approach,* pp. 47–48.
9. Barry Troyna, "Reporting the National Front: British Values Observed," in *'Race' in Britain,* ed. Charles Husband (London: Hutchinson, 1982), pp. 265–67.
10. Anthony Mark Messina, "When Parties Fail: Race and the Emergence of Extra-Party Movements in Britain," (Unpublished paper, September, 1981) p. 34.
11. Gideon Ben-Tovim and John Gabriel, "The Politics of Race in Britain, 1962–1979: A Review of Major Trends and of Recent Debates," in *'Race' in Britain,* ed. Charles Husband (London: Hutchinson, 1982), pp. 160–61.
12. Messina, "When Parties Fail," p. 35.
13. Michael Jones, *Marxism Today* (May, 1980), p. 10.
14. Samuel H. Beer, *Britain Against Itself: The Political Contradictions of Collectivism* (New York: Norton, 1982), p. 82.
15. Bo Särlvik and Ivor Crewe, *Decade of Dealignment* (Cambridge: Cambridge University Press, 1983), pp. 80–85.
16. Otto Kirchheimer, "The Transformation of the European Party Systems," in *Political Parties and Political Development,* ed. Joseph LaPalombara and Myron Weiner (Princeton: Princeton University Press, 1966), p. 178.

17. Huw Benyon and Peter McMylor, "Decisive Power: The New Tory Lot Against the Miners," in *Digging Deeper,* ed. Huw Benyon (London: Verso, 1984), p. 35.
18. Donald R. Shell, "The British Constitution in 1984," *Parliamentary Affairs,* vol. 38, no. 2 (Spring 1985), p. 142.
19. Michael O'Higgins, "Inequality, Redistribution and Recession: The British Experience, 1976–1982" (Paper presented to the Conference on the Thatcher Government and British Political Economy, Harvard University Center for European Studies, April 19–20, 1985), pp. 4–7.
20. Commission of the European Communities, *European Economy* (November, 1984, no. 22), pp. 52–53.
21. Organisation for Economic Cooperation and Development, *OECD Economic Surveys: United Kingdom* (Paris: OECD, 1986), p. 47.
22. See: "The Attack of Inflation After 31st July 1977" (Cmnd. 6882, HMSO, 1977); "Winning the Battle Against Inflation" (Cmnd. 7293, HMSO, 1978).
23. Michael O'Higgins, "Privatisation and Social Welfare: Concepts, Analysis and the British Experience," (Paper presented to the Columbia University Seminar on Privatization, May 7, 1985), pp. 11–12.
24. See: T.H. Marshall, *Social Policy in the Twentieth Century* (London: Hutchinson, 1975), p. 95.
25. Shell, "British Constitution," p. 138.
26. Ivor Crewe, "Why Labour Lost the British Elections," *Public Opinion* (June/July 1983), p. 57.

Bibliography

Industrialization and State Formation

Hobsbawm, E.J. *Industry and Empire.* Harmondsworth: Penguin/Pelican, 1983.

Ingham, Geoffrey. *Capitalism Divided? The City and Industry in British Social Development.* London: Macmillan, 1984.

Jones, Gareth Stedman. *Outcast London: A Study in the Relationship between Classes in Victorian Society.* New York: Pantheon, 1984.

Landes, David S. *The Unbound Prometheus: Technological Change and Industrial Development in Western Europe from 1750 to the Present.* Cambridge: Cambridge University Press, 1969.

Maitland, F.W. *The Constitutional History of England.* Cambridge: Cambridge University Press, 1931.

Nairn, Tom. *The Break-up of Britain: Crisis and Neo-Nationalism.* 2d ed. London: New Left Books/Verso, 1981.

Thompson, Dorothy. *The Chartists: Popular Politics in the Industrial Revolution.* New York: Pantheon, 1984.

Thompson, E.P. *The Making of the English Working Class.* New York: Vintage, 1966.

The Rise and Fall of the Postwar Settlement

Coates, David. *Labour in Power? A Study of the Labour Government 1974–1979.* London: Longman, 1980.

Gamble, Andrew. *Britain in Decline: Economic Policy, Political Strategy and the British State.* Boston: Beacon Press, 1981

Hall, Peter A. *Governing the Economy: The Politics of State Intervention in Britain and France.* New York: Oxford University Press, 1986.

Middlemas, Keith. *Politics in Industrial Society: The Experience of the British System since 1911.* London: Andre Deutsch, 1979.

Panitch, Leo. *Social Democracy and Industrial Militancy: The Labour Party, the Trade Unions and Incomes Policy, 1945–1974.* Cambridge: Cambridge University Press, 1976.

Shonfield, Andrew. *Modern Capitalism: The Changing Balance of Public and Private Power.* Oxford: Oxford University Press, 1965.

State Institutions

Ashford, Douglas E. *Policy and Politics in Britain: The Limits of Consensus.* Oxford: Basil Blackwell, 1981.

Gough, Ian. *The Political Economy of the Welfare State*. London: Macmillan, 1979.
Greenwood, John and David Wilson, *Public Administration in Britain*. London: George Allen and Unwin, 1984.
Gyford, John. *Local Politics in Britain*. 2d. ed. London: Croom Helm, 1984.
Norton, Philip. *The Constitution in Flux*. Oxford: Basil Blackwell, 1982.
Walkland, S.A. and Michael Ryle, eds. *The Commons Today*. London: Fontana, 1981.

Social and Political Forces

Butler, David and Donald Stokes, *Political Change in Britain: The Evolution of Electoral Choice*. 2d ed. New York: St. Martin's Press, 1974.
Centre for Contemporary Cultural Studies, *The Empire Strikes Back: Race and Racism in 70s Britain*. London: Hutchinson, 1982.
Coates, David. *The Labour Party and the Struggle for Socialism*. Cambridge: Cambridge University Press, 1975.
Miliband, Ralph. *Parliamentary Socialism*. London: Merlin Press, 1973.
Rose, Richard. *The Problem of Party Government*. Harmondsworth: Penguin, 1976.
Särlvik, Bo and Ivor Crewe, *Decade of Dealignment: The Conservative Victory of 1979 and Electoral Trends in the 1970s*. Cambridge: Cambridge University Press, 1983.
Wilson, Elizabeth. *Women and the Welfare State*. London: Tavistock, 1977.

Thatcherism and Contemporary British Politics

Beer, Samuel H. *Britain Against Itself: The Political Contradictions of Collectivism*. New York: Norton, 1982.
Hall, Stuart and Martin Jacques, eds. *The Politics of Thatcherism*. London: Lawrence and Wishart, 1983.
Kaldor, Nicholas. *The Economic Consequences of Mrs. Thatcher*. London: Duckworth, 1983.
Krieger, Joel. *Reagan, Thatcher, and the Politics of Decline*. New York: Oxford University Press, 1986.
Riddell, Peter. *The Thatcher Government*. Oxford: Martin Robertson, 1983.

PART III

France

Mark Kesselman

6

The Emergence of the Modern French State

The structural tensions between capitalism and democracy historically have been more evident in France than in virtually any other Western European nation. France repeatedly experienced violent revolutions in the eighteenth and nineteenth centuries, caused in part by the unresolved relationship between democratic participation within the political sphere and economic control. Far into the twentieth century, political forces openly contested capitalist organization of the economy and advocated a socialist orientation. Throughout much of the period following World War II, the French Communist Party was among the largest political parties in France, and in the 1981 presidential and parliamentary elections, French voters elected a Socialist government that included among its aims the transfer to the state of substantial segments of private industry. Rather than moving France closer to socialism, however, the shift served to strengthen the already towering state. As Stanley Hoffmann observes:

> For centuries, the drama of France as a political community has been a drama about the relations between French society and the state. The story of the successive balances and imbalances between these two is far more interesting than the story of the often accidental succession of regimes and revolutions.[1]

Principles of French State Formation

French political life has been shaped by the early development of a strong central state that sought to undermine local loyalties and foster uniform rules throughout France, thereby homogenizing and unifying unruly French society. For centuries, French kings constructed an administrative apparatus to assure order and raise taxes, as well as a military apparatus to wage war. The development of this centralized state pitted the monarchy against the nobility, which possessed independent political authority and financial resources. Eventually, after sometimes violent clashes, but more typically by tenacious and skillful efforts by royal agents, the state achieved pre-eminence.

Hoffmann suggests that under Louis XIV (1643–1715), the state

> dampened all potential conflicts not only by eliminating independent sources of power but also by domesticating the nobility, assuring a minimum of social mobility, and exerting various material and spiritual controls over the mass of the people. Moreover, the state encouraged new productive activities.[2]

Louis XIV perfected the art of reducing noble prerogatives yet by his extravagance contributed to eventual revolutionary upheaval in 1789. Known as the Sun King, he attracted leading members of the aristocracy to his sumptuous court at Versailles. The nobility was soon reduced to dependence on royal largesse, withdrawing from productive activity on the land and deriving its income from feudal dues extracted from the peasantry.

In striking contrast to England, there was little tendency in France for the nobility and gentry to gain direct control over the land and exploit it for commercial purposes. In France, land ownership was broadly distributed. In particular, peasants retained control and cultivated most agricultural land: Prior to the revolution, over half of French peasant households owned at least some of the land that they tilled. However, they were forced to transfer to the nobility half or more of their crop as feudal dues — a form of tax that they increasingly resented and which eventually sparked the peasant uprisings that were part of the French Revolution.

The antiquated tax system helped foster revolutionary pressures in another respect as well. The military adventures of Louis XIV and his successors were even more costly than aristocratic profligacy. France was the most powerful nation in Europe in the seventeenth and eighteenth centuries, and Louis XIV aggressively sponsored the deadly game of war along with the courtly game at Versailles. For most of the period from the mid-seventeenth to the mid-eighteenth century, beginning with Louis XIV's accession to the throne and continuing through the reign of Louis XV, France was at war with her European neighbors. Yet war was expensive, and, given the lack of an expanding economy and the inelastic tax base, the only alternative was to raise taxes.

France's economic stagnation during the eighteenth century forced Louis XVI to raise taxes in order to finance the royal court, the administrative apparatus, and the cost of foreign wars. By 1788, state debt was so large that interest on past loans consumed one-half of current state expenditures.[3] However, increasing taxes required the assent of the *parlements,* which were semi-judicial, aristocratic bodies that retained a veto power over certain royal decisions. The Paris *parlement* rejected the proposal and forced the king to convene the Estates General, an assembly of the three feudal orders, or estates, representing the Church, nobility, and commoners (which was known as the Third Estate). By calling for a meeting of the Estates General in 1789, Louis XVI sealed his fate — and that of the monarchy. A series of peasant and urban uprisings impelled the delegates in the Estates General to increasingly bold measures: Thus was unleashed the revolutionary process that toppled the monarchy and the entire feudal order in France.

Revolution and State Building

The French Revolution of 1789 challenged the fundamental principle of monarchical authority not only within France but also throughout Europe. France was the first European nation in which a revolution toppled the monarchy and established a republic. The National Assembly, the legislature elected by universal suffrage, abolished all feudal privileges within France, and Louis XVI was imprisoned and sent to the guillotine. The break with the old feudal order seemed complete.

The French Revolution produced the first republic in France — although it proved quite short-lived. Napoleon Bonaparte staged a coup d'état and proclaimed himself emperor in 1802. He launched a series of expansionist wars and was eventually defeated at the Battle of Waterloo in 1815.

Under Napoleon's rule (1804–15), new administrative institutions harnessed the Revolution's nationalizing thrust. France's prefectoral system of territorial administration, the *Conseil d'État* to supervise the administration, the *École Polytechnique* to train top civil servants, the tightly integrated educational system, and the Napoleonic Code of civil law were established at this time. Centuries ago, a pattern was established

by which an unruly civil society was tamed by a powerful and somewhat authoritarian state. Stanley Hoffmann has described this pattern of French political culture as the coexistence of "limited authoritarianism and potential insurrection against authority."[4]

The French Revolution marked a violent break with the French and European past. Historian François Furet suggests that the French Revolution was the moment when

> the masses had broken in on the stage of history. . . . That is why, in a sense, everything indeed "began" here: 1789 opened a period when history

> was set *adrift,* once it was discovered that the actors in the theatre of the *Ancien Régime* [old order] were mere shadows. The Revolution . . . must be seen as not so much a set of causes and consequences as the opening of a society to all its possibilities. It invented a type of political discourse and practice by which we have been living ever since.[5]

Yet two brilliant students of the French Revolution, liberal aristocrat Alexis de Tocqueville and revolutionary Karl Marx, argued that rather than negating monarchical authority, the Revolution culminated centuries of the monarchy's tenacious efforts to unify the French state and nation. Although the Revolution toppled the royal family, it strengthened the state, which was the monarchy's greatest achievement. According to Tocqueville, the essence of the Revolution was that it eliminated aristocratic privileges and strengthened the centralized state bureaucracy.[6] It might be noted, moreover, that in contrast to virtually all other nations, including ostensibly stable Britain, France had displayed astonishing political continuity until the Revolution. (A single royal family had ruled France from 987 to 1789.)

Like Tocqueville, Marx stressed the connection between the monarchy and later regimes, as well as the importance of the Revolution in furthering state-sponsored centralization in France: "The first French Revolution, with its task of breaking all territorial, urban and provincial independent powers in order to create the bourgeois unity of the nation, was bound to develop what the absolute monarchy had begun — centralisation."[7] Marx also emphasized the independent power of the French executive in the nineteenth century, with roots in monarchic rule:

> The centralised State power, with its ubiquitous organs of standing army, police, bureaucracy, clergy and judicature — organs wrought after the plan of a systematic and hierarchic division of labour — originates from the days of the absolute monarchy. . . .[8]

The French state bureaucracy has retained monarchical and aristocratic features throughout the modern era. Top positions in the state bureaucracy — especially in the armed forces, and in the diplomatic and financial corps — have often been filled by descendants of the nobility. More significant than who rules the state, however, is the state's autonomous, one might say regal, position in French society: The state has its own distinctive culture and rules of recruitment and promotion, largely impervious to democratic impulses from the legislature and grassroots social forces. Regimes with sharply divergent orientations have succeeded each other, but the state has pursued its own course.

Nationalism. The French Revolution marked the origin of popularly based nationalism in Europe. A key document that incited the common people to revolt was "What Is the Third Estate?" a fiery pamphlet written by the Abbé de Sieyès shortly before the Revolution. "What is the Third Estate?" Sieyès asked. "Everything. What has it been until now in the political order? Nothing. What does it ask? *To be Something.*" Sieyès meant that France did not consist of its monarchy and nobility — but of its common people.

A sense of nationalism, combined with a common geographic homeland, culture, and state, inspired a process of political and social mobilization to defend the Revolution from the perils of domestic subversion and foreign attack. Thus, the French people came to identify closely with the concept of the French nation, both in peace and war. The common people defended the nation because it was *their* nation, shaped through revolutionary struggle.

France spent much of the nineteenth century digesting the lessons of the Revolution. The succession of regimes and revolutions in the nineteenth century — and the twentieth as well, for that matter — can be interpreted as varied attempts to work out the tensions and problems generated by the French Revolution. Among the key issues on which we focus in the remainder of the chapter are the organization of production and class relations, France's relations to the international arena, and the constitutional framework of French politics. The story begins with the peasantry — an unlikely group to play a key role in the modern world.

A Nation of Peasants: Economic and Class Relations

Until recently, the French Revolution was typically regarded as the prototype of a capitalist revolution, in which a rising bourgeoisie threw off feudal restrictions imposed on free production and commerce. Scholars now agree that the bourgeoisie gained very little from the French Revolution and the Revolution did not usher in explosive economic expansion fueled by capitalist investment. Quite the contrary: Until well into the twentieth century, France was predominantly a nation of small farmers, and the French economy was heavily oriented toward agriculture and small-scale production. John Zysman describes the paradox: "The revolution created a modern state, but it entrenched a traditional economy."[9] Comparing England and France in the mid-nineteenth century, Marx observes, "In England industry rules; in France, agriculture. In England, industry requires free trade; in France, protection, national monopoly besides other monopolies."[10]

The fact that France had a large peasant population in the early nineteenth century is hardly unusual; so did every other European nation. However, in France, unlike other major European nations, the peasantry survived as a large and powerful element well into the twentieth century. By the mid-nineteenth century, only one-quarter of all British male workers were engaged in agriculture; in France, male agricultural workers outnumbered male industrial workers until after World War II.[11] Most French citizens lived in the countryside or small towns until the 1950s. In 1946, for example, there were sixty-one towns in Britain with over one hundred thousand inhabitants; the comparable figure for France was twenty-two.[12]

The persistence of the peasantry considerably narrowed France's potential industrial base. Some economic historians have questioned whether France ever experienced an industrial revolution such as occurred in Britain in the late eighteenth and early nineteenth centuries, and in Germany in the late nineteenth century. Since farmers meet many of their consumption needs directly, rather than purchasing commodities in the market, they provide a smaller domestic market than city-dwellers for manufactured products. Moreover, because most arable land in France was widely distributed into small landholdings, the incentive to innovate was further reduced.

Although peasants were numerous in France, they were not politically active. As Marx scornfully describes in *The Eighteenth Brumaire of Louis Bonaparte,* French peasant families lived in isolation from one another rather than forming a community or a cohesive social force. They were a conglomerate, "much as potatoes in a sack form a sackful of potatoes."[13] Under these conditions, Marx asserts, peasants could achieve political representation only when organized by an external agency, such as the authoritarian Louis Bonaparte, who led the Second Republic briefly before following his uncle's example and declaring himself Emperor Napoleon III in 1852. He was captured during the Franco-Prussian War and replaced by the Third Republic in 1870.

Because the peasantry was so numerous, politicians across the political spectrum vied for peasant support. With the exception of a few areas such as Brittany, where the influence of the Catholic church and aristocratic families remained especially powerful, peasants were generally staunch republicans, a result of the gains that they achieved during the French Revolution. However, their attachment to the land, individualistic outlook, and disdain of urban and industrial values often made peasants quite conservative. They thus represented a countervailing force to the turbulent, often radical, working class. One should beware of stereotypes about conservative peasants, however. In Provence and the southwest, for example, peasants provided an important source of support for leftist political parties. In these "red" regions, peasants advocated collectivizing land as a way to counteract falling agricultural prices and other economic hardships.[14] Yet, overall, peasants were a conservative influence in an important respect: Because all political parties, including those of the Left, looked to the peasantry for support, they were reluctant to advocate industrialization, which would have upset the rural-urban balance in France.

The Making of the French Working Class

Given the slow pace of industrialization, the process of working-class formation occurred over a very long period. The French working class in 1830 was quite heterogeneous, with little common identity and solidarity. The working class was relatively small, weak, and unable to achieve adequate political representation in the succession of regimes, dominated by small-town and rural forces, from the nineteenth century through the mid-twentieth century. As a result of repression and political exclusion, radical tendencies developed within the working class.

The character of the French working class was influenced by the relationship between trade unions — the organizations that workers formed to defend their economic interests — and socialist political parties, which aimed at political transformation. In France, unlike Great Britain and other northern European nations, trade unions remained separate from leftist parties until after World War II, when the Communist Party gained control of the *Confédération Générale du Travail* (CGT), the largest labor confederation.

The French labor movement was inclined for generations toward syndicalism, a revolutionary doctrine by which the workers seize control of the economy by direct means. This could be achieved, it was held, through a general strike, which would bring production to a halt and make workers' control possible. Such a position was less utopian at the time than it now appears, for the predominance of skilled craftsworkers made it plausible that the working class might aspire to organizing and running production.

The political orientation of the French working class was heavily influenced by revolutionary upheavals in 1830, 1848, and 1871. In every case, the working class made a key contribution and yet failed to obtain the fruits of its participation. Workers' militance was violently crushed in all three cases, and the clashes left a legacy of working-class bitterness and opposition. The Paris Commune provides the most important example.

The Paris Commune was formed in 1871, when the working class seized power to prevent the government of the Third Republic, headed by Adolphe Thiers, from capitulating to Bismarck following France's defeat in the Franco-Prussian war. When the rest of France refused to follow the example of Paris and take up arms, the Commune's fate was sealed. Thiers ordered the French army to blockade the city. After two months, when the population was impoverished and exhausted, Thiers ordered the army to enter Paris. There ensued the bloodiest civil war that France had known. The Communards were defenseless in face of the army: More than twenty thousand Communards were killed, far more than the number of victims in the Reign of Terror during the French Revolution.

During the two brief months of the Commune's existence, Paris was run according to radically democratic principles. A majority of members of the elected Commune were workers, members were paid the equivalent of a skilled worker's wages, and the recall vote was introduced to permit citizens to dismiss elected representatives. The Commune was notable less for its social reforms — for example, it abolished night work for bakers — than for the challenge that it represented by its mere existence.

As in other bloody encounters between workers and the state, the Paris Commune was a glorious moment in French working-class struggles — but a bitter defeat that symbolized the gulf between workers and the rest of the French political community. Most workers supported socialist parties, and when a unified socialist party, the *Section Française de l'Internationale Ouvrière* (SFIO), was formed in 1906 by the fusion of two rival parties, it quickly became the second largest party in the Third Republic. The potential threat that workers' opposition posed to the republic quickly faded, however, at the outbreak of World War I. The Socialist Party had pledged to oppose French entry into war, but it joined the Sacred Union, the governmental coalition that conducted the war, following the assassination of revered Socialist Party leader Jean Jaurès, who had opposed the war.

France won the war but suffered incalculable damage, in part because much of the fighting occurred on French soil: 1.4 million Frenchmen were killed, one out of every twenty-five French citizens. In World War I, as in every war in which it was involved in the nineteenth and twentieth centuries, France emerged weaker as a result of its participation in the international arena. At the same time, the working class sought — unsuccessfully — to gain the rewards for its sacrifices. The working class engaged in widespread strikes after both World War I and World War II and, as in earlier periods, was violently suppressed by the army and police.

The enormous losses that France suffered in World War I strengthened the tendency, which had developed throughout the nineteenth century, toward an inward-looking stance, a desire to escape international competition in favor of domestic stability and tranquility. After the war, France sought security by trying to extract maximum war damages from Germany and by constructing the Maginot line, an immense fortification to protect France's eastern border from Germany. (When the German army invaded France in 1940, however, it entered through Belgium, far from the Maginot line.)

The Third Republic also sought security by isolating the working class from meaningful political participation. The tension between democratic participation and economic control was uneasily resolved during the Third Republic — as it was during most periods in the Fourth and Fifth Republics — by diluting democratic participation. Much of the time, conservative coalitions succeeded in excluding the working class and its representatives from a meaningful share of political power. The working class was unable to escape from this political ghetto, mainly because of its relatively small size — itself a result of incomplete industrialization in France.

The Slow Pace of Industrialization

There have been endless discussions of why France did not become an industrial leader in the nineteenth century. Although France began the century fairly close to Britain in terms of economic output and, in fact, achieved steady growth through much of the century, by 1900, France trailed the United States, Great Britain, and Germany in industrial development. A large peasantry acted as a brake on industrialization, and the fact that France was well-endowed with fertile farmland and poorly endowed with key natural resources, notably coal, iron, and petroleum, further inhibited industrial growth. Historians have also pointed to the relatively underdeveloped entrepreneurial spirit in France. Within the ranks of the middle class, professionals, administrators, and shopkeepers outnumbered industrial entrepreneurs. In general, French manufacturers excelled in sectors that did not confer international industrial leadership — agricultural produce (notably wine) and custom-made luxury goods (silkweaving and porcelain), which did not lend themselves to mechanized production and for which mass markets did not exist.

Another factor inhibiting industrial development was the slow growth of the French population, an important reflection of Malthusian values in France. In the middle of the nineteenth century, France was the second-largest nation in Europe (after Russia). However, the British population more than tripled in the nineteenth century, and the number of Germans more than doubled, but France's population increased by less than one-half.[15] France had 15 percent of Europe's population in 1800, but only 8 percent by 1950.[16] Slow population growth meant smaller potential demand and less incentive for business firms to invest and increase productivity.

More important than technical or demographic factors, however, there was no social force in France to sponsor rapid industrial growth. Unlike Britain, where the state sought to remove restrictions on the free operation of market forces, or Prussia, where Bismarck used the state to sponsor industrialization from above, the French state aimed to "maintain an equilibrium among industry, commerce, and agriculture and attempt[ed] to insulate France from the distress and upheaval that had struck other nations bent upon rapid economic advance."[17] Dominant social and political forces in France aimed to maximize stability, not economic growth. Consequently, France had among the highest tariff barriers in Western Europe during most of the nineteenth century and early twentieth century. The purpose was not to shield French firms so that they could develop the capacity to compete internationally, but rather to protect small producers (farmers, manufacturers, and artisans) from foreign competition. Economic historian Richard Kuisel observes that "rarely, if ever, did [the French state] act to promote economic expansion, plan development, or advance economic democracy."[18]

Yet the state did not confine its economic activity to purely protectionist purposes. In a tradition dating back to Colbert, who served as finance minister to Louis XIV and who directed the creation of a French merchant marine, the state played an important role in sponsoring large-scale economic projects, especially in the nineteenth and early twentieth centuries. For example, in the 1860s, under Napoleon III, the state consolidated several small railroad companies; encouraged the formation of the *Crédit Mobilier,* an investment bank to finance railroad development; and guaranteed interest rates on bonds sold to underwrite railroad construction.

In brief, France was not an economic pioneer in the nineteenth and early twentieth centuries: Production was typically carried on in small plants, using traditional crafts methods. At the beginning of the twentieth century, nearly 50 percent of German industrial workers were concentrated in factories with over fifty workers, but only 29 percent of French workers were found in plants of this size.[19]

Economist Alexander Gerschenkron has suggested that the role of the state in fostering economic development in the nineteenth century depended on its relative position in the industrialization process.[20] There was little reason for the British state, as the industrial pioneer, to intervene to promote economic development. Because Germany was so clearly backward, both economically and politically, state action was needed to overcome the gap. France apparently fell midway between Germany and Great Britain and enjoyed the apparent luxury — eventually the illusion — of political and economic superiority; consequently, the state placed a low priority on industrial development. Whereas German output quadrupled between 1870 and 1938, French output only doubled during the same period.[21] In France, the state intervened — but to foster economic protection, not development. Zysman points out that in France, "the state was not considered an alien force to be limited, but an instrument for protecting against the unknown and guarding what one had already gained."[22]

France in the International Context

France was the most powerful European power from the sixteenth through the nineteenth centuries, as a result of its size, population, strategic location, affluence, and aggressive monarchy. However, Napoleon's defeat in 1815 marked the end of France's global ambitions. Although France continued to be regarded as the dominant continental European power until its defeat in the Franco-Prussian War of 1870–71 — and even until World War II — the nation was generally more preoccupied by domestic than international concerns. During the 1880s, Prime Minister Jules Ferry embarked on a policy of colonial acquisition, appropriating Indochina and vast areas of Africa. However, France's overseas empire was far less important to its economy than the British empire was for Britain's economy.

French international involvement produced few benefits in the nineteenth century and overwhelming costs in the two world wars of the twentieth century. Although France was the major Western European battleground in World War I, it took inadequate measures to safeguard against the resurgence of Germany in the 1920s and 1930s. Further, the Third Republic experienced a steady decline as it failed to cope with the twin crises of the Great Depression and the Nazi threat in the 1930s.

In World War II, France suffered a rapid and humiliating defeat by the German army. The armistice signed in 1940 divided France in two. Only southern France remained a formally independent nation; the north was directly administered by the German occupation forces. The war also intensified domestic conflicts that predated its outbreak: The occupied Vichy regime in the south represented the conservative forces that had felt excluded from power under the Popular Front (made up of the Socialist and Radical parties, with Communist support) and other Left-leaning governments of the late 1930s.

The Discontinuity of Constitutional Forms

In the two hundred years since the Revolution of 1789, France changed governments at a bewildering tempo: In that time France has had fifteen constitutions. Ironically, in light of the low esteem in which it was widely held, the Third Republic (1870–1940) was the most durable regime that France has known in modern times, a fact that suggests that the regime accurately reflected fundamental traits in France's political, social, and economic structure. (In a famous phrase, Thiers described the Third Republic as the "regime that divides us least.")

The (Incomplete) Republican Synthesis. According to Stanley Hoffmann, until the period following World War II, France could be characterized as a "stalemate society," which was the product of what Hoffmann calls a "republican synthesis" among social forces. Hoffmann identifies three pillars of the republican synthesis: in the economy, France was a "halfway house between the old rural society and industrialization"; within the political sphere, there was a style of authority that combined tendencies toward authoritarianism with a tendency to protest against authority; and, in the social sphere, there was the atomization of French society, a tendency toward individualism, with a corresponding paucity of associational activity.[23]

The republican synthesis was the product of blockages within French society. Hoffmann suggests that France could be characterized as a stalemate society because it was better at protecting the privileges of those forces upon whom the republican synthesis rested than at promoting modernization and change within France.

The republican synthesis imperfectly represented France's varied social forces. As a result of electoral institutions, the peasantry and traditional middle class were overrepresented and, through close links to elected officials in the all-powerful legislature, well placed to extract benefits from the state bureaucracy. Workers fared less well; their interests found a meager place in the republican synthesis.

The Left, which defended workers' interests, governed for a handful of years during the Third Republic. The most noteworthy period was during the Depression. In 1936, the Socialist and Radical parties held office with Communist Party support. Under Socialist Prime Minister Léon Blum, the Popular Front sponsored economic and social reforms, including paid vacations, the forty-hour work week, family allowances, and minimal union protection.

The Third Republic flourished for generations despite working-class opposition. However, after World War I, the conservative regime delivered diminishing advantages and increasing costs for all groups. Although France was regarded as the most powerful nation in continental Europe, it was experiencing a steady decline. Given the web of protectionism and economic stagnation, as well as the political stalemate that immobilized the Third Republic, the regime was ill prepared for World War II. The decline of the Third Republic was tragically demonstrated when France, widely regarded as the foremost military power in Europe, was quickly overrun by the German invasion in 1940.

The war years were the bleakest period in modern French history. The Vichy government was a caricature of the republican synthesis in its call for a return to the soil at the same time that it was delivering war matériel and French workers to Nazi industry. French honor was partially salvaged by the Resistance forces that operated both within France and from London. Although the Resistance was a collection of groups, leftist forces (especially Communists) were the most active within the internal Resistance. Leading the Resistance forces outside France was Charles de Gaulle, an audacious army officer who rose within the ranks of the army and was appointed to a junior cabinet position in the last government before the collapse of the Third Republic. De Gaulle was to play a leading role in French politics for the next thirty years.

Curiously, Vichy and the Resistance shared certain political goals: Both opposed the rampant individualism of the Third Republic and sought to introduce central planning and a spirit of cooperation among social forces (in Vichy's case, by authoritarian means). From the tragedy of the war years came a new political approach, based on using the state to foster economic development within a capitalist framework. The new approach reworked France's statist tradition of highly centralized government as it had evolved in the Third Republic: The tradition of state action to protect small producer groups had been substantially discredited by the severity of the Depression and the German occupation. Although remnants of this pattern survive to the present day, the major focus of state activity after the war shifted from protecting the status quo to stimulating economic expansion, despite intense political conflict and constitutional discontinuity.

The Implications for Contemporary French Politics

France emerged from the wreckage of World War II in a state of physical and political exhaustion. The economy was shattered, bitter conflicts reappeared soon after the Liberation, and traditional class cleavages intensified. The Fourth Republic, formed in 1946, was bitterly contested by major forces on the Left and Right. There was little agreement about the kind of political regime that was appropriate and desirable for France, and it appeared that France's century-long decline would continue.

Yet, during the late 1940s, despite intense conflicts that were to destroy the Fourth Republic in 1958 and the constant challenge posed by Communist Party opposition, a postwar settlement fundamentally at odds with the previously existing political culture and economy took shape. In part because of the expansion of international capitalism, but in good measure because of a change within French political and economic life, France surged ahead in a way that had not occurred for a century. The old cleavages were not eliminated, but economic expansion made them more tolerable. From a laggard in achieving capitalist industrialization, France began to be regarded as a pioneer in developing techniques of state-managed growth.

However, this time of expansion and optimism did not last indefinitely. In May, 1968, a cultural revolution shook the nation and sparked new debates that may prove as influential as the Revolution of 1789. The international economic crisis of the 1970s and 1980s again forced the French to consider issues that had been temporarily set aside during the more harmonious years of economic expansion.

NOTES

1. Stanley Hoffmann, *Decline or Renewal? France Since the 1930s* (New York: The Viking Press, 1974), p. 443.
2. Hoffmann, *Decline or Renewal?* p. 443.
3. Perry Anderson, *Lineages of the Absolutist State* (London: New Left Books, 1974), p. 111. This section also draws on Theda Skocpol, *States and Social Revolutions: A Comparative Analysis of France, Russia, and China* (New York: Cambridge University Press, 1979).
4. Stanley Hoffmann, "Paradoxes of the French Political Community," in *In Search of France,* ed. Stanley Hoffmann (New York: Harper Torchbook, 1965), p. 8.
5. François Furet, *Interpreting the French Revolution* (Cambridge: Cambridge University Press, 1981), p. 46.
6. Alexis de Tocqueville, *The Old Régime and the French Revolution* (Garden City: Doubleday Anchor, 1955).
7. Karl Marx, *The Eighteenth Brumaire of Louis Napoleon,* in *The Karl Marx Reader,* ed. Robert Tucker (New York: W.W. Norton, 1972), p. 514.
8. Karl Marx, *The Civil War in France,* in *The Karl Marx Reader,* ed. Robert Tucker (New York: W.W. Norton, 1972), p. 552.

9. John Zysman, *Political Strategies for Industrial Order: State, Market, and Industry in France* (Berkeley: University of California Press, 1977), p. 52.
10. Karl Marx, *Class Struggles (1848–1850)* (New York: International Publishers, 1976), p. 113.
11. David S. Landes, *The Unbound Prometheus: Technological Change and Industrial Development in Western Europe from 1750 to the Present* (Cambridge: Cambridge University Press, 1972), pp. 187–88.
12. Philip M. Williams, *Crisis and Compromise: Politics in the Fourth Republic* (Hamden, CT: Archon Books, 1964), p. 3.
13. Marx, *The Eighteenth Brumaire,* p. 515.
14. Tony Judt, *Socialism in Provence, 1871–1914: A Study in the Origins of the Modern French Left* (Cambridge: Cambridge University Press, 1979), passim.
15. William H. Sewell, Jr., *Work and Revolution in France: The Language of Labor from the Old Regime to 1848* (Cambridge: Cambridge University Press, 1980), p. 148.
16. Georges Dupeux, *La Société Française, 1789–1970* (Paris: Armand Colin, 1974), p. 10.
17. Richard F. Kuisel, *Capitalism and the State in Modern France* (Cambridge: Cambridge University Press, 1981), p. 15.
18. Kuisel, *Capitalism,* p. 16.
19. Kuisel, *Capitalism,* p. 28.
20. Alexander Gerschenkron, *Economic Backwardness in Historical Perspective* (Cambridge: Harvard University Press, 1962), passim.
21. Warren C. Baum, *The French Economy and the State* (Princeton: Princeton University Press, 1958), p. 16.
22. Zysman, *Political Strategies,* p. 55.
23. Stanley Hoffmann, "Paradoxes."

7

The Rise and Fall of the Postwar Settlement

France entered the postwar period humiliated and weakened from the defeat and occupation by German forces, its illusion of being a world power brutally shattered. With over two million French in prisoner-of-war camps or drafted to work in German industry, and the transportation system and productive apparatus badly damaged, it was difficult merely to provide essential services.

Jean Monnet, one of the principal architects of France's postwar renaissance, emphasized that the roots of France's difficulties lay deeper than military defeat and occupation. "It was obvious to everyone that France emerged from the war seriously weakened. Less well known, or less willingly acknowledged, was the weakness from which she was already suffering when the war broke out. This, no less than military or moral shortcomings, explained her sudden collapse. By 1938 the country was exhausted: it had lost a third of its investment capacity in a decade of crisis and social change."[1]

The Rise of the Postwar Settlement

The postwar years witnessed a fundamental restructuring of France's political economy under the Fourth Republic. Two political subsystems played a decisive role in the postwar period: The representative subsystem, centered in the National Assembly, was a forum for the clash of political parties and politicians, while the administrative subsystem, which was far removed from the legislative arena, directed bureaucratic initiatives to reshape France's political economy. To the extent that the two systems came into contact, they sought conflicting goals. Except for the Communist Party, most political forces within the representative system aimed to preserve the traditional republican synthesis, the existing balance of social and political forces. The administrative subsystem sought, not to preserve, but to undermine traditional France in order to revitalize French capitalism. The dramatic spectacle of partisan political conflict dominated public attention; the quiet process of state-led economic transformation, however, was of far more enduring significance.

Unable to resolve France's colonial burden, the Fourth Republic fell, and in 1958, General Charles de Gaulle returned to power to sponsor the Fifth Republic. The Fifth Republic was a semipresidential system in which the National Assembly was reduced to a pale shadow of its former role. In one important respect, however, the Fourth and Fifth Republics were alike: Neither succeeded in developing a framework that assured adequate representation to the French working class. Consequently, the postwar settlement in France was fundamentally incomplete and fragile.

Along with the other Western European nations analyzed in this book, France experienced a remarkable economic boom beginning in the late 1940s. However, France was unusual in three respects: the extent and durability of economic growth was especially great; the state played a key role in restructuring the economy; and organized labor was underrepresented in the mechanisms that directed the postwar settlement.

Evolution of the Constitutional Order

Soon after the euphoria of the Liberation passed, political divisions reemerged, as France scrambled to develop political institutions that would fill the vacuum created by the defeat of the Vichy regime and the end of the German occupation. The provisional government that took power in 1944 was a coalition of Resistance forces under the leadership of Charles de Gaulle. A referendum in October, 1945, asked citizens whether they preferred returning to the constitution of the Third Republic or creating a new republic, and an overwhelming majority voted to begin anew. However, when an elected Constituent Assembly met to draft a new constitution, conflicts immediately developed over what to substitute for the discredited Third Republic.

General de Gaulle, who had emerged as the leader of the Resistance forces outside France, was the first prime minister of the provisional government. De Gaulle advocated a regime that would make possible forceful leadership — the critical ingredient whose absence, in his view, produced France's decline in the 1920s and 1930s, culminating in the military disaster of 1940. However, the three major political parties that dominated the Constituent Assembly — Socialist, Communist, and Christian Democratic — preferred legislative sovereignty and opposed a strong executive on the grounds that it was undemocratic and smacked of Bonapartism. When de Gaulle failed to persuade them to accept his ideas, he abruptly resigned in January, 1946. Nonetheless, in part because of his implicit opposition to the draft constitution for the Fourth Republic (he did not publicly take a stand, but his withdrawal from active politics provided a clear message), French voters rejected the proposed constitution in a referendum.

After some slight concessions were made to de Gaulle's views, a new draft constitution was put to another referendum. This time, however, de Gaulle campaigned against the proposed constitution and actively sought to regain power. The constitution was approved by a narrow margin of one million votes: the fact that fewer citizens voted in favor than had voted *against* the first draft (there was a large increase in abstentions) indicates the Fourth Republic's slim base of support. As one scholar notes, "Plainly, it [the constitution] was accepted not on its merits but as an escape from provisional government."[2]

During its brief existence, the Fourth Republic provided a volatile, sometimes amusing, but often depressing, spectacle. De Gaulle's criticism of the republic as preventing forceful leadership appeared amply justified. The constitution delegated sovereignty to the six hundred deputies of the National Assembly, the lower house of the legislature, and placed few restrictions on the Assembly's powers. Yet, given perpetual conflicts among the many parties represented within the legislature, the National Assembly made little use of its constitutional powers. As Hoffmann describes the French multiparty system, "parties were ideological but at the same time resembled pressure groups in the sense that each one represented only a small section of the population and was tempted to behave as a spokesman for the interests of that small section."[3] Deputies spent most of their time debating lofty principles, intervening with the bureaucracy on behalf of constituents, and making and unmaking governments.

The prime minister and other cabinet ministers, known collectively as the government, owed their existence to the vagaries of parliamentary arithmetic. In order for a government to be elected and remain in office, it needed to obtain the votes of a majority of deputies. This was no easy matter, since there were numerous political parties in the Assembly, none of which had anywhere near a majority of deputies. In place of stable coalitions, tactical alliances were constantly forming and disintegrating. Moreover, a large minority of all deputies belonged to parties fundamentally opposed to the constitution, notably the Communist Party (PCF) and the Gaullist and Poujade movements. In order to gain a legislative majority, a government needed the votes of most other parties in the Assembly. Yet the prosystem parties on the center-Left and center-Right were themselves at odds. When a majority could be mustered to address one issue, it quickly dissolved when another issue arose. The result was that the Fourth Republic lurched from one ministerial crisis to the next: There were two dozen governments during the Fourth Republic's twelve-year existence.

Yet, during the years of the Fourth Republic, France experienced a national revival, which marked a striking contrast to the previous century of decline. When de Gaulle returned to power in 1958, he provided additional support for the renaissance in progress. De Gaulle created a republic to counteract what he considered the French tendency toward fractiousness: The constitution of the Fifth Republic accorded priority to leadership and left little room for democratic participation. De Gaulle's quasi-authoritarian republic was ill equipped to represent France's diverse social forces, but it was extremely effective at coordinating state efforts to pursue ambitious goals, including promoting unpopular policies necessary to achieve those goals. Although de Gaulle was credited with sponsoring the reversal of French fortunes, the origins of France's extraordinary economic revival actually predate the Fifth Republic.

Thanks to de Gaulle's personal popularity, the constitution of the Fifth Republic was ratified in September, 1958, by 80 percent of the voters, which signified a far greater popular base of support than the Fourth Republic enjoyed. The Fifth Republic addressed the perennial tension in France between democratic participation and political leadership by vastly reducing the former. Moreover, it sought to resolve the tension between capitalism and democracy by fostering rapid economic growth, in the hope that rising living standards would produce political stability. De Gaulle also exercised skillful leadership; his appeal to French *grandeur* (greatness) and independence helped ease the transition to an industrialized order.

The Enigma of Charles de Gaulle. Charles de Gaulle was a complex and contradictory figure. On the one hand, he was a faithful representative of traditional France, deeply attached to the values of order and hierarchy, which earned him the enmity of the Left. Yet, on the other hand, de Gaulle's personal leadership and the republic that he created provided the force to undermine the republican synthesis and restructure the French political economy. Stephen Cohen captures the irony that de Gaulle and the Gaullist movement functioned to hold "traditional France in place politically while building a new France."[4] Thus, at the same time that de Gaulle was closely linked to the traditional social forces of rural and small-town France, the policies that he sponsored to rationalize French capitalism severely undermined these groups.

De Gaulle was quite uninterested in economic matters for their own sake. On one occasion, when asked at a news conference why France did not modify its economic policy in a way that benefitted French business, he contemptuously remarked that French policy was not made on the floor of the stock exchange. De Gaulle's interest in economic rationalization derived from his fundamental aim of restoring France to a position of world leadership and his recognition that France could not play an important international role without a strong economy. De Gaulle described his feelings about France in the classic first paragraph of his war memoirs:

> All my life I have thought of France in a certain way. This is inspired by sentiments as much as by reason. . . . Instinctively I have the feeling that Providence has created her either for complete successes or exemplary misfortunes. . . . But the positive side of my mind also assures me that France is not really herself unless in the front rank; that only vast enterprises are capable of counterbalancing the ferments of dispersal which are inherent in her people. . . . In short, to my mind, France cannot be France without greatness [*grandeur*].[5]

In the first years of the Fifth Republic, during the late 1950s and early 1960s, there was a substantial measure of political stability. Only the Communist and Socialist parties opposed de Gaulle's leadership, but they were considerably reduced in size after 1958, because de Gaulle succeeded in isolating Left party leaders and attracting substantial numbers of working-class votes.

For several decades, France had one of the highest economic growth rates in Western Europe. Although the process originated during the Fourth Republic in the 1950s, it was sustained for two decades in the Fifth Republic. Yet de Gaulle's somewhat authoritarian style of rule eventually encountered opposition generated by the strains of rapid growth. The regime had purchased social peace by economic expansion and so was dependent on continued growth. Therefore, as the French economic miracle faltered in the 1970s, the conservative coalition ruling France since 1958 became increasingly unpopular.

Thus was laid the basis for the reversal of government and opposition (known as "alternation") that brought the Left to power in 1981. The Left's electoral success was partially a tribute to the Fifth Republic's legitimacy, since the institutional framework provided remarkable continuity and stability despite a drastic shift in the political orientation of the governing coalition. Yet, because the Left failed to restore growth or develop a new, stable political majority, there has been increased political volatility since 1981 and a shift toward the right in 1986. At the same time, it is doubtful that the Right will succeed where the Left has failed, which leaves the future of French politics open and uncertain.

The Politically Regulated Market Economy

From the first years of the Fourth Republic, a new approach developed within the administrative sphere that was in striking contrast to the partisan strife in the Third and Fourth Republics. The new approach used the state, not to protect an archaic society and economy, but to foster a modernized capitalism, based on large, productive firms, utilizing technologically advanced methods in order to invest, expand, and export.

As in the past, the state played a key role, although the focus of state activity changed drastically in the postwar period. Under the Third Republic, the state intervened to assure an equilibrium among the social forces that formed the republican synthesis. In the new scheme, the state sought to overcome conservative forces and transform France into an industrialized capitalist nation. Although some of the modernizers were Socialists, their first priority was to modernize capitalism, not reorganize the economy along socialist lines.

The working class remained excluded from the political process throughout the period until 1981: As a result of its relative weakness and ideological opposition, organized labor was given a very small role in planning the new arrangements. Although workers obtained substantial benefits from the enormous economic expansion of the postwar period, representatives of the working class in the trade union and political spheres took little part in shaping the new arrangements; further, rapid economic growth not only failed to diminish already extensive income inequalities but also intensified them. Thus, despite its enormous success in transforming the country, the French postwar settlement commanded less agreement and proved of shorter duration than its counterpart in most other European nations.

From Stalemate Society to Organized Capitalism. France entered the postwar period ripe for change yet with little indication of how it would occur. Few advocated a return to the Third Republic, and there was a brief moment of widespread consensus on the need for political, economic, and moral regeneration; however, political divisions quickly reemerged. As in the past, the state's role was central. This time, however, rather than seeking to protect the stalemate society of small producers in the countryside and towns, the state promoted the transition to a concentrated, industrialized, modern capitalism.

The Resistance forces, which ruled France after the war, ascribed responsibility for France's crushing defeat and the entire previous century of French decline to the inwardly looking, socially conservative equilibrium of the stalemate society. Rejecting the republican synthesis, they laid the groundwork for a new stance, which fundamentally altered the relationship of capitalism and democracy in France. The shift to "modern capitalism," as the new pattern was termed by economist Andrew Shonfield, remade the political economy and produced a resurgence that propelled France to the front rank of industrialized, capitalist democracies.[6]

Basic conflicts regarding the organization of production and the relationship between capitalism and democracy were not resolved. In particular, the relationship of the industrialized working class to dominant political and economic institutions persisted, splitting the Fourth and Fifth Republics, as it had divided the Third Republic. De Gaulle attempted to reduce class conflict by economic expansion and an appeal to French national glory — *grandeur,* in his terms. For a brief period after 1958, he succeeded in forging a cross-class alliance, including substantial numbers of workers, around these goals. But in the absence of mechanisms for organizing workers' representation on a collective and not simply individual basis, the project failed to achieve durable social harmony.

Other Western European nations experienced a fundamental shift in the political economy following World War II, resulting in the development of an interventionist state. Although the size and scope of the French state also increased dramatically, new tasks were grafted onto a state that habitually penetrated throughout French society. Shonfield observed that the interventionist state

> belongs to the very stuff of the French tradition. . . . In the form in which it has developed today the French method is probably the most interesting and influential expression of capitalism in its new guise. . . . [N]o other nation has so self-consciously fought to make a coherent system out of the devices which have been adopted more or less haphazardly elsewhere. And in no other nation is the new felt to fit so snugly into the old. It provides,

> therefore, some of the richest material for the analysis of modern capitalism.[7]

Compared to other Western European nations, France was distinctive in that there was the coexistence (conflictual, to be sure) of two currents: an administrative tradition, centering on the centralized state; and a democratic tradition. In the Third Republic, the two reinforced the republican synthesis of the stalemate society. Following World War II, given universal agreement on the need for change, the state was quickly able to reorient its course to pursue new goals. Richard Kuisel observes, "After the war, what was distinctive about France was the compelling sense of relative economic backwardness. This impulse was the principal stimulus for economic renovation and set France apart from other countries."[8] France was well equipped to develop the institutional capacity (ironically, in part as a result of innovations sponsored by the Vichy regime) to make the shift. Kuisel describes the change as follows:

> France resembled other capitalist countries in developing an arsenal of institutions for managing the economy. Like the others it recognized the need for fulfilling certain vital functions such as smoothing out the business cycle, easing adjustments caused by economic dislocation, promoting growth and full employment, and facilitating the general coordination of public policy. Yet France found its own way to perform these tasks. It lodged responsibility in new public institutions and staffed them with modernizers. It relied heavily on state intervention and planning. . . . The market and the liberal credo, nevertheless, survived and functioned vigorously alongside the new organs of management. The result was a Gallic style of economic management that blended state direction, corporatist bodies, and market forces.[9]

The Postwar Settlement and Planning

Most of the planners in the postwar period were activists from the Resistance whom General de Gaulle appointed to administrative positions after the Liberation. They were disdainful of the archaic character of French capitalism, impatient with rigid administrative routines, and eager to use the state to revitalize France. The key administrative agency in reorienting the French political economy was the newly created Planning Commission. However, planning should be understood in a far broader sense than the preparation of the various five-year plans. Planning was the formal expression of the state's new activist approach, which sought to associate dynamic, private business groups and state administrators in the common task of modernizing French capitalism.

Two alternatives were rejected in favor of a third course. First, as mentioned previously, a return to the stalemate society, in which there would be a balance of agriculture, small-scale manufacturing, and commerce, was rejected. It was agreed that priority needed to be accorded to modernizing the productive apparatus. The government had to choose between two impulses that had guided the Resistance program for postwar France: a modernizing thrust and a socialist, egalitarian, moral emphasis. The first pointed toward state-sponsored modernization of French capitalism; the second toward a radically different organization of production, involving substantial direct public control. The first impulse pointed toward state promotion of capitalist production; the second toward the state organizing production directly through extensive nationalization of industry. Rather quickly, the radical approach was subordinated to technocratic modernization.

Although the moderate course was chosen, the pressure from the Left for substantial reforms became too great to be ignored. In 1945–46, there was extensive nationalization of industry, including the four largest deposit banks and the Bank of France, railroads and air transport, the Renault automobile firm (nationalized in retaliation for its founder's collaboration with the Nazis), coal mines, and gas and electric production and distribution. Other reforms included the creation of plant-level committees, elected by workers, which received funds from employers to organize cultural and leisure activities for workers; the extension of the public health system to cover most citizens; and the codification of benefits for civil servants. Yet the reform impulse stopped well short of radical change: It soon became apparent that state efforts would be directed to strengthening rather than replacing French capitalism. This outcome resulted from the Left's internal divisions, the harsh material constraints imposed by wartime conditions, and the need for American assistance to rebuild the French economy — aid contingent upon France's rejecting a radical course.

The French Planning Commission pioneered in what came to be called indicative planning, which is often contrasted with the system of coercive planning practiced in the Soviet Union. In indicative planning, the state sets overall goals for the economy through a process in which public and private officials participate in establishing targets. In France, the government and the planning agency set broad goals for each plan, which specified growth rates, industries and regions to be accorded priority in obtaining state investment funds, and so on. Overall goals changed from one five-year plan to the next. Once goals for a given plan were established, they were broken down into specific targets by modernization commissions.

The key to indicative planning was that public and private officials participated side-by-side on modernization commissions to develop specific targets. The aim was to reach decisions through voluntary cooperation rather than state dictate. Perhaps even more important than the particular decisions reached was that participants exchanged useful information and developed habits of cooperation, based on an implicit technocratic consensus about the value of modernized capitalism. Planning was successful because, quite quickly, the process came to be restricted to a small and unrepresentative group. The major participants were business executives from large firms and state administrators. Trade union officials, small business representatives, farmers, and consumers were underrepresented in the modernization commissions, which thrashed out specific sectoral targets. For example, four times more business executives than labor officials were appointed to the modernization commissions. Shonfield points out, in an often-cited passage, "In some ways, the development of French planning in the 1950s can be viewed as an act of voluntary collusion between senior civil servants and the senior managers of big business. The politicians and the representatives of organized labour were both largely passed by."[10]

Planning was considered indicative, not coercive, in that private firms were legally free to seek or disregard planning goals. However, given the liberal use of state rewards for cooperation and sanctions for noncompliance, the distinction between voluntary and mandatory was often blurred. Peter Hall aptly describes the process by which "French policymakers made skillful use of the difficulties facing industry, weaving the blandishments of the Plan with material incentives and market stimuli into a rope that pulled French business from a position of economic backwardness to the forefront of the European economy."[11]

What were the planners' goals? The Planning Commission chose capitalist modernization, expansion, and international competitiveness as its major priorities. In the immediate postwar period, the most urgent need was to overcome the production bottlenecks caused by the war. The first plan defined a few specific targets and concentrated major public investments in the following areas: improving France's transportation system; boosting energy production; and rebuilding basic industries, including steel, cement, and agricultural machinery. The planners embarked on a crash program in which considerable public investments were targeted for rationalizing and strengthening these industries. Industrial development was given preference over other pressing claims, including housing construction, food production, and other consumer needs.

In later plans, however, targets became more wide-ranging, ambitious, and difficult to achieve. Planning was directed to improvements in a wider range of industries and to reorganizing public services. When the French economy became more open to and integrated with the economies of Western European and other nations in the 1970s, and when a substantial proportion of French production and consumption was tied to foreign trade, planning at the level of the French domestic economy became far more difficult.

Figure 7.1 Investment in Fixed Capital as a Percentage of Gross Domestic Production, 1896–1966

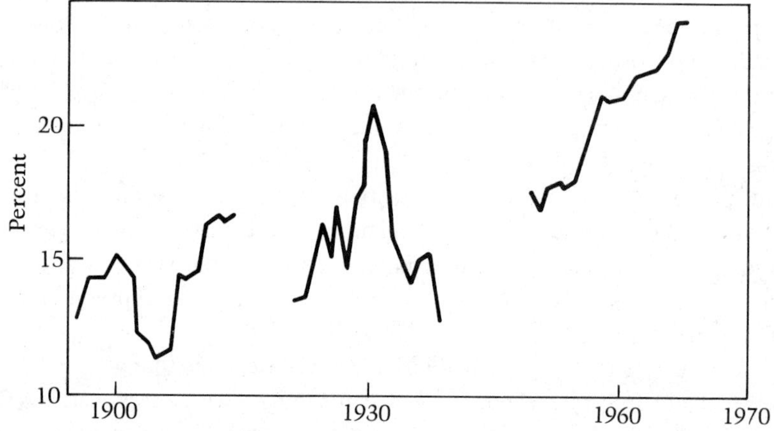

SOURCE J.-J. Carré, P. Dubois, and E. Malinvaud, *French Economic Growth* (Stanford: Stanford University Press, 1975), p. 116.

However, the primary purpose of planning was never to achieve precise quantitative targets but to restructure the French economy and transform French society. Among the specific goals was shifting the economic balance from rural, agrarian groups toward urban, industrial France. Within industry, planners aimed to replace the small, dispersed production units that characterized traditional France by consolidating production into large, concentrated capitalist firms (dubbed "national champions"). Planners also sought to make French firms technologically advanced and internationally competitive, which would permit the opening of the French economy to foreign competition and enable France to achieve a better position within the international capitalist economy.

In contrast to Britain, where governments of the Left and Right emphasized the importance of fiscal orthodoxy (thereby choking British industry), the French Ministry of Finance paid less attention to orthodox goals of restraining inflation and maintaining a strong currency. Instead, priority was accorded to industrial rationalization and expansion. Concretely, this involved deficit spending, cheap credit to industry, an expanding money supply, and frequent devaluations of the French franc (on average, once every five years).[12]

In 1958, modernizers found a powerful ally when de Gaulle returned to power. De Gaulle had been instrumental in creating the planning apparatus in 1945 while leader of the provisional government. After 1958, he provided additional support to the planning process and to capitalist modernization. De Gaulle described the plan as "an ardent obligation" and urged the French to join the twentieth century by embracing industrial values.

When de Gaulle took office in 1958, the French economy remained quite protected and inefficient despite a decade of economic growth. French producers were accustomed to operating within the comfortable shelters of high tariffs and to relying on inflation to compensate for their high production costs. This same year parliament ratified the Treaty of Rome, which created the European Economic Community (EEC) and provided for reduced tariff levels among European nations.

De Gaulle was widely expected to veto French participation in the EEC on the grounds that membership was incompatible with French national independence and in order to protect French firms from foreign competition. Instead, he wholeheartedly accepted French entry into the EEC and ordered drastic measures to prepare France for the new economic situation, including a substantial devaluation of the franc and restrictions on wage hikes. In retrospect, de Gaulle's decision was fully consistent with his overall political approach: His strategy was to strengthen France to compete better internationally, not to flee such competition.

As a result of de Gaulle's austerity program, French production costs dropped relative to those of other EEC member states and France was well-positioned to benefit from the increased intra-European trade that followed creation of the EEC. Although imports to France increased by 25 percent between 1958 and 1961, French exports rose by 71 percent. Moreover, France's international trade balance was reversed so that exports began to exceed imports.[13]

The French state pursued the most active industrial policy of all the Western European nations, with four distinct elements.[14] First, like other nations, French macroeconomic policies, including monetary, budgetary, fiscal, prices, income, public investment, and vocational training, all influenced industrial development. However, in contrast to other nations, the French state coordinated policy-making in these spheres through the decision-making process of planning, the government, Ministry of Finance, and other agencies.

The second element of industrial policy involved state incentives, including subsidies, tax write-offs, and loans, to achieve overall goals, including industrial concentration, specialization in new fields, and technological innovation. A third element of state industrial policy was specific sectoral plans, for example, in steel, machine tools, and paper products. The fourth element — the state's most vigorous intervention within industrial development — consisted of direct state creation, development, and management of new industries, including nuclear energy, high speed railroads, aeronautics, space development, and telecommunications. The French model involved the state as a (indeed, *the*) chief economic player.[15]

The Economic Miracle. During the period that Jean Fourastié designates as "the thirty glorious years" (1945–75), the planners and their allies within the bureaucracy and private sector were stunningly successful.[16] Whereas defenders of the stalemate society had succeeded in maintaining a balance between agriculture and industry throughout the nineteenth and early twentieth century, there was an intense movement off the land and into cities in the postwar period. The proportion of the labor force engaged in farming was 60.0 percent in 1850, 41.8 percent in 1901, and 38.4 percent in 1946; it dropped to half that figure (19.2 percent) by 1962 and to 14.6 percent by 1968.[17] At the same time, there was, according to historian Gordon Wright, a "rural revolution in agriculture."[18] Thanks to the mechanization of agricultural techniques, total farm output rose despite the reduction in the number of farmers.

The drastic decline of the rural population was matched by the rapid rise of the urban population. In 1946, 53.2 percent of the French lived in urban areas and 46.8 percent lived in rural *communes,* "localities," but by 1962, 63.5 percent of the French were city-dwellers and 36.5 percent lived in rural areas. The gap between the urban and rural population thus increased from 6.4 percent to 27.0 percent in less than two decades. Urban growth was especially rapid in larger cities: While the French population as a whole during this period increased by one-tenth, the number of French living in cities over fifty thousand doubled.[19]

After nearly a century of slow population growth, France grew at a comparatively rapid rate. Whereas in the eighty years prior to the end of World War II, the French population grew by only five million, in the fifteen years following the end of the war, it grew by the same number.

The newly urbanized population helped to swell the ranks of the industrial working-class: The proportion of the labor force engaged in manufacturing increased from 35.3 percent in 1944 to 43.3 percent in 1962. An even greater increase occurred in the service sector, notably teaching, health, and the state bureaucracy. Between 1944 and 1962, the service sector increased from 26.2 percent to 37.1 percent of the labor force. The French economy was rapidly transformed from a balance of agrarian and small manufacturing, like that of other southern European economies, to an industrial and service-based economy characteristic of northern Europe.

Restructuring the French economy became considerably easier when substantial benefits began to be generated. The French "economic miracle," as it was called, derived from the fact that French growth rates exceeded those of any other European nation and were second only to that of Japan. What a contrast with the 1930s, when the economy declined at the rate of 1.1 percent annually.[20]

Table 7.1 Average Growth Rates in Gross National Product, 1958–73

Japan	10.4%
France	5.5
Italy	5.3
West Germany	5.0
Belgium	4.9
Netherlands	4.2
Norway	4.2
Sweden	4.1
United States	4.1
United Kingdom	3.2

SOURCE Bela Belassa, "The French Economy under the Fifth Republic, 1958–1978," in *The Fifth Republic at Twenty,* ed. William G. Andrews and Stanley Hoffmann (Albany: State University of New York Press, 1981), p. 209.

The fruits of economic growth were quickly transformed into higher living standards, for increases in purchasing power matched increased economic output. In effect, wages were linked to price and productivity increases, so that workers had an incentive to support modernization. This was the core of the postwar settlement and made for general stability despite the grievances of particular groups and the persistence of political divisions. The average French citizen's annual income nearly tripled between 1946 and 1962, increasing from $511 to $1,358 in constant dollars.[21] This was reflected in a wholesale transformation of consumer patterns as French citizens began to enjoy the benefits of industrialization. For example, between 1946 and 1962, the proportion of homes with running water increased from 36.9 percent to 80.9 percent. The number of automobiles registered in France increased from 4.5 million in 1959 to 14 million in 1973. The number of housing units completed annually increased from 290,000 to 500,000 during the same period. In sum, after a century of economic stagnation, France experienced a sharp surge of economic expansion, the fruits of which were quite widely distributed.

The Fall of the Postwar Settlement

The decades of the 1950s and 1960s were the high point of the postwar settlement. The economy was expanding rapidly, purchasing power was increasing, and France was benefiting handsomely from the expansion of the world capitalist system. De Gaulle's semiauthoritarian rule provided a strong framework of stability, which encouraged the state-business alliance to flourish. And yet, despite the uninterrupted economic expansion, France's postwar settlement rested on a fragile basis. Conservative forces were kept relatively satisfied, but after an initial period in which about one-third of workers supported de Gaulle, the working class became united in opposition.

Political opposition was provoked by the planning process, which aimed not only to maximize economic expansion and growth but also to minimize social conflict. However, as Hall points out, the two goals were in conflict. "The reorganization of production to attain great[er] efficiency tends to intensify the social conflict that planning is also supposed to prevent."[22]

This was especially true given labor's meager role in influencing economic change. Although there was a substantial rise in wages and welfare-state programs, the state was more concerned with maximizing economic output and efficiency than with social equity. As a result, economic change not only failed to *reduce* regional and class inequalities but rather *increased* these differences.

As early as 1963, the government launched an austerity program, which imposed harsh costs on workers, to counteract inflation. When coal miners launched a strike, de Gaulle declared it illegal and threatened the miners with severe punishment. (Miners massively disregarded the warning.)

May, 1968, and the End of the Gaullist Dream

The most dramatic evidence of the postwar settlement's fragility came to the fore in the May, 1968, uprising, which followed several years of turbulence: government-imposed wage restraint; the reduction of trade union representation on the governing boards of the social security (public health) system; and the rapid expansion of universities with inadequate provision of facilities and guidance for students. The May uprising, "the nearest thing to a full-blown revolution ever experienced in an advanced industrial society," was the product of rapid economic growth without social adaptations to soften France's rigid system of authority and hierarchy.[23]

Table 7.2 Socioeconomic Background of University Students, 1975–76

OCCUPATION OF FAMILY HEAD	PROPORTION OF UNIVERSITY STUDENTS
Farmer	5.1%
Owner of business	10.4
Professional, higher executive	30.3
Lower-level executive	15.5
Clerical	8.5
Manual Worker	11.3
Other	18.9
Total	100.0%

SOURCE Gérard Vincent, *Les Français 1976–1979* (Paris: Masson, 1980), p. 149.

Beginning with university occupations at Nanterre and the Sorbonne, and a characteristically harsh government response, the May movement quickly developed into a general strike throughout France. Thousands of factories, offices, and universities were occupied; at the height of the May events, half of France's workers and a larger proportion of students were on strike. Before 1968, the highest number of work days lost from strikes in any one year in the postwar period was 5 million (in 1959); 150 million work days were lost due to strikes in May, 1968. For several days, the fate of the Fifth Republic hung in the balance. De Gaulle eventually regained control of the situation by outmaneuvering the leftist opposition and offering workers substantial concessions (an increase of 35 percent in the minimum wage, increased protection for labor unions, and the promise of paying workers on a monthly rather than hourly basis). But de Gaulle's authority was badly shaken by the uprising, and when a referendum he sponsored in 1969 was defeated, he resigned from the presidency.

Economic Crisis and Political Conflict in the 1970s

The incipient political crisis and the erosion of the postwar settlement can be dated from May, 1968; however, it was not until the mid-1970s, with the slowdown of French growth, that the political crisis became acute. Indeed, May, 1968, at first proved quite beneficial for French business: The substantial increase in purchasing power meant an increase in demand; the government provided business with additional subsidies and tax incentives in order to assist in meeting the higher wages; and a steep devaluation in 1969 had the same positive effect on French exports as had the earlier devaluation in 1958.

And yet May, 1968, also signified the new militancy of French labor, a refusal to accept workplace discipline and hierarchy in return for wage increases. The strike rate in the first years after 1968 never approached the massive level of that year, but for years it did not return to pre-1968 levels, either. Moreover, strikes in the early 1970s were highly militant and often involved seizing factories, sequestering managers, and even organizing production directly. Rather than seeking exclusively to improve wage levels, the characteristic cause of earlier strikes, workers also challenged harsh authority in the workplace, the intensification of work, and technological innovations that deskilled work and increased workplace hazards.[24]

As a result, workers gained increased rights and benefits, and the state and employers' associations sought to achieve stability through organizing collective bargaining at industrywide and national levels. For example: legislation and bargaining agreements in 1969 and 1973 codified procedures for laying off workers, granted state labor inspectors a limited veto power over layoffs, and specified that workers be given advance notice of layoffs as well as severance pay; unemployment benefits were increased, amounting in many cases to 90 percent of a worker's wage; collective-bargaining agreements were concluded on an industrywide level in the petroleum, chemical, and textile industries; and within the public sector, a network of management-union agreements included provisions for automatic wage increases. These were all attempts to restore stability and to continue on the path of economic growth forged in the earlier period. However, two developments prevented a return to the past: a political challenge from the Left, and widening economic crisis.

In the political sphere, the opposition parties on the Left, the Communist Party (PCF) and Socialist Party (renamed the PS in 1969) forged a coalition in 1972 that promised to bring them to power in the near future. The Union of the Left accepted the institutional framework of the Fifth Republic but advocated substantial economic and social changes, notably sweeping nationalization of industry.

The postwar settlement was also subject to severe economic strains in the 1970s. First, France began to exhaust the benefits that had come from her relative backwardness of the earlier period. As the substantial shift of workers out of agriculture and from rural to urban areas began to reach its limit, gains in productivity began to slow. Further, once France had caught up with advances in technology, the focus of industrial development shifted to innovation, instead of imitation.

France had benefited from international economic expansion in the postwar period, but changes in the 1970s proved damaging. First, France was especially dependent on imported petroleum and so faced a heavy economic burden when petroleum prices quadrupled in 1974, especially in combination with a sharp rise in the prices of other imported raw materials.

The restructuring of international capitalism in the 1970s proved damaging for French industry. On the one hand, the newly developing nations, such as Taiwan, South Korea, and Brazil, began to out-compete France in such basic industries as textiles, steel, and shipbuilding. Basic industries not only began to be less competitive internationally but also lost substantial shares of the domestic market to foreign competition. Hundreds of thousands of jobs were eliminated in these three industries alone (for example, more than one-third of all steelworkers were permanently laid off at this time), and entire regions were devastated by deindustrialization. Demographic trends also contributed to the squeeze on employment: France lost over 600,000 jobs after 1974, yet there were 230,000 new workers (mostly young people) seeking jobs each year.[25]

On the other hand, the French economy was battered in the 1970s by the development of a new generation of advanced technology. France was not among the world leaders in such growth industries as microelectronics, bioengineering, and robotics. U.S. and Japanese producers rapidly captured the newly created French markets in these fields. Thus, French industry was squeezed by the dual movement. At the very time that France needed to generate increased export earnings to finance the increased costs of petroleum, basic French industries were losing export markets to the fastest-growing Third World nations and importing high technology from advanced capitalist leaders. And as the international economic boom slowed in the 1970s, the French economy suffered further, along with other Western European nations.

The new trends were linked to a crisis in the French model of development, based on the state-sponsored creation of large national champions that emulated stable, industrial giants elsewhere. However, this approach was less effective in new fields, which were often dominated by smaller, flexible firms, financed by venture capital, and in close geographic proximity to similar firms and university research laboratories. Success in these fields derived from creativity, not emulation.

The success of the postwar French economy also depended upon monetary policies that provided cheap credit to business and consumers, in part financed by inflation and frequent devaluation. However, this approach became less viable as France was integrated into the international political economy. French firms had to compete with foreign firms that were subject to more stringent constraints and able to produce at lower cost; further, France was forced to pay for a substantial share of its increased exports in dollars instead of francs.

The state's response to the economic crisis in the 1970s was quite different than in comparable nations such as West Germany, which adopted austerity policies to slow growth and limit imports. At first, the conservative French governments of the 1970s responded in ways that were not conservative at all. The state forced business, rather than consumers and workers, to absorb the increased costs of the crisis. It also engaged in deficit spending to increase aggregate demand and pursued a program of extensive state investments, particularly in telecommunications and nuclear energy. Governments were slow to grasp the extent of the crisis, apparently believing that it was a temporary downturn. Further, they were under pressure from militant workers and haunted by the fear of another uprising on the model of May, 1968; the Union of the Left, the combined forces of Communists and Socialists, seemed poised to take political power if conservative governments proved unable to continue generating economic benefits.

In 1974, Valéry Giscard d'Estaing, representing centrist and conservative parties, was narrowly elected president, by a margin of less than one percent, over François Mitterrand. When petroleum prices increased later that year, Giscard d'Estaing and Jacques Chirac, his prime minister, sought to sustain domestic economic growth despite declining international demand. As a result of state policies, the French economy continued to expand at a faster rate than its Western European neighbors throughout the 1970s. For example, while real wages in France rose by 46 percent between 1969 and 1976, they were falling in other Western European nations.[26] Thus, the conservative government reacted to the growing economic crisis by sponsoring a shift in national revenue from capital to labor: While profits declined, wages and state transfer payments continued to increase. The French attempt to pursue an expansionary course in a period of declining international growth laid the basis for a more severe crisis in the late 1970s and early 1980s.

In 1976, President Giscard d'Estaing named Raymond Barre to replace Jacques Chirac as prime minister and proceeded to launch a program apparently designed to control inflation. In fact, Barre's major aim was to increase business profits at the expense of wages and to strengthen market forces in the hope that this would improve the international competitive position of French business.

The Barre plan did eventually dampen wage hikes and shift national income from wages to profits, but Barre's austerity measures also increased unemployment without restoring economic health. Given a stagnant international economy, as well as the stronger position that French workers had achieved in the preceding years, French business refused to invest. By engaging in what some termed an investment strike, business sought to undermine working-class strength. However, its actions also helped to build support for the Left. Meanwhile, the Barre government, which had promised to curtail state subsidies to industry in order to force private firms to become more competitive, tried in vain to prevent unemployment from rising. Barre, the advocate of free-market solutions, sponsored a shift from state financing for dynamic, industrially advanced national champions to bailing out lame ducks (i.e., ailing firms), in order to postpone bankruptcy and increased unemployment.[27] The policy subsidized inefficiency and further weakened France's competitive position.

The state also responded by stepping up public-sector investments. Throughout the 1970s, the state represented the only source of fresh investment: Between 1973 and 1981, public-sector investment nearly doubled but private investment declined 14 percent.[28] By demonstrating that the public sector was a better source than private business for investment funds and employment creation, conservative governments increased the popularity of nationalization — and thereby paved the way for further nationalizations after the Socialist government was elected in 1981.

Barre soon sank to record low levels of unpopularity. Were it not for bitter divisions that shattered the Union of the Left in 1977, the Right would have been voted from power in 1978. However, the Barre government stayed in power and applied its austerity measures for several more years. Barre's continued failure to stimulate domestic economic revival or reverse the steady rise of unemployment finally provided an opportunity for the Left to seek a radically new course.

A new era began in 1981, when the Socialist and Communist parties — until that point a permanent minority in the Fifth Republic —

gained power after twenty-three years of opposition. François Mitterrand won the 1981 presidential election against incumbent President Giscard d'Estaing by 52 to 48 percent of the popular vote. Immediately upon gaining election, Mitterrand dissolved the National Assembly, which was dominated by a conservative majority. The Socialist Party achieved an extraordinary victory in the ensuing parliamentary elections and gained an absolute majority of seats.

As described in the next chapters, the Socialist government proved no better able than its conservative predecessors to develop a firm basis for political stability. In 1986, the center-Right gained a narrow majority in parliamentary elections and formed a government that coexisted uneasily with Socialist President Mitterrand. Political uncertainty had returned to France.

NOTES

1. Jean Monnet, *Memoirs* (Garden City: Doubleday, 1978), pp. 232–33.
2. Philip M. Williams, *Crisis and Compromise: Politics in the Fourth Republic* (Hamden, CT: Archon Books, 1964), p. 23.
3. Stanley Hoffmann, "Paradoxes of the French Political Community," in *In Search of France,* ed. Stanley Hoffmann (New York: Harper Torchbooks, 1963), p. 25.
4. Stephen S. Cohen, "Twenty Years of the Gaullist Economy," in *The Fifth Republic at Twenty,* ed. William G. Andrews and Stanley Hoffmann (Albany: State University of New York Press, 1981), pp. 248–49.
5. Charles de Gaulle, *The Complete War Memoirs* (New York: Simon & Schuster, 1967), p. 3.
6. Andrew Shonfield, *Modern Capitalism: The Changing Balance of Public and Private Power* (London: Oxford University Press, 1969).
7. Shonfield, *Modern Capitalism,* p. 73.
8. Richard F. Kuisel, *Capitalism and the State in Modern France* (Cambridge: Cambridge University Press, 1981), p. 277.
9. Kuisel, *Capitalism,* p. 248.
10. Shonfield, *Modern Capitalism*, p. 128.
11. Peter A. Hall, *Governing the Economy: The Politics of State Intervention in Britain and France* (New York: Oxford University Press, 1986).
12. Hall, *Governing the Economy;* John Zysman, "The Interventionist Temptation: Financial Structure and Political Purpose," in *The Fifth Republic at Twenty,* ed. William G. Andrews and Stanley Hoffmann (Albany: State University of New York Press, 1981); and John

Zysman, *Political Strategies for Industrial Order: State, Market, and Industry in France* (Berkeley: University of California Press, 1977).

13. Bela Belassa, "The French Economy under the Fifth Republic, 1958–1978," in *The Fifth Republic at Twenty,* ed. William G. Andrews and Stanley Hoffmann (Albany: State University of New York Press, 1981), p. 210.
14. This section relies on Elie Cohen, "L'État socialiste en industrie, Volontarisme politique et changement socio-économique," in *Les Élites Socialistes au Pouvoir,* ed. Pierre Birnbaum (Paris; Presses Universitaires de France, 1985), pp. 219–61.
15. Zysman, "Interventionist Temptation."
16. Jean Fourastié, *Les Trentes Glorieuses ou La Révolution Invisible de 1945 à 1975* (Paris: Fayard, 1979), passim.
17. William G. Andrews, "Introduction: The Impact of France on the Fifth Republic," in *The Fifth Republic at Twenty*, ed. William G. Andrews and Stanley Hoffmann (Albany: State University of New York Press, 1981), p. 3; and Richard F. Kuisel, "Postwar Economic Growth in Historical Perspective," in *Continuity and Change in Mitterrand's France,* ed. Stanley Hoffmann and George Ross (New York: Oxford University Press, 1987).
18. Gordon Wright, *Rural Revolution in France* (Stanford: Stanford University Press, 1964), passim.
19. Andrews, "Introduction," pp. 1–10.
20. Kuisel, *Capitalism,* p. 264.
21. Andrews, "Introduction," p. 4; this section also relies on Cohen, "Twenty Years," pp. 240–50.
22. Hall, *Governing the Economy.*
23. Stephen Bornstein, "States and Unions: From Postwar Settlement to Contemporary Stalemate," in *The State in Capitalist Europe, A Casebook,* ed. Stephen Bornstein, David Held, and Joel Krieger (Winchester, MA: George Allen & Unwin, 1984), p. 64.
24. Mark Kesselman and Guy Groux, eds., *The French Workers' Movement: Economic Crisis and Political Change* (Winchester, MA: George Allen & Unwin, 1984), passim.
25. Hall, *Governing the Economy,* ch. 8.
26. Volkmar Lauber, "Acceptable Austerity? French Economic Policy under Giscard and Barre" (Paper presented at the 1981 annual meeting of the American Political Science Association).
27. Suzanne Berger, "Lame Ducks and National Champions: Industrial Policy in the Fifth Republic," in *The Fifth Republic at Twenty,* ed. William G. Andrews and Stanley Hoffmann (Albany: State University of New York Press, 1981), pp. 292–310.
28. Hall, *Governing the Economy,* ch. 8.

8

State Institutions

The Principles of French Government

Three contending principles have characterized modern French government: popular sovereignty exercised through direct democracy; legislative dominance, guided by the principle that the people's elected representatives are exclusively qualified to embody popular sovereignty; and executive rule. No one French regime has been able to achieve an adequate balance among the three. This has contributed to extensive constitutional discontinuity in France as each constitution has tended to embody a fairly extreme form of one of the three principles. For example, the short-lived Paris Commune of 1871 exemplified the practice of direct democracy by providing for the recall of political officeholders. The many French revolutions represent an even more dramatic example of direct democracy.

The constitutions of the Third and Fourth Republics accorded priority to the representative principle. The legislature was considered to be the sole embodiment of popular sovereignty. The cabinet, which consisted of the prime minister and the ministers in charge of government departments, was decidedly subordinate to the legislature. Governments were voted out of office an average of once every six months in the Third and Fourth Republics. This frequent turnover of governments tended to produce a deadlock, providing an opportunity for the bureaucracy to fill the breach and exercise power, often with the tacit or even explicit consent of the legislature and cabinet.

The Fifth Republic marked a shift from legislative to executive dominance and provided few channels for political participation and the expression of opposition. In 1986, divided control of the executive, between Left and Right, presented a more complex situation.

Like its predecessors, the Fifth Republic was initially created over the strenuous opposition of important political forces: the Communist Party (PCF); a large segment of the Socialist Party; and some influential politicians on the left associated with smaller parties. Opponents of de Gaulle's return to power in 1958 argued that he owed his position to the threat of a military coup, for army officers threatened an invasion of mainland France if de Gaulle were not approved as prime minister by the National Assembly. The Left also opposed the substantial powers accorded the president, prime minister, and government by the constitution of the Fifth Republic. In their view, this violated the principles of popular sovereignty, in which the legislature, directly elected by the people, should exercise sovereignty.

The initial divisions about the character and legitimacy of the regime gradually subsided, however. The Left was forced to abandon its opposition to the Fifth Republic because its arguments failed to produce electoral victories. François Mitterrand, who described the constitution as a "permanent coup d'état" in a fiery pamphlet in 1958, declared himself a presidential candidate in 1965 and sought election to the office that had drawn his most intense ire. In similar fashion, the Communist Party dropped its call for a basic constitutional revision and sought to reach power in a coalition with the Socialist Party. In public opinion polls, the proportion of French who approved of the basic features of the Fifth Republic increased steadily so that, by the 1980s, there was near-universal agreement on the desirability of the constitution. For example, a 1984 poll found that 86 percent of the population approved of the direct election of the president — a practice that, when first proposed by de Gaulle in 1962, elicited widespread opposition.

Thus, despite the fact that the Fifth Republic did not appear to reconcile the three principles of direct participation and democracy, legislative rule, and executive leadership, it nonetheless commanded nearly universal support by the 1970s. As a result, for the first time since the prewar period, political conflicts in France began to be played out within a widely accepted institutional framework.

The constitution of the Fifth Republic has also survived two important political tests: first, the shift in political control (alternation) from the rightist coalition that ruled since the beginning of the Fifth Republic in 1958, to the left opposition in 1981; and second, the coexistence (cohabitation) of a leftist president and a government and National Assembly

Table 8.1 Public Attitudes Toward The Fifth Republic

"For each of the following measures, which are part of the constitution, are you personally favorable or opposed?"

ISSUE	FAVORABLE	OPPOSED	NO OPINION	TOTAL
Election of president by universal suffrage	86%	6%	8%	100%
Judicial review by Constitutional Council	80	5	15	100
Use of referendum	76	12	12	100
Right of National Assembly to reverse the government	59	24	17	100
President's right to dissolve National Assembly	57	26	17	100
President's right to assume full powers in a grave crisis (Article 16)	49	37	14	100

SOURCE Jean-Luc Parodi and François Platone, "L'Adoption par les gouvernés," in *La Constitution de la Cinquième République,* ed. Olivier Duhamel and Jean-Luc Parodi (Paris: Presses de la Foundation Nationale des Sciences Politiques, 1985), p. 184. SOFRES poll, 1983.

controlled by a rightist majority after the 1986 elections. So long as political power remained the monopoly of the rightist coalition, while leftist political parties, representing nearly half the electorate, were excluded from office, the stability of the Fifth Republic was open to question. As the May, 1968, uprising graphically illustrated, the absence of political alternation polarized French society and weakened the political system through the seemingly permanent exclusion from power of politicians representing nearly half the French electorate.

An alternation of government occurred in 1981, when the Left swept the presidential and parliamentary elections and gained control of the state. Although some politicians of the Right challenged the Left's legitimacy, the constitution weathered the test with relative ease. Moreover, the Socialist government easily adapted to Fifth Republic

"What!?? The President's a Socialist and the Eiffel Tower is still standing!??" "Incredible!"

SOURCE *Le Monde, Dossiers et Documents,* May 1981.

institutions, made few institutional changes, and relinquished legislative power when defeated in the 1986 parliamentary elections.

In 1986, a period of cohabitation began when the Right won a majority in the parliamentary elections. President Mitterrand appointed Jacques Chirac, a leading conservative, as prime minister. Cohabitation raises basic constitutional issues, including: Whose policy orientation will predominate, that of the president or that of the government (the prime minister and other cabinet ministers) and parliamentary majority? How will the government manage the tensions produced by the fact that it is appointed by the president yet responsible to the parliament? How will the conflicts between the divided executive be resolved? Yet cohabitation may also reflect the French electorate's rejection of ideological and partisan polarization.

The Triple Executive

Among the most unusual features of French constitutional arrangements is what has been termed the dual executive, in which formal powers are divided between the president and government. In other European democracies, there is typically a chief of state, an office that involves purely ceremonial duties, and the bulk of executive powers is concentrated within the government. In France, the president not only is chief of state but also possesses substantial executive power. However, the president shares executive powers with the government (i.e., the prime minister and other cabinet ministers). This dyarchy, as the dual executive is sometimes called, possesses immense power within the Fifth Republic — if there is agreement at the top.

To describe the French executive as a dyarchy is somewhat misleading, in that it ignores a third powerful partner within the executive — the bureaucracy, a powerful political force in its own right. The three elements of the executive provide the motor force of the French state. Unlike the Fourth Republic, whose constitutional theory enshrined legislative sovereignty, the Fifth Republic explicitly conferred ample independent powers on the executive, going to great lengths to ensure that they could be exercised without undue legislative interference.

The President

Until 1986, the powers of the French president exceeded those of any other official within capitalist democracies. The president combined the independent powers of the U.S. president, notably command of the executive establishment and independence from parliamentary control, with the powers that accrue to the government in a parliamentary regime, particularly the power to shape the parliamentary agenda and to dissolve parliament. Although the president's powers were severely restricted in the period of cohabitation beginning in 1986, the president remains a key French officeholder.

The presidency became such a powerful office for three reasons: the towering personality of Charles de Gaulle, the founder and first president of the Fifth Republic; the ample powers conferred on the office by the constitution; and the political practices of the Fifth Republic until 1986. De Gaulle set out to design a regime that would enable political leaders to rise above party rivalry and legislative interference in order to sponsor ambitious projects for France. The president was the keystone within the constitutional edifice that he erected. Although de Gaulle partially tailored the office of the presidency to serve his own personal ambitions, he later stated (probably accurately) that he was even more concerned to create an office that would enable his successors — who would lack the legitimacy that derived from his wartime role — to be powerful leaders.

The Constitutional Presidency. The constitution of the Fifth Republic endowed the president with the ceremonial powers of the Fourth and Fifth republics, in which the president served as the symbolic chief of state. However, to these formal powers it added others that had been the prerogative of the prime minister and government in the past, as well as new powers not previously exercised in previous republics.

According to the constitution, the president names the prime minister and other cabinet officials, as well as high-ranking civil, military, and judicial officials; presides over meetings of the council of ministers (the government); conducts foreign affairs (through the power to negotiate treaties, as well as to name French ambassadors and accredit foreign ambassadors to France); and directs the armed forces. The president is authorized to communicate with parliament and request that it reconsider legislation that it has passed. The president is also granted the power to dissolve the National Assembly and call for new elections, except that once the president has dissolved the Assembly, he or she cannot exercise the power again during the newly elected Assembly's first year. The president is authorized to appoint three of the nine members of the Constitutional Council, including its president, and to refer bills passed by parliament to the Council to determine if they conform to the constitution.

Three other grants of power deserve special mention. Article 16 of the constitution authorizes the president to assume emergency powers when, in his or her judgment, the institutions of the republic, the independence of the nation, the integrity of its territory, or the execution of France's international (treaty) commitments are threatened. The constitution obliges the president to respect certain conditions: Before assuming emergency powers, the president must consult with the presidents of the two legislative chambers; and parliament must be immediately convened and cannot be dissolved while the president exercises emergency powers.

Article 11 grants the president authority to put certain proposals to a national referendum. By authorizing this direct link with the French people, the constitution sharply broke with French parliamentary traditions and practice, which had enjoined the president to remain a distant political figure, far removed from active political intervention. However, after President de Gaulle used the referendum to strengthen presidential power on several occasions, it fell into disuse. The last referendum was held in 1973.

Presidential power has been bolstered far more by Article 5, which mandates the president to safeguard compliance with the constitution: "He shall ensure, by his arbitration, the regular functioning of the governmental authorities, as well as the continuance of the State. He shall be the guarantor of national independence, of the integrity of the territory, and of respect for Community agreements and treaties." Article 5 provided a vast opportunity for presidential power by its lack of precision and by making the president the sole official charged with arbitrating and guaranteeing national independence.

The constitution creates a powerful president, at least on paper; however, there is a certain continuity with the constitutional position of French presidents of the Third and Fourth Republics. According to William Andrews, "The 1958 constitution emerged from a consensus of constituents broadly representative of the mainstream of the French parliamentary tradition and was designed to serve as the basis of a parliamentary regime."[1] The president is not granted authority by the constitution to develop policy; that key power is granted to the prime minister and government. The president's powers are in many respects those of the head of state, representing the overall unity of the state but not actively intervening within the political arena.

The fact that the president is elected for seven years and can seek reelection may not constitute evidence of extensive power. For, in French constitutional arrangements, officials with fewer political powers, including senators and members of the Constitutional Council, have longer terms.

However, given de Gaulle's personality, as well as the use he and his successors made of constitutional and political powers, the theory of a limited president above the political fray can be dismissed.

The Political President. Before 1962, the constitution provided that the president would be elected for a seven-year term by an electoral college composed mostly of mayors and town councillors, most of whom represented rural constituencies. Thus, the president did not receive a direct popular mandate from citizens but appeared as a "super-notable," as the chosen representative of the dense network of French political officialdom.

The critical change within the presidency came in 1962, once de Gaulle had extricated France from Algeria and prepared to undertake a new phase in the Fifth Republic's domestic and foreign policy. In order to obtain renewed legitimacy, de Gaulle sought a popular mandate, proposing that the president be elected directly by universal suffrage. He asserted that his proposal did not alter the president's formal powers. Few were misled, however, for a president armed with a powerful mandate from the entire nation obviously would be far more powerful than a "super-notable."

De Gaulle's proposal represented a direct provocation to France's political class and to the tradition of representative democracy that it embodied. For, given France's violent political history, independent executive leadership smacked of dictatorship. Furthermore, de Gaulle proposed to select the president by a procedure that bypassed parliament and, according to most constitutional lawyers, represented an outright violation of the constitution. Rather than invoking the machinery for a formal constitutional amendment (Article 89), which would have required gaining parliamentary approval of the change, he put the proposal directly to a national referendum (Article 11). The reason was obvious: Parliament would never have approved the proposal, as is required by Article 89, since it involved strengthening the president at the expense of other state institutions. De Gaulle triumphed handily: 62 percent of French voters supported his proposal.

The manner in which de Gaulle and successive presidents used their powers, as well as the fact that (until 1986) other political officials deferred to the president, further increased presidential power in several ways. First, in addition to the constitutional power to designate prime ministers, presidents have gained the power to dismiss them as well, thus making the government responsible not only to the National Assembly, as specified in the constitution, but also to the president. Prime ministers have made clear that they would remain in office only so long as they enjoyed the president's confidence. Second, presidents assumed the power, delegated by the constitution to the government, to intervene and develop policy in virtually any domain that they chose.

De Gaulle was the only president to benefit from the constitutional authority to sponsor referenda — and he also suffered the most damage from its use. Following the uprising of May, 1968, reviewed in Chapter 7, de Gaulle sought to bolster his weakened authority and legitimacy by calling a referendum. The questions posed, involving abolition of the Senate and creation of regional government, were less important than the symbolism of a renewed expression of popular support. However, voters rejected the referendum, and de Gaulle immediately retired from political life. Although the constitution does not require a president to link his or her fate to the outcome of a referendum, it would be difficult for a president not to follow de Gaulle's precedent.

For the first three decades of the Fifth Republic, the French presidency was virtually unchallenged as the preeminent political institution within the regime. However, events since 1986 demonstrate that presidential power derives from the political cohesion provided when the president enjoys the support of a parliamentary majority. In his first years as president, Mitterrand was confident, commanding, and preeminent. The victory of the center-Right coalition in the 1986 parliamentary elections and Mitterrand's designation of Jacques Chirac as prime minister, however, diluted the power of the presidency. Conversely, the government, which had been decidedly subordinate to French presidents until 1986, subsequently emerged as an independent political force and sponsored policies squarely at odds with Mitterrand's political orientation.

The Government and Prime Minister

The constitution of the Fifth Republic not only fails to provide a clear guide to the division of responsibilities between the president and government but also is hopelessly confused on this key issue. Vincent Wright wryly observes, "With the French Constitution of 1958 we enter the world not of Descartes but of Lewis Carroll."[2]

The government is a collective body under the prime minister's direction. The president appoints the prime minister, who is usually the leader of the major parliamentary party; and upon nomination by the prime minister, the president also appoints members of the cabinet. After the president and prime minister, cabinet ministers are the most powerful members of the executive, for they direct the bureaucracy. There are substantial differences in the power of various cabinet positions. The minister of finance informally ranks second to the prime minister through control of the budget, spending, and economic policy. Other important departments are defense, external affairs, and interior. In practice, until 1986, presidents shared with the prime minister the selection of government ministers and in some cases dictated the choice of ministers. In 1986, Prime Minister Chirac had a free hand in his choice of ministers. Nonetheless, President Mitterrand vetoed several of Prime Minister

Chirac's nominees to the cabinet, on the grounds that they had insulted Mitterrand personally or the presidential office in general during the election campaign. Mitterrand also insisted on having a say concerning the choice of defense and external affairs ministers, given his constitutional responsibilities in these domains.

President de Gaulle distrusted professional politicians and sought to sever the connection between the legislature, in which professional politicians pursued their personal ambitions, and the executive, which incarnated the general interests of the state. In order to separate the two institutions, the constitution requires that members of parliament (deputies or senators) who are appointed to the government must resign from the legislature. Although members of parliament have found a way to circumvent this prohibition, de Gaulle initiated another practice — unthinkable in the Third and Fourth Republics — to separate the legislature and the executive: He chose many cabinet ministers from the ranks of senior civil servants. Although later presidents have not relied as heavily on the civil service in choosing the government, the connection between the civil service and the political sector has remained. This pattern strengthens the autonomy of the French state and at the same time further diminishes the influence of democratic participation.

Although the president appoints the government, it is responsible only to the National Assembly: Article 49 of the constitution requires the government to resign when a censure motion, moved by at least one-tenth of all deputies, is approved by an absolute majority of the National Assembly. Although, prior to 1986, all prime ministers accepted the president's right to dismiss the government, this right is nowhere specified in the constitution. Article 8 stipulates that the president shall terminate the functions of the prime minister and other cabinet ministers when the prime minister resigns, but that is quite another matter from presidential authority to dismiss the government. This is just one of the many instances in which the constitution provides little help in resolving the potential difficulties created by cohabitation.

While the constitution provides a brief catalog of the government's powers and specifies some powers which are shared with the president, in some cases it fails to distinguish between the powers of the president and those of government. Article 20 of the constitution specifies that the government "shall determine and direct the policy of the nation. It shall have at its disposal the administration and the armed forces." Article 21 states that the prime minister is "responsible for national defense." However, the constitution also designates the president as "commander of the armed forces," thus confusing the division of military responsibility. Further, the prime minister is ordered by Article 21 to "ensure the execution of the laws," which overlaps with the directive to the president (Article 5) to ensure the regular functioning of the governmental authorities. Article 21 grants the *prime minister* the authority to make appointments to civil and military posts, yet Article 13 empowers the *president* to make appointments to civil and military posts. Other powers delegated to the prime minister and government that the president can veto include convening a special session of parliament, issuing bureaucratic decrees taken in the name of the government, and naming or dismissing high civil servants.

For nearly thirty years, the question of the precise demarcation between presidential and governmental powers did not arise, since every president was preeminent within the area of policy-making and exercised virtually unchallenged dominance over the government. In practice, presidents assumed responsibility for overall policy orientation and key policy areas, while the prime minister and government developed policy in areas of lesser importance, translated the president's overall orientation into specific policies, directed the implementation of policy, and carried on the day-to-day business of governing.

The specific policies that fell into the presidential domain differed from president to president and sometimes shifted within a given presidential term. All presidents have devoted particular attention to foreign and military policy, and intervened on any issue if it assumed dramatic political importance (e.g., bombings, natural disasters, or major policy disputes). Each president also had particular interests: De Gaulle (1958–69) pursued the politics of *grandeur,* by seeking to integrate economic and foreign policies in the quest for national cohesion and independence; Pompidou (1969–74) devoted himself to industrial policy; Giscard d'Estaing (1974–81) to liberalizing French social customs; and Mitterrand (1981 to the present) to stimulating technological and cultural innovation.

In contrast to the Fourth Republic, there has been a high degree of governmental stability within the Fifth Republic. Given the existence of a stable parliamentary majority, governments were in no danger of being voted out of office, so their duration often depended on the president's discretion. Until 1986, governments remained in office an average of about three years.

Governments have typically exercised considerable power and authority in the Fifth Republic, but almost always with the president's consent. Three prime ministers were dismissed for insubordination: President de Gaulle replaced Georges Pompidou in 1968 for failing to support his policies during the May, 1968, uprising; during Pompidou's own presidency, he removed Prime Minister Jacques Chaban-Delmas when Chaban-Delmas announced a New Society program that Pompidou considered too liberal; and President Giscard d'Estaing and Prime Minister Jacques Chirac reached an impasse (with Chirac resigning) over political differences.

Yet whatever tensions existed between the president and government prior to 1986 pale to insignificance following the center-Right's victory in the 1986 elections. President Mitterrand's appointment of Chirac as prime minister began a new era, for Chirac was a leader of the political coalition opposed to President Mitterrand's Socialist Party. Until 1986 government policies reflected and implemented the president's overall orientation; whereas in the post-1986 period Chirac's government sought to reverse several key Socialist reforms introduced in 1981–86, especially nationalization. Paradoxically, however, the period of cohabitation may lead to reduced political tensions and what some have termed the normalization of French politics — reduced ideological distance between parties — if political rivals cooperate to share power.

The Bureaucracy

The French bureaucracy is generally regarded as among the most competent and efficient in the world. Most of the over two million French civil servants, including teachers, health workers, and postal workers, do not occupy policymaking positions. Positions at the top of the administration, however, are among the most powerful and coveted in France. These positions are mostly reserved for graduates of the *grandes écoles,* selective educational institutions whose purpose is to train higher civil servants. At the top of the French academic pyramid are the *École Nationale d'Administration* (ENA), which trains generalist administrators and managers, and the *École Polytechnique,* which provides engineering and technical training. Their graduates — especially those at the top of their classes, who enter *grands corps,* or specialized elite networks — are assured attractive lifetime careers in important administrative positions.

Although the bureaucracy is widely respected for its honesty and efficiency, it has been criticized for stifling democratic participation. Despite its claim to recruit on the basis of academic merit, there is a strong class bias built into the bureaucratic structure: Few students from working-class and modest backgrounds pass the stiff entrance examinations for the top schools; further, they lack the proper accent and manner of upper-middle-class applicants.

The leftist government elected in 1981 made a modest effort to democratize access to key state positions. Under the sponsorship of the Communist minister of administrative reform, the government opened a new channel of recruitment to the *École Nationale d'Administration:* reserved places for officials with leadership experience in trade unions, voluntary associations, and local governments. Although the reform has increased the number of students from modest backgrounds, it is unlikely to have much impact on the overall structure and style of French administration.

The French bureaucracy has enormous power and autonomy, developing its policy objectives behind closed doors and pursuing them with a grand indifference to criticism: It has rightly been termed a state within a state. Because of its wide reach, the bureaucracy stifles private initiatives, discourages democratic decision making, and reinforces France's statist tradition.

Under the Fifth Republic enormous power is concentrated in the executive. When there is political cohesion unifying the three branches of the executive — president, prime minister and government, and bureaucracy — the state can act with unparalleled vigor. Indeed, the Fifth Republic enshrined such strong leadership that Maurice Duverger termed the system a "republican monarchy." Yet the period of cohabitation after 1986 suggests that in the absence of unity, the executive was forced to act with greater caution.

The Truncated Parliament

Many of the powers that the constitution of the Fifth Republic delegates to the executive were appropriated from the authority of parliament under the Third and Fourth Republics. Parliamentary power has been substantially reduced in the Fifth Republic, especially as compared with legislatures in other capitalist democracies.

The French parliament is bicameral: The two chambers are the National Assembly and the Senate. Although the powers of the indirectly elected Senate were not significantly altered from the Fourth Republic, the popularly elected lower house, the National Assembly, was stripped of most of its power. Indeed, in designing the constitution of the Fifth Republic, de Gaulle sought to humble the once-mighty National Assembly and the regime of party politics. Ironically, strong parties have developed for the first time in French history within the Fifth Republic, for reasons relating to de Gaulle's institutional reforms.

Until 1958, the National Assembly was regarded as the sole voice of the sovereign people. No other state institution could infringe on the prerogatives of the National Assembly. The National Assembly could make and unmake governments at will, legislate on any subject it chose, and intervene in any aspect of French government and administration.

In practice, however, the National Assembly was unable to exercise power in such an expansive manner, so it devised makeshift arrangements to carry on the essential tasks of government, in particular by delegating responsibility to the cabinet and administration. In considerable measure, then, de Gaulle merely codified existing practice into constitutional law when he limited parliament's role in the Fifth Republic. However, he also eliminated parliamentary discretion to delegate responsibility as well as parliament's right to intervene as it saw fit.

Under the Fifth Republic, parliament became just one state institution among others and is prohibited from acting without an explicit grant of constitutional authority. Further, the executive is granted extensive independent powers and no longer requires a grant of authority by the National Assembly. In fact, the area within which parliament is permitted to act was severely circumscribed, and even within this domain, the government is empowered to exercise tight control over parliamentary activity.

Parliament is prohibited from legislating outside a specific number of areas. Even within the area of lawmaking, the referendum procedure provides that parliament can be bypassed altogether.

Further, under Article 38, the government is authorized to request parliament to grant it special power within certain domains of lawmaking, and if parliament agrees, the government can issue ordinances having the force of law. Governments used this power to grant Algerian independence and reorganize the public health system. Although the practice had become less common in the 1970s, the Socialists — who had criticized it when in the opposition — revived its use in 1981 because of the crush of parliamentary business and obtained parliament's proxy to reform the system of unemployment benefits, extend pension rights, and shorten the work week. The Chirac government also resorted to Article 38.

Outside the specified area of lawmaking, the constitution created a new category, termed regulation, over which parliament has no power at all. Within this domain, the bureaucracy is granted power to issue rules and decrees.

Within the area in which parliament is competent, the constitution delegates to the government extensive powers to control legislative activity. The government, not parliamentary leaders, establishes the parliamentary agenda; governmental texts are accorded priority over proposals from members of parliament; and the government is empowered to restrict amendments and debate, as well as to suspend the usual procedures by which parliament deliberates. The government can call for a *vote bloquée,* "blocked vote," which requires parliament to vote on a text as a whole, including only those amendments that the governments accepts.

The government can further limit parliament's role by calling for a confidence vote either on its overall policies or on a specific legislative text. This provision applies only to the National Assembly; the government has other means to pass legislation without the Senate's approval. When the government calls for a vote of confidence, this signifies that it will resign if an adverse vote occurs. However, the government can use the threat of resignation — and the dissolution of the National Assembly that would probably follow — as a tactic to obtain parliamentary approval. When the government calls for a confidence vote on a text, the bill is considered approved unless a censure motion is passed within twenty-four hours. The procedure gives the government a further edge: In order to pass a censure motion, an absolute majority of all deputies must vote in favor. Thus, in effect, abstentions count in the government's favor. Governments have used these (and other) weapons against their own supporters, since the opposition votes against most government texts in any event. After 1986, the Chirac government repeatedly called for confidence votes to preserve its dominance despite a slender parliamentary majority and to cut off parliamentary debate.

Parliament has limited control over the budgetary process. Members of parliament are prohibited from introducing amendments to the budget whose effect is to raise expenditures or lower tax revenues. Further, unless parliament approves the budget within seventy days after it is submitted, the government is authorized to enact the budget by ordinance (though this has never occurred within the Fifth Republic).

Perhaps the most important limitation on parliament's power to control the government is the censure procedure. (We refer to censure motions introduced at the initiative of opposition parties; these should be distinguished from censure motions, discussed above, linked to confidence votes.) To begin with, parliament has no power to control or censure the president, save in the case of high treason, in which event the existing procedure is somewhat similar to the process of impeaching a U.S. president. The French president is deemed to have independent powers and is not answerable to parliament. Thus, parliament can at best direct its fire at the government. Of course, when the government and parliamentary majority oppose the president, as occurred for the first time in 1986, the president's power to dictate policy is limited.

Unequal Bicameralism

Within parliament, the National Assembly is by far the more powerful chamber. Only the Assembly possesses the power to censure the government: One-tenth of all deputies must sign a censure petition, but if the motion fails, those deputies signing the motion are disqualified from signing another during the current parliamentary session. (This limitation does not apply to censure motions introduced in response to the government calling for a confidence vote.) Since only opposition deputies are likely to sign a censure motion, this restricts the number of motions that can be proposed each year. As with the censure motion linked to confidence votes, an absolute majority of all deputies must vote for the motion in order for it pass. When this occurs, the government is obliged to resign.

The one occasion when a censure motion passed has probably deterred deputies from seeking to repeat the experience. In 1962, the National Assembly censured the Pompidou government, in connection with President de Gaulle's proposal to call a referendum to change the method of electing the president. Following the National Assembly's censure of the government, de Gaulle promptly dissolved the Assembly. The victory of de Gaulle's supporters in the ensuing elections doubtless discouraged future censure votes.

A bill can be introduced in either chamber of parliament. If passed in identical form by the two, it becomes law. If, however, the two houses vote different versions or the Senate rejects a text, the government may use its power to give the National Assembly the last word. When the two houses have voted differing texts twice, and therefore cannot reach agreement, the government may convene a joint commission of representatives from both houses to reconcile their differences. (The government is authorized to convene a joint commission after one reading by each house if it designates the bill as urgent.) If the joint commission reaches agreement and the government approves the text, then it is submitted to both houses for a vote. If passed by both houses, it becomes law. However, if the joint commission cannot reach agreement, or reaches agreement on a text that is passed by the National Assembly but rejected by the Senate, the government can submit the text to the National Assembly for a final vote. If passed by the National Assembly at this reading, the bill becomes law despite the lack of senatorial approval. Thus, in case of deadlock between the two houses, the National Assembly predominates.

The National Assembly and Senate may adopt different positions because members of the two houses are elected by different procedures.

Through the 1981 elections, and again after 1986, members of the National Assembly were chosen from single member districts by a two-ballot plurality system. At the first ballot, a candidate needs to obtain an absolute majority of those voting in the district to be elected. If no candidate is elected at the first ballot, a runoff election is held the following week. This time, a simple plurality suffices for election.

For the 1986 legislative elections, in order to minimize Socialist losses, the Socialist government introduced proportional representation (which will be discussed further in Chapter 9). At the same time, it increased the size of the National Assembly to 577.

Senators are chosen for nine-year terms by an electoral college composed of mayors and town councillors from each *département* (the ninety-five administrative districts into which France is divided). Rural interests are substantially overrepresented in the departmental electoral colleges: Although 25 percent of the population lives in villages of under fifteen hundred, 40 percent of delegates from departmental electoral colleges represent these *communes* (localities). The 23 percent of citizens living in *communes* of over thirty thousand are represented by 10 percent of the senatorial electoral delegates.[3] The Senate is thus particularly zealous in defending the conservative interests of small towns and villages.

The Senate's conservative orientation was particularly evident after 1981, when it opposed most major Socialist proposals. Since the Senate was controlled by opposition parties, they could use its limited constitutional powers to the fullest — proposing endless amendments to government bills, making maximum use of the time that the constitution authorized for the Senate to consider bills, and rejecting government bills — which forced the government to adopt legislation over the Senate's veto. Along with the Constitutional Council (described later in this chapter), the Senate was a major counterweight to the Socialist Party's control of the state. The Senate's limited power to delay the passage of legislation was nonetheless effective because the government had a voluminous agenda and was eager to pass its reform proposals quickly, while it enjoyed maximum support.

Prior to 1981, joint parliamentary commissions convened to reconcile divergent texts reached agreement in 71 percent of all cases; between 1981 and 1986, joint commissions reached agreement in only 13 percent of the cases. Twice as many bills were passed without senatorial approval as had been passed in this manner through the entire previous twenty-three years of the Fifth Republic's existence.[4] Among the bills that were passed over the Senate's opposition were some of the key Socialist proposals, including nationalization of industry and banking, reform of the press, and industrial relations reforms.

Figure 8.1 Agreement between National Assembly and Senate within Joint Commissions

SOURCE Jean Grangé, "L'Efficacité Normatif du Sénat," in *La Constitution de la Cinquième République*, eds. Olivier Duhamel and Jean-Luc Parodi (Paris: Presses de la Fondation Nationale des Sciences Politiques, 1985), p. 380.

The period until 1986 displayed a high degree of cohesion among state institutions, with the partial exception of senatorial opposition noted previously. However, contrary to the expectations of the Fifth Republic's founders, what made it possible for the state to act in a unified manner was less the intricate procedures that limited parliamentary initiative than a convergence between the presidential and parliamentary majorities. While de Gaulle had calculated that parliament would have to be kept on a short leash to compensate for the lack of a stable majority, in fact, until 1986, unity at the top was forged through common party ties. However, the partisan factor had an opposite impact when the presidential and parliamentary majorities diverged; after 1986, party rivalry maximized the chances of conflict and stalemate.

The Constitutional Council

Possibly no state institution in the Fifth Republic has varied as much from its original design or gained more power than the Constitutional Council. The Council was originally intended to be an additional instrument that the executive could use to restrain the legislature. Instead, the Council has assumed the power to restrain the executive. One study of the Council observes, "Originally an obscure institution conceived to play a role of marginal importance in the Fifth Republic, the Constitutional Council has gradually moved toward the center stage of French politics and acquired the status of a major actor in the policy-making process."[5] The most important change has been that by skillful use of its constitutional power, the Council has undertaken the power of judicial review, that is, to invalidate legislative texts that it judges in violation of the constitution. Although this development is unprecedented in French history, the Council began to exercise judicial review in a bold and continuous fashion.

Members of the Constitutional Council are named for nonrenewable nine-year terms by three political officials: the president, and the presidents of the two houses of parliament (each of whom names three members of the Council). In general, appointees are elderly political figures considered dispassionate and impartial, although they are generally political allies of their sponsors. In addition, former presidents are assigned a lifetime seat on the Council. However, when Giscard d'Estaing left the presidency after 1981, he refrained from participating in Council deliberations, on the grounds that he remained politically active. (He was elected a deputy in 1983 and sought to gain reelection as president.)

The constitution of the Fifth Republic directed the Constitutional Council to ensure the regularity of election and referendum procedures, as well as the constitutionality of laws. However, it was assumed that most of its activity would be quite routine and that its major task would be to prevent the National Assembly from encroaching on the administration's prerogatives. The founders of the Fifth Republic were principally concerned that the National Assembly needed to be restrained and did not anticipate that the Council would restrain a government from legislating its program.

The Council's expanded powers derived from three developments: In 1971, the Council expanded its jurisdiction to include judging whether laws violated individual rights; a 1974 amendment authorized the Council to examine at its own initiative any law that "appears to threaten public liberties guaranteed by the Constitution" and authorized sixty members of either house of parliament to refer cases to the Council (in addition to the president, prime minister, and presidents of the two houses of parliament); and, after the electoral victory of the Left in 1981, the Council became the principal forum in which the Right battled to prevent the Socialist government from legislating its program. Between 1981 and 1986, the Council was asked to rule on fourteen bills per year; in about half the cases, it invalidated at least a portion of the bill. Although many of the bills were of minor importance, seven were among the core elements of the Socialist reform program, including decentralization, press ownership, industrial relations, and nationalization.

The Council's ruling on the nationalization of industrial firms was among the most important and controversial of its decisions. It not only forced the government to redraft the reform and increase the compensation paid to stockholders but also represented a symbolic defeat for the government.

Inevitably, the Council became embroiled in conflict. Many on the Left charged that the Council was politically biased because its members had been appointed by conservative politicians — and most Council members were themselves former right-wing politicians. Conflict with the Socialist government transformed the Council into an active and powerful participant in government.

The Economic and Social Council

The Economic and Social Council is a consultative body composed of representatives of various interests, including business, agriculture, labor unions, social-welfare organizations, and consumer groups, as well as leading citizens from cultural and scientific fields. The Council is consulted on the five-year plan and on other bills that the government submits for its advice and acts as a liaison between social and economic interest groups. However, it has no formal powers and is prohibited from discussing the budget; it is unknown to most French and has played an insignificant role in French politics.

Local Government

Until the 1980s, French local governments were quite weak and depended on the national government. France was considered as among the most centralized regimes of any capitalist democracy, given the extraordinarily great power concentrated in the executive and the weak position of representative institutions, notably parliament, as well as of local government. Further, the local governmental structure was extremely fragmented: There are over thirty-six thousand village and city governments in France, more than the combined total of local governments in the other major Western European nations. Most French local governments are tiny: Over 90 percent of French *communes* have fewer than two thousand inhabitants and most local governments lack the technical staff and financial resources to act in an autonomous fashion. Moreover, the French structure of field administration concentrates extensive powers in the hands of national administrators stationed in the provinces to oversee local government.

Large cities enjoyed considerably greater autonomy, thanks to their greater financial, technical, and political resources. Since they raised considerable tax revenues, they could afford to hire their own technical staffs, rather than relying (as most local governments were forced to do) on national administrators for technical assistance. Moreover, the French system permitted an official to hold several elected offices. Most large city mayors simultaneously served as deputies or senators; some were even cabinet ministers — or prime minister.

The Socialist government's first major reform measure after reaching power in 1981 was a thorough overhaul of the local governmental system, as we will discuss in Chapter 10. The decentralization reform has been considered one of the Left's most successful achievements. Although other Left reforms have been reversed following the Right's 1986 electoral victory, the decentralization reform has taken firm root. For example, regional councils were directly elected for the first time when the 1986 legislative elections were held.

Para-Public Agencies

The public sector in France is extensive and sprawling, and includes not only the bureaucracy at various governmental levels but also a wide range of public and semipublic agencies. Following the reforms after the Socialist victory of 1981, more than one-quarter of all domestic production, and a higher proportion of manufactured products, were produced by state-controlled firms. One-half of the twenty largest French corporations were nationalized, including the most technologically advanced and efficient firms in such fields as electronics, automobiles, petrochemicals, steel, and consumer durables. Most telecommunications and air and rail transport were under public control. The nationalized firms were flagships of the French economy, and some rank among world leaders. Public-sector firms generally enjoy a strong reputation for efficiency and reliability.

The banking, insurance, and credit sectors were even more integrated within the public sector: 90 percent of all banks (including all the largest ones) were nationalized. (Many were sold to private owners by the Right after 1986.) Thus, the state controlled many investment decisions, both directly, through the decisions of state-controlled industrial firms, and indirectly, as a result of the credit policies of state-controlled banks and the Ministry of Finance. There is also an intricate network of state financial agencies that exercises tight control over credit and investment policy.

Many agencies promoting regional economic development, tourism, and cultural activities combine public and private funds, and are run by representatives of both sectors. The French economy has traditionally contained a large number of such semipublic agencies.

Given the strong performance of public-sector firms, some of which were nationalized before World War II and some after the Liberation, the Socialist government advocated a substantial extension of the nationalized sector in order to improve France's overall economic performance and to deal with the economic crisis. The reform measures sponsored in the early 1980s will be reviewed in Chapter 10. However, the Right made denationalization one of its major goals in the period after 1986 and rolled back many of the nationalization reforms of earlier periods.

The Policy Process

Until 1986, there was a broad continuity in the way that policy was developed within the Fifth Republic. The system was characterized by presidential dominance, and a hierarchical chain of command linked the president, government, administration, and parliament. Although the Senate, Constitutional Council, and local governments were less tightly integrated into the network, less directly subject to presidential authority, and more powerful than often recognized, they did not substantially alter the highly centralized, rationalized character of French policy-making and implementation.

The policy process provided for vigorous state intervention but allowed little room for political participation, debate, or opposition within established channels. In particular, parliament had precious little autonomy. So long as opposition parties were a minority within the National Assembly, they had few opportunities to influence policy or even express dissent. Moreover, the state-controlled television and radio networks accorded the opposition little time to present their views. During some periods, the Senate provided a forum for opposition forces. Yet it had meager power, and its debates attracted little attention.

What is noteworthy about the election of a Socialist government in 1981 is how little the policy process changed. Socialist President François Mitterrand seemed no less determined than his conservative predecessors to maintain presidential dominance: At a press conference soon after being elected, he declared, "The institutions of the republic were not created with me in mind, but they suit me perfectly." Although Mitterrand's election platform proposed shortening the president's term from seven to five years, his government never initiated the change; further, the Socialist governing style was remarkably similar to conservative governments of the past.

Perhaps the most important respect in which the period between 1981 and 1986 differed from the past was the strong party cohesion at the top levels of the state. This was the first time that the president of the republic was an active party leader and won election by heavy reliance on a mass party, as well as the first time that party leaders dominated within the cabinet. The Socialist Party's victory produced the first period of genuine party rule in France — although throughout the period 1981–86, other parties were represented in the government. (The Communist Party was in the government between 1981 and 1984, and the Left Radical Party was present through the whole period.) However, although Socialist Party officials were more visible within decision-making councils than party leaders had been in the past, the party's impact on specific policy decisions was minimal. In fact, Socialist Party officials rarely intervened to change government decisions after 1981. The Socialist Party's real value was that it delivered the votes in the National Assembly to guarantee passage of the government's reform proposals.

The most important discontinuity in the policy process in the Fifth Republic occurred after 1986, when the Right's electoral victory shattered the cohesion among decision-makers at the top. The major lesson of the transitional period beginning in 1986 is that political stability in the past depended on a stable, coherent majority that unified and integrated the policy process, enabling the president to exercise relatively unchallenged leadership. When the 1986 legislative elections produced a parliamentary majority and government with a divergent political orientation from that of the president, the entire institutional configuration was altered. The president's powers were sharply curtailed and the government, thanks to its electoral mandate, parliamentary majority, and constitutional authority (especially the power to determine policy, conferred by Article 20) emerged as the dominant institution in the policy process. However, it is unlikely that the president — elected, after all, by universal suffrage and possessing ample constitutional and political powers — would ever become a mere figurehead. At the same time, it may not be accidental that cohabitation occurred for the first time in the late 1980s; it may be part of a larger process of political and social reconciliation among contending forces in France.

Although the outcome of the transitional situation has not yet been determined, a fundamentally new era began in France in 1986. Many questions and issues that appeared resolved until 1986 have reemerged with renewed force on the institutional agenda: How are prerogatives divided between the president, government, and National Assembly? How should the parliamentary agenda be decided? Who should direct the administration? In this new situation, what should be the role of other institutions, notably the Constitutional Council?

The years since 1986 represent a period of challenge and potential crisis for the institutions of the Fifth Republic. In the present period of conflict and uncertainty, there is little chance that the state can organize a new accord to promote political stability. How will the republic confront the political-institutional conflicts born from the divided control of state institutions? For the first time in several decades, political conflicts also involve constitutional conflicts. In this respect, although much has changed in the Fifth Republic, the old saw about French politics remains valid: *Plus ça change, plus c'est la même chose,* "The more things change, the more they remain the same." An important set of factors in shaping the republic's fate is the configuration of political and social forces, to which we turn in Chapter 9.

NOTES

1. William G. Andrews, *Presidential Government in Gaullist France: A Study of Executive-Legislative Relations, 1958–1974* (Albany: State University of New York Press, 1982), p. 2.
2. Vincent Wright, *The Politics and Government of France,* 2d ed. (New York: Holmes & Meier, 1983), p. 34.
3. Françoise Dreyfus and François D'Arcy, *Les Institutions Politiques et Administratives de la France* (Paris: Économica, 1985), p. 79.
4. Olivier Duhamel, "The Fifth Republic under François Mitterrand: Evolution and Perspectives," in *Continuity and Change in Mitter-rands's France,* ed. Stanley Hoffmann and George Ross (New York: Oxford University Press, 1987). Forthcoming.
5. John T.S. Keeler and Alec Stone, "Judicial-Political Confrontation in Mitterrand's France: The Emergence of the Constitutional Council as a Major Actor in the Policymaking Process," in *Continuity and Change,* ed. Hoffmann and Ross.

9

Social and Political Forces

In 1966, French political scientist Alfred Grosser's essay on France, "Nothing but Opposition," emphasized the extent of direct protest in France.[1] Many observers, lacking Grosser's close knowledge of France, might have judged his argument as outdated. After all, granted that intense protest had occurred prior to the Fifth Republic, as well as in the first years after de Gaulle's return to power, the mid-1960s appeared to presage a new era of political stability in France.

Two years after the publication of Grosser's essay, however, France experienced the most extensive strikes that have ever occurred in any capitalist democracy. The May, 1968, uprising suggested, yet again, the fragility of political stability in France. If Grosser's title may have been somewhat overstated, Grosser was certainly correct to emphasize that protest remains a constant feature of contemporary French political culture. At the same time that state institutions in the Fifth Republic constrain participation by limiting representative bodies, notably parliament, social forces periodically challenge these institutional fetters. Given these surges of protest, it is less surprising that studies of France continue to appear with titles like *The Contentious French* and "Dissentient France."[2]

Yet French political culture is not static. Among the important changes in French politics since the 1960s have been a flowering of voluntary associations and the development of a new type of party system — one with a relatively small number of well-organized, powerful parties, united in broad alternative coalitions that aspire to govern. This chapter analyzes the important shift within the last two decades in the character of social forces and political representation in France.

The Party System

In Chapter 8, we analyzed how the constitution of the Fifth Republic was designed to assure political stability despite the absence of an underlying class or social accord. However, the period of cohabitation suggests that political stability depends as much on the existence of a cohesive party majority to organize popular support and integrate state institutions as it does on constitutional devices. A key development in the Fifth Republic was the formation of stable majority coalitions, at least until 1986. For the first time in French history, alliances that facilitated stable rule, first on the center-Right and then on the Left, developed in the 1960s and 1970s. Moreover, the coalescence of political forces made possible an alternation in office: A coalition of conservative forces ruled until 1981; a Left majority, dominated by the Socialist Party, ruled between 1981 and 1986. As described in Chapter 8, the lack of a cohesive majority since 1986 has heightened political tension and uncertainty.

Among the many ironies of the Fifth Republic is that despite de Gaulle's opposition to political parties, on the grounds that they nurture division, instability, and paralysis, the emergence of powerful political parties played a key role in buttressing cohesion, stability, and leadership within the Fifth Republic. Constitutional engineering could not have assured stable political leadership in the absence of structured and compliant political movements. In a way, during the several decades when the Center and Right controlled the presidency, Left opposition parties — which initially regarded the Fifth Republic as illegitimate — were as necessary to ensure the Fifth Republic's stability as the conservative parties that controlled the government, because especially after the May, 1968, uprising, leftist parties provided a vehicle for the expression of grievances in a relatively orderly fashion. The Left made an even greater contribution to the republic's stability after the 1981 elections by accepting the legitimacy of the Fifth Republic, working within established institutions to promote change, and sponsoring overdue reforms. The Left helped organize, integrate, and suppress social forces that might otherwise have mounted an unruly challenge to the republic. Thus, the party system helped structure both government and opposition in a nation where, in the not-so-distant past, government had been subject to continual challenge.

France is currently experiencing a political transition in which there are fundamental changes in the structure of social identities and ideological affiliations. After several decades in which the center-Right dominated the political system, keeping the Left in a state of permanent opposition and eliminating the far-Right, the Socialist victory of 1981 opened a new era. However, the fracturing of the Socialist-Communist alliance and popular discontent with the Socialist government's performance produced a rightist victory in 1986, which created the unprecedented situation of cohabitation.

Evolution of the Party System

Within the course of the Fifth Republic, there emerged — possibly for the first time in French history — strong, stable political parties that entered coalitions that significantly narrowed the alternatives offered by the political system. Two factors contributed to the narrowing of political choice in the Fifth Republic: a reduction in ideological differences among political groupings; and the pressure exerted by political and electoral institutions — in particular, the influence of presidential elections. We will first examine the evolution of the party system, then review the major parties, and analyze the parties' changing electoral fortunes.

The Fourth Republic promoted fragmentation, instability, and *immobilisme,* "paralysis." A large number of parties flourished in the Fourth Republic, but with the exception of the Communist Party (PCF), they were mostly collections of local notables who pursued their political careers within the National Assembly and maintained the loyalty of their supporters through a mixture of fiery ideological appeals and pork-barrel benefits extracted from the state bureaucracy and parliament. Although de Gaulle reserved his most scathing criticism for political parties and their leaders, the irony is that political parties did not become organized as mass-based, durable organizations until de Gaulle overthrew the Fourth Republic and sponsored a new regime.

In the first years of the Fifth Republic, most political parties were holdovers from the Fourth Republic. Except for the Communist Party and a segment of the Socialist Party, most political parties from the Fourth Republic accepted de Gaulle's return to power with resignation and apprehension. Some political leaders actively rallied to de Gaulle's banner, but most party leaders doubtless hoped (and expected) that he would quickly leave office (either voluntarily or through pressure) once the Algerian crisis was resolved. Therefore, they reasoned, there was no need to make drastic changes in the structure of political parties.

De Gaulle effected a basic change in the fluid party system in 1962 when he pushed through a referendum for popular approval for direct election of the president. He sought to reduce presidential dependence on the political class of professional politicians, who controlled political parties, served in parliament, and played an important role in the electoral college, which elected the president. The trend toward a smaller number of more structured political parties dates from the 1962 referendum, for in order to assure their political survival, party leaders learned that they needed to establish more effective, credible organizations.

The 1965 election, which elected the president by popular vote for the first time in twentieth-century France, pitted President de Gaulle against Socialist François Mitterrand. A coalition of leftist parties and forces forced the president into a runoff election, and de Gaulle was forced to campaign personally. The effect was electrifying: Political life was revitalized; henceforth, political forces within France regrouped around the issue of supporting or opposing the president as well as the president's government. Thus began the trend toward the polarization of the party system.

The electoral procedures used to elect the president and deputies to the National Assembly exerted additional pressure toward consolidation and polarization of the party system. A two-ballot procedure was used for both offices. In the presidential election, if no candidate gained an absolute majority at the first ballot, a runoff election was held two weeks later. Since the second ballot was confined to the two frontrunners from the first ballots, this provided a powerful incentive for parties to form broad coalitions to ensure that their candidate would make the runoff election.

The Center and Right Parties

In the Third and Fourth Republics, political parties on the Left were quite strong and well organized. However, because they were generally in the opposition, gaining control of the government only infrequently, their strength served to weaken political stability. Center and Right parties, on the other hand, were numerous and decentralized. In the Fifth Republic, de Gaulle succeeded in consolidating and strengthening political parties on the center-Right. The Center and Right remained consolidated into two large parties until the 1980s. The rise of the National Front (FN) on the far-Right, which was facilitated by the proportional representation system in the 1986 elections, has altered this picture. Although the two largest center-Right parties, the *Rassemblement pour la République* (RPR) and the *Union pour la Démocratie Française* (UDF, a coalition of smaller parties), ran a common slate of candidates in the 1986 parliamentary elections, they are wholly separate parties.

The RPR. The RPR (Movement for the Republic) is the descendant of the *Union pour la Nouvelle République* (UNR), which was formed in

1958 to support de Gaulle's leadership in the early years of the Fifth Republic. One observer notes, "The conditions surrounding the UNR's creation are unique among parties in democracies. The movement was defined solely in terms of allegiance to the ruling head of state, yet was ignored by him."[3] This was consistent with de Gaulle's opposition to political parties — even ones loyal to him. The UNR did not have a precise program but supported de Gaulle's personal leadership and program, including the attempt to reestablish French *grandeur* and national independence, the need for decisive political leadership within France, and the desirability of modernizing the French society and economy while retaining France's distinctive cultural heritage. Judged by its ability to maintain power, the Gaullist movement is the most successful political force in the Fifth Republic. Although it was forced to relinquish control of the presidency after 1974 and did not control the government from 1976 to 1986, it has been in high office more than any other party.

The Gaullist Party has changed enormously since its creation. At first, its leadership was recruited from close associates of de Gaulle in the Resistance who remained loyal to him throughout the Fourth Republic. Gradually, however, under the guidance of Georges Pompidou, de Gaulle's second prime minister, the Gaullist Party began to develop an existence independent of de Gaulle. In the 1960s, de Gaulle's personal popularity steadily declined, while the popularity of the UNR, which had been far lower than de Gaulle's personal standing, rose. By the late 1960s, public support for the two was at about the same level.

The May, 1968, upheaval damaged de Gaulle's popularity, and the party, under the leadership of Georges Pompidou, began to act as an independent force. In 1969, de Gaulle sought to reestablish his own personal legitimacy through a referendum on which he staked his continuation in office. When the referendum was defeated, he immediately retired from political life, and Georges Pompidou was elected president.

Pompidou died in office before serving out his full seven-year term, and with his death, the Gaullist movement suffered a severe setback. Gaullist Jacques Chaban-Delmas announced his candidacy to succeed Pompidou, but he failed to obtain the united support of the party. Jacques Chirac, a young and ambitious Gaullist politician, threw his support to Valéry Giscard d'Estaing, the candidate from the center-Right Republican Independent Party, and Giscard d'Estaing far outscored Chaban-Delmas. When Giscard defeated Socialist candidate François Mitterrand on the second ballot, he appointed Chirac as prime minister, in part because the Gaullist Party's support in the National Assembly was essential for Giscard to enact his program.

After resigning as prime minister in 1976, over personal and policy differences with Giscard, Chirac revitalized the Gaullist party, further diluting its historical connection with Gaullism. Chirac was elected mayor of Paris in 1977, after which he formed the RPR, a modernist, conservative party, with a mass base and ties to workers, technicians, and administrators. Chirac used the RPR as a vehicle to further his presidential ambitions. When he broke openly with Giscard and ran for president in 1981, the party's support helped him place third, with a respectable 18 percent of the popular vote.

The RPR, following in the Gaullist tradition, refuses to develop a detailed ideology. The party advocates rolling back many of the Socialist Party reforms, especially nationalization, and it seeks less state intervention in the economic sphere. It advocated curtailing state-welfare programs and environmental regulation, along the lines of the Reagan and Thatcher programs, for a brief period but drew back when such changes proved unpopular in France. The RPR competes directly with the National Front and has advocated repressive measures toward immigrants in an attempt to emulate the National Front.

The UDF. Created in 1978, the Union for French Democracy is an umbrella party that incorporates several parties on the center-Right. The major party leader has been Valéry Giscard d'Estaing, but the party was divided after 1981 by the rivalry between Giscard and Raymond Barre, who served as prime minister from 1976 until Giscard's defeat in 1981. Since then, Barre has sought to gain the presidency on his own, in conflict with Giscard, who nourishes similar ambitions.

The UDF is a coalition of parties, most of which date from the Fourth Republic. Although they nominate joint candidates for legislative and other elections, the constituent parties maintain a separate organizational existence. The three major parties within the UDF are the remnants of the Radical Party; the *Centre des Démocrates-Sociaux* (CDS), successor to the powerful Christian Democratic Party of the Fourth Republic; and the *Parti Républicain* (PR), which Giscard created in 1977 from the *Républicains Indépendants* (RI). These are all parties of local notables, linked to the privileged sectors of urban and rural France. The parties have little organized existence, except in election campaigns, and serve as electoral machines for their powerful leaders.

Giscard created the UDF in 1978 to strengthen his position against Chirac and the RPR. The rivalry between the two men and their parties erupted openly in 1981, when Chirac opposed Giscard for the presidency. After Chirac was eliminated at the first ballot, he refused to endorse Giscard over Mitterrand in the runoff election. Chirac's actions, which

Giscard bitterly denounced after the election as "treason," contributed to the latter's defeat.

The Right continued to be divided by political and especially personal rivalries after the 1986 elections, when Chirac, Giscard, and Barre vied for preeminence. Their political differences were probably less important than their conflicting political ambitions. Chirac gained an important advantage during the 1986 elections: In order to maximize their electoral chances, the RPR negotiated common lists of candidates with the UDF, and as the larger and better organized party, the RPR gained more well-placed candidates. In the election, it obtained 147 seats to 128 for the UDF. Chirac was appointed prime minister, and the RPR obtained the more powerful ministerial positions. Thus, Chirac positioned himself well for the presidential contest to be held by 1988.

The National Front. Until the early 1980s, there were four major political parties in France. However, the economic crisis, the failure of the Left, a rightward shift in France, and the introduction of proportional representation for the 1986 elections permitted the growth of the National Front (FN), a political force on the far-Right. The National Front exploited discontent with extensive unemployment and (largely inaccurate) perceptions of a rising crime rate, and identified a handy scapegoat — immigrant workers and their families — to blame for France's problems. One account notes that FN leader Jean-Marie Le Pen "has parlayed anti-immigrant sentiments and a general sense of insecurity into a substantial electoral following."[4] Under Le Pen's leadership, the FN elected thirty-five deputies in the 1986 legislative elections. The FN also secured 135 seats in regional councils chosen in 1986 and, in five of the twenty-two regions, elected enough representatives to hold the balance of power in selecting council presidents.

The first openly racist political party in modern Western Europe, the National Front advocated repressive measures toward immigrants residing in France, as well as expelling immigrants to their country of origin. The National Front conveniently overlooked that many of those targeted for expulsion were French citizens, either from French territories overseas or French-born offspring of immigrant parents. The National Front's electoral strength was a disquieting indication of the inability of established parties to resolve France's social and economic difficulties. Further, by adopting some elements of the FN's program and forming tactical alliances with the FN, established parties helped boost its legitimacy.

The Left Parties

Parties on the Center and Right first demonstrated the value of coalition building: By joining together under the Gaullist banner, they were rewarded handsomely by obtaining the lion's share of seats in the National Assembly through the 1970s. Parties of the Left took the first halting steps toward an alliance in 1962, when the Communist and Socialist parties supported several each others' candidates at the second ballot. The substantial increase in their parliamentary representation provided a powerful incentive to cement the alliance. In the 1965 presidential election, the Communist and Socialist parties, along with smaller center-Left parties, joined in endorsing Mitterrand against de Gaulle. Mitterrand's strong showing on the second ballot — he received 45 percent of the popular vote to de Gaulle's 55 percent — further strengthened the polarization of the party system and provided incentives for parties to ally along Left/Right lines.

The Communist and Socialist Parties: The Union of the Left. The two major leftist parties, the Communist and Socialist parties, differed so greatly that an alliance between them was at first unthinkable. Throughout the postwar period, the Communist Party proclaimed its militant opposition to capitalism and its loyalty to the Soviet Union as the homeland of socialism. The Socialist Party and the Communist Party were bitterly opposed during most of the Fourth Republic. Since most Socialist Party leaders reluctantly accepted de Gaulle's return to power in 1958 (Guy Mollet, the party's top leader, was named to de Gaulle's cabinet) while the Communist Party squarely opposed de Gaulle, the two parties were even further apart. They eventually adopted reforms which reduced their differences: The Socialist Party opposed de Gaulle in the early 1960s and shifted further to the Left in 1969; and the Communist Party became more acceptable to the Socialist Party by modernizing its program, embracing liberal-democracy, and distancing itself from the Soviet Union, an orientation known as Eurocommunism. It was at this time that the Communist Party negotiated the Union of the Left alliance with the Socialist Party.

François Mitterrand, who became the leader of the Socialist Party in 1971, favored an alliance with the Communists (PCF) and was able to gain Socialist Party (PS) support for the decision. In 1972, the two parties signed the Union of the Left alliance. Unlike earlier temporary agreements between the two Left parties, this alliance aimed to form an eventual Left government. The alliance was based on the Common Program of Government, an electoral platform which enumerated the reforms that would be implemented if the Left was chosen to form a government in 1973. (A small third party, the Left Radicals, soon joined the Union of the Left.) The Common Program specified a host of specific measures designed to stimulate economic expansion, promote social justice, and prepare the groundwork for a transition from capitalism to socialism. Among its more radical proposals was a substantial extension of the nationalized industrial and banking sectors. Although not a recipe for revolution, the Common Program went far beyond the Left's reform agenda in other capitalist democracies.

The signing of the Common Program was a political bombshell, for it held out the possibility that the united Left would replace the conservative coalition that had been in power since 1958. Although the Union of the Left failed to win the 1973 elections, both parties considerably improved their parliamentary position. The following year, the Left united around the candidacy of François Mitterrand in the presidential elections that followed President Pompidou's death in office. When Mitterrand came within one percent of winning, it appeared to be only a matter of time until the coalition was elected to power.

Yet, each party suspected — rightly, in fact — that the other was seeking to use the alliance to advance its own interests, hoping to woo the other party's supporters. Although the Socialist Party argued that it now sought a radical break with capitalism, there was ample room to question the party's commitment; similarly, the Communist Party claimed to have embraced democracy, but this was not evident from the party's authoritarian organization and continued acceptance of the Soviet Union as a socialist model. Further, although the alliance was intended to enable both parties to grow by increasing the total support for the Left, the two directly competed for votes.

The Socialist Party was better placed to profit from the alliance because of its location on the political continuum. Since there were relatively few voters to the Left of the Communist Party, the PCF could expand only by recruiting from its right flank, which involved a direct conflict with the Socialist Party. The PS, however, could recruit voters both from the Left and Center. Moreover, the Socialist Party was the more credible governing party: It had played a leading role in the Fourth Republic; its loyalty to French national interests was unquestioned (whereas many regarded the Communist Party as an agent of the Soviet Union); and it was closely integrated into the mainstream of French society.

During the 1970s, the Union of the Left alliance gained support as an alternative to the ruling rightist coalition, but it was the Socialist Party that reaped the lion's share of the benefits, in the form of increased membership and voting support. As a result, in 1977 — at the very moment when it was widely expected that the alliance would reach power in the parliamentary elections scheduled for 1978 — the PCF demanded that the Common Program be renegotiated. Given the changed balance within the alliance and the likelihood that the Socialist Party would dominate a future government, the PCF sought to obtain guarantees in advance regarding a Left government's program and the division of power. When the Socialist Party rejected their demands, the Communists shattered the alliance, and the two parties opposed each other in the 1978 elections. The Right won the elections, as it had every national election since 1958.

At this critical juncture, Mitterrand demonstrated brilliant political insight. Although many Socialists were disillusioned with the party's leftward stance, Mitterrand realized that the only chance for the Socialist Party to reach power, given the polarizing tendencies of the presidential and parliamentary electoral laws, was to maintain the appearance of a leftward orientation. Mitterrand argued that the Socialists should continue to pose as a champion of Left unity — even if its former coalition partner rejected the alliance.

Mitterrand reaped the benefits of his gamble to stay the leftward course when he ran for the presidency in 1981: He convinced millions of Communist (and other leftist) voters that the Socialist Party represented the only chance for the Left to reach power. At the same time, by holding firm in face of Communist insults in the post-1977 period, Mitterrand convinced centrist voters critical of the Giscard regime that the Socialist Party would not be a captive of the PCF. Mitterrand was elected president, and after he dissolved the National Assembly and called for new elections, an absolute majority of Socialist deputies swept into office. The Socialist Party controlled the presidency, the government, and the National Assembly. Although the Communist Party joined the government in 1981, it was given token representation: four PCF cabinet ministers out of a government numbering forty-four.

The Socialist Party had become a modern, well-organized political machine. Few had predicted that the party of aging notables and schoolteachers in the 1960s would become revitalized and appear as the vanguard of a new France in 1981. The years after 1981 could be considered the first period of genuine party government in French history. De Gaulle had maintained a studied distance from political parties during his presidency; Pompidou helped create the Gaullist Party, but the party itself had little place within governing circles.

The period from 1981 to 1984, in which a Socialist-Communist government confronted a conservative opposition, best reflected the tendency toward polarization of the Fifth Republic's presidential system.

The PCF ended its participation in government in 1984 after calculating, as it had in 1977 when it withdrew from the Union of the Left, that the costs of remaining a junior partner outweighed the benefits. When the PCF resigned from the government, the Socialist Party governed alone and was opposed by parties throughout the political spectrum.

In the 1980s, the PCF, which ranked among the largest political parties in postwar France through the 1970s, suffered a drastic loss of support. Whereas the PCF traditionally prided itself on being the party of the working class, only one fifth of all workers voted for the party in 1986 — fewer than voted for the PS or center-Right parties. (See Table 9.4, page 211.) Reasons for the PCF's decline included popular disenchantment with the Soviet Union (which the PCF supported), the PCF's dogmatism, failure to adapt to changing French society, as well as the persistence of democratic centralism, which stifled internal party freedom and repelled potential supporters. The PCF's decline weakened the entire French Left.

After 1984, there was a reversal of the political polarization in French politics. Not only did the increasing conflict between the Communists and Socialists mean the end of the neat symmetry of Left versus Right, but also, given the declining popularity of the Socialist-controlled government, it was clear that the Socialist Party would be defeated in the 1986 parliamentary elections and forced to relinquish control over the government to the center-Right parties. In an attempt to minimize its losses, the Socialist Party sponsored a basic change in the electoral system for the National Assembly.

Electoral Procedure

The 1986 election saw a return to a system of proportional representation, which had been used in the Fourth Republic. Through 1981, and after 1986, members of the National Assembly were chosen from single-member districts by a two-ballot system. This system rewarded large political parties and coalitions, since the party receiving a plurality obtained the seat. Under proportional representation, as opposed to the single-member district system in effect through 1981 and after 1986, several deputies are elected from each *département*. Each party nominates as many candidates as there are seats to be filled from the constituency, and seats are allotted to parties on the basis of their proportion of the popular vote in the *département*. Although proportional representation continues to favor large parties and coalitions, because of the way that fractional shares of seats are allotted, all parties generally receive a share of seats that more closely corresponds to the popular vote than is the case under the single-member district system. By switching to a system of proportional representation, the Socialists hoped to minimize their losses and to avoid an all-out confrontation between President Mitterrand and a rightist-controlled National Assembly.

The system of proportional representation gives political parties far less incentive to ally, since their parliamentary strength depends mostly on their proportion of the vote; it also gives a smaller bonus to large parties and party alliances. Since the Socialists could not find partners for an alliance, they hoped to use proportional representation to break apart the coalition between rightist parties or, failing that, to prevent such an alliance from reaping lavish electoral rewards. The Socialist gamble was quite successful. By instituting proportional representation, the PS obtained substantially more seats than if the two-ballot single-member district system had been used, and the center-Right gained only a slender parliamentary majority.

On regaining office in 1986, the center-Right parties promptly reestablished the former single-member district two-ballot system. Given the fact that the two major center-Right parties, the UDF and the RPR, were able to negotiate an electoral agreement, their combined votes were greater than those of the Socialist Party running alone.

In the 1986 parliamentary elections, the Socialist Party obtained 32 percent of the vote, its highest total ever except for the 1981 triumph following Mitterrand's victory. The PCF continued its downward slide

Table 9.1 Results of Voting by Proportional Representation Versus Single-member District, 1986 Legislative Elections; Seat Distribution in National Assembly.

PARTY	RESULTS WITH PROPORTIONAL REPRESENTATION	RESULTS WITH SINGLE-MEMBER DISTRICT	DIFFERENCE
PCF	34	9	+25
PS	217	203	+14
RPR/UDF	292	358	−66
FN	34	7	+27

SOURCE *Libération,* March 18, 1986, p. 24.

Table 9.2 Electoral Results, Elections to National Assembly, 1958–86 (percentage of those voting)

<table>
<tr><th></th><th>1958</th><th>1962</th><th>1967</th><th>1968</th><th>1973</th><th>1978</th><th>1981</th><th>1986</th></tr>
<tr><td>PCF</td><td>19%</td><td>22%</td><td>23%</td><td>20%</td><td>21%</td><td>21%</td><td>16%</td><td>10%</td></tr>
<tr><td>Far Left</td><td>2</td><td>2</td><td>2</td><td>4</td><td>3</td><td>3</td><td>1</td><td>2</td></tr>
<tr><td>Socialist Party</td><td>15</td><td>13</td><td>19</td><td>17</td><td>19</td><td>23</td><td rowspan="2">{38</td><td rowspan="2">{32</td></tr>
<tr><td>Left Radicals</td><td>8</td><td>8</td><td>—</td><td>—</td><td>3</td><td>2</td></tr>
<tr><td>Center parties</td><td>15</td><td>15</td><td>18</td><td>10</td><td>16</td><td rowspan="2">{21</td><td rowspan="2">{19</td><td rowspan="3">{42</td></tr>
<tr><td>Center-Right (CPR)</td><td>14</td><td>14</td><td>0</td><td>4</td><td>7</td></tr>
<tr><td>UNR→RPR</td><td>18</td><td>32</td><td>38</td><td>44</td><td>24</td><td>23</td><td>21</td></tr>
<tr><td>Far Right</td><td>3</td><td>1</td><td>1</td><td>0</td><td>3</td><td>0</td><td>3</td><td>10</td></tr>
<tr><td>Abstentions</td><td>23</td><td>31</td><td>19</td><td>20</td><td>19</td><td>17</td><td>30</td><td>22</td></tr>
</table>

SOURCE Françoise Dreyfus and François D'Arcy, *Les Institutions Politiques et Administratives de la France* (Paris: Economica, 1985), p 54; and *Le Monde,* March 18, 1986. Percentages of parties do not add to 100 because of minor party candidates and rounding errors.

by falling from 16 percent in 1981 to 10 percent of the popular vote in 1986. The PCF's disastrous showing probably signified its demise as a major political force in French politics. The PCF barely managed to outpoll the National Front, which became a significant political force only in the 1980s. The center-Right coalition of the RPR and UDF obtained a narrow electoral victory and emerged with a narrow majority in the National Assembly.

Electoral Behavior

French political parties experience quite rapid shifts in electoral support from one election to another. Yet there are underlying continuities that can be discerned over time. The French pioneered the field of electoral geography, which charts continuities and changes in the voting preferences of localities and regions. Electoral studies have demonstrated astonishing similarities in the political orientation of regions over periods of time — sometimes as long as a century in duration — although the political parties that represent a given ideological position may change.

The overall evolution of electoral patterns within the Fifth Republic might be termed the rise, fall, and rise again of rightist political parties.

Table 9.3 Presidential Elections in the Fifth Republic

CANDIDATES	DECEMBER, 1965 1ST BALLOT	DECEMBER, 1965 2D BALLOT	CANDIDATES	JUNE, 1969 1ST BALLOT	JUNE, 1969 2D BALLOT	CANDIDATES	MAY, 1974 1ST BALLOT	MAY, 1974 2D BALLOT	CANDIDATES	APRIL–MAY, 1981 1ST BALLOT	APRIL–MAY, 1981 2D BALLOT
Center-Right											
de Gaulle	43.7%	54.5%	Pompidou (UNR)	44.0%	57.6%				Chirac (RPR)	18.0%	
Opposition-Center											
Lecanuet	15.8		Poher (Center)	23.4	42.4	Giscard (Center-right)	32.9%	50.7%	Giscard (Center-right)	28.3	48.2%
Left											
Mitterrand (Socialist-Communist)	32.2	45.5	Defferre (PS)	5.1		Mitterrand (PS)	43.4	49.3	Mitterrand (PS)	25.8	51.8
			Duclos (PCF)	21.5					Marchais (PCF)	15.3	
Abstentions	15.0	15.5		21.8	30.9		15.1	12.1		18.9	14.1

SOURCE: John R. Frears and Jean-Luc Parodi, *War Will Not Take Place: The French Parliamentary Elections of March 1978* (London: Hurst, 1979), p. 6; and *Le Monde, L'Élection Présidentielle: 26 avril–10 mai 1981* (Paris: Le Monde, 1981), pp. 98, 138. Percentages of votes for candidates do not add to 100 because of minor party candidates and rounding errors.

The period of Left ascendancy was quite brief (1981–86); the Right has dominated the Fifth Republic for all but five years of its three decades of existence. Among the most important — and partially contradictory — changes in electoral patterns and the party system in the 1980s have been the following: increased volatility in voting, as evidenced in rapid voting shifts in the 1980s (to the Left in 1981, to the Right in 1986); a shift in the party system from the four, roughly equal-sized, parties (PCF, PS, UDF, RPR) that characterized the 1970s, to three large parties (PS, RPR, and UDF) and two small parties (the PCF and FN); the "presidentialization" of parties, as parties accord highest priority to electing their leader to the presidency; a decline of the overall strength of the Left, which obtained only 44 percent of the vote in the 1986 parliamentary elections; and a decline in polarization between the Left and Right in favor of more extreme political fragmentation, a result of increased tension between political parties on each side of the Left/Right divide.

In the late 1980s, changing electoral patterns have reinforced the increasing instability of French politics. Doubtlessly, the basic cause has been the inability to forge a replacement for the postwar settlement to reconcile conflict, a situation that characterizes the other capitalist democracies analyzed in this book; however, the general tendency has been intensified by the greater degree of ideological fragmentation in France. It is clear that, in the absence of a new framework, there may well continue to be volatile voting behavior, intense political conflict, and tendencies toward political instability within the French political system. Yet analysts have also discerned two trends pointing in an opposite direction. In the 1980s, there has been a *normalisation* of French politics, in which political patterns have come to resemble politics in northern Europe. The two key changes in this respect are declining ideological distance between political parties, as a result of the PCF's decline and the Socialist Party's greater moderation beginning in 1982; as well as alternation between parties of the center-Left and center-Right. A second trend, pointing in the same direction as the first, is toward ideological convergence among French citizens, which will be reviewed later in this chapter. Cohabitation could be interpreted as an institutional reflection of the new trends.

Interest Groups

Political parties, interest groups, and social movements provide outlets for expressing divisions and representing social forces. The French typically are considered to be less inclined to create and participate in such social and political organizations than are citizens of comparable capitalist democracies. However, the French are more inclined to engage in active protest — strikes, demonstrations, etc. — to manifest their displeasure and pursue their interests.

Alexis de Tocqueville analyzed nineteenth-century France in terms that seem valid today: He argued that the French demand central state intervention, rather than exercising private initiative, to regulate conflict; in the United States, by contrast, local governments and grass-roots organizations assume greater importance. A powerful current in French political thought regards interest groups as partial and partisan groupings that distort the formation of the general will; citizens should participate by acting as disinterested, public-spirited individuals, rather than as members of interest groups that pursue partisan interests.

There was a dramatic shift in popular attitudes and actions concerning interest groups in the Fifth Republic, especially in the 1980s. Whereas 13,000 new voluntary associations were created in 1960, 31,000 were created in 1980; 34,000 in 1981; 40,000 in 1982; and 47,000 in 1983. One analyst estimates that the total number of voluntary associations in France exceeds one-half million.[5] This flowering of voluntary association is doubtlessly part of a general change in cultural patterns, in which there has been an increased desire for participation. Although there are a number of powerful interest groups, including the CNPF, a peak-level employers' association, and the FNSEA, the agricultural lobby which has a quasi-monopoly over the representation of farmers' interests, the most prominent interest group, the labor movement, merits special attention.

The Labor Movement. The French labor movement is among the weakest in any advanced capitalist democracy. Aside from a brief period after World War II, when trade union membership soared, organized labor has usually recruited less than one-quarter of the working class — among the lowest proportion of any capitalist democracy. Moreover, the union movement is divided into rival confederations, each pursuing a very different strategy. The three major confederations (as well as a number of other unions) compete with each other for members at the workplace and at higher levels. The three are the *Confédération Générale du Travail* (CGT), closely tied to the Communist Party; the *Confédération Française Démocratique du Travail* (CFDT); and *Force Ouvrière* (FO), both of which are moderate unions independent of political parties. The three unions have about 1 million members apiece, although the CGT obtains the greatest support in works committee elections and is the most powerful and best organized.

French labor relations are quite archaic, and unions have been relatively unsuccessful in compelling employers to recognize the existence of unions, to bargain collectively, and to observe health and safety standards. Although French workers enjoy substantial benefits, including extended unemployment assistance and protection against layoffs, these measures were imposed on employers by the state, as a result of workers' direct action and political pressure (often exercised through unions and Left parties). French unions have been relatively less successful than unions elsewhere in extracting benefits directly from employers. From this perspective, the fact that unions encouraged frequent strikes (in the postwar period, France's strike rate was second only to that of Italy) was evidence of the weakness, not strength, of the labor movement and working class. Unable to defend their interests by institutionalized means, workers resorted to strikes and other forms of direct action.

The dominant tradition of French unionism advocated direct action. In the famous Amiens Charter of 1906, unions adopted the anarcho-syndicalist strategy of a general strike to overthrow the state, while opposing alliances with political parties within the existing system. Yet unions have failed to reconcile this goal with the growth of the welfare state, which provides widespread benefits to workers.

French unions characteristically responded with ambivalence to the welfare state. On the one hand, unions continued to proclaim radical goals, opposed all forms of class collaboration, and advocated the overthrow of the state. On the other hand, unions entered the system, bargained to maximize political and economic benefits for their members, and pursued a strategy of extracting the maximum benefits possible.

The strategy was quite successful so long as economic growth persisted into the 1970s, but as the economy stagnated, French unions experienced a crisis. The heavy industrial sectors (e.g., steel and textiles) in which union members were concentrated bore the brunt of the economic crisis at the same time that new workers entered the labor force whom unions made few efforts to recruit.

The crisis of French unionism (which in part resulted from employers' anti-union efforts) has deepened in the 1980s, despite the Left's victory in 1981. The Socialist government sponsored a drastic overhaul of the labor relations framework, but this has failed to elicit widespread worker support (either for the unions or the government). Unions have remained unable to devise new strategies to cope with the economic crisis; thus, management retains the initiative in restructuring French industry, introducing new technology, fostering part-time and temporary work (to discourage union membership), and investing abroad. Unions have advocated bold new initiatives, but they have failed to devise means, even under a Left government, to put them into practice.

The French union movement remains in deep crisis despite the fact that many of its specific demands were satisfied by the Left government. This suggests that French unions have failed to grasp what needs to be done in the current period to represent workers' interests adequately.

Social Movements

The decline of the postwar settlement left political parties and states in all capitalist democracies ill-equipped to handle the new political forces and demands that arose in the 1970s. France was no exception, although the development of French social movements was somewhat unusual.

France was the first Western European nation to experience widespread militant protest in the postwar period. In the 1970s, a range of social movements continued to derive inspiration from the May, 1968, movement. The environmental movement mounted widespread protests against France's heavy emphasis on nuclear power in the 1970s. For example, a demonstration held in 1977 at Creys-Malville, the proposed site of the world's first fast breeder reactor, drew several hundred thousand protestors. At the end of the demonstration, violent clashes developed and one participant was killed. Movements for regional autonomy in Brittany, the Basque country, and Corsica demand greater allocation of state resources to these underdeveloped areas; the teaching of local languages in the public schools; and, for some militants, independence. The women's movement, which became active in the 1970s, demanded equal rights in a nation where gender inequality was often enshrined in law. For example, married women could not open a checking account without their husband's authorization, and abortions and the dissemination of information about contraceptive devices were illegal.[6]

Despite their many differences, social movements shared a common opposition to the rigid hierarchies within French society and the state. All movements sought greater decentralization, as well as attention to the quality of life rather than industrial growth. Social movements probably had their greatest impact on the style of personal relations and daily life: People dressed more informally, teachers began to encourage discussion and debate within the classroom, and relations within the family became more informal.

Social movements were fairly successful in moving their demands onto the public agenda. For example, President Giscard d'Estaing sponsored reforms that reduced some of the most glaring instances of gender inequality. The environmental movement (or ecology movement, as it is called in France) succeeded in getting environmental protection legislation adopted.

The Socialist government accorded lavish symbolic attention to social movements, for example, creating ministries for women's rights, social solidarity, and leisure time, for the purpose of improving women's position, increasing the situation of disadvantaged groups, and enriching citizens' extra-work life. It appointed leaders of trade unions and social movements to administrative positions and provided movements with financial aid. However, by a combination of co-optation, limited responsiveness, indifference, and outright repression, the government succeeded in disarming social movements in France, especially those with Leftist leanings. Moreover, many social movements viewed the government's liberalizing reforms in the fields of the judiciary, gender relations, and labor relations as less significant than its statist approach, continued emphasis on nuclear energy, and militarism.

The 1985 Greenpeace affair illustrated the Socialist government's lack of commitment to progressive social movements. In order to prevent the Rainbow Warrior, a ship sponsored by the Greenpeace environmental movement, from interfering with French nuclear tests in the Pacific, the government directed secret service agents to sabotage the vessel. Scuba divers planted a bomb on board. The ship was heavily damaged and a crew member killed in the attack. When newspaper investigations established the government's responsibility for the attack, the defense minister was eventually forced to resign, but the government did not modify its nuclear test program.

SOURCE *Le Monde,* September 21, 1985.

Although progressive social movements were co-opted by the Socialist government, conservative groups became more vocal in protesting Socialist policies. Among the many groups that mounted antigovernment protests after 1981 were truckers, farmers, doctors, shopkeepers, business executives, undertakers, and parochial-school supporters. The result was to nourish a general climate of opposition to the Socialist government and to shift the political center of gravity in France toward the right.

Political Attitudes and Culture

Traditionally, French citizens have been quite polarized in their ideological orientations. For example, French workers have typically displayed a high level of class consciousness and resentment. In a comparison of British and French workers, Duncan Gallie found that while two-thirds of French workers identified themselves as workers, fewer than one-half of British workers did so. Nearly half of British workers judged that the disparity in living standards between workers and business executives was justified, but only about one-tenth of French workers agreed with this view. These differences also extended to attitudes toward political change: About one-fifth of British workers agreed that "many things need changing" or "the whole system needs changing," while nearly half of French workers chose these responses. Gallie concludes, "French workers were substantially more likely to identify with a wider working class, they were more resentful about class inequality, and they were notably more likely to perceive a close interconnection between the structure of political power and the persistence of class inequality."[7]

Recently, however, public opinion analysts have pointed to a decline in the extent of ideological divergence in France. The normalization of French politics is illustrated by the increasing similarity in the social base of different political party electorates, an acceptance of political alternation, and a decline in ideological differences among parties. In the 1986 parliamentary elections, the socioeconomic base of the two major political groupings, the PS and the RPR-UDF, were broadly similar, with the exception of farmers, shopkeepers, professionals, and homemakers, who strongly favored conservative parties.

Olivier Duhamel has analyzed the growth of a broad if somewhat complex consensus in political attitudes. He suggests, on the basis of extensive public opinion poll data, that the French have become socially socialist, economically liberal, and culturally conservative.[8]

Table 9.4 Socioeconomic Distribution of Voting Preferences

	PC	PS	RPR/UDF	FN	OTHER	TOTAL
Total Electorate	10	32	42	10	6	100%
Sex						
Men	12	30	40	12	6	100%
Women	7	34	45	7	7	100%
Age						
Under 25	6	40	38	9	7	100%
25–34	12	41	30	8	9	100%
35–49	10	33	40	9	8	100%
50–64	9	25	49	12	5	100%
65 and older	10	23	53	9	5	100%
Occupation						
Farmers	7	21	54	11	7	100%
Shopkeepers	5	14	61	14	6	100%
Professionals & top executives	4	32	49	9	6	100%
Middle executives	9	38	36	10	7	100%
Service workers	12	44	33	7	4	100%
Manual workers	20	34	29	11	6	100%
Not in labor force	11	29	45	9	6	100%
Unemployed	13	33	33	14	7	100%
Students	4	41	43	5	7	100%
Homemakers	6	26	52	8	8	100%

SOURCE *Libération,* March 18, 1986, p. 18.

The convergence in attitudes among many citizens, especially those who support the RPR, UDF, and PS, coexists with the persistence of strong political conflict, intensified by the institutional issue of cohabitation. One French journal termed this the paradox of "consensus within discord."[9]

In this chapter, we have analyzed the way that the party system and other social forces represent and channel participation. Traditionally, there has been a high degree of direct action and protest in France, and established channels of representation were unable to command sufficient support to institutionalize representation in an orderly fashion. In general, political participation often took the form of protest against established arrangements, rather than collaboration in decision making. The powerful and often distant bureaucracy, as well as the high degree of ideological conflict, tended to discourage a more pluralist, pragmatic pattern.

These patterns have been somewhat altered in the Fifth Republic, but there is considerable continuity as well. Social movements have been too weak to have an important impact on policymaking — but sufficiently powerful to mobilize followers to mount protests. As in the past, trade unions have taken to the streets or occupied factories when they were unable to influence policy otherwise. Although the Fifth Republic rationalized and strengthened mechanisms of decision making at the top, it did little to provide more adequate channels of popular participation. A major development, however, has been the consolidation of political parties, which has resulted in more effective channels of representation, as well as better links between social forces and the state.

Yet, in part because of the failure of both the Left and Right to devise adequate policies to resolve the economic crisis, social forces have continued to resort to direct action to protest state actions. The Fifth Republic has proved unable thus far to devise a new class accord or to achieve a balance between political participation, representation, and state decision making.

Notes

1. Alfred Grosser, "France: Nothing but Opposition," in *Political Opposition in Western Democracies,* ed. Robert A. Dahl (New Haven: Yale University Press, 1966), pp. 284–302.
2. Charles Tilly, *The Contentious French: Four Centuries of Popular Struggle* (Cambridge: Harvard University Press, 1985); Jack Hayward, "Dissentient France: The Counter Political Culture," in *Social Movements and Protest in France,* ed. Philip G. Cerny (London: Frances Pinter, 1982), pp. 1–16.
3. William R. Schonfeld, "The RPR: From a Rassemblement to the Gaullist Movement," in *The Fifth Republic at Twenty,* eds. William G. Andrews and Stanley Hoffmann (Albany: State University of New York Press, 1981), p. 83.
4. James Hollifield, "Immigrants, Race and Politics," *French Politics and Society,* no. 13 (March 1986), pp. 15–20.
5. Gérard Delfau, *Gagner à gauche* (Paris: Robert Laffont, 1985), p. 85.

6. Jane Jenson, "Struggling for Identity: The Women's Movement and the State in Western Europe," *West European Politics,* vol. 8, no. 4 (October 1985): pp. 5–18; and Wayne Northcutt and Jeffra Flaitz, "Women, Politics and the French Socialist Government," *West European Politics,* vol. 8, no. 4 (October 1985), pp. 50–70.
7. Duncan Gallie, *Social Inequality and Class Radicalism in France and Britain* (Cambridge: Cambridge University Press, 1983), p. 66.
8. Olivier Duhamel, "Libéraux-socialistes-conservateurs: les évolutions idéologiques des Français," in *Opinion Publique, 1985,* ed. SOFRES (Paris: Gallimard, 1985), chap. 6.
9. Dominique Greusard, "Le consensus dans la discorde," *Esprit,* vol. 3 (March 1986), pp. 15–25.

10

French Politics in Transition

What is the meaning of socialism in an advanced industrialized capitalist society? To what extent may a nation like France, in which the Left was in the opposition for decades, promote reforms that took generations to achieve in social democracies? What is the margin for maneuver within the current economic crisis and the prevailing situation of severe international economic competition? To what extent might socialist policies provide a framework to replace the postwar settlement?

These are not hypothetical questions: Once the Socialist Party achieved a stunning sweep of the 1981 presidential and legislative elections, these issues were at the top of the governmental agenda. What was the evolution and character of the Socialist term in office? To what extent did it constitute a transition to a new era in French politics? What lessons does it provide for understanding the transition of French politics? The period of 1981 to 1986 provides a well-delimited case for analysis: It began with the Socialist electoral sweep and ended with the defeat of the Socialists in the 1986 legislative elections. Thus began a new period of cohabitation between President Mitterrand and a conservative government.

The Emergence of the Socialist Government

The Socialists were elected in 1981 with a clear electoral majority, enormous institutional power, and an ambiguous mandate. It was not clear if they owed their victory to citizens' disgust with the Giscard regime, a desire for radical changes in France's political economy, or the hope for moderate reforms without fundamental change. Much depended, in any event, on what use the Socialist government made of its extraordinary opportunity. And that, in turn, depended on the Socialists' own goals.

In order to understand the bewildering sweep of events following the Socialist victory in 1981, it is helpful to distinguish three different Socialist goals, each of which can be considered a distinct project. The three will be described and illustrated by analyzing a major Socialist structural reform that served to promote the project. We will conclude with an analysis of the historical and theoretical implications of Socialist rule.[1]

Three Socialist Projects

Modernizing and Liberalizing French Society. In 1981, the Socialist Party campaigned on a platform calling for a national effort to modernize and liberalize French society. The Left asserted that the conservative governments that had dominated the Fifth Republic for over two decades had failed to revitalize French industry, stimulate economic growth, eliminate blockages to change, reduce inequalities, and promote local initiative. The Left argued that because the conservative coalition had been a captive of traditionally privileged groups, it was ill-equipped to eliminate the blockages of the stalemate society. Thus, the Left was forced to accomplish what should have been the goal of enlightened conservatives: the modernization and liberalization of French society.

The first socialist project can be considered liberal in both the European and U.S. sense of the term. In European political discourse, *liberal* refers to those forces who seek freedom (liberty) as opposed to traditional conservative groups, who seek to preserve privilege. Thus, liberalism is equated with the search for liberty. The Socialist government sought this goal, for example, by promoting a substantial reform of the judicial system, including: abolishing the death penalty; doing away with the Security Court, which was created during the Algerian war and which did not safeguard the rights of defendents; and strengthening women's rights. Another liberalizing reform sponsored by the Left, reviewed below, decentralized the French administrative structure.

The Left's first overall project can be considered liberal in the American sense as well. In the United States, *liberal* refers to an attempt to redistribute resources, in a moderate and pragmatic fashion, from more to less privileged groups. In this context, liberal can be distinguished from either conservative, which opposes redistribution, or radical, which seeks a sweeping redistribution. The Left promoted liberal measures, in this sense, by sponsoring an increase in welfare-state benefits, including a rise in the minimum wage, family allowances (to parents with young children), and pensions for the elderly.

Among the Left's major liberalizing reforms — and one of the most important measures sponsored in the 1981–86 period — was a series of measures to decentralize the French state and administration. The Socialist government asserted that a major cause of the rigidities in French society was an imbalance between state and society, in which a top-heavy state intervened to stifle liberty and local initiatives. Ironically, the Left, which was often criticized for being Jacobin (i.e., relying on the central state to reduce inequality in a way that threatened freedom in its turn), had criticized the Right for the excessive degree of centralization in France. In order to promote local initiative and freedom, the Left made decentralization its first major priority: Two months after gaining power, the Socialist government introduced a sweeping proposal in parliament to reduce the state's authority over local governments. The Defferre law (named for the minister of the interior), was passed in 1982. During the next several years, more than a dozen other laws were passed which aimed to strengthen subnational governments. Among the major provisions were the following: loosening the control exercised by the prefect over local governmental decisions;* transfer of the executive power within regional and departmental governments from the prefect to the elected presidents of local councils; creation of regional government; enlarging local governments' powers; and civil service reform.

The Socialist decentralization reform was relatively sweeping and successful. It represents the most substantial attempt in recent French history to revitalize subnational government. Although it is premature to judge the impact of the reform, it promises to increase the autonomy of local governments and stimulate local initiative. The Socialists have gained substantial credit for sponsoring the decentralization reform.

However, the Left did not confront one of the most complex and pressing areas that affect the autonomy of local governments: their financial base. Although the Left promised to carry out a sweeping reform of the archaic system of local taxes, it failed to do so. As a result, local governments were left vulnerable and dependent on the national government for financial help. Further, the reform was limited in that it

* Created by Napoleon, the prefectoral system involved the close supervision of French localities. The prefects, who were nationally appointed civil servants stationed in the provinces, were criticized for limiting the autonomy of French local government.

could be considered "representation without participation"; governmental powers were reshuffled among existing political officials and agencies without broadening local participation. Although the reform may elicit greater citizen participation and interest once it becomes recognized how much local governments can affect citizens' daily lives, no provision was made for increased local democracy. The reform strengthened representative and bureaucratic forms, by transferring governmental powers to elected officials and administrators at the local level, but it fell far short of promoting new forms of direct democracy and self-management within the community.

The Socialists' liberalizing reforms have partially achieved their goal of reducing rigidities and blockages within French society. Ironically, the Left was quite successful at carrying out what enlightened conservatives advocated (they had been calling for greater decentralization for years), but quite unsuccessful at achieving more ambitious projects.

Belated Introduction of Social Democracy. The French Left had traditionally been disdainful of social democracy as it evolved in northern Europe since the 1930s, because of its class compromises and acceptance of capitalism. The major Left parties, notably the Communist and Socialist parties, advocated the goal of transcending social democracy to achieve a radical rupture with capitalism. Neither French Left party ever renounced this ultimate goal, in contrast with most socialist and social democratic parties in northern Europe.

Yet as events after 1981 revealed, part of the Left's disdain for northern European–style social democracy may have been envy: Given the greater weakness and division of the French labor movement, the institutional and policy arrangements associated with social democracy were foreclosed in France. Social democracy requires a labor movement with which organized business and the state must reckon, a labor movement that has the capacity to bargain, make agreements, and enforce them on its members. The French labor movement has been divided into warring unions, and it has been unable to develop the cohesion and capacity to pursue unified goals. The French Left's performance after 1981 suggests that despite its verbal opposition to social democracy, it implicitly accepted the virtue of social democracy and wished, generations after social democracy had developed in northern Europe, to promote a social-democratic project for France.

At the core of social democracy is a compromise between the organized working class, capital, and the state, in which all partners cooperate to promote what might be described as a virtuous circle of full employment, economic growth, and welfare-state redistributive measures. This was the basis for the postwar settlement in northern Europe. The French Socialists sought to use their control of the state to stimulate economic growth and welfare-state programs through increasing welfare spending and by a sweeping overhaul of the industrial and labor relations legislation. In particular, the labor relations reform sought to organize and unify the working class and to promote more stable contractual relations between the labor movement and capital. Both goals were the object of the Auroux laws, named after Jean Auroux, the minister of labor who sponsored the reform. Among the major provisions of the reform were the following: legal safeguards for organized labor; plant-level collective bargaining; consultation with unions in new fields; and direct consultation with workers.

The Socialists' attempt to organize and rationalize labor relations can hardly be considered unprecedented or audacious. Like the decentralization reform, the innovations within the labor relations system were institutionalized long ago in other capitalist democracies. The fact that the reforms were not introduced in France until the mid-1980s testifies to the backwardness of French postwar governments. Further, although the Socialist government succeeded in getting the Auroux reforms passed and implemented, it did not achieve its goal of organizing and unifying the working class. Trade unions remain quite weak in France, they remain bitterly at odds, and collective bargaining remains underdeveloped. Moreover, other features of social democracy remain lacking, especially the virtuous circle of class compromise to promote full employment, investment, economic growth, and welfare-state redistributive programs. Thus, the Socialist government was relatively more successful in achieving its goal of liberalizing French society than in belatedly introducing social democracy in France.

Beyond Social Democracy? The Socialist government sought to resolve the crisis of capitalist democracy by radical measures, going beyond social democracy, that would promote democratic socialism in France. One of the major means that it used to promote this project was extending the proportion of production, investment, and banking within the public sector. François Mitterrand defined the project in his presidential inaugural address in 1981 as the union of democracy and socialism. If successful, this would be the first durable example of democratic socialism: Capitalist societies have had democratic methods of choosing their governments, and socialist societies have brought production under public control, but no society has succeeded in organizing its economic and political system in a thoroughly democratic fashion.

France has a tradition of state intervention and direct control of production that goes back centuries. In the recent period, the Popular Front government in 1936 and postwar governments (1944–47) sponsored the nationalization of railroads, air transport, the Renault automobile firm, coal mines, and the petroleum industry. Yet there had been no attempt in France from the late 1940s to the 1980s to further extend the nationalized sector. Whereas other capitalist democracies have nationalized a portion of their industrial and banking sector, the French Socialist government proposed going much further than any comparable nation in organizing production directly within the public sector. The quantitative extension of nationalization was intended to achieve the qualitative effect of bringing France closer toward a democratic socialist transition.

The Socialist government's nationalization reforms, reviewed in Chapter 8, included taking control of the two major French steel producers, as well as the largest producers of aluminum and glass, electronics and electrical equipment, and petrochemicals. With passage of the reforms, the most powerful, concentrated, and technologically advanced industrial firms and sectors in France were directly under state control.

Rivaling the industrial takeovers in importance was the nationalization of the remaining private French banks. (Several large banks were nationalized after World War II.) After the 1983 reform, more than 90 percent of savings deposits were in state-controlled banks. The French banking sector, under public control, accounted for the bulk of investments in France.

The Socialist government asserted that nationalization was necessary to revitalize ailing French industry, reverse French losses in industrial market shares to foreign competition, prevent foreign takeovers of French firms, improve France's international economic position, and democratize production within the public sector.

The nationalization reforms potentially served as a base to transcend capitalism. The government could have used the nationalized sector as a social laboratory for democratizing production. Workers at the shop-floor and office level, who presently execute management decisions, might have been made participants in the process of deciding key production decisions, for example, the organization of work, technological innovations, and product design. If successful, the reforms could have stimulated momentum for democratization in other sectors of French society and served as a model for other capitalist nations. However, the reforms produced few changes in the decision-making process within production. Further, the government promised that it would not disturb the autonomy of the firms (a promise it failed to keep when it issued endless instructions to firm managers — but democratizing the labor process at lower levels did not figure among the government's priorities).

Within two years of the Socialists' arrival in power in 1981, the government rapidly lost popularity. By 1984, President Mitterrand was the most unpopular president in the history of the Fifth Republic. By the 1986 legislative elections, the Socialist government had long since abandoned any thought of sponsoring new initiatives; its 1986 electoral platform emphasized what it had already achieved, but failed to propose any additional reforms. Soon after regaining office, the conservative government reversed several key Socialist reforms.

From Lyrical Illusions to a Socialism of Governance

What happened? Why did a government that reached office on a surge of popularity, armed with an ambitious reform program, fail so badly? To begin with, the Socialist government did *not* fail so badly. Many of the Socialist reforms will endure and be recognized as among the major progressive advances within twentieth-century France. The Socialist government did much to sweep away rigid obstacles to a modern, liberal society. Its economic policies began to bear fruit in the short term just at the point that the government was voted from office: In the spring of 1986, there was a sharp reversal of previous inflationary trends and a decrease in unemployment. The Socialist government demonstrated that the Left could provide relatively stable, effective government.

From the perspective of countries like Sweden or West Germany, where the Left has ruled for long periods, it would hardly be noteworthy that the French Socialists ruled for five years. However, it was unprecedented in France, where the Left typically remained excluded from office for many years, gained office for brief periods to enact a frenzied burst of reforms, and was quickly ejected from office. The Socialist government helped to establish the smooth alternation of power within the Fifth Republic and thus contributed to what some observers describe as the normalization of French politics: the decline of ideological extremism and passions, and the pragmatic acceptance of harsh realities. Yet this achievement is a reflection of the Socialists' failure when measured by their initial ambitions, for normalization occurred in part because the Socialist government abandoned its more audacious reform goals.

Generally, the Socialist government did fail in two critical respects: It failed to surmount the economic crisis in 1983–84 and, as a result, could not maintain public support; and it failed to forge a new class accord. Despite the diminution of some conflicts in France, Socialist rule revived old conflicts (for example, concerning the relationship of the state to private schools) and engendered new ones. Normalization has not resulted in political stability.

A useful way to evaluate the Socialist performance is by reviewing the three socialist projects. First, critics charged that the Socialist government not only failed to safeguard liberties but also jeopardized them, for example, by unsuccessfully attempting to increase state control over the private school system. However, on balance, the Left increased the scope of rights and liberties in France.

The Socialist government also failed to achieve its social-democratic goals. Rather than promoting economic growth and job creation, Socialist policies promoted economic dislocation and unemployment. Rather than promoting a virtuous circle of growth, redistributive policies promoted a vicious circle of inflation, international trade deficits, and a weakened franc.

The Socialists' expansionary policies were carried out at the worst moment, in terms of the international economy: Just as the French government was pumping increased purchasing power into the French economy, governments elsewhere (notably in the United States) were pursuing deflationary policies. The result was that budget deficits, the international trade deficit, and public debt soared, at the same time that domestic demand was absorbed by foreign imports and international stagnation abroad reduced the demand for French exports. The Socialist government could not maintain its expansionary policies long in face of these harsh realities: In June 1982, it shifted to a deflationary course that produced a decline in living standards for French citizens — hardly the best strategy for a leftist government's popularity.

In the long term, Socialist economic policies may have been destined to fail because its redistributive measures rested on an assumption that may no longer be valid: that there is a strong link between increased demand, new investment, technological change, new employment, and economic growth. In the current period, however, it appears that the link between investment and employment has been severed: Thanks to the microelectronic revolution, new investment — even when it is not directed abroad, as is quite likely — now tends to displace both labor and capital, thus producing a decline in total employment. Not only does the new productive technology displace workers in the traditional goods-producing industries, but it also displaces service workers, who process information, and workers who produce capital goods (e.g., robots produce new robots in the machine tool industry). The result is that additional investment creates, not new jobs, but unemployment. And as workers are laid off, total demand declines, which reduces the incentive to increase production.

The government also failed to create the organizational basis for social democracy by strengthening and unifying the trade union movement. The Auroux reforms produced some benefits for workers, but these, at least in the short run, were outweighed by rising unemployment. Moreover, employers continued their successful assault on trade unions, which dated from the 1970s. The Auroux reforms did not equip unions to respond effectively and the government, anxious to build business confidence, did little to defend the unions. Further, union rivalry increased during the Socialist period in office, especially after the Communist departure from the government in 1984.

The government was least successful in achieving its democratic-socialist project. Although the nationalized industries began to perform effectively by the mid-1980s, they could hardly be distinguished from their privately owned counterparts. Socialist industrial policy was more activist than that of President Giscard d'Estaing and Prime Minister Barre in the late 1970s, but it closely resembled the model developed in the 1950s and 1960s. In both cases, streamlining production was given priority over democratizing production.

The government's actions with respect to social movements also reflected the Socialists' reluctance to redistribute power beyond narrow limits. Socialist reforms redistributed power to local government officials, union leaders, and managers, but there was no attempt to sponsor a more drastic shift in power. The Socialists had built support in the 1970s by adopting the call for *autogestion,* "participatory democracy," which was born in the May, 1968, uprising. As they moved closer to power, however, the call was dropped. Thus, workers and most other citizens received neither additional economic benefits from Socialist rule nor increased power. It is no wonder that they turned against the Socialists.

When the three projects that the Socialists pursued in their first years provoked political resistance and economic dislocation, the government shifted direction and soon openly renounced socialist goals. President Mitterrand declared that socialism was no longer his "bible." Socialist Party First Secretary Lionel Jospin urged Socialists to relinquish the "lyrical illusions" and "intellectual arrogance" of the past, and advised them to shift from a "socialism of opposition," which sought sweeping egalitarian and radical change, to a mature and responsible "socialism of governance," which accepted the virtues of capitalism. Socialist Party officials began to praise entrepreneurial ability, market competition, and profit.

Socialist leaders asserted that the shift was dictated by fundamental changes within French society, including the disintegration of the labor movement, the inability of the state to promote economic growth, and the decline of traditional class cleavages in favor of new social identities and ideological conflicts (highlighted by the rise of the National Front). However, this argument partially confuses cause and effect, for it overlooks the Socialist government's contribution to the new trends. Although the Socialist Party and government were admittedly weakened by the new trends, their own policies and ideological pronouncements accelerated the tendency by suggesting that Left alternatives did not exist. A French political analyst speculated that Socialist policy "provoked a crisis of conscience, in which it became widely believed that it was impossible to radically change society and, therefore, even among Left voters there was a growth in neo-liberal values, including the importance of the firm, the necessity for profit, competition, and the need for risk-taking."[2]

The Conservative Backlash

The Right quickly grasped at the opportunity the Socialists' failure presented. Relying on the neoliberal approach of Margaret Thatcher and Ronald Reagan — attempting to free capital from the constraints of organized labor and state regulation — center-Right parties proposed a drastic reversal of state policies. The RPR-UDF electoral platform for the 1986 election advocated returning the banks and industries that were nationalized in 1982–83 to private control, deregulating the economy, and cutting taxes. However, in face of broad popular support for the welfare state, the center-Right stopped short of proposing substantial reductions in welfare-state programs.

The election of a conservative government introduced a period of cohabitation with the Socialist president. Although President Mitterrand seemed inclined not to contest the conservative government's right to legislate most of its proposals, some conflicts were inevitable during the period of cohabitation. What was not apparent was the manner in which French political institutions could manage the unprecedented situation that developed after 1986 nor the likely impact on the framework of the Fifth Republic.

As the 1980s draw to an end, the issue of the viability of the Fifth Republic is again on the political agenda. Although the balance among political institutions shifted away from the presidency in 1986, it is probable that the Fifth Republic will endure.

The present period of transition in France is far from over, for France remains a vibrant social laboratory. However, this is not to say that *plus ça change, plus c'est la même chose,* "The more things change, the more they remain the same," for this chapter has described immense changes in postwar France. But it does mean that as so often occurs in French history, the past will prove to be but an imperfect guide to the future.

NOTES

1. This chapter draws extensively on Mark Kesselman, "Socialism without the Workers: The Case of France," *Kapitalistate,* no. 10/11 (1983), pp. 11–41; Mark Kesselman, "The Demise of French Socialism: An Early Post-Mortem," *New Politics,* Vol. 1, no. 1 (Summer 1986); and Mark Kesselman, *The Fading Rose: Dilemmas of French Socialism* (New York: Oxford University Press), pp. 137–151. Forthcoming.
2. Alain Duhamel, "Consensus et Dissensus Français," *Le Débat,* no. 30 (May 1984), p. 24.

Bibliography

Historical Works

Hoffmann, Stanley. *Decline or Renewal? France Since the 1930s.* New York: Viking, 1974.

——— , ed. *In Search of France.* New York: Harper Torchbook, 1963.

Paxton, Robert O. *Vichy France: Old Guard and New Order, 1940–1944.* New York: W.W. Norton, 1972.

Tilly, Charles. *The Contentious French: Four Centuries of Popular Struggle.* Cambridge: Harvard University Press, 1986.

Tocqueville, Alexis de. *The Old Regime and the French Revolution.* New York: Doubleday Anchor, 1955.

Williams, Philip. *Crisis and Compomise: Politics in the Fourth Republic.* Hamden, CT: Archon Books, 1964.

Wright, Gordon. *France in Modern Times: 1760 to the Present.* Chicago: Rand McNally & Company, 1964.

Political Economy

Cohen, Stephen S. *Modern French Planning: The French Model.* rev. ed. Berkeley: University of California Press, 1977.

——— and Peter A. Gourevitch, eds. *France in the Troubled World Economy.* London: Butterworth Publishers, 1982.

Hall, Peter. *Governing the Economy: The Politics of State Intervention in Britain and France.* New York: Oxford University Press, 1986.

Kuisel, Richard F. *Capitalism and the State in Modern France.* Cambridge: Cambridge University Press, 1981.

Zysman, John. *Political Strategies for Industrial Order: State, Market, and Industry in France.* Berkeley: University of California Press, 1977.

The State and Political Institutions

Andrews, William G. *Presidential Government in Gaullist France: A Study of Executive-Legislative Relations, 1958–1974.* Albany: State University of New York Press, 1982.

——— and Stanley Hoffmann, eds. *The Fifth Republic at Twenty.* Albany: State University of New York Press, 1981.

Birnbaum, Pierre. *The Heights of Power: An Essay on the Power Elite in France.* Chicago: University of Chicago Press, 1982.

Suleiman, Ezra. *Politics, Power and Bureaucracy in France: The Administrative Elite.* Princeton: Princeton University Press, 1974.

———. *Elites in French Society: The Politics of Survival.* Princeton: Princeton University Press, 1978.

Wright, Vincent, ed. *Continuity and Change in France.* London: George Allen & Unwin, 1984.

Political Parties and Social Forces

Gallie, Duncan. *Social Inequality and Class Radicalism in France and Britain.* Cambridge: Cambridge University Press, 1983.

Keeler, John. *The Politics of Neo-Corporatism in France: Farmers, the State and Agricultural Policymaking in the Fifth Republic.* New York: Oxford University Press, 1986.

Kesselman, Mark and Guy Groux, eds., *The French Workers' Movement: Economic Crisis and Political Change.* London: George Allen & Unwin, 1984.

Ross, George. *Workers and Communists in France: From Popular Front to Eurocommunism.* Berkeley: University of California Press, 1982.

Wilson, Frank L. *Political Parties in France.* New York: Praeger, 1982.

French Politics in Transition

Ambler, John S. ed. *The French Socialist Experiment.* Philadelphia: Institute for the Study of Human Issues, 1985.

Cerny, Philip G. and Martin A. Schain, eds. *Socialism, the State and Public Policy in France.* New York: Methuen, 1985.

Hoffmann, Stanley and George Ross, eds. *Continuity and Change in Mitterrand's France.* New York: Oxford University Press, 1987. Forthcoming.

PART

IV

Federal Republic of Germany

Christopher S. Allen

11

The Emergence of the Modern West German State

The emergence of the modern West German state has been a far more complex and volatile process than that of other major Western European countries. Germany did not achieve political unification until 1871, when numerous German-speaking principalities were brought together under the principality of Prussia and its leader, Otto von Bismarck. However, the newly unified Germany proved fragile. Although Bismarck and those who succeeded him were able to rapidly attain world power at the expense of the other industrialized countries, the regime came apart after the German defeat in World War I. The parliamentary democracy of the Weimar Republic, which came to power in 1919, was also short-lived. By 1933, weakened by economic and political instability, the Weimar regime had also fallen apart, and the Nazis, led by Adolf Hitler, seized power. The German state itself was eventually broken apart and occupied by the Allies (Britain, France, the United States, and the Soviet Union) in the aftermath of World War II. By the late 1940s and early 1950s, the Allies sought to transfer governmental power back to the Germans, and in the process, two Germanies emerged: the capitalist Federal Republic of Germany (FRG), known as West Germany, and the communist German Democratic Republic (GDR), East Germany. In less than a century, Germany had been ruled by a variety of governments: feudal, imperialist, fascist, communist, and parliamentary-democratic. To understand the complexities of today's West German state, we must draw on its historical, economic, and political foundations.

The Principles of West German State Formation

Why did the emergence of the modern West German state differ so widely from its neighbors? In this chapter, we will examine the complex tensions that made West German political development both more difficult and more precarious than that of other major Western states.

One source of tension was the disparity between the concepts of nation and state. There was no unified German state until 1871, yet within the German-speaking nation there existed vibrant political and philosophical traditions (dating from the early nineteenth-century writings of Fichte and Hegel) that favored a strong, centralized public authority.[1] Each of the German-speaking principalities acted as its own subnational, sovereign state before 1871. However, there was often strident competition among the larger principalities for primacy. This deep-rooted tension among the larger principalities (between Prussia and Bavaria, for example) originated in their feudal traditions. Even after unification in 1871, nation/state tensions remained divisive, as evidenced by the pressure that nationalist movements placed on German governments prior to World War I and during the Weimar Republic. Hitler finally succeeded in unifying the German nation and state through the Third Reich from 1933 to 1945. (The First Reich was the Holy Roman Empire, and the Second was the unified Germany of Bismarck after 1871.)

A second source of tension in the formation of the West German state was the relationship between capitalism and democracy. For example, the United States developed democratic political forms in the late eighteenth century (at least for white, male property holders), well before the process of industrialization began. When industrial capitalism emerged in the nineteenth century, it was able to develop in ways that did not threaten entrenched democratic political forms based on individual rights. In Germany, on the other hand, industrial capitalism emerged much later in the nineteenth century, before full parliamentary democracy had been achieved. The timing of the introduction of capitalism and democracy in Germany is crucial for two reasons: First, in order to compete with industrial nations such as Britain, the United States, and France, the German state had to be directly involved in the industrialization process. (In effect, the state could aid industrialists without having to be held democratically accountable for its actions.) Second, the delay in introducing parliamentary democracy (until the Weimar Republic in 1919) enabled the forces pressing for democracy in Germany during this period to fuse political and economic issues. The swelling ranks of German workers not only had few democratic economic rights in the workplace but also had few democratic political rights as citizens.

By the early twentieth century, this combination of economic and political issues eventually produced the strongest socialist political party and labor movement in Europe. Socialist forces remained active throughout World War I and the Weimar Republic, until snuffed out by the rise of the Third Reich.

Post-1945 Germany may seem far more stable than in the preceding eras, yet the tensions between nation and state, and between capitalism and democracy, remain. The nation/state tension has been exacerbated by the division of Germany between East and West, and within West Germany, by the differences among *Laender,* "states." (*Laender,* "states," is the plural of *Land,* "state.") A muted tension between capitalism and democracy also remains. Despite the achievement of almost forty years of parliamentary democracy in West Germany, the lack of Anglo-Saxon style liberal-democratic foundations could still undermine individual rights within the economy, according to political sociologist Ralf Dahrendorf. The private sector remains highly centralized and is dominated by large firms. Further, the public sector is still referred to by many West Germans as *Vater Staat,* "father state." That is, West Germans expect a generous provision of welfare state benefits, but they also realize that citizens have duties and responsibilities to support the basic democratic social order.

Nationalism

In the early nineteenth century, German-speaking central Europe was governed by a number of fragmented German principalities, yet their common language and culture would eventually act as a powerful spur to the growth of German nationalism. Other countries, such as Britain and France, had already established centralized states and had become major world powers. Even the Netherlands, in spite of its size and geographical location, had enjoyed centralized political power for centuries and had grown to be an important nation in world trade from the sixteenth to the early nineteenth centuries. Prussian political elites noted this contrast between Germany and other states and hoped to achieve similar world influence with a unified Germany.

Napoleon's armies occupied many German-speaking lands (most notably the Rhineland in the West) during the first two decades of the nineteenth century. Although Prussia had consolidated many of the smaller principalities in northern and eastern portions of Germany during the eighteenth century, the growing French influence threatened its position. The defeat of Napoleon's forces by the British army at the Battle

Federal Republic of Germany
Boundaries of States
NORTH SEA
DENMARK
BALTIC SEA
Kiel
SCHLESWIG-HOLSTEIN
Lübeck
HAMBURG
Hamburg
BREMEN
Bremen
Elbe
LOWER SAXONY
BERLIN (West)
NETHERLANDS
Hannover
Weser
EAST GERMANY
NORTH-RHINE WESTPHALIA
Essen
Dortmund
Ruhr
Düsseldorf
Cologne
Rhine
Bonn
BELG.
HESSE
RHINELAND-PALATINATE
Frankfurt
Mainz
Wiesbaden
LUX.
CZECHOSLOVAKIA
SAAR
Saarbrücken
Neckar
Nuremberg
BAVARIA
Stuttgart
BADEN-WURTTEMBERG
Danube
FRANCE
Munich
AUSTRIA
SWITZERLAND
0
100 Miles
0
100 Kilometers

of Waterloo in 1815, gave the Prussians an opportunity to attain important new territorial influence. As Hans Rosenberg suggests, Prussian leaders after 1815 borrowed from Napoleon's tactics, developing an elaborate system of bureaucratic absolutism (a rigid and powerful government structure) that was heavily supported by nationalist impulses.[2] Prior to 1848, Kaiser Friedrich Wilhelm IV of Prussia skillfully employed the state ministries to exert control and provide financial support, thereby acting as a broker between the Prussian monarchy and the *Junker,* "landed elite." The Prussian state attained considerable power, as became increasingly apparent to other Germans.

After consolidating its power during the first half of the nineteenth century, Prussia was able to use German nationalism as a wedge to undermine attempts by the middle class to establish democracy during the continent-wide upheavals of 1848. The weakness of the German middle class (and the absence of a working class prior to full-scale industrialization) meant that social change in Germany would be more difficult to attain than elsewhere in Europe. Prussian leaders stemmed the spread of Western socialist and democratic movements by appealing to a sense of German separateness. By the 1860s, Bismarck was able to point to military victories over Denmark (1864), Austria (1866), and France (1870–71) as proof that government from the conservative, nationalistic Prussian "revolution from above," as Barrington Moore has called it, was the appropriate path for Germany to take in order to become a major world power.[3] Specifically, Moore meant that rapid modernization took place without the leaders losing power.

After the unification of Germany in 1871, the concept of nationalism was most effective in solidifying relationships among the formerly autonomous principalities. For example, Bavaria, which had been associated with the Austro-Hungarian Empire, tried to resist the domination of the Second Reich, as the new regime was called after 1871. However, Bismarck's skillful invocation of nationalism enabled him to overcome the resentment of the Bavarians and Rhinelanders (among others) towards the Prussian-dominated regime. In time, nationalism proved difficult to contain: The spirit unleashed by a newly unified and rapidly industrializing Germany gave rise to a pan-Germanic feeling of nationalism among German-speaking peoples in Eastern Europe. Often taking the form of militant anti-Semitism, the pan-Germanic movement espoused themes that were later repeated by the Nazis — due to the perception by some Germans that Jews had enjoyed a disproportionate share of wealth and influence in Central Europe — in justifying their claims of racial and cultural superiority.

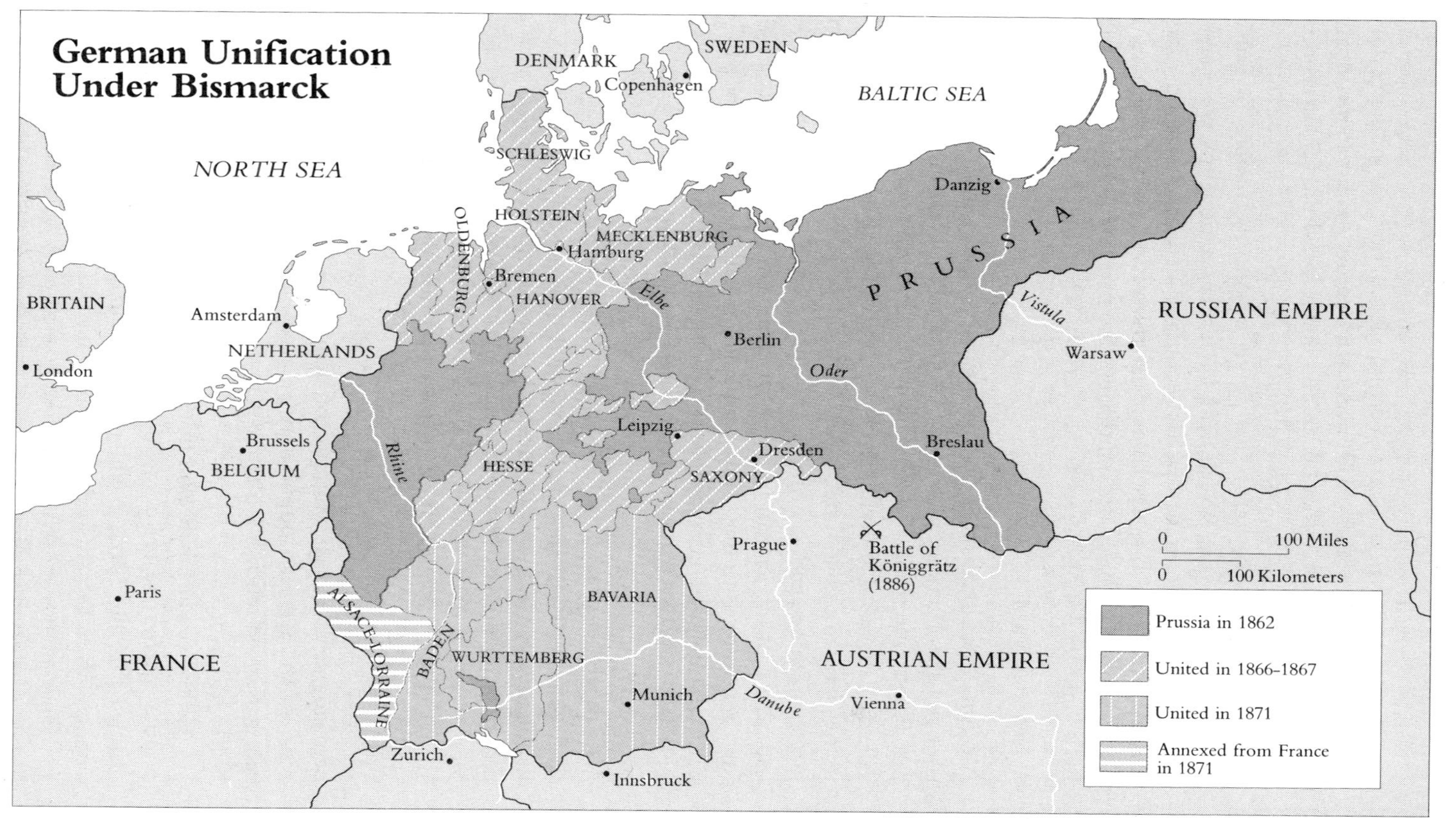
German Unification
Under Bismarck
DENMARK
Copenhagen
SWEDEN
BALTIC SEA
NORTH SEA
SCHLESWIG
HOLSTEIN
MECKLENBURG
Hamburg
OLDENBURG
Bremen
HANOVER
Elbe
Danzig
PRUSSIA
Vistula
RUSSIAN EMPIRE
Warsaw
Berlin
Oder
BRITAIN
London
Amsterdam
NETHERLANDS
Brussels
BELGIUM
Rhine
HESSE
Leipzig
Dresden
SAXONY
Breslau
Prague
Battle of
Königgrätz
(1886)
0 100 Miles
0 100 Kilometers
Paris
FRANCE
ALSACE-LORRAINE
BADEN
WURTTEMBERG
BAVARIA
Munich
Danube
Vienna
AUSTRIAN EMPIRE
Zurich
Innsbruck
Prussia in 1862
United in 1866–1867
United in 1871
Annexed from France
in 1871

With the growth of German economic and political influence during the late nineteenth and early twentieth century, German nationalism developed into a force that eventually undermined the fragile economic strength created by Bismarck and German bankers and industrialists, and disturbed the delicate balance of power among the nations of Europe. Yet, despite failure in World War I, German nationalists were able to convince many Germans that the country's defeat was caused, not by imperialist actions to secure colonies, markets, and natural resources, but by "cowardly" democratic politicians who had "stabbed the army in the back" and thereby sabotaged the German war effort.

Nazism. Nationalism was the primary sentiment behind Hitler's strength (the *N* in *Nazi* stood for *National*). Yet Nazism was more than just an extreme form of nationalism. Hitler used nationalist impulses to call for a society that went far beyond excessive patriotism: He exulted in the German imperial military tradition that had smashed rival armies in the mid-nineteenth century, and he glorified the warrior tradition that had been part of German folklore for centuries.[4] Further, in his longing for a return to a mythically glorious and racially pure German past, he used as scapegoats geographically concentrated ethnic minorities, such as Poles, Danes, Alsatians, and Jews. Even more heinous was the wave of systematic extermination, clearly the most notorious aspect of the Nazi movement, of six million Jews in the concentration camps. In fact, the Germans' strident anti-Semitism gave increased impetus to its growth in other European countries during the late nineteenth and early twentieth centuries. Hitler also used nationalism as a weapon against the Social Democratic and Communist parties during the 1920s and early 1930s. By attacking the internationalism of both branches of the left, he was able to undercut the movements' German roots, which traced back to Marx and Engels. Ultimately, the Nazis were able, via propaganda, demagoguery, and the absence of democratic opposition, to mobilize most of the German population by preaching hatred of "non-Aryan" races; thus, he unleashed the most aggressively militaristic behavior the world had ever seen.[5]

Hitler became Chancellor in 1933, after infighting among the various political parties created a vacuum into which the Nazis stepped. Hitler claimed that the Nazis could return Germany to its glorious past by saving it from the "disorderly democracy" of Weimar.

Once in power, Hitler refused to abide by the provisions of the Treaty of Versailles, which was signed at the end of World War I. After 1933, Germany began to produce armaments in large quantities, remilitarized the Rhineland, and sent aid to the Fascist army in Spain as it fought to overthrow the democratically elected Spanish republic from 1936 to 1939. The Nazis also rejected the territorial divisions of World War I. Hitler claimed that a growing Germany needed increased *Lebensraum,* "space to live," in Eastern Europe. He ordered the occupation of the German-speaking Sudetenland section of Czechoslovakia and the *Anschluss,* "union," with Austria in 1938. Hitler's attack on Poland on September 1, 1939, finally precipitated World War II.

The Nazi forces overran Poland in a matter of weeks. The Soviet Union — ill-prepared to withstand a German attack — had signed a controversial nonaggression pact with Germany during the summer of 1939. The pact had the main effect of guaranteeing to the Germans that the Soviet Union would not help the Poles fight the Nazis. After a winter of relative quiet, the Germans then turned northward and attacked Norway and Denmark, and then westward to invade the Netherlands, Belgium, and France, driving the British forces, which had entered the war after the invasion of Poland, back across the English Channel. Using the infamous *Blitzkrieg,* "lightning war," tactics perfected in Spain and Poland, the Nazis dominated a major portion of Europe by the summer of 1940. Hitler then turned his attention to the Balkan countries to the southeast, coming to fascist Italy's aid. Conquests there were just as quick and comparatively easy. The infamous German army ran roughshod over Europe, with no counter force apparently strong enough to stop it.

Hitler's grandiose visions of German world domination were dramatically heightened by these conquests. By the summer of 1941, he began to turn his attention to the only other continental power that stood in the way of his goal of total European domination: the Soviet Union. Hitler assumed that the defeat of the Soviet Union would take place as easily as his other conquests. Therefore, Hitler abrogated the Nazi-Soviet nonaggression pact on June 22, 1941, by embarking on *Operation Barbarossa,* "Operation Redbeard," the direct attack on the Soviet Union. This attack was not only the end of German military successes but also the beginning of the defeat of the Third Reich; the war in Europe finally ended in May, 1945.

The Nazis underestimated the Soviet Union in several areas. First, after gaining large amounts of Soviet territories in the summer, Hitler's attack bogged down in the fall of 1941, which meant that the early Russian winter of 1941–42 caught the German armies unprepared. In fact, Hitler was so sure that victory would be complete by the fall that he did not even equip his troops with winter uniforms. Second, the sheer size of the Soviet Union meant that German supply lines were stretched dangerously thin; armaments and supplies were slow in coming. Third, Russia had been attacked by forces from the west at different times over the course of several centuries, and Hitler badly misunderstood the capacity of the Soviet Union to withstand massive losses, to be pushed back almost to the walls of the Kremlin in Moscow (hundreds of miles inside the Soviet Union), yet still fight on. The Soviet Union suffered over 20 million war dead and still was able to stem the Nazi attack and drive the Germans back some 1,500 miles to Berlin by 1945.

Further constraining Germany during the course of the war was the entry of the United States in December, 1941. After the Japanese attacked the U.S. fleet at Pearl Harbor in Hawaii on December 7, 1941, Hitler immediately declared war on the United States. This action brought the United States into the European war as a member of the Allied forces (i.e., on the side of the British and the various European governments-in-exile that had moved to London after the Nazis had taken control of these continental European countries). The U.S. entry meant the scenario that the German generals feared most had come to pass: a two-front war. Not only was Germany bogged down in the Soviet Union after 1941–42, but the increasing resistance activity in German-occupied Western Europe also helped prepare the way for the massive Allied invasion of the continent on D-Day, June 6, 1944. By the winter of 1944–45, German forces had been driven back within their own borders and the war was clearly approaching its end. Yet even as defeat loomed for Germany in 1945, Hitler preferred to see Germany totally destroyed rather than have its national honor "besmirched" by total surrender.

The Nazi defeat in World War II effectively put an end to the grandiose claims of German superiority. In fact, with the post-war division between East and West Germany, the term *German nation* is again imprecise. Although the prospect for reunification still seems dim forty years after the war, residual German nationalism is still visible in the informal and cultural contacts between the two Germanies in the 1970s and 1980s. However, this form of German nationalism is far less threatening for its neighbors.

Economic and Class Relations

Although nationalism was a crucial factor in the formation of the German state, the nature of the country's rapid industrialization during the mid and late nineteenth century was equally (if not more) important. Germany was at a disadvantage, as compared with Britain and France, due to its fragmented political structure, and it was much slower to develop industrial capitalism. In fact, these two conditions reinforced each other. During the early nineteenth century, the various German principalities had their own currencies and customs practices, which adversely affected trade among them. In 1834, Prussia succeeded in forming a *Zollverein,* "customs union," which allowed much freer trade. The Prussian-dominated customs union was an economic forerunner of the Prussian-dominated political system that arose almost forty years later.

Once some of these restrictive barriers had been overcome, Germany was able to industrialize. But what kind of industrialization would take place? Germany had no substantial middle class, so it could not rely on individual entrepreneurs and a gradually evolving capitalism as the primary spur to economic growth. Britain had already become the leading world power with the development of its textile industry. Should Germany follow this path or try to develop other industries? Where would investment capital come from if there was no growing middle class?

It was clear that economic growth would not take place spontaneously. Germany had to rely much more on planning than on the free market to generate economic growth, and it had to move quickly if it was to compete with countries that already had a head start. Planning involved the selection of and emphasis on those key sectors of the economy (predominantly heavy industry) that could develop the few natural resources that Germany possessed. Once the customs union opened up the possibilities for trade in the 1830s and 1840s, Prussia moved quickly to help build a railway network that could link the various German principalities. The considerable iron ore deposits in the Ruhr valley and the development of a steel and a machine tool industry were crucial to this effort.

At this time, Prussian *Junker* (the estate-owning aristocracy) needed to find markets for their harvests, and the railway network proved indispensable for this purpose. Bismarck successfully brokered the interests of the *Junker* and the steel industry in what Alexander Gershenkron called the "marriage of iron and rye."[6] Germany was also able to develop two other industries quickly and effectively: Dyestuffs were derivatives of mineral deposits, which in combination became the building blocks of the large German chemical industry; and electric power generation spurred heavy industry and the development of an electrified rail and signal system.

If individual entrepreneurs were not to be the dominant actors in economic development, who were? As powerful as the Prussian state had become, it could not develop the economy by itself. Geoff Eley has pointed out that in addition to the state, the major economic forces in Germany during the nineteenth century were large banks, cartels and industry associations, and large firms.[7] In contrast, small firms dominated the capitalist system in the United States, the banks did not directly participate in industrial policy, and antitrust laws prevented cartels and strong industry associations. In Germany, explicit coordination among the state, the banks, and large firms led its transformation from a semi-feudal society to a leading industrial power by the beginning of the twentieth century.

Rapid industrialization took place at tremendous cost. Large-scale industrial capitalism required factory workers, yet in the 1850s, German society was largely made up of peasants. German industry's solution was to recruit many of these peasants and subject them to the discipline of the factory system. From mid-century to the 1890s, this huge upheaval created a working class from the remnants of the peasantry. As political sociologist Charles Sabel has indicated, these "peasant workers" quickly became radicalized.[8] Many turned to a socialist movement that had begun to grow in Germany earlier in the century under the influence of Karl Marx and Friedrich Engels, among others. This movement drew on both the adverse working conditions of industrial workers and the lack of political rights and freedoms for the working class. Trade unions were soon formed, as well as a political party: the Social Democratic Party of Germany (SPD). The SPD was founded in 1875 as The Socialist Workers Party. The name was changed to the Social Democratic Party in 1891.

Prominent leaders such as Bismarck soon became alarmed at the swift growth of these radical forces. If allowed to continue, they believed, they would undermine the nascent strength of the rapidly expanding German economy. Late in the nineteenth century, Bismarck took two decisive steps to blunt the thrust of the Left. First, in 1878, he declared the SPD partially illegal, although its candidates were still allowed to stand for the Reichstag, the Second Reich's parliament. (The party grew stronger as a quasi-underground movement until it was legalized again in 1890, but much of its radical thrust dissipated in the interim.) Second, in the early 1880s, he introduced elaborate social-welfare measures to provide a degree of relief for the most adverse effects of industrial growth. From health insurance to social security, Bismarck's government had established the first modern welfare state.[9] He did so, not against the wishes of the industrialists, but on their behalf and with their support, because most realized that economic growth required a cooperative work force.

The pattern of a strong state brokering the relationship between large, expanding industries and a growing, potentially militant working class became deeply rooted in Germany. In the turbulent first half of the twentieth century, Germany's economic and class relations either were held in place by strong state action or came apart in sharp conflicts. Periods of rapid economic growth (1900–14 and the mid-1920s) can be contrasted with times of dire economic straits (World War I, the Great Depression, and World War II).

The pattern of an economic flux has left a deep and lasting legacy in the institutions and attitudes of modern West German business, labor, and government, all of which have established elaborate mechanisms to safeguard their positions. Economist Rudolf Hilferding called this defense by business "organized capitalism."[10] German banks and businesses continued in the twentieth century the relationships that had developed during the nineteenth century, while German labor sought to extend the principles of democracy to the workplace. After World War I, a segment of German labor wanted to reestablish the militant spirit that had been blunted both by prewar economic growth and by Bismarck's earlier two-pronged strategy. The labor movement proposed a system of *Arbeiterraete,* "workers' councils," which would give members greater control of their working lives by increasing democratic rights in the workplace. By 1920, the Weimar government became increasingly conservative and changed the system: The workers' councils became *Betriebsraete,* "works councils," which were essentially company-sponsored sounding boards that gave no real power to workers. Nonetheless, this institution gave German workers a significant forum that few other labor movements in other countries were able to attain. The Weimar regime attempted to secure its position by developing what political sociologist Theda Skocpol calls "state capacity" to mediate the conflicts between powerful institutions and political parties. The upheaval of the first half of the twentieth century has heightened the sensitivity of contemporary public-sector officials (especially in the regional governments) to the need to broker powerful, conflicting interests.

Germany in the International Context

Germany lagged behind other countries in terms of international influence due to its late unification, which, in turn, had two related consequences: Its slowness in the race to acquire possessions in Africa; and its exposed geographical postition in central Europe. Thus Germany's position in the international system in the late nineteenth and early twentieth centuries was not commensurate with its growing economic and political power.

As the economy grew during the latter part of the nineteenth century, German business and political leaders faced an immediate problem: How could rapid economic growth continue if they could not be certain of obtaining needed raw materials or having access to world markets in which to sell their finished goods? Although Germany possessed considerable iron and coal deposits, it had little else in the way of natural resources. Moreover, the emphasis on the development of heavy industries, such as steel, railroads, chemicals, and industrial electronics, meant that the production of consumer goods was a lower priority. This pattern created an imbalance from which the industrialists reaped large profits while the majority of Germans did not directly benefit from the heavy-industry-led economic growth. The resultant lack of a strong domestic consumer goods economy meant that a substantial portion of what Germany produced had to be sold on world markets.

Germany had neither the colonial possessions of Britain or France nor the geographic advantages of the United States. With little influence in either North America or Asia, Germany participated in what historian Geoffrey Barraclough has called "the scramble for Africa."[11] However, Germany was a latecomer in this region and was able to obtain colonies only in Southwest Africa and Togoland, while the British, French, Italians, Spaniards, Portuguese and Belgians obtained colonies in regions of the continent with more exploitable resources.

From 1871 until World War I, German foreign policy was primarily concerned with extending its colonial influence in Africa, although it was frustrated by the presence of other world powers. German leaders turned to the rapid development of the shipbuilding industry, which would increase German participation in international commercial shipping and bolster the German navy.

Germany's position in the center of Europe was also crucial to its standing in the international community. Germany's boundaries were indistinct and uncertain compared to the generally more stable territorial boundaries of Britain and France. Britain was an island, and France was surrounded by rivers and mountains, but Germany occupied the central European plains with few natural lines of demarcation. In 1914, it was surrounded by no fewer than nine other states.

The combination of these two factors — the lack of profitable colonies and an exposed geopolitical position — with increasingly aggressive nationalism and an undemocratic political system proved to be a blueprint for disaster. World War I, originally envisioned by German leaders as a brief war to solidify the country's geopolitical position and maintain socioeconomic power for dominant elites, did neither. It turned out to be a protracted war that cost Germany both its colonial possessions and the imperial social order (the Kaiser abdicated in 1918). Moreover, the outcome of the war further intensified the nationalist impulses of many conservative and reactionary Germans. Many in the military believed that "cowardly" democratic politicians had betrayed Germany at the signing of the Treaty of Versailles on November 11, 1918. The reparations payments assessed against Germany by the Allies, along with the demilitarization of the Rhineland, were seen by many Germans as a profound slight to Germany's international position. These factors combined to undermine the Weimar Republic, and the Nazis later used such sentiments to justify their claims of superiority over other nations.

Ideology and Political Culture

Since the early nineteenth century, Germany has had a multifaceted political culture, containing many ideologies, that has added substantially to the complexity of German politics. Yet these ideologies have shared a common thread: Virtually all of them have drawn on collectivist or cooperative sentiments. Unlike the United States, in which individualism has had a dominant influence, German individualism has proved a much less significant component in the country's political culture. Even in the post–World War II era, when U.S.-style individualism has attained major importance, collectivist forms of social organization still dominate both the public and the private sectors.

Collectivist and cooperative communitarian forms have varied widely over the past two hundred years in Germany. In the early nineteenth century, Germany was characterized by the feudal/agrarian culture that had long dominated central Europe. It was essentially a social system in which rights and duties were firmly established according to hierarchical principles and the mass of peasants were subject to the direction of their lords. This system not only fostered a culture of obedience to authority but also allowed the disenfranchised to see quite clearly the subservient social position common to them all.

With its increasingly dominant position among the German states in the nineteenth century, Prussia also influenced German political culture with its state-centered emphasis that came to characterize the united Germany. The *Kulturkampf,* "cultural struggle," was a prime example of Prussian — and Protestant — dominance. Led by Bismarck, it was essentially a movement against the Catholic Church, aimed at removing educational and cultural institutions from the church and confering them on the state. This action politicized the church and many Catholic Germans; the Catholic trade union movement and the Catholic Center Party continued to play significant social roles until Hitler came to power in 1933. In fact, the modern Christian Democratic political parties — the Christian Democratic Union (CDU) and its Bavarian counterpart, the

Christian Social Union (CSU) — can be understood only in the context of this late nineteenth and early twentieth century repression that served to politicize Catholicism.

German industry also made a significant contribution to political culture during this period. Though authoritarian and profoundly undemocratic, German business proved that collectivist forms of private organization (i.e., cartels and combinations) were effective means to rapidly industrialize the previously feudal society. Nineteenth-century industry's contribution to the political culture was the spirit of organized capitalism which has had a lasting effect on German society.

The combination of the social dislocation produced by rapid industrialization and the relevance of Marxist ideology to oppressed peasant-workers produced still another significant type of political culture, one both collectivist and revolutionary. Although the radical elements of the trade unions and the SPD were effectively neutralized by Bismarck in the 1880s and by the split of the Left into Social Democratic and communist wings in the 1920s, they remain significant in contemporary West Germany through the left wing of the SPD, the alternative Greens Party, and the dwindling *K-Gruppen,* "communist groups."

Another form of German political culture arose from the frustration of the displaced lower-middle class and the *Lumpenproletariat* (rootless and discouraged workers), social groups that were unable to find a secure place in society during the economic and social transformation of the late nineteenth century. Their leaders argued for the elimination of those groups that seemed most "un-German" and a return to an idealized past in which a pure German social order could be restored: Hitler appealed to this group most successfully.

These various groups and movements were torn by a variety of cleavages — Catholicism/Protestantism, capitalism/socialism, modernism/antimodernism, and German/non-German — and clashed many times during the late nineteenth and early twentieth centuries. They all turned to the power of the state to achieve their goals, thus increasing the importance of the centralized state. These tensions (at least prior to 1945) were kept in check only by skillful leaders, such as Bismarck, and/or by powerful institutions, such as the churches, political parties, trade unions, and employer groups. When these volatile forces were not controlled, great social upheaval was the result.

The Discontinuity of Constitutional Forms

With its ascendancy in the nineteenth century, Prussia was able to unite the German principalities into a constitutional system that it controlled.

Prussian dominance was even easier to consolidate with the defeat of liberal attempts to establish democracy in 1848. After unification was completed in 1871, Germany experienced its most stable constitutional order until the contemporary era. Yet, this stability was founded on an authoritarian and undemocratic regime, which only thinly disguised the fundamental divisions in German society as it attempted to effect rapid industrialization in an essentially feudal society.

The striking feature of the Second Reich's constitutional system was its inequality, as it disproportionately rewarded the conservative *Junker* minority with predominance in the Reichstag. Even after the legalization of the Social Democratic Party in 1890, the party was not able to attain power commensurate with its voting strength until after World War I. In fact, in 1912, the two largest parties, the SPD and the Catholic Center Party, exercised virtually no power because the electoral system was tilted in favor of the Prussian elites.

World War I unleashed forces that undermined the constitutional system that had been so carefully crafted by Bismarck and his successors. The defeat of the vaunted German army and the abdication of Kaiser Wilhelm II left a constitutional breach, which was filled by a parliamentary democracy — the Weimar Republic — led by the SPD. The Catholic Center Party had obtained only 25 percent of the prewar vote, and other parties were either fragmented or, as in the case of the Prussian conservatives, discredited.

By late 1918 and early 1919, the SPD controlled the Reichstag, but it rested on shaky foundations. On the Left, opposition came from portions of the SPD that had split from the party after World War I, in response to the Russian Revolution. There was not only a strong Communist Party (with nearly 15 percent of the vote during much of the 1920s) but also an Independent Social Democratic Party (USPD) during the late teens. Consequently, the SPD did not have the full support it needed from its traditional constituency (i.e., the industrial working class) when it came to power. From the Right, the SPD had to solicit the support of reactionary and undemocratic army officers to "guarantee" German democracy (a task that was never fulfilled). In addition, many of these rightist factions argued that politicians had "stabbed the army in the back" by surrendering to the Allies before the war had come to German soil.

The Weimar government's problems were further compounded by the economic turmoil of the 1920s, the Great Depression in 1929, the postwar loss of territory to France and a newly reconstituted Poland, and the high reparations payments to the Allies. The hyperinflation of 1923, in which the German mark became almost worthless, heightened despair. During that year, wheelbarrows were sometimes needed to carry money to the bank, and many workers were paid twice a day so that they could buy food in the morning before prices went up in the afternoon.

The Weimar regime was unable to withstand such pressure. The SPD was in power only during 1919–20 and 1928–30: From 1920 until 1928, there were moderate coalition governments, which grew increasingly shaky; and after 1930, the government was led by increasingly conservative parties and coalitions. By the late 1920s, there was no stable majority coalition for any of the parliamentary-democratic parties; in fact, there were two large parties (the Communists and the Nazis) who were committed to the demise of parliamentary democracy. The inability of the SPD and the Communists to compromise — even on the tactical grounds of stopping the Nazis — cleared Hitler's path to power. By 1932, the Nazis had taken advantage of the bickering and hostility among the other parties and attained the largest share of votes in the Reichstag, although they were still short of a majority. Their most successful appeal to voters who were not fervent Nazi party members was the promise of order.

Nazism. Although the rise of Nazism signaled the end of parliamentary democracy under the Weimar regime, the Nazis initially invoked the emergency powers decree of the Weimar Constitution to justify their undemocratic actions. Although the Nazis obliterated democracy, they could claim that they had done so constitutionally. Playing on the divisions among the left-wing parties, and among the centrist and traditional right-wing parties, Hitler was able to argue that only the Nazis could provide stability. By the early 1930s, German business was concerned about issues of order and stability. Hitler gained increasing support from large firms, mainly because his rapid militarization of the economy, in defiance of the post–World War I Treaty of Versailles, proved a boon to giant chemical and steel concerns.

Once they came to power in January, 1933, however, the Nazis abandoned constitutional forms. In addition to banning trade unions and all non-Nazi political parties, they began to systematically persecute, imprison, and murder Jews. Domestically, the Third Reich was a hideously repressive system. Hitler appealed to the nationalistic instincts of the Aryan-German population, itself deprived by the effects of the Depression and disillusioned by the political squabbles of the other parties. Hitler was able to convince many (though not a majority) that his "final solution" (the expatriation and eventual killing of non-Aryans) would purify the German nation. To take such sweeping action required a bending of some Weimar constitutional procedures and a total abrogation of others. The longer he remained in power, the more Hitler abused constitutional forms. For example, he required that the *Schutzstaffeln* (SS), "elite guard," swear allegiance to him personally rather than to the country. He also required that Nazi judges disregard many of the laws that had been passed under the Weimar regime in favor of his decrees, particularly with respect to the concentration camps. Thus, by the end of World War II, in 1945, Germany's constitutional forms were in complete disarray.

The Implications for Contemporary West German Politics

This volatile legacy has produced a conventional wisdom that sees the present West German regime as precarious, with an uncertain future. These sentiments were particularly strong among such political scientists as Ralf Dahrendorf and Seymour Martin Lipset, and historian Gerhard Ritter, during the 1950s, 1960s, and 1970s. They stressed the *Sonderweg,* "German exceptionalism," and concluded that the Europeanization of West Germany (and, by implication, the stability of its democracy) was in doubt, as evidenced by such questions as "Is Bonn Weimar?"[12]

Forty years after the fall of the Third Reich, however, some of these concerns about the impending demise of West German democracy seem overstated. Germany's development may have been exceptional when compared to Britain or the United States, yet historians such as Geoff Eley have argued that Germany shared a number of similarities with many continental European states: large firms, an active state, and minimal individual rights. Nation/state and capitalism/democracy tensions remain in West Germany, but the legacy of instability has been tempered by four decades of democracy, which have provided the contemporary capitalist system with a political framework similar to those of other Western European countries. In the following chapters, we will discuss the residual tensions between Germany's undemocratic history and its postwar parliamentary system.

Notes

1. See: Johann Gottlieb Fichte, *Addresses to the German Nation* (Westport, CT: Greenwood Press, 1979); and Georg Friedrich Wilhelm Hegel, *Political Writings* (New York: Garfield Publishers, 1984).

2. See: Hans Rosenberg, *Bureaucracy, Aristocracy, and Autocracy: The Prussian Experience, 1660–1815* (Boston: Beacon Press, 1966).
3. See: Barrington Moore, *Social Origins of Dictatorship and Democracy* (Boston: Beacon Press, 1966).
4. See: Geoffrey Barraclough, *The Origins of Modern Germany* (London: Basil Blackwell, 1946).
5. For an exhaustive, yet readable, account of the Nazi period, see: William Shirer, *The Rise and Fall of the Third Reich* (New York: Simon and Schuster, 1960).
6. See: Alexander Gerschenkron, *Bread and Democracy in Germany* (New York: H. Fertig, 1966).
7. Geoff Eley, *Reshaping the German Right: Radical Nationalism and Political Change after Bismarck* (New Haven: Yale University Press, 1980).
8. See: Charles Sabel, *Work and Politics* (Cambridge: Cambridge University Press, 1982).
9. Gordon Craig, *Germany: 1886–1945* (Oxford: Oxford University Press, 1978).
10. See: Rudolf Hilferding, *Finance Capital: A Study of the Latest Phase of Capitalist Development* (London: Routledge and Kegan Paul, 1981).
11. Geoffrey Barraclough, *An Introduction to Contemporary History* (New York: Penguin, 1967).
12. Gerhard Ritter, *The German Problem* (Columbus: Ohio State University Press, 1965). German "exceptionalism" was the country's failure to follow the parliamentary, democratic path of other western societies. This legacy left many observers uncertain whether postwar West Germany would become more like other western countries. Bonn is the capitol of the Federal Republic.

The Rise and Decline of the Postwar Settlement

The Rise of the Postwar Settlement

With the defeat of the Nazi regime in 1945 and the subsequent occupation and division of Germany by the four victorious Allied powers (the United States, Britain, France, and the Soviet Union), the form of political institutions in a reconstructed Germany was not immediately clear. By the late 1940s, as the Cold War intensified, occupied Germany was caught in the middle of the struggle between East and West. In an important sense, this postwar division mirrored long-standing German uncertainties about its role as a Western, Eastern, or central European nation, uncertainties that led to war in 1870 with France and in 1914 with many Western Nations. For the United States, Britain, and France, the formation of the Federal Republic of Germany (FRG), West Germany, in 1949 was an attempt to establish a democratic form of government within the western portion of this now-divided country. Because of the Cold War, this took on added importance.

Once the pattern of parliamentary democracy within capitalism was established, the postwar political economy of the new West German republic developed in a fashion similar to those of other Western European nations (i.e., with the redevelopment of a mixed economy, and overlapping roles of the public and private sectors). It also meant the reestablishment of a parliamentary democracy that, it was hoped, would overcome the constitutional and political flaws of the Weimar regime.

Important differences distinguished the West German political economy from that of other Western states: the highly organized nature of the business community; the weak central state, combined with strong regional governments; a tradition of active worker participation within a strong labor movement; and influential quasi-public, or "para-public," institutions at all levels of society.

In this chapter, we will examine the growth of the postwar West German state by analyzing the establishment of a new parliamentary regime, an extensive system of social-welfare benefits, and a politically regulated market economy. The strong governments in the *Laender*, "states," under the new federal system have assumed responsibilities formerly performed by the central government. This return to greater regional authority is based on traditions dating from the time before German unification in 1871. We will then discuss the partial erosion of the postwar welfare state. Although massive cutbacks in social services have not occurred, unemployment has risen and some programs have been trimmed; however, the postwar welfare state has retained many of its services and most of its public support.

Evolution of the Constitutional Order

The reestablishment of a postwar constitutional order in West Germany took place under difficult circumstances. The four Allied powers controlled the country from 1945 to 1949. Britain, France, and the United States occupied the western zones, while the Soviet Union occupied the east. Each of the four powers occupied portions of the city of Berlin, which was located 180 miles inside the Soviet zone. As tensions between the two superpowers intensified, Germany's fate became less certain. In 1948, the Soviet Union attempted to cut off supplies to the western sections of Berlin; in response, the Allies supplied their zone by air with the famous Berlin Airlift. The development of separate currency systems also drove a wedge between eastern and western portions of Germany. The establishment of the deutsche mark as part of the currency reform in 1948 fundamentally integrated the western zones into the capitalist world economy.

Despite these divisions between the two Germanies, German politicians in the western zones hoped to reunite with the east sometime in the future. The Western occupation powers relinquished most controls to civilian authority in 1949 although military autonomy was not granted until 1955. The founding document for the new republic was named the Basic Law rather than the constitution, implying that no constitution would be written until reunification. The decision to choose the sleepy university city of Bonn as the capital of the new parliamentary-democratic government was a further indication that the arrangement was seen as temporary.

These decisions clearly preserved future options for a reunited Germany. The more immediate concern was how West Germany could improve upon the deficiencies of the Weimar system of government. The Bonn regime established a federal system in which the *Land,* "state," governments have considerable power. The central state possesses far fewer powers today than from 1933 to 1945, and even fewer powers than the more regionally oriented Second Reich. The federal government now is made up of a bicameral legislature: The *Bundestag* is the lower house; and the *Bundesrat* is the upper house. Particularly significant is the fact that the *Land* governments control the choice of membership in the Bundesrat and thus could represent a major obstacle to any action by the central government. The new regime is also organized under an executive system in which the chancellor, as the leader of the dominant party or coalition of parties, is the head of government, and the president (unlike under the Weimar regime) is merely a ceremonial head of state. The West German system has another unusual feature: The "constructive vote of no confidence" requires that a replacement government coalition have a majority to govern *before* the legislature can vote to bring a government down. With these and other changes, the founders of the postwar government hoped to avoid the institutional paralysis that contributed to the fall of the Weimar regime and the rise of the Nazis in its place.

With some exceptions, West Germany has had a history of strong chancellors. The first was Konrad Adenauer, who, as the leader of the Christian Democratic Union (CDU), served as the head of government from 1949 to 1963. A former mayor of Cologne in the Weimar years, he was known as *Der Alte,* "the old man." His paternalism struck a responsive chord among a majority of voters at a time when West Germany was rebuilding from the devastation of the war. His successor, Ludwig Erhard (CDU) had been economics minister under Adenauer and was widely credited with formulating the policies that produced the economic miracle of the 1950s and early 1960s. As chancellor from 1963 to 1966, Erhard was much less effective than Adenauer, however. He not only failed to respond to a slight recession in 1965 but also lacked Adenauer's decisiveness. Still weaker was Kurt Kiesinger (CDU), the chancellor of the Grand Coalition, which combined the CDU, the Christian Social Union (CSU), and the Social Democratic Party (SPD), from 1966 to 1969. Though not a resolute leader, his task was hindered by the

Table 12.1 The Executive Branch, 1949 to the present

THE FEDERAL PRESIDENTS	TERM
Theodor Heuss (FDP)	1949–1954
	1954–1959
Heinrich Lübke (CDU)	1959–1964
	1964–1969
Gustav Heinemann (SPD)	1969–1974
Walter Scheel (FDP)	1974–1979
Karl Carstens (CDU)	1979–1984
Richard von Weizsäcker (CDU)	1984–

THE FEDERAL CHANCELLORS	TERM
Konrad Adenauer (CDU)	1949–1953
	1953–1957
	1957–1961
	1961–1963
Ludwig Erhard (CDU)	1963–1965
	1965–1966
Kurt Georg Kiesinger (CDU)	1966–1969
Willy Brandt (SPD)	1969–1972
	1972–1974
Helmut Schmidt (SPD)	1974–1976
	1976–1980
	1980–1982
Helmut Kohl (CDU)	1982–1983
	1983–

SOURCE *Facts about Germany*, ed. Karl Römer (Gütersloh: Lexikothek Verlag, 1982), pp. 96–7.

increasing conflicts between the CDU/CSU and the SPD, and the strong foreign policy posture by Vice Chancellor Willy Brandt (SPD). It was also further hindered by the growth of the Extraparliamentary Opposition (APO) on the Left and by the National Democrats (NPD), a reconstituted neo-Nazi party, on the Right. While the Grand Coalition had fused the two major parties in government, it also meant that there was no authentic opposition party. However, this period of consensus government proved short-lived.

The SPD became the dominant coalition partner from 1969 to 1982. Its thirteen-year tenure was largely due to the strong leadership of Willy Brandt (1969–74) and Helmut Schmidt (1974–82). Both politicians were adept at brokering conflicts between the party's left wing and its centrist coalition partner, the Free Democratic Party (FDP). Brandt was mayor of West Berlin during the 1960s, and during his years as chancellor, he emphasized *Ostpolitik* (encouraging relations with East Germany and the Soviet bloc countries). This policy proved most popular and was continued under the leadership of Helmut Kohl (CDU) after 1982. Brandt was forced to resign in 1974, when it was revealed that one of his personal assistants was a spy for East Germany. However, Brandt remained party chairman through the mid-1980s and was a unifying figure for the party following the Christian Democrats' return to power in 1982.

Helmut Schmidt replaced Brandt in 1974 and was well regarded for his skills in managing the economy. Schmidt steered the West German economy through the first oil crisis in 1973 and through the turbulent straits of the late 1970s and early 1980s. Under his chancellorship, the West German economy outperformed other Western European economies. His primary weakness was his inability to retain a close relationship with the rank-and-file of the Social Democrats. When the FDP (the SPD's junior partner in the coalition) broke with Schmidt in the early 1980s over economic policies, Schmidt did not have sufficient support among his own party to remain in power. Helmut Kohl (CDU) replaced Schmidt in 1982, and by the mid-1980s, appeared to be a much less effective chancellor than Adenauer, Brandt, or Schmidt. (A more detailed analysis of the first years of the Kohl government will be found in Chapter 15.)

The Politically Regulated Market Economy

The Balance of Public and Private Resources. The relationship between the public and private sectors became increasingly complex after the formation of the new government in 1949. The Adenauer government created a *Sozialemarktwirtschaft,* "social market economy," which sought to rebuild capitalism with the assistance of a comprehensive, supportive, and effective public sector. For U.S. observers, however, both the social and the market components looked very different than their U.S. counterparts.

The social component included a wide-ranging welfare-state system. Even though the Nazis' abuses had clearly eroded the strong statist tradition in Germany, major welfare-state functions did remain with the central government. Moreover, the transfer of additional powers to the *Land* governments saw many of the public-sector functions, which formerly had been performed at the central level, simply shifted to the states. Further, the public sector (broadly defined) not only provided extensive welfare-state measures but also created an orderly framework within which business again could grow.

The market component of the social market economy was greatly influenced by the U.S. occupation forces, who preferred more market freedom and less state participation. They blocked SPD and trade union demands to nationalize major industries, preferring instead to break up the large firms that had the greatest involvement with the Nazi government. They reasoned that the resuscitation of capitalism required the absence of an intrusive government and the creation of small competitive firms. By the mid-1950s, however, West German industry had returned to the highly concentrated form that had prevailed since the late nineteenth century, with industries such as steel, chemicals, automobiles, and electronics each dominated by just a few large firms. The public sector not only supported such growth but also allowed banks and industry associations to coordinate firms and industries, a role that would be illegal under stronger, U.S. antitrust laws. By the mid-1950s, West German business and the CDU/CSU-led government had realized that coordination between large firms was crucial for competitive, export-led economic growth. The market pattern reflected not the U.S. model but German-style "organized capitalism."

To most U.S. political scientists and policy analysts, the relationship between the private and public sectors in West Germany remains ambiguous. When the economy shows strong growth, U.S. observers attribute this good performance to the market side, with its strong emphasis on the private sector and the comparatively weak central state. However, when the economy does not perform well, many see the cause as a too-extensive social side, with its social spending and government regulation. On balance, there exists a fluid relationship between the public and private sectors in West Germany. A series of what political scientist Peter Katzenstein has called "para-public" institutions has evolved, providing a forum within which the private and public sectors can come together and work out a range of issues. Although heavy reliance on the central state proved disastrous for Germany in the past, West German political leaders realize that the public sector must play a crucial role in an advanced capitalist society.

How did this institutional framework for cooperation between the public and private sectors shape the rapid economic growth of the 1950s and early 1960s? The so-called economic miracle rebuilt a shattered society and made West Germany the leading economy in Western Europe. How did the public sector contribute to this process?

The Politics of Growth. One striking feature of the immediate postwar years was the degree to which the large industrialists were discredited by their collaboration with the Nazis. From 1945 to 1947, when the trade unions and SPD had regrouped, they demanded that firms that had supported Hitler most heavily be taken over by the workers themselves. This demand reflected the pre–World War II goal of establishing an economic system based on worker participation, if not worker control. The Allied authorities, however, preferred to avoid such alternatives and broke up or dismantled these firms in order to render West Germany incapable of again waging war.

Both the SPD/trade union vision and the Allied goals for the West German economy proved impossible to attain as geopolitical tensions mounted between East and West. Western conservatives discredited union and SPD efforts by pointing to the negative examples of socialism in Eastern Europe. Further, the exigencies of reestablishing capitalism in the country frustrated U.S. strategies for a simplified postwar economy. The Allies preferred a strong resurgence of capitalism to serve as both a showcase for Western-style economies and a market for the products of other postwar capitalist economies in Western Europe. By 1948–49, these constraints allowed West German business elites and moderately conservative politicians like Adenauer to roll back the initial Left challenge and reestablish a German-style (rather than U.S.-style) industrial system.

The 1948 currency reform proved a crucial step in rebuilding the economy on capitalist principles, following patterns long established in Germany. It favored large property holders, discriminated against those with little savings, and sought to spur an investment-led (rather than consumption-led) pattern of growth. The deutsche mark was undervalued against other world currencies, so West German exports (a traditionally strong sector) were very successful in world markets. The demand for heavy industrial goods during the Korean War in the early 1950s generated further industrial growth.

Yet if economic policy was to emphasize exports and heavy industry, how were the needs of average Germans to be met? How too were the labor movement and the SPD, pushed aside in the late 1940s, to be

Table 12.2 The Federal Republic's exports and imports by groups of countries (*in DM millions*)

GROUP OF COUNTRIES	IMPORTS 1970	IMPORTS 1980	EXPORTS 1970	EXPORTS 1980
WESTERN INDUSTRIAL COUNTRIES	87,427	254,101	104,715	277,722
EEC countries	48,437	157,399	50,259	168,219
Other European	16,634	52,136	28,344	74,913
USA and Canada	13,917	29,293	12,618	23,656
Others	8,439	15,273	13,494	10,935
DEVELOPING COUNTRIES	17,684	69,557	14,904	51,723
Africa	6,688	23,321	3,494	14,603
America	5,343	11,191	5,114	11,490
Asia	5,611	34,332	6,224	25,552
Oceania	43	713	72	78
EASTERN BLOC COUNTRIES	4,394	17,493	5,400	19,399
Eastern Europe	4,036	15,672	4,760	17,223
WORLD TOTAL	109,606	341,380	125,276	350,328

SOURCE *Facts about Germany,* ed. Karl Römer (Gütersloh: Lexikothek Verlag, 1982) p. 216.

assimilated into a political economy that favored industrial capital? The companion policy to the economy of investment-led growth was the development of the welfare state under the social market economy. Welfare-state spending had the effect of increasing economic demand and providing essential public services. Thus, collective consumption was favored over individual consumption, an approach that harkened back to the traditions established by Bismarck seventy-five years earlier.

The West German social market economy was another source of misunderstanding for the United States. It was clearly neither a U.S.-style free market nor a Keynsian, demand-management economic policy. The politics of growth entailed a relatively strong role for the state (both central and regional), but it also involved even stronger roles for the banks and employer and industry organizations. Thus, the social market economy rapidly resuscitated the large chemical, steel, auto, and electronics firms by creating *Ordnungspolitik,* "the politics of industrial order."

The Full Employment Economy. While West Germany generally has been characterized as a full employment economy for most of the postwar period, full employment levels (i.e., less than one to two percent unemployment) were not attained until the 1960s. The economic policies favoring investment over consumption, and the weakening of the SPD and the trade union movement in the early 1950s, retarded the development of a full employment economy for at least a decade. The SPD and the unions did not have the strength — or the inclination — in the 1950s to obtain the Keynesian demand-stimulation policies that would have aided full employment.

With the social market economy portrayed as a success by resurgent German business in the mid-1950s, and with the inability of the SPD to overcome the political dominance of Adenauer's CDU-led coalition, little could be done about unemployment levels that ranged from 8 to 11 percent during the decade. Moreover, the inflow of highly skilled refugees from East Germany not only enabled productivity to rise but also contributed to an oversupply of labor. For West German business, this competition for jobs among highly skilled workers prevented costs from rising and contributed to high profits during the 1950s. For workers, however, it meant that wages remained low and that unemployment levels did not decline.

By the 1960s, several factors converged to ensure full employment that was to continue until the late 1970s. The building of the Berlin Wall in 1961 closed off the flow of workers from the East. The formation of the European Economic Community (EEC) in 1958 increased consumer demand in West Germany, as well as in all of Western Europe, and the reduction of all tariff barriers among EEC member countries greatly stimulated trade.

In fact, full employment was attained so quickly in West Germany that by the mid-1960s, there was a shortage of workers. *Gastarbeiter,* "guest workers," were then recruited from the poorer countries of southern Europe. Policymakers expected to use these workers as a cushion for the economy: bringing them in during times of economic boom and sending them home during times of recession. However, the mid-1960s boom lasted so long that by the time the economy did decline in the mid-1970s, it was difficult for the guest workers to return to homes where they had not lived for a decade or more. The presence of these foreign workers into the 1970s and 1980s (at a time of increasing unemployment) produced heightened social strain, and since neither the guest workers nor their children were entitled to West German citizenship, the problem remained unresolved in the 1980s.

The Role of Business and Union Elites. With the decline of the role of the central state, business and union elites came to play a much more influential role in politics. Even during the period of Allied occupation, business elites from banks, large firms, and industry and employer organizations played a crucial role in the reestablishment of capitalism in West Germany. Acting in the tradition of "organized capitalism,"[1] these private-sector actors worked together to protect their interests and established a conducive framework for the West German political economy. As political scientist Gerard Braunthal has suggested, the industrial organizations performed many of the functions that the central state had performed during the Second Reich.[2]

These strong private-sector institutions were instrumental in taking the teeth out of the Anti-Cartel Law of 1957, the substance of which had been borrowed from U.S. antitrust traditions. Although the law was favored by the United States and by the small, U.S.-oriented Free Democratic Party (FDP), the banks and industrial organizations succeeded in making its provisions much less restrictive for business.

Despite setbacks in the immediate postwar years, the trade unions still retained considerable influence in West German society. Although the most radical of their demands were deflected by the Adenauer governments of the 1950s, they were still able to create elaborate (if largely powerless) systems for worker participation. In 1951, they obtained provisions for *Mitbestimmung,* "codetermination," which provided for workers and union representatives to make up just under 50 percent of the boards of directors of firms in the coal and steel industries. In 1952, codetermination was extended to large firms in other industries, but union representation on these company boards amounted to only 33 percent. In 1976, under Helmut Schmidt's SPD–FDP coalition government, the codetermination law was expanded to stop just short of the virtual full-parity codetermination that coal and steel workers had enjoyed since 1951.

Unions were particularly sensitive to competing organizations within the workplace due to their experiences under the Weimar regime. In the 1920s, the presence of trade unions affiliated with the Social Democratic, Communist, and nonsocialist movements caused fragmentation and prevented the labor movement from effectively resisting the Nazis. The German Trade Union Confederation (DGB), established in 1949 and headed by Hans Boeckler, insisted on a system of union organization that was unified (i.e., no confederations explicitly affiliated with political parties) and industry-specific (i.e., one industry/one union and, more importantly, one plant/one union).

Despite weaknesses in the unions during the early years of the postwar government, they were able to rebuild by the 1960s and 1970s. Once the SPD came to power in the late 1960s, the unions became even more influential: SPD policies were much closer to the unions' than those of the CDU, and almost all DGB leaders in practice were also SPD members.

In 1972, the SPD–FDP coalition government, led by Willy Brandt, instituted changes in the *Betriebsraete,* "works councils," which were set up in all firms — union and nonunion — with twenty or more employees. Generally, the works councils dealt only with social and personnel matters; collective-bargaining responsibilities remained with the unions. The unions were suspicious of these councils, because, as parallel organizations, they could undermine the trade unions' influence. Therefore, the 1972 legislation extended trade unions' rights inside the workplace and, thereby, inside the works councils.

Welfare Policies. Welfare policies can be described as the social part of the social market economy. West Germany's social-welfare expenditures fall well within Western European standards, although they are not as generous as in the Netherlands or Scandinavia. However, public services in West Germany have dwarfed provisions in the United States since the 1950s.

From housing subsidies to savings subsidies, health care, public transit, and infrastructure, West Germany is most generous in its public spending. Even under the moderately conservative rule of the CDU-led Adenauer coalition, there was a strong commitment to adequate public services, a strategy that recalls Bismarck's efforts to use public services to forestall radical demands. Similarly, the unions and the SPD's demands for increased public spending ensured that the Left was incorporated into the political order during the 1950s and early 1960s. By the late 1960s, when the SPD came to power (and the welfare state had expanded further), elements of the Left believed that the welfare state had defused the most radical social demands and enabled the social order to avoid fundamental change.

Table 12.3 Social-welfare disbursement (*in DM millions*)

TYPE OF DISBURSEMENT	1975	1980
Total	334,019	449,473
Pensions insurance	143,339	188,621
Health insurance	61,631	86,536
Accident insurance	7,180	9,963
Employment promotion	18,416	22,655
Child benefits	14,693	17,605
Public service supports	10,900	13,239
Supplementary insurance	3,301	4,447
Continued payment of wages and salaries in sickness	18,000	27,150
Contractual and voluntary employer disbursements	7,800	10,430
War victims benefits	11,135	13,400
Social support	8,617	13,944
Public youth aid	3,705	5,876
Education support	2,890	3,322
Housing benefits	1,779	2,046
Public health service	1,280	1,472
Asset-building	13,376	11,935
Tax easements	28,292	37,862
Others	9,646	10,975

SOURCE *Facts about Germany*, ed. Karl Römer (Gütersloh: Lexikothek Verlag, 1982) p. 265.

The Decline of the Postwar Settlement

The Structure of Decline

The erosion of the social-welfare arrangements that characterized the postwar settlement has been far less pronounced in West Germany than in other large, industrialized states. During the mid-1970s, when unemployment grew from one to two percent to roughly four percent, and when some social-welfare measures were capped (but not reduced), West

Germans spoke of the "crisis" of the welfare state. Yet non-German observers were hard pressed to find indications of crisis. Clearly, the West German state has used repressive security measures against some social groups, particularly those thought to be sympathetic to terrorists during the late 1970s, but the contraction of substantial welfare-state benefits has not even begun to approximate that of the United States and Britain in the 1980s.

Inflation. The West German governments have been most successful in keeping inflation under control. If anything, political leaders in the 1970s and 1980s have been criticized for being too preoccupied with this issue at the expense of unemployment, which crept to 9 percent by late 1982. Due to the fears of the hyperinflation of the 1920s, this issue has always been identified by private- and public-sector leaders as the linchpin of stable economic growth.

There was some concern in the mid-1960s when unemployment rose to near 6 percent at the same time that a small, neo-Nazi party (the NPD) emerged, but the NPD then nearly disappeared. Overall, the West German governments (both CDU-led and SPD-led) have made inflation-fighting a top priority. During the oil crises of 1973–74 and 1979, oil-poor West Germany allowed inflation to creep no higher than 7 percent. Significantly, the country was also able to maintain its level of welfare-state spending. In the United States during the same periods, inflation rose and social-welfare spending was cut.

Declining Growth. In 1980 and 1981, Chancellor Helmut Schmidt was portrayed in the U.S. press as a leader who was able to provide both economic growth and social equity. At the time, the West German economy was expanding and unemployment was still only 4 percent (a figure U.S. economists have always considered full employment). In fact, the political economy was called the *Modell Deutschland,* "German model," and it was seen as a society that rivaled the Japanese in economic success during the 1970s.[3]

Recession arrived in West Germany, however, in 1981 and 1982 (as it did in the United States and throughout the industrialized world), and the German model seemed to be considerably tarnished. The recession hastened the collapse of Schmidt's SPD–FDP coalition. Schmidt was compelled by his party's left wing to stimulate the economy with expansionary measures, while being pulled in the opposite direction by his coalition partners, the small Free Democratic Party, who argued for reduction in social spending and the strategic contraction of the economy. In late 1982, the FDP jumped ship and formed a coalition with the CDU/CSU. Despite a moderate decline in growth, however, unemployment in West Germany was only slightly higher than in the United States, and it remained the lowest of all the major Western European countries during the early 1980s. On a closer examination of the West German economy, it is clear that reports of a generalized decline are much mistaken.

Certain fulcrum industries — those that still employ a sizable proportion of the work force and represent a major portion of the gross national product (GNP) — have performed well through the 1970s and early 1980s, and retained their strength in world markets. The industries that fall into this category are chemicals, luxury automobiles, machine tools, and industrial electronics. West Germany's strategy for international competitiveness was, not to develop new high-technology industries, but to employ high-technology *processes* in these comparatively old-fashioned industries. Economist Michael Piore and political sociologist Charles Sabel have called such process innovation "flexible system manufacturing" because it emphasizes the high skill levels and flexibility of the work force, thereby enabling these industries to find crucial niches in world markets.[4] Mercedes and BMW automobiles are the most visible examples of the success of this strategy in the U.S. market. The major question for the German economy in the mid-1980s was whether this flexible system model could be employed in enough fulcrum industries to generate improved macroeconomic performance.

Institutional Pressures on the Welfare State. During 1977 and 1978, a small band of radicals, known officially as the Red Army Faction (RAF) but more commonly called the Baader-Meinhof gang, assassinated several prominent people, among them a banker and an industrialist. The SPD–FDP government responded, some thought, too harshly. The left wing of Chancellor Schmidt's SPD party was among the critics, who charged that the state had taken excessive measures to monitor individuals believed sympathetic to the terrorists and that violations of individual rights were overlooked in the quest to capture the terrorists. Subsequently, some left-wing SPD members defected to non-party *Buergeriniativen,* "citizen action groups," and to the Greens Party, which was formed in the late 1970s. Those who remained became very dissatisfied with Schmidt, and their criticism of his leadership partially eroded his capacity to keep the FDP in the center-Left coalition beyond the fall of 1982. With the FDP pulling to the right and many in his own party pulling to the left, Schmidt's support eroded rapidly and his resignation soon followed.

Continued high unemployment (by German standards), and the costs of support for workers who have depleted their benefits, have presented a difficult dilemma for the welfare state during the 1980s. These issues cost the Schmidt coalition considerable support, and it was replaced by a CDU-led coalition in 1982. The CDU/CSU–FDP coalition government, led by Helmut Kohl, has shouldered the cost of sustaining the long-term unemployed through general welfare funds. However, a more serious structural problem lies beyond the immediate issue of cost: How can West Germany's elaborate vocational education and apprentice system absorb all of the new entrants into the labor market? In a country that prides itself on its skilled work force, this issue could undermine one of the strong points of the German economy: the continued supply of skilled workers.

Decomposition of the Blue-Collar Working Class. West Germany has relied heavily on its skilled blue-collar workers throughout the postwar period. There has been little decomposition of this segment of the working class due to their importance in the flexible system production processes of such industries as machine tools, automobiles, chemicals, and industrial electronics. Although there has been some evidence of partial decomposition in weaker industries, such as steel and shipbuilding, where there have been major job losses, working-class decomposition is far less pronounced than in either Britain or the United States.

West Germany has seen only a small growth of service sector jobs, unlike the United States, where a large proportion of the new jobs are in services. The right wing in West Germany has argued that the country should emulate the United States by creating new jobs in this area. The left wing has countered with the assertion that most service sector jobs in the United States are low-paying jobs at fast-food restaurants with few benefits. They argue that the strains placed on society by this plan for employment growth, in the form of inadequate economic demand (due to low wages) and increased social spending (due to lack of fringe benefits), would represent a net loss for West German society. The plan for high productivity, high-wage unionized employment has sustained the economy for many years. The U.S. "solution," they believe, is the wrong choice.

Erosion of the Postwar Settlement

The Labor Movement: Mobilization and Fragmentation. As in most industrialized countries, West Germany's labor movement was comparatively weak in the 1950s. With virtually full employment in the early 1960s and the passage in 1963 of a new trade union program at a major conference of the German Trade Union Confederation (DGB), the unions were in a much stronger collective-bargaining position. The tightened labor market forced employers to raise wages in order to attract employees. The trade unions' 1963 program moved towards a coming to terms with the CDU-led social market economy, emphasizing wages rather than fundamental social transformation.[5] Although trade unions in other Western European countries, like France and Italy, also became more influential in the late 1960s, their goal was primarily social transformation rather than wage reform.

Events in the mid-1960s intensified the mobilization for increased wages. In 1966, during a slight increase in inflation, West German unions signed a three-year wage agreement that would provide only a moderate increase over the term of the contract. When the small inflationary trend disappeared in 1967 and German businesses began earning record profits, the unions were locked into a collective-bargaining contract in which wage increases lagged considerably behind. In 1969, the West German unions, led by *IG Metall* (the metalworkers' union, which represented over one-third of organized labor), mobilized to gain back wages that had been lost to the employers' high profits.

By the early 1970s, trade unions also began to emphasize qualitative issues. Under pressure of a rank-and-file movement around working conditions in a Ford automobile plant in Cologne (led predominantly by the plant's large contingent of foreign workers) the unions (particularly IG Metall) began to emphasize the alienating working conditions characteristic of mass production industry. The unions connected the qualitative issues with their earlier historical concerns regarding worker control in the late 1910s and early 1920s. Although this tendency began to grow within the labor movement, it remained a minority current during the 1970s and early 1980s.

By the mid to late 1970s, unemployment began to rise, particularly in some heavy industries, such as steel and shipbuilding. The unions began to turn their attention toward measures to reduce the rate of unemployment, which increased to 8–9 percent by 1982. While high unemployment generally has divisive effects on trade unions, West German unions remained far less fragmented than trade union movements in other countries with much higher levels of unemployment, although some disagreements did arise. The organizational structure also prevented union fragmentation, as unemployment often causes unions to compete with each other over scarce jobs. Unlike Britain, where unions are divided along craft lines, and France, where they are divided along political lines, the more highly unified West German system — with only one major labor federation, the DGB — has prevented almost all interunion rivalry.

New Social Movements. New social movements emerged in West Germany in the late 1960s. Those who joined these movements felt that the SPD had drifted to the Right on some issues between 1966 and 1982, by becoming a party of government rather than a party of opposition. At various times during this sixteen-year period, movements sprang up to challenge what was considered to be a betrayal of left-wing causes by the Social Democrats.

From 1966 to 1969, the SPD participated in the Grand Coalition with the CDU–CSU. Many in the left wing of the party believed that the more conservative CDU/CSU would impede the SPD's ability to fulfill important socialist goals. More important, the Grand Coalition left the government without a sizable party of opposition. Subsequently, an Extraparliamentary Opposition (APO) was formed in the late 1960s. The APO feared the SPD would become increasingly supportive of U.S. actions in Southeast Asia, as it was now a party of government. The university educational system, which remained remarkably elitist, restrictive, and authoritarian, was also a major APO concern. When young West Germans demonstrated in the late 1960s for increased access to the university system, the SPD was unable to pass reforms. After the 1969 election, the SPD became the dominant coalition partner and the FDP replaced Christian Democrats in the coalition. The SPD was able to institute some moderate reforms, but to some the party's left-wing supporters, the damage was done. Some believed that the constraints of coalition politics inhibited the struggle for fundamental change and they preferred to remain outside the SPD. Others, however, rejoined the party after its electoral victory in 1969, with hopes of reaching their goals through the system.

In the mid-1970s, the Brandt government issued a Radicals Decree, which sought to prevent political extremists from obtaining civil service jobs. This decree was intended primarily to ward off CDU/CSU criticism that the SPD was soft on communism and that the Brandt government was allowing too many communist teachers into the country's classrooms. However, the decree had the effect of alienating those left-wing SPD members who were trying to work within the system. In the late 1970s, the Schmidt government promulgated similar laws in order to investigate leftists who were suspected of being sympathetic toward the Red Army Faction terrorists. These measures drove former SPD members to informal, localized, citizen action groups, which acted outside of the party system.

These citizen action groups received further support from opponents of nuclear power. Because West Germany had to import almost all of its energy resources, the industrial sector (and the SPD) became enthused about the development of nuclear power in the 1960s. In the 1970s, as concern grew over the inadequate waste-disposal system, opposition to nuclear power intensified, and antinuclear groups demanded that some alternative source of power be found. The SPD, constrained by its position on this issue, did not speak out against nuclear power and so, once again, seemed to turn away from its left-wing constituency.

These social movements grew increasingly influential in the early 1980s. Elements of the citizen action groups became core supporters of the Greens Party, which was formed in the late 1970s. In 1982, the combined presence of these groups — the Greens and the social movements outside the SPD — contributed to the final exhaustion of the SPD as a party of government. Willy Brandt, reflecting during the early 1980s on these developments, termed these movements "the SPD's lost children," meaning that the SPD ought to have listened and incorporated their concerns into party policy.

Although increasingly important in West Germany, these social movements were not usually associated with what French sociologist Serge Mallet has called the "new working class" phenomenon that had been identified in other countries. Political scientist Ronald Inglehart has named the West German social movements "post-materialist," in the sense that their concerns were not traditional Marxist materialism.[6] In fact, they have not relied on class as a primary category in which to define themselves, as many tend to be university-educated children of the middle class. They have thus not been able to create an identity strong enough to challenge the highly skilled working-class structure of West Germany. If there is a "new working class" in West Germany, it remains within the trade unions as members have increased their skills to engage in flexible system manufacturing. The still dominant working-class culture of West Germany has acted as a barrier to the "post-materialist" social movements' attainment of further influence.

Volatility of the Electorate. The electorate has been, for the most part, remarkably stable, although some fringe parties have attained the 5 percent share of the vote necessary to participate in government, most notably the neo-Nazi NPD and the Greens. Otherwise, the electorate has stayed within the so-called "two-and-a-half" party system, with the Christian Democrats (CDU/CSU) on the right, the small Free Democratic Party in the center, and the Social Democratic Party (SPD) on the left.

From 1949 until the early 1980s, this two-and-a-half party system was solidly entrenched. The Christian Democrats were the leading party in coalition with the FDP from 1949 until 1966 (with the exception of the 1957–61 period, when they enjoyed a majority. The period from 1966 to 1969 was known as the Grand Coalition because the two major parties, the CDU/CSU and the SPD, combined to form the government. At that time, the FDP was the only opposition party. Eventually, the two large parties disagreed, so after the 1969 elections, the SPD and FDP formed a new coalition government. This center-Left coalition lasted until 1982, when the SPD and the FDP parted company over economic policy. The centrist FDP decided to "face right" and tipped the balance of power back towards the Christian Democrats, led by Helmut Kohl.

No wide swings in the election results have occurred from one voting period to another. From the mid-1960s until the early 1980s, the two-and-a-half parties showed little change in votes received. The CDU/CSU's share of the vote ranged between 43 and 47 percent; the SPD's share was between 38 and 44 percent; and the FDP's between 6 and 11 percent. This electoral stability is particularly noticeable when compared with the growth of the new Social Democratic Party in Britain and tremendous volatility in the electoral performance of French political parties.

By the early 1980s, this pattern was altered by a degree of party dealignment. In some countries, like the United States, individualism has increased and voters have tended to abandon party affiliations. In West Germany, however, electoral volatility took collective rather than individualistic forms, resulting in the formation of a new party, the Greens.

Dealignment and the Emergence of the Greens. Support for the Greens is best described as *diverse.* Its following is drawn from a variety of sources: the locally based citizen action groups; the environmental movement; religious groups dissatisfied with organized Catholicism and Protestantism; the peace movement; and the successors of marginal Marxist sects. Despite its rapid rise, the Greens Party remains much less organizationally coherent than the other political parties in West Germany.

A crucial issue for the Greens has been electoral support. Under West German electoral law, a party must receive at least 5 percent of the vote in order to earn seats in the legislature. In the 1983 election, the Greens obtained 5.6 percent of the vote, which, for the first time, allowed them representation in the Bundestag. This electoral success presented a major dilemma to the Greens, however. Support for the Greens had grown from disillusion with the party system; it was an "antiparty" party. So, when it had the opportunity to accept twenty-seven seats in the same Bundestag that it had criticized since its formation, the party was divided by a major internal dispute: The fundamentalists wanted to use the parliamentary forum against the system; and the realists wanted to use this opportunity to try to attain some concrete results. By the mid-1980s, the realists seemed to have gained the upper hand in the debate. In addition, as a party with legislative seats, the Greens were eligible to receive federal funds, which enabled the party to finance its activities.

In 1985, the Greens went a step further toward becoming a traditional party by entering into a coalition with the SPD in the state of Hesse. This Red-Green coalition raised a number of crucial questions: How durable would such a coalition be? Would it be a model for other German states? Would a similar coalition be possible for the 1987 national elections? The answers to these questions remained unclear in the mid-1980s, though the success of the Greens has caused the other parties to become more sensitive to Greens issues and to include some Greens themes in their own platforms.

The New Right and Neo-Conservatism. Unlike Britain, France, and the United States, West Germany has seen little right-wing activity in recent years. In 1969, the neo-Nazi NDP received 4.3 percent of the vote, but its support had declined markedly by the 1972 election, and the party has not been a force in West German politics since that time. Further right-wing activity has taken the form of occasional street demonstrations by smaller neo-Nazi sects. In Frankfurt, in 1985, one of these meetings was broken up by a small contingent of leftists, and a street battle ensued. This conflict was reminiscent of the major altercations between Nazi and Communist Party militants at the end of the Weimar regime, but it was isolated and insignificant in comparison. Right-wing resentment of Turkish guest workers and their families has occasionally resulted in violent incidents, especially with the rise in unemployment during the 1980s, but they remain a marginal problem in West German society.

West Germany, perhaps more than most countries, remains sensitive to the dangers of fascism, for the Nazi period left a deep and lasting legacy. Although major political actors are keenly aware of the dangers of such movements and the fragility of advanced industrialized societies, some disquieting signs remain. Observers point out that the 1933–45 period is inadequately taught in West German schools; further, the SPD voiced only mild opposition to the 1985 Reagan/Kohl visit to the cemetery in Bitburg in which Nazi SS troops are buried. Despite West Germany's continued reluctance to thoroughly confront the horrors of the Nazi era, there seems to be little danger of a return of Nazism.

A Minor Rightward Shift in the Policy Agenda. Helmut Kohl's accession to power in late 1982, as the leader of the center-Right CDU/CSU–FDP coalition, represented the third governmental shift from Left to Right in a major industrialized country in three years. In 1979, the Conservative Party of Margaret Thatcher replaced Labour's James Callaghan as prime minister in Britain, while in 1980, Republican Ronald Reagan replaced Democrat Jimmy Carter as president of the United States. In both of these countries, the policy agenda swerved sharply to the right, and attacks on the welfare state, conservative economic policies, and increased hostilities toward labor movements were prevalent. The 1983 national elections in West Germany, which confirmed Kohl's coalition government, were seen as a *Wende,* "turnaround," by many observers. Some even wondered whether Helmut Kohl would become Germany's Ronald Reagan.

If anything, by the mid-1980s, Helmut Kohl had become Germany's Gerald Ford. The policies of the center-Right coalition represented only a gentle moderation in direction, rather than a sharp veer to the right. The Kohl government's policies can be likened to the moderately conservative Republican policies in the United States during the Nixon and Ford years. In 1985, West German policies indicated a continuity with previous SPD policies under Schmidt.

In sum, a greater degree of stability has exisited during the post–World War II period than at any other time in West German history. Conflicts and tensions related to the role of the state and between unions and employers are still present, but private and public institutions have proved adept in keeping most issues within bounds. For example, the welfare state has experienced much less upheaval than in most other Western European nations; the country's economic troubles have been comparatively well managed by business and political leaders; the Left has been unable to use the issues of persistent unemployment as a rallying cry for fundamental structural or institutional change; and even Helmut Kohl has been unable to emulate the policy direction of his fellow conservatives, Margaret Thatcher and Ronald Reagan. The pattern, then, has been one of forcing most contentious issues toward the center.

Part of the reason for this stability is the ability of economic and political leaders to balance the private and public sectors. Nineteenth-century German history shows the important role that the state played in the unification of the country and the development of an industrial economy, yet twentieth-century German history shows the dangers in placing too heavy a reliance on centralized state authority. Even the Left has now realized that it must maintain a strong presence in both public and private sectors. Social-welfare measures are important for their constituents, but so too are the institutions that workers have obtained within the workplace. Consequently, the lesson of West Germany's pre–World War II undemocratic legacy and its post–World War II parliamentary system is that a balance must be struck between the public and private sectors.

Notes

1. Rudolf Hilferding, *Finance Capital: A Study of the Latest Phase of Capitalist Development* (London: Routledge and Kegan Paul, 1981).
2. See: Gerard Braunthal, *The Federation of German Industry in Politics* (Ithaca: Cornell University Press, 1965).
3. See: Andrei S. Markovits, ed., *The Political Economy of* Modell Deutschland (New York: Praeger, 1982).
4. Michael Piore and Charles Sabel, *The Second Industrial Divide* (New York: Basic Books, 1984).
5. For a comparative treatment of West German trade unions during the postwar period, see: Andrei S. Markovits and Christopher S. Allen, "West Germany," in *Unions and Economic Crisis: Britain, West Germany and Sweden,* ed. Peter Gourevich et al. (London: George Allen and Unwin, 1984).
6. See: Ronald Inglehart, *The Silent Revolution: Changing Values and Political Styles Among Western Publics* (Princeton: Princeton University Press, 1977).

13

State Institutions

Principles of West German Government

When the West German government was established in 1949, the primary goals of the founding fathers were to work toward eventual reunification of the two Germanies and to avoid repeating the failure of Germany's only other experiment with democracy, the Weimar Republic.[1] Unable to accomplish immediate unification, the *Grundgesetz,* "Basic Law," was the founders' compromise. It symbolized the temporary nature of disunited Germany. However, their goal of ensuring a lasting democratic order was a more complicated problem. Two fundamental institutional weaknesses had undermined the Weimar government. Provisions for emergency powers enabled leaders to arbitrarily centralize authority and suspend democratic rights. Further, the fragmentation of the political party system prevented stable majorities from forming in the Reichstag. This instability encouraged the use of emergency powers to break legislative blocks.

The founders of the postwar regime sought to remedy the abuse of centralized power by establishing a federal system in which the *Laender* were given considerable powers, particularly administrative powers. Although the federal Bundestag (lower house) became the chief lawmaking body, the implementation of many of these laws fell to the *Laender* governments. Under the Basic Law, many functions that had formerly been centralized during the Imperial, Weimar, and Nazi periods — the educational system, the police, and the radio and television networks — became the responsibility of the states.

There was little opposition to this significant shift from a centralized to a federal system. The Third Reich's abuse of power with respect to Jews, political parties, trade unions, and human rights in general had created strong sentiment for curbing the state's repressive capacities. In addition, West German leaders, influenced by the presence of U.S. advisors, were inclined to support a federal system. Further, the development of a federal system was, not a departure, but a return to form. Prior to 1871, the various regions of Germany formed a decentralized political system. The regional states had developed such autonomous institutions as banks, universities, vocational schools, and state administrative systems.

The new system overcame party fragmentation and the inability to form working majorities by several methods. The multiplicity of parties, characteristic of the Weimar Republic, was partially overcome by the institutionalization of the 5 percent rule, which required that all political parties receive at least 5 percent of the vote in order to obtain representation in any government. In the late Weimar period, sharp conflict among parties opened the door for the Nazi rise to power; however, under the 5 percent rule, smaller parties have tended to disappear, with most of their adherents gravitating toward the three major parties. Further, the Bundestag is more likely to achieve working majorities than the Weimar government, for several reasons. Election laws require that the interval between elections must be four years (except under unusual circumstances). This gives an elected government the opportunity to implement its electoral goals and to take responsibility for its success or failure. The electoral system itself was changed from proportional representation under the Weimar system (which proved unstable) to a combination of proportional representation and single-member electoral districts. The constructive vote of no confidence, which requires that any vote to unseat a government must also be a vote to install a new majority government, has been a positive component of the postwar government. Under the Weimar constitution, negative majorities often garnered enough votes to unseat the chancellor but did not provide a mandate to install a replacement. In addition, the chancellor's powers are now more clearly defined, and the president is merely the ceremonial head of state. Under the Weimar constitution, the president could be called upon to wield emergency powers. Hitler used this rule to manipulate the system under the aging President Hindenburg in 1932–33. In the current system, the president has been stripped of broad power.

The principles of the West German government contained in the Basic Law apparently have given the regime a solid foundation. Since the system has survived for almost forty years, it is clear the founders' most important goals have been fulfilled. A return of Nazism seems unlikely, and the tensions between capitalism and democracy appear much less strident. Political scientist Ralf Dehrendorf has stated that until the arrival of the current republic, Germany had been a premodern country. After 1949, it seemed much more like other Western industrialized countries. The remaining sections of this chapter will look more closely at its political institutions.

The Executive

The division of authority between the head of government (the chancellor) and the head of state (the president) was firmly established in the Basic Law. For example, criticism of the chancellor for the government's policies is not perceived as an assault against the state itself. In this sense, the division of the executive branch was crucial in gaining respect for the new West German state at a time when most of its neighbors remained suspicious of its past.

The distinction between executive functions can be contrasted with the confluence of the roles of head of state and head of government in the office of president of the United States. The implications of this combined role have not always been positive: Both Lyndon Johnson and Richard Nixon hid behind their position as head of state, suggesting that criticism of their policies was unpatriotic.

The West German chancellor is elected by a majority of the members of the Bundestag. In practice, this means that the chancellor's ability to be a strong party or coalition leader is essential for the success of the government. In the United States, there is a separation of power between the executive and legislative branches; in West Germany, the power of the two branches is fused. It is virtually impossible for the chancellor to function without a working majority in the Bundestag.

A government is formed after a national election, or in the case of a chancellor's resignation between elections, after a majority of the Bundestag has nominated a chancellor. The new leader consults with other party (and coalition) officials to make up the cabinet. These party leaders have considerable influence in determining which individuals receive ministries. In the event of a coalition government, between two or more parties, party leaders often earmark, even before the election, potential cabinet ministers. The coalition partners then negotiate the policies the coalition will pursue and the choice of ministers for the cabinet. Once

Figure 13.1 State Structure of the Federal Republic of Germany

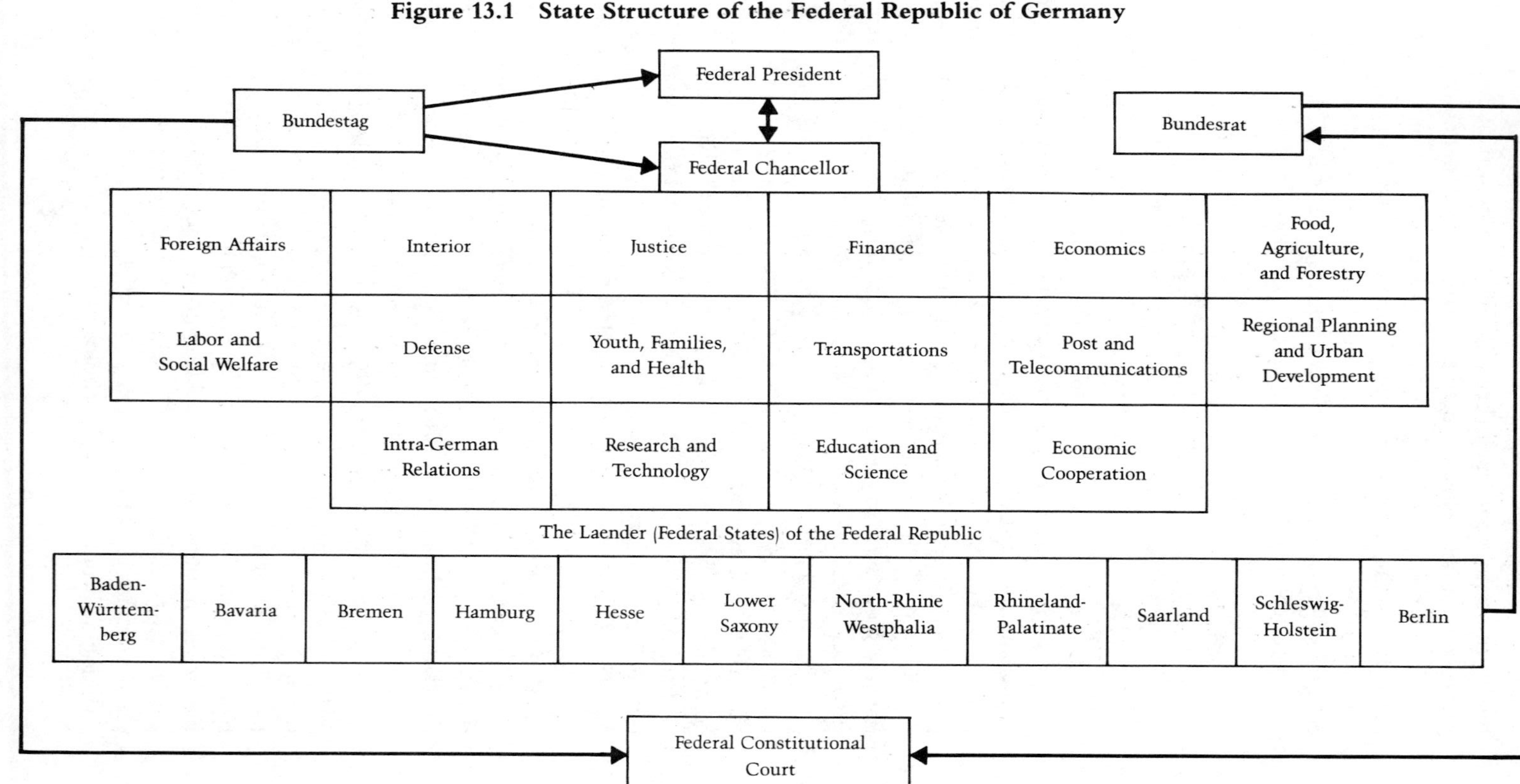

the cabinet is formed, however, the chancellor has considerable authority to govern, due to the power of the *Bundeskanzleramt,* "Federal Chancellery," which is, in effect, the "first among equals" of all the cabinet ministries. The Chancellery is the administrative office through which the chancellor oversees the entire government and mediates any conflicts among the other ministries. Thus, the Chancellery is a kind of superministry, with wide-ranging powers in many areas, somewhat similar to the Office of Management and Budget in the United States.

The office of the chancellor has played a pivotal role in the postwar era. Its clearly defined role within the federal framework has made it a far more effective office than in the Weimar period. By requiring that the chancellor be the head of the majority party or coalition, the government is able to avoid manipulation in the way that Hitler used Hindenburg to attain power for himself. Further, the chancellor's more limited role within the federal system has constrained the ability of the central government to take sweeping action. Many West Germans see this limitation of centralized executive power as a welcome improvement.

The Legislature

The Bundestag

The lower house of the legislature, the Bundestag, consists of 496 seats, 248 of which are elected in single-member districts and 248 of which are elected by proportional representation from lists compiled by the political parties. This system represents a compromise between the British and American tradition of a single legislator representing one district and the method more common in continental Europe of a group of party members representing a given region based on the percentage of the party's vote in that region. In practice, this hybrid system, which is known as personalized proportional representation, requires citizens to cast two votes on each ballot: one for an individual member of a political party, usually, but not always, from the district; and one for a list of national/regional candidates grouped by party affiliation. Thus, this system has the effect of personalizing list voting, for list-system voters sometimes find it hard to identify their representative in the Bundestag. The party list also creates stronger, more coherent parties, resulting in more stable governments. In the U.S., fragmented, individualistic parties have made gaining and holding effective majorities difficult on a given group of issues. In contrast, Willy Brandt's SPD–FDP coalition governments had extremely narrow margins, and it was only the strength of the party discipline that enabled Brandt to remain in power.

The political parties are also ideologically coherent. Each Bundestag member almost always votes with fellow party members, which contributes to unity in the parties' positions over the course of a four-year legislative period and enables the electorate to discern each party's stance on a range of issues. Consequently, all parties and their representatives in the legislature are more likely to be held accountable by voters based on their positions on the issues. This clear distinction among the parties is one reason that West Germany has had much higher rates of electoral participation (85 to 90 percent at the federal level) than the United States (52 to 53 percent in presidential elections). Some observers have argued that German citizens vote in such high numbers out of habit or duty. Given the remarkable stability in voting patterns from election to election, it is more likely that high electoral participation is due to clear party ideology. Further, West German voting participation rates compare favorably with other Western European countries. Electoral turnout in the United States is exceptionally low among industrialized countries.

The tradition of strong, unified parties in the Bundestag has had some drawbacks, however. The hierarchical party system relegates newer members to a comparatively long time in apprenticeship as backbenchers. (Senior party members sit in the front benches of the Bundestag, as in other European legislatures, leaving the rear seats for newly elected members.) This system does educate younger members into party ideology. However, it also frustrates particularly ambitious young legislators, especially since senior members of the party wield a disproportionate amount of influence. This dominance of the party elders increases when their party is in power, because the Federal Chancellery often controls the Bundestag with respect to setting legislative agendas and making key decisions. Most laws, in fact, originate with the Chancellery and with the ministries, rather than with the Bundestag or Bundesrat, so party discipline tends to channel committee discussion well within the broad position that the party itself has taken. The structure of the Bundestag discourages action by individual legislators, a practice that is more prevalent in U.S. legislative bodies due to the lack of party cohesiveness.

The chancellor and the party leadership can lose touch with the backbench members of their party. For example, Schmidt took positions — on failing to stimulate the economy and on allowing the stationing of additional U.S. missiles on German soil in the early 1980s — to which the majority of the SPD was strongly opposed in the early 1980s. Thus, when the FDP attacked Schmidt from the right on economic issues, his own party's rank and file also criticized him. Ultimately, any party leadership in government that fails to respond to its membership, its voters, or both, will be forced to resign or will lose in the next election.

The Bundesrat

As the upper house of the legislative branch, the Bundesrat occupies a position somewhere between the U.S. Senate and the British House of Lords. Though slightly less powerful than the Senate, it is considerably more powerful than the Lords. The Bundesrat is the mechanism by which the federal system actually works. It is the institutional intersection of the national and the state governments, and it consists of members of the eleven *Laender* governments. Each *Land* sends from three to five representatives to the Bundesrat, depending on its population.

The political composition of the Bundesrat at any given time, therefore, is determined by which parties are governing the *Laender*. Each of the eleven *Laender* cast their votes in a bloc, depending on the views of the party or coalition in control at the time. Consequently, the party controlling the majority of the *Land* governments can have a significant effect on legislation passed in the Bundestag. Because *Land* elections usually take place between Bundestag electoral periods, the Bundesrat majority can shift during the course of a Bundestag legislative period.

The Bundesrat must approve all legislation passed in the Bundestag. If the Bundesrat should vote against a particular bill, the Bundestag need only pass the measure again by a simple majority to override the Bundesrat's veto. If, however, a two-thirds majority of the Bundesrat were to vote against a bill, the Bundestag would have to pass it again by a two-thirds margin. In practice, however, the blocking capacity of the Bundesrat is only a serious problem when the legislation is concurrent, that is, when the state and national governments have overlapping responsibilities in administration. If a party or coalition has a stable majority in the Bundestag, however, then the Bundesrat's obstruction can be overcome. For example, during most of his term, Willy Brandt faced a one-vote minority in the Bundesrat. Because his SPD–FDP coalition also had a slim but firm majority in the Bundestag, however, he was able to stay in power.

The Bundesrat introduces comparatively little legislation. More bills are introduced in the Bundestag, though the majority of laws originate from the executive office (through one of the ministries). However, the Bundesrat's administrative responsibilities are considerable. Most of the members of the Bundesrat are also *Laender* government officials, and they are considerably experienced in the implementation of particular laws. Their expertise frequently is called upon in the committee hearings, which are open to all Bundesrat members.

The Bundesrat's strong administrative role is a crucial component of the government. In different ways, this system avoids the shortcomings of both the fragmented legislative practices of the United States and the overly centralized policies of previous German governments. Because the Bundesrat is also concerned with shaping the framework of implementation, its role is more purposeful than that of the U.S. Congress, where laws that overlap or contradict previous legislation are frequently passed. For example, the Bundesrat coordinates the link between regional and national economic policies, vocational education systems, and a major television network (ARD). Unlike the Imperial and Weimar systems, in which Prussia dominated, the Bundesrat tends to be closer to the concerns and needs of the entire country and provides a forum for understanding how national legislation will affect each of the eleven *Laender*.

The Judiciary

The role of the judiciary has always been and continues to be a strong one. The historically deep involvement of the state in most political and economic matters necessitates an extensive set of rules to define its wide-ranging powers. This historical relationship between the state administration and the judiciary was an extremely close one, yet it engendered many abuses. During the Imperial period, the court system was used to safeguard the privileged position of those in power (e.g., failing to rule against the Reichstag voting system, which allowed the small number of Prussian estate owners to have a majority of power). During the Weimar period, the courts ruled against the workers' councils' demands for increased power within the workplace. Hitler abused the court system extensively during the Nazi regime, inducing it to make a wide range of antidemocratic and repressive decisions, such as banning non-Nazi parties, allowing the seizure of Jewish property, and allowing millions to be sent to the concentration camps.

The founders of the postwar government were most concerned that the new judicial system avoid these earlier abuses. One of the first requirements was that the judiciary explicitly safeguard the democratic rights of individuals, groups, and political parties, stressing some of the individual freedoms long associated with the U.S. and British legal systems. In fact, the Basic Law contains a more elaborate and explicit statement of individual rights than exists in either the U.S. Constitution or the British common law.

Yet the West German legal system does not follow the models. The Anglo-Saxon legal system is characterized by adversarial relationships between contending parties, in which the judge (or the court itself) merely provides the arena for the struggle to take place; the courts are essentially a neutral arbiter of an ad hoc system of laws. In West Germany, on the other hand, the judiciary is an active administrator of the law and has a different relationship with the state in the adjudication of cases. This judicial system, perhaps the most far-reaching in Western Europe, relies on the "capacity" of the state (as political sociologist Theda Skocpol terms it) to identify and implement certain important societal goals.[2] If the task of the state is to create the laws to attain these goals, then the judiciary must safeguard their implementation. In both defining the meaning of very complex laws and implementing their administration, West German courts have far greater power than their counterparts in the United States. Their role in shaping policy was most evident in the 1976 ruling on increased codetermination (worker participation) rights. The court allowed the unions to obtain near-parity on the boards of directors but stated that full union parity with the employers would compromise the rights of private property.

The court system has three branches. The criminal/civil system, which is headed by the *Bundesgerichtshof,* "Federal High Court," is a unified rather than a federal system and, therefore, is not subject to the *Land* governments' control. The Federal High Court not only handles criminal and civil cases but also hears disputes between the federal government and the *Laender* (and among the *Laender* themselves) and makes decisions that are clearly political. The *Bundesverfassungsgericht,* "Special Constitutional Court," deals with matters directly relating to the Basic Law. Its most notable decisions in the 1950s included banning both the ultra-right Socialist Reich Party and the Communist Party as forces hostile to the Basic Law. During the early 1970s, when the Radicals Decree was promulgated, the Special Constitutional Court ruled on several individuals who lost their jobs because they were seen as "enemies of the constitution." During the terrorist wave of the late 1970s, this court again was pressed into service to pass judgment on the undemocratic actions of the terrorists. The *Bundesverwaltungsgericht,* "Administrative Court," is the third branch of the court system and consists of the Labor

Court and the Finance Court. The Administrative Court is more concerned with the implementation of particular laws than the other two courts. In contrast to the Bundesrat, which concerns itself with the implementation of the law within geographical boundaries, the Administrative Court deals with functional boundaries and serves as a middle-level institutional layer linking national governmental institutions and individual laws.

Regional and Local Government

Regional and local governments have enjoyed substantial authority and autonomy in the postwar federal system. This tradition of strong public-sector involvement in economic growth and development dates back to the years before the unification of Germany. In the late eighteenth and early nineteenth centuries, cities and states developed governmental systems that provided for their material and social needs. The cities of Bremen and Hamburg remain city-states; even today they have overlapping municipal and *Land* governments. Because each of the cities and states had different material needs and social circumstances, local governments could do a more effective job of fulfilling needs than a central state. While Bismarck's welfare-state measures brought economies of scale to those programs that needed to be implemented on a national basis, regional and local governments continued to provide for certain specific needs.

West German regional and local governments differ from those in the United States in their capacity to raise revenues by owning enterprises, dwarfing those abilities of equivalent governments in the United States. For example, there is a wide degree of local and regional ownership of revenue generating enterprises. This has been due, in part, to the historical patterns of public-sector involvement in the economy but has also sprung from the belief that these levels of government are the stewards of the public good. The maintenance of art museums, theater companies, television and radio networks, recreational facilities, and housing complexes are seen as local and regional measures crucial to the quality of life in modern West German society. Even during the recession in the early 1980s, there were remarkably few cutbacks in either the ownership of public enterprises or various types of social spending.

West German regional and local governments also differ from those in the United States in the nature of their politics. In the United States, state and local politics often revolve around personalities or issues of only narrow parochial interest. This is partially due to the fragmentation of the U.S. political party system in which national parties often have very little to do with local issues. In the Federal Republic, state and city politics are organized on the same basis as the national parties, though they are not dominated by national politics. Rather, voters are able to see the connection among local, regional, and national issues in ways that enhance both unity and diversity in the political system. Because the parties take positions and establish platforms for state and city elections, voters can discern the differences between parties, not just between personalities. Not surprisingly, voter turnout in West German state and city elections is very high, particularly when compared with equivalent U.S. elections.

Para-Public Agencies

Para-public agencies exercise both public and private responsibilities; they shape, direct, implement, and diffuse West German public policy. The central state was discredited in the late 1940s, due to the excesses of Nazism and to the U.S. occupation authorities, who had a strong affinity for the private sector. West Germans faced a dilemma: How would they rebuild their society if a strong public-sector role was ruled out? The answer was to return to those nineteenth-century institutions that blurred the differences between the public and private sectors. These institutions have played a crucial role in the West German political economy, one that has been long unrecognized.

Political scientist Peter Katzenstein has written extensively about para-public agencies, which he calls "detached institutions."[3] He sees them primarily as mediating entities that reduce the influence of the central state. Katzenstein finds that they tend to work best in areas of social and economic policy and less well in their interaction with the university system. Among the most important para-public agencies are the Chambers of Industry, the Council of Economic Advisors (known as the Five Wise Men), and the institutions of worker participation (Co-determination and the Works Councils). Even parts of the welfare system are run on a para-public basis, since the distributional system is organized along functional lines in welfare associations. The Federal Reserve System is the most influential of these para-public agencies: It received some 35 billion deutsche marks from the federal government in 1984. The Federal Reserve was established during the 1920s and is an extremely powerful institution with close contacts to the commercial banks. In 1972, Karl Klasen, as the head of the system, was able to force the well-known economist Karl Schiller out of the Brandt cabinet. Schiller's position, according to Klasen, meant that there was "too much power in the government and not enough in the Fed."

The Policy Process

This chapter has detailed the functions and performance of the country's major governmental and quasi-governmental institutions, many of which are perceived as overly legalistic and bureaucratic. From the founders' efforts to establish representative institutions, a system of complex relationships among the executive, legislative, and judicial branches, and of overlapping jurisdictions among the central state, the regional and local governments, and the para-public agencies has evolved. Can this system produce effective policies?

During the past thirty-five years, governmental policies have been seen as both useful and appropriate by a majority of the population a majority of the time. The period after 1980, however, has tempered some of this support. Persistent unemployment and minor cutbacks in some welfare-state benefits have concerned those who fear the eventual creation of a "two-thirds society," in which the majority has access to welfare-state benefits, but a significant minority remains excluded. However, the policy process in West Germany has proved far more stable than in other Western European countries. Certainly the common experience of working for reconstruction during the 1950s supported this pattern, as did the desire to institutionalize democracy in a country that has had far too little democratic experience in the past. This spirit of working towards a common social goal is reflected in the concept of state "capacity," the belief held by *Beamten,* "civil servants," that they are working for the public good. While West German civil servants have had a reputation for being inflexible and rigid in the performance of their duties, they have retained a sense of pride and importance in their work. Further, there are certain crucial functions, they believe, that can be performed only by the public sector.

These views of the state's proper role are also shared by the public at large, regardless of the party in power. Thus, the West German state continues to perform functions that have been "reprivatized" in both Britain and the United States in the 1980s. A strong confidence in the policy process of the system endures among almost all political parties and interest groups. The trade unions frequently lobby both conservative and socialist governments for additional programs or benefits, referring to the state as *Dieser, unser Staat,* "this, our state." This view differs fundamentally from the current attitude in the United States, where politicians speak of "getting the government off the backs of the people."

Notes

1. For two important accounts of the initial uncertainty about the stability of German democracy after World War II, see: Gerhard Ritter, *The German Problem* (Columbus: Ohio State University Press, 1965); and Ralf Dahrendorf, *Society and Democracy in Germany* (New York: Anchor, 1969).
2. For a theoretical discussion of this theme, see: Theda Skocpol, "Bringing the State Back In: Strategies of Analysis in Current Research," in *Bringing the State Back In,* ed. Peter B. Evans, Dietrich Rueschemeyer, and Theda Skocpol (Cambridge: Cambridge University Press, 1985), pp. 3–43.
3. See: Peter Katzenstein, *The Semi-Sovereign State* (Philadelphia: Temple University Press, 1987). Forthcoming.

Social and Political Forces

The Party System

In earlier chapters we have seen that the party system in West Germany has been not only comparatively stable but also tightly organized and ideologically coherent. In this chapter, we will look more closely at the parties to examine their institutional evolution, their coalition patterns, and their general political strategies.

Table 14.1 Elections to the Bundestag (1949–83) (percentages of list vote)

	1949	1953	1957	1961	1965	1969	1972	1976	1980	1983
CDU/CSU	31.0	45.2	50.2	45.3	47.6	46.1	44.9	48.6	44.5	48.8
SPD	29.2	28.8	31.8	36.2	39.3	42.7	45.8	42.6	42.9	38.2
FDP	11.9	9.5	7.7	12.8	9.5	5.8	8.4	7.9	10.6	6.9
Greens	—	—	—	—	—	—	—	—	1.5	5.6
Refugee parties	4.0	9.1	8.0	2.8	—	0.1	—	—	—	—
Communist parties	5.7	2.2	—	1.9	1.3	0.6	0.3	0.4	0.2	0.2
Neo-Nazi parties	1.8	1.1	1.0	0.8	2.0	4.3	0.6	0.3	0.2	0.2
Other parties	16.4	4.1	1.3	0.2	0.3	0.4	—	0.2	0.1	0.1

SOURCE Peter J. Katzenstein, *The Semi-Sovereign State* (Philadelphia: Temple University Press, 1987.) Forthcoming.

The Communist Party

West Germany is one of the few Western industrialized countries that does not have a significant communist party. This absence is all the more striking given the importance of the *Kommunististische Partei Deutschlands* (KPD) during the Weimar period. The KPD split from the Social Democratic Party (SPD) in 1919, following the success of the Russian Revolution. Similar splits took place in most labor, socialist, and social democratic parties at that time. During the 1920s, the KPD received as high as 15 percent of the vote and represented a major challenge to the SPD from the left as the latter struggled with the reins of government during the early Weimar years. For most of the 1920s, the KPD was a rather dogmatic communist party, following quite closely the dictates of the Communist Party of the Soviet Union. Not surprisingly, the KPD frequently attacked the SPD, declaring its members "social fascists" for their lack of revolutionary vigor in confronting the Nazis. In fact, this disagreement between the two Left parties, SPD and KPD, enabled the Nazis to undermine the Weimar regime and seize power.

Following World War II, the KPD reappeared only briefly in West Germany and eventually disappeared in 1956, when it was banned by the Special Constitutional Court. Several factors were responsible for its demise. Prior to Hitler's rise to power in 1933, a major area of KPD support was in the northeastern part of Germany. After World War II, this area became the German Democratic Republic (GDR), or communist East Germany. Within the newly defined West Germany, there remained a much smaller constituency for the KPD. In addition, the onset of the Cold War in the late 1940s seriously eroded its support in West Germany, although the party did receive 5.7 percent of the vote in the first postwar election in 1949. However, the intensity of anticommunist sentiment was particularly damaging to the KPD in West Germany. The accounts given by refugees and expellees upon their emigration — stories of forced migration of ethnic Germans from what was now Poland to the newly formed East Germany, confiscation of property, and general ill-treatment by the Soviet occupation armies — further impeded the KPD's ability to garner support during the early 1950s. West German leaders took advantage of these accounts to propagandize against communism.

Some members of the KPD organized the *Deutsche Kommunistische Partei* (DKP) following the 1956 ban, but the new Communist Party received even less support than the KPD. In 1968, the ban on the KPD was lifted, and its name was appropriated by Maoists and the New Left. It had a brief period of influence during the social turbulence of the late 1960s, but it split in the early 1970s, and a Marxist-Leninist KPD appeared. By the late 1970s, there were numerous tiny communist parties and sects, none of which came close to achieving even 5 percent of the electoral vote. By the early 1980s, many of the sects had officially disappeared, with many former members occupying a minority wing within the Greens.

The Social Democratic Party

As the other, more influential party of the Left in Germany, the *Sozialdemokratische Partei Deutschlands* (SPD) has had a longer and more durable history. The SPD was founded in the 1860s in response to rapid German (Prussian) industrialization, survived Bismarck's attacks in the 1880s, and grew to be the largest party in the Reichstag by 1912. The party was badly split by World War I, however, with the more evolutionary wing supporting the war and the Imperial government, and the revolutionary wing viewing the war as an opportunity to defeat capitalism in all countries. In the latter view, support of bourgeois governments' war efforts represented a fundamental betrayal of the international working class. Following World War I, the evolutionary Socialists who controlled the SPD helped it become the leading party of the Weimar Republic during the early years of the regime. The revolutionary Socialists joined either the KPD or the short-lived Independent Socialists (USPD), a party that only lasted until the early 1920s. Such splits among the left-wing parties proved fatal for the SPD in the Weimar period. The lack of a united Left prevented a clear response to growing economic and social turmoil and thereby indirectly helped the Nazis find a path to power.

When the SPD reemerged after 1945, it was initially in a strong position to play a dominant role in rebuilding West Germany. Industrialists and the conservative Weimar parties had been discredited due to their relationship with the Nazis, and the SPD retained its evolutionary commitment to both democracy and socialism. In the immediate postwar years, the SPD, under the leadership of Kurt Schumacher, led the call for nationalization of industry under democratic control, provision of welfare-state measures to rebuild the country, and a return to the participatory workplace structures (e.g., the workers' councils) that had been curtailed by the early Weimar governments.

Despite its strong influence from 1945 to 1948, the SPD was able to attain only 30 percent of the electorate from 1949 until the early 1960s. Some critics observed that the party's inability to achieve wider influence resulted from its continued emphasis on its working-class origins and reliance on a Marxist-based ideology. Observers more sympathetic to the SPD believed that the Cold War, the Communist GDR just to the east, and the economic miracle of the 1950s all played major roles in reducing the party's influence. In any event, the SPD — although a major party — was politically frozen out in the 1950s: The party formed municipal governments in a few of the major cities and regional governments in several traditionally socialist northwestern *Laender,* but it attained little national influence.

In an attempt to broaden its constituency, the SPD altered its party program at a 1959 party conference in Bad Godesberg. Yielding its heavy reliance on Marxism, the SPD sought to become what political scientist Otto Kirchheimer has called a "catch-all party."[1] The SPD neither relinquished Marxism completely nor ceased to be a party representing the working class. It also began to see itself as able to attract support from groups outside the traditional working class: service-sector workers, elements of the middle class, professional employees, and less conservative members of the Free Democrats or Christian Democrats. The Bad Godesberg conference transformed the SPD into a party more like other Western European social democratic parties.

This change in strategy proved successful. The SPD's percentage of the vote in the national elections of 1961 and 1965 increased to 36 percent and 39 percent, respectively. The 1965 election provided the party with enough strength to enter the government in 1966 as a member of the Grand Coalition with the CDU/CSU. The change in overall SPD strategy also brought to national prominence such regional leaders as Willy Brandt, who was the mayor of West Berlin during the early 1960s, and Helmut Schmidt, who was one of the leaders of the SPD in Hamburg. Yet, in moving away from a strongly Marxist philosophy, the party angered many left-wing supporters who felt that the SPD had compromised its long-standing principles. These suspicions were confirmed when the SPD entered into the Grand Coalition with the CDU/CSU. According to the left-wing SPD members, there was no longer an effective opposition party, so many leftists became part of the Extra-parliamentary Opposition (APO) during the late 1960s. The APO mobilized against the Grand Coalition's support of the U.S. policies in Vietnam, the elitist and inaccessible higher education system, and the distortion of social priorities that accompanied economic growth of the late 1960s. By 1968, the APO became an increasingly thorny problem for the government, especially for the SPD.

This pressure on the SPD, as well as a general incompatibility between the SPD and the Christian Democrats, brought about the demise of the Grand Coalition and the call for new elections in 1969. The SPD increased its share of the vote to 42.7 percent and thus was able to propose a new coalition government with the FDP, which had received 5.8 percent of the vote. (Although the two parties had less than 50 percent of the popular vote, they attained a bare majority of the apportioned Bundestag seats after the parties with fewer than 5 percent of the vote were discounted.)

The center-Left SPD–FDP coalition appeared shaky at first — the coalition held a slim majority until its reelection in 1972 — but it was able to stay in power for thirteen years. The SPD brought to the coalition its concern for increased social-welfare spending, and the FDP brought its support for increased individual freedom of expression at a time when youth in all industrialized societies were raising these issues. However, the one factor that helped to cement together the interests of these two dissimilar parties for such a long time was the strong performance of the West German economy. In fact, the coalition came apart in the early 1980s when an economic recession prevented the increased social spending demanded by the SPD's left wing and induced the FDP to define individualism less in terms of free expression and more in terms of an antistatist, free-market economic position.

The Free Democratic Party

The political views of the postwar FDP have drawn on the remnants of the nineteenth-century liberal movement that was defeated in the failed bourgeois revolution of 1848. The FDP philosophy is Germany's closest equivalent to the individualistic emphasis of British and American liberal parties. (Here *liberal* is used in the European context to mean an emphasis on the individual as opposed to an activist state tradition. We do not mean "liberal" in its U.S. sense, which has come to be associated with personal freedom for individuals [i.e. "permissiveness"] and a relatively active — by U.S. standards — welfare state.)

Due to Germany's strong collectivist traditions, the FDP's liberalism won comparatively little support during the pre-1945 period. Since 1945, however, the party's political influence has been disproportionately greater than its electoral strength of 5 to 10 percent of the voters, mainly due to the discrediting of the central state after the Nazi abuses, the role of the U.S. occupation forces and their preference for free-market economic arrangements, and the effects of the Cold War. These factors increased the influence of nonleftist parties in the eyes of both the Allied powers and the West German people.

The FDP's perspective is an expression of two ideologies, broadly characterized here as economic liberalism and social liberalism. During the postwar period, the FDP has relied on both of these philosophies to ally with the two major political groupings, the CDU/CSU and the SPD. In fact, the FDP has been out of the cabinet only twice since 1949: during the CDU/CSU majority from 1957–61, and during the Grand Coalition from 1966–69. Moreover, the FDP has almost always had control of either the Economics Ministry or the Foreign Ministry during the various coalition governments.

The party has carefully nurtured its centrist position in West German politics by utilizing one or another of its political leanings to soften the ideological profile of the major party with which it is allied at the time. For example, during the latter years of the center-Left Schmidt governments in the late 1970s and early 1980s, the FDP acted as a strong counterweight to the SPD's rank-and-file demands for more public spending. In fact, many SPD members described the FDP as the "tail that wagged the (SPD) dog." On the other hand, after 1983, during the center-Right Kohl government, the FDP resisted the CDU/CSU's attempts to increase the government's domestic surveillance of West German citizens.

By adopting a strategy of coalescing with first one major party and then the other, the FDP occasionally has been accused of lacking strong political conviction. Critics view the FDP as a small collection of notables whose adherence to the party has been as a vehicle to gain important cabinet posts. Each time this accusation is made — generally after a change of government — it seems that the FDP will so disillusion its voters as to fall below the 5 percent of the vote necessary for representation in the Bundestag. In fact, during the early and mid-1980s, the FDP failed to reach the 5 percent minimum in several *Land* elections. However, West German voters generally have been reluctant to give either of the two large party groupings an absolute majority, and they turn to the FDP as a buffer against the ideological extremes of the SPD and the CDU/CSU.

The Christian Democrats

The Christian Democrats combine the Christian Democratic Union (found in all *Laender* except Bavaria) and the Christian Social Union (the affiliated Bavarian grouping). Unlike the parties mentioned above, the CDU/CSU originated immediately following World War II, when most nonleftist parties wished to avoid the bickering and divisiveness of the Weimar period and establish a counterweight to the SPD (and, at first, the KPD). Just as the Left was divided during the Weimar regime, so too were the centrist and non-Nazi rightist parties fragmented during the 1918–33 period, forming a variety of groupings: the Catholic Center Party; a nationalist party; a conservative party; and parties representing farming interests. To the right of all of them were, of course, the Nazis.

The moderate leaders of the nonleftist parties feared that after the war, the SPD (with or without the KPD) would represent a partially united Left, while the forces of the Right would be both fragmented and discredited due to their close ties with the Nazis. Consequently, several of these moderate conservatives proposed the creation of a Christian party grouping, which would not only finally unite Catholics and Protestants in one confessional (Christian) party but also serve as a catch-all party of the center-Right, incorporating the various nonleftist elements (including "rehabilitated" ex-Nazis).

A key component to the success of this strategy was the presence of a moderately conservative leader who would be both effective at brokering the interests of the various moderate and conservative groups and personally untainted by a close association with the Nazis. The most obvious choice was Konrad Adenauer, the former mayor of Cologne. Nicknamed *Der Alte,* "the old man," Adenauer had a generally favorable record of opposing the Nazis prior to 1933 and remained untainted by the Nazis during the Third Reich. He was also politically experienced enough to hold together the various conservative factions. This combination of attributes benefitted the CDU/CSU from 1948–49 on, for two reasons: the Allies preferred to deal with dependable, nonleftist political leaders; and the CDU/CSU had to attract the support of the voters from the smaller, conservative parties in order to win the required 5 percent of the vote.

Programmatically, the CDU/CSU performed these tasks through the *Sozialemarktwirtschaft,* "social market economy." The social market economy was neither a social-democratic system (such as contemporary Sweden) nor a pure market economy (as expounded by Ronald Reagan and Margaret Thatcher), but it blended elements of both forms to create a society that was not only capitalist but also had a paternalistic sense of social responsibility. In fact, this synthesis joined the interests of a wide range of the party's supporters. The most active supporter of the market side of the equation was Adenauer's economics minister for most of the 1950s (and later chancellor), Ludwig Erhard. Favoring the social side were the Christian trade unionists, whose ideology derived both from the Catholic tradition that celebrated the value of human work and the Protestant work ethic.

Drawing together these diverse perspectives, the party proved successful throughout the 1950s and early 1960s. Yet as Adenauer aged and as economic conditions changed in the early 1960s (e.g., the tightening of the labor market due to the building of the Berlin Wall in 1961 and the beginnings of a brief recession during 1961–63), he was replaced by Ludwig Erhard. As chancellor, Erhard was less effective than as economics minister, because his emphasis on the pure market side of the social market economy proved an inadequate remedy to increasing problems. Many industrialized countries had moved toward Keynesian demand-stimulation policies, and Erhard was reluctant to depart from his 1950s strategies. A more serious recession in 1966 forced Erhard from power and ushered in the Grand Coalition, led by Kurt Kiesinger, a Christian Democrat. Kiesinger was a weak chancellor and was soon eclipsed by the novelty of SPD participation and by the more dynamic presence of Grand Coalition Vice-Chancellor and Foreign Minister, Willy Brandt.

After the SPD and FDP established their center-Left coalition in 1969, the CSU/CSU spent thriteen years as the opposition party. During this period, the popularity of SPD policies and the unpopularity of the CDU/CSU leadership prevented the Christian Democrats from mounting a strong challenge to the SPD–FDP coalition. It was not until the SPD–FDP coalition collapsed in 1982 that the CDU/CSU returned to power with the FDP. However, the party's return had more to do with the failings of the SPD than any new, positive program of the Christian Democrats.

The Greens

In the 1980s, the realists (who thought it important to enter political institutions to gain access to power) won the upper hand in the Greens Party over the fundamentalists (who remained unalterably opposed to any collaboration with existing parties). The Greens' entry into a coalition with the SPD in Hesse state government in 1985 generated strong debate regarding the possibility of coalition with the SPD in other *Laender* and at the federal level. The Greens would have to examine some basic issues if they were to consider coalition with the SPD at the federal level, which was the only real coalition possibility.[2] Would it remain outside the party system and function only as a protest party, or would it, by joining forces with the SPD, attempt to attain some of its goals? The second option was no guarantee of long-term success, as all of the other parties began to include environmental and qualitative issues in their party programs. Moreover, in early 1986, SPD leaders stated that for the 1987 election, they would try to attain an absolute majority for themselves and thus bypass the Greens. While it seemed unlikely that this would occur, the Greens' position remained uncertain as the 1987 election approached.

Electoral Behavior

Voter participation is the most frequently cited aspect of electoral behavior in West Germany. It is considered high by Western European standards, and exceptionally high by U.S. standards. Since 1949, the participation rate in West Germany has averaged between 85 and 90 percent in federal elections and only slightly lower in regional and local elections. High voter participation in other countries is normally seen as an indication of a commitment to democracy, yet in Germany, it has been considered a commitment to duty. Some social scientists have, in fact, equated participation with political instability and cited the short-lived Weimar Republic as a prime example of high voter participation leading to undemocratic political outcomes. These social scientists examined voting patterns during Weimar and noted participation rates averaging between 80 and 90 percent, leading them to question the political stability of the postwar government.

Political sociologists, such as Seymour Martin Lipset[3] and Ralf Dahrendorf,[4] have been the leading proponents of this view. They have correlated the high voter participation during the Weimar years with the regime's high degree of political instability, and they have concluded that high participation is not necessarily a benchmark for democracy. In fact, both scholars have asserted that German voters participated in such high numbers out of traditionally strong nationalist feelings of obligation rather than out of any strong commitment to the workings of democracy. They implied that this sentiment has continued in the postwar period.

This explanation, however, does not apply to contemporary West Germany, particularly since the high level of participation has lasted almost three times longer than Weimar. Moreover, both Lipset's and Dahrendorf's survey data rely heavily on pre-1965 information. Not only have the high voting patterns continued from 1949 through the mid-1980s without political instability, but participatory democracy has also been attempted in several other social institutions. The upheavals of the late 1960s, primarily concerning the democratization of society, exemplify this trend. The mobilization of the student movement, the left-wing SPD members' attempts to work within the system, and the increased desire among workers for improved methods of participation would seem to call the Lipset/Dahrendorf argument into question. In each of these cases, the motivation for participation was not duty or obligation, but to increase democratization.

The Labor Movement

As a social force, the labor movement in West Germany has a more significant role than its counterparts in most other major Western European countries. As mentioned in Chapter 12, the trade unions' strong role has been enhanced by the works councils and codetermination (worker participation) arrangements. The labor movement has also enjoyed minimal interunion conflict: The one union/one industry and one union/one plant policies have corrected the problem of divisiveness that characterized the Weimar years.[5]

There are only seventeen unions in the largest West German labor organization, the *Deutsche Gewerkschaftsbund* (DGB), "German Trade Union Confederation," as compared with over one hundred in the U.S. AFL–CIO and over three hundred in the British Trades Union Congress. These seventeen unions have a total membership of 7.7 million workers, and the largest and most influential union is the *IG Metall,* "Metalworkers Union," which represents close to one-third of total union membership. *IG Metall* has organized all industries in which metal is used or fabricated, including steel, shipbuilding, machine tools, automobiles, and electronics. Even beyond its numerical strength, its presence in so many sectors has given *IG Metall* the dominent position in the union movement. The second largest union is the *Gewerkschaft Oeffentliche Dienste, Transport und Verkehr* (OeTV), "Public Service, Transport, and Communications Workers Union," which has been a visible presence in West German society, as many of its workers have direct contact with the public. Other influential unions include: the *IG Chemie, Papier und Keramik,* "Chemical, Paper, and Ceramics Workers Union," and the *Gewerkschaft Handel, Banken, und Versicherung* (HBV), "Trade, Bank, and Insurance Workers Union." There are also three smaller confederations outside the DGB, representing civil servants, salaried middle managers, and Christian workers, but they have much less influence than either the DGB or its affiliated unions.

The strength of the West German unions extends beyond the fact that they represent some 35 to 40 percent of the country's work force. They have maintained a strong social presence in the country as well, as evidenced by their informal influence both in the works councils and in other para-public institutions, such as those dealing with vocational education. The DGB also owns the fourth-largest bank in West Germany, the *Bank fuer Gemeinwirtschaft,* and the second-largest life insurance company, the *Volksfuersorglishche Lebensversicherung.* The unions' reputation during the 1980s, however, has been marred by an ongoing scandal involving *Neue Heimat,* a trade-union-owned housing construction company that has been the largest in West Germany. Some *Neue Heimat* officials had embezzled and misappropriated the company's funds.

The system of collective bargaining is both strong and flexible in its approach to labor issues. Since the late 1960s, wage-bargaining is undertaken on a yearly basis. The union in the strongest position, usually *IG Metall,* bargains with the employers first, while less-powerful unions follow *IG Metall's* lead. The unions engage in *Manteltarifverhandlungen,* "framework bargaining," on larger and more fundamental issues only once every five years. In 1984, *IG Metall* attempted to set a thirty-five-hour workweek through these framework negotiations. This dual system allows the unions to focus on wages without getting locked into unfavorable long-term contracts, and it provides the opportunity to address more qualitative, basic issues.

The Organization of Business

Compared to U.S. business, which stresses small firms competing in a largely domestically oriented economy, the West German business community is very tightly organized. In addition to the highly structured banking sector, West German employers and industries have created a series of associations to represent their collective interests. In the absence of strong state action in planning or economic policy, the *Verbaende,* "employer and industry associations," have become strategic economic actors. Comparable organizations in the United States generally act only as lobbying organizations or as interest groups, but their West German counterparts have a very different role. By implementing *Rahmenbedingungen,* "framework policies," and *Ordnungspolitik,* "the politics of industrial order," the associations have been instrumental in shaping and framing the external environment (i.e., relations with government and foreign competitors) for their members. In their ability to act at the "mesoeconomic" (industry) level, and not just at the microeconomic (firm) or macroeconomic (the entire economy) levels, they can address issues that are too difficult for firms to deal with on their own. And because their solutions deal with an effective response to the needs of certain industries, they have established considerable legitimacy among firms in the private sector.

The associations have earned a reputation for effectiveness in the private sector, especially in the following areas: performing market research for specific exporting industries, examining the raw-materials needs for an entire industry; acting as a mediator with the banks and the governments; and aggregating the interests of the employers in a given industry to enable them to negotiate with the trade unions that are organized on an industry basis. Significantly, these institutions are neither statist nor pure market: They are not government institutions, but they have tremendous power to act collectively and thereby guide the outcomes that the market will produce.

There are three main associations that organize West German business. the *Bundesverband der Deutschen Industrie* (BDI), "Federation of German Industry," has the most comprehensive view of the West German business interests. With its headquarters in Cologne, the BDI is organized into thirty-nine industry associations, which are further subdivided into several hundred branch and regional organizations. Together with the banking system, these industry-specific institutions represent a powerful tool used by West German business to identify and act upon its long-term needs. Political scientist Gerard Braunthal has pointed out that over 85 percent of West German firms (for a total of almost one hundred thousand) are members of the BDI.[6]

The *Bundesvereinigung der Deutschen Arbeitgeberverbaende* (BDA), "Federation of German Employers' Associations," addresses more practical, short-term needs. Located adjacent to the BDI in Cologne, the BDA is primarily concerned with collective-bargaining issues, conduct of employer actions during strikes, and legal issues surrounding such disputes. Over 80 percent of all German employers are represented in the BDA, including foreign multinationals. The BDA discourages its members from negotiating separately and thereby weakening the collective power of organized business. In 1979, the German Trade Union Confederation (DGB) accused the BDA of establishing boundaries that its members were not to exceed in their negotiations with the trade unions.

The *Deutscher Industrie und Handelstag* (DIHT), "Association of German Industry and Commerce," represents small business and thousands of craft producers. This institution provides a needed counterbalance for smaller businesses against the large firms represented by the BDI and BDA. Although many observers have identified large firms as the primary motor for growth in West Germany, economic performance has also depended heavily on the ability of small business to produce high-quality, specialized products.[7] The DIHT acts as the umbrella organization for the Chambers of Commerce, organizations that themselves are significant in both shaping regional economic policies and coordinating (with the participation of the unions) the vocational education system. The DIHT is organized regionally, with over sixty offices, and all small businesses are required to join.

Taken together, these associations have been a powerful force in aggregating the interests of West German business. They also represent the distinctly West German model of "organized capitalism," which does not fit the standard categories of market-dominated or state-dominated economy. While these institutions work within the constraints of a world market system, they differ profoundly from U.S. standards of free markets, in which antitrust legislation prohibits such collaboration among business associations. Rather they shape the market and guide its outcomes, and although their actions are codified in the elaborate West German legal system, they are not directed or controlled by the public sector.

Interest Groups

In West Germany, interest groups are seen as having a social responsibility that transcends the immediate interests of their members. In line with Germany's public law tradition, which gives private organizations a degree of social responsibility, interest groups are seen as part of the fabric of society and are virtually permanent institutions. They are especially valued for their ability to evolve and adapt to new issues. Unlike the U.S. system, which emphasizes competition in policy debates, this system creates a bounded framework within which interest groups will eventually come to an agreement on policy.[8] Moreover, they are encouraged to represent the aggregate interests of all their members, which ensures an institutional longevity that surpasses interest groups in most other industrialized countries. But how does the West German state mediate the relationships among interest groups?

Peter Katzenstein observes that in West Germany, "the state is not an actor but a series of relationships" and that these relationships are solidified in "para-public institutions."[9] The para-public institutions encompass a wide variety of organizations: the *Bundesbank* (Federal Reserve Bank), the institutions of codetermination, the labor courts, the social insurance funds, and the employment office. Katzenstein writes that these organizations are defined by law as "independent governance by the representatives of social sectors at the behest of or under the general supervision of the state." In other words, interest groups in West Germany are combined with certain quasi-governmental agencies; together, they perform a para-public role.

Employer associations and trade unions are the key interest groups within West Germany. Other, less influential, groups include the Protestant and Catholic churches; the *Deutscher Bauernverband* (DBV), "Farmers Association;" the *Handwerk Verein,* "Association of Artisans;" the *Bundesaerztekammer,* "Federal Chamber of Physicians;" and the now nearly defunct *Bund Vertriehenen Deutschen* (BVD), "League of Expelled Germans," which has represented the interests of emigrants from East Germany and Eastern Europe. Each of these groups has been tightly integrated into various para-public institutions to perform a range of important social functions, which, in other countries, might be performed by state agencies. These organizations are forced to assume a degree of social responsibility that goes beyond what political scientist Arnold Heidenheimer has called the "freewheeling competition of 'selfish' interest groups."[10]

These interest groups and the para-public agencies within which they function attempt to contain social conflict through multiple, small-scale "corporatist" institutions.[11] The West German corporatist variant in the 1980s is much more regionalized and industry-specific and much less centralized than earlier national-level forms of corporatism. Yet this interest group/para-public system is subject to the same problems that have plagued economy wide corporatism in other, more centralized, industrial societies, such as Sweden and France. A partial failure of certain interest groups and institutions to resolve conflict and represent their members led to the rise of social movements during the 1960s and 1970s, particularly concerning university reform, wage negotiations, and foreign policy. The Greens Party, which was formed in the 1980s, is a prime example of a movement that arose out of the inability of existing institutions to address, mediate, and solve contentious issues.

Social Movements

In the 1960s and 1970s, various social movements emerged in West Germany in response to issues of university reform, the role of radicals in the center-Left SPD–FDP government, nuclear power, and deployment of U.S. missiles in the country. These issues found political expression first through political organizations, such as the Extraparliamentary Opposition (APO); the *Jungsozialisten (Jusos)*, the youth wing of the SPD; the various *K-Gruppen* (small communist parties and/or sects); and, later, in the citizen action groups and the peace movement. In the late 1970s and early 1980s, these diverse social movements found expression in a political party, the Greens. Common to these groups was their desire to democratize the various public, para-public, and private institutions, as well as the existing political parties. The evolution of these issues into causes of significant social turmoil owes much to the failure of institutions to deal with the various demands raised by the new social movements.

By the late 1960s, the elitist educational system proved to be hopelessly unable to accommodate the influx of young people who were born after the war. Political scientist Joyce Mushaben has argued that at a time when the college-age group was expanding rapidly, the entrenched university and government bureaucracies resisted enlarging the capacity of the system.[12] It was only through the pressure of the APO, the student movement itself, and the more sympathetic SPD–FDP coalition government after 1969 that the university system was able to quadruple its student population by the mid-1970s.

The exclusion of radicals from certain positions in the SPD–FDP coalition government represents another example of institutional failure. Leftists who chose to work within the system were frustrated in their attempts to obtain employment in the public sector. Significant numbers of individuals were denied employment in a variety of professions because their backgrounds were deemed too radical by the government. In large measure, the failure of the center-Left Brandt government to open up its doors to include these individuals caused them to abandon the SPD for the new social movements and, eventually, the Greens.

The controversy over nuclear power and the deployment of additional U.S. missiles on the West German soil gained momentum in the mid-1980s, inspiring the formation of other movements to address additional issues. Because the SPD leadership had turned away from its left wing in the 1970s, it was insulated from the consequences of its decision to support nuclear power and the deployment of additional U.S. missiles. The SPD's eventual decision to oppose missile deployment came after Schmidt had lost power and, thus, too late to stem the tide of support that the Greens were able to attain on this issue. Many observers have argued that the growth of these new social movements has been due to the inability of various existing institutions and political parties to respond to "post-industrial" demands. However, the extent of influence of these movements remained unclear in the mid-1980s.

Political Culture

The pre-1945 political culture has changed in a number of significant ways in the postwar era. First, increased U.S. influence has tempered, although not overcome, the collectivist emphasis and brought individualist themes to West German politics. Second, extreme political forms — Nazism, and Soviet-style communism — are no longer significant in West German society. Third, the integration of West Germany into international institutions such as the EEC and NATO has helped solidify its position within the community of industrialized nations and thereby increased the Westernization of its political culture.

However, distinctly German characteristics remain. For a country that has experienced forty years of economic growth, expansion of social welfare, and institutionalization of parliamentary democracy, there remains a great deal of anxiety concerning political and economic stability. The collapse of Weimar and the rise of the Third Reich remain an important part of West Germany's political culture. In the 1960s and 1970s, political sociologists Lipset and Dahrendorf expressed uncertainty regarding West Germany's genuine commitment to democratic values.[13] Underlying such claims was the fear that any economic downturn could unleash antidemocratic forces demanding the restoration of social order on authoritarian terms.

Despite the accomplishments of German society since 1945, West Germans continue to express a pessimism that often seems misplaced to many non-Germans. Business's sensitivity to fluctuations in the world economy, the middle class's fear of inflation, strong apprehension by workers over persistent unemployment, and anxieties expressed by the Greens and alternative social movements over nuclear proliferation all represent examples of an uncertainty that pervades West German society. In some respects, however, these uncertainties may have made West Germany more adaptable to change in the 1970s and 1980s. As a variety of institutions — public, private, and para-public — become increasingly concerned with minimizing social disruption, they have also become more flexible and less authoritarian.

In sum, social forces in West Germany have been much more supportive of the political system during the years of the Bonn republic than during the Weimar regime. The political party system has seen its two most extreme parties disappear, and electoral behavior has supported democracy in far greater measure than at any other time in the country's history. Yet conflict has not disappeared: business and labor remain contentious, though they have created an institutional structure that seems to channel most conflicts constructively; and the para-public institutions try to mediate the concerns of interest groups and social movements in ways that include all elements of society. Some observers in West Germany, however, note that these institutions are not always completely responsive. Lastly, the political culture seems to have matured considerably since 1945, although the residual pessimism that remains seems unwarranted by the country's comparative economic and political successes.

NOTES

1. See: Otto Kirchheimer, "The Vanishing Opposition," in *Political Oppositions in Western Democracies,* ed. Robert Dahl (New Haven: Yale University Press, 1966).
2. See: Gerard Braunthal, "Economic Perspectives, Ideology, and Coalition-Building: Prospects for an SPD-Green Coalition" (Paper presented at the Conference of Europeanists, Washington, DC, October 18, 1985).
3. See: Seymour Martin Lipset, *Political Man* (New York: Anchor, 1960).
4. See: Ralf Dahrendorf, *Society and Democracy in Germany* (New York: Anchor, 1969.)
5. For a more extensive discussion of the labor movement, see: Andrei S. Markovits and Christopher S. Allen, "West Germany," in *Unions and Economic Crisis: Britain, West Germany and Sweden,* ed. Peter Gourevich et al. (London: George Allen and Unwin, 1984).
6. See: Gerard Braunthal, *The Federation of German Industry in Politics* (Ithaca: Cornell University Press, 1965). For a discussion of the industry associations for specific industries, see: Philippe Schmitter and Wolfgang Streeck, eds., *Private Interest Governments* (Beverly Hills: Sage, 1985).
7. For a discussion of "flexible specialization" in German industry, see: Michael Piore and Charles Sabel, *The Second Industrial Divide* (New York: Basic Books, 1984); and Horst Kern and Michael Schumann, *Das Ende der Arbeitsteilung?* (Munich: Beck, 1984).
8. For an interesting debate on the capacity of existing institutions to adapt, contrast the "positive" view: Albert O. Hirschman, *Exit, Voice, and Loyalty* (New Haven: Yale University Press, 1970); with the "negative" view: Mancur Olsen, *The Logic of Collective Action* (Cambridge: Harvard University Press, 1969).
9. See: Peter Katzenstein, *The Semi-Sovereign State.* (Philadelphia: Temple University Press, 1987). Forthcoming.

10. See Arnold Heidenheimer, *The Governments of Germany,* 3d ed. (New York: Crowell, 1971).
11. For an overview of the general debate on corporatism, see: Philippe C. Schmitter and Gerhard Lembruch, eds., *Trends Toward Corporatist Intermediation* (Beverly Hills: Sage, 1979). This earlier work concentrated on societal level and macro forms of corporatism. Schmitter's later work: Philippe C. Schmitter and Wolfgang Streeck, *Private Interest Governments;* comes closer to a description of the contemporary "meso," or intermediate-level corporatism found in West Germany.
12. See: Joyce Marie Mushaben, "The State v. the University: Juridicalization and the Politics of Higher Education at the Free University of Berlin, 1969–70" (Ph.D. dissertation, Indiana University, 1981).
13. See: Lipset, *Political Man;* and Dahrendorf, *Society and Democracy in Germany*.

15

West German Politics in Transition

The word *transition* implies a sense of movement or change from previous patterns. Over the long term, West Germany has made a major transition from the Imperial, Weimar, and Nazi periods. There are two important manifestations of this transition: first, the diminished role of the central state and the growth in influence of state governments, as well as para-public and private institutions; and, second, the solidification of a Western-style parliamentary democracy. Over the short term, West Germany has experienced comparatively little change during the period from the late 1960s to the mid-1980s.

The Emergence of the Kohl Government

In early October, 1982, the center-Left SPD–FDP government of Helmut Schmidt collapsed. The official cause of the coalition's demise was the desertion of the centrist FDP from the SPD, which was largely due to disagreements regarding economic policy. By late September, the CDU/CSU, led by Helmut Kohl, had made it clear that it would consider the possibility of embracing the FDP to form a new government. However, under the Basic Law's "constructive vote of no confidence," the FDP could not vote to bring down the existing coalition unless a center-Right

CDU/CSU–FDP coalition was assured. On October 2, 1982, the FDP joined the CDU/CSU, and thirteen years of center-Left government had come to an end.

The conservative press, as well as the center-Right coalition itself, nicknamed this change in government *Die Wende,* "the turnaround." The change in coalition caused sympathetic observers to believe that a major change in policy and ideological direction was also in the offing. For the previous two election campaigns, the CDU/CSU had used variants of the phrase "freedom instead of socialism" as an electoral slogan against the SPD, giving the impression that the new center-Right government would follow this ideology.

Recent changes of government in two of West Germany's major allies, Britain (1979) and the United States (1980), also implied that a turnaround would occur. In both countries, parties on the respective Left wings of the political spectrum had exhausted their effectiveness and were replaced by parties and leaders who first preached conservatism and then acted upon it. West German observers believed that political trends in their country would take a similar turn.

Two factors prevented a genuine turnaround from taking place as the Kohl government came to power: One was constitutional, and the other was programmatic. The nature of the change from a center-Left to a center-Right government was somewhat irregular in terms of constitutional procedures, because the prevailing practice for a change in regime was through the electoral mechanism. However, the Basic Law does provide for a change of government through the constructive vote of no confidence. In fact, the rise to power of the Grand Coalition in 1966 involved such a change, and the 1972 elections were held a year ahead of schedule because the Brandt-led SPD–FDP coalition was placed under extreme pressure from the Rainer Barzel–led CDU/CSU. The Brandt government had intentionally lost its majority in the Bundestag and wanted an election for a renewed popular mandate.

In late 1982, the new Kohl government, in an attempt to assure that its position was constitutionally legitimate, called for new elections in March, 1983. Kohl argued that he needed a popular mandate to implement new policies, and the FDP itself also felt the need for an electoral legitimation of its change in direction. Due to these constitutional concerns, the center-Right Kohl government had to mobilize for an election only five months after attaining office. In contrast, Kohl's fellow conservatives, Margaret Thatcher and Ronald Reagan, were able to implement new policy directions because they moved quickly as soon as they attained office. The Kohl government did not have the same opportunity to make major and rapid changes in policy directions.

The failure to make a sharp policy turnaround was also the result of programmatic factors. The Kohl government felt it needed a mandate because the center-Right coalition had developed no clear policy program. The "freedom instead of socialism" slogan was a rather vague concept on which to build a government. For one thing, the shift of the FDP from a left-facing to a right-facing direction took place relatively quickly in 1982; just two years earlier, during the 1980 elections, Schmidt had glowingly praised the role of the FDP as the anchor of the SPD–FDP coalition. Although the CDU/CSU benefited from the FDP's rapid shift in loyalties, it came to power more by default than from any distinct sense of its own purpose. In essence, the turnaround only denoted the end of the center-Left Keynesian synthesis rather than the beginning of a conservative mandate. Thus, neither before nor after Kohl's victory in the March, 1983, election was there a sharp push for the wholesale dismantling of the welfare state. In short, the lack of a clear policy program precluded any real turnaround.

While Willy Brandt's SPD–FDP government took office in 1969 in a wave of reform euphoria and Helmut Schmidt came to power in 1974 as an "economic helmsman" coming to the bridge as recession set in, Helmut Kohl's emergence as chancellor had no comparable theme. In fact, both inside and outside West Germany, journalists and social scientists overstated the degree to which there had been a true turnaround: The transition of West German politics in the mid-1980s was more apparent than real. This lack of programmatical clarity made the search for a new political accord among the center-Right parties all the more difficult to achieve.

Contemporary Politics: The Search for a New Accord

The 1983 election campaign served to obscure the lack of clear policy direction. The results showed that the new center-Right government was able to solidify its majority, but it did so by relying in large measure on electoral slogans promising a turnaround in government and attacking the socialism of the SPD. The CDU/CSU achieved almost 49 percent of the popular vote, while the FDP received 7 percent. The SPD, under the caretaker leadership of Hans Jochen Vogel, dropped to its lowest electoral total since 1961, achieving only 38 percent of the vote. The Greens made a major breakthrough with 5.6 percent of the vote, achieving seats in the Bundestag for the first time. On the face of these results, the center-Right coalition seemed to have attained the needed mandate. The reality was more complicated.

Far more significant than the electoral returns was the conflict among the three parties — CDU, CSU, and FDP — who were the nominal victors. Because there had been no agreement on a definitive set of policies prior to the election, strains that soon developed among the three parties had a centrifugal effect on the coalition.

The FDP was primarily concerned about electoral survival. In the five months between joining the CDU/CSU-led coalition and the election itself, the FDP had grown fearful that many of its voters, particularly those on the left wing of the party (i.e., the social liberals), would desert the party and leave it short of the 5 percent necessary for representation in the Bundestag. The party had already lost representation in several *Land* governments in state elections during 1982 and was wary of losing its presence on the national level.

The CDU also had reason for concern if the FDP did not make the 5 percent electoral threshold. In fact, Kohl decidedly did *not* want the CDU/CSU to attain an absolute majority, for fear of giving increased power to the CSU leader, Franz Josef Strauss. Kohl and Strauss had been at odds for many years over leadership of the Christian Democratic movement. In 1976, Strauss was the CDU/CSU chancellor candidate and had lost decisively to Helmut Schmidt's SPD–FDP coalition. Kohl was Schmidt's challenger in the 1980 election and suffered a similar fate. There have been important policy differences between the two men, particularly on such issues as relations with the Soviet Union, internal security, and labor law reform. In general, Kohl has been characterized as moderately conservative, while Strauss — on most, but not all, issues — has been further to the Right. However, a great deal of the animosity is personal. Kohl, from the state of Rhineland-Palatinate, and Strauss, from Bavaria, have very different leadership styles and their interaction frequently has been strained.

Kohl was successful in ensuring that the FDP attained the 5 percent of the vote necessary for representation in the Bundestag. He was thus able to gain allies within the coalition, as FDP leaders Hans Dietrich Genscher and Martin Bangemann were not Strauss supporters. Ironically, Kohl's tactics concerning the FDP (to prop up the centrist party in order to use it as a wedge against the CSU right wing) were a mirror image of the tactics used by Helmut Schmidt against the SPD left wing in 1980. At that time, Schmidt, fearful of the militancy of his party's left wing, urged some SPD voters to consider giving their second vote (i.e., the one for the party list) to the FDP for the "good of the coalition." Kohl essentially made the same case to some CDU voters on behalf of the FDP.

Yet in minimizing the threat from Strauss, Kohl created a new set of problems. By directly aiding the FDP, Kohl played into the hands of the economic liberals (fiscally conservative, in U.S. terms) who were in a dominant position within the party. These individualistic free-marketers subscribed to the theory that the Western European (and West German) recession was part of a broader "Eurosclerosis" (decline of Europe). In their view, West Germany was crippled by the lack of U.S.-style high technology, absence of venture capital, rigid labor laws, and an onerous welfare-state burden. Even CDU and CSU members began to pay more attention to these arguments, in light of the apparent U.S. successes under the Reagan administration in 1983 and 1984. During 1985, for example, the Kohl government sponsored conferences on how to attract and develop venture capital.

As this minority, "pure free-market" position developed within the coalition, the government's goal of a coherent economic policy became more difficult to achieve. In early 1986, the Kohl government, under pressure from the economic liberals, demanded that the labor law be altered to prevent workers who were locked out in the course of a labor dispute from receiving unemployment benefits. This change forced unions to pay strike benefits to locked-out as well as striking workers, thereby inhibiting the unions' ability to engage in strikes. This demand flew directly in the face of German "organized capital" and "social market economy" concepts. More traditional forces within the CDU and CSU (and within the business and banking communities) argued that West German economic policy should rely on prevailing financial and institutional patterns rather than emulate the United States, whose economy had a wholly different structure. To the extent that the West German economy bounced back somewhat in 1984 and 1985, this traditional viewpoint was correct.

These strident debates within the coalition had the effect of inhibiting the development of a distinct policy direction. One leading Christian Democrat stated in mid-1985 that the government's economic policy was "lacking in concepts."[1] Yet, as the economy improved slightly by mid-decade (despite persistently high unemployment, which continued to hover at the 8 percent mark), the government was quick to accept some of the credit for the improved performance without shouldering the blame for the joblessness.

Several other issues placed stress on the coalition during its first few years in office. In order to improve internal security, CDU Interior Minister Friedrich Zimmerman attempted to increase computerization of data on the activities of West German citizens. The FDP, still passionately committed to individual rights, resisted this effort strongly, and the resulting disagreement proved a source of embarrassment to the government coalition. A scandal developed in 1984 surrounding the CDU defense minister, Manfred Woerner, who was accused of withholding information regarding the homosexual liaisons of a West German army general. The FDP's concerns for personal freedom clashed with Christian views of traditional morality. In the spring of 1985, Chancellor Kohl and U.S. President Reagan's visit to a cemetery in Bitburg where a number of Nazi SS troops are buried caused tensions among coalition members, as well as substantial international consternation. Together, these actions called into question the capacity of the Kohl coalition government to take unified and effective action in a number of areas.

The government could claim some success, however, in withstanding the massive public demonstrations in the fall of 1983, when additional U.S. missiles were installed in West Germany. The government was also able to push through the beginnings of the American Strategic Defense Initiative (SDI), also known as "Star Wars," against the opposition of the SPD and the Greens. FPD party leader Martin Bangemann originally resisted the policy, but Kohl and the CDU were able to overcome his opposition.

For the most part, the search for a new political accord during the first few years of the Kohl center-Right coalition has proved a fitful one.

(Cartoon: Leger/Kölner Stadt-Anzeiger)

The tensions within the coalition made smooth patterns of agreement difficult; moreover, the lack of a clear policy trajectory from the outset, due to the need for one party to counter the interests of another, opened the door for further disagreements as new issues arose. However, the coalition was fortunate in that economic performance improved, although the government itself could not rightly claim credit for the positive change. Had there been no economic improvement, the center-Right coalition would have been much more unpopular and likely would have become increasingly divided.

Institutional Implications

While there was some economic improvement, the center-Right coalition had not produced a turnaround in the economy. In other Western European countries, the central state has played a stronger role in conducting policy in certain areas, but responsibility for the maintenance of short-term political and social continuity had evolved to other actors within West German society, namely, state governments and the wide variety of private and para-public institutions.[2] When these institutions worked well, the country was able to withstand uncertainty and tension without falling apart. This section examines three institutions — the banks, the *Land* governments, and the trade unions — as they have addressed three separate policy areas: venture capital, regional policies, and persistent structural unemployment. We will assess these institutions' short-term successes as well as their potential medium- and long-term limitations.

The Banks and Venture Capital

A standard criticism of the West German economy during the early 1980s pointed to its apparent inability to provide an adequate supply of venture capital for the development of high technology. The U.S. strategy was to allow the market to produce a variety of venture-capital firms for small high-technology companies. This "financially resource-intensive" model resulted in a number of spectacular successes as well as several dismal failures. The French and Japanese governments, on the other hand, encouraged their economics and research ministries to work together to provide the resources for new, high-technology investment. These countries also experienced both successes and failures.

West Germany avoided adopting either the pure market or statist approaches: The structure of West German capital financing, with its weakly developed stock market, precluded choosing the U.S. approach; and primary reliance on the *Bundesministerium fuer Forschung und Technologie* (BMFT), "Federal Ministry for Research and Technology," was problematic. Under pressure from the economic liberals, the government did not want this ministry to develop the wide-ranging capacities of its French and Japanese counterparts. The government also discouraged direct BMFT support because prevailing West German law on public-sector funding for such research required grant-receiving firms to include direct participation in the research by the often union-dominated works councils. Many firms preferred to have total control over this aspect of their business.

Consequently, West Germany has tended to rely for venture capital on a traditional source, namely, the large banks, which claim as their primary function the allocation of large amounts of capital. The Deutsche Bank, West Germany's largest, has established five in-house venture capital firms, given them seed capital to develop potentially successful ventures, and mobilized the full resources of the bank behind the ventures that appear the most promising, thereby wasting as few resources as possible.[3]

The major limitations of this approach involve questions of efficiency and political access. By the mid-1980s, it remained unclear whether a large institution like the Deutsche Bank could efficiently and quickly fund projects in the rapidly growing high-technology field. The banks, in turn, have argued that West Germany needs to apply high technologies in traditional industries (e.g., chemicals, automobiles, machine tools, and industrial electronics) rather than develop high technology for its own sake. The fact that industrial workers and the general public had no institutional political access to the decision-making process concerning the development of new technologies could be a problem. Not only would the banks be making explicitly political decisions, the exclusion of popular forces from the process could also provoke a technology backlash.

The Land *Governments and Regional Policy*

Part of the reason for the exhaustion of the center-Left SPD–FDP government in 1982 lay in the inability of the national government's policies to respond to the increasingly diverse structural problems within the economy. A sharp disparity in the performance of various industries had arisen, and the application of broad macroeconomic policies no longer had the same overall effect. Moreover, this imbalance involved more than just a few industries: Sectors such as steel, shipbuilding, and textiles were in deep decline; microelectronics and biotechnology were struggling to gain a foothold; and "fulcrum sectors," such as chemicals, automobiles, machine tools, and industrial electronics, were still relatively strong but undergoing major restructuring. In the late 1970s and early 1980s, the macroeconomic emphasis of the Schmidt government did not stress measures to differentiate among the needs of the various industries. After 1983, the Kohl government further discouraged explicit action by the national government.

This particular problem of imbalance did not involve just certain industries; the industries needing governmental assistance or promotion are concentrated in specific regions of the country, creating opportunities for the *Land* governments to become directly involved. In the absence of explicit industrial adjustment policies from the Kohl government, the *Laender* themselves began to produce programs geared to their particular regional needs. These *Land* governments had long histories of autonomy, and their ability to create concrete strategies of industrial adjustment in the mid-1980s represented an increase in their influence. Despite the successes of some regional governments, their diverse policies began to undercut the sense of common purpose that had been so important for social stability during the 1950s, 1960s, and 1970s.

The most active regional governments were the two southern *Laender:* Baden-Württemberg and Bavaria. Ironically, both states had long been governed by the CDU and the CSU, respectively. Both *Laender* had West Germany's lowest unemployment levels (that is, 4 percent and 6 percent in the mid-1980s) and consequently tended to have nonconfrontational relations with the trade unions. These two *Land* governments developed a plan to direct their support toward such areas as financing, vocational education, and export promotion. Northern *Laender* (e.g., North Rhine–Westphalia, which was governed by the SPD), tried to effect Social Democratic variations of these strategies, which gave greater input to the trade unions in the implementation of adjustment measures. Specifically, the SPD's close connection to the unions gave the latter influence on such issues as severance pay, retraining assistance, and alternative strategies that were more in line with union concerns. The SPD minister president for the *Land,* Johannes Rau, hoped to use any regional success achieved to his advantage in his candidacy for SPD chancellor in the 1987 federal elections.

The major limitations of these regional strategies lay in the very fact that they remained at a subnational level. The long-term danger was that due to the absence of framing, or coordinating, policy measures originating from the national government, West Germany might become a two-thirds society, in which a majority does well, but a marginalized minority is abandoned, without access to power or resources. The two northern *Laender* of Bremen and Lower Saxony had mid-1980s unemployment levels of 12 percent and 15 percent with apparently few opportunities to significantly reduce these levels. In sum, the success of regional policy seemed to be accompanied by a decline in a sense of common purpose, which had long been crucial to West Germany's social cohesion.

The Trade Unions and Structural Unemployment

From the early 1960s until the mid-1970s, West Germany enjoyed nearly full employment. During this fifteen-year period, unemployment rarely exceeded one to two percent. Yet when the oil crisis hit industrialized societies in the mid-1970s, unemployment increased to 4 – 5 percent; the second oil crisis of 1979 was followed by a prolonged recession in the early 1980s, and unemployment jumped again to 8 – 9 percent.

The usual response by trade unions is to demand that the government institute public works programs to aid the unemployed. The DGB and its constituent unions did just that, with moderate success, until 1978. However, the FDP's increased resistance to government spending gave the Schmidt center-Left government little room to maneuver. With the onset of the turnaround in late 1982, unions realized that they could not expect major expansionary measures from the CDU/CSU–FDP coalition.

As a result, the unions implemented the second part of the collective-bargaining law, the *Manteltarifvertrag,* "framework bargaining round," which once every five years allows the unions to bargain over broader, nonwage issues. *IG Metall* advocated reducing the workweek from forty to thirty-five hours, with no reduction in pay, as a way to reduce unemployment. If employers wanted to maintain production at previous levels, they would be forced to hire additional employees to offset the hours lost by the reduction in work time. After a metalworkers' strike during the late spring of 1984, the workweek was reduced to an average of 38.5 hours. The settlement did not produce the expected employment gains, however, for the reduction of only one-and-one-half hours per week was not enough to affect the employers' hiring patterns. Moreover, because the employer-union agreement did not stipulate how the workweek would be reduced, employers tended to increase production without hiring additional workers. The union had not bargained over plant production procedures, which was the only way that it could have forced the employers to add new positions.

The larger problem for *IG Metall* was that although it made creative use of one institution, it neglected the use of others. It had used the collective-bargaining laws to address a deficiency in governmental policy, but it did not adequately use the plant-level institutions of worker participation, the works councils, to place additional demands on how the workweek would be constituted. *IG Metall* had considerable influence inside the works councils of the Baden-Württemberg metalworking firms but neglected to play this card; it assumed that achieving an agreement for a reduction in the workweek was a guarantee of increased jobs and did not realize that an increase in jobs would also require challenging the employers' practices inside the plant.[4]

In conclusion, various regional and para-public institutions can work well, and through them, a number of social goals can be fulfilled. However, in the absence of more comprehensive, supportive, and framing policies at the national level, the fragmentary approaches taken by these institutions may not be sufficient to achieve as wide a range of objectives as would otherwise be possible.

New Policy Implications

Since 1945, governmental policies that have veered sharply to the Left or to the Right have not survived; consequently, any future West German governmental programs will likely fall within a familiar range.

The implementation of right-wing policies would first depend on a shared vision among the three parties of the Kohl government. The differences among the CDU, CSU, and FDP certainly will not soon disappear; in fact, their distinct positions may well be of short-term electoral help in appealing to a wide range of voters on the center-Right, who would be ill-disposed to vote for just one of these parties. Yet the CDU/CSU–FDP coalition's failure to agree on a course for West German conservatism may have serious medium- and long-term policy consequences. West Germany is a middle-rank industrial power; it must find a secure niche among the world's nations to survive. This may mean emulating smaller countries in Western Europe that have long understood the need to develop national policies for ensuring political stability.[5] The drifting economic policy of the current governing coalition will not ensure a strong West Germany in the future. Certainly the various institutions outside of the national level (regional and para-public) have taken some of the pressure off the Kohl government. However, too great a reliance on such institutions may prove costly when the construction of responsive national policies proves necessary.

The current center-Right government is plagued by an ideolological ambivalence about the proper role of the state. The FDP and those Christian Democrats who espouse conservative British and U.S. policies are predisposed to a reduced role for the public sector and for collective institutions in general. However, long-established patterns of conservatism reflect a more balanced relationship between the private and public sectors. This current ambivalence in eroding a conservative consensus may prove disastrous for the coalition and, perhaps, for the country.

The possibility of the ascendancy of a centrist government in the near future would involve the creation of either another SPD–FDP coalition or another CDU/CSU–SPD Grand Coalition. The former, at least in the mid-1980s, is most unlikely, and the latter would likely prove short-lived. A left-wing government could take two forms: an SPD majority or a "Red-Green" (SPD–Greens) coalition. Although only one party has received an absolute majority in the history of the republic — the CDU/CSU from 1957 to 1961 — the SPD hoped to achieve that feat in the 1987 federal elections. Both SPD leader Willy Brandt and chancellor-candidate Johannes Rau stated in early 1986 that they would prefer to govern without the Greens. In the 1985 *Land* elections in both North Rhine–Westphalia and Saarland, SPD candidates Johannes Rau and Oskar Lafontaine achieved absolute majorities. The SPD leadership hoped to repeat this success in the 1986 *Land* election in the economically depressed state of Lower Saxony, but fell short. As the 1987 election approached, the SPD hoped to use these examples to convince the voters that the party could benefit all of West Germany rather than just a few fortunate regions.

The SPD's electoral strategies were part of a broader self-assessment undertaken after the party left government in the fall of 1982. The SPD realized that it needed another formal party conference that would do for the party in the late 1980s and early 1990s what the Bad Godesberg program did for the party in the 1960s and 1970s. The predominant issue, particularly for Brandt, was how to retain a base among its traditional supporters — blue- and white-collar workers — while appealing to its "lost children" among the Greens. The success of this strategy remained to be seen in the mid-1980s; however, in the likely event that the SPD fails to achieve an absolute majority at the national level, a coalition with the Greens would be the only other left-wing option.

Although the SPD and the Greens worked together in some *Laender,* most notably in Hesse, the relationship between the two parties remained uneasy in the mid-1980s. The right wing of the SPD and the fundamentalist wing of the Greens, which represented major portions of the two parties, distrusted each other in important policy areas. While they generally agreed in their opposition to additional U.S. missiles on West German soil, they were sharply split on ecology and the economy. The Greens supported a decentralized economy, with a reliance on alternative, small-scale forms of production and a purist position on the abolishment of nuclear power. The SPD favored qualitative economic growth but argued that large West German firms and institutions should be subject to increased popular control, rather than broken up into smaller units. The SPD also favored moving away from a reliance on nuclear power, but it asserted that a sudden break would destabilize the economy.

Whatever Left policy direction might emerge, the wide-ranging left-wing must overcome resistance from business. The SPD–FDP coalition was able to achieve power mainly because the presence of the FDP legitimated the SPD for the business community. The possible reaction of business to either of the two left-wing government options remained uncertain in the mid-1980s; it might depend a great deal on the political constitution of governments in other Western European countries. If other major Western European countries also elect left-wing governments, the constraints faced by either an SPD majority or a Red-Green coalition might be somewhat different. One factor that has inhibited a broader left-wing movement in Western Europe has been the inability of the left-wing parties in the four major Western European countries — Britain, France, Italy and West Germany — to lead their respective governments at the same time. Yet even in such a hypothetical situation, a left-wing government in West Germany would still likely face considerable political obstacles from the business community.

Thus, any of the three options — Right, center, or Left — would face difficulties. Yet whichever of the three paths is to be taken, it will be made smoother by the multifaceted capacities of the country's various and powerful institutions, which would keep the transition within recognizable post-1945 bounds.

This assessment of the various political possibilities facing West Germany is particularly significant with respect to the short-term and long-term aspects of the current period of transition. In the short term, the range of possible policy options has narrowed considerably. Compared to the right-wing option in Britain or the potential left-wing option in Italy, West German politics have dramatically constrained the possibility of extreme outcomes. In that sense, the short-term transition in West Germany has not been extensive since the mid-1960s. In the long term, however, the transition has been substantial; the comparison between the pre- and post-1945 watershed is striking.

Transitional Tensions

The tension between nation and state, while still not resolved, given the continued division of Germany between East and West, is much less contentious than it was prior to the Third Reich. In fact, if some form of reconciliation is to take place between the two Germanies, it is likely to be gradual and to involve such forms as cultural exchanges and economic relations. Moreover, the postwar settlement, which introduced the modern welfare state and integrated West Germany into the family of Western European nations, also has acted as a sharp brake against serious conflict on nation/state issues. To the extent that the *Land* governments in West Germany have increased their autonomy, concerns over nationalism will likely diminish. If there is residual tension on this score, it concerns the growing disparity among the regions. Autonomy among the *Laender,* especially under Kohl, seems to have deflected attention away from national issues and may prevent the development of a national consensus in some areas.

The tension between capitalism and democracy has also been much smoother during the postwar period. Of particular importance is the role of skilled workers in the chemical, automobile, machine tool, and industrial electronics industries. These workers are seen as a natural resource, and the capacity of the unions and the various levels of government to enhance their craft skills via vocational education has been a particularly innovative development at a time when trade unions are under sharp attack in many other industrialized countries. Yet one should not over-estimate the apparent harmony among employers and unions due to the institutions of worker participation: The trade unions may be strong, but the power of organized capital, in the form of banks and associations, appears to be stronger. Moreover, considerable conflict remains, as evidenced by the six-week strike in the metalworking industries in 1984 and the sharp discussion in early 1986 over the cessation of unemployment benefits to workers locked out due to a strike by fellow workers. Although parliamentary democracy has found a solid base in West Germany for almost forty years, some tension between the role of the state and the rights of individuals remains. Despite attempts to democratize West German society, the role of the state remains entrenched in many areas.

Nonetheless, West German politics has made a substantial transition since 1945. Residual tensions remain, but they have been effectively kept in check by the powerful public and para-public institutions, and West Germany is firmly embedded among Western industrialized parliamentary democracies.

NOTES

1. CDU Official Olga Wilde, interview, Bonn, June 16, 1985.
2. See: Philippe Schmitter and Wolfgang Streeck, eds., *Private Interest Governments* (Beverly Hills: Sage, 1985); and Peter J. Katzenstein, *The Semi-Sovereign State* (Philadelphia: Temple University Press, 1987). Forthcoming.
3. See: "Der Riesen-Monopoly der Deutschen Bank," *Der Spiegel,* February 5, 1985, pp. 40–66.
4. For an excellent discussion on relations between *IG Metall* and the works councils, see: Kathleen Thelen, "Dilemmas of Dualism: *IG Metall* and the Works Councils" (Paper presented at the International Studies Association Convention, Anaheim, CA, March 29, 1986).
5. See: Peter J. Katzenstein, *Small States in World Markets* (Ithaca: Cornell University Press, 1985); and Gosta Esping Andersen, *Politics Against Markets* (Princeton: Princeton University Press, 1985).

Bibliography

Barraclough, Geoffrey. *An Introduction to Contemporary History* (New York: Penguin, 1967). Excellent book showing Germany's late — but intense — participation in nineteenth-century imperialism; also important for situating Europe in the world economy of the twentieth century.

———. *The Origins of Modern Germany* (London: Basil Blackwell, 1946). Tour-de-force of German history from the tenth to the twentieth centuries.

Braunthal, Gerard. "Economic Perspectives, Ideology, and Coalition-Building: Prospects for an SPD-Green Coalition" (Paper presented at the Conference of Europeanists, Washington, DC, October 18, 1985). Concise treatment of the possibilities of an SPD-Greens coalition.

———. *The Federation of German Industry in Politics* (Ithaca, NY: Cornell University Press, 1965). First major book on the politics of West German business after World War II.

Dahrendorf, Ralf. *Society and Democracy in Germany* (New York: Anchor, 1969). Famous work by a leading German liberal on the uncertainty of West German democracy.

Eley, Geoff. *Reshaping the German Right: Radical Nationalism and Political Change after Bismarck* (New Haven: Yale University Press, 1980). An important work showing that nineteenth-century late industrialization was due as much to the skills of German capitalists as to Bismarck's leadership.

Evans, Peter B., Dietrich Rueschemeyer, and Theda Skocpol, *Bringing the State Back In* (Cambridge: Cambridge University Press, 1985). Important series of articles on the capacity of advanced industrialized states to undertake structural and societal change.

Fichte, Johann Gottlieb. *Addresses to the German Nation* (Westport, CT: Greenwood Press, 1979). Overview of the philosophy of this important nineteenth-century German thinker.

Gerschenkron, Alexander. *Bread and Democracy in Germany* (New York: H. Fertig, 1966). The classic account of Germany's late industrialization.

Hegel, Georg Friedrich Wilhelm. *Political Writings* (New York: Garfield Publishers, 1984). Recent English-language sampler of Hegal's political philosophy.

Hilferding, Rudolf. *Finance Capital: A Study of the Latest Phase of Capitalist Development* (London: Routledge and Kegan Paul, 1981). Classic account of the banks' domination of the German political economy during the late nineteenth and early twentieth century.

Hirschman, Albert O. *Exit, Voice, and Loyalty* (New Haven: Yale University Press, 1970). Trailblazing work on institutional and organizational adaptation.

Inglehart, Ronald. *The Silent Revolution: Changing Values and Political Styles Among Western Publics* (Princeton: Princeton University Press, 1977). Major work on the politics of new social movements.

Katzenstein, Peter. *The Semi-Sovereign State* (Philadelphia: Temple University Press, 1987). Forthcoming. Major new work on West German political economy showing the crucial role of para-public institutions, which were essential for West Germany's adaptation to the postwar period.

———. *Small States in World Markets* (Ithaca: Cornell University Press, 1985). Deals with capacity of small European states to combine political stability with economic flexibility. Katzenstein argues that of the larger countries, West Germany comes closest to the small-state model.

Kirchheimer, Otto. "The Vanishing Opposition," in *Political Oppositions in Western Democracies,* ed. Robert Dahl (New Haven: Yale University Press, 1966). Well-known treatment of the "catch-all party" phenomenon.

Lipset, Seymour Martin. *Political Man* (New York: Anchor, 1960). Questions whether high participation is effective for democracy and introduces theme of "working-class authoritarianism."

Markovits, Andrei S., ed. *The Political Economy of* Modell Deutschland (New York: Praeger, 1982). Excellent series of articles on the success of the West German economic model during the 1970s.

Markovits, Andrei S., and Christopher S. Allen. "West Germany," in *Unions and Economic Crisis: Britain, West Germany and Sweden,* ed. Peter Gourevich et al. (London: George Allen and Unwin, 1984). The German portion of a two-volume work on Western European trade unions in the postwar period.

Moore, Barrington. *Social Origins of Dictatorship and Democracy* (Boston: Beacon Press, 1966).

Olsen, Mancur. *The Logic of Collective Action* (Cambridge: Harvard University Press, 1969). Critical analysis of institutions' capacity to adapt and evolve in a positive manner.

Piore, Michael, and Charles Sabel. *The Second Industrial Divide* (New York: Basic Books, 1984). Major work on the new system of "flexible system manufacturing," on which the German labor movement relies to maintain its workplace and political strength.

Ritter, Gerhard. *The German Problem* (Columbus: Ohio State University Press, 1965). Historical critique of Germany's shortcomings over many centuries.

Rosenberg, Hans. *Bureaucracy, Aristocracy, and Autocracy: The Prussian Experience, 1660–1815* (Boston: Beacon Press, 1966). Excellent short summary of the Prussian legacy.

Sabel, Charles. *Work and Politics* (Cambridge: Cambridge University Press, 1982). Important work outlining the foundations of the West German labor movement's response in the 1980s.

Schmitter, Phillippe C., and Gerhard Lembruch, eds. *Trends Toward Corporatist Intermediation* (Beverly Hills: Sage, 1979). Major treatment of corporatism at a national level.

Schmitter, Philippe, and Wolfgang Streeck, eds. *Private Interest Governments* (Los Angeles: Sage, 1985). Important book on the political influence of business within specific sectors of the economy.

Shirer, William. *The Rise and Fall of the Third Reich* (New York: Simon and Schuster, 1960). An exellent, popular account of the Nazi period.

PART

V

Italy

Stephen Hellman

16

The Emergence of the Modern Italian State

The Principles of Italian State Formation

The Legacy of Late Unification and Development

No country's political and economic development is free of problems, but few, if any, of the larger European nations faced as many serious difficulties in as short a time as did Italy. Unification was late, and it threw together an extremely diverse group of kingdoms, principalities, and dependencies. All of these areas lacked the principal resources for an industrial revolution. The North imposed a monarch, constitution, development policy, and ruling class that were at best ill-suited, and at times terribly inappropriate, to the needs of the rest of the country — particularly the South. Unity was imposed, often by force, against the opposition of the Catholic Church. The political system that evolved out of this tangle of problems side-stepped the development of broadly democratic rules and institutions in favor of keeping together a disintegrating regime. Reforms came too late to neutralize the polarization and fragmentation that had been at work for half a century, and the regime identified with the Liberal Party collapsed less than five years after World War I; five years after *that,* a full-fledged dictatorship was in place.

The Risorgimento

Like most of the rest of Europe, Italy was swept by several strong waves of nationalism in the first half of the nineteenth century, but these met with little initial success. At mid-century, the North remained divided between the Kingdom of Sardinia in the West (Piedmont and Liguria) and under Austrian occupation in the northern and eastern sectors (Lombardy and Venetia). In the North-Center, a number of small duchies and principalities led an uneasy existence. Across the entire middle of the boot, dominating most of central and some of northern Italy, were the Papal States, covering most of the area of the modern regions of Emilia-Romagna, Umbria, and the Marches, as well as parts of Latium. Just south of Rome, and embracing all of southern Italy plus the island of Sicily, was the Kingdom of the Two Sicilies — surrounded, as one of its rulers once put it, "by salt water on three sides and holy water on the fourth."[1] This was an extremely backward regime whose kings were descendants of the Spanish Bourbon monarchy.

The revolutionary upsurges of 1848 had led to local constitutional reforms and to short-lived republican governments in Venice and Rome, which were crushed, respectively, by the Austrian and French monarchies. More significantly, the revolutions led the Piedmontese king to send his army into Lombardy to drive out the Austrians — an act that excited Italian patriots and brought many of them north to join what they saw as a war of liberation. The Austrians, however, were victorious and quickly reestablished their rule.

The mainly middle-class movement of national resurgence, known as the *Risorgimento,* seemingly had little to cheer about as the second half of the century began. Its ranks included a wide range of views, from radical and anticlerical republicans to conservatives who thought that a confederation of the main states under the presidency of the pope was a realistic goal until the country was much more economically and politically mature. Earlier failures, however, laid the groundwork for future successes. The king of Piedmont, Victor Emmanuel II, and his skilled prime minister, Cavour, made clear that the elimination of Austrian influence remained a top priority, and they worked to reinforce Piedmont economically and diplomatically. The more moderate nationalists, attracted by Cavour's enlightened liberalism and the realistic possibility of success, joined together to back unification of the country under the Piedmontese monarch.

As would prove to be the case several times over the next decade, events were shaped by outside intervention. French arms proved decisive in forcing the Austrians to cede part of the northern territories to Victor Emmanuel II in 1859. In exchange, the Piedmontese gave the French the regions of Nice and Savoy. This made Napoleon III look the other way when the smaller principalities — and such important areas of the Papal States as Emilia and Romagna — revolted against their rulers and were annexed by Piedmont in 1860.

Victory for the Moderates. Later in 1860, the initiative temporarily slipped from the hands of the Piedmontese moderates. Giuseppe Garibaldi, undoubtedly the most colorful figure of the *Risorgimento,* landed with a thousand volunteers in western Sicily. Acting independently, but encouraged by the more radical leaders of the *Risorgimento,* he scored surprising military victories over the Bourbons. This in turn led to popular insurrections in major southern cities, and soon most of southern Italy as far as Naples was in Garibaldi's hands. The more democratic and republican of the nationalists had hoped to use the South as a bargaining chip to achieve the most advanced possible constitution for the new, unified state. But Cavour swiftly outmaneuvered Garibaldi and the more progressive forces. He moved the Piedmontese army south, annexing most of the Papal States but steering wide of Rome, with its French garrison. He also swiftly organized plebiscites by which the newly-liberated southern territories were joined to Victor Emmanuel's regime. In the end, what the Piedmontese did not win outright or gain due to foreign intervention came to them in fairly painless fashion.

A national parliament, elected by very limited suffrage, proclaimed the Kingdom of Italy in March, 1861. The first king of the new state, in a gesture that summarized for many the Piedmontese attitude toward the rest of the country, made no symbolic concessions and continued to call himself Victor Emmanuel *the Second.* In a similar vein, no new constitution was drawn up. The *Statuto albertino,* won by the Piedmontese in 1848, was extended over the whole country. (The constitution was named for King Charles Albert of Piedmont, Victor Emmanuel II's father.) It was a relatively enlightened document, but far less democratic than the ill-fated Roman and Venetian republican charters of 1848. It provided for a constitutional monarchy while leaving extensive powers in the hands of the king.

The remainder of the modern state, except for Trento and Trieste (which would be obtained at the end of World War I), was annexed with the assistance of Prussian military might. In 1866, Italy joined the Prussians in a war against Austria and obtained Venetia in spite of a conspicuous lack of success on the battlefield. In 1870, after Prussia defeated the French at Sedan, the garrison protecting Rome was withdrawn, and Italian troops were finally able to reclaim Italy's historic capital. This

0 100 Miles
0 100 Kilometers
AUSTRIA
SWITZERLAND
ALTO ADIGE
Bolzano
TRENTINO
FRIULI-VENEZIA GIULIA
Trento
ALPS
VALLE D'AOSTA
Aosta
LOMBARDY
Milan
VENETO
Venice
Trieste
Turin
PIEDMONT
Po
YUGOSLAVIA
Genoa
EMILIA-ROMAGNA
Bologna
LIGURIA
FRANCE
APPENINES
Florence
Ancona
Ligurian Sea
TUSCANY
MARCHE
Perugia
Adriatic Sea
Elba
UMBRIA
Corsica
L'Aquila
ABRUZZI
LATIUM
Vatican City
Rome
MOLISE
Campobasso
Bari
CAMPANIA
APULIA
Naples
Potenza
BASILICATA
SARDINIA
Gulf of Taranto
Tyrrhenian Sea
Cagliari
CALABRIA
Catanzaro
Palermo
MEDITERRANEAN SEA
SICILY
AFRICA
Boundaries of Regions
Italy

forcible annexation was viewed as a terrible insult to the church. Pope Pius IX, who had already shown his hostility toward liberalism, declared himself a prisoner in the Vatican and refused the symbolic guarantees offered by the new state. In a country where 99 percent of the population was nominally Catholic, the Vatican's rejection of the new regime created terrible problems. The more religious citizens and leaders had to follow the pope's lead, and thus remained outside, or on the margins of, Italian politics for many years. The more secular and modern elements, who were central to the *Risorgimento,* deeply resented the pope's rejection of all compromise. Many of those who already held anticlerical attitudes (such views were especially strong in the former Papal States, which had been very despotically governed) were thus reinforced in their views.

Even so rapid a summary reveals a great deal about the problems the new Italian state would face. Unification very suddenly brought together extremely diverse areas, with different social systems, cultures, and even languages — for most of the common people spoke regional or local dialects. The *Risorgimento* was a limited process in several senses: its protagonists were mainly from the very small middle classes; diplomacy and foreign action were decisive in its most significant victories; and it was more the extension of one region's hegemony over the rest of the country than the bonding together of a nation from its component parts. The largest social group, the peasantry, had been excluded from the movement and did not figure very prominently in the plans of those who now guided the state. The most important social institution, the church, had to be pushed aside for unification to take place, and it assumed a very hostile position toward the regime. Finally, the new leaders were in no hurry to extend democratic participation in a society in which somewhere between three and four of every five people were illiterate.

Economic and Class Relations

Especially in the first decades of the new state's existence, the economic policies put in place by Italy's leaders were a faithful reflection of their regional origins, class outlook, and classically liberal ideology. Even the politicians who were not members of the dominant Liberal Party embraced this ideology to a considerable degree. Liberalism, for these moderates, meant establishing the conditions for a (relatively) free market economy, in which property rights would be secure and the citizenry free from arbitrary interference from state or church. But the immense

The Unification of Italy, 1859–1870

problems facing Italy soon led those who governed the country to rethink their opposition to a more active economic role for the state. At the same time, the ruling elite was loathe to interfere with property relations already in place when changes would threaten the established social order. Because so large a portion of Italy was composed of peasants under highly oppressive conditions of land tenure, this extreme caution concerning the social question, as issues involving class relations were delicately known, left the new state with a legacy that would eventually contribute to its demise.

This social conservatism is nowhere more apparent than in the new state's agrarian policies, which avoided any hint of reform. The state had seized more than 2.5 million acres of land from various religious orders, particularly in the former Papal States, but in the South as well. It proceeded to sell these holdings, mainly to the urban and rural middle classes. It also left intact the large landholdings (*latifondia*) of the South, with their oppressive, often absentee, landlords. Peasant riots and rebellions in the South in the 1860s were brutally repressed by what increasingly became yet another army of occupation. It is an appalling, but telling, commentary on the unification of Italy to note that more people were killed in these episodes of "brigandage" — which were really extended guerrilla wars — than in all the wars of the *Risorgimento*.[2] To cement the link with the new and old landowning classes of the Center and South, a tariff to protect the cereals grown on their inefficient holdings was introduced — by a group, let us remember, that was otherwise strongly committed to liberal principles of free trade.

Once the southern landlords knew their own immediate interests were protected, they left the northern economic elite to pursue its own development policies. Not surprisingly, these policies favored northern — especially Piedmontese — industrial and agricultural production, at the expense of practically every other region of the country. Just as unification saw the monarchy and the *Statuto albertino* extended to the rest of the country, it also brought the "Sardinian" tariff to all Italy. This very abruptly lowered the protection previously enjoyed by struggling new industries in the more backward areas of the country. The tariff was intended, not to help nascent industry elsewhere in the country, but to open new markets for the more advanced industries of the North. That the industrial development of much of the rest of the country was actually *hurt* by this policy was clearly of little concern not only to the northern industrialists, but also to many of the true believers in "free" trade.

For a time, Cavour's successors (he died in 1861, shortly after the new state was created) followed the path originally set out by the founding moderate coalition. But by the mid-1870s, the drawbacks of limited state intervention in a country that had so much ground to make up were becoming increasingly apparent. The state, to this point, had restricted itself to imposing a very heavy tax burden on its citizens, which did little to win the allegiance of a largely alienated public.[3] It also undertook a series of public works projects, but some of these, such as the railroads, received decisive contributions from foreign and domestic industrial and financial interests. By the end of the 1870s, the great advances of the new German state were seen in many influential quarters as perhaps a more appropriate model for a new state to follow. Over the next decade, taxes were lightened and tariff barriers were erected at the same time that the state became a more active economic protagonist. By the end of the 1880s, Italy's new course was firmly set.

Class Structure and Class Relations

For all the discussion of industrialization and the development of heavy industry, it would be highly misleading to think of Italy, or even the North, as highly industrialized in the years prior to World War I. There were, to be sure, growing areas of modern industrial concentration in the North, especially around Turin, Genoa, and Milan. In the period immediately preceding World War I, there were about five million people employed in the industrial and transport sectors of the economy. But the country on the whole was overwhelmingly agricultural, and much of the industry that did exist was based on agricultural production. At the turn of the century, agriculture accounted for 51 percent of the gross national product and industry a scant 20 percent. Only 15 percent of the work force was engaged in industry, and that is with industry defined to include very small producers who often employed no workers at all.[4] In fact, it was not until 1930 that industrial output passed that of agriculture, and it was not until the *1950s* that there were more people employed in industry than in agriculture.

Equally important are Italy's staggering emigration figures in the first half-century following unity (and especially between 1871 and 1911). If the population of the country rose by roughly ten million up to World War I, we should keep in mind that the natural growth rate would have more than doubled this increase. In peak years, well over a half-million people left Italy (eight hundred thousand emigrated in 1913): the *net* emigration figures (i.e., subtracting those who returned), show a loss of six million people between 1901 and 1913.[5] Such massive migration, of course, affected the entire country but was greatest in agricultural areas, especially in the South. The outflow of so many people — most of them younger and able-bodied — had a distorting effect on the population that remained. The reduction of the potential work force also served as a social safety valve that was usually welcomed by both the local and national elites.

The agrarian question was made acute by the fact that the largest category (five million) of those employed on the land were *braccianti,* "day laborers." Not all were entirely without land, and a great many were in the South.[6] But there is one area in Italy where an extremely large number was to be found under very special conditions: in the Po Delta region, which is mainly in Emilia-Romagna. This is one of the only areas in Europe where the socialist movement encountered significant success in penetrating the countryside. This very early site of intensive and extensive commercial exploitation of the land was the source of one-third of Italy's agricultural production. The same conditions that generated such efficient exploitation of a fertile basin created a large and highly radical agricultural proletariat. Their collective form of work and the frequent, dramatic changes they witnessed in their own environment (radical crop changes, land reclamation and irrigation projects, and so on) gave these laborers a dynamic view of social change, and made them receptive to the most radical ideological appeals, including anarchism. Their protests and strikes triggered most of the strike waves in northern and central Italy in the 1880s and 1890s.

Because socialism had taken root by the end of the nineteenth century, it spread with relative ease into neighboring areas of central Italy dominated by *mezzadria,* "sharecropping," when they were drastically disrupted after the turn of the century. For a long time, *mezzadria* was able to survive in its various forms. But the ruling class's own policies supporting cash crops and the commercialization of agriculture rapidly undermined this highly traditional and stable form of land tenure, dramatically, and irrevocably, radicalizing class relations in the countryside as a result. The central Italian countryside furnished the most violent and sustained episodes of class warfare in Italy in the twentieth century, which is why the most brutal face of Italian fascism was also found in the countryside of Tuscany, Emilia-Romagna, and Umbria in the early 1920s. These three regions even today are known as the red areas of the country, and they continue to provide the Left with more support than anywhere else in Italy.

What of the South, with its legacy of misery, injustice, corruption, and repression? Although the southern part of Italy, known as the Mezzogiorno, would witness some local organization, the mass of peasants in this area were unable to present themselves in united fashion. Their characteristic activities would remain the communal riot and the occasional large-scale land occupation (which, in exceptional circumstances, involved tens of thousands on a regional basis). This reflected the extremely complicated and stratified condition of southern agriculture. Rare indeed were pure types of smallholders, sharecroppers, or day laborers. The typical southern peasant was (and remains) a mixed figure, who combined *several* of these roles on highly fragmented and poorly productive holdings. This fragmentation has historically undermined the emergence of class solidarity in the South, save for those isolated pockets that witnessed the industrialization or development of homogeneous forms of land tenure.

The Growth of the Organized Workers' Movement

By the middle of the 1880s, there were already the seeds of an organized workers' movement in Italy, beginning in Milan, the countryside of Lombardy, and the Romagna. The Italian Workers' Party was created in 1882 and by 1895 had evolved into the Socialist Party (PSI). By 1891, the first *camera del lavoro,* "chamber of labor," had been created. The chambers were broad-based, territorial rather than trade, organizations that corresponded well to the unconcentrated nature of industry (and the urban work force). They also strongly influenced the solidaristic tactics that came to characterize the movement as it matured: sympathy strikes and other acts of solidarity by neighboring workers, craftsmen, and even shopkeepers have been typical in Italian labor disputes. At the same time, *fasci* appeared in Sicily.[7] The most successful of these varied collectives drew their members from mining and agriculture, and were bonded by a strong local identity and deep sense of alienation from national politics.

By the turn of the century, the PSI was already badly divided along ideological lines. Faced with profound divisions from its foundation, the PSI simultaneously subscribed to maximum and minimum programs: the former committed it to the ultimate goal of overthrowing capitalism; the latter to a series of immediate reforms to improve wages and working conditions. As in many other socialist parties of the period, PSI unionists and elected officials tended toward reformism, while rank-and-file organizations usually assumed more radical and uncompromising positions. This tended to lead even more moderate leaders to adopt rather inflammatory rhetoric simply to hold onto their positions.

Through the first decade of the 1900s, the more moderate elements had control over the party, but in 1912, the left wing of the party took over. One of the most militant factions was led by Benito Mussolini, a fiery orator and journalist who was eventually expelled for his support of Italy's entry into World War I. His nationalism and penchant for action without much regard for doctrine would soon earn him a following on the Right.

Meanwhile, and not surprisingly given the active involvement of so many Socialists in the union movement, tensions between reformists and revolutionaries (also known as maximalists because of their commitment to the maximum program) were found within the union movement. Reformism finally carried the day in 1906, with the founding of the *Confederazione Generale del Lavoro* (CGL), "General Labor Confederation," and victory over the more radical tendencies within the unions. The CGL naturally took a proworker stance toward organized politics but studiously avoided direct affiliation with any single party. It never had a real opportunity to flourish until the period immediately following World War I. From roughly 350,000 members in the prewar period, its membership leaped to over one million in 1919 and to 2.2 million in 1920, but it fell by half in the following year because of capitalist retrenchment and economic crisis.[8] By the next year, the Fascists were in power, and with union-busting a top Fascist priority, the CGL's fate was sealed.

Italy in the International Context Through World War I

Italy's location, late entry into the community of nations, and relative lack of development has made her a peripheral actor on the stage of European politics. On the positive side, this has meant a much less onerous colonial heritage than that which burdened the other European powers. Even without grandiose aspirations, however, Italy's rulers had to be highly attuned to European developments following unification. After all, the country's borders had recently been determined in various interactions with France, Austria, and Germany (Prussia), and Italy's major markets also were found just beyond the Alps.

The new Italian state initially followed Piedmont's foreign policy, which favored Britain and France. But early French protection of the church and later tensions over areas of North Africa with sizable Italian minorities (especially Libya and Tunisia) strained Franco-Italian relations. These tensions were exacerbated by Italy's increasing use of economic protectionism, which led to trade wars that Italy could ill afford.

Indeed, there were times when a shooting war between Italy and France seemed possible. In the early 1880s, Italy joined the Triple Alliance with Prussia and Austria. This was a blatantly anti-French agreement, aligning Italy with her one natural enemy, Austria. The Hapsburg Empire continued to occupy some unmistakably Italian areas (most notably Trento and Trieste) and others that the Italians claimed (Istria, parts of Dalmatia, and the city of Fiume, all of which are in Yugoslavia today). Occasionally, embarrassing episodes, fanned by extreme nationalists, complicated relations between these somewhat reluctant allies over the next few decades.

The fact that Italy was, at best, a second-rate power did not completely dash its aspirations to join the same league as the more powerful European states. These ambitions affected industrial policies and drove several governments to undertake colonial and imperial adventures in Africa. Aware that the Royal Army had not exactly covered itself with glory in the wars of the *Risorgimento,* and increasingly aware that the Italian state enjoyed little public respect or prestige, Italian leaders undertook what Lenin aptly called "the imperialism of ragged wretches."[9] The term especially fit the Italian context, for the Right often mobilized the support of land-hungry peasants with visions of rich and abundant farmland awaiting them (in Libya and the Horn of Africa!). Starting in the mid-1880s, Italy sent expeditionary forces into Eritrea and Ethiopia. Several tragic defeats (in 1887 and 1896) became symbols exploited by nationalists, whom the more restrained leaders of the country tried to ignore.

Giovanni Giolitti was the dominant figure in Italian politics through the first decade of the new century. He was not an imperialist, and under him there was a great improvement in relations with France. He moved away from the rigid adherence to the Triple Alliance which had been Italian policy for several decades. However, his consummate tactical skills were not limitless. In 1911, in part to offset the Right's fury over a suffrage reform that did away with all property and educational restrictions, he declared war on Turkey. Italy won a quick victory and with it a colonial claim to Libya. This was initially a very popular move, but it also showed the limits of Giolitti's highly manipulative vision. He had sincerely counted on drawing the Socialists, led at the time by the reformists, into his government. The war doomed that slim hope. The PSI, spurred by strong anti-imperialist sentiments, turned sharply to the left in its 1912 congress.

When World War I broke out, Italy remained neutral, which in fact was consistent with Italian policies in Europe over the previous fifteen years. Yet within a year, Italy had signed a secret agreement with the Western Allies: in exchange for declaring war on Austria, Italian claims to Trento and Trieste would be granted at war's end. In May, 1915, in a move that pleased only the hard-core nationalists, Italy entered the war against her former ally. A declaration against Germany came a year later. Although the Italian front was certainly secondary by the standards of 1914–18, it visited all the horrors of trench warfare on the millions (mostly peasants) who were conscripted. Approximately six hundred thousand Italians died at the front, which often came perilously close to the Po Delta.

The war extended Italy's border to the Brenner Pass in the North and to Trieste and Istria on the Adriatic, but this hardly satisfied the nationalistic Right. The Italian delegation, in fact, abandoned the postwar peace talks when it became clear that their more ambitious claims would not be entertained, thus further legitimizing the aggressive Right. Substantial segments of the urban middle class, and numerous veterans, felt that the country's national destiny had been thwarted by an unjust postwar settlement. Workers and peasants trudged home much less inflamed by patriotic passion. During the worst moments of the war, the government had promised them greater justice at home when victory was achieved. With the war at an end, they were returning in a mood that was far from passive — and many peasants came back with a newly acquired sense of solidarity and appreciation of large-scale organization and cooperation.

Wars are notorious for exposing the flaws in the political systems that wage them, and they are particularly harsh on countries that lose. It is indicative of Italy's rickety underpinnings that even though the Liberal regime emerged from the slaughter of World War I on the winning side, its days were numbered.

Liberal Italy's Political Contradictions

Since we know what brought the Liberal regime down, it is relatively easy to pinpoint the system's key political failure. It developed neither the culture nor the mechanisms that could attract mass support or regulate modern class conflict. To be sure, it is not easy to design or put such mechanisms into place. But the existing system was so retrograde that it had trouble even recognizing the demands of the emerging social classes as legitimate. The ruling elites had devised a political arrangement that was, at best, suited to the middle of the nineteenth century.

They had also inherited a set of institutions and tensions that greatly complicated their tasks. The *Statuto albertino* gave the king much more executive power than a modern constitutional monarch ought to have. The monarchs who followed Victor Emmanuel II were far from gifted or enlightened individuals, and their close ties to and affection for the armed forces often created problems for Parliament. The *Statuto albertino* also declared Roman Catholicism to be the official state religion, but the Vatican adamantly refused to recognize Italy and forbade believers to take part in any political activity. Finally, though Italy was an extremely diverse country, the state was highly centralized, even concerning local matters. The country's leaders were often motivated by fears about the disintegrative potential of too much local autonomy, particularly in the South. As a result, they chose to do nothing to alter a structure that ordinary citizens of all classes experienced as distant, arbitrary, and oppressive. This certainly was not the way to win public support for the new state.

Trasformismo *and the Absence of a Bourgeois Party*

Trasformismo refers to the practice of building a majority in Parliament by winning over enough deputies, of whatever tendency, by whatever means prove most effective. In the Italian context, this could range from sponsoring special, pork-barrel projects to buying the support of corrupt local bosses. What is ultimately transformed is the very meaning of the historical differences between parties, groups, and traditional ideologies: if a leader absorbs former enemies into the government itself, so much the better.

Invention of this practice is usually attributed to Agostino Depretis, a comrade-in-arms of Garibaldi and deputy of the Historical Left in the old Piedmontese parliament, who became prime minister in 1876. But *trasformismo* really was a requisite of the political system that existed at the time and was practiced and approved by all of the major political actors in the period prior to the rise of the mass parties. To function most effectively, *trasformismo* requires a limited franchise — or very effective control over local politics — along with a highly personalized style of representation. The local notable, or a trusted deputy, is the mediator between the home district and the political center.

This system of representation is one of the main reasons why the ruling elite was very slow to extend the franchise, a reform even enlightened conservatives had come to see as necessary by the 1880s. It also slowed and even blocked the emergence of a more modern, ideologically coherent party (or parties) of the middle classes and more progressive capitalists. The ruling elites continued to rely on local power-brokers long after their most modern and powerful supporters — the northern commercial and industrial interests — had organized themselves and begun to exert direct pressure on the machinery of the ever-expanding state. The politicians' endless wheeling and dealing, often with backward landlords whose interests ran counter to their own, alienated many entrepreneurs and convinced them the entire political system was ineffective. The landlords also were increasingly impatient with a system that they saw as too indulgent of the organized workers and peasants. In short, the classes that underpinned the original post-*Risorgimento* coalition were increasingly alienated from what were supposed to be their own structures of political power.

The polarized mass politics that followed Giolitti's 1911 electoral reform and World War I put the finishing touches on the old system of local power bases. This period also demonstrated that vast segments of the dominant Liberal Party were not such great devotees of democracy when it stopped serving their immediate interests. The local elections of 1920 showed how rapidly the old system could erode. The PSI was the main winner, which the reactionaries took as direct evidence of the failure of democracy. Even more moderate factions within the traditional ruling parties were faced with the disturbing fact that their entire network of influence and patronage had been upended in a great many areas. The scale of this shift was immense. Between the local elections of 1914 and 1920, city halls with Socialist governments increased from 300 to over 2,100. (There are just over 8,000 municipalities in Italy.)[10]

The Biennio Rosso *(1919–20)*

The breaking point for the Liberal regime came in the *biennio rosso,* the "red two years," that followed the war, when mass politics arrived with a vengeance. Demands for change that had long been pent up now swept across the country, in both institutionalized and more spontaneous, explosive ways. Italy's two truly mass parties, the PSI and the church-linked Popular Party (PPI), grew by leaps and bounds, and gained more than half the votes cast in the 1919 general elections. Union membership (and strikes) grew astronomically. Landless peasants occupied massive, uncultivated tracts in the South, forcing the government to improvise very hasty, but extensive, distributions. Day laborers and sharecroppers agitated for, and won, so many significant improvements that the new contracts came to be called the Red Pacts. On two separate occasions, hundreds of thousands of northern workers occupied their factories, and at least in some areas (Turin, for instance), a revolution even seemed possible.

The Red Pacts included some changes that undermined the entire system of domination inherent in sharecropping, for example guarantees of tenure on the land and a peasant voice in determining which crops would be planted. The landlords accepted this at the time because they had to, but they immediately began looking for ways to break the contracts and revert to the previous system. They eventually found the means in the Fascist squads, which created true reigns of terror in the countryside of Emilia-Romagna and Tuscany.

The factory occupations of April and October, 1920, appalled the industrialists and the urban middle class, for they also represented a direct threat to the established order. Except for a few exceptionally militant areas, however, the organized workers' movement had shown that it was not prepared for a real showdown with either the state or big industry. The second occupation actually saw a vote held by the National Council of the CGL on whether a revolution should be proclaimed! Predictably, the answer was no.[11] The utter frustration and disgust of the most militant Socialists led them to break with the moderate majority of their party in 1921 to form the Communist Party (PCI). Yet frightened and angry bourgeois were now looking, among other places, to the extreme Right for help, since they felt the state could not be counted on to maintain order.

The Roman Question

The church not only was adamantly opposed to liberalism as a doctrine but had also governed one-seventh of the territory and population of the future Italian state. As noted earlier, anticlericalism was a potent political force in Italy in the late nineteenth century, and with the Vatican's continued hostility, antireligious measures often became governmental policy. Some areas of the country had deep religious traditions, but there were many where it is not an overstatement to speak of widespread hatred for the church as an institution. Deep ideological revulsion on both sides of the divide aggravated memories of misgovernment in the Papal States or resentment of the local priests' favoritism of landlords, as was common in the countryside of central Italy.

The church's *non expedit* or non-cooperation, decree of 1874 forbade Catholics to participate in the politics of the new state either as politicians or as citizens, and it remained in force through the end of the nineteenth century. By the first decade of the new century, however, these strictures were relaxed, thanks to a less intransigent pope (Pius X) and to the suffrage reform, which threatened great increases for the Socialists. In the 1913 elections, held under nearly unrestricted male suffrage, pragmatism of a rather cynical variety finally triumphed. Catholics, with the church's agreement, struck deals with moderate Liberals. In exchange for Catholic votes, these Liberals — whose party was formally anticlerical — promised not to support measures opposed by the church. When this arrangement (the Gentiloni Pact) was discovered, it drove an even wider wedge between the Left and Prime Minister Giolitti; in fact, it did little for the Liberals' credibility along all the points of the political spectrum.

By the next general election (1919), universal male suffrage and proportional representation were in force, and the Popular Party was in the field. It won just over 20 percent of the vote. The PPI, a forerunner of Christian Democracy, mobilized the Catholic urban and rural middle classes, as well as workers in some of the religious areas in the North. Its varied social composition was often evident in its strong internal divisions, and these — particularly the more radical positions — made the Vatican extremely uncomfortable. Ambivalent as it might have been, the church's open support of a political party finally made the *non expedit* a dead letter. This did not indicate a deep change in the Vatican's attitudes toward democracy, however; as soon as Mussolini came to power and indicated he was ready to compromise with the church and extend financial aid to it, Pope Pius XI began to back away from the PPI. He deserted it altogether in 1924, when a pro-Fascist group seceded to form its own Catholic party.[12]

Fascism's Rise to Power

The Liberal system's bankruptcy was revealed, and its fate sealed, when it handed power over to Mussolini following the famous March on Rome late in October, 1922. The march itself was an act of intimidation, in which tens of thousands of Fascists paraded through the capital, demanding power for their party. Power was achieved legally, although with only 32 of 530 seats in Parliament, the Fascist Party (PNF) obviously needed a lot of outside support. It received support from everywhere (the PPI included) except the Left.[13] The representatives of the old regime had calculated that they could restrain Mussolini, but they soon discovered their error. "Semifree" elections in 1924 gave the Fascists an overwhelming majority, and by 1925–26, the country was ruled by a dictatorship.

Italian fascism, *as a movement,* combined so many diverse elements and claims that it is not easy to sort them out; this very complexity and inconsistency helps explain its broad appeal. Mussolini openly showed his contempt for the old political system. Most important, he convinced people he would act decisively to change things — especially to put an end to the "red menace" once and for all. The Left was on the defensive domestically and hopelessly divided internally, but it was not a negligible social force. Its rhetoric, often a substitute for action, convinced masses of people, not just a few reactionaries and vested interests, that a violent revolution might be just around the corner.

The Fascist regime spanned a full quarter of the history of the modern Italian state, and much of its legacy was unequivocally negative. Its militaristic adventures (e.g., the conquest of Ethiopia, the Spanish Civil War, and most of all, the alliance with Hitler in World War II) ultimately disgraced Italy and brought horrible suffering to millions, including, of course, the Italians themselves. A generation of dictatorship that ends in disgrace and defeat also does nothing to legitimize the state or to nurture democratic traditions among the masses. Italy's entire legal and administrative apparatus, centralized and autocratic enough under the *Statuto albertino,* emerged from fascism with these oppressive aspects greatly accentuated.

Political Trade-offs. As with so many aspects of fascism, one needs to distinguish what the regime claimed it was doing from what it actually did. Its ambitions were openly totalitarian: Society was to be regimented from top to bottom, with no political structures other than the PNF mediating between the citizen and the state. The arrangement was unabashedly hierarchical, with the *Duce,* "Leader," the living embodiment of all Fascist virtues, at the very top. As in all such systems, the final result was to be nothing less than the remaking of citizens in a new image: tough and uncorrupted by the materialistic softness that liberal democracy (or capitalism, for the really radical Fascists) represented.

In practice, Mussolini was a mediator and maneuverer rather than a dedicated ideologue. As a result, most of Italy's deeply rooted structural and institutional problems continued under the dictatorship; for example, the regular army personally swore allegiance to the king, who remained head of state. This was not a purely abstract consideration, because it was eventually the monarch and his general staff who deposed Mussolini in 1943 when the Allies began to march up the peninsula after liberating Sicily. On another level, party-state tensions existed throughout the dictatorship, in spite of the unity between the two that one might have expected and that certainly was claimed. Mussolini inherited a top-heavy state structure and centralized it even further. At the same time, local party officials were notorious for turning their areas into personal fiefs, and *il Duce* tolerated this as long as these leaders did not grow overly ambitious or directly challenge his popularity.

Fascism and the Church. A significant trade-off was the Concordat with the church that Mussolini signed in 1929. The Vatican gained considerable scope for action, and it did not hesitate to use, and try to expand, this opportunity. The church's role in public education is the best known of the privileges it was granted, but in fact it was able to extend and consolidate its presence throughout society with a host of welfare and social activities. It could do this because, as the official state religion, it had a free hand in all religious activities — and the definition of *religious* was effectively open to negotiation. Further, the church was often so aggressive in pursuing its interests that it came into direct conflict with the state machinery or with Fascist officials who were less accommodating than Mussolini.

In return, the state and regime gained legitimacy from the ecclesiastical authorities, which meant approval from parish pulpits every Sunday. And the Vatican's approval of specific policies actually helped generate enthusiastic support for the regime. This certainly proved to be the case for some of Mussolini's foreign adventures: Pope Pius XI and most of the church hierarchy strongly applauded the conquest of Ethiopia when the bulk of world opinion (save for the Nazis) was aligned against Fascist aggression, which took on overtly racist tones and included such barbarities as the use of poison gas. The pope also applauded Mussolini's involvement on the side of Franco in the Spanish Civil War, referring to it as a crusade against communism.

Industrial Concentration and Increased State Intervention. The Fascist regime extolled the virtues of small producers in agriculture and industry while pursuing policies that favored the largest firms in each sector. At first, these policies were primarily indirect. "Self regulation," Mussolini's early policy, really meant letting market forces take their course, and those forces strongly favored the largest, strongest firms. Similarly, the number of cartels increased greatly under fascism, but this was already an established trend in Italy and elsewhere in the capitalist world. Even in the early stages of the regime, Mussolini followed established traditions with subsidies to many of the largest firms in the country, particularly those in armaments and related industries.

The Great Depression and Mussolini's increasingly aggressive foreign policy finally put an end to even the fiction of self regulation by the late 1930s. The world crisis pushed every country toward more protectionism, but Mussolini soon announced a policy that effectively took protectionism to its logical conclusion: autarchy, or complete economic self-sufficiency. Although autarchy is quite consistent with a strongly nationalistic ideology, it was adopted for more immediate reasons: The League of Nations imposed economic sanctions on Italy following the invasion of Ethiopia in 1935. Mussolini intended to carry on with his militaristic foreign policy, which required the arms that only a heavy industrial sector could provide. If other countries were going to try to dictate policy to him, he would show them that Italy could go it alone.

Given Italy's shortages of many key raw materials, these political decisions forced the state to become much more involved in economic affairs. Scarce resources had to be found or replacements developed; they had to be distributed to the key industries; and the funds to do all this — in the midst of the crisis — somehow had to be acquired. The mechanism that emerged out of these requirements was a crude approximation of planning, which really amounted to further reinforcement of the cartels and firms that were already in place. Resources were disproportionately channeled, and market shares were distributed to the largest and strongest enterprises as a matter of declared policy.

The Istituto per la Ricostruzione Industriale (IRI). IRI was created in 1933 as a holding company for bank stocks the state had been forced to buy in order to keep some of the largest financial institutions afloat. Because the state continued to buy up crippled companies, and because the autarchic policy would not allow it to let the market shape the Italian economy freely, Rome had to become increasingly involved in the ownership, and eventually the management and restructuring, of these troubled firms. At the very least, self-protection dictated involvement: to recoup some of its investment (for the original intent was to resell the stocks it had bought), the state had to see to it that companies became viable again. For the more ambitious believers in the autarchic economy, the implications were, of course, far more profound: one simply could not abandon important segments of the economy to ruin.

By 1937, IRI had been made a permanent holding company geared to furthering the policies of rearmament and autarchy. By 1940, about one-fifth of all the capital assets in all the joint-stock corporations in Italy were controlled by IRI, and important sectors of the economy, such as iron, steel, shipbuilding, and banking, were effectively monopolized by the state.

The End of Fascism: The Implications for the Republic

Whatever slim chance the monarchy had of survival into the postwar era was dissipated by the way it came to terms with the Allies. In the forty-five days in 1943 between the deposition of Mussolini on July 25 and the announcement of the armistice with the Allies, the king and his new government had been completely indecisive. Most damaging of all was the failure to give the army clear instructions concerning the Germans. This was meant to reassure Hitler's generals, but it had the opposite effect. Hence, while Victor Emmanuel III negotiated the surrender, German troops poured into Italy, Allied bombs continued to fall on Italian cities, and the army desperately tried to figure out what to do.

The armistice of September 8 found the Germans prepared while the Italians were little more than sitting ducks. Many garrisons were captured and shipped to German prison camps. Some groups tried to resist and were massacred by the thousands. The bulk of the army simply disintegrated, the king and his ministers fled behind Allied lines, and the Germans dug in on the peninsula all the way south to Rome. The war in Italy would drag on until just two weeks before the final German surrender in May, 1945. In October, 1943, the new government declared war on Germany. This was a last-ditch effort by the monarch to save himself and a response to Allied promises to take Italy's actions into account in the final postwar settlement. The declaration of war did have the positive benefit of legitimizing the Resistance on the broadest possible basis, and many monarchists made an honorable contribution to the struggle against the Germans and what remained of the Fascist regime in the North, where Mussolini had been set up by the Nazis. The anti-Fascist parties, united in the Committee of National Liberation (CLN), wanted nothing to do with the king, but Allied pressure and the unexpected shift of the Communists finally convinced them to wait until the war was over to settle the institutional question on the future of the monarchy and the form of the new government.

The Resistance was a brutal conflict that often took on overtones of civil war in the North. Its symbolic importance for the country, especially for the Communists and the Left in general, cannot be stressed enough.

Since the Fascists and Nazis were quick to denounce all partisan activities as those of "Communist bandits," this largely successful effort to salvage national pride and honor relegitimized the Left as both a prodemocratic and a patriotic force. Further, the main German lines of defense happened to run along the Appenine Mountains right through the areas of the country with the strongest "red" traditions (i.e., Tuscany and Emilia-Romagna).

The war-time experience also helped perpetuate the historic North-South division of the country. The South was spared the brutal German occupation and the unifying liberation struggle. It was, in short, once more cut off from any direct role in some of the country's most significant moments.

The institutional question was far more than a debate about what the *form* of the postwar regime would be; it revealed a lack of consensus about the very meaning of the Italian state to its citizens and profound disagreement about the *content* of the regime, even among many who favored a republic. Unity against a foreign invader and a totally discredited dictatorship was one thing; unity in favor of a new set of institutional arrangements was quite another, as internal jockeying in the CLN throughout the Resistance showed very clearly. Both the Liberal and the Fascist regimes were discredited. What could the emerging political elites do to win mass support and more successfully entrench democratic institutions and practices?

In light of who these elites were, the answers were not entirely favorable for representative democratic institutions. There was a variety of secular and democratic groups who ranged politically from the Left to the Center-Left, but the main political protagonists and the very deep social and ideological divisions that would face the new regime became clear early on. The Communists and Socialists dominated the Left, and the Socialists often sounded even more radical than the Communists. The Resistance had remobilized the class cleavages of the North-Center, and the organizations of the Left, parties and unions alike, were attracting literally millions of new members.

The only other mass party was Christian Democracy (DC), which grew out of the old Popular Party and was very closely aligned with the church. Thanks to the Concordat, the church was reintegrated into Italian national life; its privileges under fascism gave it a tremendous head start in establishing a presence throughout postwar Italian society. Though the church had distanced itself from Mussolini, it could hardly be considered a modern democratic force — yet its head start and formidable resources made the DC the logical pole of attraction for those who were seeking a realistic political alternative to the Left.

Fascism also bequeathed to Italy an economy under more direct state control than that of any other capitalist society. It had been an interventionist state earlier, but the tendency was greatly magnified under Mussolini. This could, in theory, represent an advantage for those who faced the daunting problem of simultaneously reconstructing a war-shattered society and helping to develop an economy that still employed more people in agriculture than industry. Could a coalition be found that agreed on how to use this potentially formidable instrument, or would the regime be fundamentally divided about whether the state holdings should be used at all?

Finally, and lending greater urgency to many of these questions, it must be remembered that for all the glory of the Resistance, Italy had been liberated by the Allied armies. At war's end, they occupied the country, and it was clear that Italy's future lay solidly within the Allies' sphere of influence. While the Allies honored their promise to recognize the contribution of the Italians in the Resistance, it was also plain that they had their own ideas about the country's future and their own favorites among the players. Their interference in the postwar settlement in Italy would be much less than in Germany, but their role — particularly the role of the United States — would be far from negligible.

NOTES

1. Luigi Barzini, *The Italians* (New York: Athenium, 1964), p. 241, quoted in: Sidney G. Tarrow, *Peasant Communism in Southern Italy* (New Haven: Yale University Press, 1967), p. 21.
2. Denis Mack Smith, *Italy: A Modern History* (Ann Arbor: University of Michigan Press, 1969), pp. 69–75.
3. Giuliano Procacci claims that no one in Europe was so heavily taxed. See: Giuliano Procacci, *History of the Italian People* (Hammondsworth, England: Penguin, 1968), p. 333.
4. Procacci, *History of the Italian People,* p. 391.
5. Official census data cited in George H. Hildebrand, *Growth and Structure in the Economy of Modern Italy* (Cambridge: Harvard University Press, 1965), pp. 112–17.
6. The figure refers to the 1911 census and is cited in Adrian Lyttleton, "Landlords, Peasants and the Limits of Liberalism," in *Gramsci and Italy's Passive Revolution,* ed. John A. Davis (New York: Barnes & Noble, 1979), p. 129.
7. Derived from the Latin, *fasces,* a Roman symbol of strength in unity represented by a bound bundle or sheaf of rods. The fascist movement eventually gave the same term far greater notoriety.

8. Daniel L. Horowitz, *The Italian Labor Movement* (Cambridge: Harvard University Press, 1963), p. 75.
9. Quoted in: Procacci, *History of the Italian People,* p. 352.
10. For the 1914–20 electoral figures, see: Frank M. Snowden, "From Sharecropper to Proletarian: The Background to Fascism in Rural Tuscany, 1880–1920," in *Gramsci and Italy's Passive Revolution,* ed. John A. Davis (New York: Barnes & Noble, 1979), p. 165.
11. By 591,243 to 409,369, with 93,623 abstentions. See: Martin Clark, *Antonio Gramsci and the Revolution that Failed* (New Haven: Yale University Press, 1977), pp. 168–69.
12. Charles S. Maier, *Recasting Bourgeois Europe* (Princeton, NJ: Princeton University Press, 1975), p. 548.
13. Paolo Farneti, "Social Conflict, Parliamentary Fragmentation, Institutional Shift, and the Rise of Fascism: Italy," in *The Breakdown of Democratic Regimes: Europe,* ed. Juan J. Linz and Alfred Stepan (Baltimore: The Johns Hopkins University Press, 1978), pp. 23–26.

17

The Rise and Fall of the Postwar Settlement

In a society where the strongest representatives of labor are excluded from the governmental and industrial decision-making processes, a term like *postwar settlement* clearly has a limited meaning. In Italy, as in France, it was clear by the late 1940s that each country would develop within the Western sphere of influence, within a more or less liberal-democratic institutional framework, and without much concern for the main representatives of the working class. The settlement in these countries was a lopsided sort of truce: the Left enjoyed political freedom and such influence as it could muster in the field of labor relations, with the tacit understanding that it was condemned to the role of *permanent* opposition. This was certainly a better situation than the Italian workers' movement had endured under fascism, but the Left had expected much more at war's end. In this chapter, we will describe how it came to be relegated to the margins of Italian political and economic developments and how the Christian Democrats and the seemingly disorganized and ragtag forces grouped around them managed to score such a decisive victory.

The Rise of the Postwar Settlement

The Evolution of the Constitutional Order

Italy emerged from the ravages of war and the Nazi occupation of the North with a delicate and uncertain political equilibrium. The Resistance had not only relegitimized the Left but also had given it a dominant position in the North and Center. The Resistance had also radicalized both the leadership and the rank-and-file in the areas that had been in the midst of the heaviest fighting and the most brutal repression. From 1945 onward, there was much talk of the "wind from the North," directed by the radical northern Committees of National Liberation (CLN), that would sweep away both the political and the economic structures of the old regime in favor of a thoroughgoing revolution. (The CLNs represented the six parties taking part in the Resistance and excluded only the Republican Party (PRI), which refused to serve while the monarchy still existed.)

In the North, the Left had unquestioned hegemony. Moreover, although the Socialists were divided between moderates and radicals, the majority favored close collaboration with the Communists. There was talk in both parties about the need to unify the workers' representatives into a single party in this period, and after 1946, they presented themselves to the voters in a single list as the Democratic Popular Front (FDP). The Communists had been extremely conciliatory since their leader, Palmiro Togliatti, had arrived in liberated territory in March, 1944, and had broken the impasse over the institutional question by announcing that the Communist Party (PCI) would support the monarchist government in its fight against fascism and nazism. Since Stalin had just recognized the government, this maneuver should not have come as a complete surprise. It was, however, only the first of several key junctures that would see Communist moderation outflank and at times enrage the rest of the Left in the name of national unity.

As dedicated as Togliatti apparently was to long-term collaboration with the DC, only the leftmost fringes of the Catholic party appear to have harbored similar desires. Like all the mass parties of Christian inspiration at the end of World War II, the DC's platform and behavior quickly shifted from an emphasis on reform (necessary in the immediate aftermath of the war) to a more cautious, conservative posture that reflected the interests and fears of the bulk of its supporters. Its social bases of support were far too diverse to give rise to any coherent platform, but its favored status in the eyes of both the church and the United States, combined with its immense strength among the smallholding peasants and the urban middle classes, ensured that it would not be striking radical poses. The Christian Democrats tolerated cooperation with the Communists and Socialists only as long as they were compelled to do so by the political balance of power.

The Vote of June 2, 1946. Italy's first exercise in truly universal suffrage abolished the monarchy and also elected, by proportional representation, a Constituent Assembly that was to serve as a temporary parliament and to write a republican constitution within eighteen months. The vote contained several surprises. Turnout was exceptionally high at 89 percent. The monarchy managed to garner 10.7 million votes, or nearly 47 percent, in spite of its association with fascism and the shameful vacillation in 1943 that had contributed to the army's disintegration. Ominously, the monarchy was soundly defeated in the North and Center but carried the Mezzogiorno, emphasizing yet again the depth of the country's historical divisions.

These divisions were, if anything, even more apparent in the vote for the Constituent Assembly. In spite of the DC's great strength in the Catholic North-East, there was a left-wing majority from the top of the boot down through the red zones, with the Socialists slightly stronger than the Communists, especially in the major industrial areas of the North-West. Counting the tiny Action Party, which had been highly influential in the Resistance and within the CLN and which would soon disband, the Left had just over 41 percent of the vote. (See Table 17.1.) The DC emerged as the country's strongest single party with 35 percent;

Table 17.1 The Voting on June 2, 1946, and April 18, 1948

	1946 (CONSTITUENT ASSEMBLY)			1948 (CHAMBER OF DEPUTIES)		
	VOTES			VOTES		
PARTY	('000)	PERCENT	SEATS	('000)	PERCENT	SEATS
Communists	4,357	18.9	104	8,137	31.0	183
Socialists	4,758	20.7	115			
Action Party	335	1.5	7			
Social Democrats				1,858	7.1	33
Republicans	1,003	4.4	23	652	2.5	9
Christian Democracy	8,081	35.2	207	12,713	48.5	305
Liberals	1,561	6.8	41	1,005	3.8	19
Monarchists	637	2.8	16	729	2.8	14
Extreme Right*	1,212	5.3	30	527	2.0	6
Others	1,025	4.4	13	599	2.3	5
TOTALS	22,968	100.0	556	26,220	100.0	574

NOTE *Uomo Qualunque,* "Common Man," in 1946: Italian Social Movement (neo-Fascists) in 1948.

SOURCE Giuseppe Mammarella, *Italy After Fascism* (Notre Dame, IN: University of Notre Dame Press, 1966), pp. 116, 194.

it was the only party to show roughly uniform strength across the entire country. But the DC's support was hardly compact: it had been forced to avoid a clear recommendation on the question of monarchy versus republic. On the Right, the combined strength of the Liberals and, unexpectedly, the odd *Uomo Qualunque,* "Common Man," formation represented a warning to the DC from the middle classes not to press too far in its collaboration with the Left. The UQ tended to reject all the major parties, and was highly suspicious of parliamentary institutions. It rapidly faded from the scene in the late 1940s.

As had become increasingly evident in the politics of the preceding year, the three mass parties, with three-quarters of the vote between them, were destined to be the major actors in the system for at least the short run. The Liberals, the dominant force in pre-Fascist Italy, were reduced to a mere 7 percent and would only touch that figure once more, in the early 1960s, before declining to near-insignificance. It would be nearly impossible — and extremely unwise — to work out a constitution or an effort at a lasting settlement over the strong objections of either of the two major poles of the political system (i.e., the PCI–PSI or the DC). Neither society nor the political sphere presented a coherent, clear-cut coalition favoring the many changes that had to be undertaken. This standoff explains many of the peculiarities and apparent inconsistencies and contradictions of the republican constitution.

The Constitution. Although Italy has undergone several regime changes, the republican constitution is only the second basic law of the land since unification, for the *Statuto albertino* had managed to survive fascism. Since its drafting spanned the most tumultuous period in the republic's political history, it is not at all surprising that the constitution reflects both the ideological tension and the shifting balance of power within the Constituent Assembly (and the country) between mid-1946 and early 1948.

From its opening preamble, which announces that "Italy is a democratic Republic founded on labor," it is clear that this is an unusual document. One of Italy's foremost legal experts summed up its basic dilemma neatly when he said that the Right blocked any truly radical changes the Left wanted to impose but allowed the Left to include the *promise* of a revolution in the final draft.[1] Thus, several articles (41 and 42) proclaim the right to private property, but they immediately add that this right is not absolute; it may give way to broader social needs. In other articles, the qualifier comes from the opposite side of the spectrum. For example, Article 40 guarantees the right to strike but adds that strikes must be carried out within the boundaries of the laws that regulate them. While union membership is similarly guaranteed, the unions themselves must be organized on democratic principles in order to be recognized by the authorities. Numerous commentators have pointed out that the constitution is filled with extremely broad principles but no means to guarantee their enactment. Examples include Article 34, which asserts that eight years of education is both compulsory and free, and Article 38, which includes the right of the disabled to education and vocational training.

There is much in the document, and the debate that generated it, that invites cynical winks and snorts of laughter. Consider, for example, that in the debate over the relative powers and responsibilities of the two houses of the legislature, the Chamber of Deputies and the Senate, the Communists bolstered their arguments with citations from George Washington and Benjamin Franklin, while the Christian Democrats rebutted them with lengthy citations from that fountainhead of Christian doctrine, Josef Stalin![2] But the underlying debate was deadly serious, and when one considers that governmental collaboration between the three major parties ended during the drafting of the constitution, it is remarkable that they were able to hammer out a compromise that obtained an 81 percent majority when the final draft was approved in December, 1947. (Mindful of the fate of the first draft of the new French Constitution just a few months earlier, the Italian legislators decided not to submit their handiwork to the electorate for its approval.)

Yet one is tempted to conclude that precisely *because* it is a tension-ridden, contradictory, and incomplete document, the Italian Constitution is the most that could have been produced under such difficult circumstances. The Left may only have gotten its broad principles enshrined in many of the articles but all the promises of social justice and equality — as well as the achievement of numerous concrete freedoms — enabled the Communists and Socialists to identify quite strongly with the "Democratic Republic, born in the Resistance." They would be able to say, quite correctly, that the Left's decisive contribution made this one of the most progressive constitutions in the Western world, and they would also be able to attack the DC, over the next generation, from the standpoint of defenders of constitutionalism. We will see in our discussion of Italy's institutional arrangements that for years the ruling party stalled or sabotaged many of the more innovative aspects of the constitution.

The Lateran Pacts and Article 7. One of the greatest shocks to emerge from the Constituent Assembly was the inclusion, *without amendment* and with the decisive support of the PCI, of the Lateran Pacts in Article 7 of the constitution.[3] Pope Pius XII had made clear his intent to safeguard the church's privileges in the republic, and all the non-Catholic forces were eager not to complicate the already daunting challenge of reconstruction by reopening old wounds. Giving the pacts *constitutional* status, however, was more than most non-Catholics could accept. The PCI had originally announced that it would oppose enshrining the pacts in the constitution, and the Communists' turnabout was therefore one of the most dramatic events in this period.

The explanation offered by the PCI stressed its desire to avoid polarizing the country and alienating much of the peasantry and even many workers. Togliatti also undoubtedly hoped that a goodwill gesture toward the church might extend the tripartite experiment. Instead, within two months of voting for the pacts in March, 1947, the Communists found themselves relegated to the opposition by Prime Minister Alcide De Gasperi. Within a year, the pope declared it a sin to uphold Marxist doctrine; by 1949, active Communists and Socialists were excommunicated. Togliatti might have been in a conciliatory mood, but as soon as the tide turned in their favor, neither the DC nor the church was so inclined. The country would be split in two, but with the Right and the church on the offensive. The Communists, who would soon be denouncing the "clericalization" of Italy, paid a heavy price for their conciliatory stance.

Although technically forbidden by the pacts to get involved in Italian politics, the church under Pius XII disregarded this injunction. It simultaneously pursued its material interests in ruthless fashion, insisting that *all* its financial activities were religious and therefore tax-exempt. And the Vatican also took its privileged position as the state religion very seriously, going so far as to encourage state persecution of evangelical Protestant sects, often using Fascist codes that defined them as "harmful to the race." These persecutions began in the late 1940s and continued through the early 1960s.[4]

The most potent social leverage provided by Article 7 were the Church's guarantees in the spheres of education and marriage. Article 36 of the Concordat stated that integral to *public* education is "the teaching of Christian doctrine in the form received by the Catholic tradition." This meant that time would be set aside each week in all public schools for religious instruction. Moreover, both the texts and the teachers had to be approved by the diocesan authorities, and if approval was withdrawn from a teacher, he or she could not continue to teach that material.[5] With respect to marriage, the Concordat established the right of ecclesiastical courts to render decisions that the civil courts would then declare valid (Article 34); in other words, the state delegated part of its jurisdiction to the church. The courts would increasingly reclaim the state's sovereignty in the 1970s, by which time a divorce law had finally been passed as well. But, as these examples should make clear, Article 7 gave the church immense power in Italian affairs for more than a generation.

The DC's Triumph. Even during the peak period of collaboration at the end of the war, the DC was under tremendous internal pressure to end its alliance with the Left. Relations between the coalition partners steadily worsened, paralleling but by no means simply mimicking the degeneration in East-West relations. De Gasperi increasingly refused even to listen to the Left's demands for more radical economic reforms. Instead, in his capacity as Minister of the Interior (he had insisted on this post as well as the prime ministership), he rapidly rid the prefectures, police, and military structures of CLN appointees; replacements were often those who had served under the Fascists. These actions frequently caused riots led by the Left, and considerable force was used to quell the protests.

The situation degenerated in 1947. After a trip to the United States, where he received promises of copious aid and was urged to get the Left out, De Gasperi returned to find a perfect excuse for the governmental crisis he had long sought. In January, the Socialists, fragmented into numerous factions, had split over the question of relations with the Communists. The left and center of the Socialist Party (PSI), themselves divided over the question of an eventual fusion with the PCI into a single workers' bloc, remained, but two right-wing factions seceded to form what eventually became the Social Democratic Party (PSDI). They commanded the loyalty of about a third of the membership but nearly half (50 of 115) the deputies in the Constituent Assembly.

So uncertain was the climate that De Gasperi could not find immediate support for a new coalition in spite of the schism. He was finally successful in May, 1947, and then only in part. He created a minority *monocolore* (one-party) government. His cabinet was bolstered by the presence of Luigi Einaudi, an internationally respected conservative economist with very strong ideas about the proper economic policies for Italian reconstruction. The cabinet received a vote of confidence thanks to the support of all the parties of the Right.[6] A scant year after the 1946 referendum, tripartism had come to an end. More dependent on conservative (and reactionary) forces than ever, the DC would soon abandon any pretense of carrying out the extensive social reforms it had once promised. Italy's social structure, ideological traditions, and political balance of power left almost no room at all for intermediate positions in the Left-Right polarization that was to split Italian society for the next ten to fifteen years.

The new reality, and the Left's inability to counter any of De Gasperi's basic policies, soon convinced the PSDI and PRI that they had to join the government. The Liberal Party (PLI) also formally entered the enlarged cabinet at the end of 1947, and the first Centrist government was born. As with all the governing formulas attempted by the Italians, this would prove strife-ridden and unstable, but these three political satellites would remain firmly in the DC's orbit and provide it with support over the next thirteen years — which would see thirteen different governments (see Table 17.6 at the end of this chapter). They would preside over the reconstruction and the period of unprecedented economic growth that came to be known as the "miracle."

The End of the Left's Illusions. What was the Left doing as these events transpired? It was, of course, agitating and mobilizing against the government's actions, but it was also confidently waiting for De Gasperi and Einaudi's policies to fail dismally, at which point it expected to pick up the pieces and carry on with its proposals for extensive reforms — and perhaps even achieve full political power. When these overconfident expectations failed to materialize, the Communists and Socialists found their position badly weakened. The working class originally had strong *political* representation, but that had been undermined when the Socialists split. Meanwhile, the workers' *economic* position steadily deteriorated, and the trade unions soon discovered that they had very limited margins of maneuver.

But the Left, to the discomfort of many Socialists, was hampered above all by its close identification with the Soviet Union as the Cold War developed and created an increasingly bipolar world. So-called analyses of capitalism's imminent demise or of the Marshall Plan as designed simply to rearm the West and prepare for war against the Soviet Union may have served Stalin's purposes, but they hardly won converts to the PCI or PSI. And then, just prior to the critical 1948 Italian general elections, the Left in Czechoslovakia, which had originally won power in fair elections, installed a Stalinist regime rather than face the voters a second time.

The Czechoslovakian events added intensity and venom to an already vicious campaign. The vote of April 18, 1948, saw the combined PCI–PSI list obtain 31 percent, which was a remarkably strong showing under the circumstances. (See Table 17.1.) Nonetheless, it was a crushing defeat that stunned the Left's leaders, who had anticipated at least a renewed standoff. The rank-and-file were even more stunned, for many had genuinely believed that victory (and revolution) was at hand. There was no doubt as to the winner of this contest: for the only time in the history of the Republic, one party won an absolute majority of the seats and did nearly as well in the percentage of the vote (48.5 percent). The DC had drawn strong support from all social classes, and it did well in every region of Italy. In a climate of complete polarization, it had attracted many votes from its own coalition partners as well as from the extreme Right.

Courageously resisting pressures from the Vatican, the parties of the extreme Right, and his own right wing (which was easily as reactionary as the extreme Right), De Gasperi reconstructed another centrist government. Although a devout Catholic himself, and hardly a radical democrat, De Gasperi and most of his close collaborators did not share Pius XII's preference for a clericalized, semiauthoritarian state.

The Left withdrew to lick its wounds, defend itself as best it could, and make the best of an extremely difficult situation. The Communists would in fact soon make important inroads in the South, where land-hungry peasants would undertake massive agitations and land occupations that led to a limited land reform. In the North, while the leadership knew that no dramatic surprises were being hatched in PCI headquarters, many militants continued to nurture the dream of X-Hour, when the party would give the word and some sort of revolution would take place (perhaps aided by the Red Army). Having tried the parliamentary democratic road to power and failed to achieve it, they could not believe that their leaders were going to accept defeat.

The Left's insurrectionary dreams were soon dashed to pieces. On July 14, 1948, Togliatti was gunned down on the steps of Parliament by a right-wing extremist. As he hovered near death, spontaneous general strikes broke out all over the country. In many areas in the North and the red zones, events took on a semi-insurrectionary tone: Police stations and communication centers were seized by armed ex-partisans, factories were occupied, and remnants of the old CLNs suddenly reappeared in isolated areas. Extremely violent clashes took place between demonstrators and the police and armed forces (broadly referred to as "the forces of order" in Italy), with estimates of thirty dead, hundreds wounded, and seven thousand arrested. At the end of these events, the government estimated that 30 million workdays had been lost.[7] Reacting to events only after they had already taken place, the party and union leadership declared a protest strike and frantically attempted to regain control of the situation. They did, and when shouts from monster rallies called on party leaders to "give us the go-ahead," the masses were told to stay calm.

The government, led by its archconservative interior minister, Mario Scelba (but supported by many others, including Catholic unionists), counterattacked, claiming that the PCI had attempted an insurrection and arresting hundreds of militants and politicians. The use of deadly force against left-wing and lower-class protest, always a hallmark of Italy's "forces of order," would be extensive over the next fifteen years. At the same time, and more ominously for the long run, the Catholic unionists used the July 14 attack as the excuse they needed to split the previously unified trade union movement. At the end of the war, a single trade-union confederation, the General Confederation of Italian Labor (CGIL), dominated by the Left, had been created. Its unity, always fragile, obviously could not last once the Left was expelled from the government. The Catholic unionists' schism had, in fact, been expected for some time. They would soon create the Italian Confederation of Trade Unions (CISL). The CISL remained closely identified with the DC through most of the 1960s and, for nearly fifteen years after the split, it was known for its willingness to sign "sweetheart" contracts with management. A year after the Catholics seceded, so did the Social Democrats and Republicans. They eventually formed the Italian Labor Union (UIL), which has always been the smallest of the major confederations but which has been quite strong in some areas and among certain categories of employees. By 1950, the trade unions were deeply divided along partisan lines that persist even today.

The Political Economy of Development: From Reconstruction to "Miracle"

Italy entered the postwar period with a host of serious structural problems and deficiencies caused not only by the war but also by the country's late development and the legacy of fascism. Even during tripartism, a number of policies — opposed strongly by the Left — had been set into motion. These in turn laid the groundwork for a satisfactory economic recovery and, eventually, for a truly impressive period of growth in the 1950s and 1960s. This does not mean that a rational master plan was followed; on the contrary, the lack of foresight ultimately undermined many of the system's achievements and guaranteed that when the contradictions finally did emerge, they were extremely intense.

Reconstruction Policies. Inventories at war's end showed that Italian industry, save for the heaviest sectors, was not as badly damaged as many had feared. The reason was partly because the Germans did not have the time either to dismantle or destroy the physical plant and partly because, during the Resistance, armed workers had defended their factories in the belief that socialism would follow hard on the heels of liberation. The labor movement may have had limited economic leverage, but its *political* strength remained considerable for some time. In the immediate aftermath of the war, this political strength translated into numerous concessions that the organized workers' movement was able to extract for itself and for the lower classes as a whole, including: guarantees against layoffs; wage indexation; seats on management boards; and highly subsidized basic commodities, starting with bread.

The country's leading economists, led by Einaudi, were students of nineteenth-century economic theory. None of this government spending or demand-side Keynesian nonsense for them! They wanted a strong currency, free trade, an end to inflation, and a balanced budget, and they were quite prepared to obtain their goals at the expense of the working class and the unemployed. Other West European countries might build their growth on the basis of a full-employment economy; the Italians intended to proceed on the basis of low wages, a large surplus-labor pool, and limited social spending. Italy's policies were so out of line with those of other West European countries, at least into 1948, that they drew open criticism from officials charged with carrying out the Marshall Plan. Among other things, the Italians were diverting Marshall aid intended for investment and to avoid deflation, in order to bolster their foreign reserves by hundreds of millions of dollars.[8]

The State and Private Sectors. This strong distaste for state intervention has generally been seen as a negative legacy of fascism. Of course, it does not mean that Einaudi and the Liberals dictated all economic policy, although their influence on monetary policy was immense. Others of a more interventionist bent (De Gasperi among them) went along with the idea of free trade because they were convinced that this would hasten European integration. Still, it is striking that in the midst of a postwar inflation and already high unemployment, classical deflationary measures — guaranteed to choke investment and thus dampen internal demand while encouraging business to slow production and increase layoffs — were followed. Credit was squeezed; subsidies and other public expenditures were cut, not only to reduce the government's bill but also to hold down consumption; efforts were made to raise taxes; and layoffs and other "rationalizing" measures in industry were encouraged to raise productivity and keep wages down even further. By the end of 1947, with the Left safely out of the government, the deflation was in full swing. Unemployment, which had been steadily rising with inflation since 1946, continued to creep upward after prices began to fall. By 1948, it was officially set at 2.1 million, a figure that would remain remarkably constant for almost a decade.[9]

Other forces favored at least a measure of long-range planning. The Marshall Plan required some indication of where and how the hundreds of millions of dollars that it intended to furnish in aid would be spent. (A total of $1.3 billion, most of it in outright grants, was eventually provided.)[10] More than this, however, several farsighted initiatives were set in motion by selectively directing credit to more dynamic firms and by using the extensive state holdings that were inherited from fascism. Against the protests of both the protected oligopolies and the free-marketers, immense investments were poured into the modernization of key industries, such as steel and chemicals. The state would not use IRI, the country's largest industrial employer, simply to keep employment up (which is what the Left and the unions wanted), but on the other hand, it had no intention of selling its holdings, as the Right demanded. The government kept its shares in IRI holdings but did not demand dividend payments, which thus had to be paid only to private shareholders. By this shrewd tactic, public-sector entrepreneurs were able to plow back a significant part of profits in the interests of the most rapid expansion possible. In the words of one astute observer,

> It was another one of the characteristic Latin conspiracies in the public interest, of which France, in particular, has provided some outstanding examples. In Italy such things have to be done with greater stealth, because there is neither the instinctive French respect of the high public official, nor any of the confidence in his moral purpose.[11]

The postwar period would also witness the expansion of state holdings. The *Ente Nazionale Idrocarburi* (ENI), the National Hydrocarbons Agency, was established in 1953 under the leadership of Enrico Mattei, a Christian Democrat and former partisan commander. Mattei oversaw the rapid development of Italy's petroleum resources: he set about building refineries, branching into the petrochemical industry, and striking deals with foreign governments to guarantee future sources of fossil fuels. His activities upset foreign and domestic competitors alike.[12] When Mattei was killed in a plane crash in 1962, rumors circulated (and a movie was made) suggesting that this was more than a routine aeronautical accident.

These public-sector initiatives meshed extraordinarily well with developments in the most dynamic parts of the private sector, which tended to be the manufacturers of durable consumer goods. *The* key firm was Fiat, which became Europe's largest auto manufacturer by the late 1960s and whose share of the Italian automobile market through the 1960s was on a scale comparable to that of General Motors, Ford, and Chrysler *combined* in North America. Fiat's decision in the early 1950s to make a cheap, small car (the "600") is generally seen as the decisive step in making the economy produce for a mass market. Italy's industry would expand enormously following this strategy, and the country would become a society of mass consumers. There were also numerous other export-oriented, less conservative entrepreneurs whose firms were either directly or indirectly involved in providing state-of-the-art goods at low prices to an increasingly affluent European public. By the mid-1950s, these companies were poised for maximum expansion, and they, too, viewed Italy's internal market — and not just the rest of Europe — as a fair target. Thanks to earlier public-sector intervention, abundant steel, fuel, chemicals, and other goods were already being produced in quantities that enabled expansion to take place without the hitches and bottlenecks that would have occurred had the free-marketers won the earlier debate. The groundwork for what would come to be known as the "economic miracle" was complete.

The Economic "Miracle". If we measure "miracles" in terms of truly extraordinary growth, then the Italian version was limited to 1958–62, when the gross national product (GNP) grew at a rate of over 6 percent per year, with a peak of over 8 percent in 1961. But, in fact, throughout the 1950s and 1960s, the Italian economy expanded at a rate exceeded in Western Europe only by West Germany.[13] GNP doubled between 1950 and 1962, and even the slowdown to the end of the 1960s averaged a very healthy 4 percent a year. It was the remarkable steadiness of Italian growth, and the country's avoidance of the more violent fluctuations suffered by neighboring economies, that helped register such an impressive record. The spurt in growth that began in the late 1950s also — finally — chopped down the very high rate of unemployment that had declined slowly since the late 1940s. By the early 1960s, unemployment had gone as low as 2.5 percent, and it stayed quite low through the decade.[14]

Italian society was radically and irrevocably altered in this period. None of the statistics can really render the *qualitative* changes this previously poor and agricultural country underwent in twenty years. In the early 1950s, a parliamentary committee of inquiry into poverty in the country described the living conditions of two-thirds of Italian families as "modest" by the limited standards of the time: one family in eight lived in "utter destitution"; one house in ten had a bath; less than half of all Italians had an indoor toilet; and fewer still (38 percent) had indoor running water that was drinkable.[15] By the 1960s, and especially by the 1970s, although it still lagged behind the other major Western European countries, Italy had attained an overall economic profile and standard of living comparable to that of advanced capitalist nations. The proportion of illiterates or those who had not completed elementary school was no longer 59 percent of the entire population over six years of age, as it had been in 1951, but only half that in 1971, and almost all these people were old.[16] Industrial workers surpassed the entire agricultural population in the 1960s, and the latter finally fell to a fifth of the total work force by the 1971 census (See Table 17.2). New car registrations had been a quarter million in 1960 and reached a million in 1968.[17] Even by other measures of consumption, such as televisions or telephones per capita, by 1971 the Italians were on a scale roughly comparable with the other large Western European countries.[18]

Unresolved Contradictions of the 1960s. As we have seen, Italian development benefited greatly from the timely intervention of central policymakers and from aggressive managers in the public sector of the economy. None of this, however, should be confused with rational planning. The Italian achievement was the setting loose of numerous healthy forces that dragged much of the economy along with them. The miracle, therefore, built on the country's preexisting strengths. In Italy, this means, above all, that the real engine of growth was in the North, while the South, as usual, represented the caboose. In spite of serious and extremely expensive initiatives, in 1971 the South's *relative* standing was actually marginally worse by almost all measures than it had been twenty years earlier. Of course, we need to keep this in perspective: Per capita income rose two-and-a-half times in the Mezzogiorno in this period, thus eliminating much of the abject misery that once characterized the area, but it rose even more rapidly in the North[19] — despite the fact that so many southerners had moved north or out of the country altogether. It is worth noting that the very high (and understated) unemployment rates of 7 to 9 percent in the 1950s up to the miracle would have been nearly *doubled* had there not been a steady exodus of workers out of the country in the previous decade. Between 1946 and 1955, net emigration totaled 1.6 million.[20]

Table 17.2 Employment in Italy, by Sector of The Economy, 1951–81

Economic Sector	1951 Employees ('000)	1951 Percent	1961 Employees ('000)	1961 Percent	1971 Employees ('000)	1971 Percent	1981 Employees ('000)	1981 Percent
Agriculture	8,640	43.9	6,272	30.7	3,875	20.1	2,759	13.3
All Industries	5,803	29.5	7,138	34.9	7,617	39.5	7,727	37.2
All Services*	5,250	26.6	7,017	34.4	7,803	40.4	10,265	49.5
TOTALS	19,693	100.0	20,427	100.0	19,275	100.0	20,752	100.0

*Includes government.

SOURCES For 1951: Kevin Allen and Andrew Stevenson, *An Introduction to the Italian Economy* (London: Martin Robertson and Co., 1974), p. 104; thereafter: Italian Confederation of Trade Unions, *CISL 1984* (Rome: Edizioni Lavoro, 1984), p. 56.

Given the overwhelmingly rural nature of the population at the time, reform efforts in the South were originally directed toward agriculture. A land reform begun in 1950 distributed considerable acreage from expropriated *latifondia* to poor peasants, but in very small, usually uneconomical, plots. On a far more ambitious scale, the *Cassa per il Mezzogiorno,* "Fund for the South," was also created in 1950 and would ultimately spend billions of dollars in an effort to develop Italy's most backward regions. There is some evidence since the 1980s that the billions poured into the Mezzogiorno — by the European Economic Community (EEC) and private Italian firms, as well as by public-sector enterprises — have begun to bear fruit. But for too long a period, and certainly for the period through the peak years of the miracle, southern development was only further distorted by the northern-driven expansion and by the DC's use of the state as a patronage agency.

The tumultuous and spontaneous nature of Italian growth in this period also created, or aggravated, many problems in the North. The mass migration of workers into the major urban centers, first from the surrounding countryside, then from the South, put intolerable strains on housing and social services, particularly education, health and transportation. The proportion of the population living in cities of over one hundred thousand inhabitants rose from about one-third in 1951 to nearly one-half by 1971, with major centers like Turin, home of Fiat, doubling in size. It was often enough for a *rumor* to circulate that Fiat was about to begin hiring: Within days, the main train station in Turin would be filled with desperate southerners, often with cardboard boxes serving as suitcases, milling about and sleeping on the benches.

The Labor Movement

Organized Labor's Weaknesses. The workers did not willingly accept the marginal role into which they were thrust from 1947 on, but a highly unfavorable combination of political and economic circumstances kept them in a totally subordinate position until the early 1960s and weak until the 1970s. Further, the left-wing union leadership made a number of serious errors that greatly compounded its difficulties. A quick summary of all these factors will make it easier to understand why the tide turned in the 1960s and why the explosion of the late 1960s was so violent, protracted, and radical.

Economically, labor market conditions remained unfavorable through the peak period of the miracle. It is certainly no accident that successful strike activity turned dramatically upward in 1962, which marks the end of the biggest expansionary cycle in growth and the achievement of effective full employment. But market conditions alone would never have marginalized the movement so thoroughly, especially a movement that had been so powerful at war's end that it was able to wring numerous concessions out of employers and government alike. As we have seen, the complete exclusion of the Left was a necessary precondition for the government to carry out fully its reconstruction policies, and the division along *political* lines of the originally united labor confederation further weakened the entire labor movement. Although the Communist-dominated CGIL continued to be considerably larger than its only serious competitor, the DC-linked CISL, its broader political isolation, combined with the unfavorable market for labor, meant the CGIL could be ignored.

In fact, as Table 17.3 shows, the CGIL steadily lost ground to the CISL through the 1950s and most of the 1960s, mainly because of its own dramatic losses in membership. However, the CGIL has always organized far more workers than the CISL in the crucial industrial sec-

Table 17.3 Total Union Membership, Excluding Pensioners, in the Two Major Confederations for Selected Years, 1950–82

	CGIL ('000)	CISL ('000)	UIL ('000)
1950	4,314	1,094	*
1955	3,741	1,166	*
1960	2,212	1,158	*
1965	2,158	1,318	*
1970	2,513	1,674	*
1976	3,551	2,537	1,016
1979	3,527	2,510	1,188
1982	3,286	2,410	1,181

*Reliable figures for the UIL are not available for this period.

SOURCES For 1950–70: Guido Romagnoli, ed., *La sindacalizzazione tra ideologia e pratica. Il caso italiano 1950–1977,* vol. 2 (Rome: Edizioni Lavoro, 1978), Table 1.2. For 1976: Guido Romagnoli, "Sindacalizzazione e rappresentanza," in *Le Relazioni sindacali in Italia. Rapporto 1981,* ed. Guido Baglioni et al. (Rome: Edizioni Lavoro, 1982), Table 2. For 1979–82: ed. Baglioni et al., *Le Relazioni sindacali in Italia. Rapporto 1982–83* (Rome: Edizioni Lavoro, 1984), Table 2.

tor.[21] The CGIL's decline in the 1950s was hastened by an open policy of union-busting and the overt repression of union and left-wing militants. In the event that workers did not understand what was in store for "troublemakers" and "agitators," management regularly harassed and fired activists or exiled them to isolated areas of the factories, often to perform tasks that were physically obnoxious or completely mind-numbing.

This took a terrible toll of the union, as the membership decline demonstrates. But the CGIL itself committed major errors throughout the reconstruction period and the first half of the 1950s. These had the effect of isolating it further from developments on both the shop floor and in the society at large. The CGIL shared the belief that capitalism was on its last legs. It was also committed to a strongly centralized organizational structure because of a deep commitment to "class unionism." Finally, and crucially, the Communists were committed in this period to use *all* their mass organizations as "transmission belts" to carry out the *party's* major priorities. In a period of isolation, the PCI's temptation to use the union as a megaphone was even greater than usual. Thus, even when the union addressed workers' concerns, it did so on a generic level, organized from the top down. Agitations tended to be either defensive (e.g., against plant shutdowns) or were pitched at the highest national — or even international — level. Examples of the latter included protests against Italian membership in NATO, or peace marches.[22]

Finally, when the CGIL's organizational decline became severe and it began to lose its leadership position in elections in key factories, especially Fiat, it started to correct its earlier errors and even dropped the transmission belt concept of party-union relations. It by no means abandoned its class unionism, but taking a page from the CISL's practices, it did begin to pay considerably more attention to local conditions as well.

The Tide Begins to Turn. Nineteen sixty-two marked a critical turning point in Italian labor relations. The end of the unfavorable labor market saw an extensive and successful series of strikes by an increasingly militant labor force. For the first time since the beginning of the 1950s, wage settlements outstripped increases in productivity — and they did so by a considerable margin. Moreover, in spite of persisting political divisions, the unions showed an increasing awareness that unity of action could bring them impressive benefits. Finally, the union leaders discovered that management was far from united: Rifts quickly opened between public and private sector firms and, within the private sector, between those with relatively high labor costs and those that were more capital-intensive.

These trends would take another six or seven years to mature, for in 1963, the economy suffered its first serious downturn since the end of the 1940s. There were complex reasons for this, not the least of which was the length and intensity of the miracle's boom, which generated a trade imbalance and inflation. The drop was seriously aggravated by a capital strike, as investors reacted to rising labor militancy and the newly created Center-Left government. Hundreds of millions of dollars' worth of *lire* were withheld from normal investment channels, and much of this money found its way illegally across the Swiss border.[23] When the government responded to rising imports and an increasingly unstable *lira* with classical deflationary policies, the initial crisis became a recession in 1964–65. The resulting temporary rise in unemployment and dampening of militancy, followed by a strong recovery through the end of the decade, marked a brief setback for the unions and encouraged the conservatives within government, as well as the bulk of management, to believe that they had fully regained the upper hand and could block any serious reform efforts with little trouble.

Divisions *within* the CGIL also threatened the labor movement with serious setbacks in the 1960s. If the labor market was driving the unions toward collaboration, the political arena was generating immense strains between the Communists and Socialists. (This, of course, is one of the reasons why the more progressive business elites and most of the DC felt it essential to push ahead with the Center-Left.) The entry of the PSI into the government in 1963, with the declared purpose of isolating the PCI and undermining its working-class support, created extreme conflict in a union confederation in which the two parties were supposed to work side-by-side. In early 1964, the Left wing of the PSI broke away to form the Socialist Party of Proletarian Unity (PSIUP), which in turn hastened the Socialists' rapprochement with the PSDI: The two eventually (re)united in 1966. The CGIL's success in remaining united during this period was a remarkable achievement that is a testimony to the strong desire for unity among both the leadership and the rank-and-file of the union. By 1969, with the most militant Socialists thoroughly disgusted by the Center-Left, and with the PSI and PSDI once again going their separate ways, the crisis had passed. An unusually large number of labor contracts had expired and were simultaneously scheduled for renewal that year. Given the resurgence of militancy over broader social issues as well as wages and working conditions, people began to speak in the spring of how hot the autumn was likely to be. In fact, it marked the decisive turning point of the entire postwar period.

Politics from the Miracle to the Hot Autumn

Centrism would take nearly a decade to die, and its agonies would reveal how vulnerable Italian democracy remained in this period. In 1953, De Gasperi tried to guarantee a solid majority in the upcoming elections by altering the proportional electoral system. The "swindle law," as it was immediately dubbed by the opposition, would have given any alliance of parties 65 percent of the seats in the Chamber of Deputies if it obtained a bare majority of the valid votes cast. The centrist alliance, which had received 62 percent in 1948, missed its goal by fifty-seven thousand votes (out of 27 million).[24] In 1960, Ferdinando Tambroni, a Christian Democrat, accepted votes from the extreme rightwing neo-Fascist Italian Social Movement (MSI) to keep his *monocolore* caretaker government in office, but he was obviously maneuvering to curry favor with the Right and stay in power. Without consulting his party, he gave the MSI permission to hold a national congress in Genoa, an anti-Fascist stronghold. Only after massive demonstrations and riots left ten people dead was Tambroni forced from office and into political obscurity. It took these dramatic events to drive home the point that the door to the Right was firmly closed. Thereafter, DC Secretary Aldo Moro pressed insistently for a DC-PSI alliance.

Yet it would *still* require more than three years for the Socialists, who had been steadily drifting away from the Communists, to join a government as full-fledged participants. As the DC and PSI moved closer together, the Liberals moved to the Right and lost their left wing in the process. They made it quite clear that they would not be party to any coalitions that included the PSI, so their shift made it all the more imperative for the DC and PSI to come to terms.

The 1950s also saw the end of the church's most blatant period of direct involvement in Italian politics, for Pope Pius XII died in 1958 and was succeeded by Pope John XXIII. While Pope John XXIII's contribution to opening up the church, and to a relaxation of political tension in Italy, is unquestioned, it is important to emphasize that this did not occur overnight. In 1960, as the Tambroni affair was unfolding, and again in 1963, on the eve of the Socialists' entry into the government, *l'Osservatore Romano,* the official newspaper of the Vatican, intervened in a heavy-handed fashion in the DC's internal struggles.[25]

This by no means freed the DC from conservative, and even reactionary, forces within its own power bloc. The small farmers' association, which was an immensely powerful interest group run by a DC power broker, was vituperatively anti-Left and, indeed, anti-working class. The same was true of the civic committees of Catholic Action, Italy's largest lay Catholic organization, whose leadership issued veiled threats to create a "truly Christian" party every time the DC leaned toward a rapprochement with the Socialists.

The Evolution of the DC's System of Power. The most significant political development of the 1950s, in terms of its implications for the entire Italian system, undoubtedly involves the evolution of the ruling party. Beginning in 1954 with the secretaryship of Amintore Fanfani, the DC proceeded to establish a more independent organizational base for itself. Fanfani sought to provide his party with power bases that did not rely solely on its major support structures: southern notables, the church, private industry's financial contributions, or American largesse. This meant, in practice, a two-pronged strategy: first, to build and reinforce an independent party structure; second, to use the many public resources at hand to build a patronage structure that would both support the party organization and serve as an independent source of funding and favors for the party faithful — beginning with members of his own faction. Most importantly of all, this provided the DC with the glue that held together its extremely heterogeneous constituencies.

Given the abundant opportunities the Italian system provided for such exploitation, ranging from communications, to aid, to welfare agencies, and to the massive state sector of the economy, and given as well a political elite that had no qualms about using these opportunities for narrowly partisan purposes, the groundwork was laid for what one analyst calls "the occupation of power" by the DC.[26] This colonization of the state and para-state apparatuses would accelerate throughout the period of the economic miracle and the Center-Left as well.

Because these were periods of steady economic growth, the wasteful and inefficient use of public resources was not immediately apparent. As we shall see in our discussion of the crisis of the 1970s, these practices continued and contributed immensely to Italy's crushing public-sector deficits and the slowness with which the country could recover from the inflationary spiral of the 1970s.

The Politics and Political Economy of the Center-Left. In spite of all the enthusiasm it generated among its supporters and the fear it engendered among Communists and conservatives alike, the Center-Left did not come close to delivering on the many promises it had held out. It began with a flurry of reforms that quickly died out as conservative interests inside and outside the DC increased their resistance. The Socialists were weakened at the outset by the loss of their left wing in 1964 and further demoralized when their unification with the PSDI and presence in government actually cost them votes in 1968. (See Table 17.4.) Enmeshed in parliamentary maneuvering and in the patronage system, the Socialists were junior partners of the DC. They would eventually change their line, but even their exit from the Center-Left proved painful and did not bring immediate benefits.

The Communists' opposition to the Center-Left reflected their fear of greater isolation, as well as their serious concern about the aggravation of divisions within the working class at a time when there were finally

Table 17.4: Vote Obtained by Italian Parties in General Elections, 1953–1983 (Percentage Obtained by Each Party List, Chamber of Deputies)

PARTY	1953	1958	1963	1968	1972	1976	1979	1983
NSU/DP	—	—	—	—	0.2%	1.5%	0.8%	1.5%
PDUP	—	—	—	—	0.7	w/DP	1.4	w/PCI
PCI	22.6%	22.7%	25.3%	27.0%	27.2	34.4	30.4	29.9
PSI	12.7	14.3	13.9	14.5[a]	9.6	9.6	9.8	11.4
PSIUP[b]	—	—	—	4.5	1.9	—	—	—
PR	—	—	—	—	—	1.1	3.5	2.2
PSDI[c]	4.5	4.6	6.1	[a]	5.1	3.4	3.8	4.1
PRI	1.6	1.4	1.4	2.0	2.9	3.1	3.0	5.1
DC	40.1	42.4	38.3	39.1	38.7	38.7	38.3	32.9
PLI	3.0	3.6	7.0	5.8	3.9	1.3	1.9	2.9
Extreme Right[d]	12.8	9.6	6.9	5.8	8.7	6.1	5.9	6.8
OTHERS	2.7	1.4	1.1	1.3	1.1	0.8	1.2	3.2
TOTALS	100.0	100.0	100.0	100.0	100.0	100.0	100.0	100.0

a. Result of united PSI-PSDI list
b. Split from PSI in 1964
c. Split from PSI in 1947, reunited 1966–69
d. Includes MSI (Neo-Fascists) and monarchists until 1972; MSI thereafter

KEY NSU/DP = United New Left/Proletarian Democracy
PDUP = Initially "Il Manifesto"; later Democratic Party of Proletarian Unity
PSIUP = Socialist Party of Proletarian Unity
PR = Radical Party
PSDI = Italian Social Democratic Party
PRI = Italian Republican Party
PLI = Italian Liberal Party
MSI = Italian Social Movement

positive developments in the opposite direction. Encouraged by their electoral advances in 1963 and 1968, the Communists did all they could to mobilize dissent against the limits on the reforms that were enacted, particularly against those that were stalled by bickering within the governing coalition.

The unions, particularly the CGIL, but increasingly the CISL as well, also refused to go along with the government's calls for restraint. It is unlikely that any incentives could have persuaded them to accept the wages policy (i.e., to link their raises to increases in productivity) that was discussed with increasing frequency in the mid-1960s. Moreover, the unions were deeply upset by the way the 1963 recession had been handled. In spite of the presence of their ostensible ally, the PSI, in the government, the familiar old measures had been adopted: credit restrictions, deflation, and unemployment. This was hardly guaranteed to win working-class allegiance and deeply hurt the PSI's credibility. As it also forced the unions to settle for much less in the 1966 round of contract negotiations, it generated resentment and a desire for revenge for the next round, which would begin in 1968 but reach a peak in the autumn of 1969, when an unusually large number of contracts were simultaneously up for renewal.

The Fall of the Postwar Settlement

The Hot Autumn

Although there actually was a *hot autumn* of 1969, the term has come to serve as shorthand for the extensive mobilization and struggles that convulsed Italian society from 1968 through 1970. The cycle of trade union mobilization actually lasted until 1972, beyond the round of formal contract negotiations. The period witnessed, and indeed began with, mass mobilizations and demonstrations by students and other social forces not linked to the workers' movement. It was, in fact, the *breadth* of these struggles, along with their intensity and longevity, that makes them a watershed in postwar Italian history. With them, the patterns that had governed political, economic, and social relations in Italy since 1947–48 came to an end.

Labor's Position. The unions' rediscovered unity, along with their combativeness and growing organizational strength, put them in an extremely strong position in relation to management and, temporarily at least, in a powerful and unprecedented role as a direct negotiator with the government. The unions' leverage was greatly aided by a labor market that continued to be highly favorable and by a divided, confused, and demoralized management front. Radically egalitarian and participatory ideas were widespread at the end of the 1960s, and these found fertile ground in a movement with a strong class tradition, which by 1969 had spread to the CISL and UIL. These ideas were most deeply entrenched in the unions that represented the cutting edge of the hot autumn: those from the large factories of the North, with huge unskilled and semiskilled work forces. In short, the labor movement found itself in an exceptionally powerful position, and its demands were quite radical. Its own internal organization, the nature of collective bargaining, and relations between the labor movement and the state were, as a consequence, profoundly altered in the 1970s.

Internally, the unions moved on two fronts. Unity of action never evolved into a single CGIL–CISL–UIL confederation, as many had hoped, for political suspicions remained too great. However, the unions increased their independence from the parties and signed the Federation Pact in 1972. At the same time, the factory councils were institutionalized at the grass roots. They strengthened a more participatory form of representation, for the workers' representatives were chosen by *all* workers in a factory or shop, including those who were not in the union, and the delegates were also subject to recall. These councils helped perpetuate decentralized, factory-by-factory bargaining well into the 1970s, which kept the initiative in the hands of low-level militants rather than under the centralized control of the labor movement leadership. These decentralized, bottom-up struggles were also one of the hot autumn's most distinctive features: They went far beyond demands over wages and working conditions and often challenged management prerogatives and capitalist control over the workplace.

The workers obtained extremely advantageous contracts through the first half of the 1970s. Wage settlements continued to stay ahead of productivity. Overtime was restricted and had to be negotiated with the unions, which frequently pressured management to hire more workers. It became extremely difficult to lay off or even transfer workers, irrespective of economic requirements. Further, workers who were laid off had the benefit of the Wage Integration Fund, which makes up partial or total lost salary during "temporary" layoffs (which might be truly temporary, but which might go on for years). Some of the most controversial demands of the unions, and those most strongly resisted by most of management, concerned workers' involvement in actual investment decisions. It was one thing for this to occur in the public sector, but private capitalists have always considered their freedom to invest sacrosanct. With timely tax concessions and other incentives and guarantees from the state, however, the unions were instrumental in some factories' promising to build new plants in the South and in less densely congested areas of the North and Center.

The contracts were also notable for their extremely egalitarian content. Lump-sum, rather than percentage, increases were won; job classifications were drastically reduced; and blue- and white-collar categories were given the same raises. Separate wage scales based on sex, age, or geographical areas of the country were eliminated. Most notable of all was the automatic cost-of-living increase, or *scala mobile,* "escalator," which not only was established as a lump-sum payment every few months but also included limits on higher salaries. With the high inflation rates of the 1970s contributing to the equalizing effect, wage differentials were drastically cut down over time.

Politically, beginning in 1968, the unions made a decisive contribution to important national reform legislation. In addition to the abolition of wage differentials, they led a series of general strikes for a generous and advanced pension plan. However, the most important piece of strictly working-class legislation was the Workers' Statute of 1970, which formally sanctions the workers' rights as citizens inside the factory. It guarantees union activities in the workplace, including time off for delegates and other officials to perform their duties, and allows leaves of absence to do full-time union work or to assume elected political office. Considering that a dozen years earlier, a worker could be harassed or fired simply for appearing with a left-wing newspaper in his or her pocket, the change — and the altered balance of power — is easily appreciated.

The confederations negotiated with the government on a number of issues, most notably housing and medical services. After a housing initiative was drafted, however, it was sabotaged in Parliament. This underscored the limits of an agitational and pressure-group approach to legislative questions and of trying to apply the labor-management model to the political sphere. Because of their efforts to maintain a distance between themselves and the parties — a necessity if united action free of partisan suspicion was to continue — the unions soon realized that they needed *political* representation more than ever. Most labor leaders concluded that as long as the major political representative of labor, the PCI, remained on the margins of power, hopes for serious, wide-ranging reforms would remain blocked. Even the CISL and UIL leaders, while remaining suspicious of the Communists, accepted this reasoning.

The Politics of (Apparent) Stagnation. In spite of the unprecedented mass mobilization from 1968 onward, the parliamentary balance of power remained remarkably, and for the Left, depressingly, stable. Many of the old assumptions and systems of social relations had broken down, but the political system seemed as immobilized as ever. To be sure, the struggles had generated or hastened the realization of numerous reforms, but these changes had also generated a monumental backlash, particularly among the urban and rural middle classes who were among the DC's main mass constituencies. Most ominously, in the main cities of the South, there were also distressing signs of mass disaffection, which were ably exploited by the neo-Fascists. By 1970, faced with the first of numerous episodes of right-wing terror, the DC was already beginning to backpedal to cover its right flank. By the early 1970s, the PCI had also begun to worry about the threat of a reactionary backlash and had begun to moderate its own strategy and to issue warnings to the workers' movement not to alienate all other strata in society.

The 1972 elections seemed to bear out the most sober analyses. A host of smaller left-wing groups presented themselves at the polls, hoping to reap the harvest of radical opinion that they all assumed existed in the wake of the hot autumn. Some were made up of militant Catholics, whose goal was to attract workers who had previously voted for the DC and who might be reticent to cast a ballot for the PCI or PSI. While these groups, along with the PSIUP, did draw a million votes (3 percent), their electorate was so fragmented that they failed to elect a single deputy. (The PSIUP dissolved itself soon afterward.) At the same time, the MSI greatly improved its showing, while the DC, rushing to the Right, held its own. With the Communists and Socialists failing to improve their positions, the Right emerged with the advantage in Parliament: the old centrist coalition of the 1950s once more existed on paper, with a majority of fifteen seats. When the Socialists refused to join another paralyzed and discredited Center-Left coalition, Giulio Andreotti formed a neo-centrist government. Thus, the most radical and sustained mobilizations in the history of the Republic had seemingly produced a reedition of a totally discredited formula from the past.

The PSI had been pushed Left by the hot autumn and by the renewed break with the PSDI. It had paid dearly for its subordinate collaboration with the DC, and it would no longer allow the Communists to monopolize the opposition, largely at the PSI's expense. Therefore, after 1972 it announced that only the direct participation of the entire Left in government (i.e., the PCI must be included) could really resolve Italy's structural problems. With a clear eye on the renaissance of the French Socialists, the PSI set about trying to establish the conditions for such a Left alternative. It hoped to see the Left grow, but with the Communists stagnant or even perhaps receding to the PSI's advantage. This was an ambitious, and highly risky, operation. The PCI was nearly three times the size of the PSI and far less discredited in public opinion. If the PCI changed enough to legitimize itself to a larger public (and this was what the PSI desired as well), the major beneficiary of any shift might well prove to be the PCI.

The Historic Compromise. In response to the backlash against the Left and convinced by the 1972 elections that all the major parties had a solid lock on their constituencies, PCI Secretary-General Enrico Berlinguer steered his party on a decidedly moderate course. In 1973, after the military overthrew an elected leftist government in Chile, Berlinguer spelled out a new strategy that he had in fact been developing for more than a year.[27] This strategy, dubbed the "historic compromise," was a far cry from the Left alternative sought by the Socialists. In its most ambitious form, the historic compromise proposed long-term collaboration between the PCI, PSI, and DC, though the real emphasis was on the PCI and DC. These parties were seen as the embodiment of the truly progressive forces in Italian society. They also represented such a large majority that stability would be guaranteed. With many references to the period of tripartite cooperation in the immediate postwar period, Berlinguer indicated that the Communists would moderate their own — and the workers' — demands in exchange for limited, but serious, reforms. With the institutions of the Republic in jeopardy, he proposed an emergency government of all constitutional parties to confront the immediate problems facing the country. He then clarified the PCI's position on many issues that might worry more moderate voters, offering, for instance, reassurances that the Communists truly accepted democratic institutions and that they accepted the existence of NATO for the foreseeable future.

Berlinguer's initiative thus ran in the opposite direction of the Socialists'. It was a brilliant stroke for two entirely separate reasons. First, it forced the DC to respond to the PCI's offer of a way out of a seemingly paralyzed and degenerating situation: "Let us all work together," the

PCI was in effect saying, "for a package of reforms the country must have. No one will get everything he wants, but we will at least serve the country's interests and break this stalemate." Second, the enunciation of the historic compromise accelerated the PCI's already considerable evolution away from the Soviet Union and many of the practices and dogmas that had weighed the Italian Communists down in the past.

For all its brilliance, the historic compromise was fatally flawed. Had it represented a *short-term* solution — like the Grand Coalition in West Germany in 1966–69 — to the immediate problems of the country as well as to the legitimization of the PCI as a party of government, it might well have generated a dramatic change in the political balance in Italy by the end of the 1970s. Berlinguer clearly believed in its long-term effectiveness, however; he and his advisors therefore misread the profound changes in the mid-1970s. At a time when the DC's base was more conservative than ever, they insisted on emphasizing the ruling party's progressive constituencies and on overestimating the DC's capacity and desire for change.

The entire strategy was based on a fundamentally pessimistic and static misreading of the underlying dynamics of Italian society. It assumed that the major parties, especially the DC and PCI, embraced almost all the vital and progressive forces in the system and that they would continue to do so. And it did this precisely at a time when civil society was showing increasing signs of being *less* linked to the established parties than ever before. For all these reasons, when the previously rigid party alignments and subcultures began to erode in the mid-1970s, the Communists misread the signs. Instead of understanding that a new, secularized public demanded quick action on numerous issues, they interpreted the results according to their old formulas. The PCI believed its new support came from people who were convinced of the correctness of the historic compromise and of the need to collaborate with the Christian Democrats. Events soon proved how wrong the Communists were.

The Political Breakthroughs and Partial Realignments of the Mid-1970s

Evidence that the profound changes in society were finally going to have repercussions at the ballot box came suddenly, dramatically, and unequivocally. The referendum of 1974, which tried to repeal the divorce law, and which the Left had feared, revealed that Italian public opinion was far less backward than had been assumed. The church, pretending to speak for the mass of Italians, found itself humiliated when it ended up on the short end of a 60–40 percent vote to retain divorce. Only the very religious North-East had cast a clear vote to follow church teachings, while Sicily, presumed land of darkness and superstition, had narrowly voted in favor of retaining divorce. Major northern cities like Turin had 80 percent majorities. The Christian Democrats, who had suffered the additional embarrassment of campaigning with the neo-Fascists, were stunned: The vote for abolition was a full 7.5 percent below the DC–MSI electoral total. Equally surprised, but utterly delighted, were the Communists. For the first time in the history of the Republic, *they* were the largest party on the winning side of a convincing majority. This did not, however, lead Berlinguer to reconsider his analysis.

The local elections of 1975 confirmed that there had been a deep shift in the electorate. The DC's support fell dramatically to 35 percent, equaling its historical low of 1946. At the same time, the PCI vote rose to a totally unprecedented 33 percent, with rises approaching 10 percent in major cities. By the time new local governments were set up, more people in the country were governed locally by the Communists than by the DC. After nearly thirty years of a seemingly immobile electorate, two shocks in two years made it seem as if anything was now possible. There was extensive speculation that the next general elections might even see the DC overtaken by the PCI. Buoyed by their own relative improvement in the local voting, the Socialists precipitated early elections in 1976 with the hope of reaping even greater benefits. They had reluctantly been participating in Center-Left coalitions to keep the disastrous neo-centrist formula, which had lasted a year, from being attempted again.

The 1976 vote saw the Communists, and the Left, even further reinforced. The Left had increased its total by 7 percent over 1972, and that was the precise size of the PCI's gain. With 34.4 percent of the total, the PCI touched its historical high point, and in an impressive fashion. Even in the South, where the PCI had traditionally been weaker, it managed to come close to its overall showing. To the Socialists' dismay, they remained at just below 10 percent. To the dismay of the whole Left, the DC had yet again held its own, but it had only done so at the expense of its minor partners. The traditional four-party centrist bloc and all the parties Left of the Social Democrats were now of equal strength at 47 percent each. As long as the Socialists refused to govern without the PCI, the situation was totally stalemated.

The Rationale for Austerity. By the middle of the 1970s, the Italian economy was showing many of the troubled symptoms familiar to all the advanced capitalist societies. In some areas, particularly inflation, Italy's specific problems manifested themselves early and combined with the so-called oil shock of 1973 to create especially serious difficulties. With its own natural resources long since consumed, the country's near-total reliance on imported fuel, and consequent susceptibility to sudden price rises, is evident from a glance at Table 17.5's inflation figures for 1974 and 1980 (there was a second shock in 1979). Unemployment had also begun to rise in the middle of the decade, which contributed to the further decline in the exceptional radicalism of the labor movement, for the union leadership was increasingly reasserting its control over its own rank-and-file. Through the first half of the decade, restraint would have been impossible to achieve — and restraint was obviously what the Communists, and the unions, had to promise if PCI participation in the government was to be realized.

Table 17.5 Broad Performance of the Italian Economy Between 1970 and 1985

	1970	1971	1972	1973	1974	1975	1976	1977
Percent Change of Real GDP over Previous Year	5.3	1.6	3.2	7.0	4.1	−3.6	5.9	1.9
Percent Rise in Consumer Prices over Previous Year	5.0	4.8	5.7	10.8	19.1	17.0	16.8	17.0
Percent of Total Labor Force Unemployed	5.4	5.4	6.4	6.4	5.4	5.9	6.7	7.2

	1978	1979	1980	1981	1982	1983	1984	1985
Percent Change of Real GDP over Previous Year	2.7	4.9	3.9	0.1	−0.3	−1.2	2.6	2.3
Percent Rise in Consumer Prices over Previous Year	12.1	14.8	21.2	17.8	16.5	15.0	10.8	9.4
Percent of Total Labor Force Unemployed	7.2	7.7	7.6	8.4	9.1	9.8	10.4	10.4

SOURCE Real GDP and Consumer Prices through 1984: OECD and ISTAT figures cited in CISL, *CISL 1984* (Rome: Edizioni Lavoro, 1984): 28, 32. Unemployment figures: *ISTAT, Annuario Statistico, 1983,* (Rome: 1984): Table 292 for 1970–82. All others: Ferruccio Marzano, "The Report on Italy's Economic Situation in 1984," *Journal of Regional Policy* 5 (April–June, 1985): 208–209

The worst, most structurally rooted, aspects of the crisis were plain to see in the increasing fiscal crisis of the Italian state. Italy had increasingly taken on the trappings of a modern welfare state, which generates its own difficulties even under optimal conditions. Extremely generous and expensive benefits had been slapped onto a terribly inefficient bureaucratic and fiscal structure, which could neither deliver services effectively nor pay its own way. The dimensions of the problem can perhaps best be communicated with a simple comparison: The famous Reagan budget deficit caused great alarm in the United States when it broke the $100 billion barrier in the early 1980s; at about the same time, the Italian deficit, without colossal defense outlays and in an economy that hardly bears serious comparison to the United States, reached $53 billion.

The social security system, especially as it regards pensions, sheds light on several crucial aspects of the crisis.[28] As previously noted, the pension reform of the late 1960s was very advanced. Men can retire at sixty years of age (women at fifty-five), or after forty years of employment. The pension itself is based, not on what the worker contributed to a fund, but on his or her average income in the last five years at work. Moreover, the workers' share of the contribution is very low. Soon after the initial reform, pensions were fully indexed, and minimum pensions were established for those unable to benefit from the new provisions. Coverage was soon extended to public-sector employees.

These benefits would obviously cause state spending to rise dramatically in any event. But as they came in the early 1970s, with a strong middle-class backlash developing and the DC rushing to cover its right flank, benefits were extended to other strata of the population — the groups the Christian Democrats were trying to placate. The traditional middle classes (peasants, small businessmen, shopkeepers) had not enjoyed decent social security benefits previously, and now the DC rushed to provide them with at least moderate coverage. The ruling party further sweetened the package by requiring very low contributions from these groups in relation to the benefits provided. Many pensions remain low, and few pensioners enjoy the generous maximum provisions that exist on paper (though this will change in the future). But in the first half of the 1970s, four million people were added to the pension rolls and expenditures on pensions rose by a factor of 2.5.

How did the Italian state pay for its expenditures? It avoided a good deal of expense by making employers pay a very high share — over half — of the contributions going to the fund for industrial workers. No other advanced capitalist country approaches this proportion. The consequences of this practice are easy to imagine: Employers who pay what is expected suffer crippling disadvantages in costs and thus lose ground to their competition; the incentive to cheat, or to decentralize production and pay lower wages and benefits to unorganized workers, is very great indeed.

Where the state could not, or would not, make others pay, it went into debt, which is why the deficit has risen at such an astounding rate. It raised taxes and even partially reformed the tax laws, which did bring in more revenue, but increased revenue was outstripped by the rise in spending. The reason for this gap is well known: Tax evasion is something of a national pastime in Italy, and it is notorious among the self-employed middle classes and indeed among all groups that have to declare their income (rather than having taxes withheld from a salary). In the words of *The Economist,* certainly no enemy of private enterprise, Italy is "a country where cheating on taxes by the self-employed is regarded as their entrepreneurial privilege."[29] Since these groups overwhelmingly support the DC and its traditional coalition partners, governments have rarely tackled the problem of evasion with much zeal.

As with many of the degenerations of Italian public life, the dimensions of tax cheating can reach amusing levels. In the early 1980s, for example, the average Italian employer's declared income was lower than that of the averge employee. This led to numerous ironic headlines and cartoons and to considerable public outrage. It also speaks volumes about the cowardice of the Italian political elite, and why so much of the public holds its leaders in such contempt. It also helps explain why the tax revolt, which is usually thought of as a middle-class phenomenon, is characteristic of blue- and white-collar workers in Italy: They have their taxes withheld and, therefore, pay the full (high) rate that exists on paper.

In Lieu of an Alternative: National Unity

Given the numerical standoff in Parliament, it became impossible to ignore Berlinguer's calls for broad collaboration. The DC made sure it conceded the bare minimum possible, however. It would accept PCI support and consult with the Communists over the government's program and day-to-day operations. The PCI would also get the symbolic offices to which its size entitled it: the presidency of one of the houses of Parliament, a proportional share of committee chairs, and so on. The DC would *not* permit, under any circumstances, formal Communist representation in the cabinet. In two consecutive *monocolore* governments led by Andreotti between 1976 and 1979 (which were called Governments of National Unity because they were supported — or not opposed —by all parties except for the extreme Left and Right), the byzantine formulas at which Italian politicians are expert obtained new variants. After 1977, the PCI was in the majority but not in the government. Communist abstention in 1977 was characterized as a "non no-confidence vote," i.e. they did not oppose, but they could not fully support, the cabinet. After a cabinet crisis in 1978, the PCI actually voted positively for the second Andreotti cabinet. (As the confidence vote took place on the day DC Chairman and former Prime Minister Aldo Moro was kidnaped by the Red Brigades, the vote was intended as an act of solidarity.)

Because they were obsessed with legitimizing themselves as a respectable and serious governing party, the Communists accepted this situation as the best option available. They gave maximum publicity to the often extremely limited achievements of the government, including some rather dubious reforms that remained limited largely to the paper on which they were written (e.g., on industrial reconversion and youth employment, as well as a very sweeping, but vague, Programmatic Accord signed by all members of the majority). The Communists were unwilling to single out one or two key reforms and insist on specific action within a given period, which might well have won them a strong measure of public sympathy, especially on a highly symbolic issue like serious tax reform. Instead, they attempted to create the broadest consensus possible, particularly with the DC. They simultaneously counseled the unions to accept wage restraint and to exercise flexibility on many contract items, for inflation had risen to well over 15 percent and unemployment was also showing an alarming upswing.

In strictly institutional terms, the PCI could feel that its presence made a considerable difference. Communist pressure pushed the scandal-ridden president, Giovanni Leone, out of office, and PCI votes were decisive in electing his extremely popular successor, Sandro Pertini. The Communists also held to a hard-line position in refusing to negotiate with Moro's kidnapers at a time when the other major parties were vacillating. Their contribution to stabilizing a highly uncertain climate, and their contribution to consolidating Italy's democratic institutions and practices, should not be lightly brushed aside. Indeed, in an era when the declining role of representative institutions was being loudly announced in the West, it is notable that the Italian Parliament's role — its "centrality," in the jargon of Italian politics — was enhanced. For this, too, the PCI deserves a good deal of credit.

In the end, however, the PCI, under increasing pressure from its own rank-and-file, simply lost its patience with the endless maneuvering, bickering, and stalling that comes of any attempt to collaborate with the Christian Democrats. Unfortunately for the Communists, their decision to present an ultimatum to include them in the government or do without their support came too late. By 1979, the Communists had consumed the considerable goodwill held by their own previous supporters and had wasted what was once their trump card: the assertion that the PCI was *not* a party like the others. Events had shown that the PCI was all too similar to the others and far from immune to the endless power-brokering that consumes so much of Parliament's energy.

The unions, for many of their own reasons but with considerable resistance from more militant organizations, followed a parallel path in the late 1970s.[30] The government in power after 1977 was likely to be the best they could hope for. They therefore formally sanctioned the restraint they had been showing and adopted a platform known as EUR, named for the Roman suburb in which the agreement was passed, with the understanding that continued moderation would result in significant action by the government on reforms. All informed observers agree that this restraint was real: Industrial conflict and the rate of wage increases dropped sharply in 1977–78, and concessions were made on the *scala mobile* and on several items relating to increasing productivity. But some of the paper reforms mentioned above were crucial to the unions, and their non- or partial implementation quickly led to widespread disillusionment. On others, including a very important modification in the structure of pensions, unionists stood by in frustration as the DC and the minor coalition parties, pressured by their own constituents, gutted and finally blocked the law altogether.

The Center-Left Reborn: The Pentapartito. The Communists' ultimatum came in 1979, precipitating new elections when the DC (predictably) refused to admit the PCI into the cabinet. But by this time, the Socialists had yet again changed their line. This shift was in large measure the outcome of a series of changes that had taken place through the mid-1970s. Bettino Craxi, from 1976 the Socialist party secretary, had been revamping both the strategy and the entire leadership of the PSI.[31] Craxi promised the electorate stability and governability for five years. In short, he was prepared to rejoin a majority without insisting that the PCI be included. Since it was the PSI's previous refusal to participate without the PCI that had led to the impasse of the mid-1970s, it was obvious that the end of the parliamentary stalemate was at hand. In the actual voting, the PSI did not receive the additional support Craxi had asked for. The PCI vote declined, by 4 percent, for the first time in the entire postwar period, and the Socialists remained stable at just under 10 percent. (See Table 17.4.) Very little movement of the vote occurred between

Table 17.6 Governments of the Italian Republic, 1946–85

PRIME MINISTER (PARTY)	PARTIES IN CABINET	DATE FORMED
De Gasperi II (DC)	DC, PCI, PSI,* PRI	7/46
De Gasperi III (DC)	PCI, PSI, DC	2/47
De Gasperi IV (DC)	DC + independents	6/47
De Gasperi V (DC)	DC, PSDI,** PRI, PLI	5/48
De Gasperi VI (DC)	DC, PSDI, PRI	1/50
De Gasperi VII (DC)	DC, PRI	7/51
De Gasperi VIII (DC)	DC	7/53
Pella (DC)	DC + independents	8/53
Fanfani I (DC)	DC	1/54
Scelba (DC)	DC, PSDI, PLI	2/54
Segni I (DC)	DC, PSDI, PLI	7/55
Zoli (DC)	DC	5/57
Fanfani II (DC)	DC, PSDI	7/58
Segni II (DC)	DC	2/59
Tambroni (DC)	DC	3/60
Fanfani III (DC)	DC	7/60
Fanfani IV (DC)	DC, PSDI, PRI	2/62
Leone I (DC)	DC	6/63
Moro I (DC)	DC, PSI, PSDI, PRI	12/63
Moro II (DC)	DC, PSI, PSDI, PRI	7/64
Moro III (DC)	DC, PSI, PSDI, PRI	2/66
Leone II (DC)	DC	6/68
Rumor I (DC)	DC, PSI-PSDI, PRI	12/68
Rumor II (DC)	DC, PSI	8/69
Rumor III (DC)	DC, PSDI, PRI	3/70
Colombo (DC)	DC, PSI, PSDI, PRI	8/70
Andreotti I (DC)	DC	2/72
Andreotti II (DC)	DC, PSDI, PLI	6/72
Rumor IV (DC)	DC, PSI, PSDI, PRI	7/73
Rumor V (DC)	DC, PSI, PSDI	3/74
Moro IV (DC)	DC, PRI	11/74
Moro V (DC)	DC, PRI	1/76
Andreotti III (DC)	DC[a]	7/76
Andreotti IV (DC)	DC[a]	3/78
Andreotti V (DC)	DC, PRI, PSDI	3/79
Cossiga I (DC)	DC, PLI, PSDI	8/79
Cossiga II (DC)	DC, PSI, PRI	4/80
Forlani (DC)	DC, PSI, PSDI, PRI	10/80

Table 17.6 Governments of the Italian Republic, 1946–85 (*continued*)

PRIME MINISTER (PARTY)	PARTIES IN CABINET	DATE FORMED
Spadolini I (PRI)	DC, PSI, PSDI, PRI, PLI	6/81
Spadolini II (PRI)	DC, PSI, PSDI, PRI, PLI	9/82
Fanfani V (DC)	DC, PSI, PSDI, PLI	12/82
Craxi (PSI)	DC, PSI, PSDI, PRI, PLI	8/83
Craxi II (PSI)	DC, PSI, PSDI, PRI, PLI	8/86

NOTES *For the sake of simplicity, the Socialists are always referred to as PSI, even though their name was different when they were united with the PSDI prior to January, 1947 and during 1966–69. In the latter period, the united party is designated as PSI–PSDI.

**The Social Democrats became the PSDI at the beginning of the 1950s; they kept the name Unified Socialist Party until the early 1970s following the second split with the Socialists in 1969. They are always referred to as the PSDI in this table.

[a]Externally supported by the PCI, PSI, PSDI and PRI

SOURCES For De Gasperi II–IV: Giuseppe Mammarella, *Italy After Fascism* (South Bend, IN: University of Notre Dame Press, 1966), Chapters 5 and 7. For De Gasperi V to Rumor IV: P.A. Allum, *Italy — Republic Without Government?* (New York: Norton, 1973) p. 118. Thereafter: compiled by the author from newspaper articles.

the Left and Center-Right blocs: The Left lost about one percent. The PSI did join the *pentapartito,* a new five-party coalition, which was identical to the old Center-Left formula, except that it now included the Liberals.

The 1970s thus ended on a different note from that on which the decade had begun, save for a distressing similarity in the composition of the governing coalition. The Communists were back in the opposition and more isolated than they had been in a long time; the working class and the unions were increasingly weakened, as the entire economy went into the most serious slide of the entire postwar period; and the DC, seemingly immune to a serious setback at the polls, remained at the center of a battered, but safe, system of power that even many of the ruling party's own leaders recognized was responsible for some of the country's most intractable problems. For those who had hoped for a radical alteration of the old political equilibria in the wake of the hot autumn, the picture was especially bleak. We will see in the final chapter of this section that the 1980s did not represent merely a return to form for Italy, and that the DC *is* capable of losing votes in a general election and even of being shunted out of the office of prime minister. But the ability of the old equilibria to persist, albeit in weakened form, under shocks and pressures that might well have led to changes of regime in other societies, is testimony to both the resilience and the problems of the Italian political system.

NOTES

1. Piero Calamandrei, cited in: P. Vercellone, "The Italian Constitution of 1947–48," in *The Rebirth of Italy 1943–50,* ed. S. J. Woolf (New York: Humanities Press, 1972), p. 124.
2. Mario Einaudi, "The Constitution of the Italian Republic," *American Political Science Review,* 42 (August, 1948), p. 662.
3. The Lateran Pacts, or Accords, consisted of three separate documents. The first was a treaty establishing the Vatican as a sovereign city-state headed by the pope. The second, and by far the most important, was the Concordat, which made Catholicism the official state religion of Italy and provided the church with its social and legal privileges. The third was a large indemnity paid by the Italian state to the Vatican for property seized during the *Risorgimento.*
4. Carla and Stefano Rodotà, eds., *L'articolo 7 e il dibattito sul Concordato* (Rome: Savelli, 1977), p. 19. Numerous interesting excerpts of the debates on the floor of the Assembly are provided on pp. 30–75.
5. Rodotà, *L'articolo* 7, p. 18.
6. For extensive discussion of the politics of the postwar period, see: Giuseppe Mammarella, *Italy After Fascism: A Political History 1943–1965* (Notre Dame, IN: University of Notre Dame Press, 1966): esp. part 2. See also: Norman Kogan, *A Political History of Italy* (New York: Praeger, 1983).
7. The figures are cited in: Massimo Caprara, *l'Attentato a Togliatti* (Rome: Marsilio Editore, 1978), pp. 74, 100.
8. Alan S. Milward, *The Reconstruction of Western Europe 1945–51* (Berkeley: University of California Press, 1985), pp. 78–79, 98, 197–98.
9. George H. Hildebrand, *Growth and Structure in the Economy of Modern Italy* (Cambridge: Harvard University Press, 1965), p. 157.
10. Kevin Allen and Andrew Stevenson, *An Introduction to the Italian Economy* (New York: Harper & Row, 1975), p. 10.
11. Andrew Shonfield, *Modern Capitalism* (Oxford: Oxford University Press, 1969), pp. 186–87.
12. Eugenio Scalfari, *L'Autunno della Repubblica* (Milan: Etas Kompass, 1969), pp. 44–53 and following.

13. Gisele Podbielski, *Italy: Development and Crisis in the Postwar Economy* (Oxford: Clarendon Press, 1974), pp. 15, 100.
14. Allen and Stevenson, *Introduction to Italian Economy,* p. 109.
15. Allen and Stevenson, *Introduction to Italian Economy,* pp. 11–12.
16. Official census figures quoted in: *CISL 1984* (Rome: Edizioni Lavoro, 1984), p. 18.
17. Scalfari, *L'Autunno della Repubblica,* p. 58.
18. For example: 180 televisions per 1,000 population (versus 293 in Britain and 272 in West Germany), or 174 telephones (versus 269 and 226, respectively). Allen and Stevenson, *Introduction to Italian Economy,* p. 28.
19. Podbielski, *Italy,* pp. 136–37.
20. Hildebrand, *Growth and Structure,* p. 117.
21. Guido Romagnoli, ed., *La sindacalizzazione tra ideologia e pratica. Il caso italiano 1950–1977,* vol. 2 (Rome: Edizioni Lavoro, 1978), Table 2.2. The relationship in industry has been just short of 2:1 in the CGIL's favor since the late 1960s. The CISL climbed to about one million (claimed) industrial members by 1980.
22. For a summary of the unions' programs and platforms in the first decade following the war, see: Peter Lange, George Ross, and Maurizio Vannicelli, *Unions, Change and Crisis: French and Italian Union Strategy and the Political Economy, 1945–1980* (London: George Allen and Unwin, 1982), pp. 100–117.
23. Mammarella, *Italy After Fascism,* pp. 352–53.
24. Mammarella, *Italy After Fascism,* 254–55.
25. Giuseppe Tamburrano, *Storia e cronaca del centro-sinistra,* rev. ed. (Milan: Feltrinelli, 1973), pp. 30–31, 246.
26. Ruggero Orfei, *L'Occupazione del potere. I democristiani '45–'75* (Milan: Longanesi, 1976).
27. For a discussion of the origins of the strategy, see: Stephen Hellman, "The Longest Campaign: Communist Party Strategy and the Elections of 1976," in *Italy at the Polls. The Parliamentary Election of 1976,* ed. Howard R. Penniman (Washington, DC: American Enterprise Institute, 1977).
28. The following discussion is drawn primarily from: Salvati, "The Italian Inflation," pp. 543–59; Allen and Stevenson, *Introduction to Italian Economy,* pp. 121–26; and Maurizio Ferrara, "Le promesse impossibili del Welfare State: il caso italiano," *Il Mulino* no. 300 (July/August, 1985), pp. 531–37.
29. "Will *la dolce vita* turn sour?" *The Economist,* January 5, 1985, p. 58.
30. On the unions' program, see: Lange, Ross, and Vannicelli, *Unions, Change and Crisis,* pp. 165 and following. On internal opposition to

the program, see: Miriam Golden, *Austerity and Its Opposition: Communism, Corporatism, and the Italian Labor Movement* (forthcoming). On the general economic climate and the constraints under which the unions acted, see: Michael Salvati, "The Italian Inflation," in *The Politics of Inflation and Economic Stagnation,* ed. Leon Lindberg and Charles S. Maier (Washington, DC: The Brookings Institution, 1985), pp. 515–17.

31. Gianfranco Pasquino, "The Italian Socialist Party: Electoral Stagnation and Political Indispensability," in *Italy at the Polls, 1979,* ed. Howard R. Penniman (Washington, DC: American Enterprise Institute, 1981), pp. 143–59. See also: David Hine, "The Italian Socialist Party Under Craxi: Surviving But Not Reviving," in *Italy in Transition: Conflict and Consensus,* ed. Peter Lange and Sidney Tarrow (London: Frank Cass, 1980), pp. 133–48.

18

State Institutions

⯭ *The Principles of Italian Government*

The Italian Republic has a parliamentary government elected by proportional representation. The electorate votes for parties, which must form a government that will command majority support in each chamber of Parliament. The President of the Republic, after consulting with the leaders of all parties, designates the most likely prime minister (technically, the President of the Council of Ministers). The designee then constructs a cabinet by consulting the leaders and important figures of the various parties that will support the proposed government. If votes of confidence are forthcoming in both the Chamber of Deputies and the Senate, the government is sworn into office and remains in office until a political crisis makes clear that the government no longer commands the coalition's support. At that point, the prime minister notifies the president, who can charge the incumbent, or designate someone else to form a new government. If no coalition can muster majority support, or if the normal term (five years) of Parliament draws to a close, the president, after further consultations, dissolves the legislature and calls an election to be held within six to eight weeks.

Several aspects qualify the purity of the Italian parliamentary system. Italian bicameralism, as we will see, is unique. The entire adult population over eighteen years of age is automatically registered to vote and casts its ballots for the Chamber of Deputies. Suffrage for the Senate is restricted to those twenty-five or older, and a senator must be forty years old to be elected. Further, the electoral system is not a pure proportional ballot. Parties present lists in the multimember districts in which they wish to stand; most compete in every district. Votes that are left over after all seats in a district are assigned go into a national remainder and are distributed proportionally. If, however, a party cannot collect enough votes in any single district sufficient to elect one member, it wins no seats at all. Finally, a pure list system elects candidates in the order in which they appear on the ballot. The Italian system permits a limited preference vote. Voters may write in a few names or list numbers of the candidates they favor; when the votes are counted, candidates are declared elected in the order of the preference votes they have received. Hence someone whose name appears well down the list can jump to the head of the line. The preference vote is used throughout the country, but it is especially common in the South. Parties that are highly factionalized (the DC is the prime example) are susceptible to extensive infighting for these votes.

The Peculiarities of Italian Political Instability

The life of the average government since the Republic was formed has been just less than one year (see Table 17–6). While *cabinets* rise and fall with alarming regularity, the same parties and indeed the same people almost always end up in the key ministries of each successive cabinet. As we saw in the last chapter, this is a result not of the *instability* of Italian society and the party system but of their remarkable historical *stability*. A consistent 40 percent of the seats in Parliament have been held by parties that are excluded from consideration as potential cabinet partners. Therefore, coalitions have been required between quite heterogeneous partners, with a single party — Christian Democracy — at the center of every government.

This situation of stable instability, in which all the maneuvering to find the 50-plus percent of parliament's votes takes place within the 60 percent of acceptable partners, has profoundly shaped the contours of Italian politics. Save for a few historic junctures where a new subordinate partner had to be added to the ruling coalition, the political scenario has been depressingly similar: the same politicians divide up the same ministerial portfolios with very limited variations. The utter predictability of the situation has generated a long-term tendency for the main governing parties to jockey constantly for marginal positional advantages in relation to their coalition partners and with respect to internal rivals within the same party. The mathematical certainty about who will hold power has made it extremely difficult for any government to enact serious legislation, for the resistance of just a few key figures can bring the government's support below 50 percent — or precipitate a crisis and cabinet reshuffle, which can consume weeks or even months. The same certainty has made Christian Democracy into a party not like any other in Italy or Europe. The DC's role has been undermined since the mid-1970s, but it is still three times the size and infinitely more entrenched in power than its next-largest coalition partner, the PSI.

The Executive

The President

The president is elected by secret ballot of a joint session of both chambers of Parliament, with an additional sixty representatives from the regions. (See pp. 394 to 396). On the first three ballots, a two-thirds majority is required; from the fourth ballot, a simple majority suffices. The term of office is seven years. The constitution says nothing about whether a president may be reelected, but the assumption has been that this is possible. In the last six months of a presidential term, the power to dissolve Parliament and call elections is suspended: this precaution against possible abuses of power is known as the white semester. The other constitutional powers of the president include designation of a prime minister and use of a suspensive veto, which sends a law back to Parliament unsigned. This veto can be overridden with a simple majority vote, however. The most important presidential power by far is the ability to name a potential prime minister, for there are often several plausible contenders for the role.

The office of the presidency has emerged as a flexible one, highly dependent on the incumbent. Until the late 1970s, it appeared that the dignity of the office was on a downward slide; successive elections were increasingly drawn out and bitter. In 1978, Giovanni Leone, a singularly mediocre DC power broker, was forced to resign under a cloud of scandal. He was replaced by an elderly Socialist, Sandro Pertini, a highly principled figure who spent his youth in Fascist prisons and exile. It was widely assumed that Pertini might not survive his term, but everyone knew he could be relied on not to tarnish the office any further. In fact, this outspoken, profoundly humane maverick quickly became the most popular political figure in Italy; he is probably the *only* political office-holder in the Republic's history to be loved by a broad spectrum of the public. When he stepped down in 1985, the presidency had been immeasurably enhanced. Francesco Cossiga, who succeeded Pertini, is one of the few untarnished Christian Democrats of national stature; his election, for the first time in a generation, was a model of speed and decorum.

Pertini was not only outspoken but also an activist president within the limits of the job, as had been several predecessors. He was appreciated much more by the common people than by many politicians, who thought he was abusing his powers. He also spoke out frequently on matters of corruption, and made clear that he thought those in power bore heavy responsibility for delays in implementing reforms.

The Prime Minister and the Cabinet

The constitution's framers tried to ensure the collective responsibility of the government: the cabinet, not the prime minister, must obtain Parliament's confidence. In fact, the realities of Italian politics have given key ministerial figures considerably more leverage than most of the framers would have thought possible. A recent study shows that in the first thirty years of the Republic, more than one-third of *all* cabinet and subcabinet positions were held by only thirty-one people![1] Some of those whose names still crop up in major struggles or as candidates for high office were stalking the corridors of power in the 1940s.

One of the side effects of such permanence in power has been that politicians often take a very proprietary attitude toward their ministry. This has created a small group with formidable ability and no small amount of expertise in several areas. (It has also allowed opportunists and maneuverers of no special talent to rise and remain at great heights, but this is hardly a purely Italian problem.) This situation renders nearly impossible the creation of coherent or coordinated policies. Powerful and ambitious ministers often have a vested personal, factional, or party interest in seeing a rival's plans fail, for in such a system, almost all of the leading politicians in the governing coalition are rivals.

Because of the overriding need to divide positions between parties and factions, Italian cabinets are not only badly divided at the outset but also terribly cumbersome. Every minister is a member of the cabinet, and there are at least twenty ministers with a portfolio and another five or six without portfolios. There are two subministers (undersecretaries) for each portfolio — and politics demands that these officials represent different parties or factions than the minister. This is a formula that maximizes the representation of diverse interests and the distribution of patronage and influence, but it can interfere with coherent policy-making. Fortunately, the subministers do not actually attend cabinet meetings; however, the presence of two dozen or so ministers of many persuasions is a far cry from the tight model of a limited number of key leaders that prevails in the British system and those patterned on it.

There are additional anomalies in the Italian executive, some the result of conscious design. For instance, there are three different ministries with major economic responsibilities: Finance is responsible for raising revenues; Treasury for spending and debt management, and Budget and Planning for, among other things, coordinating the other two. In reality, Treasury is the most powerful ministry, for it actually holds the purse strings of the other ministries. Numerous interministerial committees are supposed to coordinate policy among the governing partners, but they encounter the same obstacles that plague the entire cabinet system.

The Prime Minister. The Italian prime minister is one of the weaker heads of government in Western Europe, in part by constitutional design, but especially because of the nature of coalition government in Italy. A strongly united dominant party, or even an uncontested leader of a dominant party, could make things easier. Instead, the importance of the prime minister has declined as the DC and its system of power have weakened. The first half of the 1980s saw a predominance of non-Christian Democratic prime ministers, which was unthinkable through the 1970s. No matter how forceful, dynamic, or politically courageous prime ministers of whatever party may be, however, they ultimately must face the fact that the major political debts of the ministers in power are to their own parties and factions and not to the head of government.

The weaknesses of the executive branch are of course well known, and reforms are frequently suggested. Hints of truly radical reforms, for instance, along French or U.S. presidential lines, inevitably generate howls of protest and sober commentaries about secret designs for a Second Republic or about paving the way for another Mussolini.

The Legislature

The Constituent Assembly, as the creature of the mass parties and with fresh memories of executive abuses under both the Liberal and Fascist regimes, went out of its way to vest the legislature with maximum powers. Many observers would say that the founders were all too successful. As is frequently the case in Italy, however, the problem does not lie in the design of the institutions, but in the way they have come to operate in the give-and-take of the country's politics.

Parliament's Powers — and Anomalies

In addition to voting governments into and out of office, and the wide latitude in passing laws that is typical of a parliamentary system, the

Italian Parliament has a number of additional powers: in joint session, it elects (and may impeach) the president of the republic; it chooses a third of the members of the Constitutional Court and of the Superior Council of the Judiciary, the two highest judicial bodies in the country; and it may amend the constitution, through a cumbersome process. The president must consult with each chamber before dissolving it and calling elections. There are also several checks on parliamentary abuses of power. One is judicial review, about which more will be said in the next section, and another is the abrogative referendum: if half a million citizens sign a petition, or five of twenty regional councils pass a motion, a public vote is held to preserve or abolish controversial legislation. Though written into the constitution in 1948, neither option was possible until 1970, because it took that long to institute the enabling legislation for referenda and to establish the regions.

One of the curiosities of the Italian system is that it presents a case of pure bicameralism: The two chambers have *identical* powers. This is the result of a compromise between the DC and the Left, in which neither side got what it really wanted, and the machinery that was put in place is monstrously cumbersome. For instance, despite the equal status of the two chambers, there is no standing committee to reconcile different versions of similar legislation; therefore, each chamber must pass the identical bill before it becomes law. At times this can mean that slightly altered proposals shunt back and forth, dragging out passage of the final product. Of course, when the political will exists, the major party leaders can easily get together and hammer out a compromise. Since this will is often lacking, however, most observers agree that the bicameral arrangement is not only an absurdity but also an unnecessary impediment in a system that has enough obstacles to efficiency and rationality.

Though Parliament lacks a joint conference, it has a number of standing committees whose areas of competence parallel the major ministries. As in other legislatures, these bodies can take proposals and amend them beyond recognition or simply bury them and refuse to refer them to the floor of the Chamber or the Senate. But Italian committees are unique in their ability to pass directly into law (or kill) a wide range of legislation without referral back to the floor of Parliament. When a committee receives a bill under these conditions, it meets "with deliberative powers" (*in sede deliberante*). Since the committees are quite large and their seats are distributed in proportion to their parties' seats in Parliament, they can be considered miniparliaments of between twenty and fifty members, depending on their chamber and area of competence. Moreover, should the cabinet, a fifth of the committee members, or a tenth of the members of the chamber so demand, the bill can be brought to the floor and voted up or down without debate. Through the mid-1970s, the overwhelming majority of all legislation was passed by committees. Largely for this reason, the Italian Parliament has generated far more laws than any other European legislature in the postwar period. Moreover, laws passed in this fashion tend to receive unanimous, or near-unanimous, votes.[2] However, the bulk of the laws passed in this way are *leggine,* "little laws," which are special interest or pork-barrel legislation. In combination with another of the anomalies of the Italian system — the absence of limits on the number of bills that private members could submit in either chamber —the prodigious output of Parliament usually avoided the truly important issues facing the country. The situation improved in the 1970s, when a number of rule changes gave both Parliament and the committees more power. The most important changes made it mandatory to consult *all* parties in setting the parliamentary agenda, and in referring issues to committee. Simultaneously, committees were given more powers to hold hearings, to subpoena bureaucrats, and to hold their deliberations in public.[3] The number of private member bills was also limited. In the period of maximum cooperation between all major parties — the National Unity episode of 1976–79 — Parliament functioned with notable efficiency. But even in the preceding five years, the improvement was notable. In the polarized climate of the 1980s, however, the situation deteriorated once more.

Any discussion of committee deliberations must include the role of the opposition in Italy, specifically the role of the major opposition party, the PCI. First, the unanimous or near-unanimous votes in committee on the vast majority of laws passed *in sede deliberante* indicates that the PCI votes with the governing parties far more often than against them and that legislation proposed by the PCI is by no means rejected out of hand. Second, any party with 10 percent of the seats in the legislature, or 20 percent of those in a committee — and the PCI has had both throughout the postwar period — could easily block much of the output of *leggine* and even obstruct Parliament's operations altogether by forcing issues to the floor of the Chamber or Senate, yet the PCI has never done this.[4] In fact, Parliament did not even discuss its generally lax rules on obstructionism (in the form of filibustering or presenting infinite amendments to a bill) until the late 1970s. When it did so, it was reacting to initiatives of the small but highly disruptive Radical Party, not those of the PCI. The Communists have consistently shown that, so long as they are not pushed to the margins of the political system, they are quite willing to compromise and expedite the operations of Parliament.

Another important feature of the Parliament is that a secret ballot must be held on final votes for bills in the Chamber of Deputies. Although this procedure is not strictly required in the Senate, it is frequently used there as well. This was also one of those compromises designed to limit the complete dominance of possibly tyrannical party leaders. The result, however, is a curious twist in the system of representative government that keeps citizens from knowing how their elected representatives vote. The secret ballot is really a license to sabotage one's own party or coalition with impunity. Italians call this "sniping," and it probably reaches its height in presidential elections. But many a government has suffered serious embarrassment, and even disruption, when the votes were tallied. A favorite pastime of close observers of Parliament is to subtract the votes a coalition actually receives from those one would expect if all its members voted as they were supposed to and then speculate on who the snipers might be.

In spite of undeniable improvements and the passage of significant reform legislation since the 1970s, all is not well on the parliamentary front, and it appears that parliamentary instability is increasing. Until 1972, every legislature ran its legal course of five years before being dissolved, and even the dissolution of 1972 was well-planned, designed to head off a referendum on divorce, which most party leaders feared far more than elections.[5] Since then, however, not a single legislature has run its full term. Further, the period required to form a cabinet during a crisis has doubled since the mid-1960s, and executive decrees, or decree laws, are used more frequently. Decree laws are supposed to be employed only in emergencies, and they expire unless Parliament enacts them within sixty days of their declaration. This provision is intended to force the legislature to act, and though it was never applied before the early 1970s, it has been thoroughly abused thereafter. Since the mid-1970s, between 20 and 25 percent of *all* government-proposed laws that have passed in Parliament originated as decrees,[6] and the figure has been rising in the mid-1980s.

The Judiciary

The Slow Implementation of the Constitution

Like the rest of the Italian political system, the judicial branch has been plagued by blatant (and cynical) political manipulation since the first days of the Republic. Moreover, for a full generation, the top echelons of this branch of government openly rejected most of the constitution's innovations. Like the rest of the system, the judiciary has changed, but this has been a tortured, contradictory process that often simultaneously illustrates the best and the worst of Italian politics.

Article 104 of the constitution affirms the judiciary's independence from all other branches of government. This departure from Italian legal tradition was inspired by the ease with which fascism had run roughshod over Liberal Italy's legal structures. Although the DC defended judicial autonomy in the Constituent Assembly, it promptly abandoned the principle once it came to power. Some of the institutions most necessary to establish the independence of the courts were blocked until the late 1950s: the ruling party simply stalled the creation of the Constitutional Court and the Superior Council of the Judiciary as long as it could.

During the same period, the highest-ranking appeals judges in the system (most of whom were appointed under fascism) interpreted the constitution on extremely narrow grounds. They drew rigid distinctions between the programmatic, or abstract, articles and those that were enforceable legal strictures. These highly conservative judges never reconciled themselves to the principle of judicial review and often flouted the rulings of the Constitutional Court once it was established. They greatly delayed the evolution of the legal and judicial system until, by the end of the 1970s, they had largely faded from the scene.

A major reason for leaving the previous system of justice intact through the late 1950s of course had nothing whatever to do with legal principles. This period coincides with the strongest phase of the effort to push the Left to, or even beyond, the margins of normal political life. A Fascist penal code made the task much easier. Since the 1931 code was intended to outlaw *all* political activity, it does not take much imagination to realize how much the labor movement could be obstructed and harassed by the state's legal apparatus.

Pressures from above and below finally forced the system to change. The Constitutional Court eventually did establish itself as a relatively autonomous body that would not hesitate to strike down national or regional laws that contravened the constitution. It also moved quickly to strike down huge sections of the penal code. Because of Parliament's notorious immobility, the Constitutional Court has on occasion also helped by eliminating old laws and codes to such an extent that legislators have been forced to act. This tactic was highly effective in extending women's rights and in reforming family law. In general, the Constitutional Court's activism and relative independence (in spite of the fact that its members are appointed according to political criteria) have made it one of the more respected political institutions in the country. This is much less true of the higher levels of the regular criminal courts, which frequently seem to sabotage investigations being carried on by lower levels when the evidence points in politically embarrassing directions.

Changes in the judiciary also have been stimulated from below as increasing numbers of judges entered the system at the lower levels. By the 1960s, young recruits brought social ferment to the profession. The stranglehold of the highly conservative old guard was gradually broken, and it was replaced by a mixture of civil service rules (e.g., tenure, relatively automatic promotion based on seniority) in a highly politicized and sometimes militant setting. The judiciary is presently divided into three organized political factions: conservatives are well represented; the moderate center-left group is largest; and the Left is smallest (a reflection of the powerful discrimination that occurred during the first twenty years of the Republic). Since the 1970s, strikes and job actions have not been uncommon among judges.

Delayed Reform. To say that the system of justice in Italy is in crisis seriously understates the matter. Every advanced capitalist democracy faces serious problems in this area, but the Italian case truly seems to be more acute. Texts written more than a decade ago wondered how the system had managed to survive into the 1970s, and matters have gotten much worse since.[7] There is irrationality at the very heart of things: a Fascist legal code, modified but never abrogated, coexists with a progressive democratic constitution; structures that evolved under a highly centralized state must contend with principles like judicial review, with its assumptions of the separation of powers; and, above all, a fragmented and immobile political system invades every aspect of Italian public life and seems to either obstruct or render ineffective serious reform proposals.

In 1984, following one failed attempt at reform, an outline of a new code emerged from Parliament to begin the tortuous route through the lawmaking machinery. If the new framework is not a civil libertarian's dream, it does represent quite an advance over the remnants of the 1931 code. The proposal makes both pretrial investigations and trial deliberations far more open than they are at present and entrenches the principle of the equality of the accused and the prosecution (as the constitution has insisted since 1948). Preventive detention is weakened, conditional liberty or any system of bail — the lack of which has been a scandal in Italy — is extended, and the formerly all-powerful role of the public prosecutor is greatly limited.

There are deep-seated problems that institutional reforms can hardly touch, but anything that would improve the present situation is long overdue. Cases are so backlogged, the machinery grinds so slowly, and the system is generally so inefficient that the intolerable becomes the norm. For example, lawyers regularly stall their clients' cases, knowing that every three or four years an amnesty will be issued to clear the docket; those unfortunate enough to be jailed for minor offenses frequently serve the equivalent of the maximum sentence before they ever come to trial. Meanwhile, the system has a reputation of letting the "big fish" get away: investigations take blatantly false paths for years; powerful judges shift the venues of investigations to sabotage them; decisions are rendered for extremely obscure motives; and so on. The public may not hold judges in low esteem, but it certainly does not have high expectations of the legal system. In a country that produces a sarcastic remark for almost every occasion, few are as telling as, "Italy is the cradle of the law and the grave of justice."

Local Government

There are three main levels of subnational government in Italy: *comuni* (the general Italian term for all municipalities, towns, and cities), provinces, and regions. As *political* entities, the *comuni* were by far the most important through the 1970s, and they remain the liveliest site of local politics in the country. In terms of *administrative* importance, however, the provinces historically have been the major subdivision of the country, linked directly by the prefect — a member of the national bureaucracy — to the Ministry of the Interior in Rome and run at times like colonial offices. Because their boundaries are often arbitrary, and institution of the regions seem to make them unnecessary, there is strong feeling that the provinces should be eliminated altogether. The regions, although steeped in history, had no formal status until the formation of the republic, and only the Special Regions had any significant powers until the 1970s. Since then, by far the most interesting developments in local government have occurred at the regional level.

The Communes

There are roughly eight thousand *comuni* in Italy. The large size of the average *comune* means that towns are generally populous enough to reproduce most of the parties, and the partisan conflict, that are found at the national level. Towns with more than five thousand inhabitants vote according to proportional representation; the number of councilors varies (from twenty to eighty) according to the size of the *comune*. Where there are less than five thousand inhabitants, the party or parties that win a majority obtain three-fourths of the seats. With the exception of the smallest municipalities, the patterns of national politics are reproduced at the local level, with a variety of strictly local lists more strongly represented. The very high levels of voter turnout in general elections (around 90 percent) are nearly matched in the local elections, which occur every five years, on a schedule that must not conflict with general elections.

Before the regional reforms, *comuni* were often heavily monitored by the prefects, who had immense powers at their disposal: They could veto budgets; dissolve local *giunte*, "cabinets;" and install prefectoral commissions of nonpolitical specialists if local crises dragged on too long. Still, there were always areas of clearly-defined powers, and possibilities for other initiatives, that ambitious local politicians could exploit. In fact, in spite of the extremely centralized nature of state structures, local governments have been an effective way of channeling state resources to the grass roots of society. *Giunte* run by the Left have proven to be quite skilled at working the system, and the central bureaucracies have been willing to collaborate with competent local politicians, whatever their party.[8]

Since the institution of the regions, oversight has been shifted to committees, which work in tandem with the prefects. The addition of this new layer of government, many of whose tasks remain obscure or overlap with preexisting layers, has brought considerable confusion and has prompted one informed observer to note that "the communes appear to have exchanged a meticulous, overdemanding master for a slovenly, unpredictable one."[9] Others are much less pessimistic and point to advances at the local level such as a much greater decentralization of power that has given Italians far more say over local affairs than they ever enjoyed earlier.

The Regions

One need look no further than the PCI's strength in the red zones (45–50 percent of the vote) for an explanation of why the DC dragged its heels implementing the regions. This was not the only instance of constitutional sabotage by the ruling party, but it was the most nakedly partisan in motivation. In fact, it was only when the PSI insisted that the ordinary regions be established as a precondition for the Center-Left that the mechanisms began slowly to grind. A sense of the speed of

Italian reforms can be had by noting that the first Center-Left government was voted into power in 1963: the regions were constituted and Regional Councils elected in 1970; their full powers, which were cut back considerably from original plans, were finally voted in 1975 and devolved in 1978. Cynics commented at the time that having bankrupted the state, the DC was finally willing to divide it up more equitably.

Two types of regions were anticipated by the constitution. The five Special Regions, which were mainly established in the 1940s, consist of the two major islands Sardinia and Sicily, and three areas on the northern border of the country with strong French, Germanic, and Slavic cultural characteristics.[10] The fifteen *ordinary* regions were the source of all the foot-dragging. Like the larger city governments, Regional Councils vary in size according to population and are elected for five-year terms by proportional list systems.

Like the *comuni,* the regions are closely controlled by Rome, which disburses about 90 percent of the money they are permitted to spend and which further specifies where the bulk of these funds must be spent. The central government also created a new administrative position, the regional commissioner, to act as a sort of super-prefect and to oversee the work of the Regional Council: commissioners may exercise a suspensive veto similar to that of the President and Parliament over the Councils' legislation. Major regional legislation must follow nationally established guidelines, which take the form of parliamentary framework laws, which establish the boundaries on a given issue within which the regions may *then* legislate in accordance with their special requirements. With the establishment of the regions, certain areas of competence passed from Rome to the regions, and so did many bureaucrats. The underlying idea of shifting these bureaucrats, originally proposed in Article 117 of the Constitution, is a noble one: to limit duplication in the public administration. While this certainly has had the effect of limiting many opportunities for local patronage, it has also projected throughout the country the arrogance that all too often is a hallmark of the central bureaucracy.

As an intermediate level of government, the regions are resented by local governments (especially the *comuni*) and resisted by the national government and the central ministries of the bureaucracy. The regions are most often accused of usurping the cities' specific tasks, instead of focusing on the coordination and planning role that was the main rationale for their creation. There is some truth in these charges, for most regional governments hastened to duplicate the national pattern of ministries in their own bureaucracies as soon as they were created, and many of them have proven as reticent to delegate operations to the *comuni* as

Rome was to delegate to them. On balance, however, most lower-level criticism of the regions is the product of local resentment of lost influence.

The regions tend to reproduce the country's historical cleavages in their own operations. By almost all relevant measures — from how efficiently they deliver services to whether they even manage to spend the funds that have been earmarked for their use — the southern regions lag behind the rest of the country, while the red regions and the northern industrialized areas show the most initiative. It is also interesting to note that in the period 1975–85, there were six more or less solidly red regions: Piedmont, Liguria, and Latium were added to the historic triumvirate (Tuscany, Emilia-Romagna, and Umbria). The drop in the PCI vote at the end of the 1970s, and the increasing tension between Communists and Socialists through the 1980s, reduced the number of left-wing governments at all levels. By 1985, with the PSI again forming local coalitions with the DC and its partners in the national government, there were leftist *giunte* only in Tuscany and Umbria, and even there, PCI–PSI relations were often deeply strained. Emilia-Romagna had a *monocolore* PCI government.

Public Administration and Para-State Agencies

If few institutions enjoy much public respect in Italy, it is safe to say that the bureaucracy is especially reviled. Everyone complains about how slow and inefficient their own government's bureaucracy is, but Italians do appear to have an edge, if it can be called that, over the rest of the advanced capitalist countries. Centralized and inflexible traditions, outmoded recruitment, grossly inadequate pay and working conditions (and a ridiculously short working day), ironclad job security, and practically every other shortcoming known to complex organizations are all combined in Italy's public administration. Its problems are so widely acknowledged that a Ministry for Bureaucratic Reform has long been a political and administrative fixture — and the butt of innumerable sarcastic comments. The administrative system of the Italian state hardly ends with the formal ministerial bureaucracies and the career civil servants who staff them, however. Its most unique aspects are found in the state-owned firms, holding companies, autonomous agencies and enterprises, and special institutions that saturate the country.

This sprawling structure is not only highly politicized *and* extraordinarily fragmented but also the key to understanding the present impasse in the entire political system, for it is in the bureaucracy that the Christian Democrats, beginning in the early 1950s, consciously built a base that was autonomous from the Vatican, from business interests, and from the United States. As long as the DC could overwhelmingly dominate its coalition partners, it doled out extremely thin slivers of the political pie; as the party's hegemony weakened, it was forced to provide its partners with wider shares. Ultimately, the struggles and stalemates from the late 1960s onwards even saw some control pass to the organized labor movement and the PCI. But the system is the DC's creation, and the DC retains the largest portion of it, although the Socialists have made important inroads since the 1980s. The system was fragmented from the very beginning, not so much because of the (limited) sharing of power *between* coalition partners, but because the DC itself was divided internally and this immense spoils system further stimulated the creation of independent power bases within the ruling party. Forty uninterrupted years at the center of the system, at least thirty of which have been spent carving it up, have created a dynamic that may now be next to impossible to reverse.

The Regular Public Administration

Although figures for the number of state employees in Italy are high, the problem does not lie in the absolute size of the bureaucracy. Once the various categories of employees in medicine, education, the postal service, the military, and all the state-owned industries are subtracted, the total of 400,000 is comparable to other Western European countries of similar size. Indeed, the total public sector is actually *smaller* than that of Britain, France, or West Germany when measured on a per capita basis.[11] The main problem lies in the organization of various ministries: They seem designed to maximize inefficiency and demoralization through the ranks; they are overcentralized and rule-bound; promotion disregards merit and rewards seniority (and political connections); and the pay and working conditions are terrible. As a result, absenteeism is widespread, second jobs are more the rule than the exception, and the service rendered is arrogantly delivered and appallingly slow. It is also widely believed that corruption is rampant. Further, like the judicial branch, in the first generation of the Republic the bureaucracy's upper reaches were staffed with people appointed under fascism, which helped entrench an attitude of intolerance toward ordinary citizens.

The civil service, with a few exceptions, remains highly fragmented and riddled with political influence. Each ministry sets its own entry requirements and supervises its own examinations. This long-standing tradition of many autonomous, centralized little empires has been further reinforced under the Republic, as many ministries were "colonized" by the ruling parties, frequently by one or two power groups within the DC. Especially for the more important upper-level appointments, where lengthy essays and oral exams are the allegedly objective basis on which candidates are judged, applicants with the right connections find it quite easy to get past the hurdles. This colonization not only perpetuates the fragmentation at the top of the system but also penetrates to the grass roots, making the bureaucracy an effective patronage machine but a much less satisfactory mechanism for the delivery of services. The results are disastrous all along the line: division, incoherence and infighting at the center, and wretched service on the delivery end.

State Enterprises, Autonomous Agencies, and Special Institutions

A good number of public agencies have counterparts nearly everywhere in the advanced capitalist world, although these agencies enjoy an astonishing degree of independence in Italy. State monopolies in Italy may cover a few unusual sectors (salt and bananas come to mind), and some public corporations in Italy may have slightly different structures elsewhere, but the state-run, nonstock corporation is a stranger to few modern capitalist societies. In Italy, the key industries of this type, such as the railroads and telephone and telegraph services, date back to the turn of the century.

Health, pension, social security, and welfare agencies and institutions are also commonly nationalized services, although in most advanced societies, many of them are under direct ministerial control. In Italy, they evolved as autonomous agencies, parallel to many Catholic (and other) institutions. They are organized under the umbrella of the Ministry of Labor and Welfare, but the major institutions maintain autonomous control over the investment of their own funds, which amount to billions of dollars. They operate under strict controls, but their potential leverage over the economy is immense. The largest agency is the Social Security Institute (INPS), and for at least twenty years, there has been discussion and halting steps toward reorganizing and making more efficient the entire range of welfare agencies under INPS. This process has accelerated since the mid-1970s, but it has been fiercely resisted by thousands of local mini-agencies, representing a variety of special interests.

State Participation and Holding Companies. The *Istituto per la Ricostruzione Industriale* (IRI) was not disbanded nor its holdings privatized at war's end; its role in the economy steadily expanded, and *other* holding companies, most notably ENI, were also created as the state extended its economic activity. Ironically, there were strong echoes of the origins of IRI in the late 1960s and early 1970s: when many companies began to suffer from the effects of the hot autumn and the general economic downturn, a *new* group of holding companies was established to help troubled firms.

Holding companies own, in the name of the state, controlling shares of stock in enterprises that are run according to the rules governing private companies. These holdings are then grouped into super holding companies, such as IRI and ENI, which in turn are responsible to the Minister of State Participation. This multitiered arrangement is by design: Government is to exercise a broad planning and oversight function, but the firms must be free to operate in the marketplace and to respond quickly to its pressures. The holding and super holding companies direct and coordinate specific sectoral policies and monitor the individual firm's performance.[12] In practice, however, the system has never worked this way and has become increasingly distorted over time. Coordination and planning have never been forthcoming from the minister, who historically has tended to follow the holding companies' recommendations. More importantly, the lower reaches of this system have become increasingly permeated by strictly political, and often narrowly factional, managerial appointments and investment and production decisions.

The reason for this politicization is that the stakes are truly enormous: State-controlled enterprises in Italy account for entire sectors of the economy, half of all fixed investments, over three-quarters of all banking and credit institutions, and one-quarter of the country's industrial employees. The margins for abuse and outright corruption are great, but so is the possibility to help structure the economy in a direction more in line with one's own vision.

Broader social principles may occasionally find their way into important decisions, but the picture is far more often one of narrow partisanship or the indiscriminate distribution of "goodies" to key power groups' numerous, and contradictory, constituencies. Squabbling over the increasingly debt-ridden system has escalated as the DC's grip has slipped. Since 1979, the Socialists have made it clear that they intend to put their hands on every possible lever of power; it is a sign of the changing equilibria that two of the DC's historically uncontested fiefs — the Ministry of State Participation and the Chair of ENI — have recently passed to the PSI after years of paralyzing political conflict. Although the PSI has portrayed itself as decisive and action-oriented, it has thus far followed the DC's example, using most positions of power primarily to consolidate and extend its own political networks.

Policy Processes: Continuity and Transition

With its strong unitary tradition and bureaucratic structures, its extensive involvement in the economy, and a single party that has completely dominated the executive branch since the foundation of the regime, the Italian Republic would appear to have most of the components needed for a decisive and coherent system of government. Instead, the system functions in almost exactly the opposite way, as it has done practically from the start: only in the late 1940s through the mid-1950s, when the DC had uncontested leaders who also served as prime ministers, can we speak of a truly strong executive. The political system is by no means thoroughly paralyzed, but it addresses most major issues with excruciating slowness and tends to generate legislation, especially in the economic sphere, that seems more intent on avoiding offense to constituents and clients than on achieving some clearly defined policy.

In strictly economic terms, Italy was in many ways extremely well-served by the lack of a strong commanding hand on the helm of the economy. The incredible adaptability of the Italian private sector, particularly the very numerous smaller firms, has long been admired for enabling Italy to adjust so rapidly to changing market conditions. Even the state sector was left to pursue autonomous economic policies for much of the postwar period. It is only one of Italy's many ironies that the fragmentation and lack of coordination in its governing bodies and immense public sector led to a policy that was, in practice, far more laissez-faire than in many societies with much larger private sectors and a much less explicit commitment to economic planning. This hands-off policy may not have made the machinery of government function better nor addressed major social injustices, but it did allow the country's entrepreneurial spirit to flourish.

Laissez-faire, however, is a notoriously risky *political* approach, especially when conditions change dramatically in a short time span. The paralysis and fragmentation of the policy-making process in Italy were evident even when the labor movement was on the defensive, the Left was completely isolated, and the economy was in its most robust phase of expansion. For the existing system, the crunch came following the late 1960s, when previously excluded groups (e.g., the entire workers' movement, women, young people, pensioners) forced major breaches in the system that had earlier repelled their demands. Simultaneously, the expanding economy, which had enabled the system, to that point, to pay at least most of its bills, suffered a sharp downturn.

As the 1970s proceeded, the DC found the parliamentary arithmetic, the social climate, and its own slipping bases of power all working against it. Therefore, the party increasingly turned to the technique it had always employed in distributing benefits internally: *Lottizzazione,* the proportional distribution of patronage, was extended to those political and social forces (especially the PCI and the unions) whose social leverage was greatest and whose political demands could no longer be denied. This arrangement was not only a response to political and social pressures but also a shrewd survival tactic; it peaked when the PCI's votes were necessary for the government to continue in office (1976–79), and it has ebbed and flowed considerably since then.

Institutional reform has been in the works since the early 1980s. A parliamentary committee has aired a great many proposals, and debate on the topic was at first surprisingly serious. Most of the (weakened) reform proposals address the functioning of Parliament and the relationship between the executive and legislative branches. Although few would disagree that Italy's institutions could use a major overhaul, many think that any rush to strengthen the executive or make Parliament "efficient" should be avoided. For all its problems, the Italian political system has generated many serious reforms since the late 1960s. The system's responsiveness to mass pressure originating outside Parliament resulted in the reform of pensions, the passage of the Workers' Statute, and the passage of advanced divorce and abortion laws. Citizen participation in a dizzying number of grass-roots assemblies in neighborhood councils, local public health clinics, school districts, and workplaces also indicates a degree of democratization and grass-roots participation rare in the West.

On this note, we now turn to a closer examination of the numerous political and social forces in Italy in order to obtain a more detailed picture of their relative strengths and how they have been changing.

Notes

1. Mauro Calise and Renato Mannheimer, *Governanti in Italia: Un trentennio repubblicano, 1946–1976* (Bologna: Il Mulino, 1982).
2. Giuseppe Di Palma, *Surviving Without Governing: The Italian Parties in Parliament* (Berkeley: University of California Press, 1977), chap. 2.

3. The changes are discussed in Robert Leonardi et al., "Institutionalization of Parliament and Parliamentarization of Parties in Italy," *Legislative Studies Quarterly,* III (February, 1978), pp. 161–69.
4. Raphael Zariski, *Italy: The Politics of Uneven Development* (Hinsdale, IL: The Dryden Press, 1972), p. 245.
5. To prevent excessive disruptions of parliamentary operations, referenda may not be called in either the first or the last years of a legislature's normal term. They also may only be held between April and June. Hence, if all else fails, a well-timed dissolution can stall a referendum by two full years, which is precisely what happened in 1972.
6. Riccardo Motta, "L'attività legislativa dei governi (1948–83)," *Rivista italiana di scienza politica,* XV (August, 1985), p. 265.
7. P. A. Allum, *Italy: Republic Without Government?* (New York: Norton, 1973), p. 184; Raphael Zariski, *Italy: The Politics of Uneven Development,* chap. 9; esp. p. 319.
8. Sidney Tarrow, *Between Center and Periphery* (New Haven: Yale University Press, 1977), esp. chap. 3 and 6.
9. Zariski, "Approaches to the Problem of Local Autonomy: The Lessons of Italian Regional Devolution," *West European Politics,* 8 (July, 1985), p. 72.
10. The three are, respectively, Aosta, Trentino-Alto Adige, and Friuli-Venezia Giulia.
11. Frederic Spotts and Theodore Weiser, *Italy: A Difficult Democracy* (New York: Cambridge University Press, 1986), p. 129.
12. M. V. Posner and S. J. Woolf, *Italian Public Enterprise* (Cambridge: Harvard University Press, 1967), esp. pp. 30–40, 121–28.

19

Social and Political Forces

Italian Politics: Between Subcultures and Secularization

Any discussion of Italian politics in the postwar period must begin with the domination of the two major parties (Christian Democracy and the Communists) and the deeply rooted "white" (Catholic) and "red" (Marxist) subcultural traditions that have been their primary source of strength. Subcultural factors, although weakened, explain why certain structures and types of actions have lasted so much longer in Italy than in other advanced capitalist democracies.

These divisions are by no means equal in strength or geographical distribution. Catholicism historically has been a more powerful and diffused social force in Italy than have the various manifestations of Marxism, and its entrenchment was given a very helpful boost by Mussolini and by the republican constitution. Further, the strong subcultures have always been geographically limited to areas that sometimes surprise people unfamiliar with Italian history and politics. The red areas are found, not where the largest factories and blue-collar work force are concentrated, but in the central regions of Emilia-Romagna, Tuscany, and Umbria. The white areas, where the church and religion are most deeply rooted, are found mainly in the North-East and eastern Lombardy. (See map on page 404.) Political subcultures in Italy also have cut across classes more than is often appreciated. While this is not so surprising for the white areas, for Catholic social thought rejects class conflict, it is far more striking to discover that the Left subculture has a fairly broad class base

The Political Geography of Italy

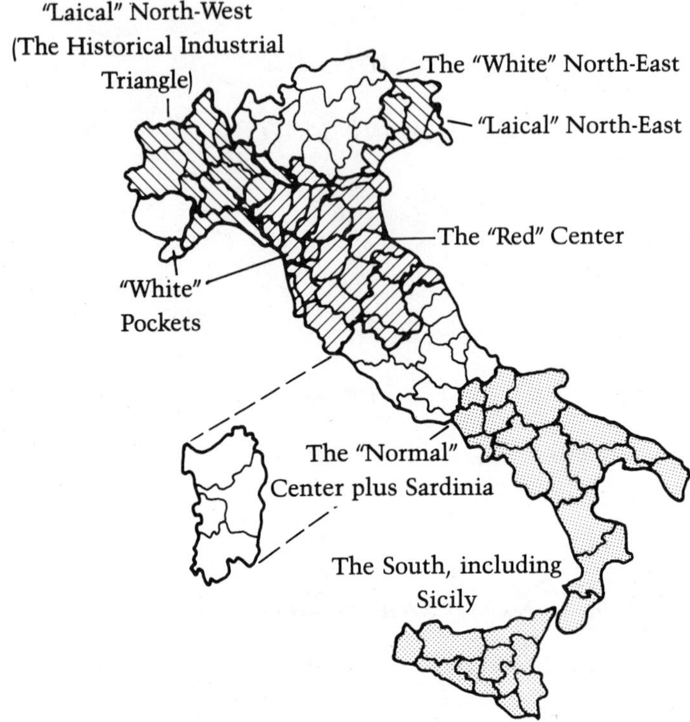

Lines mark provincial boundaries

as well, due to agrarian (and anticlerical) origins. This is why Italian socialism and communism have been far less obsessed with the factory proletariat than have their counterparts in many other countries, such as France.

There are other divisions in Italian society. Class divisions run very deep in Italy, even though they have been mitigated by religious and regional factors. Perhaps the most important division of all is between North and South. While it is an oversimplification to speak of a southern culture or political style, the area's dependent development and the resulting distorted class and social structures have had an undeniable effect on its modern political institutions.

Far weaker are the variants of modern "bourgeois" subcultures, such as secular liberalism and conservatism, which never managed to acquire mass bases as they did in most of the rest of Western Europe and North America. These secular forces were stunted by *trasformismo,* were repressed by fascism, and then delegated much of their role to the DC after 1945. Their political expressions have survived and evolved in the form of the minor, so called laical parties of the center.

In order to understand the configuration of political and social forces in Italy since World War II, the starting point must be the strong political subcultures and their organized presence in society. Most of the dramatic transformations of Italian society since the 1960s involve the success or failure of these older patterns, and the parties that represent them, at adapting to new developments.

The Party System

For anyone used to the relative simplicity of a two, three, or four-party system, Italy's eight or nine significant parties (there actually are several more!) challenge the memory as well as comprehension. The Left is divided between Communists and Socialists but has been dominated by the Communists since the 1940s. The Center, really the Center-Right, is about the same size and is occupied by Christian Democracy and three small lay parties. There is a small but persistent extreme Right which used to contain monarchists and neo-Fascists, but which has consisted only of the latter since a unification brought them all together in 1972. Figure 19.1 represents the present array of parties in traditional Left-Right terms.

Figure 19.1 also shows the dilemma of Italy's governing coalitions. The DC and its smaller partners are forced by parliamentary arithmetic to join together in coalitions that leave very little room for maneuver. The PSI has played a pivotal role since the 1960s in light of the impossibility of including the neo-Fascists (MSI) in any coalition. The presence of the neo-Fascists would drive all parties Left of the DC into the opposition and might well split the DC itself. This is the leverage that lies behind the PSI's success in demanding far more power than its vote merits.

The ideological distance between the parties has shrunk since the 1960s: All the parties have tended to move toward the center. This has made it somewhat easier to bring together parties that used to be openly hostile toward one another (e.g., the Liberals and Socialists) and has contributed to the DC's decline and the reinforcement of the smaller lay parties. In 1976, when moderates feared that the PCI might overtake the DC in votes, they voted overwhelmingly for the ruling party and reduced the three minor lay parties to a historic low of 7.8 percent and thirty–

Figure 19.1 Representation of Italian Parties as of 1983 General Elections

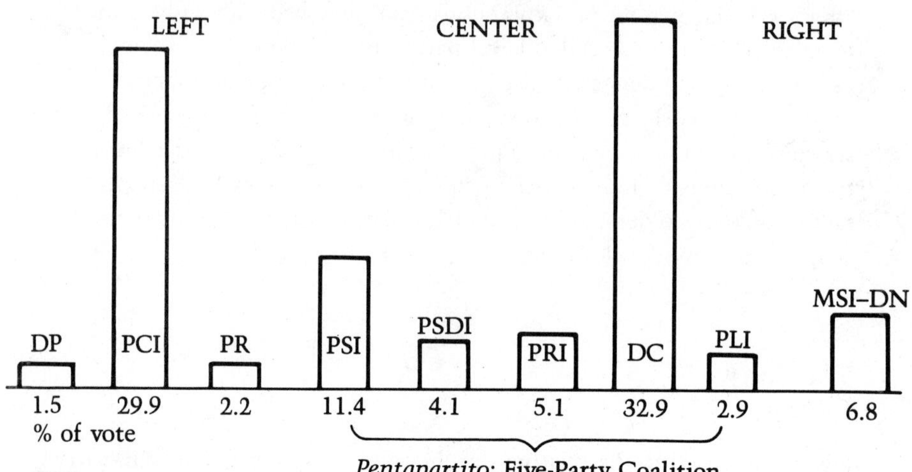

KEY:
DP–Proletarian Democracy
PCI–Communist Party
PR–Radical Party
PSI–Socialist Party
PSDI–Social Democratic Party
PRI–Republican Party
DC–Christian Democracy
PLI–Liberal Party
MSI–DN–Italian Social Movement/National Right

four seats. By 1979 and 1983, PCI strength had peaked and safely declined to around 30 percent. Reassured, the moderate voters returned to the smaller lay parties, which won 12.1 percent of the vote (and sixty–eight seats) in 1983. (See Table 17.4.)

By the 1970s, the previously static party system was changing rapidly. Were these changes the accumulation of quantitative trends, such as increasing secularization, education, urbanization, and so on, or were they more qualitative, with old classes losing their centrality in society and "new subjects" raising "post-materialist" demands?[1]

Electoral Shifts Since the 1970s

By the standards of most other societies, changes in Italian voting patterns have been limited. One notable shift *between* blocs took place in 1976 when the overall vote of the Left, stuck for three decades at around 40 percent, shot up to 47 percent. This single election coincided with the extension of the vote to eighteen-year-olds, leading observers to point out that the shift was not as dramatic as many thought, for youth in Italy vote disproportionately for the Left. Thus, what looked on the surface like a massive flow of votes out of the center was really not such a radical break with tradition.[2]

Italy has a very stable core of voters, especially for the major parties. Small family farmers and white-collar government workers generally vote for the DC, and blue-collar workers, especially in the dense proletarian quarters of the large northern cities, favor the PCI. Although political subcultures persist, they have weakened, and the once-solid red or white vote is definitely shrinking as a proportion of the total.

Vote-shifting *within* blocs definitely has increased since the mid-1970s. This phenomenon, linked to expanding education and urbanization, goes hand in hand with the decline of subcultural voting. Educated and more politically sophisticated urban voters, drawn not only from white-collar and professional strata but also from the working class, tend to make decisions on the basis of specific policies and thus are far more likely to change their vote from election to election.[3] Their support was crucial to the PCI's successes in 1975 and 1976, and to its decline in 1979. They also were instrumental in the DC's decline in the major cities in both 1979 and 1983.

Through most of the 1970s, almost everyone of voting age in Italy exercised the franchise: The turnout rate regularly hovered between 93 and 94 percent. The rate has now fallen to just under 90 percent, which is still far higher than in most countries. Until the end of the 1970s, the decrease in voting seemed to be uniform across Italy, with abstention rates much higher, as usual, in the South than elsewhere. In the 1980s, however, there was a notable increase of both abstentions and spoiled ballots everywhere *except* the South, particularly in the large urban industrial centers of the North.[4] The turnout in these areas remains over 90 percent, as compared with 80 to 85 percent in the South.

Christian Democracy (DC)

Italian politics mystify those who see simple connections between social change and electoral behavior. For nearly thirty years, some of the most tumultuous socioeconomic changes to occur anywhere in Western Europe barely rippled the general profile of Italy's major parties and, indeed,

Figure 19.2 Vote for Major Italian Parties in General Elections, 1953–83

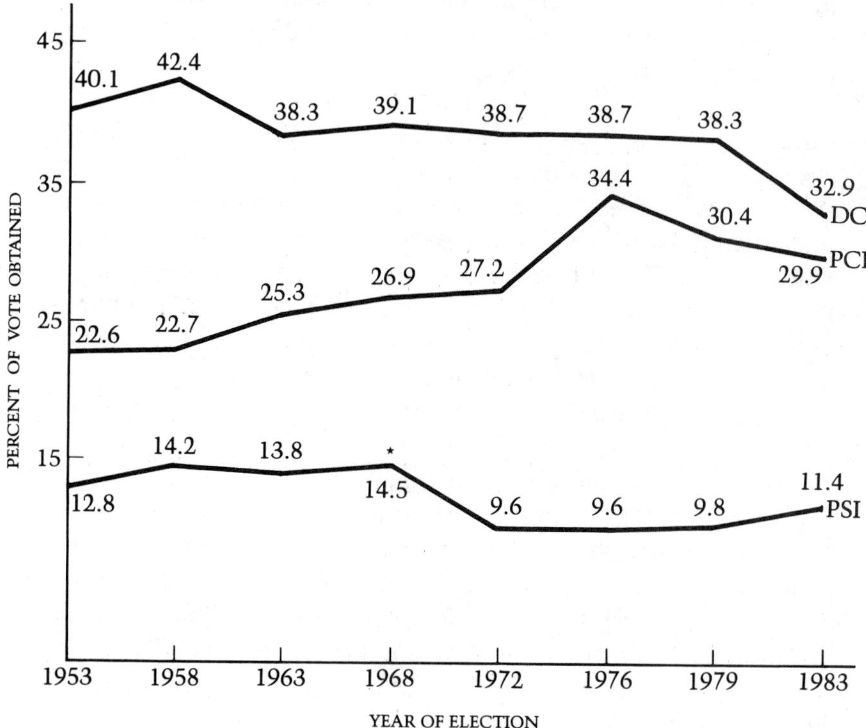

* The PSI ran united with the PSDI in 1968.

most of its minor parties as well. Consistently high voter turnout and proportional representation no doubt understate change, but even they cannot account for such striking continuity. If the electoral patterns of the country as a whole show remarkable stability, the pattern of the largest party, Christian Democracy, is most remarkable of all. Through all the turmoil and transition of the thirty years between 1953 and 1982, the DC's share of the vote hovered between 38 and 40 percent; only a rise to 42 percent in 1958 broke this pattern. Throughout the 1960s and 1970s, its total wavered less than a single percentage point in five consecutive elections. (See Figure 19.2.) Divided into about ten factions, of which at least five are significant, the Christian Democrats themselves were often surprised by their ability to emerge unscathed from internal wars and a seemingly unending series of crippling scandals. A serious examination of the electoral fortunes of the DC over the past thirty years requires an explanation, not of the dramatic drop that occurred in 1983, but of the incredible consistency that preceded it.

The most persuasive explanation for its performance lies, ironically, in what many see as the greatest obstacle to the party's internal coherence — its catch-all, multiclass, composite nature, which allows the DC to be all things to all people. This may deny Italy a true conservative party, but it did enable the DC (at least until 1983) to make up in one area when it lost in another. There is, however, considerable evidence that its present crisis is extremely serious.

The DC's bases of support throughout the postwar period have rested on four factors: religion; anticommunism; patronage; and the "halo effect" from being in power during a time when Italy became a prosperous, highly developed country. None of these factors is about to disappear, but all of them have faded, and some have declined significantly. The halo effect, for instance, counts most among voters who remember the wretched poverty and chaos of the immediate postwar period, but by 1979, new voters were children of the economic miracle. Similarly, it could be argued that so many scandals over the years, combined with dimmer economic prospects in the 1970s, have worked systematically against the DC as the party in power, especially among younger people. Serious questions have been raised about the ruling party's future because almost all trends suggest a very deep erosion of its ability to attract or hold the allegiance of young voters.

Religion, for example, continues to count heavily among those who vote for the DC. No other party in Italy has more than a third of its supporters attending church regularly, yet the figure for the DC soars to twice that. As the church has become less directly involved in Italian politics since the early 1960s, however, its ability to orient voters has also waned. Moreover, church attendance has been steadily dropping in the general population: from over 50 percent in the 1950s, the figure for those who attend regularly has dropped to 25 percent. Further, the social group that historically was the backbone of DC strength, smallholding farmers, also has been dramatically reduced as has the agricultural population in general.

Anticommunism has always been crucial to the DC's appeal, since the main opposition party is the largest communist party in the western world. This fact has helped the DC attract many conservative and moderate voters who would otherwise have been alienated by its close ties to the church. Ever since the end of the worst period of the Cold War, and particularly since the PCI's growth in the 1970s, public opinion polls show a steady drop in the strongest anticommunist attitudes. Those who continue to fear the PCI will be most prepared to support the DC as the strongest "dike" against communism; however, this group, like the most religiously observant, continues to shrink as ideological tension declines.

Finally, even the DC's ability to rely on patronage and clientelism has diminished of late, although this should not be exaggerated. But as DC hegemony has waned, its dominance of the machinery of political patronage has unquestionably declined. Hence, just as it needs greater access to patronage, it has its hands on fewer levers of power.

Continued Sources of Strength. While the factors that have undercut Christian Democratic strength may be formidable, Italy's largest party is hardly about to fade from the scene or even be reduced to the status of a minor party. The church is no longer such a dominant force in Italian politics, but it remains extremely influential. While its message is muted, it still puts very strong emphasis on what it always refers to as "the political unity of all believers," and it will never completely withdraw its support from the DC.

One should also not underestimate the DC's formidable organizational capacities. It may not resemble the traditional mass parties on which it was originally modeled, and its claim to 1.3 million members may be somewhat inflated, but its presence in society is far from negligible. This presence is greatest in the Catholic North-East, where the DC has been most able to draw on the church's influence and the myriad organizations rooted in the Catholic subculture. These organizations (e.g., cooperatives, peasant associations, unions, Catholic Action, etc.), rather than a strictly autonomous party machine, have been the true source of the party's strength in the white zones. Moreover, as the DC "colonized" the state, a number of extremely powerful agencies and institutions fell into its hands, and these have become independent power bases for various party factions. The ability to use IRI, ENI, banking institutions, and the mass media to fund political activities and provide a dense network of patronage jobs is a key factor in the DC's amazing persistence.

The DC is thus a mass party but not a party of mass mobilization. It does not mobilize a potentially cohesive social group (say, small farmers and property holders and businessmen, agricultural labor, or workers and technicians) in the interests of a coherent policy. On the contrary, a coherent policy would threaten party unity and undermine the power of the party bosses who dispense patronage to their diverse clients. Rather, one of the purposes of the clientelistic mass party is to maintain a socially *disorganized* constituency.

The Communist Party (PCI)

After a long period in the wilderness, the PCI came tantalizingly close to obtaining recognition as a fully legitimate, governing party at the end of the 1970s. This was not simply a result of political arithmetic: the party, under Enrico Berlinguer's leadership, had clarified a great number of points in its strategy and doctrine that, until then, had made it suspect even in the eyes of some of its own supporters. The PCI became increasingly critical of the Soviet Union, openly acknowledged the permanent value of democratic processes and institutions, and became much more open internally. These factors, combined with the strong desire for change throughout society, increased party membership by 300,000 (to 1.8 million) between the end of the 1960s and 1976, and saw its electoral support rise 7 percent in the same period. Since then, its strategy has been dramatically altered, its votes and membership have slipped, and it has been pushed into the political wilderness once again. While it is in far better shape than any other nonruling communist party, the heady days of the 1970s are behind it.

An Electoral and Strategic Dilemma. Until 1979, the PCI had never lost votes in a general election. It had crept up steadily in the 1950s and 1960s, and then gained impressively in the 1970s. Given the previous stability of voting patterns in Italy, it is easy to understand why people thought the old equilibria had been demolished. In 1979, however, the party dropped a full 4 percent, and it slipped another half point in 1983. Suddenly, rather than the steady improvement that seemed inevitable just a few years earlier, by the early 1980s many people were speaking of the party's "natural ceiling" of around 30 percent. The great leap of 7 percent in 1976, in this view, was, not the larger step up the ladder of success, but the one-time-only opportunity that was lost.

Still, the long-term trends do not look as threatening to the PCI as they do for the DC, in the sense that the Communists' problems are less structural and more strategic and political. Younger voters have generally tended to support the Left, and the PCI's share of the youth vote has been quite high (e.g., an estimated 40 percent (or more) in 1976). Even after its disappointing performance of the late 1970s, the PCI is still expected to attract about a third of the youth vote. But since 1979, the "newer" political formations, such as the Radical Party, or the more militant small parties of the Left have made inroads into the votes of younger people.

Since the late 1970s, the PCI has had to contend with stagnation and political isolation. The Communists acquired working-class support steadily through the 1970s, as Catholics defected from the DC and as the Socialists dropped their efforts to reinforce their links with the working class, striving instead to become a modern reform party. Even more importantly, the public perception of the PCI as more strongly oriented toward the working class has increased since the party moved back into the opposition in 1979 and tried to reassert its distinct identity, which had been compromised during its collaboration with DC-led governments in the middle of the 1970s.[5]

The dilemma for the PCI is that as long as it is menaced by political isolation, its natural inclination is to fall back on its *social and organizational* strong points: the red regions and the blue-collar suburbs. Yet a strong mobilization of the party in defense of the workers alienates many non-working-class groups that might otherwise be inclined to give the PCI greater support, as they did in the 1970s. The Communists need, and have not yet been able to find, a line of action that enables them to hold their traditional bases of support while winning over enough new strata to tip the political balance back in their favor. This is what happened at the beginning of the National Unity period, but two political factors have changed significantly since then: the Socialists stopped insisting on PCI participation in a national coalition; and, in the late 1970s, the PCI disappointed those who believed the Communists would make the political difference to force the DC and its partners to change policies.

The Socialist Party (PSI)

The Socialists enjoyed a very brief moment as the largest party of the Left, and the second largest party in Italy, in the 1946 vote — until they lost their moderate wing when the Social Democrats seceded in 1947. Since that time, they have been preoccupied with consolidating and expanding a distinctive political niche for themselves. Their strong left wing and class identity were badly eroded in the early 1960s, when the party split a second time upon joining the DC in the Center-Left. An attempt to recoup the loss by reuniting with the Social Democrats between 1966 and 1969 failed: The two parties did far worse combined than when they had been separated; moreover, the turn to moderation could not have come at a worse time. The PSI tried to revive its leftist identity through most of the 1970s, all but begging the PCI to help construct a Left alternative to the DC. But the Communists snubbed this appeal, while pursuing their historic compromise with the DC. The

PCI's rather contemptuous treatment of the PSI at the time contributed to the ill will that has since been a constant obstacle to cooperation on the Left. The PSI also discovered in the 1970s that the PCI and the smaller parties were attracting the stray votes on the Left. From the late 1970s on (just as the Communists began to make overtures to *them* to join together against the DC) the Socialists have turned more decisively toward the center. Thus, the PSI has been plagued not only by bad timing but also by a tendency to make abrupt shifts that neither of its larger political neighbors nor, apparently, the voting public, seem to appreciate. Although the two major parties combined have lost nearly 10 percent of the vote since the middle of the 1970s, the PSI has only gained about 2 percent, while dramatically worsening its relationship with each.

The PSI is a party full of contradictions. Its politically precarious position, and its lack of heavy ideological baggage, has made it much more sensitive to changes taking place in Italian society. This was true in the 1960s as much as in the 1970s, but its ability to act in a way that would take advantage of these changes has, to date, never amounted to much. Thus, it lost most of its close ties to the working class after promising the workers serious reforms under the Center-Left. And while it boldly announced that it would become the modern reform party of all the new classes and strata of modern capitalism, voting returns through the 1970s showed that the PSI was losing support in the most economically advanced areas of the country and gaining votes — largely through patronage — in the South. Its crass pursuit of positions of power, and the very large number of local leaders implicated in scandals from the late 1970s on, also have made the claim to modernity suspect. Finally, while verbally disdaining the importance of traditional organizational structures, the PSI maintains a party structure with a (claimed) membership of half a million.

The "Laical" Center, or Moderate Parties

The moderates have spent most of the postwar period in a position totally subordinate to the DC. At one time or another all of the lay parties have been threatened with extinction, but thanks to proportional representation and the unpredictability of Italian politics, each has managed to come back from the precipice. Collectively, they have fared quite well since the mid-1970s. While it is almost impossible for very small parties to elect senators, the lay center parties have run a joint list of candidates in a limited number of Senate districts since the late 1970s. Their recent rise in strength has been far more impressive than that of the Socialists, and their strength in the Chamber of Deputies is nearly equal to that of the PSI while their combined popular vote actually exceeded the Socialists in 1983. Although these parties do not enjoy the same cohesion as the PSI since Bettino Craxi took that party firmly in hand, they should in theory expand in the future. The problem will be twofold: Which parties will adapt most successfully, and How much room will there be if the PSI's migration into the same political space should prove permanent?

The Social Democratic Party (PSDI). Because the PSI has always been larger and could lay claim to the glorious history of Italian socialism, the PSDI has never had a very distinctive identity, though it has been a party of government since breaking away from the Socialists in 1947. Next to the DC, the Social Democrats have been in more governments, and had more ministers, than any other party. They have managed to hold onto a limited space in the political spectrum, as a centrist party more than a moderate leftist party. After the ill-fated reunification and renewed split with the PSI, the Social Democrats' share of the vote declined steadily through most of the 1970s; however, along with the other minor centrist parties, they have recently recovered some of their support, apparently at the expense of the DC.

The social base of the PSDI is older and less urban than that of the other parties, and its leadership, at least for the past generation, has been notably mediocre (and more scandal-ridden) compared to the Liberals and Republicans. Although they really have little in common with the large Social Democratic parties of northern and western Europe, the PSDI obviously makes a great effort, especially at election time, to associate itself with these larger, more successful parties.

The Republican Party (PRI). The Republicans have tended to enjoy the (largely deserved) reputation as the most modern of the minor lay parties. They fashioned a technocratic image in the 1960s and earned respect as the party that told the country — and the DC — hard economic truths. The PRI first proposed the Center-Left coalition and was an early proponent of bringing the PCI into government, in order to exact serious reforms from governments dominated by the DC. The Republicans have been favored by some of the more dynamic sectors of public and private capitalism in the country, and they also enjoy disproportionate support among the more educated white-collar strata.

The PRI also fell to very low levels of support in the 1970s, but not to the point of threatened extinction (below 2 percent), where they had hovered prior to the mid-1960s. They did remarkably well in local elections late in the 1970s as scandals swept over the DC and the Socialists. When the first non-DC prime minister in the postwar period was finally chosen in 1981, it was Giovanni Spadolini, the head of the PRI. The choice obviously did the PRI no harm, for in the next elections, its vote rose from 3 to 5 percent.

The Liberal Party (PLI). Heirs of Cavour and Giolitti, the Liberals are generally considered the most conservative of the small centrist parties. Historically, they have been identified as the party of big business. There were occasions when their more conservative, but wholly respectable, image served them well, particularly in the early 1960s, when their opposition to the Center-Left brought their support to a postwar high of 7 percent — at the expense of the DC. Thanks to their opposition to the PCI (they refused to join the National Unity governments of 1977–79) and the general flow of votes back to the smaller parties, they have inched forward from near oblivion (1.3 percent) in 1976, but they remain in a very precarious position at just under 3 percent.

The Extreme Right

The Neo-Fascist Italian Social Movement (MSI). The MSI has had the extreme Right of the spectrum largely to itself since 1972. In deference to its minor allies — and to public opinion — it took the name *Movimento Sociale Italiano–Destra Nazionale* (MSI–DN) when the fragments of the remaining monarchist parties joined the neo-Fascists because it was clear the monarchists alone could no longer hope to elect any deputies. But the DN, "National Right," has always been a free-rider. This became clear between 1976 and 1979, when more than half the MSI–DN's parliamentarians broke away to form a more "respectable" right-wing party, the DN. This schism was a reaction to the often uncomfortably close relationships between MSI militants and right-wing terrorists in Italy and Europe. But in the 1979 elections, the DN could not reelect a single one of its 17 deputies, and it failed to reach 250,000 votes. In contrast, the MSI raked in 2 million votes to remain Italy's fourth largest party; in 1983, its total rose to 2.5 million. The explicit appeal of the MSI is that of the classical hard-line law-and-order party of the Right. It has been ambivalent about how fully it accepts constitutional democracy, though it is perfectly clear that it does not accept the Republic as presently constituted. Rather, the most respectable and articulate wing of the party speaks of an authoritarian democracy with a very strong president. At the same time, there is a side to the MSI that the leadership has always been loath to disown completely: The (often obscure) links to terrorism mentioned above, and the more open involvement of many younger militants in episodes of vigilantism and in occasional bloody conflicts with some of the groups of the extraparliamentary left.

The MSI has always been strongest in the South, and through the 1970s, its support in the largest cities of the North declined steadily. In 1983, however, the bulk of its new support came from the North, and specifically from the largest cities. For those who read the drop in participation and the increase in spoiled ballots as signs of a rising disgust with *all* parties, this gain represented yet another confirmation of a limited, but significant, trend.

The New Left

Since at least the middle of the 1960s, radical leftists have believed that the PCI's increasing drift toward moderation was opening up room on its left for more militant forces. Indeed, the fact that no group or party that could even roughly be described as left of the PCI elected a single deputy in 1972 prompted the Communists to adopt a moderate line. In addition, the 3 million votes won by the MSI in 1972 convinced the PCI that the threat from the Right was more serious. Space on the extreme Left eventually did open, though slowly, and with serious weaknesses and divisions.

Democratic Party of Proletarian Unity (PDUP). At the risk of oversimplification, we can divide the New Left in terms of its attitude toward the PCI. One group, which did not see the PCI as hopelessly compromised or as an obstacle to any future advance of the Left in Italy, coalesced around former Communists associated with the journal (later a daily paper) *Il Manifesto* and eventually created the Democratic Party of Proletarian Unity (PDUP). The party achieved some influence, though more in the intellectual realm than through political activity. Most of the prominent *pduppini*, as its members were called, argued that while the PCI's strategy was wrong, any future Left alternative would have to be built around the Communists. Hence, the PCI had to abandon the historic compromise and assume a more militant posture. The PDUP ran with the hard-line new leftists on a joint list in 1976 and fared quite poorly: the entire list obtained 1.5 percent of the vote. In 1979, the PDUP ran separately, quite consciously aiming its appeal at disgruntled PCI supporters, with some success: it obtained half a million votes on its own (1.4 percent) and six seats. In 1983, with the PCI in the opposition and no longer espousing the historic compromise, it ran on a joint list with the PCI. By then, most of its members had rejoined the PCI.

Proletarian Democracy (DP). DP is an even more heterogeneous formation that groups together a few of the hard-line figures from the union movement and many of the more militant remnants of the radical movements of the late 1960s and 1970s. DP has been consistently harsh in its assesment of the PCI and contests elections by outflanking everyone else on the Left. Its support for whatever group appears to be most radical at the moment has at times created problems for DP, since some of these upsurges (most notably in the late 1970s) included strong anti-union and even anti-working-class sentiments. This was especially problematic for that part of the DP's leadership that had risen from the extremely militant, pro-working class groups and organizations spawned by the hot autumn and its aftermath.

With the field left open by the PDUP's alliance with the Communists in 1983, DP picked up nearly a quarter of a million votes, which brought it to well over half a million total votes, and, more importantly, seven seats (as compared with none in 1979). Thus, after three elections, the New Left would appear to be quite small but relatively well established. Not at all surprisingly, it draws very strong support from the youngest age groups in the electorate.

The Radical Party (PR). Although the Radical Party appeals to the same social groups as the parties of the New Left, namely, young people and professional and white-collar strata, it is far more difficult to categorize the PR by standard Left-Right criteria. The PR is more of a "movement-party" than a political party in any strict sense of the word. It originated in the 1950s as a break-away from the PLI, arguing that the Liberals were betraying their secular heritage by subordinating themselves to the DC and ignoring crucial issues of civil liberties. After several false starts, the PR finally found a strong identity in the late 1960s and took up the banners of several issues that most other groups and parties were ignoring: women's rights; civil rights (of a libertarian sort); conscientious objection; and ecology. It also emphasized the question of the advanced capitalist countries' responsibilities to the Third World. The PR is the closest thing to a Greens or ecological party in Italy: in the mid-1980s, it actually ran as a Greens party in local elections. (See Chapter 12 for further information about the Greens.)

The Radicals first won limited parliamentary representation in 1976, with four seats, but their really dramatic breakthrough came in 1979, when they obtained over 1.25 million votes and eighteen seats. Especially impressive in 1979 were the inroads the PR made into the Communist vote in the North, increasing their share by more than four percentage points in all the largest cities. In Rome and the South, the increases were even more impressive than in the big cities, although they were less obviously at the expense of only the PCI. In each case, the Radicals were able to tap different types of protest vote. They deserve our attention because of their ability to exploit widespread dissatisfaction with considerable competition — everyone from the Socialists and lay parties of the center to the Marxist small parties on the Left. This success, particularly via a campaign that was almost strictly a mass media phenomenon, showed that there is a potential political space in Italy for a new, more modern form of protest politics.

It would appear that 1979 was an exceptionally fortunate period for the Radicals, with an immense area of dissatisfaction opened by *all* the established parties, and with the PCI heavily compromised by its collaboration with the DC. Since its peak in 1979, the PR slipped from 3.5 percent nationwide to just over 2 percent of the vote in 1983.

The Organized Labor Movement

As we saw in Chapter 17, trends that had been under way in the 1960s came to a head not only in the hot autumn of 1969 but also in a drawn-out, extremely intense cycle of labor struggles between 1968 and 1972. The result of these struggles was a series of very important changes in the system of industrial relations in Italy, as well as long-delayed reforms. The hot autumn also inspired newly found unity and militancy in the previously divided unions — CGIL, CISL, and UIL. Although the unions were weak numerically when compared to the powerful organizations of northern and central Europe, their ability to speak for a highly mobilized working class, combined with the disarray of both management and the ruling parties in Parliament, decisively tipped the balance of power in their favor. In the face of such militance, the Socialists, from within the Center-Left coalition, were forced to insist that reforms be enacted. Even more importantly, the intensity of the mobilization and its immediate political consequences — enabling the PCI to gain working-class support while the PSI stagnated — persuaded the PSI that it would not remain in government with the PCI on the outside.

Labor's High Point: The 1970s

The unions achieved impressive gains in the 1970s, as discussed in chapter 17. It is, however, important to recall how *radical* many of these achievements were, for the direct challenge to management's prerogatives reveal a great deal not only about the balance of power in the factories (and streets) but also about the nature of the labor movement.

To understand the widespread militance of the unions, one must remember the radical, egalitarian, and antiauthoritarian thrust of almost all the struggles of the late 1960s, especially in Italy. A younger, more militant work force had come to the factories, and many union leaders, along with the rank-and-file, were intent on challenging the capitalist organization of labor. Many of these workers came from deskilled and degraded positions in the factories.

A significant series of developments also took place in the internal structures of the organized labor movement as a direct outgrowth of the mobilization of the 1960s. The newer generation of workers was not as fiercely divided along ideological lines as were their immediate predecessors. They had not lived through the bitter struggles of the Cold War, and they saw how divisions in the labor movement hurt earlier contract settlements. An initial step toward reunification was a unity-in-action pact, followed in the early 1970s by the formation of the Unitary Federation among the three major confederations. Although there was far too much residual resistance and suspicion for a single organization to emerge out of this action, it was viewed as a first step. Even in the most radical and pro-unity sectors of the working class (the metalworkers), old divisions persisted. In most other sectors, the tensions and divisions were even greater. Still, limited unity was a notable step after a full generation of formal schism.

Political Repercussions. Among the most striking outcomes of the hot autumn was not only an extremely drawn out and intense struggle in the factories, but one which took on a distinctively *political* form. This followed from the radical nature of the struggles for reforms: to address so many related social issues was to think in terms of broad reforms that only the government could address. The only way for the unions to overcome their historical political divisions and cooperate with a minimum of trust was to distance themselves from their host parties. In the late 1960s, they formally drew up incompatability rules which banned overlapping leadership roles in both a union and a party — that is, a Christian Democrat, Communist, or Socialist union leader who also held a high party post had to choose one role or the other. The union leaders were sure that, united, they could negotiate more effectively with the government than could the individual parties. The parties, especially the Communists, who saw themselves as the workers' main spokesmen, were always very uncomfortable with what they viewed as the unions' usurpation of their political role. But they had to accept this situation as the price of union unity.

By the middle of the 1970s, the PCI's forbearance seemed to have paid off in its favor. The Communists' political strategy emphasized collaboration and compromise; the National Unity period, in turn, made it much easier for the three union confederations to collaborate. By the end of the 1970s, however, the political collaboration had broken down and relations between the PCI and PSI became strained, generating tensions not only between the three confederations but also *within* the CGIL where Communists and Socialists must coexist. Further, by the end of the 1970s, labor's advantages had faded due to the massive economic crisis and the restructuring measures that many firms had undertaken to counteract the workers' earlier gains. By the 1980s, the tables had been turned once more, and a newly isolated PCI and badly split union movement were groping for a new identity and for new means to reinforce their eroded positions.

The Church

No discussion of Italian social and political forces since the war can ignore the immense, and decisive, role this unique institution has played. Provided with the opportunity to intervene decisively in postwar Italy, the church under Pope Pius XII did not hesitate to exercise it, often harshly. Even many Christian Democrats who favored a more modern state neither integrated with nor under the moral sway of the Vatican were deeply uncomfortable with their dependency on the church and its institutions. But at the peak of the Cold War, they found it to be a potent, and convenient, ally. By papal decree, militant Communists and Socialists were excommunicated; it was declared a sin even to vote for, or otherwise support, Marxist doctrine. In many cases, pressure was put on parents who were leftist activists by denying their children the sacraments. Social intervention was also critical in the "recommendation" of the parish priest from a migrant's home village. This letter would attest to the holder's good nature and political reliability, as well as to his not being a union activist. Migrants who came to the big cities of the North to work in the factories could be sure of rapid insertion into the labor force when they carried the endorsement of their local clergyman. The church was supposed to stay out of politics, but it did not, and its own pronouncements and the activities of the clergy — including twenty-five thousand parish priests — represented a formidable organizational network.

Most formidable of all was the extraordinarily capillary network provided by the lay organization, Catholic Action. At its peak under the leadership of Luigi Gedda, and indeed throughout the 1950s, it numbered 3 million members and was dedicated to bringing Catholic values into every aspect of Italian life. It was ferociously anticommunist and established "civic committees" in practically every hamlet of the country; these committees became, in effect, the territorial power bases of the DC.[6] Many observers, including Catholics with a more secular understanding of modern politics, saw ominous implications in relying too heavily on an organization so clerical in its outlook. This was in fact one of the main reasons the DC tried to establish an autonomous organization of its own, under Fanfani, in the 1950s.

Catholic Action is in fact a whole series of church-related organizations under whose umbrella *all* lay organizations are lumped. This includes everything from the formerly gigantic smallholder's association, to the formidable Christian Workers' Association, the ACLI, to the Catholic university students' and various youth associations. This extraordinarily dense network was already largely in place upon the fall of fascism. Even when it was displaced, gradually and in piecemeal fashion, as the DC's "shadow organization," some of the associations under its umbrella continued to serve as recruitment agencies for the ruling party among their constituents or in their respective areas of competence.

The Church took an active and direct role in the political process in numerous ways. Local clergy, from the parish priest to the bishop, reviewed candidates for local DC lists and passed judgment on their suitability for public office depending on what the clergy took to be their degree of religiosity and open support for favorite church issues.[7] The hierarchy made no bones about its intentions: It would be happy with nothing less than a clericalized or "confessional" state, one in which society was shaped according to Catholic doctrine. Well into the 1960s, there were many examples of blatant interference by the Vatican in the formation of governments and the election of the President of the Republic. Fascist legislation regarding censorship of material considered offensive either to the church's reputation, its moral standards (nudity or suggestiveness in magazines, films, or theater), or its dogma (e.g., information on contraception as well as the availability of contraceptives) was retained and amplified to placate the religious authorities.

Direct interference faded with the death of Pius XII, whose anticommunism was matched only by his authoritarian methods and integralist beliefs. Both John XXIII and Paul VI, although different in many ways, recognized that it was better for everyone to put more distance between the Vatican and the DC, and also between church and state. There was, to be sure, a brief step backward in the early 1970s when the divorce issue arose, and in the early 1980s over abortion — but one cannot realistically expect the church to ignore fundamental issues of doctrine.

Under John Paul II, as one might expect of a non-Italian pope, the direct involvement of the Vatican in the country's internal affairs has tended to lessen. Yet precisely because he is a foreigner, this pope has left much of the initiative on Italian matters to the lower levels of the church. Many cardinals, bishops, and parish priests have maintained a discreet distance, but some have not. In the aftermath of the DC's decline in 1983, for example, many church leaders felt the time had come to involve themselves more actively, and they did so in the local elections of 1985. The DC improved its showing at that time, and many observers attributed this to the renewed activism of so many clerics.

Of course, even in the peak years of its involvement, the church always had to act under severe constraints. If it went too far, it knew it could divide Catholic opinion — which could eventually be fatal to its own privileged position. Thus the most important consideration for the Vatican, in the final analysis, has always been the political unity of Catholics. Even when the pope had no qualms about intervening directly in political affairs, and strongly wanted to push Italy to the right, there were never serious challenges to the DC as *the* political expression of Catholicism. This means that in spite of the formidable organizational resources at their disposal, Catholic groups would never get the church's go-ahead to set up a truly clerical party. The fate of Catholic Action shows the limits on autonomous Catholic political behavior quite clearly. In spite of millions of members and what appeared to be a power base so strong, committed, and independent that there were rumors that Catholic Action's Cold War leadership might set up a right-wing party to challenge the DC, this of course never materialized. Without *active* church support, as Raphael Zariski points out, "Luigi Gedda was just a paper tiger."[8]

Social Movements

Italy has a long history of spontaneous social outbursts and movements, including uprisings that have at times seemed insurrectionary. Massive land occupations in the immediate postwar period forced the government to speed up its limited land-reform program; ten people were killed during uncontrollable urban protests when the Christian Democrats flirted with the neo-Fascists in 1960; and in 1970, when it was announced that Catanzaro was to become the capital of the region of Calabria in the deep South, thousands of people took to the streets in the rival city of Reggio Calabria. The protest quickly turned into rioting with strong anti-Left overtones. What these phenomena have in common with the so-called new social movements that have appeared since the late 1960s is that they have arisen outside of, or quickly escaped the control of, traditional political forces. Where they differ is that the "new" movements — and this, after all, justifies the adjective — have also raised demands, or offered political actors, that did not fit easily into the platforms and constituencies of the traditional parties.

Italy provided especially fertile ground for extreme forms of the new movements, in the sense of being either more explosive or more drawn out. Almost all serious reforms were initially delayed or sabotaged, which aggravated underlying social conditions and political evolution. Further, until recently, the dominant parties succeeded in blanketing the social sphere very effectively: Their effort to organize everything, and to spawn groups that could capture and channel social activity, left limited room for the development of autonomous interest groups or structured citizens' movements.

Workers' and Urban Movements

In terms of size and impact on society, by far the most significant movement in recent times has been the workers' activism that began in the 1960s and peaked during the hot autumn. Although the unions eventually absorbed the workers' new demands, it was first necessary for the unions themselves to change, both structurally and in terms of their programs.

Because of the highly explosive social and political context of the late 1960s, the boundaries between the labor movement and broader social movements were almost nonexistent. As a result, the workers' movement took up the banner of all sorts of social reforms, such as housing, transportation, and medical and other social services. Along with the struggles inside the factories, the major cities witnessed the growth of extensive urban protest movements that lasted well into the mid-1970s. Among other things, these movements helped to discredit Christian Democratic rule in the big cities, while leading to several important political reforms.

The urban movements often focused initially on the severe shortage of decent housing at affordable prices, which led to sometimes spectacular, large-scale occupations of public housing projects. They also focused on other services, such as schools, health, parks, and day-care centers. At their peak, these movements became involved with numerous groups of the extraparliamentary Left, who often helped organize extremely effective "guerrilla" actions, such as boycotting telephone and utility bills and refusing to pay mass transit fares. To the acute embarrassment of the PCI, which was trying to portray itself as a responsible alternative party on the local level, many Communist militants joined these activities.

Student and Youth Movements

Student and youth movements have taken several completely different forms in Italy. In the 1960s, they had a distinctly leftist and highly ideological and politicized character. They often first took shape around protests against the Vietnam War, an event that was especially important in radicalizing many young people from Catholic backgrounds, putting them side-by-side politically, for the first time, with youths from entirely different backgrounds. These student movements reached their first, fairly amorphous, peak in 1967–68, and eventually furnished activists for the many extraparliamentary formations that had arisen (or, in some cases, had been revitalized) by the end of the 1960s. They provided critical contributions to factory and urban struggles, and trained many militants and future leaders for the organizations of the traditional Left. A 1979 study of Communist militants shows, for example, that nearly one-quarter of all militants in the party, and over one-third of those who joined in the 1970s, had some experience in various movements or groups (excluding the unions) prior to joining the PCI.[9]

A totally different youth and student movement surged later in the 1970s, and enjoyed notoriety as the Movement of 1977. This movement, although far more limited in size than that of the 1960s, made a significant impression for several reasons. It was, broadly speaking, antipolitical, and, it had an extremist, nihilistic fringe that was inclined to violence and that attacked all parties, as well as the unions and the more privileged sectors of the working class. These tendencies were the most extreme expression of widespread frustration among young people who understood all too well that the economic crisis left them with few prospects of any kind of stable employment, let alone the type of job to which they aspired. In separate instances in Rome and Bologna during 1977, demonstrating students were killed by gunfire from the forces of order.

This points up yet another, and perhaps the most significant, aspect of the movements of this period. With the Communists extolling cooperation with the DC and demanding to be included in the government, there was, in effect, no significant opposition party during this extremely tense and difficult time. As a result, this period saw the most extreme forms of activity arise on the fringes of the protest movements — very famous wall posters and photos of the period show demonstrators armed with pistols firing at the police. This was also the time that the activity of the left-wing underground and terrorist groups, such as Front Line and the Red Brigades, reached its peak. These groups were never part of a large movement, but they definitely enjoyed diffused sympathy among many of the more disillusioned and frustrated young people, especially before the terrorism escalated. The underground had originally bombed symbolic targets or kidnapped so-called enemies of the people. They soon were "kneecapping" and then murdering their targets (former Prime Minister Aldo Moro was the most notorious of these cases, but victims also included left-wing trade unionists, journalists, and politicians). The existence of the armed fringes and the terrorists, as well as the spread of violent tactics, divided many of the groups on the extreme Left. Their reactions ranged from strong denunciation, to "understanding" analyses, to elaborate rationalizations of the violence.

Ultimately, the most interesting thing about the terrorism is that it lasted so long (some fringes still persist). In part, this reflects the inability of the Italian police and more broadly defined forces of order to do more than wade into demonstrations, but it also reflects the much deeper and more serious crisis of Italian institutions and society when compared to other Western countries. At the same time, it is notable that Italy did not panic and enact a range of measures as repressive as those introduced by the West Germans when they were faced with a much less serious threat.

The Women's Movement

The Left had long paid attention to women as a specific social group, although it did so primarily in traditional leftist terms. In the terminology of the modern women's movement, the old parties of the Left spoke mainly of women's *emancipation* from the inequalities of the workplace and a deeply Catholic society. The new movement, often to the incomprehension of the Left, also wanted to raise questions of *liberation* from a social and political structure that was permeated by sexist, patriarchal behavior and values. Since the organizations of the Left — old and new — were also targets, they were often hostile to the feminists' initial complaints. In fact, the feminist movement of the 1960s and 1970s in Italy originated in the extraparliamentary Left, which preached egalitarianism but relegated female members to (at best) secondary roles.

The PCI and the unions were slow to appreciate the strength and depth of the feminist challenge. At first, they dismissed feminists as a middle-class, privileged fringe: Feminists within the organizations kept up the pressure, however, and events, especially the momentous 1974 referendum on divorce, followed by the 1975 local and 1976 national elections, rapidly converted the unpersuaded. In fairness to the traditional Left, it should be pointed out that the great victories on divorce and abortion would never have been so lopsided if the Left had not fully mobilized its forces in support of the pro-women's positions. Further, once the leadership of the PCI and unions did appreciate the importance, and justice, of the feminists' demands, they pushed their own rank-and-file to accept the new ideas.

The ideas of the women's movement have penetrated Italian society with astonishing speed, at least in the urban centers. This is, after all, a country where as recently as the 1970s, adultery was a crime *only a woman* could commit. Since the latter part of the 1970s, the women's movement in Italy, as elsewhere, has fragmented. There remain specific umbrella organizations that can occasionally mobilize women around specific issues, the most broadly based of which is the Women's Liberation Movement (MLD), which split from the Radical Party in the late 1970s. The general direction of activities, however, has tended to be more inwardly directed over the past decade, with large numbers of study groups, collectives, and local, single-issue activities attracting most feminists' attention.

Ecological Movements

The Radical Party (PR) is, in certain respects, the Italian equivalent of the Greens in both its environmentalist and its pacifist positions. In fact, the PR did not present lists in local elections until 1985, at which time it actually ran with a Greens label and achieved a modest result (2 percent). This was in part a function of the fact that it competed with *other* Greens lists for environmentalist support in the largest cities.

As a broader social movement, the environmentalist phenomenon has been strong in the larger cities, but with a few specific exceptions (e.g., protests against industrial pollution or the siting of a proposed nuclear reactor), it has not undertaken a mass mobilization effort, as has been the case in some northern European countries. At first glance, this appears anomalous, for Italy has unquestionably suffered more ecological disasters than any other country in Europe. Earthwork dams slapped together by greedy contractors have a tragic record of failure, and several mountain villages have literally been swept from the map within recent memory; unlimited speculation (and poor regulations or corrupt enforcement) have ruined some of the most beautiful scenery and undermined the terrain in many of Italy's major centers, such as Naples; Venice continues to sink into the Adriatic Sea as the water from beneath the city is pumped out to service industries whose pollutants dissolve the stonework on buildings and monuments even faster than they settle into the water; and in the Seveso disaster, a cloud of dioxin forced the evacuation of an entire small city near Milan. Recent survey research shows that while barely one percent of Italians list ecological issues as *the* most important problem facing the country, more than one in ten (mainly the young and more highly educated) put the environment among the three most important issues on the national agenda.[10]

Political Culture: Continuity And Change

Political culture is generally defined in terms of citizens' attitudes toward their own role in politics and toward the authority structures and institutions of their countries. It is thought to be a more stable measure of the underlying attitudes of the general population compared, say, to a survey that asks about current events. Since the concept was first used in the late 1950s, Italy has generally been found to have a political culture that is described in terms that are at best unflattering: Distrust, apathy, fragmentation, isolation, and alienation.[11] Moreover, survey data are especially difficult to interpret since a very high percentage of respondents will not discuss political preferences with an interviewer. For example, in 1959, 48 percent of all respondents either refused to tell their choice in the previous year's election or claimed that they did not vote or that they could not remember for which party they had voted! In view of what we know about Italy's voting rates and the stability of partisanship, these responses are clearly evasive. Although the PCI obtained 23 percent of the vote in 1958 (the PSI won 14 percent), only 4 percent of the respondents to the 1959 survey admitted to voting for the PCI (5.5 percent for the PSI).[12] While such reticence is less widespread today, most studies still show a refusal or nonresponse rate between 25 and 30 percent, while the PCI, which now solidly commands around 30 percent of the vote, rarely arrives at 20 percent among those who do answer.

How should one interpret this reticence? Is it proof of an ingrained cynicism or alienation from politics, or is it not better understood as a rational response to an unknown and, therefore, potentially threatening situation? In a country where the loss of one's job, not to mention denial of the sacraments and outright excommunication by the church, were once the penalties for belonging to the "wrong" parties, a very strong degree of caution is appropriate, however disappointing it is to those who want to know more about public opinion.

At the same time, we should remember that there has been, along with growing secularization, an increasing fluidity and volatility in partisanship and voting behavior. The rise in the number of nonvoters and ballot spoilers in the past few elections is equal to a good-sized small party by Italian standards. A limited but significant space has opened up to the left of the PCI, while the area from the Socialists through the lay center parties not only accounts for nearly a quarter of the electorate but also has shown the greatest fluidity and turnover. Ideas and behavior do not follow directly from broader social changes, but they do follow eventually, with fits, starts, and lags. As we have demonstrated in this chapter, deeply entrenched institutions and traditions may filter and delay changes, but in the final analysis, they cannot stop them.

NOTES

1. Ronald Inglehart, *The Silent Revolution* (Princeton: Princeton University Press, 1974) presents the argument and empirical evidence that the modern strata in advanced capitalist countries are typified more by "post-materialist," quality-of-life concerns than by the traditional and redistributive values that have been central concerns since the Industrial Revolution.
2. Giacomo Sani, "The Italian Electorate in the Mid-Seventies: Beyond Tradition?" in *Italy at the Polls: The Parliamentary Elections of 1976,* ed. Howard R. Penniman (Washington, DC: American Enterprise Institute, 1977), pp. 81–122.
3. Arturo Parisi and Gianfranco Pasquino, "Changes in Italian Electoral Behaviour: The Relationships Between Parties and Voters," in *Italy in Transition,* ed. Peter Lange and Sidney Tarrow (London: Frank Cass and Co., 1980), pp. 14–15.
4. Leonardo Morlino, "The Changing Relationship Between Parties and Society in Italy," *West European Politics,* 7 (October, 1984), pp. 54–56.
5. Biorcio and Mannheimer, "Scandagliando il voto di maggio," *Politica ed Economia* XVI (June, 1985), p. 11.

6. Gianfranco Poggi, *Catholic Action in Italy: The Sociology of a Sponsored Organization* (Stanford, CA: Stanford University Press, 1967).
7. Arturo Carlo Jemolo, *Church and State in Italy: 1850–1950* (Oxford: Basil Blackwell, 1960), Chap. VIII.
8. Raphael Zariski, *Italy: The Politics of Uneven Development,* p. 222.
9. Stephen Hellman, "Militanti e politica nel Triangolo industriale," in *L'identitá comunista. I militanti, le strutture, la cultura del Pci,* ed. Aris Accornero et al. (Rome: Editori Riuniti, 1983).
10. Biorcio and Mannheimer, "Elettorato e fratture culturali," p. 43.
11. Gabriel A. Almond and Sidney Verba, *The Civic Culture: Political Attitudes and Democracy in Five Nations* (Princeton, NJ: Princeton University Press, 1963), p. 402; Joseph La Palombara, "Italy: Fragmentation, Isolation, and Alienation," in *Political Culture and Political Development,* ed. Lucian W. Pye and Sidney Verba (Princeton, NJ: Princeton University Press, 1965), pp. 282–325.
12. Giacomo Sani, "The Political Culture of Italy: Continuity and Change," in *The Civic Culture Revisited* ed. Gabriel A. Almond and Sidney Verba (Boston: Little, Brown and Co., 1980), pp. 283–85.

20

Italian Politics In Transition

In the wake of the tumultuous 1970s, the *Pentapartito,* the ruling five-party coalition, invites sarcasm. It is, after all, simply the Center-Left with the rather irrelevant addition of the Liberals. Indeed, one might say that the net result of the tortuous political history of the Republic since the elections of 1948 has been to expand the governing coalition from the original four parties to include the Socialists. Of course, this ignores an immense number of changes that have taken place despite the astonishing continuity in the political system — and especially the governments — of Italy. It also offers some insight as to why the Italians are so quick to label their various political experiments: They must keep the (same) players straight as they shift roles; the new labels at least provide the illusion of change where none may exist. While the system is obviously blocked in some fashion, the consistent electoral returns — and the lack of courage and imagination on the part of elected representatives — have prevented the formation of clear alternatives.

The 1980s have brought a shift in the balance of power within the governing coalition significant enough to allow serious discussion of a change in the center of gravity of the political system. At the same time, the balance has not really shifted much, and a great deal will depend on which of the contending forces is most astute in turning the new situation to its own advantage. In the mid-1980s, the balance of power was still very much unsettled, but the outlines of the conflict were clear. We now turn to a discussion of the major actors as they tackle the formidable problems that continue to plague Italy.

The Emergence of the Craxi Government

In 1983, the DC's drop in support stunned almost everyone, most of all the Christian Democrats, even though, in fact, there had been considerable shifts in the DC's vote in 1979. Losses in 1979 were notable in the large urban centers of the North and the previously solid Catholic areas of the Northeast, but these earlier losses had been offset by gains in the South. In 1983, there were no offsetting gains and the drop was heavy everywhere, especially in the South and the Northeast. Already demoralized by intense internal conflict and a series of scandals, the DC was forced, as it had been in 1981 when Spadolini (PRI) became prime minister, to relinquish leadership of the government to another party.

Bettino Craxi, the dynamic, ambitious leader of the PSI, thus became the first Socialist prime minister of the Republic. Craxi established a high profile for himself, using the mass media to reach the new middle classes that are the PSI's prime targets (see Chapter 19). He came to office speaking in terms of tackling deep economic problems while making the country more governable by reforming Parliament. His party's rise of 1.6 percent in 1983 was not a striking victory, especially given the combined losses of the DC and PCI, but he moved quickly to legitimize himself as a decisive, "can-do" politician, gambling that this would bring even further support to the PSI while both the DC and PCI were weakened and demoralized. This strategy has given him longevity in office: In early 1986, he achieved the distinction of presiding over the longest-lived government in the Republic's history. Yet Craxi's very desire to remain prime minister was a source of tension between the PSI and the DC. The two parties had agreed to share the prime ministership during the course of the legislature elected in 1983, but as the term wore on, Craxi, sensing his strengthened position, consistently refused to open serious discussions concerning any changes. The Christian Democrats could not risk a serious crisis over what would appear to be their greed for high office, but the ill will generated by these events guarantees strained relations between the major coalition partners.

The Communists and the Labor Movement

Since abandoning the historic compromise and returning to the opposition, the PCI has been in a very uncomfortable position. It is by no means a purely working-class party, yet it needs to consolidate its support among the workers in order to make the case that, as the main representative of the working class, it is indispensable to the government.

(For similar reasons, the rulers of the *Pentapartito* have tried to bypass the Communists and deal directly with the trade unions.) In wooing the workers and Communist militants, however, the PCI has alienated other social groups. This in turn makes any dramatic increase in support less likely and traps the PCI in a closed circle. The party has responded in two ways: first, by taking a hard-line on domestic (especially economic) issues while expanding internal party democracy; and second, by continuing to criticize the Soviet Union. This is an effort to appeal, respectively, to workers and to the middle class. This show of flexibility may well pay off for the Communists in the long run, but it has not resolved their short- and medium-term problem of isolation.

The PCI's transition was rendered more difficult by the death of Enrico Berlinguer in 1984 at the age of 62. This may seem ironic, for Berlinguer was the author of the discredited historic compromise strategy. But he was also the party's uncontested leader. Given the Communists' traditional caution, he provided the continuity and reassurance the party needed as it steered into uncharted waters. He died during the campaign for the 1984 European elections, and in those elections a large sympathy vote brought the PCI back to the levels of its 1976 vote. In 1984, the Communists even surpassed the DC, albeit in an election that didn't really count with respect to the balance of power in Parliament. This was yet another blow for the DC, but it did little to overcome the PCI's isolation.

The Labor-Management Front. While developments in the political arena were undermining the unity of the trade union confederations, equally dramatic changes in labor market conditions increasingly eroded the victories of the 1970s. The end of the decade brought a full-fledged crisis to Italy: declining growth, rising inflation and unemployment, a balance of payments crisis, and runaway state spending. Symbolically, the turning point came in 1980 at Fiat, the country's largest private employer and scene of many historic victories and defeats for the labor movement. This time, a thirty-five day strike ended in a serious setback for the militant metalworkers: twenty-five thousand workers were laid off by the automotive giant in a major restructuring of its largest factories. The strike collapsed when white-collar (and some skilled blue-collar) workers, along with supervisory personnel, marched through the streets of Turin, demanding to return to work. Faced with deep divisions within its own ranks, as well as a hopeless bargaining situation, the union settled for very weak terms and called off the strike.

The economic crisis, combined with labor's obvious weakness, enabled management to present an increasingly united front. Even the state and private-sector employers' groups began to coordinate their previously independent negotiating strategies. Emboldened by Fiat's victory and desperate to recoup earlier losses to labor, the major private employers' association (*Confindustria*), moved in the early 1980s against a number of union guarantees. A prime target was the *scala mobile* (automatic cost-of-living "escalator"), which the unions had earlier considered untouchable once it was included in the 1975 national contract. Aware of their vulnerability, the unions worked out a bargaining platform that included numerous concessions to business. In fact, one reason the union leadership accepted so much government mediation in the negotiation of a national contract was their calculation that the government could make up part of what they conceded to management. The final agreement, reached early in 1983, was named the Scotti Accords, for the Labor Minister who mediated the negotiations. The Accords included a modification in the *scala mobile* and a temporary ban on wage bargaining at the factory level, among other things.[1]

The PCI, which was entirely cut out of these negotiations, used its working-class activists and the more militant elements in the unions to agitate for as many changes as possible in the final set of union demands. The party endorsed these demands late (and grudgingly). The PCI was deeply concerned by what it saw as too many union concessions, and it was all too aware of the ease with which it had been marginalized from these crucial consultations. Therefore, the Communists stepped up their pressure on the unions in anticipation of the next round of negotiations. At the same time, the non-Communist unionists, especially those close to the DC and PSI, increasingly charged the PCI with violating union autonomy from the parties, in hopes of arriving at a settlement that left the Communists out in the cold. Union unity was unraveling, and PCI–PSI relations had reached their lowest point. Six months after the Scotti Accords were signed, Craxi became prime minister and the stage was set for a showdown among the forces claiming to represent the workers.

The Search for a New Equilibrium

As the leader of the smallest of Italy's three major parties, Bettino Craxi cannot accept the current balance in Parliament: This would mean accepting the PSI's inferior status as permanent. Craxi has sought to avoid the same fate the party had suffered under earlier incarnations of the Center-Left by demonstrating that the PSI could make a difference and that a well-defined majority in Parliament could be more effective than the nebulous, all-party, National Unity arrangement or the recent DC-led majorities. Craxi has attempted to impose a strict interpretation of majority rule in Parliament, which means, above all, that he has imposed far more isolation on the PCI than the Communists are willing to accept. Beginning with the rule changes of the early 1970s, the PCI had in fact been consulted regularly, and it did not expect that its return to the opposition would result in such thorough marginalization. The Socialists, in contrast, claim that this clarification of the role of government and opposition has made for more efficient decision-making.

Given this struggle between the PSI and PCI, it is perhaps fitting that it would come to a head over the question of labor relations. Following the precedent set in the 1983 Scotti Accords, Craxi arranged another round of tripartite negotiations between government, labor, and management, once again leaving the Communist Party with no formal role in the discussions.

The 1984 Labor Negotiations

The second round of negotiations thus began under conditions that almost guaranteed disagreement. The PCI would only accept a settlement in which its own contribution was unmistakable. The CISL and UIL, as well as the Socialists in the CGIL, were equally clear that this would be unacceptable to them. Craxi, meanwhile, had to show that he could come up with an agreement without relying on the PCI's good offices: otherwise, the argument that the PSI, alone, made a difference in governing Italy would not stand. Finally, labor-management relations were also tense: *Confindustria* was as eager as ever to be rid of the *scala mobile*, and labor and management had not stopped arguing about how to calculate the escalator according to the 1983 Accords.

In February, 1984, the government proposed a compromise it called the best possible under very strained circumstances. Its most controversial provision committed the unions to a cost-of-living increase based on the *projected*, rather than the real inflation rate. In other words, a ceiling was fixed for the *scala mobile*. The Communist majority of the CGIL refused to accept this; the Socialist minority of the CGIL, the CISL, and the UIL all announced that they would sign the agreement. When Craxi found that he would not have the approval of all three major confederations, which is what such accords require, he issued an "emergency" executive decree, which made the agreement legally binding for sixty days, by which time Parliament would have to pass it through normal legislative channels. Arguing (with some reason) that the decree was both inappropriate and unconstitutional, the PCI announced it would do everything it could to block its passage, including obstructionism in the Chamber of Deputies.

The next months saw relations within the labor movement and between the PSI and PCI deteriorate even further. With the Communist faction of the CGIL refusing to sign the agreement, the tenuous unity of the Federation Pact of 1972 had obviously run its course. Not only did the CISL, UIL, and CGIL then go their separate ways, but strains within the CGIL also came close to a breaking point. In Parliament, the PCI, aided by the small leftist formations, was successful in obstructing the passage of the decree within the required sixty days — at which point Craxi issued a *second* decree, which Parliament passed. The Communists announced that if the real inflation rate exceeded the government's optimistic projections, they would "go to the masses in defense of working people" in order to see that justice was done. They would, in other words, resort to a referendum to try to win back what Craxi's "dictatorial" decree had taken from the workers. Craxi, meanwhile, was clearly delighted with the way events had unfolded, for he had isolated the Communist unionists and shown that even in the area of labor relations, the PCI was not the essential actor it claimed to be.

When the gap between the government-imposed ceiling and the workers' projected earnings under the old *scala mobile* proved to be 2 percent, the PCI went ahead with its threat to call a referendum, flanked by the Communist component of the CGIL. Once again, the only other active campaigners were from *Democrazia Proletaria* and the smaller groups of the far Left. This fact left many Communists very uncomfortable, while many of their supporters in the CGIL were equally uncomfortable with the heavy-handed way the party had intervened and, essentially, forced the union to go along with its action. In June, 1985, the referendum to abrogate the decree-law failed, though by a narrow margin — 46 to 54 percent. This enabled the Communists and the far Left to claim a moral victory, since their share of the parliamentary vote was barely above 30 percent. It was, however, a defeat that pointed out that *no one* could now claim to speak for *all* working people. *Confindustria* took the offensive in view of such sharp divisions in the labor movement, and announced one day later that it was not going to honor the 1975 *scala mobile* agreement when it expired later that year.

The 1984 Revisions to the Concordat

Early in 1984, the government proposed for parliamentary approval a commitment to sign a new Concordat with the Vatican. This proposal passed the Chamber of Deputies with an overwhelming majority, although some parties made a point of abstaining or absenting themselves from the hall when the question was finally called. Several critical items remained to be decided; indeed, the government had brought the question to Parliament before initialing any of the outstanding issues. Craxi was eager to be associated with such a momentous step in church-state relations and had insisted that the matter be put at the top of the parliamentary agenda.

The two most important outstanding issues involved religious instruction and the taxation of church property. A third question — the Italian courts' automatic recognition of marriage annulments — was a serious point of contention until the early 1980s, when the Constitutional Court finally ended it. The tax question promised to drag on for a very long time, while progress was apparently being made on religious education, so Craxi prudently settled for an agreement that, though far from ideal, was much more streamlined and modern than the 1929 Concordat.

Late in 1985, the Christian Democrats executed the sort of maneuver for which they are famous. The DC Education Minister announced that she and the responsible Vatican representative had signed an agreement that settled the matter of religious instruction in the schools. The problem was that she had not submitted a draft agreement to Parliament first, as had been promised for all outstanding matters pertaining to the Concordat. While the agreement did bow to lay party demands in its reassurances that teachers would be required to have "a new professional qualification," it also set deadlines that made it impossible to provide alternatives to religious instruction for the next academic year.

The announcement was met with an uproar.[2] More than a half-dozen separate motions were immediately announced in Parliament, ranging from simple requests for clarification to outright motions of censure against the minister for failing to consult Parliament. When it became clear that the minister might be forced to resign, the DC's leadership informed Craxi that they would not let her be forced out of office. In short, Craxi had to make the question one of confidence *in the government* in order to circumvent direct criticism of the minister. (Motions of confidence take precedence over all other matters and supercede amendments or motions of censure on the same question.) The DC threatened to withdraw its support from the government, which would precipitate a crisis and cause Craxi to lose the prime ministership. Under these circumstances, Craxi had little choice but to bow to the threat, enraging his minor lay-party coalition partners. The DC had plainly outmaneuvered the non-Catholic forces in the coalition on an issue it did not want to subject to intensive public debate.

The Precarious Balance: Socialists and Christian Democrats

The case of the Concordat is only one illustration of the tensions that exist between the two parties whose collaboration has been essential to most of the coalitions in Italy since the early 1960s. Each party needs the other, especially since the DC lost so heavily in 1983, but each also has its own agenda. The DC would like to recoup its losses in order to regain unquestioned preeminence as *the* party of government; it would also like to keep the Socialists in a permanently subordinate position. The Socialists know they hold the balance of power, but not by much: their goal continues to be to increase their own support to make their own leverage within future coalitions even greater than at present.

Thus the DC tries to get the Socialists to commit themselves to continued collaboration and to distance themselves from the PCI. Even if the Christian Democrats' desire for more access to local patronage were not part of their calculations, this broader strategic design would explain the DC's insistence in the 1980s that local left-wing governments be dissolved wherever possible. This was, in fact, a demand they made of the PSI before agreeing to Craxi's prime ministership. It also explains why the Socialists will never break completely with the Communists. As we have seen, maneuvering between the two giants of the Italian party system is a highly risky tactic with which, historically, the PSI has fared none too well. It is the PSI's only option, however, to which Craxi has committed himself far more openly and aggressively than any of his predecessors.

Craxi (or his successor), therefore, must push the DC as far as the situation will permit and take as much for his own party as is possible. The ultimate threat is that if the Christian Democrats prove too recalcitrant, the PSI will come to some sort of agreement with the PCI, which would be delighted to break its isolation. But any move to the left by the Socialists leaves them open to twin dangers: the accusation that they are pure opportunists; and the fear of moderate voters, who tend to rush to support the DC when the Left is seen as too close to national power.

The Strange Fate of the Grande Riforma

These considerations help us understand why perhaps the major theme of both the 1979 and especially the 1983 electoral campaigns has to a very large extent faded from view. The *Grande Riforma,* "Great Institutional Reform," was supposed to render Italy more governable and unblock an intolerable situation, but once it began to be examined seriously, in a joint Chamber-Senate Committee, a barrage of self-serving objections was quickly laid down by all interested parties. The major parties also chose to use the commission, and the broader discussion of Italian institutions, to maneuver and send obscure signals to each other. Craxi, who made the *Grande Riforma* a centerpiece of the PSI's platform in 1983, beat something of a strategic retreat on the issue as soon as he became prime minister. The perquisites of power and patronage proved far more attractive than any serious alterations to the status quo.

Under the circumstances, it is surprising that even a partial consensus emerged. There is strong agreement that the redundancy of the two chambers of Parliament must be eliminated and an apparent consensus that the prime minister's role in forming governments should be strengthened. On practically every other issue — and a great many were discussed, ranging from the internal organization of parties and unions, to the electoral system, to the secret vote in Parliament — there was too much disagreement and a reluctance to disrupt current arrangements.[3] Many proposals relating to citizen action were dealt with in a fashion that suggested a desire to keep things as they are and avoid new channels of participation or guarantees of citizens' rights. A Communist proposal to allow consultative referendums was shelved; there was agreement that the rules governing the present, abrogative form of referendum should be stiffened; suggestions concerning a sort of ombudsman were quickly shunted aside. As with many aspects of Italian institutional behavior, it was a highly informative, if not very inspiring, performance.

A (Moderately) Autonomous Foreign Policy: Italy and the Middle East

Throughout the entire postwar period, Italy has tended to keep a low and generally noncontroversial profile in foreign affairs. Italian foreign policy can usually be counted on to follow U.S. guidelines — to a degree some critics consider slavish. If there is an exception to this pattern, it has been with regard to North Africa and the Middle East. Many politicians have argued, with some accuracy, that Italy's avoidance of postwar decolonization crises, such as those suffered by Britain and France, provide a special opportunity to act as a bridge between Europe and the developing countries generally, and those that ring the Mediterranean in particular.[4]

There is, of course, a good deal of self-interest behind this apparent magnanimity. A country with few natural resources undoubtedly finds it easy to be considerate of oil-rich neighbors, and Italy has actively helped several of these neighbors exploit their deposits (and spend their reserves on everything from construction projects to high technology). At the same time, the Italians *do* feel they have a special relationship to that part of the world, and it takes no more than a glance at a map of the Mediterranean to understand why. Thus, for both materialistic and idealistic reasons, Italian attitudes and policies toward the Middle East have sometimes "tilted" toward the Arab countries, and toward the plight of the Palestinians. It is especially significant that these attitudes are found within the DC as well as on the Left.

On rare occasions, Italy's efforts to be evenhanded run afoul of U.S. foreign policy goals in the Middle East, especially when the U.S. assumes a more aggressive or interventionist posture. Several dramatic episodes in the 1980s illustrate this potential for tension.

One case involved Lebanon. Following Israel's 1982 invasion, the U.S. put enormous pressure on its Western allies to contribute troops to a "peacekeeping" force in Beirut. The Italians grudgingly went along, but their soldiers scrupulously observed a strict neutrality among all contending Lebanese factions, limited their involvement to humanitarian and goodwill actions, and refused to be drawn into conflictual situations. The Americans, in contrast, quickly made clear that they supported the officially-constituted Lebanese government, which some Christian and most Moslem factions considered a puppet of the Israelis and the U.S. The Italians — much to their major ally's annoyance — repeatedly criticized the American lack of neutrality. Their stance appears to have paid off, for the Italians were spared all but limited harassment, while the U.S. and French garrisons suffered constant attacks, including devastating suicide bombings that eventually forced them to withdraw. The Americans were clearly defeated, while the Italians could claim to have pulled out with both their dignity and persons intact.

Evenhandedness and fear of offending any Arab faction had a less positive outcome late in 1985 when the Italian cruise ship Achille Lauro was hijacked by Arabs whose exact political affiliation remains obscure. The hijackers murdered an American tourist. The Egyptian plane on which they were making their escape was intercepted in international airspace by U.S. jet fighters, who forced the plane to land at a NATO airbase in Sicily. There the Americans turned the hijackers and the suspected planner of their operation over to stunned and embarrassed Italian authorities. Because the interception of the Egyptian plane was a violation of international law, but mainly because the Italian authorities wanted as little to do with the affair as possible, they reacted with a rapidity that is otherwise unknown in Italian courts. The hijackers were arrested and charged, but the alleged mastermind was released on grounds of insufficient evidence.

These events quickly erupted into a crisis that nearly ended Craxi's reign as prime minister. The Americans were furious at the haste with which the alleged ringleader had been freed; they claimed that they had not even had a chance to present the evidence that would have incriminated him. (The Italians eventually issued a warrant for his arrest and condemned him to prison *in absentia,* lending credence to the U.S. charge.) Many Italians, in turn, deeply resented what they saw as a typical U.S. recourse to force, along with the misuse of a NATO base on their territory and heavy-handed intervention in the internal affairs of a supposed ally. Craxi and Foreign Minister Andreotti, a Christian Democrat noted for his pro-Arab views, used this rare outburst of offended national pride to deflect much of the criticism that arose over the release of the suspected ringleader. Craxi's hand was further strengthened by strong PCI support for his actions.

None of these developments pleased Defense Minister Spadolini, who is more pro-American and pro-Israeli than most of his coalition partners; he also holds to a harder line on international terrorism. Claiming that he had not been consulted on a matter that obviously involved his ministry, Spadolini resigned, and for a time it appeared that his Republican Party would not join any government led by Craxi. The well-known animosity between these two leaders did nothing to help solve the problem. After several weeks of political consultations and maneuvers, the *Pentapartito* was reconstructed and a crisis was avoided. But the episode was a classic illustration of the way ideological and policy differences, as well as personal rivalries, have been a perennial source of cabinet instability. A further domestic side-effect of the Achille Lauro affair was increased rapprochement between the PSI and the PCI. Craxi was grateful for Communist support, and he also was able to use this support and the resulting improved relations between the two parties as an implied threat against those of his coalition partners who felt he had already remained in office too long.

If the Italian leadership thought it had somehow side-stepped the broader issue of international terrorism by its actions in the Achille Lauro affair, further tragic events much closer to home soon proved otherwise. Later in 1985, a bloody attack in the main concourse of Rome's international airport left several dozen people dead or wounded. While the Italians would continue to take far less belligerent actions than the Americans, they could not simply repeat diplomatic niceties and hope terrorists would strike elsewhere when their own citizens were being massacred (and when their vitally important tourist industry was put in jeopardy). However reluctantly, they were forced in subsequent months to make statements and take precautionary or retaliatory actions — for instance with regard to Libya — that they would greatly have preferred to avoid. And as long as the U.S. has an administration that insists on taking a hard and highly vocal line on international terrorism and its assumed promoters and sponsors in the Middle East, the Italians are going to find themselves in an extremely awkward position with respect to their senior ally.

New (and Old) Policy Directions

Because Italy faces so many serious problems, she has never lacked for grandiose schemes to attack them. Far more often than not, these schemes have remained on paper, or they have been sabotaged before they could even become formalized. At best, they have been partially implemented and distorted by vested interests within Parliament, the bureaucracy, or the political system. Therefore, one learns to treat the announcement of bold new plans with considerable skepticism, especially when the prime minister who announces them is known for his love of the limelight and is head of a party that remains a junior partner in the ruling coalition. The DC may have been shocked and put on the defensive in the 1980s, but it has an unmatched instinct for protecting its own interests, which are threatened by any significant change.

Despite these serious qualifications, recent Italian governments have undertaken a number of initiatives that attack several of the most serious structural problems in the economy. They have not, however, attempted broad reforms that go to the roots of these problems. We have already examined the new approach to labor relations, which would have to count as one of the most notable, if as yet inconclusive, departures of the 1980s. By the mid-1980s, a strong economic recovery was underway, and numerous parties tried to claim credit for it. But since most of the rapidly rising indicators (private capital investment, personal savings, productivity) cannot easily be tied to governmental policies, the real credit may belong primarily to the small- and medium-size capitalists who find ways to compete successfully *despite* the obstacles that political leaders put in the way. In this final section, we will review the most nagging structural problems facing the Italian government and indicate, where appropriate, the measures that have been taken to address them.

The Economy in the 1980s

The Public Sector. Although Craxi has not shrunk from demanding a greater share of leadership positions for Socialists in the public sector, economic necessity has limited the use of patronage in filling such positions. Changes at the helm of both IRI and ENI have, in fact, resulted in dramatic turnarounds in both holding companies. They have been made more responsive to political control and immediate market conditions and have rid themselves of unprofitable enterprises that had accumulated during the 1970s. Because of their public role, they have been forced to act cautiously, making great efforts to transfer laid off workers to more profitable firms within the system. Finding a politically acceptable formula for economic success was difficult enough in the years of steady growth, but digging these economic giants out of the crises of the late 1970s and early 1980s has been a far more daunting challenge.

IRI, for example, has adopted a policy of selling off state-held stocks (although the state has, to date, ensured that a controlling share in the companies remains in its own hands). Aided by a booming stock market, this policy has proven, at least through the mid-1980s, to be a very successful way of generating investment funds without digging deeper into the Treasury. At ENI, privatization has been much more limited, but the various holdings have been forced to become more responsive to the marketplace. Since this change of strategy coincided with the very steep drop in the price of oil in the early 1980s, ENI's more aggressive approach could turn out to be problematic. As the agency responsible for guaranteeing continuous supplies, ENI was able to deal in a buyer's market and to cut costs drastically, but as an agency that must also develop sources of fuel, ENI must hope that the price does not fall too much, for its own (considerable) investments will be jeopardized. Through the mid-1980s, the turnaround was impressive: losses averaged a billion dollars a year in 1982 and 1983; by 1985, the holding reported profits just shy of half a billion dollars.[5]

Runaway State Spending and Deficits. This problem threatens to get completely out of control, for Italy's difficulties are on a different plane than those of other advanced capitalist countries. Interest on the public debt is now twice the average for the advanced capitalist countries and costs Italy about 10 percent of its gross domestic product (GDP), while the debt itself approaches the equivalent of the entire GDP. The already huge gap between public spending and taxes, which had become out of line with other West European countries at the end of the 1970s (when spending was 46 percent and taxes were 38 percent, for a gap of 8 percent of GDP), has grown to staggering levels. By 1984, government spending had risen to 59 percent of GDP. Although revenues collected through taxation had also increased notably, to 42 percent, the gap had thereby *doubled*. Through 1985 and into 1986, the situation had worsened, by all experts' accounts.[6] No one has a convincing blueprint for solving this problem, but it is evident that both the bureaucracy and the system of taxation are, as they always have been, prime candidates for structural reforms. The problem, now as in the past, is to find a government and a governing majority with the courage to do something about it. As always, suggestions for reform abound, and numerous ministers, seemingly with great sincerity, announce forthcoming austerity measures and the end of extravagant subsidies for special interest groups. Then the very powerful entrenched interests and lobbies dig in, and such minor progress as is made usually does little more than slow the speed at which the problem mounts.

The Private Sector. Immense state deficits mean that high interest rates are unavoidable, and high interest rates ultimately discourage expensive capital investments. Since Italian interest rates are already high, many experts worry that rising deficits may soon create structural blocks against the investment boom that began in the early 1980s. Following a pattern evident in most other advanced countries, the boom has taken place against a backdrop of steadily *rising* unemployment. This is a sure sign of continued economic restructuring, which has displaced large numbers of previously protected workers, and, in turn, has prompted organized labor to offer considerable wage concessions in the hope of influencing the way the restructuring of industry occurs.

However, the forces at work in the economy are beyond the conscious control of labor or any distinct group of firms. Indeed, the private firms most hostile to organized labor, led by *Confindustria,* are willing to let market forces dictate the course of events. The unusually dynamic small industrial firms expanded at an unprecedented rate in the 1970s, costing Italy far fewer industrial jobs than in most advanced countries, and the industrial sector, in fact, grew between the censuses of 1971 and 1981. By the middle of the 1980s, however, the number of industrial jobs lost was being counted in hundreds of thousands per year[7] — far more than even the vigorous small industries or the "submerged economy" can handle.

The broader implications of these developments is not encouraging for the organized workers' movement. A boom that continues under these conditions cuts the unions' support. It also undermines the PCI's claim to a role in governing the country: Who needs the Communists when the workers are weak and on the defensive? It will, moreover, aggravate tensions between the DC and PSI, for the Christian Democrats will probably demand the prime ministership at a certain point so *they* can claim some of the credit for a remarkable recovery.

While the Italian industrial sector continues to show the flexibility for which it has long been famous, the agricultural sector's plight can no longer even be described as in a tailspin: It has crashed, victim of the same market forces that have helped industry thrive. There are, to be sure, modern agricultural sectors that are competitive with the most advanced producers in the world, but if one asks the basic question of whether Italy is able to provide its own food, the answer is a resounding no. With very few exceptions, the decline in the agricultural population, so dramatically represented in Table 17.2, has meant the depopulation of the countryside, the abandonment of farming, and the migration of the rural population to the cities. Most of those left on the farm receive various subsidies and remain marginal figures in Italian society. Of all European countries in the early 1980s, only Greece and Portugal had less acreage on the average farm and a more fragmented system of holdings than Italy. Even Spain, with a far larger agricultural sector (and an economy less than two-thirds the size of Italy's), had larger average-sized farms and fewer very small holdings.[8]

As a result, Italy has had to import food, which, combined with the need for imported oil, means a structural trade imbalance or, at the very least, a trade balance that is profoundly weakened. In the postwar period, Italy made up for the built-in imbalance in several ways: through aggressive export policies, tourism, and money sent home by the millions of people who had emigrated. This pattern promises a difficult future for the country, as advanced Third World countries compete for Italian export markets, which have become increasingly saturated with consumer goods: shoes; leather goods, textiles, and jewelry. In fact, in 1980, the volume of Italian exports shrank for the first time since World War II, though it has since expanded greatly as the investment boom took hold. Although tourism remains a strong source of foreign currency (and jobs), the 1970s saw, for the first time in the history of modern Italy, more immigration than emigration between two censuses. This no doubt reflected two converging trends: the decline of the formerly abundant agricultural population, and the inability of modern capitalist economies to create jobs at the previous rate. It also underscores how Italy's fundamental problems are aggravated by a changing national and international economy.

Unemployment. As we saw in Table 17.5, the level of unemployment has risen steadily in Italy; it is very close to the West European average. Youth unemployment, however, has been much higher than the average since the 1970s and higher than that of any other West European country, except Spain. As much as one-third of the labor force under twenty-five years of age is estimated to be out of work, although many young people have part-time or full-time jobs in the underground or submerged economy, where working conditions, wages, and benefits cannot compare to those enjoyed by the organized work force. Officially, though, the labor force and unemployment are growing as women join the work force at a far faster rate than in the past. (One of the legacies of a more traditional rural society was that while it was acceptable for women to work in the fields, their departure for factories and cities was discouraged.)[9] Therefore, unemployment can be expected to increase more rapidly than general economic growth until the rate of female participation in the work force levels off. With the traditional outlet of emigration now greatly reduced, this is yet another source of strain on the Italian economy.

Finally, it should be apparent that the nature of the restructuring that has been under way, as well as the persistence of the nagging structural problems of the Italian economy, do not favor the South. While the Mezzogiorno is not completely bypassed when the country moves ahead, it does not keep pace with the more advanced areas. Even during the unprecedented expansion of small industrial firms during the 1970s, the least developed areas of the country lagged far behind the North.[10] Other trends, such as the emptying of the countryside, the influx of women into the labor force, and the reversal of the historical flow of labor out of the country, leave the outlook for the South exceptionally bleak. With its major cities already far below the standards of any modern society, the potential for upheaval — from natural catastrophe (e.g., earthquakes or epidemics)[11] to demagogic manipulation by the extreme Right to the "politics of riot" — remains alarmingly high. The state is paying a tremendous price for its earlier systematic neglect and manipulation of the South, as disproportionate welfare, pension, and bureaucratic expenses all attest. However, any serious tampering with the present arrangement would threaten the precarious balance by which millions of families live and thereby risk a very serious, and unpredictable, social and political reaction. Whatever model emerges for Italy at the end of the twentieth century will be held back and deeply conditioned by this tragic reminder of the country's previous failures.

NOTES

1. For a good summary of these developments, see: Gino Giugni, "Recent Trends in Collective Bargaining in Italy," *International Labour Review,* no. 123 (September/October, 1984), p. 602. See also the discussion in: Miriam Golden, *Austerity and Its Opposition: Communism, Corporatism, and the Italian Labor Movement* (forthcoming), chap. 3.
2. The above is drawn from various accounts in the Italian press between December 15, 1985, and mid-January, 1986.
3. Gianfranco Pasquino, "The Debate on Institutional Reform," in *Italian Politics: A Review, Volume I,* ed. Robert Leonardi and Raffaella Y. Nanetti (London: Frances Pinter, 1986).
4. In return for a ten-year trusteeship over Somalia, Italy renounced all colonial claims at the end of World War II. For more details, see Zariski, *Italy: the Politics of Uneven Development,* pp. 323–28.
5. Robert Suro, "Turnaround at Italy's E.N.I.," *New York Times,* March 17, 1986, p. D6.
6. Ferruccio Marzano, "The Report on Italy's Economic Situation in 1984," *Journal of Regional Policy,* 5 (April/June, 1985), p. 211.
7. Marzano, "Report on Italy's Economic Situation," p. 209.
8. Tassos Haniotis and Glenn C.W. Ames, "U.S.–EEC Agricultural Trade and the Impact of the Second Enlargement," *Journal of Regional Policy,* 5 (April/June, 1985), p. 172.
9. In 1970, only 25 percent of women between the ages of fifteen and sixty-four were in the labor force, the lowest figure by far in Western Europe, except for Portugal. Economists agreed that this was a significant factor in explaining Italy's very small work force. Compare: Gisele Podbielski, *Italy: Development and Crisis in the Postwar Economy* (Oxford: Clarendon Press, 1974), pp. 122–25. By 1975, the women's participation rate had risen to 35 percent; by 1982, it was 41 percent: *CISL 1984* (Rome: Edizioni Lavoro, 1984), p. 64.
10. Aris Accornero et al., "La geografia industriale tra due censimenti," *Politica ed Economia,* XIII (June, 1982), pp. 41–43.
11. Palermo was seriously damaged in an earthquake in 1968, while Naples suffered a cholera epidemic in 1973. In 1980, a very severe earthquake struck near Naples, driving more than one hundred thousand refugees into that already overcrowded city.

Bibliography

Allum, P.A. *Italy—Republic Without Government?* New York: W.W. Norton, 1973.

Although the coverage of this textbook ends in the early 1970s, the material provided is exceptionally thorough, particularly with reference to the central state institutions. The author's distinctive point of view makes this far more than a run-of-the-mill textbook.

Barkan, Joanne. *Visions of Emancipation: The Italian Workers' Movement Since 1945.* New York: Praeger, 1984.

A very well-written, comprehensive introduction to the unions and parties of the left. A very good overview that clarifies an often highly complex situation.

Barnes, Samuel H. *Representation in Italy: Institutionalized Tradition and Electoral Choice.* Chicago: University of Chicago Press, 1977.

Strong evidence is presented regarding the continuity of political identification in Italy, showing how there have been consistent electoral results not only during the entire period of the Republic, but since the first real elections around the time of World War I. Party names may have changed, but Barnes shows how the various traditions (Left and Catholic, particularly) have persisted.

Blackmer, Donald L.M. *Unity in Diversity: Italian Communism and the Communist World.* Cambridge: MIT Press, 1968.

A highly detailed, very solid account of the international dimension of the PCI from the postwar period through the mid-1960s.

——— and Sidney Tarrow, eds. *Communism in Italy and in France.* Princeton, NJ: Princeton University Press, 1975.

Some of the material is out of date, but the strong historical dimension of many of the chapters and the comparative analyses in the chapters by Tarrow and Blackmer remain very useful.

Chubb, Judith. *Patronage, Power and Poverty in Southern Italy: A Tale of Two Cities.* Cambridge: Cambridge University Press, 1982.

The two cities in the title are Palermo and Naples, which are analyzed in depth. The book also provides an excellent, up-to-date account of the South and the DC's character as a mass party of patronage.

Davis, John A., ed. *Gramsci and Italy's Passive Revolution.* London: Croom Helm, 1979.

An excellent collection of essays and historical case studies tracing Fascism's rise and its bases of support, with particular emphasis in most essays on the agrarian dimension. Very useful as well for an understanding of the Left's sources of strength as well as its greatest weaknesses.

Evans, Robert H. *A Venetian Community, an Italian Village*. Notre Dame: University of Notre Dame Press, 1976.
One of the only works available in English that provides a detailed discussion of the Catholic subculture and how it affects the everyday lives of Italians.

Farneti, Paolo. *The Italian Party System*. London: Frances Pinter, 1985.
A book valuable for its historical discussion of the evolution of the Italian party system, with a lot of detailed information on the parties as organizations as well as in Parliament and as electoral machines.

Galli, Giorgio and Alfonso Prandi. *Patterns of Political Participation in Italy*. New Haven, CT: Yale University Press, 1971.
This book summarizes a four-volume study of politics in Italy in the 1960s. It provides a very detailed portrait of party politics in a period when the subcultural dimensions of politics were still highly stable. The main focus is on the Communists and Christian Democrats.

Horowitz, Daniel L. *The Italian Labor Movement*. Cambridge: Harvard University Press, 1963.
A detailed historical study of the unions, going back to their origins in the nineteenth century, but ending in the early 1960s.

Jemolo, A.C. *Church and State in Italy, 1850–1950*. Oxford: Basil Blackwell, 1960.
A classic historical work whose pessimistic conclusions reflect the peak period of church influence over Italian society and politics. A must for anyone who wants to go into the subject in any detail.

Kertzer, David I. *Comrades and Christians. Religion and Political Struggle in Communist Italy*. Cambridge: Cambridge University Press, 1980.
A very interesting study of Italian Communism's operations at the grass roots level in the red zones. The study focuses on a single neighborhood in Bologna.

Kogan, Norman, *A Political History of Italy: The Postwar Years*. New York: Praeger, 1983.
A detailed political history that carries through the end of the National Unity period and into the early 1980s.

Lange, Peter and Sidney Tarrow, eds. *Italy in Transition: Conflict and Consensus*. London: Frank Cass, 1980.
Originally appeared as a special edition (Vol. 2, No. 3, 1979) of *West European Politics*. An exceptionally good collection of articles, focusing on the major parties, political economy, and state of Italian political institutions at the end of the 1970s.

———, George Ross, and Maurizio Vannicelli. *Unions, Change, and Crisis: French and Italian Union Strategy and the Political Economy, 1945–1980*. London: George Allen & Unwin, 1982.
The section on Italy provides a very thorough account of union strategy since World War II. Recommended for the student with more familiarity with (and interest in) the topic.

LaPalombara, Joseph. *Interest Groups in Italian Politics*. Princeton, NJ: Princeton University Press, 1964.

A very valuable early study of a topic that remains underresearched. The concepts developed in this work are still useful. The book captures the essence of the relationship between DC power and the Italian state when the DC was at its peak.

Leonardi, Robert and Raffaella Y. Nanetti, eds. *Italian Politics, A Review*. Vol. 1. London: Frances Pinter, 1986.

An up-to-date collection of articles on the most recent developments in Italian politics. Currently planned to be published each year with an emphasis on the most important events of the preceding twelve months.

Lyttelton, Adrian. *The Seizure of Power: Fascism in Italy, 1919–1929*. London: Weidenfeld and Nicolson, 1973.

The best study available of the rise and first years of the Fascist regime.

Mack Smith, Denis. *Italy: A Modern History*. Ann Arbor: University of Michigan Press, 1969.

The best-known general history of the country in English. This book is especially useful for those with an interest in the personalities and maneuvers of the Risorgimento (on which Mack Smith has written extensively).

Mammarella, Giuseppe. *Italy After Fascism*. Notre Dame: University of Notre Dame Press, 1966.

Most useful for its political history of the immediate postwar period. A more detailed account of the reconstruction and De Gasperi phase than later books provide.

Penniman, Howard, ed. *Italy at the Polls: The Parliamentary Elections of 1976*. Washington, DC: American Enterprise Institute, 1977.

———, ed. *Italy at the Polls, 1979*. Washington, DC: American Enterprise Institute, 1981.

Both volumes consist of good collections of articles by top-ranked experts on these crucial elections. They go considerably beyond the elections as well, analyzing changing party strategies, public opinion, the media, and the workings of Italian political institutions.

Poggi, Gianfranco. *Catholic Action in Italy. The Sociology of a Collateral Organization*. Stanford, CA: Stanford University Press, 1967.

The necessary starting point for anyone with an interest in the social presence of Roman Catholicism in Italy, as well as how that presence translated into power (and problems) for the Christian Democrats.

Procacci, Giuliano. *History of the Italian People*. Hammondsworth, England: Penguin Books, 1973.

A lively and entertaining history written with emphasis on social forces. The bulk of the book, reflecting Procacci's specialization in earlier historical periods, dwells on pre-Risorgimento events.

Tannenbaum, Edward R. *The Fascist Experience: Italian Society and Culture, 1922–1945*. NY: Basic Books, 1972.

A very helpful survey of almost all aspects of Italy under the Fascist regime, with detailed descriptions of the efforts of Mussolini to organize the entire society according to fascist ideals. A good starting point for further research on the regime.

Tarrow, Sidney. *Between Center and Periphery*. New Haven: Yale University Press, 1977.

A study of local politics set within the broader framework of how the Italian state operates, and how skillful local politicians find ways to "work the system" and perform some functions the broader party and political system cannot carry out. The book is also valuable as a source of information on municipal politics (and mayors) in Italy.

——— *Peasant Communism in Southern Italy*. New Haven: Yale University Press, 1967.

A good concise introduction to both the PCI and the Mezzogiorno, as well as a fascinating study of how the Communist Party ended up being changed more by its environment than vice-versa.

Urban, Joan Barth. *Moscow and the Italian Communist Party: From Togliatti to Berlinguer*. Ithaca, NY: Cornell University Press, 1986.

In spite of the title, this study actually begins with the 1920s, and traces the often tortured, tension-ridden relationship between the PCI and the Soviets through the 1980s.

Woolf, S.J., ed. *The Rebirth of Italy 1943–50*. New York: Humanities Press, 1972.

Easily the best single volume on the subject, this collection emphasizes the economic and foreign policy aspects as well as the evolution of the political institutions.

Zuckerman, Alan S. *The Politics of Faction: Christian Democratic Rule in Italy*. New Haven: Yale University Press, 1979.

One of the very rare studies available in English of the DC as a party and as a system of power.

PART VI

Sweden

Jonas Pontusson

21

The Emergence of the Modern Swedish State

With only 8.3 million inhabitants, Sweden is tiny by comparison to the other countries treated in this volume. (The least populous of the others is France, with 54 million inhabitants.) So, why bother with Sweden? The Swedish case warrants our attention mainly because of the strength of the Swedish labor movement.

The Principles of Swedish State Formation

Sweden is the most highly unionized of the advanced capitalist countries. Unions organize roughly 85 percent of the labor force in Sweden, as compared to 55 percent in Great Britain, 50 percent in Italy, 35 percent in West Germany, and less than 20 percent in France and the United States. Most union members in Sweden belong to either of two national federations: one for blue-collar unions (*Landsorganisationen,* or LO for short); and one for white-collar unions (*Tjänstemännens centralorganisation,* or TCO). Swedish unions seldom compete for the same constituency, and their organizational structure, especially in the LO unions, is highly centralized.

While TCO is politically neutral, LO has always been closely tied to the Social Democratic Party, which enjoys the electoral support of the vast majority of blue-collar workers. LO and the Social Democratic Party constitute the two basic components of what the Swedes call *arbetarrörelsen,* "the labor movement." Though they would prefer to be called nonsocialist, the three parties to the right of the Social Democrats are commonly referred to, even by their own supporters, as the bourgeois parties.

The Swedish Social Democrats have enjoyed a longer and more stable tenure in government than any other party operating in the context of free and competitive elections. From 1932 to 1976, Sweden had but three prime ministers, and they were all Social Democrats.[1] In view of the Social Democrats' close ties to the unions, and the exceptionally high level of unionization, it seems safe to claim that in no other advanced capitalist country has labor had as much influence over the postwar development of the political economy. Sweden thus represents a test case of the achievements (and limits) of labor reformism.

During their long tenure in government, the Social Democrats built a remarkably comprehensive welfare state. At the same time, the postwar boom turned Sweden into one of the world's richest countries in terms of income per capita. Swedes and foreign observers alike came to view Sweden as a model of labor peace and social progress in this period.

The Swedish Model

The notion of a "Swedish model" encompasses two rather different images of postwar Swedish politics: On the one hand is the image of bipartisan consensus and, on the other, the image of a gradual extension of Social Democratic hegemony.* The dominant image of Sweden in the 1950s and 1960s was that of a consensual polity; class conflict was said to be in decline, and traditional ideologies no longer relevant. Labor had come to recognize free enterprise (under private ownership) as the most efficient way to organize production, and the business community had come to recognize the need for government intervention to address social problems. As a result, both groups adopted a pragmatic, problem-solving approach to public policy. What Marquis Childs referred to as Sweden's "middle way" (between laissez-faire capitalism and state socialism) rested on reasonableness and willingness to compromise.[2]

*The term "hegemony" was coined by Antonio Gramsci, an Italian Marxist of the interwar period, to convey the idea that a ruling class cannot rely solely on repression to maintain its dominance; it must also gain the consent of dominated classes through material concessions and/or ideological appeals. The term is here used to convey that the electoral support of Swedish Social Democracy extends beyond the working class, that Social Democratic rule has involved alliances with other political forces, and that the Social Democrats have largely been able to define the issues and terms of political debate in postwar Sweden.

The other image of postwar Swedish politics projects a strategic model for reformist socialists rather than a bipartisan model of modern politics. This is the image of a reformist labor movement that has gradually advanced its position in relation to the political representatives of private capital and thus prepared the ground for a peaceful transition to socialism. In this image, class conflict never disappeared; rather, it was transformed by the political ascendancy of social democracy. The labor movement accepted the framework of capitalism as a tactical concession, recognizing the prevailing balance of power, but never abandoned its ambition to transform the system.[3]

The consensual image of Swedish politics could no longer be sustained in the 1970s. A wave of wildcat strikes in 1969–70 shattered Sweden's reputation as the land of labor peace, and industrial relations have remained much more conflictual than they used to to be. In 1980, a general strike/lockout paralyzed the Swedish economy for three weeks. Party politics also underwent a marked polarization in the course of the 1970s. In particular, a proposal put forth by LO to transform a share of corporate profits into collectively owned stocks, administered by *löntagarfonder,* "wage-earner funds", became a source of intense political controversy in the late 1970s and early 1980s, with the critics charging that LO's proposal would pave the way for Eastern European-style socialism.

The debate over wage-earner funds challenges the image of Social Democratic hegemony as well as the image of bipartisan consensus, for wage-earner funds became a mobilizing issue for the Right rather than the Left. Recent developments thus invite us to rethink postwar Swedish politics.

The interpretation of Swedish politics presented here seeks to move beyond the conventional juxtaposition of consensus and ideological conflict. Rather, substituting the term *compromise* for *consensus* helps to demonstrate that the Swedish political economy is characterized by class-based ideological divisions *and* by a persistent bias towards compromise. Far from being mutually exclusive, these features have often reinforced each other. For example, the leadership of the labor movement has commonly appealed to working-class solidarity to legitimate wage restraint and other concessions deemed necessary to secure the economic and/or political conditions for continued Social Democratic rule. The crux of understanding Swedish politics since the 1930s, therefore, is understanding the dynamic relationship between conflict and compromise, on the one hand, and the connection between industrial relations and party politics, on the other. We will now turn to the foundations of modern Swedish politics: preindustrial class relations; the pattern of industrialization; and the introduction of parliamentary democracy.

Sweden
Boundaries of Counties
ATLANTIC OCEAN
Kiruna
Luleå
Umeå
Östersund
Härnösand
Gulf of Bothnia
FINLAND
NORWAY
Falun
Gävle
Helsinki
Oslo
Uppsala
Västerås
Karlstad
Örebro
Stockholm
Mariestad
Nyköping
Norrköping
Linköping
Göteborg
Jönköping
Visby
BALTIC SEA
Växsjö
Halmstad
Kalmar
DENMARK
Kristianstad
Karlskrona
Copenhagen
Malmö
U.S.S.R.
0 100 Miles
0 100 Kilometers

Preindustrial Class Relations

The political success of social democracy in Sweden was made possible by a timely alliance with a separate party representing small- and medium-sized farmers, the Agrarian Party.

Following the elections of 1932, the Social Democrats managed to break with the succession of weak minority governments of the 1920s by striking a deal with the Agrarian Party. In return for an increase of agricultural tariffs, which the labor movement had traditionally opposed, the Agrarian Party supported the Social Democratic government's program to combat unemployment through public works. The Agrarian Party formally joined the government as a junior partner in 1936 and again assumed this role in the 1950s.

The coalition between the Social Democrats and the Agrarians came about in response to the Great Depression, but the availability of this alliance option for the Social Democrats must be understood in terms of the traditional economic and political independence of the Swedish peasantry.[4]

Feudalism and Absolutism

The feudal system of agriculture combined subsistence and manorial farming. The peasants lived off plots of land that they leased from noble landlords. In lieu of paying rent, they worked a specified number of days for the landlord. Though manorial farming accounted for the bulk of agricultural output in the late Middle Ages, feudalism was much weaker in Sweden than on the European continent. In 1500, roughly half of all the cultivated land in Sweden was owned by peasants.

The geography of Sweden helps explain the weakness of feudalism: Forests cover the northern two-thirds of the country; and forests, hills, and lakes are prominent features of the southern landscape. Except for a few regions, the arable land was simply too scattered for large-scale manorial farming. Geographic isolation, reinforced by the harsh climate, also meant that the peasantry did not need feudal lords for military protection.

For most of the late Middle Ages, Sweden was ruled by Danish kings. Many Danish nobles owned land in Sweden, and close ties between the Danish and Swedish nobilities existed at the time. Led by dissident nobles, the independent peasantry played a critical role in the drawn-out struggle against Danish rule. The foundations of the Swedish nation-state were laid in 1520–23, when a peasant army organized by Gustav

Vasa expelled the troops of the Danish Crown once and for all, and Gustav Vasa was elected king. In the next couple of decades, the new king instituted a hereditary monarchy, and engineered a Lutheran Reformation that subjected the Church to royal authority (and expropriated much of its wealth).

Through its role in the overthrow of Danish rule, the independent peasantry gained representation as a separate estate, that is, a distinct segment of the population entitled to a voice in the running of the government. Whereas most other countries had three estates (clergy, nobility, and commoners), Sweden thus ended up with four estates (burghers and independent peasants being represented separately). Among the states of Renaissance Europe, Sweden was also unique in that it had a conscript army. As Perry Anderson puts it, the Swedish Crown "could afford a conscript army . . . because the soldiers thus recruited had never been serfs: their legal and material condition was compatible with loyality in the field."[5]

Through military conquest, Sweden acquired vast territories along the eastern and southern shores of the Baltic Sea and emerged as one of the great powers of Europe in the seventeenth century. Claiming absolute authority, successive monarchs diminished the powers of the estates and created a centralized state machinery in this period. The era of military expansion ended with a series of defeats in 1709–18, and the overseas territories were gradually lost. The House of Nobility became the effective seat of government in the mid-eighteenth century, but a coup by the king restored royal absolutism in 1772. A constitutional monarchy was finally established in 1809, after Sweden suffered a most humiliating military defeat at the hands of the Russians and lost Finland, which had been a Swedish dominion since the twelfth century. As part of the last phase of the Napoleonic Wars, Sweden forced Denmark to give up Norway in 1814. This was the last time that Swedish troops were deployed abroad, and the country has enjoyed peace ever since. In granting Norway independence in 1905, Sweden abandoned all ambitions to be a great power.

The Crown bought the military services of the nobility with new land grants in the seventeenth century. However, it reclaimed most of the land thus distributed in 1680, from which time onwards the nobility was gradually transformed into an urban administrative elite. While the nobility effectively monopolized positions of responsibility in the state, the economic basis of its power eroded. The sale of land owned by the Crown and the government-sponsored consolidation of peasant plots into larger landholdings in the eighteenth and nineteenth centuries led to the formation of a distinct class of small- to medium-sized farmers, engaged in commercial agriculture. However, as the land was divided up among a growing number of children, the smallest farms became inadequate even for subsistence farming. Thus the transformation of agriculture in this period generated a rural proletariat.

The number of propertyless males living in the countryside increased fourfold from 1750 to 1850, and the problem of rural poverty assumed massive proportions in the nineteenth century. Emigration served to diffuse this explosive situation: Between 1860 and 1910, more than 750,000 Swedes, about one out of five, emigrated to the United States.

Early Parliamentary Politics

Under the constitution of 1809, the state administration was solely responsible to the king; the power of taxation was vested in the annual meeting of the estates, the *Riksdag;* and other legislative powers were shared by the king and the representatives of his subjects. Based on the principle that different segments of the population should be represented separately, the system of estates representation was abandoned in 1866. The *Riksdag* was now reorganized as a bicameral body, elected by all citizens eligible to vote. Enacted in response to political developments abroad, the 1866 reform was designed to preempt more radical reform.

To begin with, the 1866 reform did not bear directly on the constitutional prerogatives of king and *Riksdag*. Throughout the nineteenth century, the cabinet consisted of ministers appointed by the king on an individual basis. Virtually all these ministers were career civil servants, and most came from aristocratic families. It was not until 1906 that the first partisan cabinet was established; and the principle of parliamentary government (that the views of the cabinet should correspond to those of the parliamentary majority) did not become firmly established until the introduction of universal and equal suffrage in 1919.

Under the parliamentary reform of 1866, the suffrage was restricted to men with fixed property or with a certain minimum income. In effect, less than 25 percent of all males above the age of twenty-one were entitled to vote. Moreover, voting rights were graduated, so that the very wealthy commanded a great number of votes. The 230 members of the second chamber all served for the same four-year terms and were elected directly by the voters, but the 150 members of the first chamber served staggered, individual terms of eight years and were elected indirectly, with county and city councils serving as electoral colleges. Anyone eligible to vote could run for the second chamber, but one had to be at least thirty-five years old and own a considerable amount of property in order to run for the first chamber.

The electoral system ensured that the nobility would dominate the first chamber completely and that representatives of small- and medium-sized farmers would dominate the second chamber. Prior to the 1890s, parliamentary politics revolved around differences between the Conservatives of the first chamber and the Agrarians of the second. Both of these 'parties' were very loosely organized. The major differences between them concerned taxation and defense organization. The Conservatives and the Agrarians converged around the issue of tariffs in the 1880s, and the issue of democratic reform subsequently brought about the disintegration of the Agrarian bloc. While the more progressive elements joined the Liberal party, which was formed at the turn of the century, most farmer-parliamentarians joined the Conservative bloc.

The tradition of independent farmer politics remained, however, and the Agrarian Party was reconstituted as a modern mass party in the wake of the First World War. Like its parliamentary predecessor, the new Agrarian party contained a wide range of political opinion. Conservative sentiments dominated at the outset, but the Agrarian Party was from the beginning distinguished from other political parties by its emphasis on the immediate interests of a well-defined constituency and its lack of a strong ideological profile. This orientation made it possible for the party to ally with the Social Democrats in the 1930s.[6]

The Industrial Revolution

The Swedish system of industrial relations is distinguished by strong and cohesive employer organizations as well as by strong unions. There is a crucial asymmetry between the electoral-parliamentary arena and the industrial arena: Whereas the dominance of social democracy has fed on and contributed to divisions among the bourgeois parties, the strength of employers and that of unions have reinforced each other. The highly organized and centralized character of industrial relations can be attributed to the Swedish pattern of industrialization.

The Swedish Pattern of Industrialization

By Western European standards, Sweden industrialized late and very rapidly. While the Swedish economy was still essentially agrarian in 1870, industry's share of the gross national product had surpassed that of agriculture by the turn of the century. The value of manufactured goods increased twentyfold from 1870 to 1914, and the industrial labor force doubled from 1870 to 1890 and again from 1890 to 1920. Industrial employment did not exceed agricultural employment until the 1930s, however.

The Industrial Revolution in Sweden was first and foremost a response to the increase of international demand for raw materials that accompanied industrialization in other countries. Swedish industrialization occurred in two stages. The first wave of industrialization, almost entirely concentrated on the export of lumber, iron, and steel, began in the late 1850s and peaked in the 1870s. Saw mills mushroomed along the northern coast of the Baltic, and the old iron mills (*bruk*) of central Sweden flourished during this period. Isolated mill towns dominated by a single, patriarchal employer constituted the social setting of early industry, and geographic dispersal has remained a prominent characteristic of Swedish industry.

The second wave of industrialization, roughly from 1890 to 1914, differed from the earlier period in several respects. Production for export continued to play the dominant role, but a domestic market for industrial goods began to develop. With the emergence of the paper and pulp industry and the engineering industry, which produced a variety of machines and equipment, the composition of Swedish exports shifted from raw materials to finished goods. Drawing on indigenous technical innovations and relying on the steel industry for material inputs, the engineering industry catered to domestic as well as international demand for industrial machinery and other investment goods, and quickly became the flagship of modern Swedish industry. Located mainly in urban areas, the engineering industry accounted for about 25 percent of the industrial labor force by the turn of the century, and its relative significance has continued to increase in the course of the twentieth century.

While the first phase of industrialization was largely financed by foreign capital, through the merchant houses of Stockholm and Gothenburg, the development of the new industries of the 1890s was based on domestic capital. As in Germany, banks assumed a key role in mobilizing domestic savings, dispersed among a large number of small savers, for industrial purposes. The big commercial banks that emerged during the second phase of industrialization were actively involved in the affairs of their corporate clients, and each of these banks became the organizational nexus of a distinctive constellation of industrial firms and capitalist families. Most notably, Stockholm's Enskilda Bank served as the vehicle for the ascendancy of what remains the most powerful (but no longer the richest) capitalist family in Sweden, the Wallenbergs.

The structure of Swedish industry has remained quite stable since World War I. While the relative importance of engineering products has grown steadily, heavy industries based on Sweden's major natural resources — wood and iron — have remained an important source of export revenues. During the postwar period, the output of the engineering industry has shifted towards consumer durables (electrical appliances and automobiles), and chemical products have emerged as a major new industry.

While there has always existed a large number of small industrial firms, the export-oriented segments of Swedish industry were from the very beginning highly concentrated and have become even more so in the course of the twentieth century. In 1976, the twenty largest export firms accounted for 55 percent of Swedish exports. The performance of any one of these firms directly affects the balance of trade.

Early Industrial Relations

Along with the absence of any major ethnic or religious cleavages, the pattern of industrialization favored the formation of a well-organized and class-conscious labor movement in Sweden.[7] The homogenous working-class culture of the mill towns and the concentrated character of early export industries facilitated union-organizing efforts. Perhaps more importantly, the pattern of industrialization encouraged the formation of all-inclusive, industrial unions, as opposed to craft unions. Being late-comers, Swedish industrialists could borrow technology and production methods from abroad, and they quickly moved beyond the craft-production stage. Except for a few industrial sectors, organizing skilled workers in defense of craft privileges was a much less viable strategy in Sweden than in countries that industrialized earlier. By 1907, 48 percent of all industrial workers belonged to unions and 45 percent of the workers affiliated with LO, the national federation of blue-collar unions formed in 1898, belonged to industrial unions. (The remainder was equally divided between craft and mixed unions.)

The defense of local autonomy has traditionally been a core feature of craft unionism, so the absence of a strong craft tradition in Sweden undoubtedly contributed to the integration and centralization of the union movement. The early dominance of industrial unionism, however, did not automatically lead to centralization. In the formative period, union locals enjoyed a great deal of autonomy relative to the national unions, and LO's powers and functions were very limited. In large measure, the impetus behind the centralization of authority within the union movement has come from the employers.

The Engineering Employers' Association and the Swedish Employers' Association (*Svenska Arbetsgivarföreningen,* SAF) were created in 1902 for the purpose of enforcing employer unity in the face of growing union strength. Both organizations were highly centralized, and from the beginning, they sought to bargain on behalf of their members. The Engineering Employers' Association, which joined SAF in 1917, initiated the basic employer strategy prior to the 1930s: meeting local strikes with large-scale lockouts, thereby forcing the national unions and LO to restrain wage demands. Rather than seeking to crush the unions, the employers sought to institutionalize collective bargaining on their own terms. Berndt Schiller captures the logic of the employer strategy most concisely:

> Through uniformity of contracts, which would include all in the same industry in the kingdom, the employers wished to create a "straight line" against the workers and prevent the trade unions from gradually trying to move forward on the issue of wages and other working provisions.[8]

The cohesion and militancy of the employer movement can also be seen as a consequence of the pattern of industrialization. Export dependence has made it imperative for Swedish employers, especially the employers of the relatively labor-intensive engineering industry, to keep wages in check. The export-oriented engineering firms specialized in a rather narrow range of products from the beginning and typically have not competed with each other directly. In general, the commonality of interests among employers appears to have been greater in Sweden than in countries with an older and more diversified industrial structure. At the same time, the small number of employers in each industry (due to the country's small size as well as economic concentration) has facilitated employer coordination in Sweden.

In view of Sweden's record of labor peace in the postwar period, it is tempting to argue that the high degree of organization among employers as well as among workers has itself made bargaining and compromise necessary. Prior to the 1930s, however, strong unions and employer organizations clashed with each other more or less continuously. Indeed, the number of working days lost due to strikes and lockouts exceeded that of virtually all other industrialized countries in the first three decades of the twentieth century. The decline of industrial conflict in Sweden was quite sudden, and it coincided with the Social Democrats' gaining control of the government. As Walter Korpi argues, the political realignment of the 1930s changed the conflict strategies of both unions and employers. It opened the possibility for the unions to pursue their interests by political means rather than by strikes and deprived the employers of government support for their aggressive use of lockouts.[9]

The Evolution of the Constitutional Order

Arguably, the coordination between the two wings of the labor movement, the LO unions and the Social Democratic Party, constitutes the single most important factor behind the success of labor reformism in postwar Sweden. In large measure, this arrangement boils down to the willingness of the unions to subordinate the short-term economic interests of their members to the long-term political interests of the labor movement as a whole. The political orientation of the Swedish labor movement can be linked to the early dominance of industrial unionism and the centralization of authority within LO. Since they aim to represent all workers in an industry, industrial unions tend to be more political than craft unions, and as we shall see, the LO leadership has served a very important coordinating function within the labor movement. Yet these features of union organization are as much a consequence as a cause of the unions' emphasis on class interests and politics, as opposed to sectional interests and wage bargaining. To understand the strategic orientation of the Swedish labor movement, one must appreciate the role that the struggle for political democracy played in its formation.

The Formation of the Labor Movement

The demand for equal and universal suffrage figured prominently in early union organizing. Most union organizers were socialists, and the organizational boundaries within the labor movement were at first indistinct. It was primarily union activists who came together to form the Social Democratic Party in 1889, and the party served as a coordinating body for the unions until LO was established ten years later. LO's first constitution required affiliate unions to join the Social Democratic Party and stipulated that two (out of five) members of LO's executive council should be appointed by the party. To attract workers who did not yet support the Social Democratic Party, these requirements were quickly replaced. The new system allowed union locals to decide whether or not to affiliate with the party, and individual members had the option to contract out (a system that is still in effect).

The LO unions staged a three-day general strike in support of universal suffrage in 1902. It is in the context of this strike that the employers' efforts to institutionalize collective bargaining must be understood: The employers were essentially trying to separate industrial conflict from the struggle over political reforms, and up to a point, this strategy was quite successful. By forcing LO to moderate the wage demands of its affiliate unions, however, the employers undermined LO's authority within the union movement. Rank-and-file unrest grew as the economy entered a protracted crisis in 1907. When the employers once again threatened LO with widespread lockouts in 1909, LO responded by calling a general strike. The general strike became a test of endurance and ended in a total defeat for the unions. The LO unions lost more than half of their membership. They had regained the prestrike membership level by 1917, but it was not until the 1930s that the LO leadership would again assume an active leadership role within the union movement.

The defeat of 1909 illustrated the inherent advantages enjoyed by the employers in the industrial arena and thereby reinforced the strategic importance of political reforms for the labor movement. In the long run, the general strike turned out to be no more than a temporary setback for the labor movement. The decline of union membership had less devastating consequences for the labor movement's ability to mobilize support than might have been expected, because the labor movement was never synonymous with the unions. Catering first and foremost to the needs of workers living in isolated mill towns, the labor movement organized consumer cooperatives, mutual aid societies, sports clubs, adult education, and popular entertainment. Belonging to the labor movement thus meant a great deal more than being a union member and voting for the Social Democratic Party.

The formation of the labor movement must be seen as part of a broader process of social mobilization, coinciding with the emergence of other *folkrörelser,* "popular movements," most notably the temperance movement and various revivalist religious movements. Like the labor movement, these popular movements mobilized the lower strata of society against hierarchy and privilege. The temperance and revivalist movements appealed primarily to farm laborers and poor farmers, but also gained considerable support among industrial workers in the mill towns. Overlapping membership of the labor movement and other popular movements became quite common. According to Lars Engqvist, a leading Social Democrat, "The greatest achievement [of the popular movements] lay in the field of popular education. They trained their members not only in the techniques of democracy and how to chair a

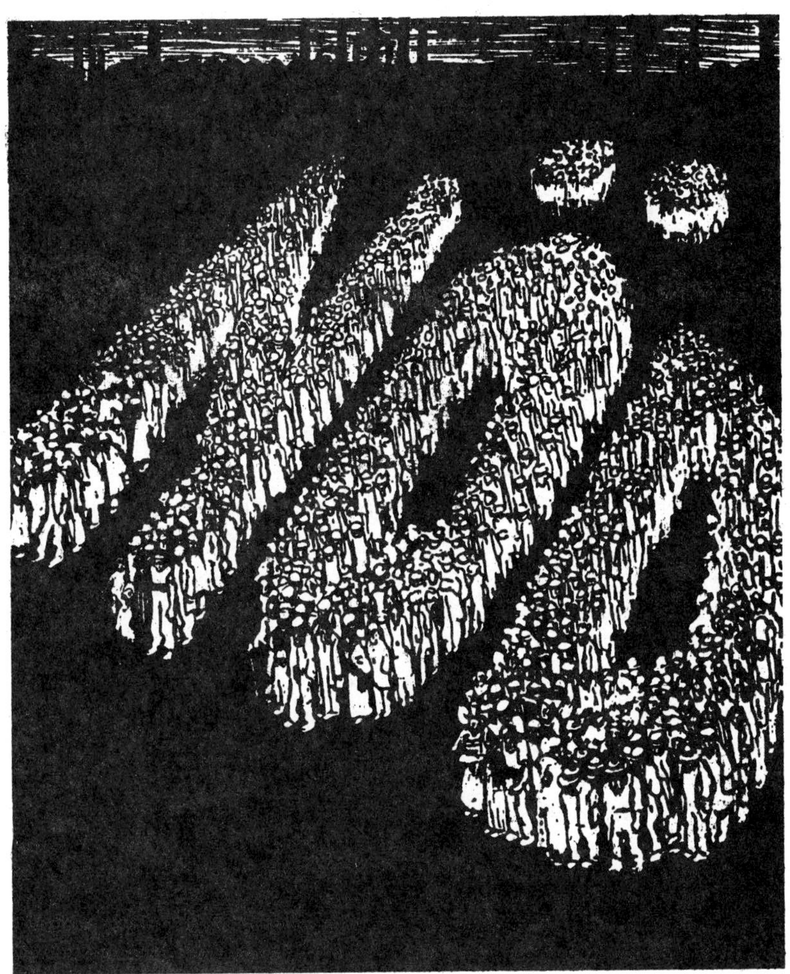

The general strike of 1909. The battle-cry was *nöd* — misery.

SOURCE International Center of the Swedish Labour Movement, *The Swedish Labour Movement,* rev. ed.: Stockholm.

meeting, they provided them with knowledge and the cultural experiences that society would otherwise have denied them."[10]

The Democratic Breakthrough

The popular movements supported the demand for universal suffrage. In fact, the mobilization in favor of universal suffrage was itself a popular movement that encompassed the other movements. Supported by temperance activists and revivalists as well as free-trade industrialists, the newly formed Liberal Party allied with the Social Democrats in the two-pronged struggle for parliamentary government and universal suffrage.

As the contrast with Britain illustrates most clearly, the timing of political developments in Sweden contributed to labor strength. In Britain, most male workers had the right to vote and the Liberals had established a strong electoral base within the working class prior to the formation of the Labour Party (1906). In Sweden, by contrast, the Social Democratic Party was formed before the Liberal Party and could appeal to first-time working-class voters on the basis of its role in the struggle to give workers the right to vote. At the same time, the broad-based coalition behind the demand for universal suffrage lent legitimacy to the nascent labor movement and effectively precluded a repressive state response to its growth. As Steven Koblik suggests, the interaction with other popular movements enabled "the labor movement in Sweden, particularly the Social Democratic Party, [to avoid] the experience of its sister party in Germany, which was isolated from non-labor elements of German society."[11] Through the struggle for universal suffrage, the Social Democrats built an electoral base that extended beyond industrial workers to farm laborers and other lower-class strata.

In the face of growing demands for democratization, the aristocratic governing elite sought to preempt radical change through compromise. In 1907, a Conservative government introduced an electoral reform that extended the franchise to almost all men, eliminated differential voting rights in elections for the second chamber, and substituted proportional representation for the existing system of winner-take-all elections. Proportional representation was intended to curtail leftist gains as a result of the extension of the suffrage. Along with indirect elections and differential voting rights in local elections, it ensured that the Conservatives would continue to dominate the first chamber.

The decisive struggle over democratization came to focus on the character of the first chamber. Popular discontent grew in the course of World War I, and radical forces within the labor movement gained strength, especially in the wake of the Russian Revolution. Food riots and political demonstrations created at least the appearance of a revolutionary situation in 1917–18, and the collapse of the German empire made the Conservatives acutely aware of the precariousness of their position. In this context, the first chamber accepted the principle that both chambers should be elected on the basis of equal and universal suffrage (for women as well as men). The first elections based on equal and universal suffrage were held in 1919.

The peaceful achievement of parliamentary democracy vindicated the reformist orientation of the Social Democratic leadership. In 1917, the left wing of the Social Democratic Party split to join the Communist Third International, but many left-socialists subsequently rejoined the party. Formally constituted in 1921, the Communist Party has never seriously challenged the dominant position of the Social Democrats within the labor movement.

The peaceful achievement of parliamentary democracy was contingent on specific events, but the impact of these events must be understood in the context of the distinctive features of Swedish social development noted earlier. In Castles' words, the fact that the aristocracy "was primarily urban in both location and cultural values, and that their influence was grounded more in service to the monarch than in independent ownership of land, gave it a weak basis for resistance to movements aiming at the democratisation of the polity."[12]

The Implications for Contemporary Swedish Politics

Though their names have changed, the five parties that have been represented in parliament during the postwar period had all been established by 1921. From Left to Right, these parties are: the Communist Party (known as the Left Party-Communists since 1967); the Social Democratic Party; the Agrarian Party (or, since 1957, the Center Party); the Liberal Party (known as the People's Party since 1934); and the Conservative Party (known as the Moderate Unity Party since 1969).[13]

In a sense, the compromise whereby the Conservatives accepted universal suffrage in return for proportional representation anticipated the postwar settlement between labor and business. By making it more difficult for the Social Democrats (or any other party) to gain a parliamentary majority of their own, proportional representation itself contributed to the bias in favor of compromise that has characterized Swedish politics since the 1930s.[14]

During their forty-eight plus years in government since 1932, the Social Democrats have held a parliamentary majority of their own for only six years (1941–44 and 1969–70). The Social Democrats governed in coalition with the Agrarian Party from 1936 to 1940 and again from 1951 to 1957. During the war, the Liberals and the Conservatives joined them in a four-party national emergency government. For the remainder of their tenure in government, the Social Democrats have relied partly on Communist support (or abstention) and partly on issue-specific deals with the parties of the center (i.e., the Agrarian/Center Party and the Liberals) to get their legislation through parliament.

The possibility that a defeat for the government would lead to the formation of a bourgeois government usually has ensured Communist support for any Social Democratic legislation opposed by the bourgeois parties. Even when Communist support has been sufficient to pass legislation, however, the Social Democrats typically have sought to strike a deal with either or both parties of the center, in order to avoid being too closely associated with the Communists and to make sure that their reforms would survive a reversal of government and opposition. The option of an alliance with the Communists has itself been a source of leverage for the Social Democrats in bargaining with the parties of the center, and the ideological differences between these parties have facilitated Social Democratic rule. While the Agrarian/Center Party, as the champion of agricultural interests and environmentalism, has supported interventionist economic measures that the Liberal Party has opposed in the name of the free-market economy, the Liberal Party has supported welfare measures that the Agrarian/Center Party has opposed on account of their costs.

Table 21.1: Swedish Governments since 1932

	PRIME MINISTER	PARTIES IN THE CABINET
1932–36	Per-Albin Hansson	S
1936–39	Per-Albin Hansson	S, A
1939–45	Per-Albin Hansson	S, A, L, C
1945–46	Per-Albin Hansson	S
1946–51	Tage Erlander	S
1951–57	Tage Erlander	S, A
1957–69	Tage Erlander	S
1969–76	Olof Palme	S
1976–78	Thorbjörn Fälldin	A, L, C
1978–79	Ola Ullsten	L
1979–81	Thorbjörn Fälldin	A, L, C
1981–82	Thorbjörn Fälldin	A, L
1982–86	Olof Palme	S
1986–	Ingvar Carlsson	S

S = Social Democrats
A = Agrarians (Center Party since 1957)
L = Liberals
C = Conservatives

Rooted in the experience of democratization, the party system is characterized by two seemingly contradictory features. On the one hand, it is dominated by the cleavage between the socialist parties (Social Democrats and Communists) and the bourgeois parties (Agrarians, Liberals, and Conservatives). On the other hand, the bourgeois bloc is fraught with divisions, some of which predate the socialist/bourgeois cleavage. The tension between these two features of the party system have been critical to the political success of Swedish social democracy. At the same time that the Social Democrats have been able to mobilize working-class support by evoking the ideology of class struggle, they often have been able to play the bourgeois parties against each other and to strike compromises with either or both parties of the center (the Liberal Party and the Agrarian/Center Party).

Notes

1. In the interest of accuracy, it must be noted that the Social Democratic tenure in government was interrupted briefly in 1936. The Social Democratic government resigned over the issue of defense spending in June, 1936, and the Agrarian Party formed a minority government until the September elections, commonly referred to as the "vacation government."
2. Marquis W. Childs, *Sweden: The Middle Way* (New Haven: Yale University Press, 1936). See: Richard Tomasson, *Sweden: Prototype of a Modern Society* (New York: Random House, 1970), for a more recent treatment of Sweden in this genre.
3. The best examples of this view are John Stephens, *The Transition from Capitalism to Socialism* (London: Macmillan, 1979); and Winton Higgins and Nixon Apple, "How Limited Is Reformism?" *Theory and Society,* vol. 12, no. 5 (1983), pp. 603–30. The work of Walter Korpi (see Bibliography) sometimes conveys a similar image of the Swedish labor movement.
4. The independence of the peasantry stands out as a distinctive feature of preindustrial class relations in all the Scandinavian countries. The following discussion has been inspired by and draws on Francis Castles, *The Social Democratic Image of Society: A Study of the Achievements and Origins of Scandinavian Democracy in Comparative Perspective* (London: Routledge & Kegan Paul, 1978), chap. 3, and Timothy Tilton, "The Social Origins of Liberal Democracy: The Swedish Case," *American Political Science Review,* vol. 68, no. 2 (June, 1974), pp. 561–71.

5. Perry Anderson, *Lineages of the Absolutist State* (London: Verso, 1979), p. 182
6. The deal with the Social Democrats was accompanied by a leadership change within the Agrarian Party. As constituted in 1921, the Agrarian Party was the product of the merger of two separate farmers' parties organized during World War I. On early parliamentary politics, see: Dankwart Rustow, *The Politics of Compromise* (Princeton: Princeton University Press, 1955).
7. The following discussion draws heavily on Geoffrey Ingham, *Strikes and Industrial Conflict: Britain and Scandinavia* (London: Macmillan, 1974), esp. chap. 4.
8. Berndt Schiller, "Years of Crisis, 1906–1914," in *Sweden's Development from Poverty to Affluence, 1750–1970,* ed. Steven Koblik (Minneapolis: University of Minnesota Press, 1975), p. 214.
9. This is one of the main points of the work of Walter Korpi. See: Walter Korpi, *The Democratic Class Struggle* (London: Routledge & Kegan Paul, 1983), chap. 6.
10. Lars Engqvist in *The Swedish Labour Movement* (Stockholm: International Center of the Swedish Labour Movement, n.d.), p. 7.
11. Koblik, "Introduction," in *Sweden's Development,* (ed.) Koblik, p. 179.
12. Castles, *Social Democratic Image,* p. 137.
13. For the sake of simplicity, we will here refer to the parties by their generic names (not those in parentheses). The change of name must be respected in the case of the Agrarian/Center Party; as we shall see, the party's social base has been profoundly transformed since 1957. Also, it should be noted that the Agrarian/Center Party stands to the right of the Liberal Party on many issues. While electoral support for the Social Democrats and the Communists has been fairly stable during the postwar period, the distribution of electoral support among the bourgeois parties has changed greatly. See note 14, chapter 24.
14. Compare: Peter Katzenstein, *Small States in World Markets* (Ithaca: Cornell University Press, 1985), chap. 4.

22

The Rise and Fall of the Postwar Settlement

Electoral gains and an alliance with the Agrarian Party enabled the Social Democrats to form a government with a stable parliamentary majority in the 1930s. The Social Democrats' breakthrough altered the balance of class power in favor of labor, yet private businessmen remained in control of strategic economic decisions that would determine the fortunes of the new government. The Social Democrats had abandoned their ideological commitment to the wholesale nationalization of industry during the 1920s, and their alliance with the Agrarian Party precluded any nationalization measures.

Some form of accommodation between labor and business became imperative for both sides. The Social Democratic leadership clearly recognized this fact. In a speech to an association of businessmen in 1938, Ernst Wigforss, the Minister of Finance and chief ideologue of the Social Democrats, urged the business community to abandon the notion of an imminent reversal of government and opposition and, instead, to engage in a "discussion [with the government] based on the possibility of concessions, accommodations, and compromises." On the other hand, Wigforss assured his audience that "the representatives of political power admit the necessity of maintaining favorable conditions for private enterprise in all those areas where they are not prepared without further ado to replace private enterprise with some form of public operations."[1]

The settlement between labor and business that eventually emerged did not eliminate conflicts of interest, but it provided a broadly accepted framework for resolving such conflicts. Three basic principles defined this settlement: first, the government should promote economic growth and full employment but should avoid detailed intervention in corporate affairs; second, the public provision of welfare should be expanded to secure a more equal distribution of the benefits of economic growth; and third, industrial relations should be regulated jointly by unions and employers, without government interference.

In its broad contours, the postwar settlement conformed to similar settlements in other advanced capitalist countries, such as Britain, in which labor emerged as a major political force in the postwar period. But the Swedish labor movement was better able to turn the settlement to its own advantage than most other labor movements, especially the British. The first half of this chapter describes labor's achievements within the framework of the postwar settlement; the second half examines the problems and pressures that have led both labor and business to seek to redefine the terms of their accommodation.

The Postwar Settlement and Labor's Reformist Achievements

The Basic Agreement signed by LO and SAF in 1938 represents a cornerstone of the postwar settlement. This agreement set out detailed procedures for collective bargaining and resolving disputes over contract provisions, and LO and SAF assumed responsibility for securing labor peace. The employers abandoned their traditional demand for legal restrictions on the right to strike, and LO accepted the requirement that any contract signed by one of its affiliates would recognize management's authority to hire and fire workers and assign their duties at work.

The other components of the postwar settlement took the form of tacit understandings instead of formal agreements and did not become clearly defined or broadly accepted until the second half of the 1940s.

The Politics of Economic Policy in the 1930s and 1940s

Though social democracy is usually identified with the welfare state, the achievement and maintenance of full employment represents the linchpin of its political success in postwar Sweden. The political significance of full employment must be understood against the background of the experience of mass unemployment in the interwar period: From 1921 to 1939, the rate of unemployment among union members never dropped below 10 percent, surpassing 25 percent in the depression of 1921–22 and again in the depression of the early 1930s.

The Social Democrats made substantial gains in the 1932 elections on the basis of their program to combat unemployment through public works, partly financed by government borrowing. Having formed a minority government, they managed to strike a deal with the Agrarian Party whereby the latter agreed to support job-creation measures in return for agricultural tariffs. The job-creation measures introduced in 1933 were in fact quite modest, and most economists agree that the ensuing recovery was primarily due other factors (most notably, the currency devaluation of 1931 and the demand for Swedish iron and timber generated by German rearmament). In contrast to previous bourgeois governments, however, the Social Democrats did take visible actions to combat unemployment and could thus claim credit for the improvement in the employment situation that occurred in the second half of the 1930s.

It was not until World War II that the government began to engage in deficit spending on a major scale, and the rate of unemployment finally dropped below 10 percent. By the end of the war, the bourgeois parties had also come to accept the idea that the government could and should promote full employment through the stimulation of aggregate demand in the economy (by means of deficit spending and/or keeping interest rates down). In this respect, the consensus regarding the principles of economic policy that emerged in the course of the 1940s represented a victory for the labor movement. In other respects, however, this consensus represented a retreat for the labor movement.

The concept of planning provided the ideological foundation of the Social Democrats' approach to economic policy in the 1930s and 1940s. Broadly conceived in terms of more active state intervention in the economy, planning would involve general government measures to promote not only economic expansion and productivity increases but also selective measures to steer the process of economic development in accordance with the interests of labor and society at large. It thus provided the link between short-term policy measures and the long-term goal of moving towards an economy in which social needs rather than private profits would determine what is produced. Though no longer committed to the wholesale nationalization of industry, Social Democratic leaders entertained the possibility that planning might involve the nationalization of strategic sectors. They also spoke of the need to extend public influence over the system of corporate finance. These ideas were put forth most forcefully in the postwar program that LO and the Social Democrats adopted in 1944.[2]

The labor movement's planning offensive in the immediate postwar period was partly motivated by the belief that the experience of wartime regulations had legitimized the idea of planning in the eyes of the business community. Actually, the issue of planning served to unite and mobilize the business community and the bourgeois parties in opposition to the government in 1945–48. Organized business launched a heavily ideological campaign against planning, equating planning with the demise of free enterprise and democracy, and put the Social Democrats on the defensive. The Social Democrats held their own in the 1948 elections (polling 46.1 percent as compared to 46.7 percent in 1944), but the Communists' share of the vote dropped sharply (from 10.3 percent to 6.3 percent), and the socialist bloc, taken as a whole, suffered its first setback since 1928.

Though the Social Democrats were able to retain control of the government, the experience of the immediate postwar period illustrated the limits of their political dominance and served as a warning against radical reform initiatives. As one observer puts it, "The 1948 elections represent a turning point in Swedish politics . . . it is a different, more pragmatic Social Democracy that continues to govern."[3] Unwilling to go it alone with the Communists, the Social Democrats abandoned their ambitions to nationalize industry and institutionalize selective state intervention in industry. Planning now came to mean economic forecasting. The formation of a new Social Democratic/Agrarian coalition government in 1951 confirmed this retreat.

The Foundations of the Welfare State

Though the origins of the Swedish welfare state predate the political ascendancy of social democracy, the development of social insurance and other forms of public welfare provision lagged behind Britain and the continental countries prior the 1930s. The underdevelopment of the welfare state enabled the Swedish Social Democrats to take credit for basic welfare reforms that had already been introduced in other countries. More importantly, it enabled them to shape the development of the welfare state according to their ideological preferences.

As a number of recent comparative studies suggest, the expansion of the welfare state characterizes the postwar era in all the advanced capitalist countries, yet these welfare states vary greatly in qualitative terms as well as in scope.[4] The welfare state constructed by the Swedish Social Democrats is distinguished by its comprehensive character. Whereas welfare reforms in many other countries, most notably the

United States, have been viewed in terms of residual aid to the poor and most needy, the Swedish Social Democrats have emphasized the principle that welfare benefits should be provided as a matter of citizens' rights. From the very beginning, they sought to move away from means testing (i.e., an examination of each applicant's income and needs) and to provide standard benefits for all eligible citizens.

The Social Democrats increased public pension benefits and introduced public unemployment insurance, family allowances, housing subsidies, and a statutory two-week vacation in the 1930s. These reforms were relatively modest, however, and it was really in the second half of the 1940s that the breakthrough of welfare reformism occurred. Along with its advocacy of economic planning, the postwar program of the labor movement proposed a series of major social reforms designed to bring about a more equal distribution of income and opportunities. In marked contrast to the almost complete failure of labor's planning offensive, most of these reform proposals were passed by parliament within a few years, and some of them were passed unanimously. All three of the bourgeois parties voted for government bills to increase public pension benefits and family allowances in the second half of the 1940s. The bourgeois parties also supported the principle of a comprehensive national health insurance, but for practical reasons, the implementation of this reform was delayed until the early 1950s.

Educational reform constituted another major plank in the postwar program of the labor movement, and here, too, labor's reformist ambitions were largely shared by the parties of the center (i.e., the Liberals and the Agrarians). Under the traditional system, most children attended only seven or eight years of *folkskola,* "elementary school," but children slated for *gymnasium,* "secondary school," attended separate, lower-secondary schools, *realskola,* from grade four or six onwards. Partly because secondary education was only available in urban areas, this system contained a strong class bias. Legislation passed in 1950 paved the way for the gradual introduction of a unitary system of elementary education for nine years, a reform that was completed in the 1960s.

The Social Democrats came to power with a two-pronged strategy of reform: They wanted to extend democratic control of the economy and to introduce social reforms designed to redistribute income and improve the living conditions of working people. By the late 1940s, the second prong of this strategy entirely overshadowed the first. To use John Stephens' terminology, the focus of labor reformism shifted from "production politics" to "consumption politics."[5] This reorientation was a product of the broad-based support for welfare reforms as well as the intense opposition to planning in the immediate postwar period.

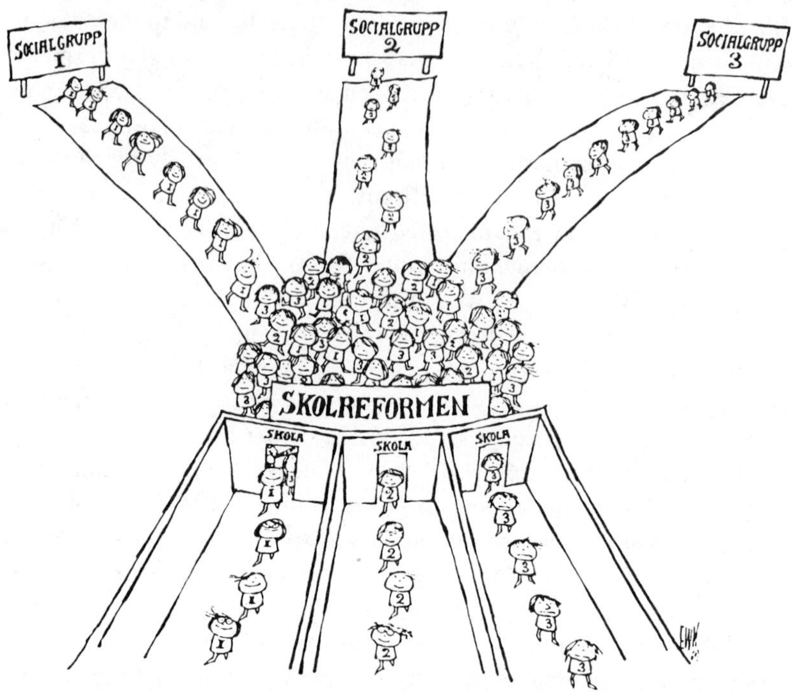

For statistical purposes, the Swedish population is divided into three "social groups" based on educational qualifications and income. This cartoon illustrates that the unitary school system has not had much effect on social stratification.

SOURCE Ingrid Wahlund and Thord Wallén, *Min arbetsplats och samhället* (Stockholm: TCO and Brevskolan, 1982).

The 1959 Pension Reform

The welfarist consensus of the 1940s was by no means complete. The finance of welfare reforms and the level of benefits provided remained issues of contention. The struggle over pension reform in the second half of the 1950s represents a watershed in postwar Swedish politics, as it pitted the labor movement against organized business and the bourgeois parties in a heated debate that revealed persistent differences with regard to the basic principles of the welfare state. At the same time that it split the coalition between the Social Democrats and the Agrarian Party, the issue of pension reform enabled the Social Democrats to mobilize new electoral support and thereby retain control of the government.

Created in 1913, the old system of public old-age insurance was based on the principle of flat-rate contributions and benefits. All senior citizens received the same pension from the government, regardless of their previous income. Despite several increases by Social Democratic governments, the amount of this *folkpension,* "people's pension," remained very modest in the 1950s. Civil servants and other white-collar employees enjoyed additional pension benefits provided by their employers, as did some skilled workers, but most workers depended entirely on their public pensions and experienced a very sharp drop in their income at the time of retirement. To eliminate such disparities in pension coverage, the labor movement, and LO in particular, advocated that the basic flat-rate pensions be supplemented by earnings-related pensions provided through an obligatory public insurance scheme. Under this proposal, which quickly came to be known by the acronym ATP (for *allmän tillägspension*), the basic and supplementary pensions would together represent 60 to 70 percent of a person's average income during his or her fifteen best years of employment.

Passed by a one-vote majority in 1959, the ATP reform represented a departure from the philosophy of earlier Social Democratic welfare reforms. Whereas most of the earlier reforms rested on the idea of establishing a minimum standard (or raising the minimum standard), the ATP reform rested on the principle of income maintenance.[6] In LO's assessment, the preservation of preretirement income differentials was necessary to prevent white-collar and skilled workers from gaining additional retirement income through collective bargaining. In other words, the labor movement accepted inequality of pension benefits to secure equality of pension rights.

This shift in philosophy corresponds to a shift in the coalition that supported Social Democratic rule. Having previously relied on an alliance with small- and medium-sized farmers, the so-called red-green coalition, the labor movement now turned to an alliance with new white-collar workers, a wage-earner coalition.[7] Several provisions of the ATP reform were consciously designed to appeal to the interests of the growing, and increasingly unionized, white-collar strata, and the effect of the reform was to provide these strata with a direct, material stake in the welfare state. Thus, the struggle over pension reform served to mobilize electoral support for the Social Democrats among white-collar as well as blue-collar workers (see chapter 24). Recognizing the popularity of the ATP reform among at least some white-collar strata, the Liberals endorsed the reform shortly after its passage, and the other bourgeois parties followed suit within a couple of years.

The build-up of public pension funds was one of the most contentious issues in the debate over the ATP reform. The public pension funds created in 1959 quickly became the dominant source of supply to the credit market but, through legal restrictions on their use, did not become the mechanism of investment steering that business had feared. Among other things, the 1959 legislation prevented the funds from owning corporate stocks. The labor movement was much less concerned with the extension of public investment than with improving and equalizing pension coverage, and so was willing to compromise on the fund issue in order to allay the fears of the business community and avoid further political polarization.[8]

The Expansion of the Public Sector

Following a decade without any major reforms, the 1959 pension reform set the stage for a new phase of welfare-state expansion in the 1960s and early 1970s. As a percentage of the gross domestic product, social expenditures by the state doubled from 1962 (10.9 percent) to 1972 (20.3 percent).[9] The impetus behind this development was two-fold: the outcome of the struggle over pension reform, and the acceleration of economic growth in the 1960s, encouraged the Social Democrats to pursue further reforms; and growing public awareness of persistent inequalities of income and opportunity in the course of the 1960s led to increasing criticism of the Social Democrats for not having done enough on this score.

Though welfare-state commitments were extended in a number of areas, the expansion of the welfare state in the 1960s was first and foremost a matter of improving the benefits and services provided under existing programs. Aside from increasing cash benefits, this deepening of the welfare state occurred through extensive public investment in social infrastructure (for example, the construction of new hospitals and schools) and the expansion of public-sector employment. The number of people employed by the government increased from 417,000 in 1960 to 985,000 in 1975, and most of this increase took place within the education sector and the so-called care sectors (child care, health care, and care for the aged and handicapped, etc.).

The public pension funds created under the auspices of the ATP reform helped finance public investment in social infrastructure in the 1960s. The funds also played an important role in the ambitious housing program that the government adopted in 1964, promising that one million new dwelling units would be constructed in the next ten years. Housing policy came to constitute a critical nexus between the social and economic policies of social democracy in the 1960s: By promoting the rapid expansion of modern, low-rent apartment housing, the government sought to raise the living standards of the working class and, at the same time, attract workers to the urban areas of the south, where economic expansion created new jobs.

Taxation increased along with government spending, and lower income strata were forced to shoulder a larger share of the tax burden in the 1960s and 1970s. While personal income taxation by the central government remains quite progressive, the income taxes charged by local government authorities are proportional (i.e., everyone pays the same percentage rate), and the central government has increasingly come to rely on indirect taxation as a source of revenue. (The value-added sales tax, which was introduced in 1960, is currently about 23 percent.) The system of taxation has thus become less progressive as the welfare state has become more comprehensive. The reason for this apparent paradox is quite simple: Because the number of people with high incomes is relatively small, taxing them does not provide sufficient revenues to finance the continued expansion of welfare programs.

In its most advanced, Swedish version, the welfare state redistributes income (or means of consumption) primarily through the universalistic provision of benefits and services and only secondarily, if at all, through taxation. For the Swedish Social Democrats, the primary purpose of the welfare state has always been to ensure that certain basic social needs are met irrespective of income. Through the direct provision of social services (as opposed to cash benefits), they have sought not only to sever the connection between income and consumption but also to remove the profit motive from the provision of such services. In this sense, the reformist project of Swedish social democracy might be characterized as socialist, but the public sector, as presently constituted, represents at best a bureaucratic kind of socialism. Moreover, the Social Democratic project depends on a thriving capitalist economy that is capable of sustaining full employment and real wage increases and thereby extending the revenue base of the welfare state.

The Full-Employment Economy

The Social Democrats' argument in favor of economic planning in the immediate postwar period was based on the premise that the problem of unemployment would reappear with the return to peacetime conditions. Over the long run, the postwar settlement was acceptable to the labor movement because it turned out that full employment could be realized without planning and detailed state intervention in the development of industry.

Except for the recession of 1951–52, the Swedish rate of unemployment in 1950–80 typically ranged between 1.5 and 2.5 percent, and never exceeded 3 percent, a figure well below what many U.S. economists consider to be the natural rate of unemployment. Full employment was achieved at the same time that the labor force expanded through immigration and the entry of women into the labor force. As Table 22.1 shows, Sweden had one of the lowest rates of unemployment among the advanced capitalist countries in the 1960s and 1970s; it also had one of the highest rates of employment. The rate of employment among women increased more rapidly than in any other country, and Sweden ranked first on the rate of female employment as well as the overall rate of employment by the end of this period.

Table 22.1 Swedish Employment Statistics in Comparative Perspective (1960–80)

	LABOR FORCE AS PERCENTAGE OF THE TOTAL POPULATION AGED 15–64			FEMALE LABOR FORCE AS PERCENTAGE OF TOTAL FEMALE POPULATION AGED 15–64			UNEMPLOYED AS PERCENTAGE OF LABOR FORCE		
	1960–66	1967–73	1974–80	1960–66	1967–73	1974–80	1960–66	1967–73	1974–80
Sweden	73.6%	74.3%	79.2%	53.3%	59.2%	69.9%	1.5%	2.2%	1.9%
European OECD Countries	68.9	67.4	66.8	44.1	44.3	47.4	2.6	3.4	5.7
All OECD Countries	68.7	68.1	68.4	45.7	47.2	51.0	3.1	3.4	5.4

SOURCE Anna Hedborg and Rudolf Meidner, *Folkhemsmodellen* (Stockholm: Rabén & Sjögren, 1984), p. 139.

Having been a country of mass emigration prior to World War I, Sweden became a country of mass immigration during the economic boom of the 1950s and 1960s. In contrast to West Germany and other countries with guest worker programs, Sweden granted permanent residence status and full eligibility for welfare benefits to all immigrants, most of whom came from Finland, Yugoslavia, Turkey, and Greece. The right of entry was restricted in the early 1970s, but immigration continued. By the early 1980s, the country had some 800,000 foreign-born residents, out of a total population of 8.3 million.

As part of the extension of welfare-state commitments in the 1960s and early 1970s, the government introduced a number of measures designed to promote equality between immigrants and native Swedes and to enhance the educational opportunities of the children of immigrants in particular.[10] Though the official treatment of immigrants has been exemplary, the status of immigrants in Swedish society remains inferior to that of native Swedes on many counts. Remarkably few immigrants occupy positions of prestige and power.

Since the early 1960s, the government has promoted the entry of women into the labor force through legislative measures pertaining to income taxation and maternity leaves (more recently, to paternity leaves as well) and, most importantly, through the provision of subsidized day-care arrangements.[11] The concrete demands of women and the labor movement's ideological emphasis on work as a socializing experience have directed this policy orientation, but the promotion of female employment can also be seen as part of the effort to extend the revenue base of the welfare state.

Most of the women who entered the labor force in the 1960s and 1970s were employed by the government. As suggested earlier, the expansion of the public sector was made possible by high employment and wage increases in the private sector, especially in the export-oriented industrial sector. Though the basic causes lie elsewhere, the government deserves at least some credit for achieving stable and sustained growth in the postwar period.

The strategic reorientation of the labor movement in the late 1940s might be characterized as a move away from production politics, towards a more strictly welfarist strategy for reforming society, but this should not be taken to mean that the Social Democrats abandoned any ambitions to influence the development of industry. The point is, rather, that they sought to do so by means that did not challenge private control of investment and the autonomy of corporate management, and for purposes that conformed to the dictates of international market forces. Corporate tax policy illustrates this point.

Though corporate profits have been subject to a nominal flat-rate tax of 55 percent during the postwar period, the system of investment funds provides tax exemption for profits that firms set aside for future investment in return for government control of the release of these funds. Generous depreciation allowances also enable firms to reduce their effective tax burden. According to one estimate, the effective rate of profits taxation of Swedish industry averaged only 18 percent in 1973–75. Critically, the tax breaks provided to business are contingent on the reinvestment of profits, favor more profitable firms, and encourage firms to increase their productivity by substituting machinery for labor.

The government has primarily used the release of investment funds to encourage firms to invest during economic downturns. It began to

A Swedish view of what it is to be a housewife.

SOURCE Ingrid Wahlund and Thord Wallén, *Min arbetsplats och samhället,* TCO and Brevskolan (Stockholm, 1982).

employ investment fund releases more selectively for purposes of regional and industrial policy in the 1960s, but this practice has remained remarkably circumscribed.

Significantly, selective state intervention in the Swedish economy has focused on labor markets rather than on capital markets. Combining selective measures to stimulate the demand for labor in particular localities or industrial sectors with various efforts to help workers adjust to changes in the demand for labor (most notably, relocation subsidies and retraining), active labor market policy became the hallmark of the Swedish model in the 1960s. According to its Social Democratic proponents, active labor market policy would not only facilitate growth, but would also increase the opportunities available to the individual worker and reduce his or her dependence on any particular employer. As a result of the expansion of labor market policy, workers would no longer have to tolerate bad working conditions and unsatisfactory jobs.

Organized business and the bourgeois parties initially resisted the expansion of government spending on labor market policy. Aside from the costs involved, they objected to the undue interference with market forces and the discretionary powers of the administrative agency responsible for labor market policy, the Labor Market Board. An official commission of inquiry working in the first half of the 1960s yielded a broad-based consensus regarding the principles of active labor-market policy, however, and this consensus has been reinforced by the practical collaboration of union and employer representatives on the Labor Market Board. Active labor-market policy did not seek to challenge the terms of the postwar settlement; rather, it leaves the restructuring of industry to corporate investment decisions and essentially deals with the consequence of such decisions.

Solidaristic Wage Bargaining

The achievement of full employment strengthened the bargaining position of organized labor in the postwar period, and the policies pursued by Social Democratic governments have contributed further to union strength in a number of tangible ways. At the most concrete level, the unemployment insurance introduced in 1934 took the form of public subsidies to union unemployment funds and provided a direct incentive for people to join unions. At the other extreme, access to the policy-making process appears to have enhanced the legitimacy of the unions.

The combination of full employment and Social Democratic control of the government not only strengthened the unions but also forced them to assume responsibility for the wage restraint required to sustain the international competitiveness and continued expansion of Swedish industry. Having assumed responsibility for the peaceful resolution of contract disputes through the Basic Agreement of 1938, LO became directly involved in wage bargaining in the postwar period.

LO was initially reluctant to assume an active role in wage bargaining, and the centralization of wage bargaining was, in effect, imposed upon the unions by the employers and the government. By the mid-1960s, however, LO had become thoroughly committed to the idea of central LO/SAF negotiations. Whereas the employers perceived such negotiations as a means to secure wage restraint, the unions viewed them as a means to pursue a solidaristic wage policy in which the unions would collaborate to improve the relative position of low-wage workers. Though the goal of wage solidarity had become widely accepted by the late 1940s, prominent figures within LO, most notably (but not only) representatives of high-wage unions, held that wage bargaining could not serve as a redistributive mechanism, for wage restraint by well-paid workers would simply result in higher profits for their employers.

The low-wage unions within LO insisted on some degree of wage solidarity as a condition for their acceptance of wage restraint in the 1950s. The LO research department emerged as the low-wage unions' most important ally in their push for a solidaristic wage policy. Gösta Rehn and Rudolf Meidner, the chief economists at the research department, argued, and ultimately convinced the LO leadership, that solidaristic wage policy would serve the interests not only of the low-wage unions but also of the labor movement as a whole.[12] Solidaristic wage policy would serve to reconcile full employment and price stability by promoting the restructuring of industry. On the one hand, increasing the wages of low-paid workers would squeeze the profit margins of less-efficient firms and force them to rationalize their production or go out of business. On the other hand, the wage restraint of high-paid workers would increase the profit margins of more efficient firms or sectors and hence encourage expansion. The net effect of this selective profit squeeze would be to raise average productivity in the economy and thereby make it possible to increase the real wages of all workers.

Though solidaristic wage policy challenges the market allocation of wage increases, it does not challenge the market allocation of investment. Like the system of corporate profits taxation, solidaristic wage policy promotes the restructuring of industry by reinforcing market-determined profit differentials. It speeds up the process of industrial change but does not alter the direction determined by market forces or corporate choices. In this sense, the strategy of promoting industrial change through solidaristic wage-bargaining represents a retreat from labor's planning ambitions in 1930s and 1940s.

The strategy of promoting industrial change through solidaristic wage-bargaining involved an implicit alliance between organized labor and the most dynamic segments of business, at the expense of less competitive (typically smaller) firms. In a slightly different vein, this strategy can also be seen as a formula for reconciling different interests within the labor movement. While unions in growth sectors accepted wage restraint in return for policies that promoted the expansion of these sectors and that avoided subsidizing inefficient production, unions in declining sectors accepted the phase-out of jobs in return for higher wages and active state intervention to help workers adjust to the process of industrial change. For LO, active labor-market policy was a necessary complement to solidaristic wage-bargaining.

Wage drift typically favors better-paid workers and has served to counteract the solidarity of central agreements.* Nonetheless, LO

*"Wage drift" refers to wage increases over and above those stipulated by collective bargaining contracts. Such increases occur mainly through changes in piece rates and other forms of productivity incentives.

achieved a substantial reduction of wage differentials among its members from the mid-1960s to the late 1970s. This achievement attests to the ability of unions and workers to go beyond the short-term maximization of individual gains posited by conventional economics.

The Erosion of the Postwar Settlement

A number of interrelated developments since the late 1960s have undermined the postwar settlement between labor and business and rendered industrial relations as well as electoral politics more polarized and unstable. The protracted, worldwide economic crisis that began in the mid-1970s played an important part in this decline, but the erosion of the postwar settlement must, in part, be explained in terms of strains and pressures generated by the experience of rapid economic growth in the 1950s and 1960s.

New Political Issues

The 1960s marked the high point of political consensus in the postwar period. At the very time that the notion of a Swedish model gained currency, however, the shortcomings of this model were becoming apparent. Along with the rediscovery of inequality, regional decline and environmental pollution emerged as major public concerns in the course of the 1960s.

The postwar expansion of the Swedish economy entailed a massive concentration of economic activity in the urban areas of the southern third of the country and in the three big cities (Stockholm, Gothenburg and Malmö) in particular. From 1960 to 1970, the net population loss in the so-called forest counties (roughly, the northern two-thirds of the country) averaged about 12,000 per year. While the workers who moved south experienced many adjustment problems, the deindustrialization of the north eroded the economic base of social services as well as the marketplace power of the workers who stayed. The much-vaunted affluence of the 1960s made these problems more apparent — and less tolerable.

Labor's postwar strategy focused on increasing employment and productive output, and the leadership of the labor movement firmly believed that the geographic concentration of industry was an essential part of the process of economic development. The government sought to encourage and facilitate the relocation of the work force through the promotion of housing construction, as well as active labor-market policies. The government introduced a regional development program in 1964, but the purpose of this program was to address the immediate employment problems of declining regions rather than to promote long-term development, and the funds allocated for it were very modest.

Not suprisingly, many people blamed the government (i.e., the Social Democrats) for the problems associated with urbanization and regional decline. For the New Left, which emerged from the student movement in the second half of the 1960s, the issue of regional decline illustrated the Social Democrats' failure to prioritize human needs over corporate profits and to democratize economic decision making. Though the New Left failed to establish an electoral foothold, its critique of the so-called consumer society and its emphasis on quality-of-life issues greatly influenced the climate of public opinion in Sweden. The Communist Party, in particular, seized upon the themes of the New Left to challenge social democracy and recruited a new generation of activists from within the student movement.[13]

To the right of the Social Democrats, the Agrarian Party renamed itself the Center Party in 1957, and subsequently emerged as the champion of active government efforts to promote a more regionally balanced pattern of economic growth. For the Center Party, regional policy issues served as a means to shore up its traditional support in rural areas and, at the same time, to capitalize on the growing importance of environmental and other quality-of-life issues to urban voters. Presenting itself as the party of decentralization and environmental protection, the Center Party increased its share of the vote in every election from 1962 (13.1 percent) to 1973 (25.1 percent). Most of this increase occurred at the expense of the other bourgeois parties, but the Center Party also made inroads into the Social Democrats' share of the electorate. In 1973, the Center Party came out against nuclear power, which became the dominant issue in the elections that brought the bourgeois parties to power in 1976.

Labor Market Developments

At the same time that new political issues undermined the electoral dominance of social democracy, labor market developments in the late 1960s and early 1970s marked the beginning of a weakening of LO's ability to control the process of wage bargaining. A wave of wildcat strikes in the winter of 1969–70 shattered Sweden's reputation as the land of labor peace. The longest and most militant of these strikes, which occurred at the state-owned mines in Kiruna, the northernmost town in Sweden, challenged the government's as well as the LO leadership's claim to represent the workers.

Though unofficial strike activity continued in the 1970s, it did not again assume the proportions of 1969–70 and was, in fact, quite limited by comparison. More importantly, LO's ability to deliver wage restraint and to promote wage solidarity has been undermined by the growing importance and militancy of white-collar unions since the mid-1960s. In retrospect, it seems clear that the success of centralized wage-bargaining in the 1950s and 1960s hinged on the fact that the bargaining process involved only two major players, LO and SAF.

Postwar growth was accompanied by a major expansion of white-collar employment, and Social Democratic policies encouraged the unionization of white-collar employees. At the same time, the egalitarianism of the postwar period, and of the 1960s in particular, undermined the legitimacy of the income differentials between white-collar and blue-collar work. As the best-paid LO members have become increasingly concerned with their income position relative to white-collar employees, they are less inclined to exercise wage restraint in the name of solidarity within LO. While some white-collar unions have shown a willingness to coordinate their wage bargaining with LO, competition among them has constrained this type of coordination. The smaller of the two white-collar federations, SACO-SR, which represents mainly well-paid public-sector employees, demonstrated its willingness to strike in defense of income differentials in 1966 and again in 1971.[14]

Interunion rivalries generated inflationary wage pressures in the early 1970s and thereby contributed to the sharp economic downturn in the second half of the decade. The economic crisis in turn rendered the problem of interunion wage rivalries more intractable for LO. Whereas solidaristic wage policy had previously been a matter of redistributing wage increases, it now became a matter of redistributing income losses.

The Economic Crisis

As Table 22.2 indicates, Swedish industry fared worse than its foreign competitors in the second half of the 1970s. The growth of output came to a complete halt, and labor productivity grew more slowly than in other countries. Two factors accounted for the exceptionally low productivity growth: the slump in investment; and government subsidies that encouraged firms to keep redundant workers employed.

Table 22.2 The Performance of Swedish Industry in Comparative Perspective (1960–80)

	ANNUAL GROWTH OF INDUSTRIAL OUTPUT (VALUE ADDED)			ANNUAL GROWTH OF INDUSTRIAL OUTPUT (VALUE ADDED) PER EMPLOYEE		
	1960–67	1967–73	1973–80	1960–67	1967–73	1973–80
Sweden	5.3%	4.5%	0.2%	5.3%	5.6%	0.8%
European OECD countries	5.4	6.6	1.7	4.8	5.8	2.6
All OECD countries	6.1	6.1	2.3	4.4	5.2	2.7

SOURCE: Anna Hedborg and Rudolf Meidner, *Folkhemsmodellen* (Stockholm: Rabén & Sjögren, 1984), p. 141.

The industrial crisis that began in the mid-1970s was rooted in long-term changes in the world economy. The liberalization of trade, the rise of new competitors, and the reduction of shipping costs in the 1960s fundamentally altered the competitive environment of Swedish industry. In particular, the competitive position of Sweden's raw materials-based industries (lumber, paper and pulp, iron ore, iron, and steel), which had served as the engine of early industrialization, deteriorated markedly. Their decline was temporarily halted by the worldwide raw materials boom of 1973–74, but subsequently assumed crisis proportions.

The advanced sectors of Swedish industry (engineering and chemical products) have also come under increasing competitive pressure since the mid-1960s, and the character of corporate responses to international market forces in these sectors has accentuated the problems that the decline of basic industries pose for the labor movement. Like the firms in declining sectors, the firms in advanced sectors have sought to cut costs by substituting machinery for workers and to improve their financial position by avoiding debt-financed capacity expansion. Moreover, the big engineering firms have engaged in product specialization and direct investment abroad to strengthen their marketplace position. On the average, direct investment abroad by Swedish firms corresponded to 21 percent of domestic industrial investment in the 1970s.

Needless to say, the LO economists who argued that solidaristic wage policy could be used to promote the restructuring of industry did not intend for the profits generated by the wage restraint of high-paid workers to be invested abroad. Labor's postwar strategy rested on the premises that corporate tax breaks and solidaristic wage restraint would translate into new investment in the advanced sectors of industry and that this expansion would generate new employment at roughly the same pace as jobs would be lost in declining sectors. Selective state intervention in the process of industrial change therefore could be restricted to the promotion of labor mobility. Since the mid-1960s, however, employment has been lost in virtually all industrial sectors, even when output has grown.

A serious unemployment problem was avoided in the 1970s through government subsidies and, above all, continued expansion of public-sector employment. But this strategy of maintaining full employment entailed further tax increases at a time when real wages were beginning to stagnate and subsequently decline. As in many other countries, popular resentment of the tax burden fueled the resurgence of conservatism in the 1970s.

The Radicalization of the Labor Movement

In response to new challenges in both the industrial and the political arena, the labor movement launched a series of new reform initiatives from 1967 to 1976.[15] First, the labor movement adopted a more interventionist approach to industrial policy in the late 1960s, and the government introduced a number of institutional reforms designed to extend public control over economic development in general and over industrial investment in particular. Second, LO launched a labor law offensive in the early 1970s, seeking legislation to strengthen union and employee rights at the workplace and to extend the scope of collective bargaining to issues concerning work organization, personnel policy, and corporate investment decisions. Finally, the LO congress of 1976 endorsed a proposal for collective profit-sharing that would gradually transfer ownership of large firms from private shareholders to so-called wage-earner funds.

The point of these reform initiatives was both to help business adjust to changes in the world economy and to democratize the sphere of production. The reform offensive of 1967–76 thus marked a return to the kind of two-pronged reform strategy that labor tried to pursue in the 1930s and 1940s and a radical departure from the terms of the postwar settlement. In the end, labor's reform initiatives resolved neither the economic problems at hand nor the electoral difficulties of social democracy. We will discuss these reform initiatives and their fate in more detail in Chapter 25.

The Bourgeois Tenure in Government

The electoral victory of the bourgeois parties in 1976 introduced a new element of instability into Swedish politics. The bourgeois tenure in government (1976–82) saw no less than four different cabinets. The first cabinet included all three bourgeois parties — Conservative, Center, and Liberal — and split over the issue of nuclear power in 1978. It was succeeded by a Liberal minority government, which sometimes drew on Social Democratic support in parliament. Following the 1979 elections yet another tripartite cabinet was set up, but it split less than two years later, when the Conservatives refused to support a tax reform package agreed upon by the Center Party, the Liberals, and the Social Democrats. The last bourgeois cabinet consisted of ministers drawn from the Center and Liberal parties.

The 1976 reversal of government and opposition, which ousted the Social Democrats and brought the bourgeois parties to power, did not immediately result in any major reorientation of government policy. To improve the competitiveness of Swedish exports, the bourgeois parties undertook several devaluations in 1976–77. At the same time, however, they continued the expansion of subsidies to industry, active labor-market programs, and public-sector employment; and meticulously avoided any measures that might be interpreted as an effort to roll back the welfare state. In return, LO continued to exercise wage restraint.

Committed to cutting taxes, the bourgeois parties relied on borrowing to finance the continued growth of government spending. So, in effect, they pursued a socialist spending policy and a bourgeois tax policy. The mounting government deficit set the stage for the introduction of spending cuts in the fall of 1980. Though meek in comparison with those of Thatcher or Reagan, the austerity measures of the bourgeois parties during their last two years in power nonetheless marked a significant move away from the traditional approach to macroeconomic management, and did result in increased unemployment. By the time of the 1982 elections, the rate of unemployment had risen to a postwar record of 3.5 percent.

The Reorientation of Business

Organized business played an important role in the rightward shift after the 1979 elections. The reform initiatives introduced by the labor movement in the late 1960s and early 1970s challenged the power of capital and served to mobilize and politicize organized business in much the same way as labor's planning offensive in the immediate postwar period.

Organized business launched a massive campaign against wage-earner funds in the late 1970s. At the same time, the employers themselves began to challenge the terms of the postwar settlement by seeking to mobilize public opinion against the continued expansion of government spending, arguing that it represented an obstacle to economic recovery.

SAF argued in the 1980 wage negotiations that any wage increases must presuppose public-sector cutbacks. In view of the substantial decline of real wages that had already occurred, the unions could not possibly accept the proposed wage freeze, and the ensuing deadlock resulted in a general work stoppage, mainly a lockout, that paralyzed the entire economy for ten days. More working days were lost in this conflict than at any time since the general strike of 1909. In the end, the government intervened to prevail upon the employers to accept rather substantial wage increases.

The immediate outcome of the 1980 conflict marked a temporary setback for the employers, but their call for public-sector cutbacks was soon heeded by the bourgeois parties in power. The 1980 conflict also represents a turning point in the development of collective bargaining. Challenging the principle of wage solidarity, the employers have sought to decentralize wage bargaining since 1980.

The Postwar Settlement and Beyond

Premised on private ownership of the means of production, the postwar settlement prescribed joint regulation of industrial relations by unions and employers, business-led adjustment to international market forces, and public provision of welfare. The settlement rested on a certain balance of power: The labor movement did not think that it could dislodge private business from its dominant position in the economy, and the business community did not think that it could dislodge labor from its dominant position in the polity.

The accommodation between labor and business was struck prior to the economic boom of the 1950s and 1960s, but the boom sustained it by creating a situation of positive-sum conflict; i.e., a situation in which everyone made some gains, and distributive conflict revolved around how large the gains of different groups would be. Favorable economic circumstances enabled the labor movement to realize its reformist ambitions without challenging the power and prerogatives of private business. As the world economy changed, the conditions for labor reformism became less favorable and the postwar settlement came under increasing strain.

We can distinguish two periods in the erosion of the postwar settlement. The first period, from the late 1960s to the mid-1970s, is characterized by the emergence of environmental and other quality-of-life issues and by the radicalization of the labor movement. The second period, since 1976, is characterized by the business community's challenge of the welfare state and solidaristic wage policy, and by a general rightward shift in the policy agenda.

The erosion of the postwar settlement does not signify the outbreak of class warfare. The bias towards compromise built into the Swedish political economy remains, especially now that the Social Democrats have regained control of the government, but there no longer exists a clearly defined and broadly accepted framework for bargaining between labor and business. In the absence of such a framework, the politics of compromise threatens to become the politics of stalemate.

NOTES

1. Cited in Walter Korpi, *The Democratic Class Struggle* (London: Routledge & Kegan Paul, 1983), p. 48.
2. *The Postwar Program of Swedish Labour* (Stockholm, 1946). For a more detailed discussion of the politics of planning in the 1930s and 1940s, and postwar economic policy, see: Jonas Pontusson, "Labor Reformism and the Politics of Capital Formation in Sweden" (Ph.D. dissertation, University of California, Berkeley, 1986).
3. Bengt Owe Birgersson et al., *Sverige efter 1900,* 9th ed. (Stockholm: Bonnier Fakta, 1981), p. 198.
4. Michael Shalev, "The Social Democratic Model and Beyond," *Comparative Social Research,* vol. 6 (1983), pp. 315–51, provides a convenient and insightful overview of the literature on comparative welfare-state development. For useful comparative treatments of the distinctive features of the Swedish welfare state, see: Norman Furniss and Timothy Tilton, *The Case for the Welfare State* (Bloomington: Indiana University Press, 1979); and Gösta Esping-Andersen, *Politics Against Markets: The Social Democratic Road to Power* (Princeton: Princeton University Press, 1985).
5. John Stephens, *The Transition From Capitalism to Socialism* (London: Macmillan, 1979).
6. Compare: Hugh Heclo, *Modern Social Politics in Britain and Sweden* (New Haven: Yale University Press, 1974), chap. 5.
7. Compare: Esping-Andersen, *Politics Against Markets,* chap. 3.
8. Jonas Pontusson, *Public Pension Funds and the Politics of Capital Formation in Sweden* (Stockholm: Swedish Center for Working Life,

1984), provides a detailed analysis of the organization and investment practices of the pension funds created in 1959.

9. Social expenditures continued to grow in relation to the gross domestic product through the early 1980s, but beyond a certain point, their growth was increasingly due to the slowdown of the economy rather than the extension or deepening of the welfare state.
10. In 1975, Sweden became the first country in the world to allow noncitizens to vote and run for office in local elections, so long as they have been permanent residents for at least three years. Since the early 1970s, only political refugees, relatives of previous immigrants, and citizens of other Nordic countries can immigrate to Sweden.
11. See: Mary Ruggie, *The State and Working Women: A Comparative Study of Britain and Sweden* (Princeton: Princeton University Press, 1984).
12. Gösta Rehn and Rudolf Meidner first presented their arguments in a report to the LO congress of 1951, published in English as *Trade Unions and Full Employment* (London: George Allen & Unwin, 1953). Compare also the report to the 1961 congress, *Economic Expansion and Structural Change* (London: George Allen & Unwin, 1963). For a comprehensive treatment of the theory and practice of solidaristic wage policy, see: Andrew Martin, "Trade Unions in Sweden," in *Unions and Economic Crisis: Britain, West Germany, and Sweden,* ed. Peter Gourevitch et al. (London: George Allen & Unwin, 1984), pp. 190–359.
13. See: Donald Hancock, *Sweden: The Politics of Postindustrial Change* (Hinsdale, IL: Dryden Press, 1972), chap. 5.
14. SACO-SR stands for *Sveriges Akademikers Centralorganisation-Statstjänstemännens Riksförbund* (Confederation of Professional Associations). The organization of white-collar unions is discussed further in chapter 24.
15. Compare: Andrew Martin, "Trade Unions," and/or Martin, "Sweden: Industrial Democracy and Social Democratic Strategy," in *Workers' Self-Management in Industry,* ed. David Garson (New York: Praeger, 1977), pp. 49–96.

23

Swedish State Institutions

Sweden has been a constitutional monarchy since 1809, and a parliamentary democracy since 1919. The constitution of 1809 survived the introduction of parliamentary government and universal suffrage. Following many years of preparatory deliberations, the leaders of the four major parties agreed on the principles of a new constitution in the late 1960s. Adopted by parliament in 1974, the new constitution essentially codified the practices of Swedish government since World War I, and formally reduced the role of the monarch to ceremonial duties.[1]

Whereas party leaders had previously formed cabinets at the king's invitation, the new constitution assigned the task of nominating a new prime minister to the Speaker of parliament. It dropped the provision that the cabinet could only promulgate laws in the presence of the king or the crown prince and introduced the possibility that parliament might require the cabinet (or individual ministers) to resign through a formal vote of no confidence.

This chapter provides an overview of the institutional arrangements of government in Sweden. It treats the executive, legislative, and judiciary branches of the central government, then deals with local government authorities, and, finally, explores the role that interest groups have come to play in the policy-making process at the national level.

The Executive

The executive branch of the central government might be viewed as three concentric circles. At the core there is the *regeringen,* "cabinet," or "government" in the narrow sense, officially known as the king-in-council until 1974. The next circle represents the departement, "ministries"; and the outer circle represents a large number of *ämbetsverk,* administrative boards or agencies (e.g., the Labor Market Board), and *affärsverk,* commercial state agencies (e.g., the Postal Service).[2]

Cabinet and Ministries

Headed by the prime minister, the cabinet traditionally has included a few ministers without direct responsibility for any ministry. In recent years, the office of ministers without portfolio has evolved into what the British would call junior ministers (i.e., ministers assigned specific duties within a ministry). Altogether, the Palme cabinet of 1982–85 consisted of the prime minister, a deputy prime minister, thirteen heads of ministries, and five junior ministers.[3]

The cabinet performs four basic functions: First, it submits legislative proposals to parliament and promulgates laws passed by parliament; second, the cabinet issues ordinances that specify how the laws should be enforced and guides the activities of local authorities and central administrative agencies; third, it hears certain appeals against decisions by the state administration; and finally, the cabinet makes appointments to top-level civil service posts.

The entire cabinet meets once a week for a formal decision-making session, but hardly any substantive discussions take place on these occasions. Though the agenda may include upwards of six hundred items, formal cabinet meetings seldom last more than an hour. In effect, these meetings simply record government decisions. The cabinet often meets informally — typically, over lunch — to discuss forthcoming legislative proposals and other matters of political importance, but most of the decisions recorded by formal cabinet meetings are actually made by individual ministers in consultation with the senior civil servants in their ministries and, perhaps, with the prime minister's office. Unless the political stakes are significant, matters that bear on the concerns of several ministries are likely to be decided in interministerial conferences rather than in meetings involving the entire cabinet.

The preparation of government bills for submission to parliament is a slow and deliberative process. Following a tradition that dates back to the nineteenth century, the government usually begins any major legislative initiative by appointing a public commission of inquiry to investigate the problems that the government wants to address and to make legislative recommendations. Virtually all commissions of inquiry include at least one ranking civil servant with some relevant expertise. Whereas commissions were almost entirely composed of civil servants in the nineteenth century, it has become increasingly common for the government to use commissions of inquiry as a means to elicit outside expertise as well (e.g., by appointing academic economists as either advisors or full-fledged commission members). Also, commissions of inquiry have come to serve as a mechanism of preliminary consultation, and sometimes outright bargaining, between the government, the opposition parties, and various interest groups. The mix of party and interest group representatives varies greatly, depending on the political circumstances and the issue at hand, and some commissions consist entirely of nonpartisan experts.

In what is known as a *remiss* procedure, the cabinet elicits official commentaries from government authorities and interest groups before it considers a commission's legislative recommendations. The cabinet's deliberations in turn provide the basis for the drafting of legislative proposals by the ministry most directly concerned with them. Should the ministry's draft bill diverge significantly from the commission's recommendations, it too might be sent out for comments by interest groups and government agencies before the cabinet finally approves (or amends) the bill.

In urgent matters (e.g., whether or not to bail out firms on the verge of bankruptcy), the cabinet relies on ministerial staffs rather than commissions of inquiry for preliminary investigations and policy recommendations. In such cases, ministerial memorandums may be circulated for official commentaries, but the *remiss* procedure is sometimes completely abandoned.

The prime minister plays a very influential role in the process by which the cabinet arrives at collective decisions. The second most important figure in the cabinet is undoubtedly the Minister of Finance, who is responsible for the government's overall economic policy and the government's budget. Responsibility for the government budget forces the Ministry of Finance to take an interest in the activities of the other ministries, and provides leverage in dealing with them.[4]

The preparation of the government budget is almost inevitably a source of some conflict between the Ministry of Finance and the other ministries. Under Social Democratic rule, party discipline and ideological consensus within the cabinet have contained or attenuated interministerial conflicts of this sort. Under the bourgeois coalition governments of 1976–82, interministerial conflicts became intertwined with partisan conflicts and, hence, became less manageable or, at least, more visible to the public. According to opinion polls, even bourgeois voters tended to think that these governments were less effective than previous Social Democratic governments.

Administrative State Agencies

While independent government agencies or boards exist in other countries treated in this volume, the Swedish case is distinguished by the fact that the administrative machinery of the central government is almost entirely organized in this manner. The only ministry that performs significant administrative functions is the Ministry of Foreign Affairs; the other ministries are primarily concerned with policy-making and, consequently, have very small staffs. The largest ministry in 1978 (other than Foreign Affairs) employed no more than 180 people.

Altogether, there are some seventy to eighty central government agencies. The most important nonmilitary agencies include the National Police Board, the Social Insurance Board, the Board of Health and Welfare, the Housing Board, the Board of Education, the Environmental Protection Board, the Customs Authority, and the Labor Market Board. Typically run by career civil servants, agencies carry out the various activities stipulated by laws and ordinances and apply the policy principles enunciated by parliament and cabinet to individual cases (as, for instance, with the allocation of subsidies or issuance of licenses). They are responsible directly to the cabinet and enjoy a great deal of autonomy; further, it is unlawful for a minister to try to influence individual decisions by administrative agencies.[5]

The autonomy of government agencies is rooted in a long tradition, dating back to the seventeenth century, when collegial boards were established to meet the administrative requirements of the absolutist-military state. Controlled by the aristocracy, these boards came to serve as institutional checks on the arbitrary exercise of royal authority. As part of an ongoing effort to rationalize the state bureaucracy in the twentieth century, collegial management by ranking civil servants was abandoned, and power was concentrated in the hands of the agency head, the director general. More recently, lay boards, which commonly include representatives of interest groups most directly affected by the agency's activities, have been appointed to direct the activities of many government agencies. With a board of directors composed entirely of union and employer representatives, the Labor Market Board has been a trendsetter in this respect, but it still represents an extreme case.

In principle, the division of labor between ministries and agencies is clear-cut: The ministries formulate government policy, and the agencies implement it. But in practice, this distinction is somewhat blurred. For ministries sometimes assume administrative duties, and agencies often make discretionary decisions that influence the actual effects of a policy. In the case of the Labor Market Board, policy-making functions have explicitly been delegated to an administrative agency.

The Bureaucratic Elite

The cabinet steers the activities of government agencies by means of laws, ordinances, and budgetary allocations, and also hears appeals of decisions made by such agencies. The power to appoint ranking civil servants to head government agencies provides yet another potential mechanism of cabinet control. In comparison with the Italian Christian Democrats and other parties that have controlled the government for a long time, however, the Swedish Social Democrats have not colonized the state bureaucracy to any significant degree. While successive director generals of the Labor Market Board have been closely identified with the Social Democratic governing elite and many lower-level bureaucrats at the board have been recruited from the labor movement, the Labor Market Board is exceptional in this respect, as in many others.

In general, top-level positions in ministries and government agencies are filled from within the bureaucratic elite on the basis of merit and seniority, and without much regard to the appointee's political views. Typically, three chief officers serve directly under the minister, and only one of these positions, known as secretary of state, is a political appointment. Like the rest of the ministerial staff, the other chief officers retain their jobs when the government changes hands. Since the 1960s, it has become more common to appoint experts with some kind of partisan affiliation to serve in the ministries as advisors. When the Social Democrats returned to power in 1982, economists previously employed by LO assumed such positions in the Ministry of Finance, the Ministry of Industry, and the Ministry of Labor. Still, career civil servants retain their dominant role in the ministries as well as the administrative agencies.

Until the 1930s, the bureaucratic elite was a bastion of conservatism and, by and large, its political orientation has remained bourgeois. Out of seven hundred civil servants employed in the ministries and the prime minister's office in the late 1960s, about fifty were members of the Social Democratic Party and seventy to one hundred voted for the party, according to one estimate.[6]

It is possible to speak of the emergence of a distinctive, Social Democratic governing elite in the postwar period, but it is important to recognize that this elite never displaced the existing governing elite. Since there is very little evidence to suggest that bourgeois bureaucrats have actively tried to sabotage Social Democratic policies, perhaps one could argue that the political neutrality of civil service made it unnecessary for the Social Democrats to politicize top-level appointments. On the other hand, the political views of career civil servants have undoubtedly influenced government policy in many subtle ways. The cohabitation of these governing elites constitutes an important, and often neglected, aspect of the politics of compromise in postwar Sweden.

The Legislature

According to the new constitution, *Riksdagen,* "parliament," is the supreme policy-making body in Sweden. It alone has the authority to levy taxes and it must approve all state expenditures. Parliament shares with the government (i.e., the cabinet) the power to promulgate constitutional, civil, and criminal laws. In addition to these legislative powers,

Figure 23.1 Distribution of parties in Parliament, 1912–69

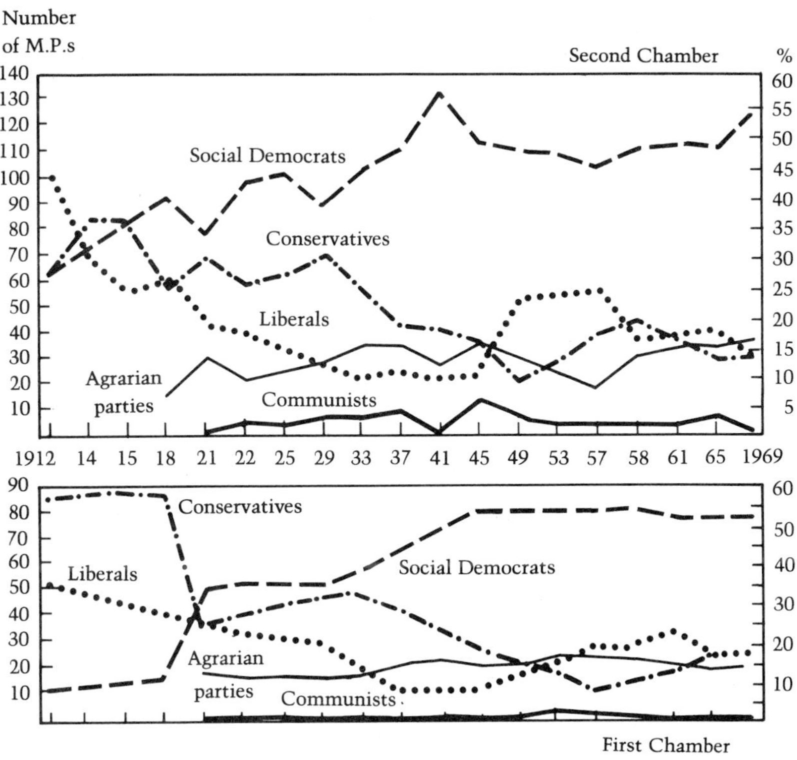

SOURCE Stig Hadenius, *Swedish Politics During the 20th Century* (Stockholm: Swedish Institute, 1985), p. 106.

parliament appoints the prime minister and supervises the government. Parliament's control functions include the appointment of four ombudsmen, charged with keeping an eye on how government agencies enforce the laws and hearing complaints from the public, and twelve auditors, who supervise the central government administration itself.

The Organization of Parliament

From 1866 to 1970, parliament consisted of two chambers with equal legislative powers: The first chamber had 150 seats (151 as of 1959), and the second chamber had 230 seats (233 as of 1965). While the members of the second chamber were elected directly and all served the same four-year terms, the members of the first chamber were elected indirectly, with county and city councils serving as electoral colleges, and served for staggered individual terms of eight years.

Along with the extension of the franchise, single-seat parliamentary constituencies were abandoned in favor of proportional representation in 1907–09. The country was then divided into twenty-eight constituencies, each assigned a number of seats corresponding to its share of the population of eligible voters. The parties presented a list of candidates in each of these constituencies and were awarded seats in proportion to their share of the popular vote.

Table 23.1 The Distribution of Seats in the Unicameral Parliament, 1970–present

	COMMUNISTS	SOCIAL DEMOCRATS	CENTER PARTY	LIBERALS	CONSERVATIVES
1970–73	17	163	71	58	41
1973–76	19	156	90	34	51
1976–79	17	152	86	39	55
1979–82	20	154	64	38	73
1982–85	20	166	56	21	86
1985–	19	159	44	51	76

SOURCES Walter Korpi, *The Democratic Class Struggle* (London, Routledge & Kegan Paul, 1983), p. 239; and *Inside Sweden,* October, 1985.

Under the bicameral system, all legislation had to be passed by both chambers of parliament. If the two chambers disagreed with respect to appropriations or expenditures, the matter would be settled by a joint vote. Other types of legislation would be referred back to joint committee for reconsideration and dropped from that parliamentary session if no compromise could be reached.

As part of the constitutional reform effort of the late 1960s, parliament was reorganized on a unicameral basis and parliamentary terms shortened to three years. The first unicameral parliament was elected in 1970 and had 350 seats. The 1973 elections resulted in a perfect tie between the socialist and bourgeois blocs (175–175), and certain questions had to be settled by the drawing of lots in 1974–76. To ensure a parliamentary majority, the number of seats was reduced to 349 before the 1976 elections.

The parliamentary reform also perfected the principle of proportional representation by introducing so-called compensatory seats. Of the current 349 seats, 310 are allocated on the basis of the outcome of elections in twenty-eight constituencies. The remaining 39 seats are allocated so as to ensure that each party's total number of seats corresponds to its share of the national vote. At the same time, however, the reform curtailed the proliferation of small parties by stipulating that a party must receive at least 4 percent of the national vote in order to win any seats at all.[7]

The parliamentary reform was intended to make the political system more responsive to the citizenry. In retrospect, it seems clear that it also had a destabilizing effect on the political system. The old parliament provided a more stable basis of government, because staggered, indirect elections to the first chamber and the long duration of first-chamber terms served to reduce, or at least delay, the impact of electoral shifts. Despite the electoral ascendancy of the Social Democrats, the bourgeois parties dominated the first chamber in the 1930s. In the 1950s, the situation was the opposite: Though their electoral support declined, the Social Democrats continued to enjoy a majority in the first chamber by virtue of their strong electoral performance in the 1940s. Many observers have suggested that the introduction of a unicameral parliament has altered the dynamics of parliamentary politics, forcing the government and the opposition parties to make policy decisions on the basis of possible short-term electoral consequences rather than the long-term interests of the country. The destabilizing effect of the parliamentary reform does not explain the polarization of Swedish politics in the 1970s, however. Instead, the answer lies in the erosion of the postwar settlement and the electoral decline of social democracy.

Politics in Parliament

In the parliamentary system of government, the parliament is the supreme policy-making body, but the cabinet is the prime mover in the policy-making process. Under normal circumstances, party discipline renders the exercise of parliamentary authority rather perfunctory, because the actual formulation of government policy occurs elsewhere — in the ministries and the cabinet — and whatever compromises may be necessary to pass a government bill have already been made by the time the bill reaches the chamber floor.

So long as the government enjoys a clear partisan majority, the passage of its bills is a foregone conclusion. Needless to say, this does not mean that all the members of the majority always agree. Rather, members of the majority, instead of voting with the opposition and thereby endangering the government's survival, seek to influence government policy through the party platform or informal contacts with party members in the cabinet.

When the government submits a bill to parliament, the opposition parties usually prepare motions in which they outline how they think the matter should be handled. At the beginning of each parliamentary session, any member of parliament may submit motions on any subject, and it is primarily members of the opposition who take advantage of this opportunity. Unless the government decides to endorse a motion from the opposition, which would be a very rare occurrence, such motions invariably fail to pass.

The tendency for party government to render parliamentary deliberations perfunctory is most obvious in the British case, for the simple reason that most postwar British elections have resulted in a one-party majority in the House of Commons. The Swedish Social Democrats, though by far the largest party in parliament, have held a clear majority of their own on only two occasions (1941–44 and 1969–70). While Communist support, or even abstention, usually has been sufficient for a majority and has seldom required any major concessions, the Social Democrats have preferred parliamentary alliances to their right. Since the break-up of the coalition with the Agrarian Party, Social Democratic governments usually have sought to make issue-specific deals with one or both of the parties of the center (i.e., the Center Party and the Liberal Party), in order to avoid being too closely identified with the Communists and to make sure that their legislation would survive a reversal of government and opposition.

During the bourgeois tenure in government, the Liberals and the Center Party formed minority cabinets in 1978–79 and 1981–82 that relied on compromises with the Social Democrats whenever Conservative support was not forthcoming.[8] At the same time as party politics have become more polarized, the narrowness of government majorities since 1973 has made bargaining and compromise between government and the opposition a prerequisite for effective government.

Bargaining between government and the opposition sometimes occurs during the course of deliberations in parliamentary committees. Altogether, there are sixteen standing committees of parliament, each specializing in a specific policy area. These committees issue recommendations as to whether the chamber should approve, amend, or reject government bills and motions by members of parliament. Their deliberations are not a matter of public record and consequently provide a context in which party representatives can adopt a more pragmatic posture or take tentative positions. Most likely, however, any significant compromises between government and opposition will have been made — or at least set up — at an earlier stage in the legislative process, either in a commission of inquiry or an informal meeting among the party leaders.

Though the outcome is usually predetermined, parliamentary debates provide an important opportunity for the opposition to criticize the government and for the government to explain its policies to the public and the opposition. Parliament (meaning the chamber in session,) is a forum of public debate rather than a policy-making body, yet the composition of the chamber determines who makes government policy.

The Judiciary

The Swedish system of civil and criminal justice is three-tiered. At the lowest level, there are some one hundred *tingsrätter,* "district courts," which settle the vast majority of cases. Six *hovrätter,* "courts of appeal," constitute the intermediate echelon, and the *Högsta domstolen,* the "Supreme Court," represents the last recourse for appeal in civil and criminal cases.

Except in libel cases, there are no jury trials in Sweden. In district courts, verdicts are usually passed by a judge in consultation with *nämndemän,* "lay judges," elected by municipal councils and serving on an occasional basis (at least ten days per year for a six-year term). In the appellate courts and the Supreme Court, cases are heard by a panel of professional judges, and verdicts are decided by majority vote.

Along with the system of civil and criminal justice, there is a separate system of administrative justice. It, too, is three-tiered. *Länsrätter,* "county administrative courts," hear appeals against decisions by public authorities concerning such matters as assessment for taxation, granting of business licenses, consignment of alcoholics to special care institutions, etc. The decisions of county administrative courts in turn may be appealed to four *kammarrätter,* "administrative courts of appeal," and ultimately to *Regeringsrätten,* the "Supreme Administrative Court," which exercises its authority on behalf of the cabinet. In addition, the judiciary includes several specialized courts, most notably the Labor Court, which settles disputes over the interpretation and implementation of collective-bargaining agreements.

The cabinet appoints all professional judges. With few exceptions, such judges must be trained as jurists. In contrast to some other liberal democracies, most notably the United States, the appointment of judges is essentially an apolitical matter, and the career pattern of judges is similar to that of other high-ranking civil servants in Sweden.

Judicial appointments are apolitical because the judiciary wields little political influence. Under the parliamentary system of government, the parliament is the supreme law-making authority and the judiciary is essentially an administrative organ of parliament. The idea that the courts might overturn legislation passed by parliament is quite incongruous with this system, for anything that parliament decides is, by definition, lawful.

The judiciary is not entirely without political influence, however. Three members of the Supreme Court and one member of the Supreme Administrative Court form the *Lagrådet,* the "Law Council." Any proposed legislation concerning civil or criminal law must be submitted to this council for review before it is formally submitted to parliament, and the government may choose to submit other legislative proposals to the Law Council as well. The council's recommendations are not legally binding, but they matter a great deal. Politics dictate that the government must either shelve or rewrite a bill opposed by the Law Council.

The office of *justitieombudsman,* "justice ombudsman," or JO, is undoubtedly the most unusual and well-known feature of the Swedish system of justice. Indeed, the word *ombudsman* is one of Sweden's few recent contributions to the English language. The constitution of 1809 provided for an ombudsman, appointed by parliament, to serve as a public advocate and watchdog over the state administration. As the state administration has increased in size and importance during the postwar period, the office of the justice ombudsman has been expanded to comprise four ombudsmen, each specializing in a certain area of state administration.[9]

A person who thinks that she or he has been mistreated by any government authority may file a complaint with the justice ombudsman.

The ombudsman investigates all such complaints and sometimes initiates investigations. If it is concluded that a public official has misused authority, the ombudsman will issue a public reprimand to the official in question. The ombudsman may also take the official to court, but this happens only rarely. The role of the ombudsman is not so much to correct wrongs committed against individual citizens but rather to protect the rights and freedoms of citizens in general. From this perspective, it is considered advantageous that verdicts (without compensation) can be reached without lengthy legal proceedings.

Local Government

Local governmental authorities play an important role in Sweden; indeed, their spending accounts for more than two-thirds of total government spending. Yet the bulk of spending by local government authorities is mandated by the central government, and a large portion is financed by grants from the central government.

Sweden is divided into twenty-three *län,* "counties," which are in turn divided into *kommuner,* "municipalities." By incorporating several municipalities into one, the number of municipalities has been reduced from nearly 2,500 to about 285 in the postwar period.[10] At the county level, there are two kinds of governmental authority: the *länstyrelsen,* "county administrative board," and the *landstinget,* "county council." Whereas the county administrative board is an organ of the central government, the county council is an elected body, with its own administrative apparatus.

While some central administrative agencies have their own local organization, most rely on the county administrative boards to carry out various tasks on their behalf. Perhaps most importantly, the county administrative boards are in charge of tax assessment and collection for the central government. They are also responsible for the coordination of regional policies and for physical planning.

The status and organization of the county administrative boards is similar to that of central administrative agencies. Each county administrative board is headed by a *landshövding,* "county governor," who is the counterpart of an agency's director general, and a board of directors. As of 1977, the cabinet only appoints the county governor, and the other members of the county administrative board are appointed by the county council. The county administrative boards are in no direct sense accountable to the county councils, however.

County councils and municipal governments are organized in a manner prescribed by parliament (most recently in the Local Government Act of 1977). At each level, an assembly of directly elected representatives (*landstingsfullmäktige* and *kommunfullmäktige*) constitutes the authoritative policy-making body. In the past, the members of these bodies were elected for four-year terms in the even years between parliamentary election years (e.g., local elections were held in 1962 and 1966; parliamentary elections, in 1964 and 1968). As part of the parliamentary reform that took effect in 1970, the terms of local office were changed so that local and parliamentary elections now coincide.

At both the county and the municipal levels, the assembly of elected representatives appoints a number of committees charged with specific tasks, as well as an executive committee responsible for directing the local government administration and coordinating and supervising the work of the other committees. The role of the executive committee is similar to that of the cabinet at the national level, but all parties must be represented on the executive committee in proportion to their share of assembly seats if a minority so requests. Consequently, party government is rare at the local level.

The activities of local government fall into two broad categories: activities that local governments choose to undertake, and activities mandated by parliamentary legislation. The latter account for 75 to 80 percent of total spending by county and municipal governments. Partly as a result of parliamentary legislation, the activities of the county councils have been almost entirely concentrated on the provision of health services and medical care — activities that most municipalities are too small to sustain on their own. In contrast, municipal governments perform a wide range of functions, as parliamentary legislation makes municipal governments responsible for utilities, public sanitation, emergency services, public transportation, education, child care, care for the elderly and disabled, social assistance to the poor, recreation and cultural amenities, and a number of lesser activities.

As this brief description suggests, many of the core programs of the Swedish welfare state have been organized under the auspices of local government. Not surprisingly, local governments led the way in the expansion of the public sector in the 1960s and 1970s, but, again, parliamentary legislation provided the principal impetus behind the growth of local government spending. The central government helped finance the growth of local government spending through program-specific grants as well as general grants designed to compensate for differences in the tax base of local authorities.

Creating municipalities large enough to sustain the expansion of welfare-state activities at the local level constituted an integral part of

Figure 23.2 Public Administration in Sweden, 1983.

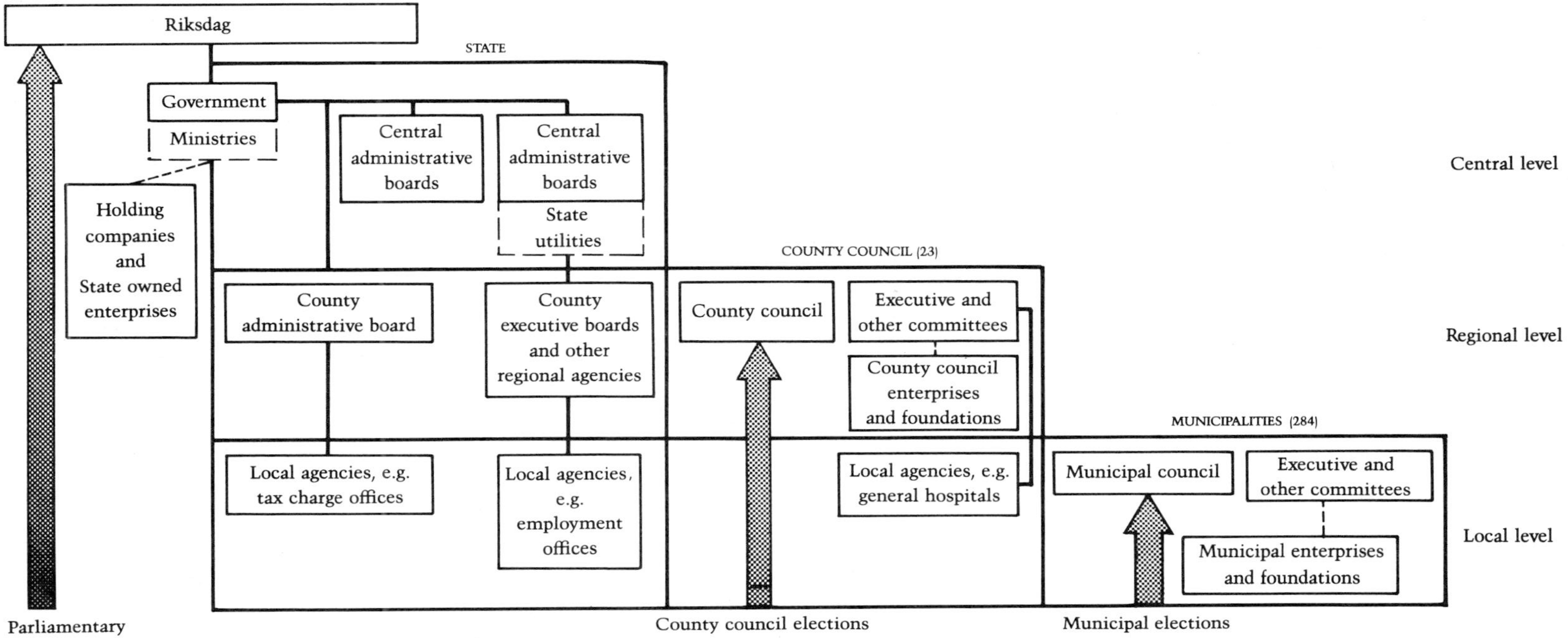

SOURCE Agne Gustafsson, *Local Government in Sweden* (Stockholm: Swedish Institute, 1983), p. 17.

the postwar strategy of Swedish social democracy. The first postwar reform of municipal boundaries, passed by parliament in 1952, sought to ensure that no municipality would have fewer than two thousand residents. The next reform, passed in 1962, proposed to raise this threshold to eight thousand by means of voluntary consolidation. Many small municipalities refused to merge, however, and parliament made amalgamations mandatory in 1969. As of 1983, 41 percent of all municipalities had more than twenty thousand residents, and about 77 percent of the population lived in these municipalities.

The reform of municipal boundaries reduced individual citizens' direct access to local government officials. Due to the increased size of their constituencies and the increased range of their activities, the members of municipal executive committees have increasingly become full-time politicians. Some observers argue that such developments have undermined the Swedish tradition of local democracy; others argue that the boundary reform has revived local politics.

In the past, municipal government tended to be devoid of political issues and dominated by prominent members of the community. As the size of municipalities has increased and local elections now coincide with parliamentary elections, local politics have become more like national politics in that party organizations and ideological differences among parties play a more important role. Though the principle of proportional representation on executive committees continues to apply, party discipline and majority rule have become more prominent features of decision making by local governmental bodies since the 1960s.

The traditional, consensual basis of local politics constituted an important underpinning of the bias towards compromise in national politics. The increasingly partisan character of local politics has contributed to the polarization of national politics since the late 1960s.

Interest Groups and Corporatism

Returning now to policymaking at the national level, there is an institutional dimension to the politics of compromise in postwar Sweden that has yet to be explored: the various mechanisms that serve to integrate socioeconomic interest groups, unions, and business organizations into the policy-making process. Sweden is commonly cited as an example of what political scientists call *corporatism,* a situation in which bargaining between the government and a relatively small number of well-organized interest groups has, at least partially, displaced parliamentary politics as the determinant of state policy. In *pluralism,* interest groups exert pressure on policymakers from outside; in corporatism, interest groups are permanent participants in the policy-making process, directly involved in the implementation of state policy.

In his classic book *Modern Capitalism,* Andrew Shonfield projects the conventional image of policymaking in Sweden by recounting the frustration of a British trade union leader returning from an organized visit to Sweden:

> "All they can tell you when you ask them how they do it," he said, describing some particularly difficult decisions which involved the concerted action of competing interest groups, "is: 'We has a meeting.' *We has a meeting!* I'd like to see how they'd make out with our blokes over here."[11]

Though interest groups wield a great deal of influence, we must qualify the notion that state policy in Sweden is invariably a product of direct, more-or-less formalized bargaining among labor, business, and the government. We can distinguish three mechanisms whereby interest groups have been integrated into the policy-making process in postwar Sweden: first, ad hoc consultations with the prime minister and/or other members of the cabinet; second, representation on public commissions of inquiry and the *remiss* procedure discussed earlier; and third, representation on advisory committees in the ministries and on the boards of administrative agencies.

In the 1950s and 1960s, the government regularly organized conferences with representatives of labor and business at Harpsund, the prime minister's country residence. These conferences took the form of consultations rather than negotiations, however. They promoted mutual understanding among the persons involved but very seldom resulted in anything that could be described as a binding agreement. The bourgeois parties and the New Left nevertheless strongly criticized "Harpsund democracy" as a departure from the principle of popular sovereignty. The New Left further criticized the practice as a form of class collaboration. Since the late 1960s, neither organized business nor the labor movement have shown much interest in organized (and publicized) meetings of this kind.

As suggested earlier, public commissions of inquiry have often served as a forum for informal negotiations between the government and various interest groups, and also between the government and the opposition parties. It is important to note, however, that public commissions sometimes fail to reach a consensus, and the government may ignore the views that key interest groups present in their *remiss* statements. Three successive commissions failed to come up with a compromise solution to the problem of pension reform in the 1950s, and parliament finally passed the Social Democratic proposal with a one-vote majority. More recently, the public commission appointed to investigate the issue of wage-earner funds ended in total disarray. Despite the fact that LO was the only major interest group that advocated wage-earner funds and that all business organizations were vehemently opposed, the new Social Democratic government proceeded to introduce wage-earner funds legislation in 1983 (see Chapter 25).

In both these cases, the legislation that the government submitted to parliament modified earlier proposals put forth by the labor movement in order to allay the fears of the opposition, and the fears of the business community in particular. In this sense, the term *compromise* might be used to describe the outcome of the struggles over pension reform and wage-earner funds, but these were *not* explicit compromises worked out through bargaining with organized business or the bourgeois parties. They were, rather, unilateral concessions, based on the government's assessment of public opinion and its recognition of the need for collaboration with business in other matters.

The Labor Market Board represents the best example of a *corporatist* state agency in Sweden. Not only is its board of directors made up entirely of union and employer representatives, but such representatives also participate in the actual administration of labor market policy through advisory committees.[12] As indicated earlier, however, the Labor Market Board is a rather unusual agency. In most other cases, the participation of interest group representatives is restricted to the board of directors; interest groups are less well represented at the board level and have neither the information nor the expertise that would enable them to direct the agency's activities in any detailed fashion.

In some instances, the significance of board representation for interest groups appears to be almost entirely symbolic. For example, the public pension funds established in 1959 all have tripartite boards of directors. Yet the legal rules governing the investment practices of these funds and the regulation of credit markets by the Central Bank leave them with very little choice about how to invest. Insofar as some choice exists, it has been exercised by the funds' executive director. The boards of directors meet only a few times a year and do little more than approve investments that have already been made.[13]

Much of the literature on corporatism predicts that, having emerged in one policy arena, corporatist policy bargaining will spill over into other policy arenas. However, the Swedish case does not really bear out this prediction. Quite the contrary, it highlights the uneven development of corporatism. While the supply of labor became subject to detailed state intervention and corporatist policy bargaining in the postwar period, the supply of capital remained beyond the reach of corporatist arrangements. For the most part, private business has retained unilateral control over investment decisions, which define the parameters of bargaining between labor and business.

The Swedish case also belies the literature on corporatism insofar as the current scholarship projects a continued extension of corporatist bargaining at the expense of parliamentary bargaining. Rather, parliamentary politics regained prominence as the electoral margin between goverment and opposition diminished in the 1970s. The Swedish case strongly suggests that it is wrong to view corporatist and parliamentary bargaining in mutually exclusive terms; these dimensions of the politics of compromise exist alongside each other.

Notes

1. The constitution comprises three separate enactments, known as *grundlagar,* "basic laws": the Instrument of Government, the Freedom of the Press Act, and the Act of Succession. Basic laws are distinguished from regular laws in that they must be passed by two sessions of parliament with an election between them. Governing the organization and procedures of parliament, the *Riksdag* Act is a complement to the constitution, but not itself a basic law.
2. The activities of commercial state agencies are supposed to be self-financing, but deficits are covered by and surpluses absorbed into the government budget. The outer circle of the executive branch also includes a number of state-owned corporations, which do not enter into the budget.
3. The ministries in this cabinet were as follows: Agriculture; Finance; Housing; Labor; Education and Cultural Affairs; Industry; Health and Social Affairs; Justice; Transport and Communications; Foreign Affairs; Foreign Trade; Defense; and Public Administration. The tasks of the junior ministers were as follows: Immigrant and Equality Affairs; Energy; State Enterprises; Social and Health Services; and Cultural Affairs, Mass Media, and Comprehensive Schools.
4. The Ministry of Finance was headed by the same person, Gunnar Sträng, from 1955 to 1976. Sträng gained an exceptional position of power in the course of this tenure, especially after the much younger Olof Palme became prime minister in 1969. Under the bourgeois parties, the Ministry of Finance was temporarily divided

up into two ministries (Economy and Budget), controlled by different parties.

5. In the past, parliament could only pose questions regarding state administration to members of the cabinet. Under the new constitution, it can go straight to the heads of state agencies, but the questions must concern policy (not particular cases). Compare: Pierre Vinde and Gunnar Petri, *Swedish Government Administration* (Stockholm: Prisma/Swedish Institute, 1978).
6. Åke Ortmark, *Maktspelet i Sverige* (Stockholm: Wahlström & Widstrand, 1968), pp. 85–87.
7. There is an exception to this rule: A party that receives 12 percent of the vote in a single electoral district can compete for constituency seats even if it receives less than 4 percent of the nationwide vote. So far, no party has made it into parliament under the 12 percent rule.
8. The minority cabinet of 1978–79 was actually a strictly Liberal cabinet but cooperated closely with the Center Party on most issues. The Liberal party held only thirty-nine seats in parliament at the time!
9. Modeled on the justice ombudsman, several other kinds of ombudsmen have been established in the postwar period: a business ombudsman (to promote competition), a consumer ombudsman, and an equal opportunities ombudsman. These offices are appointed by the cabinet rather than parliament.
10. As part of the most recent boundary reform, traditional distinctions between rural municipalities, towns, and cities were abolished. This section draws primarily on Agne Gustafsson, *Local Government in Sweden* (Stockholm: Swedish Institute, 1983).
11. Andrew Shonfield, *Modern Capitalism* (London: Oxford University Press, 1969), p. 199.
12. Compare: Gösta Rehn, *Cooperation between the Government and Workers' and Employers' Organizations on Labor Market Policy in Sweden* (Stockholm: Swedish Institute, 1984).
13. Compare: Jonas Pontusson, *Public Pension Funds and the Politics of Capital Formation in Sweden* (Stockholm: Swedish Center for Working Life, 1984).

24

Social and Political Forces

Swedes are more apt to exercise the right to vote than the citizens of any other liberal democracy (except for those countries with some form of compulsory voting). In 1965–80, voter turnout averaged 90 percent.[1] The high turnout suggests that the party system articulates voter preferences rather well and that most voters believe that voting makes a difference. Proportional representation plays an important role in this context, for it has served to curtail the parliamentary dominance of social democracy as well as to provide a broad range of choice for the electorate.

The five parties that are currently represented in parliament had all been established by 1921, and no other party has been represented in parliament since 1940.[2] The stability of the Swedish party system is remarkable, especially in comparison with the other Scandinavian countries. Left-socialist parties emerged in Denmark and Norway, as well as in several other Western European countries, during the 1960s, but not in Sweden. Nor did Sweden experience the sudden electoral ascendancy of populist antitax parties, as occurred in Denmark and Norway in the early 1970s. Furthermore, the growing importance of environmental concerns has failed to provide the basis of a new parliamentary party, as it has done elsewhere, most notably in West Germany.[3]

A constitutional provision introduced in 1970 requires that a party must gain 4 percent of the popular vote to gain parliamentary representation. This provision constitutes a certain obstacle to the emergence of new parties, but the absence of new parties must be seen, more fundamentally, as an expression of the ability of the existing parties to co-opt new political issues and constituencies. This integrative capacity hinges on two features of the political system: the organizational network supporting the Social Democrats, and party competition within the two parliamentary blocs.

We have rejected the distinction between parties and interest groups as the organizing principle for this chapter. Instead, the chapter first treats the organizations that are part of the labor movement and then deals with the bourgeois parties, white-collar unions, and organized business. We will then briefly explore the weakness of new social movements and the ideological hegemony of social democracy in postwar Sweden.

The Labor Movement

Arne Geijer, the late president of LO, once said: "We probably do not have better ideas, programmes, or visions within the labor movement in Sweden than in many other countries, but we have an organization that many others lack."[4] The labor movement is essentially an organizational network. The main pillars of this network are *Landsorganisationen,* LO, and the *Socialdemokratiska Arbetarpartiet,* the "Social Democratic Party" (or SAP for short).

LO and The Blue-Collar Unions

LO is a federation of blue-collar unions, formed in 1898. It included a large number of craft unions at the outset, but industrial unions quickly assumed a dominant position, and in 1912, LO adopted industrial unionism as its official organizing policy. Over time, most craft unions affiliated with LO were absorbed into industrial unions, and industrial unions combined to form larger and more powerful organizational units. Today, LO consists of twenty-four national unions, with a combined membership of just over two million (95 percent of the blue-collar labor force). The Metal Workers' Union has traditionally been LO's largest affiliate, but the Municipal Workers' Union became the largest affiliate in the 1970s. In 1981, five unions accounted for 70 percent of the combined membership of the LO unions.[5]

At the local level, the LO unions are organized geographically and in the workplace. The national congress, held every three or four years is the highest decision-making body of each union and elects the union's president and executive board.

Federal LO congresses are held every five years. Between congresses, the highest decision-making body in LO is the General Council, which meets at least twice a year and where affiliated unions are represented in proportion to their membership. LO's daily activities are run by four executive officers and supervised by an executive board that is composed of the executive officers and eleven members elected by the congress. The executive board invariably includes the presidents of the largest unions.[6] In addition to research and administration, LO runs a network of educational facilities for trade union activists. The branches of different LO unions coordinate their activities through LO's district organizations. Just as LO represents the national unions before the central government, the LO districts represent union branches before local government authorities.

LO's powers were initially quite limited: It administered financial support for workers locked out by their employers but could not initiate industrial action and did not have any funds to support striking workers. The founders of LO did not intend for it to become directly involved in collective bargaining. The disastrous general strike of 1909 actually represented a breach of LO's constitution. It was not until 1930s that LO again began to assume a more directive role.

The Basic Agreement of 1938 stipulated that responsibility for the maintenance of peaceful industrial relations ultimately rested with LO and SAF. In the wake of this agreement, the LO congress of 1941 adopted a new constitution that enhanced LO's authority over its affiliates as well as the authority of the executive boards of the LO unions. Among other things, a central strike fund controlled by the executive board of LO was established.

The Basic Agreement of 1938 and the 1941 constitution set the stage for LO's coordination of wage bargaining through central agreements with SAF. The significance of the formal sanctions provided by the 1941 constitution should not be exaggerated, however. The denial of strike funds and the expulsion of an affiliate union represent measures of last resort that have never been used to enforce wage settlements. Negotiations with the employers must first be authorized by the General Council, and LO's pursuit of a solidaristic wage policy has been predicated on consensus among the major national unions. The decentralization of wage bargaining in recent years reveals the weakness of LO in the absence of consensus among its affiliates.

The Social Democratic Party

Except for a rather major setback in 1928, the Social Democratic Party's share of the popular vote increased in every parliamentary election from the time of the foundation in 1889 through the 1930s. In the extraordinary wartime circumstances of 1940, the Social Democrats polled 53.8 percent of vote. They have never again done as well.

The electoral performance of the Social Democrats in the postwar period can be summarized as follows: After a sharp downturn in 1944, electoral support for the Social Democrats tended to stagnate or even decline slightly (see Table 24.1). The Social Democratic share of the vote was down to 44.6 percent by 1956. The struggle for pension reform in the late 1950s reversed the trend, and the Social Democrats scored a postwar high of 47.8 percent in 1960 and another postwar high of 50.1 percent in 1968.[7] After 1968, however, a new period of decline set in. With 42.7 percent of the vote, the Social Democrats did worse in 1976 than in any parliamentary election since 1932. The trend was again reversed in 1979, and the Social Democratic electorate now appears to have settled at a new plateau of around 45 percent.

Table 24.1: The Distribution of Votes in Parliamentary Elections, 1910–1985 (including selected elections prior to 1968)

	COMMUNISTS	SOCIAL DEMOCRATS	AGRARIAN/ CENTER PARTY	LIBERALS	CONSERVATIVES	OTHERS
1910	—	16.8%	—	42.5%	40.1%	0.6%
1917	8.1%*	31.1	8.5%	27.6	24.7	0.0
1932	3.0	41.7	14.1	11.7	23.5	6.0*
1936	3.3	45.9	14.3	12.9	17.6	6.0*
1940	3.5	53.8	12.0	12.0	18.0	0.7
1948	6.3	46.1	12.4	22.8	12.3	0.1
1956	5.0	44.6	9.4	23.8	17.1	0.1
1960	4.5	47.8	13.6	17.5	16.5	0.1
1968	3.0	50.1	15.7	14.3	12.9	3.1
1970	4.8	45.3	19.9	16.2	11.5	2.2
1973	5.3	43.6	25.1	9.4	14.3	2.4
1976	4.8	42.7	24.1	11.1	15.6	1.8
1979	5.6	43.2	18.1	10.6	20.3	2.2
1982	5.6	45.6	15.5	5.9	23.6	3.8
1985	5.4	44.7	12.4	14.2	21.3	2.0

*The votes received by the left Socialists in 1917 have been attributed to the Communist Party (yet to be formed). Most of the votes listed under "Others" for 1932 and 1936 were received by a splinter Communist Party.

SOURCES Walter Korpi, *The Democratic Class Struggle* (London: Routledge & Kegan Paul, 1983), p. 237 and *Inside Sweden,* October, 1985.

The Social Democratic Party is a "labor party" in the twofold sense that it enjoys the electoral support of the large majority of workers (67% in 1979) and that it acts as the political wing of the labor movement. The fact that the industrial working class ceased to grow in the postwar period partly explains the electoral stagnation of social democracy. At the same time, however, the Social Democrats' share of the blue-collar vote has tended to decline.

The LO unions play a critical role in mobilizing working-class support for the Social Democrats. As noted earlier, the boundary between union organizing and political activism was quite blurry in the formative period of the labor movement. It remains common practice for union branches to affiliate with the Social Democratic Party collectively, with individual members being provided the opportunity to opt out of collective affiliation. In 1983, the Social Democratic Party had 1.2 million members (20 percent of the electorate), and roughly three-quarters of them were affiliated through their union.

In contrast to the British Labour Party, the unions do not cast bloc votes at party congresses. Above the local level, there exist no formal ties between the party and LO, but the LO leadership has always consisted exclusively of outspoken Social Democrats. Indeed, LO leaders have been much less concerned with asserting independence from the party than, for instance, the leaders of the communist-dominated union confederation in France. Prior to the introduction of state subsidies to political parties in 1965, Social Democratic election campaigns depended almost entirely on union contributions. Representatives of LO participate, as a matter of course, in all programmatic discussions within the Social Democratic Party, the LO president is a member of the party's executive committee, and Social Democratic prime ministers have always consulted with the LO leadership on a regular basis.

The Social Democratic Party also relies on other organizations affiliated with the labor movement to mobilize political support. The Social Democratic Youth League and the Social Democratic Women's League are directly affiliated with the party and are represented on its executive committee. Other organizations dominated by Social Democrats include the Union of Cooperative Societies (*Kooperativa Förbundet,* or KF), the Workers' Education Association (*Arbetarnas Bildningsförbund,* or ABF), the Cooperative Housing Association (*Hyresgästernas Sparkasse- och Byggnadsförening,* or HSB), the Intercompany Sports Association (*Rikskorpen*), the Young Eagles (*Unga örnarna*) (an alternative scouting organization), and the major tenants' and senior citizens' organizations (*Hyresgästernas Riksförbund* and *Pensionärernas Riksorganisation*).

The organizational network of the labor movement has perpetuated a strong sense of class identity among Swedish workers and has provided stability to the Social Democratic electorate. According to one poll, 70 percent of the children of Social Democratic voters themselves vote for the party. The organizations affiliated with the labor movement have not only served to deliver votes, however; they have also served to articulate popular sentiments and thereby keep the Social Democratic leadership in tune with societal changes.

One might argue that the welfare state has to some extent replaced the organizational network of the labor movement as the basic mechanism whereby the Social Democrats mobilize political support. Among white-collar workers, public-sector employees are more likely to vote for the Social Democrats than private-sector employees. Also, senior citizens have emerged as an important Social Democratic constituency in recent years. Had senior citizens been disenfranchised, the bourgeois parties would have won the 1985 elections by a rather comfortable margin.

The Communist Party

When Swedes speak of the labor movement, they are usually thinking of the Social Democratic organizations mentioned above, but the term also encompasses the Communist Party. Prior to the 1960s, the Communist electorate was even more heavily working class in its social composition than the Social Democratic electorate.

The historical role of the Swedish Communist Party has been that of an oppositional force within the labor movement. The most serious Communist challenge to the Social Democratic leadership of the labor movement occurred towards the end of World War II. While the Communist Party polled 10.3 percent of the popular vote in the parliamentary elections of 1944, and 11.2 percent in the local elections of 1946, Communists and other oppositional trade unionists gained control of the Metal Workers' bargaining delegation and launched a full-scale strike in 1945. The Metal Workers' strike failed, however, and the onset of the Cold War quickly reduced the Communists' electoral strength. Since 1948, the Communist Party's share of the vote in parliamentary elections has ranged between 3.4 percent in 1958 and 5.6 percent in 1979 and 1982.

The Communist Party's relationship to the Soviet Union has been a source of internal division as well as public suspicion ever since its foundation in 1921. The pro-Moscow current prevailed within the party until the 1960s, but the advocates of a more independent path gained strength from the mid-1950s onwards. The party chairperson elected in 1964, C.-H. Hermansson, initiated a strategic reorientation that anticipated the Eurocommunism of the 1970s (which advocates criticism of human rights violations in Eastern Europe, pursuit of a national road to socialism based on pluralist democracy, and cooperation among West European communist parties). The party adopted many of the themes of the New Left in the second half of the 1960s and renamed itself *Vänsterpartiet Kommunisterna,* the "Left party-Communists," or VPK, as part of an effort to recruit members and voters from the student movement and other new social movements. The most obvious reason why the new radicalism of the 1960s did not yield a left-socialist party, as it did in Denmark and Norway, is that the Swedish Communist Party was relatively large and open to new ideas.

The social base of the Communist Party has changed fundamentally since the 1960s. The average Communist voter is today as likely to hold a white-collar as a blue-collar job. Support for the Communist Party among white-collar strata is heavily concentrated among public-sector employees, especially among teachers and social workers. The transformation of its social base does not appear to have significantly improved the Communist Party's overall electoral prospects, however.

The Bourgeois Parties

The bourgeois parties are less well organized and lack the movement-party qualities of the Social Democratic and Communist parties. The old Agrarian Party formed part of the organizational network of the farmers' movement, and its successor, the Center Party, continues to enjoy close ties to agricultural interest groups and cooperative organizations. The importance of this constituency for the Center Party diminished greatly in the course of the postwar period, however. Most bourgeois voters have few direct contacts with "their" party, except perhaps during election campaigns.

As Table 24.1 shows, the distribution of electoral support among the bourgeois parties has undergone dramatic alterations, while the overall electoral balance between the socialist and bourgeois parties has been relatively stable during the postwar period. Leaving the most recent elections aside (to be discussed in Chapter 25), we can divide the postwar period into three subperiods, each characterized by the electoral ascendancy of a different bourgeois party.

The Liberals

Polling 22.8 percent of the vote in the 1948 elections, the *Folkpartiet,* "Liberal Party" (literally, "People's Party"), nearly doubled its electoral support and replaced the Conservatives as the largest opposition party. The Liberals did even better in the next two elections and came to set the tone of bourgeois politics in the first postwar decades. With a strong traditional base among middle-income white-collar strata as well as small businessmen, the Liberals were well situated to benefit electorally from the ongoing shift of employment out of agriculture and into service industries. Moreover, they were ideologically better able to adjust to the new circumstances of the 1940s than were the Conservatives.

Under the leadership of Gunnar Ohlin, the Liberal Party quickly espoused the Keynesian principle that the government should seek to promote full employment through demand stimulation, and endorsed the social reforms proposed by the Social Democrats. At the same time, it strongly opposed planning and detailed state intervention in economic and social life and sought to project itself as the champion of individual freedom, in contrast to the collectivism of the labor movement as well as the hierarchy of the old class society.

The struggle over pension reform in the late 1950s proved to be a turning point in the electoral fortunes of the Liberal Party. The party's share of the vote dropped precipitously in the 1958 and 1960 elections and continued to decline in the 1960s. It stabilized at around 10 to 11 percent in the 1970s but then dropped to 5.9 percent in 1982, and many observers began to speculate whether the Liberal Party might fall below the four percent of the popular vote required for parliamentary representation.

The Center Party

Most of the electoral losses that the Liberals suffered from 1958 to 1973 translated into gains for the *Centerpartiet,* the reincarnation of the Agrarian Party. As noted earlier, the Agrarian Party left the government over the issue of pension reform in 1957 and changed its name to the Center Party shortly thereafter.

In the 1960s, the Center Party emerged as the champion of environmental protection and active government efforts to promote more regionally balanced economic development. The party thus sought to shore up its support in rural areas and, at the same time, to mobilize new support among urban white-collar workers on the basis of quality-of-life issues. This strategy proved extremely successful: The Center

Party increased its share of the popular vote from an all-time low of 9.4 percent in 1956 to an all-time high of 25.1 percent in 1973. While the Center Party's share of the farm vote increased from 49 percent in 1956 to 68 percent in 1973, the farm vote as a percentage of the party's electorate dropped from 77 percent to 21 percent. The Center Party gained blue-collar as well as white-collar and small business voters from the Liberal Party and also made some inroads into the Social Democratic electorate.

Seeking to capitalize on the growing popular concern with environmental issues, both the Center Party and the Communists came out against the development of nuclear power in the early 1970s. In the election campaign of 1976, the leader of the Center Party, Thorbjörn Fälldin, pledged to phase out nuclear power, a promise that may have tipped the electoral balance in favor of the bourgeois parties. Since his coalition partners were firmly committed to nuclear power, however, Fälldin was unable to deliver on his promise. The three-party coalition government that came to power in 1976 ultimately fell apart over the issue of nuclear power.

Following the 1979 elections, the bourgeois parties agreed to settle the issue of nuclear power by means of a popular referendum. The Center Party and the Communists joined forces behind a proposal to phase out nuclear power over ten years. Two other proposals were put to the electorate: one supported by the Social Democrats and the Liberals, and the other by the Conservatives. Both of these proposals stated that the eleven nuclear power plants that were already built or planned should be allowed to come on-line and operate for the duration of their life span (about twenty-five years) but that no further development of nuclear power should take place.

The proposal supported by the Social Democrats also included a provision concerning the need for public ownership and supervision of nuclear power plants. The Social Democrats clearly did not wish to run on the same ticket as the Conservatives, but many voters nonetheless deserted them in the referendum. Whereas the Social Democrats and the Liberals together polled 53.2 percent of the vote in the 1979 elections, their proposal polled only 39.1 percent in the referendum. The Center Party/Communist antinuclear proposal pooled 38.7 percent (as compared to 23.7 percent for the Center Party and the Communists in 1979), and the Conservative proposal drew 18.9 percent of the vote (compared to 20.3 percent for the Conservatives in 1979).

The importance that the issue of nuclear power came to assume in the 1970s, and the rather peculiar line-up of the political parties in the 1980 referendum, led many observers to speak of the emergence of a new axis of political divisions, cutting across the Left/Right axis. The issue of nuclear power lost its prominence and the Center Party's electoral support declined sharply in the first half of the 1980s, however. The Soviet nuclear accident in the spring of 1986 has brought the issue of nuclear power back to the centerstage of Swedish politics, but it is too early to tell what the political fallout of the accident will be (whether support for the Center Party will revive, for example).

The Conservatives

Some voters deserted the Center Party because they were disillusioned with its failure to deliver on the issue of nuclear power. However, the decline of the Center Party must first and foremost be seen as part of a repolarization of party politics along the Left/Right axis after the referendum and as a consequence of the economic crisis in the late 1970s. The Conservatives, known since 1969 as the *Moderata Samlingspartiet,* "Moderate Unity Party," surpassed the Center Party in 1979, to become, once again, the largest opposition party. From 1970 to 1982, the Conservatives had gained support in every election and increased their share of the vote from 11.5 percent to 23.6 percent.

In the course of this ascendancy, the Conservatives became increasingly outspoken in their criticism of the Social Democratic welfare state, shifting their ideological emphasis from traditional conservative themes to a more individualistic and market-oriented approach, commonly referred to as neoliberalism. The Conservatives thus became a channel for antitax and antiwelfare sentiments, and they preempted the kind of parties of popular discontent that emerged in the other Scandinavian countries in the 1970s. Following the 1979 elections, the Conservatives increasingly came to define the terms of the policy debate among the bourgeois parties, and both the Center Party and the Liberals moved rightward in order to recover their losses or at least preempt further losses to the Conservatives.

In many instances, the Swedish Social Democrats have benefited from the fragmentation of the bourgeois bloc.[8] Had the bourgeois parties formed a united front in the debate over pension reform in the late 1950s, for example, they could very well have defeated the Social Democratic proposal and thereby brought about a reversal of government and opposition. On the other hand, this fragmentation has been an asset for the bourgeois parties in the sense that it has enabled them to appeal to a wider range of voter preferences. In the 1970s, the Conservatives appealed to antitax and antiwelfare sentiments, the Center Party appealed to environmentalist concerns, and the Liberals appealed to social responsibility (increased aid to developing countries being one of their main planks). It is hard to imagine that any single party could have accomplished this.

White-Collar Unions

White-collar employees rarely belong to the same unions as blue-collar employees in Sweden, and no white-collar unions belong to LO. Instead, there are two separate federations of white-collar unions: *Tjanstemännens Centralorganisation,* the "Central Organization of Salaried Employees," or TCO; and *Sveriges Akademikers Centralorganisation-Statstjänstemannens Riksförbund,* the "Central Organization of Professional Associations," or SACO-SR. Whereas TCO seeks to represent all white-collar employees, SACO/SR is primarily an organization of white-collar employees with academic degrees.

As Table 24.2 illustrates, the unionization of white-collar labor began later and progressed more slowly than the unionization of blue-collar workers. Legislation introduced by the Social Democrats in 1936 codified

Table 24.2 The Growth of Union Membership in Sweden

	MEMBERSHIP (IN THOUSANDS)			UNIONIZATION RATES	
	LO	TCO	SACO-SR	BLUE-COLLAR	WHITE-COLLAR
1900	44	—	—	12%	—
1920	280	—	—	31	—
1930	553	—	—	45	24%
1940	971	—	—	66	35
1950	1,278	272	37	76	47
1960	1,486	394	58	78	50
1970	1,680	658	100	80	63
1975	1,918	881	122	89	72
1980	2,127	1,033	174	—	—

SOURCE Anders Kjellberg, *Facklig organiseringi tolv länder* (Lund: Arkiv, 1983), pp. 269–79.

the right of all employees to organize and bargain collectively, clearing the legal obstacles to the unionization of civil servants and providing a major boost to white-collar unions in general.

A federation of public-sector white-collar unions was established in 1937 and merged with the federation that already existed for the private sector, forming TCO in 1944. SACO was formed in 1947 and merged with SR, an organization of civil servants, in 1973. The distribution of membership among these organizations has remained fairly constant as the rate of unionization has increased. Today, TCO has a membership of slightly more than one million, and SACO-SR has a membership of about 180,000.

TCO

TCO consists of twenty-three national unions. Like LO, it is committed to the principle of industrial unionism (i.e., its affiliates organize employees according the type of employer for whom they work rather than the type of work that they perform). Formally speaking, TCO's organizational structure is very similar to LO's, but in reality, TCO is much less unified and centralized than LO.

Two differences between TCO and LO stand out. First, TCO does not bargain with employers on behalf of its affiliates. For the purposes of collective bargaining, the TCO unions have been grouped into three separate cartels: one for bargaining with the central government (TCO-S), another for bargaining with local government employees (*Kommunal tjänstemannakartellen,* or KTK), and the third for bargaining with private employers (*Privattjänstemannakartellen,* or PTK). Generally speaking, the private-sector cartel, which includes unions affiliated with SACO-SR, has been less prone to cooperate with LO in wage bargaining than the public-sector cartels.

Second, TCO differs from LO in that it is not affiliated with any political party; rather, TCO's membership spans the entire spectrum of political opinion. Since the 1960s, the Social Democrats have come to play an increasingly prominent role within the TCO leadership, especially within the public-sector unions, but they have avoided partisan initiatives that might split the organization. TCO actively seeks to influence government policy, but only insofar as government policy bears directly on the interests of TCO members. Of course, the interests of TCO members are themselves a matter of interpretation.

Because the TCO membership constitutes a major electoral constituency for both parliamentary blocs, TCO has come to occupy a pivotal role in Swedish politics. Neither the Social Democrats nor the parties of the center can afford to alienate TCO.

SACO-SR

The significance of SACO-SR fades by comparison to TCO. SACO-SR represents a much smaller segment of the labor market and a more homogeneous political consitutency. Its members occupy the upper echelons of the wage hierarchy, and their immediate interests as well as their socio-cultural background make them strongly disposed to voting for the bourgeois parties. SACO-SR is LO's natural foe, for it exists to defend income differentials, and in the late 1960s and early 1970s, it was willing to strike for this purpose. Since some TCO unions compete with SACO-SR for the same constituency, the latter's wage militancy has served as a constraint on the coordination of wage bargaining between LO and TCO.

Organized Business

Sweden has an exceptionally well-organized and cohesive business community as well as strong unions. There are some nine hundred business organizations in Sweden, but it is sufficient, for our purposes, to discuss only two of them: *Svenska Arbetsgivarföreningen,* the "Swedish Employers' Association," or SAF, and *Industriförbundet,* the "Federation of Industry."

SAF and the Federation of Industry

SAF was formed in 1902 as a federation of employers' associations that had previously organized in response to the emergence and rapid growth of unions. Set up to administer a mutual insurance scheme that would compensate affiliated firms for economic losses suffered due to strikes, SAF quickly assumed a more active role, coordinating the wage bargaining for its members.

The Federation of Industry was formed as an umbrella organization of trade associations in 1910. Most Swedish firms belong to a trade association as well as to an employers' association. Whereas the latter represents the firm's interests as an employer and deals primarily with unions, the former represents its interests as the producer of a particular product (or range of products) and seeks to influence government policy, to provide various services to its members, and sometimes to regulate relations among affiliated firms.

SAF consists of thirty-six employers' associations, with a combined membership of about 37,000 firms. The firms that belong to SAF together employ some 1.3 million people, or 85 percent of total employment by private business. SAF thus represents a large and varied segment of the business community. By comparison, the Federation of Industry represents a smaller and more homogenous constituency, for its membership is restricted to manufacturing industry. Some 3,100 firms are affiliated to the federation through twenty-six associations. Yet these firms together employ 750,000 people and account for more than 75 percent of Swedish industrial production. In other words, the average size of a firm belonging to the Federation of Industry is much larger than the average size of a firm belonging to SAF.

Generally speaking, business organizations are more highly centralized and less concerned with democratic procedure than unions. The highest decision-making body in SAF is the General Assembly, which meets once a year. Contrary to LO congresses, there is seldom any substantive debate at these meetings. Like corporate shareholder meetings, the General Assembly typically approves the reports of the executive board in a rather perfunctory fashion, and its main purpose is to appoint members of the board.

The executive board wields formidable powers under the SAF constitution. Any collective bargaining agreement signed by a firm or employers' association affiliated with SAF must be approved by the executive board before it can go into effect. While the board can order a general or partial lockout, no member can engage in offensive action against the unions without its approval. Firms that are struck or that engage in approved lockouts receive financial assistance, financed through dues and an indemnity that affiliated firms must pay in case of need. Firms that defy the directives of the executive board are not only denied financial assistance but also subject to fines and the ultimate sanction of expulsion.

Prior to World War II, SAF and the Federation of Industry were closely allied with the Conservative Party. Immediately after the war, segments of the business community began to support the Liberal Party instead. Though both parties continued to receive substantial financial contributions from big firms as well as individual capitalists, SAF and the Federation of Industry distanced themselves from the opposition parties and adopted a posture of partisan neutrality in the era of the postwar settlement.

At the same time as the employers' resistance to union wage demands became more intransigant, the new SAF leaders appointed in 1976 broke with the tradition of apolitical pressure-group politics. In recent years, organized business, and SAF in particular, has engaged in a number of mass-media campaigns—for nuclear power, against government spending, and against wage-earner funds—that resemble the tactics used by organized business in the planning debate of the immediate postwar period. This politicization can be seen as a response to the labor movement's turn towards reform initiatives that have challenged the prerogatives and power of business. It can also be seen as a response to the bourgeois tenure in government. The policy continuity that characterized the reversal of government and opposition in 1976, and the continued expansion of government spending under the bourgeois parties, made business wary of relying on the bourgeois parties as its representatives in the political debate.

New Social Movements

In most of the advanced capitalist countries, the period since the mid-1960s has witnessed the political mobilization of new social groups and the emergence of new political issues outside the framework of traditional party and interest group politics. The new social movements include, most notably, the student and antiwar movements that emerged in the second half of the 1960s and their successors: the women's movement and the ecology movement of the 1970s, as well as the peace movement of the early 1980s. It is commonplace to assert that the emergence of these movements signifies the decline of parties and that the new social movements threaten the long-term political stability of the advanced capitalist countries.[9] From a Swedish perspective, such claims appear to be exaggerated.

Sweden has experienced the same kinds of new social movements as have most other Western European countries, but none of these movements has assumed the proportions that they have assumed elsewhere. At the same time, Swedish political parties have quickly picked up on the issues raised by new social movements. The movements seem to have contributed to a more issue-oriented electorate, which is less inclined to vote for the same old party as a matter of habit, but which has largely failed to generate lasting organizational and cultural alternatives to traditional parties and interest groups. Many of the activists in new social movements ultimately have become involved in more traditional forms of political activism. Most notably, many student activists in the late 1960s joined the Communist Party (others undoubtedly joined the Social Democratic Party).

The dynamics of party competition brought environmental issues to the fore of the public debate in the 1970s. The Communists and the Center Party both sought to distinguish themselves from their political rivals by championing so-called green issues and thereby preempted the emergence of a strong, extraparliamentary ecology movement. Yet the Center Party retreated on the issue of nuclear power in order to continue governing with the Liberals and the Conservatives after the nuclear power referendum in 1980. In the absence of well-organized movement with this issue as its primary concern, the widespread popular opposition to nuclear power manifested in the referendum subsequently dissipated.

Similarly, the labor movement can be said to have partly preempted and partly co-opted the women's movement in Sweden. LO's solidaristic wage policy promotes equal pay for equal work, and the resulting wage structure has benefited women. By 1979, the average hourly wage of women employed in industry had reached nearly 90 percent of that of men. The corresponding figure for Britain was less than 75 percent. As Mary Ruggie argues, the position of Swedish women in the labor force differs from that of British women in two other respects as well:[10] first, Swedish women with preschool children are three times as likely to work; and second, Swedish women enjoy more secure employment. In Britain, the rate of female unemployment increased more rapidly than the rate of male unemployment during the economic downturn of the mid-1970s, but this was not the case in Sweden. Along with solidaristic wage policy, Social Democratic child care and labor market policies have promoted the economic equality of women.

On the other hand, Ruggie also shows that Swedish women have *not* made significantly greater inroads into traditional male occupations than British women have: Qualitative gender issues (e.g., issues pertaining to the division of labor in the family) seem to have assumed a more marginal role in Sweden than in many other countries. The Swedish labor movement has promoted women's equality, but it has viewed women's equality almost exclusively in economic terms.

The peace movement, finally, is rather weak in Sweden by comparison with West Germany, Britain, Belgium, or the Netherlands. Since Sweden is not a member of the North Atlantic Treaty Organization (NATO), the peace movement has lacked the organizing focus that the deployment of nuclear missiles has provided in these other countries. Further, the objectives of the peace movement have been less controversial and are largely shared by all parties other than the Conservatives. In a sense, the Swedish political environment is too friendly to progressive causes to allow new social movements to emerge as independent political forces.

The Ideological Hegemony of Social Democracy

While the stability of the Social Democratic electorate is most impressive, it seems justifiable to ask, Why has the Social Democratic Party (or the socialist bloc as whole) never again achieved the level of support that it commanded in the elections of 1940 and 1944? One explanation is that the labor movement's integration into the political system reduced its capacity to mobilize support. Walter Korpi argues that the bourgeois parties adopted reformist programs in response to the political success of social democracy in the 1930s and 1940s and, thereby, preempted further electoral gains. In other words, the political dominance of social democracy in the postwar period has manifested itself through a leftward shift in the "center of political gravity" rather than a transfer of electoral support to the Social Democrats.[11]

Anyone who visits Sweden will quickly recognize that the influence of Social Democratic thinking extends beyond the 45 percent of the adult population who vote for the Social Democrats. To a remarkable extent, the Swedish Social Democrats have been able to define the problems on the political agenda and the terms in which these problems have been discussed by all major political parties. It is in this sense that social democracy might be described as the *hegemonic* force in postwar Swedish politics.

The public sensitivity to even small fluctuations in the rate of unemployment is perhaps the best illustration of Social Democratic hegemony. The opinion polls suggest that the bourgeois parties lost the 1982 election because they had allowed the rate of unemployment to reach a postwar record of 3.5 percent. By strongly criticizing the Social Democrats for allowing the rate unemployment to go above 3 percent in the recession of 1972–72, the bourgeois parties had, in a sense, helped set the stage for their own defeat. The contrast with Britain is striking: In 1983, Margaret Thatcher scored a landslide election victory despite the fact that the rate of unemployment had increased from about 6 percent to over 13 percent since she came to power in 1979.

The circumscribed character of Social Democratic hegemony in postwar Sweden must also be noted, however. Korpi's thesis of a leftward shift in the political spectrum after World War II ignores the fact that the labor movement retreated from its ambitions to extend democratic control over business at the same time that the bourgeois parties accepted welfare reformism and the principles of Keynesian economic management. Though most Social Democratic leaders consider themselves to be socialists, the idea of socialism has not figured in Social Democratic efforts to mobilize support beyond the activist core of the labor movement. Rather, the Social Democrats have always presented themselves as the champions of reforms *within* capitalism. The essential content of Social Democratic hegemony was perhaps best articulated by Per Albin Hansson (prime minister from 1932 until his death in 1946), who likened the society that the Social Democrats strove for to that of *det goda folkhemmet,* "the good family," in which the strong family members help the weak.

In many ways, the 1960s marked the high point of Social Democratic hegemony within Swedish society. The decade of the 1960s was characterized by welfare-state expansion in all the advanced capitalist countries, and the idea that Sweden represented the vanguard of the movement towards a more just and rational society served as a vehicle for the extension of Social Democratic hegemony among white-collar strata.

The welfarist consensus of the 1960s rested on rapid economic growth, and has subsequently become more precarious. Whereas the Liberals and the Center Party competed primarily with each other and the Social Democrats in the 1960s and early 1970s, they now compete primarily with the Conservatives, and even the Social Democrats have moved rightward on certain issues.

The erosion of Social Democratic hegemony in recent years can be seen as a consequence of long-term societal changes as well as economic stagnation. The organizational network and culture of the labor movement, which developed in the context of a geographically decentralized pattern of industrialization that gave rise to homogeneous working-class communities, constituted the foundation upon which the Social Democrats built their following in society at large. Arguably, the rapid urbanization of the postwar period has weakened the organizational foundation of Social Democratic hegemony. While survey data indicate that workers living in big city suburbs are nearly as likely to vote for the socialist parties as workers living in mill towns, their relationship to the labor movement is more indirect, and these urbanized workers are obviously exposed to a wider range of other cultural and ideological influences.

The long-term prospects of Swedish social democracy are not as good as they used to be. It is by no means predetermined that the erosion of Social Democratic hegemony will continue, however, for the struggle for ideas and voter allegiance ultimately depends on the choices that political actors make.

Notes

1. Walter Korpi, *The Democratic Class Struggle* (London: Routledge & Kegan Paul, 1983), p. 56. Unless otherwise noted, this is the source for the figures on voting behavior that follow.
2. Left-socialists held more parliamentary seats than the Communists in the 1930s. The Liberal Party split over the issue of prohibition in the 1920s but was reunited in 1934.
3. *Miljöpartiet,* a Greens party, was formed in the early 1980s but received only 1.7 percent of the vote in 1982 (1.5 percent in 1985). The only other major party without parliamentary representation is the Christian Democratic Union (*Kristlig Demokratisk Samling,* KDS), which was formed in the early 1960s. Its share of the vote has ranged between 1.4 percent (1976 and 1979) and 1.9 percent (1982).
4. Cited in *The Swedish Labour Movement* (Stockholm: International Center of the Swedish Labour Movement, n.d.), p. 3. This pamphlet contains a lot of information about the organizations affiliated with the labor movement, and conveys how the Swedish Social Democrats perceive themselves.
5. The five largest unions were as follows: the Municipal Workers' Union (540,000 members); the Metal Workers' Union (448,000); the State Employees' Union (203,000); the Construction Workers' Union (159,000); and the Union of Commercial Employees (155,000). See Table 24.2 for an overview of LO's membership growth.
6. While the other members of the executive board are elected every five years, the four executive officers, collectively known as the secretariat, serve until they retire (at age sixty-five) or resign. Elected in 1983, the current LO president, Stig Malm, became president at a much younger age than his predecessors (forty-six). He will not reach retirement age until 2002!
7. Somewhat like the elections of 1940, the circumstances of the 1968 elections were extraordinary. The Soviet invasion of Czechoslovakia occurred in the middle of the election campaign. Though the Swedish Communist Party criticized the invasion, it suffered heavy

losses to the Social Democrats as a result. More generally, the Social Democrats seem to have benefited from voters' seeking domestic stability at a time of international tension. In the preceding local elections of 1966, the Social Democrats polled only 42.2 percent of the vote.

8. Francis Castles, *The Social Democratic Image of Society: A Study of the Achievements and Origins of Scandinavian Social Democracy in Comparative Perspective* (London: Routledge & Kegan Paul, 1978), emphasizes the importance of the fragmentation of the Right to the success of Scandinavian social democracy.
9. Compare: Suzanne Berger, "Politics and Antipolitics in Western Europe in the Seventies," *Daedalus,* vol. 108, no. 1 (Winter 1979), pp. 27–50.
10. Mary Ruggie, *The State and Working Women: A Comparative Study of Britain and Sweden* (Princeton: Princeton University Press, 1984).
11. Korpi, *Democratic Class Struggle,* chap. 3.

25

Swedish Politics in Transition

A number of developments have undermined the postwar settlement between labor and business in Sweden. The rapid economic growth of the 1960s resulted in regional decline, deteriorating working conditions, and other social problems; and generated political pressures for increased economic planning and employee participation in corporate decision making. By the end of the 1970s, however, the central problem confronting the labor movement, and politicians of all stripes, was no longer how to ensure that economic growth would conform to social needs but rather how to restore growth.

The Swedish Social Democrats have always been keenly aware that welfare reformism ultimately hinges on sustained economic growth. Since the onset of stagflation (increased inflation and reduced growth) in the mid-1970s, state expenditures have increased because welfare benefits are pegged to consumer prices, and because the number of people eligible for targeted welfare programs (such as unemployment compensation, rent subsidies, and social assistance) has increased. At the same time, the revenue base of the welfare state has decreased as the size of the labor force has contracted (or at least stopped expanding) and real wages have fallen. The hard choice imposed by this economic squeeze — to cut back benefits or increase taxes — was partly postponed by government borrowing. But borrowing cannot continue indefinitely. During their brief tenure in power, the bourgeois parties more or less exhausted this solution. Consequently, the need for renewed economic growth has become ever more important.

Two developments since the late 1960s have undermined the labor movement's traditional strategy of promoting economic growth. First, the growth of white-collar unions and the wage rivalries between white-collar and blue-collar workers have made it more difficult for LO to exercise solidaristic wage restraint. Second, increased foreign investment by big business has weakened the link between wage restraint, on the one hand, and increased domestic investment and employment, on the other, thereby further undermining the legitimacy of wage restraint in the eyes of well-paid LO members.

The labor movement's initial response to this cluster of problems was to propose a series of reforms that would extend democratic control over the economy and promote growth through public investment in industry and collective profit-sharing. Partly in response to labor's socialist offensive, and partly in response to changes in the competitive environment of export firms, organized business began to challenge the terms of the postwar settlement in the second half of the 1970s. In electoral politics, this bourgeois offensive manifested itself through the resurgence of the Conservatives and their increasingly assertive criticism of the welfare state.

The policies of the Social Democratic government that took office in 1982 and the significance of the most recent elections (in 1985) must be understood against the background of these successive offensives by Left and Right.

The Socialist Offensive

Between 1967 and 1976, the labor movement put forth a series of new reform initiatives that challenged, in one way or another, the power and prerogatives of private business. We can distinguish three phases in this reform offensive.[1] In the late 1960s, the labor movement launched an *active industrial policy* to extend government control of industry. In the first half of the 1970s, it proposed and mobilized support for legislation that would promote *industrial democracy* by strengthening union and employee rights and influence at the workplace. Finally, the LO congress of 1976 endorsed a proposal for collective profit-sharing that would gradually transfer the ownership of large firms from private shareholders to *löntagarfonder,* "wage-earner funds."

It should be emphasized that these reform initiatives were not launched according to some preconceived strategy to transform society.

Rather, they were conceived separately, in response to the immediate problems confronting the labor movement.

Active Industrial Policy

Rank-and-file union activists as well as leftist intellectuals began to criticize the Social Democrats' market-oriented approach to economic policy in the mid-1960s. The outcome of the local elections of 1966 jolted the party leadership into taking this criticism seriously. Suffering heavy losses to the Communists and the Center Party, the Social Democrats polled a smaller share of the popular vote (42.2 percent) in these elections than they had done in any election since 1932.

Following the 1966 local elections, the Social Democratic leadership seized upon the idea of an active industrial policy as a means to reassert the party's distinctive ideological profile. The government quickly undertook a number of institutional reforms designed to extend public control over economic development in general and over industrial investment in particular. The Board for Technological Development and the state-owned Investment Bank were established, along with a separate Ministry of Industry in 1967–68. The government also adopted a policy of actively promoting the expansion of state enterprise and created a holding company to coordinate the activities of state-owned firms. At the end of this industrial policy offensive, in 1973, the government set up a separate pension fund, known as the Fourth AP Fund, to invest public pension savings in the stock market.

The themes of labor's industrial policy offensive in the late 1960s were similar to its planning offensive in the immediate postwar period. On the one hand, the Social Democrats argued that business needed active state support to adjust to changes in the world economy and to compete more effectively. On the other hand, they argued that state intervention was necessary to ensure that corporate adjustment strategies conformed to the interests of labor and of society at large.

The Social Democrats viewed the active industrial policy as an extension of the tripartite (government-business-labor) collaboration that had been institutionalized in the arena of labor market policy, but the business community was not at all inclined to welcome selective state intervention in the supply of capital. In the course of the 1970s, industrial policy increasingly became a matter of ad hoc responses to the competitive troubles of particular firms or sectors. The terms of state aid were worked out through negotiations between corporate management and the Ministry of Industry. To the extent that labor participated at all in such negotiations, it was represented by local unions, which typically assumed the role of lobbyists for their firms. In general, industrial policy-making has pivoted on direct state-business relations, and bypassed corporatist arrangements for interest representation. Far from providing labor with direct influence over industrial restructuring, the growth of industrial policy weakened organized labor's role in the policy-making process.[2]

Industrial Democracy

The focus of labor reformism shifted from industrial policy to industrial democracy in the early 1970s. The wildcat strikes of 1969–70 highlighted the fact that many workers were unhappy with their working conditions and revealed a major gap between the national union leadership and the rank-and-file. In LO's view, this gap was due to the centralization of wage bargaining, which had undermined the representative functions and authority of local union organizations. Having previously sought to extend employee rights and influence at the workplace through negotiations with SAF, LO turned to legislation as a means to extend the scope of collective bargaining to issues having to do with workplace conditions, personnel policy, and other corporate decisions affecting the labor force, and thereby to provide union locals with a new role that would not interfere with the implementation of solidaristic wage policy.

TCO quickly came out in support of LO's push for industrial democracy, which ensured that the Liberals and the Center Party would be favorably inclined towards industrial relations reforms. Though the 1973 elections resulted in a hung parliament, with the bourgeois parties and the socialist parties holding exactly the same number of seats, an impressive series of prolabor industrial relations laws were passed from 1972 to 1976.

Capping the labor law offensive, the Co-Determination Law of 1976 effectively abolished managerial prerogatives by requiring management to negotiate with the unions over any corporate decisions that would affect the work force. The Co-Determination Law also provided for increased union access to company records and gave the unions "priority of interpretation" in contract disputes involving nonwage issues (i.e., the union interpretation prevails until a dispute is settled by the Labor Court).

According to Prime Minister Olof Palme, the new labor laws represented "the greatest diffusion of power and influence that has taken place in our land since the introduction of universal suffrage."[3]

Though experiences vary, the labor laws have not lived up to the labor movement's expectations. While the Co-Determination Law required management to subject any corporate decisions that would affect the work force to collective bargaining, it did not require management to reach an agreement with the unions. Thus far, the employers have strongly resisted the extension of industrial democracy through collective bargaining.[4]

Wage-Earner Funds

Going beyond the principle of co-determination, the LO congress of 1976 endorsed the idea of a gradual collectivization of ownership through the build-up of wage-earner funds. This idea had been discussed loosely at the LO congress of 1971, which decided that a committee of experts should be appointed to pursue it further. The committee, headed by Rudolf Meidner, submitted its report to the 1976 congress.[5] In essence, it proposed that firms above a certain size (fifty or one hundred employees) should be required to issue new stocks corresponding to 20 percent of their annual profits and that these stocks should be owned by funds representing wage-earners as a collective group. The shareholder voting rights of the funds were to be partly exercised by union-appointed fund boards and partly by representatives of the employees of the firm in question.

The idea of wage-earner funds was first and foremost conceived as a means to facilitate solidaristic wage policy. The Meidner committee assumed that it would be easier to get well-paid workers to exercise wage restraint if profits generated by restraint were socialized. As the economic crisis deepened in the second half of the 1970s, LO increasingly emphasized that collective profit-sharing would serve not only as a means to reduce wage differentials among LO members by lowering wages at the upper end of the scale but also as a means to increase profit margins, business savings, and investment. In effect, LO promised that workers would accept a smaller share of national income in return for a share of the wealth thereby created.

For LO, wage-earner funds also represented a way to ensure that wage restraint translated into increased investment and employment in domestic industry, and to extend labor's ability to influence the restructuring of industry. From this perspective, the idea of wage-earner funds can be seen as a response to the shortcomings of labor's industrial policy and industrial democracy offensives. Indeed, several LO publications in the early 1980s argued that firms partly owned by the workers would be more apt to collaborate with the government and that the introduction of wage-earner funds was necessary to enable unions to participate more fully in industrial policy making as well as corporate decision making.[6]

Following lengthy discussions between LO and the Social Democratic Party, a new wage-earner funds proposal was put forth in 1981. The new proposal reduced the scale of collective profit-sharing and introduced a number of modifications designed to reassure the business community. Most importantly, it eliminated the provision that firms would be required to issue new stocks, something which the bourgeois parties had construed as confiscation. Under the new proposal, collective profit sharing would instead take the form of a profits tax, the revenues of which would be used by regionally organized wage-earner funds to purchase corporate shares. Private shareholders would be free to choose whether or not to sell shares, and the value of their assets of their holdings would almost certainly increase.

Even the 1981 wage-earner funds proposal implied a very significant change in the ownership structure of Swedish industry, however. According to the opponents of wage-earner funds, this change would be for the worse, because the funds would be unable to make the tough economic decisions necessary for Swedish industry to keep up with international competition and would end up protecting employment at the expense of efficiency. At the same time, the critics asserted that wage-earner funds would concentrate power in the hands of union bureaucrats rather than democratize economic decision making and that this concentration represented a threat to pluralistic democracy as well as free enterprise.

The controversy stirred up by the proposed wage-earner funds lent a confrontational cast to Swedish politics reminiscent of the planning debate in the immediate postwar period and the pension reform debate in the late 1950s.

The labor movement clearly lost the struggle for public opinion in the debate over wage-earner funds that followed. According to exit polls, 33 percent of all voters in 1976 favored wage-earner funds, 43 percent were opposed, and 24 percent were undecided. Shortly before the 1982 elections, the polls showed that 15 percent of all voters were in favor, 57 percent opposed, and 27 percent undecided. Among Social Democratic voters, support for wage-earner funds dropped from 57 percent in 1976 to 31 percent in 1982, while negative reactions increased from 16 percent to 27 percent.[7]

The tactical and principled differences between LO and the leadership of the Social Democratic Party weakened the effort to mobilize popular support for wage-earner funds. They did so by exacerbating the basic problem of popularizing what was necessarily a complicated, and rather technical, scheme. It is not entirely unfair to say that many voters still did not quite understand the idea of wage-earner funds after six years of debate. By contrast, the message of the campaign against wage-earner funds was simple and consistent ("No to collective funds!").

Quite clearly, the Social Democrats won the 1982 elections despite rather than because of the issue of wage-earner funds. For all the intensity of the debate over wage-earner funds, the majority of voters considered other issues, most notably rising unemployment, to be more important.

The Social Democrats seem to have expected that their return to power in 1982 would lead the opponents of wage-earner funds to adopt a more pragmatic outlook and thus set the stage for a compromise solution, but this did not turn out to be the case. When the new government invited some twenty-five organizations to participate in consultations over wage-earner funds and related issues, every single business organization declined the invitation. The bourgeois parties announced beforehand that they were not about to engage in any form of negotiations, and the TCO leadership showed up only to inform the government that it would neither support nor oppose any forthcoming legislation.

The political deadlock over wage-earner funds thus persisted. Under pressure from LO, the government nevertheless proceeded to introduce legislation, passed with Communist support in 1983, that set up five wage-earner funds, to be built up over a six-year period through a special payroll tax and a tax on excess profits. Assuming that stock prices increase at the rate of inflation, their combined assets will correspond to about 5 percent of all stocks registered at the stock exchange by the end of 1990. Since only a small number of corporations are registered at the stock exchange, and since stock prices are likely to increase at a faster rate than inflation, the reform's effects on the structure ownership will be even more limited than this figure suggests. Further, the current legislation makes no provision for the build-up of wage-earner funds beyond 1990. While the government can, of course, introduce further legislation on this score, the prime minister and the minister of finance have both asserted that they consider the 1983 reform to be a one-shot deal.

From a socialist perspective, the 1983 reform could perhaps be justified as a first step in a broader effort to restore the reform momentum that existed prior to the bourgeois tenure in government. But this clearly was not how the new Social Democratic government viewed the matter. The introduction of wage-earner funds did not form part of a new reformist agenda. Rather, it was an isolated reform undertaken in conjunction with an economic policy package that represented a continuation of austerity measures designed to increase corporate profits. The primary motive behind the reform seems to have been to secure LO's acceptance of this policy orientation.

The Bourgeois Offensive

Much like the planning offensive in the immediate postwar period, labor's reform initiatives in 1967–76, and the issue of wage-earner funds in particular, served to mobilize and politicize the business community. SAF and the Federation of Industry initiated the mass-media campaign against wage-earner funds between 1979 and 1983, and financed most of the advertising component of this campaign. Aided by the editorial views of the major newspapers and by the ambiguities of the labor movement's case for wage-earner funds, the campaign against wage-earner funds had a great impact on public opinion.

Among the bourgeois parties, the Conservatives assumed the leadership of the campaign against wage-earner funds. Along with the growing resentment of high taxes among bourgeois voters, the debate over wage-earner funds benefited the Conservatives electorally (their share of the vote increased from 15.6 percent in 1976 to 23.6 percent in 1982) and contributed to a marked rightward shift in the terms of debate within the bourgeois bloc.

Going beyond a defensive mobilization against wage-earner funds, organized business also began to mobilize public opinion against government spending in the late 1970s. In the 1980 wage negotiations, SAF tried to tie wage increases to public-sector cutbacks in the wage negotiations of 1980. In the short term, this strategy failed; the unions fought it, and the bourgeois government intervened in the ensuing strike/lockout to prevail upon the employers to accept wage increases. Under pressure from the Conservatives and the business community, however, the government reoriented its economic policy and introduced public-sector cutbacks shortly after the labor market conflict of 1980.

Since 1980, the employers have directly challenged LO's solidaristic wage policy and sought to decentralize wage bargaining. In the 1960s and 1970s, the employers accepted the reduction of wage differentials as the price that had to be paid for LO to exercise wage restraint. They apparently believe that this kind of trade-off is no longer necessary (i.e., that market forces will impose the necessary wage restraint).

Within SAF, the effort to decentralize wage bargaining was spearheaded by the engineering employers, who enjoyed a veritable profits boom in the early 1980s and were, in effect, able to pay higher wages than provided for by peak-level agreements. At the same time, the engineering employers found it difficult to recruit skilled labor and felt that economywide bargaining impeded their efforts to increase labor productivity.

In the wage negotiations of 1983, the engineering employers managed to strike a separate deal with the Metal Workers' Union. The average wage increase provided by this agreement did not significantly exceed the LO-SAF agreement, but the break-away by the Metal Workers represented a serious breach of unity among the LO unions. To avoid a similar situation, LO reluctantly agreed to across-the-board industry-level negotiations in 1984. For the first time since 1956, no central LO-SAF agreement was signed in 1984. At the government's urging, LO and SAF agreed to a 5 percent cap on wage increases in 1985, and in 1986 signed a central agreement that included supplementary wage increases for low paid workers. It would be premature to say that the traditional system of wage bargaining has been restored, however. The engineering employers went along with central negotiations in 1986 for essentially tactical reasons, and remain committed to the idea of separate industry-level negotiations.

The business community's offensive against public spending and solidaristic wage policy can be interpreted in two different ways. It might be seen as an opportunistic response to the reversal of government and opposition in 1976, and the weakening of labor's marketplace power due to the economic crisis. Alternatively, the bourgeois offensive might be seen as an expression of long-term changes in the interests of business. One might argue that the business community's interests in domestic demand stimulation have weakened as it has become increasingly dominated by export firms and as the activities of these firms have become increasingly multinational. Similarly, the employers' efforts to decentralize collective bargaining might be explained in terms of changes in world competition that make a more flexible organization of production imperative.

The New Social Democratic Government

When the Social Democrats returned to power in 1982, full employment once again became the primary goal of government policy. The new government has increased the budgetary resources available to the Labor

Market Board for temporary public works and job training. In many other respects, however, the policy reorientation that began during the bourgeois tenure in government has continued under the Social Democrats.

While in opposition, the Social Democrats criticized the spending cuts introduced by the bourgeois parties and advocated an expansionary fiscal policy to stimulate economic recovery. Back in power, they proceeded to implement their own cuts and to maintain what in effect amounted to a hiring freeze in the public sector. Instead of stimulating domestic demand, the Social Democrats opted for currency devaluation as the key to economic recovery. By devaluing the Krona by 16 percent, the new government boosted the profit margins of export firms and cut domestic purchasing power. A number of subsequent government measures were also designed to improve corporate profits and otherwise encourage private investment. Along with the collective wage-earner funds, the Social Democrats retained, with some modifications and a new name, the system of tax-subsidized individual savings funds that the bourgeois parties had introduced.

Given the massive government deficit that the bourgeois parties had run up, the Social Democrats had little choice but to adopt a restrictive fiscal policy. The imperative of bringing the deficit under control does not entirely explain the new government's approach to economic policy, however. Even though the Social Democrats promised more active and forward-looking policies to promote industrial development in the 1982 election campaign, the new government has not developed any consistent approach to promoting advanced sectors. Instead of substituting an offensive industrial policy for a defensive one, the Social Democrats have retreated from the idea of selective state intervention in the process of industrial restructuring.

Whereas the bourgeois parties introduced some minor cuts in welfare benefits, Social Democratic spending cuts have not affected benefits directly. Rather, the cuts have been made by reducing public investment and personnel and administrative costs. From a short-term perspective, the Social Democrats have effectively defended the welfare state, but cuts in public investment and employment must ultimately affect the quality of the services provided by the welfare state. Indeed, a certain deterioration is already noticeable.

Reversing this gradual erosion of the welfare state depends on sustained economic growth, but under capitalist auspices, growth in turn presupposes a redistribution of income from wages to profits and perhaps also increased income differentials among wage earners. This is the dilemma that the wage-earner funds were supposed to resolve. In essence, the labor movement proposed to increase corporate profitability and investment without making the owners of the corporations richer. Thus, market forces would no longer be at odds with the redistributive aims of the welfare state.

In the second half of the 1970s, reformist socialists cited the Swedish labor movement's advocacy of wage-earner funds to support the thesis that welfare reformism can create the conditions for a gradual and peaceful transition to socialism.[8] In retrospect, the debate over wage-earner funds stands out as a turning point in Swedish politics — but the turn that occurred was to the Right rather than the Left. Though a watered-down proposal for wage-earner funds was indeed introduced, the labor movement retreated from its earlier ambitions to democratize the sphere of production, and the debate contributed to a rightward shift of the policy debate, not only within the bourgeois bloc, but also within the labor movement.

Back to the Middle Way?

While the bourgeois parties tried to turn the 1985 elections into a referendum on wage-earner funds, the Social Democrats sought to direct the electorate's attention to other issues, emphasizing the competence of their government and the relatively strong performance of the economy since 1982. The Social Democratic strategy worked: The bulk of the Social Democratic voters who opposed wage-earner funds stuck with the party. With 44.7 percent of the vote (compared to 45.6 percent in 1982), the Social Democrats were able to retain control of the government. Whereas Communist abstention was sufficent in 1982–85, however, the government now depends on the support of another party to get its legislation through parliament.

The most significant result of the 1985 elections was that the Liberals staged a major comeback at the expense of the Conservatives. Only a few months before the elections, the polls indicated that the Conservatives might gain as much as 27 to 30 percent of the vote. In fact, the Conservatives' share dropped from 23.6 percent to 21.3 percent. While the Center Party's share of the vote continued to decline (from 15.5 percent to 12.4 percent), the Liberals' share increased from 5.9 percent to 14.2 percent.[9]

In the election campaign, the Conservatives went beyond the united bourgeois front against wage-earner funds to advocate a *systemskifte*, "change of system," of their own. Specifically, they proposed to dismantle wage-earner funds, cut taxes, reduce the public sector, foster private alternatives to public services, introduce commercial television, eliminate the tax deduction for union dues, and abolish collective union affiliation with the Social Democratic Party. Perhaps the polls made the Conservatives overconfident. In any case, their campaign rhetoric made many bourgeois voters uneasy. Advocating a more moderate, neoliberal approach, the youthful new leader of the Liberal Party, Bengt Westerberg, represented an attractive alternative.[10]

In the context of the labor's weakening power in the marketplace, and the employers' offensive against the unions, a bourgeois government dominated by the Conservatives would have marked a decisive turn to the Right in Swedish politics. Therefore, the victory of the Social Democrats in 1985 might be seen as a return to the middle-of-the-road politics that characterized Sweden in the 1960s. While the electoral ascendancy of the Conservatives has been checked, the Social Democrats have now, after two successive victories, reestabished themselves as the party of government. At the same time, labor has retreated from its socialist offensive in the 1970s.

Since the late 1960s, both labor and business have challenged the terms of the postwar settlement, but neither has been able to impose a new settlement. We have argued here that the postwar settlement rested on a certain balance of power: The membership strength of the unions and Social Democratic control of government partly offset the systemic power of private business. At the same time, proportional representation and the electoral strength of the bourgeois parties among farmers and white-collar strata prevented majority rule by the Social Democrats, and the organizational cohesion of the employers curtailed the exercise of union power in the marketplace. Finally, the dependence of the Swedish economy on world markets made it necessary for any government to cater to the interests of export industry.

The basic components of this configuration of power are still in place, and consequently, the bias towards compromise persists. While the employers have sought to exploit divisions among the unions, they have made no effort to create a union-free environment. Compared with unions in most other advanced capitalist countries, the Swedish unions have weathered the economic crisis remarkably well. The rate of union membership has remained steady; even the Conservatives have refrained from challenging the legitimacy of organized labor directly.

On the other hand, three factors distinguish the current situation from that of the 1960s and render the prospects of labor reformism problematic. First of all, the world economy of the 1980s is much less favorable than in the 1960s, and economic growth seems likely to be more erratic in the years to come. Perhaps more importantly, the dynamics of international competition seem to have changed in ways that make the goals of the labor movement — full employment, income redistribution, and public-sector expansion — more difficult to realize even if the economy grows.

Second, the new Social Democratic government confronts an opposition that is very different from that of the 1960s. The Conservatives still remain the largest opposition party, and as indicated earlier, the other bourgeois parties have moved rightward in recent years. The Liberals regained voters from the Conservatives in 1985 in part because they had adopted a softer version of the themes developed by the Conservatives in the previous period.

Third, the authority of LO within the union movement has weakened. In the past, LO has not only delivered the wage restraint necessary to maintain macroeconomic stability but also served as a mediator between the unions and the government. As we have seen, many of the new reforms that sustained the forward momentum of labor reformism in the postwar period were initiated by LO and virtually imposed on the Social Democratic governing elite. Along with developments in collective bargaining, the failure of the labor movement's push for wage-earner funds has weakened LO's political influence.

In the 1985 election, the Social Democrats ran as the party of government rather than as a party of reform. This kind of appeal has served the British Conservatives very well, but it does not seem to represent a viable long-term strategy for a party that depends on the working class as its core constituency. In the absence of a new reform agenda, the bourgeois offensive might well resume. But what would a new reform agenda look like, short of another challenge to private ownership? While the bias towards compromise persists, the middle way is hard to find in the 1980s.

Epilogue

Prime Minister Olof Palme, the dominant figure in Swedish politics since the late 1960s, was assassinated on February 28, 1986. This was the first political assassination in Sweden since King Gustaf III was assassinated in 1792, and will undoubtedly lead to a tightening of security for leading politicians (Palme was entirely unprotected at the time). Palme was succeeded as prime minister and chair of the Social Democratic Party by a long-time collaborator, Ingvar Carlsson. The change of prime minister is unlikely to affect the substantive policy orientation of the government.

NOTES

1. For an overview, see: Andrew Martin, "Trade Unions in Sweden: Strategic Responses to Change and Crisis," in *Unions and Economic Crisis,* ed. Peter Gourevitch et al. (London: George Allen & Unwin, 1984), pp. 190–359; or Andrew Martin, "Sweden: Industrial Democracy and Social Democratic Strategy," in *Workers' Self-Management in Industry,* ed. David Garson (New York: Praeger, 1977), pp. 49–96.
2. Most of the features that distinguish industrial policy from labor market policy predate the reversal of government and opposition in 1976. See Jonas Pontusson, "Labor Reformism and the Politics of Capital Formation in Sweden" (Ph.D. dissertation, University of California, Berkeley, 1986).
3. Martin Carnoy and Derek Shearer, *Economic Democracy* (Armonk, NY: M.E. Sharpe, 1980), p. 261.
4. *Labor Market Reforms in Sweden* (Stockholm: Swedish Institute, 1979), shows how the new labor laws worked in the first few years and how they were perceived by workers.
5. For an abridged, English version, see Rudolf Meidner, *Employee Investment Funds* (London: George Allen & Unwin, 1978).
6. Compare, for example, *Co-determination through Collective Agreements and Legislation* (Stockholm: LO, 1982).
7. These figures come from Gösta Esping-Andersen, *Politics Against Markets: The Social Democratic Road to Power* (Princeton: Princeton University Press, 1985), p. 307; and *The Debate on Collective Wage Earner Funds in Sweden* (Stockholm: Federation of Swedish Industries, 1983), p. 2.
8. Compare, for example, Walter Korpi, *The Working Class in Welfare Capitalism: Work, Unions, and Politics in Sweden* (London: Routledge & Kegan Paul, 1978); John Stephens, *The Transition from Capitalism to Socialism* (London: Macmillan, 1979); and Winton Higgins and Nixon Apple, "How Limited Is Reformism?" *Theory and Society,* vol. 12, no. 6, 1983, pp. 603–30. Jonas Pontusson, "Behind and Beyond Social Democracy in Sweden," *New Left Review,* no. 143, 1984, pp. 69–96, develops a theoretical critique of this school of thought.
9. For the 1985 elections, the Center Party ran common slates with the Christian Democrats, who received 1.9 percent of the vote in 1982. The Center Party's own electorate shrunk to less than 10 percent in 1985 (as compared to 25.1 percent at its peak in 1973). The party leader, Torbjörn Fälldin, resigned shortly after the 1985

elections. He has been succeeded by Sweden's first female party leader, Karin Söder.

10. The Conservative party leader, Ulf Adelsohn, resigned in June 1986. His successor has yet to be chosen.

Bibliography

Castles, Francis. *The Social Democratic Image of Society: A Study of the Achievements and Origins of Scandinavian Social Democracy in Comparative Perspective* (London: Routledge & Kegan Paul, 1978). This book contains an insightful discussion of the historical reasons for the dominance of social democratic parties in the Scandinavian countries as well as a general assessment of what these parties have accomplished in government.

Childs, Marquis W. *Sweden: The Middle Way on Trial* (New Haven: Yale University Press, 1980). A journalistic account of Swedish politics in the late 1970s, providing a good sense of political culture and some of the major personalities involved; however, the text is now somewhat dated.

Esping-Andersen, Gösta. *Politics Against Markets: The Social Democratic Road to Power* (Princeton: Princeton University Press, 1985). A very interesting comparison of welfare-state development and the divergent political fortunes of social democratic parties in Scandinavia.

Hancock, Donald. *Sweden: The Politics of Postindustrial Change* (Hinsdale, IL: Dryden Press, 1972). The standard textbook on Swedish politics in English; it is comprehensive, but quite out of date.

Ingham, Geoffrey. *Strikes and Industrial Conflict: Britain and Scandinavia* (London: Macmillan, 1974). An important book on the historical origins of industrial relations systems.

Korpi, Walter. *The Working Class in Welfare Capitalism: Work, Unions, and Politics in Sweden* (London: Routledge & Kegan Paul, 1978). An important interpretation of the Swedish experience of labor reformism, based on survey data of worker attitudes towards work, unions, and politics.

———. *The Democratic Class Struggle.* (London: Routledge & Kegan Paul, 1983). A careful analysis of voting behavior and a further elaboration on the interpretation set forth in *The Working Class in Welfare Capitalism* [above].

Lindbeck, Assar. *Swedish Economic Policy* (Berkeley: University of California Press, 1974). A very detailed and rather technical treatment of the objectives, instrumentalities, and effects of economic policy in postwar Sweden.

Martin, Andrew. "Trade Unions in Sweden: Strategic Responses to Change and Crisis," in *Unions and Economic Crisis: Britain, West Germany, and Sweden,* ed. Peter Gourevitch et al. (London: George Allen and Unwin, 1984), pp. 189–359. By far the most comprehensive and incisive English-language treatment of the theory and practice of solidaristic wage-bargaining.

Ruggie, Mary. *The State and Working Women: A Comparative Study of Britain and Sweden* (Princeton: Princeton University Press, 1984). Focusing on issues pertaining to women's participation in the work force, this book shows how the Swedish welfare state differs from the British and links the differences to the greater power of labor.

Samuelsson, Kurt. *From Great Power to Welfare State: 300 Years of Swedish Social Development* (London: George Allen and Unwin, 1968). The standard Swedish history text in English.

Scase, Richard. *Social Democracy in Capitalist Society: Working-Class Politics in Britain and Sweden* (London: Croom Helm, 1977). An interesting comparison of social structure and working-class consciousness.

Essentially Descriptive Works Published by the Swedish Institute

Forsebäck, Lennart. *Industrial Relations and Employment in Sweden* (1980).

Gustafsson, Agne. *Local Government in Sweden* (1983).

Hadenius, Stig. *Swedish Politics During the 20th Century* (1985).

Lindström, Eric. *The Swedish Parliamentary System* (1982).

Vindé, Pierre and Gunnar Petri. *Swedish Government Administration* (1978).

PART VII

THE SOVIET UNION and selected nations of Eastern Europe

Joan DeBardeleben

26

The Emergence of the Soviet State

⯭ The Principles of Soviet State Formation

The Russian Revolution, in October 1917, ushered in not only a radical change in Russian government but also a new force in the international political system. For the first time in history, a Marxist party took control of the reigns of state power. This revolution did not occur, as Karl Marx and Friedrich Engels had expected, in an industrial country of Western Europe, such as Germany, France, or England. Rather, it shook Russia, a country where some 80 percent of the population were peasants, most tilling the soil for a subsistence living.

The victorious Marxist group, the Bolsheviks, faced many problems as they attempted to construct a socialist and, finally, a communist society. Some were the result of the backwardness of the country at the time of the revolution; for example, Marx and Engels had assumed that a socialist revolution would be carried out by a strong urban proletariat (working class), which would first revolt against the exploitive and inhumane working conditions in capitalist factories. The proletariat would replace the bourgeoisie (the capitalist ownership class) as the ruling class and would proceed to construct a more equitable and democratic society. For Marx and Engels, socialism (also called the "dictatorship of the proletariat") would be the first step on the road to communism; it would be democratic because both political and economic power would rest in the hands of the majority, namely, the working class. Society as a whole, rather than private capitalists, would own the means of production (e.g., factories, machines, land). Thus, political democracy would be reinforced by economic democracy in an industrial society. In Russia, however, the working class was small: Factory workers made up only about 5 percent of the population in 1917. Thus, if this class were to follow the prescribed course, it would rule as a minority over recalcitrant elements from other social classes, such as the peasantry, the old gentry, and the bourgeoisie. Furthermore, it was not clear that the small and immature working class could direct the necessary social changes to transform society. Rather, this class was to be led by a party that included only a minority of the proletariat and that was headed, not by workers, but by individuals from the intelligentsia.

Although Marx did not provide much guidance on what should follow the revolution, his writings suggest that once the power of the proletariat was secure, the next step would be the elimination of class divisions. All citizens would be equal working participants in communist society, sharing both the burdens and benefits of labor, for communist society would be a classless society. The elimination of class conflict depended, however, on material abundance; capitalism itself, according to Marx and Engels, would have laid the economic and technological foundation for overcoming material scarcity. Marx and Engels recognized that capitalism, despite its social injustices, was highly efficient and productive. Yet Russian capitalism in 1917 was hardly developed enough to provide that material foundation for a future socialist or communist society: Despite the rapid industrial takeoff of the late 1800s and early 1900s, industrial output was still far below that of most Western European countries; levels of literacy, especially in the countryside and among women, were low; and, by almost any measure, the Russian standard of living was also well below that of Western Europe. Thus, before the Bolsheviks could hope to build a society free of class competition, they would have to overcome the economic backwardness inherited from the capitalist period. They might have to fill in for the capitalists, at least for a time, in order to progress to the next stage. Could this be done without resort to coercion? Who would bear the costs and burdens of the industrialization effort, which the working class had largely borne during industrialization under capitalism? If the relative backwardness of Russia in 1917 proved a difficult starting point for the Bolsheviks as they attempted to build a socialist and, finally, a classless communist society, why did they ground their revolution in a theory that, on the face of it, seemed of little direct relevance to an agrarian

The Soviet Union
Boundaries of Union Republics
ARCTIC
IRELAND
UNITED KINGDOM
NORTH SEA
NORWAY
NETHERLANDS
BELGIUM
FRANCE
DENMARK
SWEDEN
BARENTS SEA
Novaia Zemlia
KARA SEA
WEST GERMANY
EAST GERMANY
FINLAND
BALTIC SEA
WHITE SEA
Tallinn
ESTONIA
POLAND
AUSTRIA
CZECHOSLOVAKIA
LITHUANIA
Riga
LATVIA
Leningrad
Vilnius
Minsk
BELORUSSIA
HUNGARY
YUGOSLAVIA
Pechora
Moscow
Kiev
RUMANIA
MOLDAVIA
UKRAINE
Gor'kii
Ob'
Kishinev
Odessa
Khar'kov
BULGARIA
Don
Volga
RUSSIAN SOVIET FEDERATEI
BLACK SEA
Volgograd
Novosi
TURKEY
GEORGIA
Tbilisi
ARMENIA
Yerevan
CASPIAN SEA
KAZAKHSTAN
ARAL SEA
Baku
SYRIA
AZERBAIDZHAN
UZBEKISTAN
TURKMENISTAN
Alma-Ata
Tashkent
Frunze
KIRGHIZIIA
IRAQ
Ashkabad
Dushanbe
TADZHIKISTAN
IRAN
AFGHANISTAN
PAKISTAN
INDIA
0 800 Miles
0 800 Kilometers

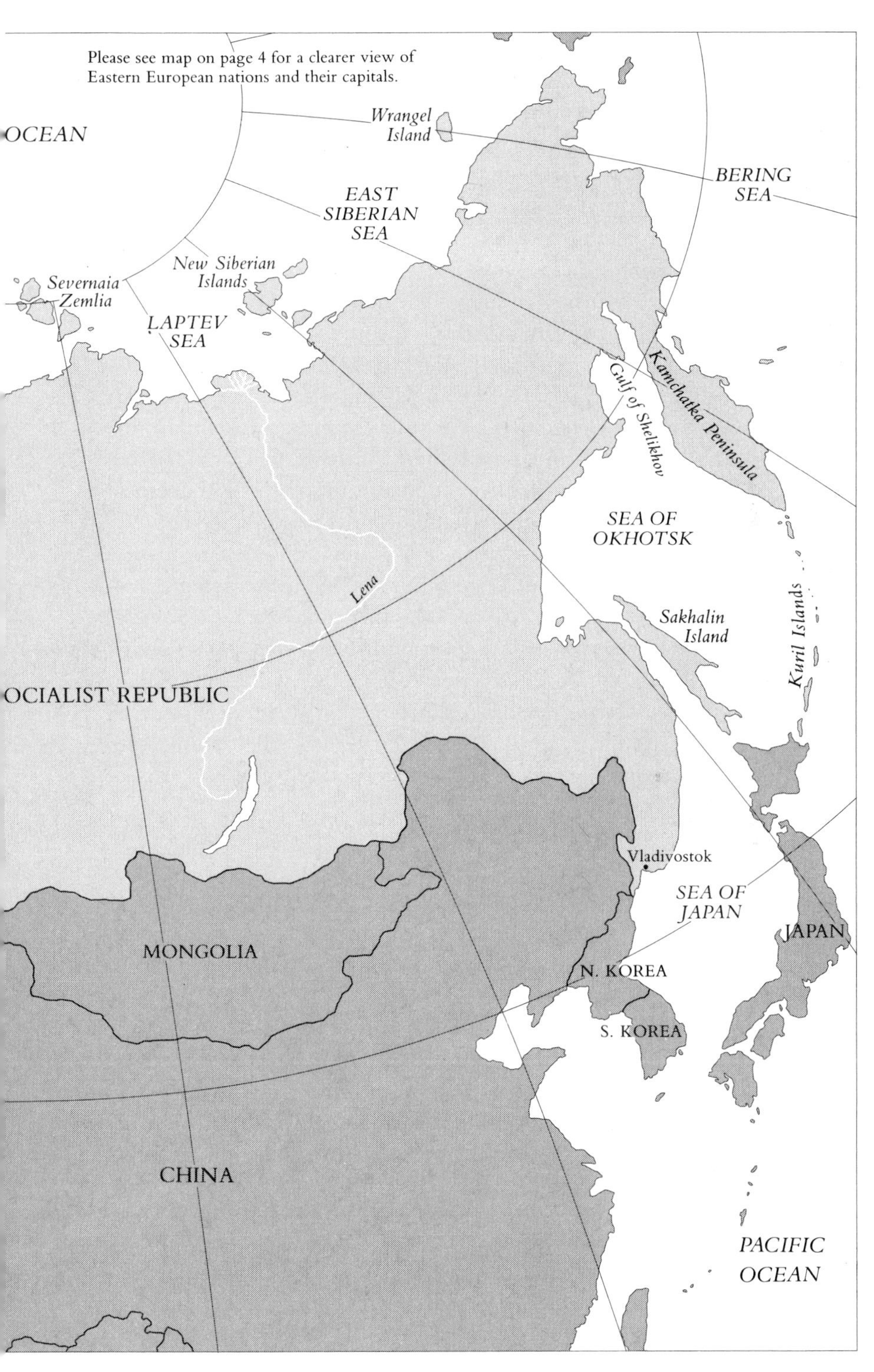
Please see map on page 4 for a clearer view of Eastern European nations and their capitals.
OCEAN
Wrangel Island
BERING SEA
EAST SIBERIAN SEA
New Siberian Islands
Severnaia Zemlia
LAPTEV SEA
Kamchatka Peninsula
Gulf of Shelikhov
SEA OF OKHOTSK
Lena
Sakhalin Island
Kuril Islands
OCIALIST REPUBLIC
Vladivostok
SEA OF JAPAN
JAPAN
MONGOLIA
N. KOREA
S. KOREA
CHINA
PACIFIC OCEAN

peasant society? How could power fall into the hands of such a group, anyway, when even in Western Europe, where conditions seemed so much more propitious, no Marxist party had been able to win power? We will attempt to address these questions in this and the following chapter as we explore some of the unique conditions in prerevolutionary Russia that paved the way for the Bolshevik Revolution of 1917 and some of the problems that ensued from the revolution.

If some of the problems confronting the Bolshevik Party were rooted in the particular circumstances facing Russia in 1917, others might have faced any Marxist party in any country. The new leaders were forced to conduct their social experiment with little theoretical or practical guidance. How could *social* ownership of economic resources be made genuine? Would it simply be *state* ownership? If so, would a new class of bureaucrats, running the state-owned industries and farms, simply replace the former capitalist and tsarist elite? Furthermore, would it be possible to construct a society that was at once both socialist and democratic? Much depends on one's understanding of the term *democracy;* as we shall see, the Soviet Marxist definition is quite different from the liberal definition predominant in Western Europe. In the following chapters, we will elucidate some of the difficulties that confronted the Soviets as they attempted to build a society worthy of being called both democratic and socialist. To offer a broader perspective, we will also examine the different ways in which some of the Soviet Union's Eastern European allies have addressed the same problems. First, we will examine the Russian Revolution itself and attempt to understand why Russia became the first socialist state.

The Old Order

Up until the Bolshevik Revolution of 1917, Russia had taken a separate developmental path from Western Europe, which may account for the different political outcomes in the twentieth century. In Russia, social classes were able to wield much less autonomous power in relation to the state, and the state took on a much more extensive role in furthering industrialization. Certain cultural patterns, such as collectivism (an emphasis on group over individual values) and a continuing close link between the Russian Orthodox church and the tsarist state, also differentiated Russia from Western Europe. Finally, the political leadership had suffered repeated setbacks in the international sphere, partly because

Russia's domestic structures were too weak to support a successful foreign policy. Foreign policy debacles in turn sparked domestic unrest; for example, Russia's involvement in World War I became the final catalyst for the fall of the tsarist regime.

The State and Social Classes

In prerevolutionary Russia, all social classes had developed in dependence on the strong tsarist state. In the sixteenth century, the tsar Ivan the Terrible began the process that finally subordinated the nobility to the state; by the reign of Peter I (1689–1725), every nobleman was required to perform lifetime service in the military corps or state bureaucracy in exchange for the right to exploit land and labor. Thus, the landed class became also an administrative class. Not until 1762, during the reign of Peter III, were the nobles formally freed from compulsory state service. However, the *dvorianstvo* (Russian nobility) still did not become a strong political force; furthermore, they were dependent on the state for control of the labor force, the serfs, who were bound in servitude to their masters. (The holdings of the nobility were scattered, and many nobles lived in virtual poverty.) Serfdom, which had developed gradually over the previous centuries, was fully developed by the middle of the seventeenth century. In most regions, the *dvorianstvo* did not develop an entrepreneurial spirit to improve and commercialize agriculture but was able to live off the labor of the dependent peasant class.

In 1861, Tsar Alexander II emancipated the serfs, but this was a dubious benefit. The peasant became a legal person, free from the landlord's authority. But the freed peasants were obligated to pay redemption fees to the state (which had compensated the previous landowners) for forty-nine years to gain ownership of the land; they also remained bound to the land and to the *mir,* the "peasant commune", which still engaged in periodic repartition of land strips among families in the community. The *mir* also had legal ownership of the land and was collectively responsible for the redemption payments as well as for providing military recruits for the government. Only wealthy peasants could buy their way free. Not until 1907, with the Stolypin reforms, were redemption payments abolished and measures taken to replace the peasant commune by private cultivation. Peter Stolypin, president of the tsar's Council of Ministers, hoped that a more truly independent and prosperous peasant class would soon take on the attributes of a conservative petite bourgeoisie in the countryside: As beneficiaries of the tsarist reforms, this class was to provide a stable foundation of political support for the regime and help to improve agricultural productivity. World War I interrupted this process in 1914, and the regime was so severely shaken by the international crisis that revolutionary forces were able to topple it in 1917, before Stolypin's blueprint had a chance to prove itself.

Might Russia have followed a path similar to that of Western Europe had the war not intervened? This, of course, is a question we will never be able to answer definitively, but there was no substantial bourgeoisie or other social base to provide a political foundation for constitutional government and liberalism, as had developed in most Western European countries. Once the tsarist government fell in February, 1917, the peasants contributed to the revolution by seizing the lands remaining in large estates.

Meanwhile, in the late nineteenth century, industrialization was taking off in Russia. From the very beginning, the key impetus came not from an indigenous bourgeois class, but from the state itself and from heavy injections of foreign (especially French, English, German, and Belgian) capital in the form of joint-stock companies and foreign debt incurred by the tsarist government. For example, about 75 percent of the output of coal and pig iron depended on French capital. In 1900, over 70 percent of capital invested in industrial joint-stock companies in mining, metallurgy, engineering, and machinery was of foreign origin. Percentages were lower in other sectors of the economy, but still above 25 percent in lumber; chemicals; leather processing; and cements, ceramics, and glass.

The large role of state and foreign capital in the Russian industrialization effort had significant social consequences. Although many workers were employed in small private workshops, on the whole factories were larger than in Western Europe or North America. In 1914, over 40 percent of the workers were employed in factories with one thousand workers or more (as compared to just over 30 percent in 1901).[1] Many of these factories were run by absentee owners, who did not develop personal relations with their workers. A small, but restless, working class was developing in the cities; meanwhile in the countryside, traditional patterns still survived. It seemed Russia suffered the injustices of two worlds — the bondage and dependence of the peasantry, and the inhumane and impersonal oppression of the large capitalist factories. Most members of the small working class retained their link to the countryside: They were worker-peasants, often making their way back to the village on weekends or holidays to help out with the harvest, supplementing family income with their factory earnings.

The tsarist state did not legalize trade unions until 1906, and then their activities were carefully circumscribed. By 1914, they were largely ineffectual, but at the end of the nineteenth century there was increasing evidence of worker discontent in the form of numerous illegal strikes, especially in the large urban centers. In 1905, worker discontent produced a major state crisis, with widespread strikes in the cities and uprisings in rural areas. The tsar responded by establishing a constitutional monarchy, with an elected legislative branch. However, the powers of the Duma, the elected assembly, were gradually restricted in the following years. Through increasing repression, the tsarist state was able to maintain its dominance over Russian society.

Russian Political Culture

Russia was converted to Orthodox Christianity in 987. The Russian Orthodox Church took on an increasingly independent status after Constantinople (Byzantium), the center of Orthodoxy, fell to the Turks in 1453. The tsarist state was intimately connected with the Orthodox church, which provided a kind of official religion or ideology for tsarism. As early as the sixteenth and seventeenth centuries, the notion spread in influential circles that Russia was the Third Rome, meaning that only in Russia was true Christianity still embodied in the Church's doctrine and rituals; Russia was the rightful world center of Christianity, as the Roman and Byzantine churches (the First and Second Romes) had been corrupted by heretical doctrines. In the 1660s, a schism shook the Russian Orthodox church, as its head, Patriarch Nikon, sought to reform church rituals and statutes. The Old Believers, who had followers among both peasants and rich merchant families, rejected the reforms as embodiments of the anti-Christ, thus alienating the official Orthodox church from broad segments of the Christian population. Nonetheless, the tradition of an official state religion was firmly entrenched in Russian history and may bear some resemblance to the present Soviet state's claim to a monopoly on correct political doctrine.

Russian political culture was also firmly linked to autocracy, which legitimized the strong dependence of social classes on the state and the right of the state to intervene in a broad range of social affairs. The tsar's secret police maintained firm control over the independent secret societies that demonstrated fledgling opposition to the regime in the nineteenth century, and strict censorship was imposed. At the same time, a series of popular uprisings, which had been a feature of Russian history since the seventeenth century, reflected the alienation of the peasantry from the prevailing patterns of authority.

Russian patriotism, embodied in the idea of Moscow as the Third Rome, was also important. By the nineteenth century, tsarist control extended into central Asia (bordering on what is now Iran, Iraq, and Afghanistan) and to the Pacific coast in the north and east (see map on page 561). The empire included a mosaic of diverse ethnic groups: Russians were the dominant population group in the empire, and a significant proportion was also Slavic (e.g., Polish, Ukrainian, Belorussian). The official commitment to nationalism implied both Russian dominance and justification of expansionism in the national interest.

Another important element of traditional Russian culture was collectivism, reflected most clearly in the *mir,* "peasant commune," which regulated the most important aspects of the peasant's everyday life. *Mir* in Russian means both "world" and "peace," exemplifying the association in the peasant's mind between the security of the immediate social environment and the whole world. The state supported formation of the peasant commune in the eighteenth century in part because the *mir* facilitated collection of taxes from the peasantry. The *mir* periodically redistributed strips of land within the commune, depending on changes in family circumstances. This served as an obstacle to the improvement of agriculture, for the peasant family felt little inclination to make sacrifices for land with which it would soon part. The commune reinforced preindustrial values; it survived until Stalin's industrialization campaign in 1929.

International Pressures

Standing relatively unprotected between Europe and Asia, Russia had been subject to repeated intrusions and challenges for centuries. The Mongol invasion of 1237 led to about 250 years of subjugation. From the late 1400s, the principality of Moscow engaged in expansion by conquest. Land hunger and a desire for geopolitical security as well as for access to seaports and trade routes were important motives. By the seventeenth century, the Russian empire extended east to the Pacific coast in Siberia (see map on page 561). Russia's defeat in the Crimean War (1854–56) helped to convince tsarist officials that Russia's inferior military position could be rectified only if Russia were strengthed economically. Serfdom was holding back Russia's development, for it bound the peasants to a backward form of agrarian subsistence and allowed the nobility to maintain its old lethargic lifestyle. The state's desire to remain an international power compelled the regime to consider emancipation of the serfs, even if the nobility opposed the reform.

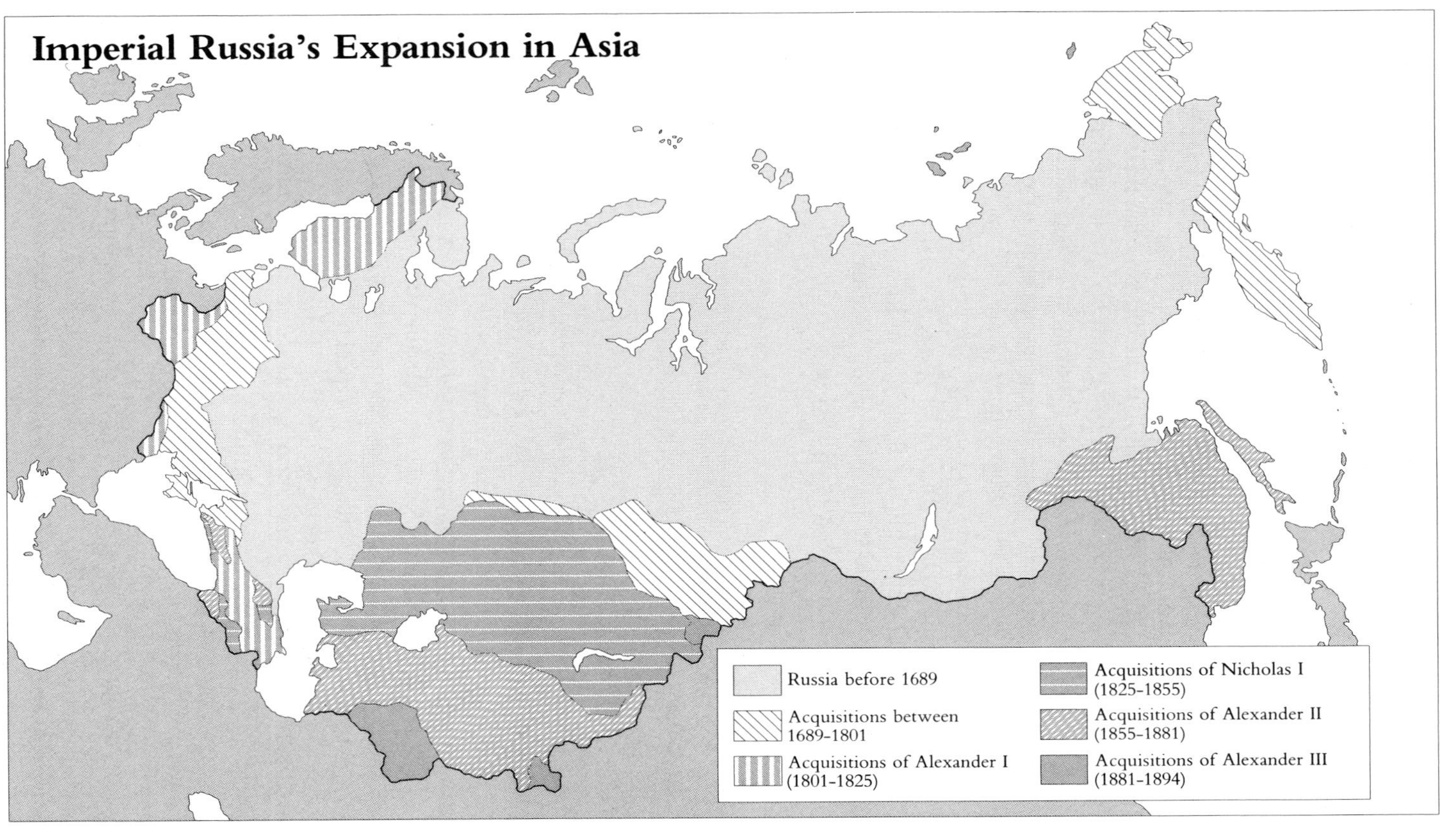
Imperial Russia's Expansion in Asia
Russia before 1689
Acquisitions between 1689-1801
Acquisitions of Alexander I (1801-1825)
Acquisitions of Nicholas I (1825-1855)
Acquisitions of Alexander II (1855-1881)
Acquisitions of Alexander III (1881-1894)

Despite the industrial takeoff in the late nineteenth century, the Russo-Japanese War of 1904–05 put strains on the system, as did the failed revolution of 1905. Russia also entered World War I ill-prepared, which caused widespread food shortages and rising prices both in the country and in the city. Further, the Russian army suffered repeated setbacks at the hands of the Germans, triggering disillusionment among the soldiers. Soldiers of peasant background rubbed shoulders with more politicized urban recruits. In this way, some of the peasants came into contact with the revolutionary ideas circulating among factory workers.

War was clearly a catalyst for revolution (as in later communist revolutions, such as in China and Yugoslavia). World War I bared the weak spots in the tsarist economic and political structures, and the incompetence of the regime in handling the war left a power vacuum into which revolutionary forces could enter. The bourgeois and liberal forces, which had dominated the evolution of Western European polities, proved too weak and too inflexible to fill the gap in Russia. To understand why a Marxist party should come out on top, we need to examine the revolutionary movement as it had developed in the nineteenth century.

The Revolutionary Movement

The Russian revolutionary movement of the nineteenth century originated among the nobility. Following their emancipation from state service in 1762, the gentry had the leisure to travel frequently to Europe, where they came into contact with the ideas of German idealism and the French Enlightenment. Sons and daughters of the gentry were educated in Russian universities and were exposed to new ideas through intellectual circles and journals. Some began to question their own place in society, giving rise to the classic "superfluous man" portrayed so frequently in Russian literature of the time. The superfluous man found no purpose or place for himself in society and often drifted into lethargy and stagnation. Other offspring of the nobility worked with the *zemstvos,* organs of local government, which, among other things, engaged in various social-welfare activities. Finally, some responded by commitment to revolutionary ideologies and organizations, seeking to alter the backward and oppressive Russian institutions. In time, these individuals came to form the basis of the Russian revolutionary intelligentsia, which was linked more by attitudes than by social background, although most had studied for at least some period of time at a university. Sons and daughters of peasants, artisans, clergy, or civil servants also joined the ranks, so that by the mid-1800s the intelligentsia, which was to form the core of the revolutionary movement in Russia, was made up of *raznochintsy*, individuals of diverse social class rank, united by their disillusionment with the injustices of the existing order.

From Populism to Marxism

Initially, the revolutionaries were not Marxists. In fact, Marx's and Engels' writings did not receive much attention (from revolutionaries or the tsarist censors) until the last few decades of the nineteenth century. The earliest uprising of the gentry, the Decembrist movement of 1825, was based in the military corps and involved demands for a constitutional monarchy. Indeed, throughout the nineteenth century and up to 1917, the "liberal" intelligentsia, including elements of the small bourgeois class and of the gentry, continued to voice such demands. This element, however, was too weak to set the tone of the revolutionary movement.

Most revolutionaries of the 1840s to 1880s were populists. Populism was a diverse movement, united by its faith in the peasantry and in the *mir* as a unique and indigenous basis for building socialism in Russia. Some elements in the populist movement felt that only conspiratorial action, assassination, and terrorism could topple the tsarist order before the communes were destroyed by the incipient capitalism that was gradually beginning to disrupt traditional relations in the countryside. Drastic action by a revolutionary elite might be required. Members of these revolutionary circles often exhibited a fanatical and total commitment to the cause, disavowing all other values. Contrary to their expectations, however, even the assassination of Tsar Alexander II in 1881 elicited neither a peasant rebellion nor a collapse of the old order. Rather, many peasants had a romantic attachment to the tsar as their protector. The new tsar, Alexander III, simply responded to the attack with increased repression.

Other populists took a different approach: They wanted to educate the peasants to realize the necessity of revolution. To do this, hundreds of students went to the villages to bring their revolutionary message directly to the peasantry during the "To the People" movement of the 1870s; however, the peasants were suspicious of these strangers, and the young intelligentsia became disillusioned with possibilities for a peasant-based revolution. Populist ideas, however, received continued expression in the Social Revolutionary Party, which was founded in 1900. As the intrusion of capital and Western values seemed increasingly inevitable, many revolutionaries turned to Marxism. Even Lenin's older brother had participated in a (failed) plot to assassinate the tsar and was sentenced to death. The young Lenin disavowed these methods and embraced Marxism.

The first Marxist organization, the Emancipation of Labor Group, was formed in 1883. Unlike the populists, the Marxists placed their hope for revolution in the urban proletariat. They had little faith in terrorism and assassination; rather, they sought to lead a full-scale revolution in the socioeconomic foundation of society. They saw removal of individual leaders as a superficial measure; as the assassination of Alexander II had demonstrated, the ruling class would simply install new leaders to replace those who had been eliminated. The Marxists wanted to turn ownership and control of the factories over to the workers as a whole. The working class, however, was a small minority in tsarist Russia; thus, a role for the revolutionary intelligentsia in the movement would also be assured for they would best understand the demands of revolutionary change. Marxism may have been attractive to the intelligentsia for other reasons as well. Marxism recognizes the inevitability and desirability of social change and industrialization; this ensures the necessity of science and education, endeavors appreciated by the intelligentsia. In embracing Marxism, the Russian intellectuals also expressed their ambivalence to Western culture: In many ways, the intelligentsia saw the West as more progressive and advanced than Russian society, with its backward and oppressive institutions, but in other ways, they felt repulsed by the inhumane factory conditions which Western capitalism had spawned. They had a certain hope for Russia's potential, for socialist revolution might allow Russia to become an example for Western Europe. If a workers' revolution was to occur in Russia, however, some alterations would have to be made in the interpretation of Marxism.

Leninism

Marxism did not seem to be directly and immediately applicable to Russia. The working class was small, and capitalism was only beginning to push out feudal relations in the countryside. Yet the intelligentsia was attracted to the theory. Some workers, introduced to Marxism by political activists, may have found the radical tenor in the party appealing. The Marxist party, the Russian Social Democratic Labor Party (RSDLP), formed in 1903, was soon riddled with conflict over the correct application of Marxism in Russia. The two major factions in the party, the Bolsheviks and the Mensheviks (meaning "majority" and "minority", respectively, in Russian), emerged with independent newspapers and largely separate organizations by 1917, despite repeated efforts at reunification. The most influential Marxist revolutionary by 1917 was Vladimir Ilich Lenin (born Ulianov), who was the leader of the Bolshevik organization, which was finally to take power. Lenin reinterpreted key elements of Marxist theory so that they better fit Russian reality.

First, why should one expect a workers' revolution in a backward country like Russia? Following the ideas of such theorists as Rosa Luxemburg, John A. Hobson, and Rudolf Hilferding, Lenin developed his famous theory of imperialism. He believed that the more advanced capitalist countries of Western Europe had been forced to invest capital in the more backward capitalist countries like Russia in order to assure continuing profit levels. These profits, extracted from imperialist ventures, could be used by the owners in the more advanced capitalist systems to buy off their own working classes through improved working conditions and wages. The Western European working classes, therefore, had lost some of their revolutionary fervor, and the social-democratic parties that represented them had become increasingly reformist, abandoning social revolution for simple amelioration of conditions. Meanwhile, backward capitalist countries like Russia became victims of imperialism. Factories were large and conditions oppressive. Because the indigenous Russian bourgeoisie was weak, it had not been able to push forward basic democratic reforms like genuine constitutionalism and freedom of political expression and organization. On the other hand, the bourgeoisie had also not been able to consolidate its power as effectively as its counterparts in Western Europe. Therefore, the apparatus of legitimation, that is, the mechanisms to bring the population to accept the existing order of things, had not been fully developed. Despite some legal reforms, there was little real amelioration in working conditions. Lenin concluded that Russia was the weakest link in the capitalist chain: The oppression was particularly severe, but control by the capitalist class was less firmly embedded in society. The bourgeoisie had to rely on the tsar's crude instruments of political repression to inhibit organization of the working class. Revolution could come more easily in Russia than in Western Europe, and once it did, according to Lenin, it would stimulate the German working class to follow the Russian example. Russia would experience the first revolution, but it would then spark further revolutions in Western Europe. Subsequently, the newly established proletarian governments in Western Europe could offer material assistance to their Russian comrades, who still would have to cope with a backward, largely agrarian economy.

Second, how and why should a workers' revolution occur in a country with such a small proletariat? Normally, according to Marxist theory, a bourgeois democratic revolution should precede a socialist workers' revolution. But because the indigenous Russian bourgeoisie was so weak, Lenin believed that the working class, with the help of the peasantry, would have to take on a greater role in toppling the tsarist government and in struggling for "bourgeois" rights. Once a bourgeois democratic revolution had occurred, then the working class must realize that its interests were no longer congruent with those of the capitalist class, which would want to take as much profit from the workers' hands as possible. At this point the working class must step forward and push the revolution to its next stage: dismantling private capitalist ownership patterns and replacing them by collective working-class control.

Russian Marxists disagreed about the actual timing of these two phases of the revolution. Some, like Leon Trotsky, felt that the two revolutions, the bourgeois democratic and the proletariat socialist, could and should be telescoped into one, producing a situation of permanent revolution. On the other hand, the Mensheviks generally took a more gradualist approach, believing that there must indeed be two distinct phases. Finally, Lenin seemed to stand somewhere between, impatient with and distrustful of the bourgeoisie, but also skeptical of Trotsky's permanent revolution idea. In practice, however, when 1917 came and the tsarist regime was toppled, Lenin saw that mass discontent made an almost immediate grasp for power feasible. He thus seemed to adopt, in practice, Trotsky's notion of telescoping the bourgeois and proletarian revolutions into virtually one phase, separated in time by only a few months. For Lenin, the revolutionary coalition must also include the peasantry, for they suffered both from the remnants of feudalism in the countryside, as well as from the incipient effects of capitalist intrusion into peasant markets.

The Revolutionary Party. On a more practical level, revolution required a revolutionary party. In 1902, Lenin laid the groundwork for Bolshevik party organization in his famous work, *What Is To Be Done?*, in which he amended traditional Marxist thinking with his idea that "the history of all countries shows that the working class, exclusively by its own efforts, is able to develop only trade union consciousness."[2] That is, without appropriate ideological leadership, the proletariat would not see the systemic source of its repression, namely, the whole ownership and control system of capitalism. Rather, workers might focus on the particular factory owner or seek simple material improvements in working conditions — shorter hours, better pay, improved safety conditions. Western European experience seemed to confirm Lenin's conviction that the working class needed a conscious vanguard to lead it to a proper revolutionary understanding. This vanguard would necessarily include many members of the intelligentsia, for they had the capability and opportunity to perceive the broader sources of exploitation more clearly than the worker, who, however revolutionary his sentiment might be, had only a limited view of the situation as a whole. Lenin's vanguard notion suggested that the party should be led by an elite group, the most conscious of the members, and that all party members must possess a superior political awareness. Thus, the party would not be an open, broad-based organization (as would the trade unions) but would be limited to those who had made an active commitment to the cause and who understood revolutionary dynamics. This pattern was to continue after the revolution and into Soviet rule: Substance, not procedure, was emphasized, and it became more important to hold the correct viewpoint than to resolve disputes through established democratic procedures. There was some disagreement between the two major factions in the party, the Mensheviks and the Bolsheviks, over how strict membership requirements should be for the party, but essentially both groups concurred in endorsing a vanguard concept.

Did introduction of the vanguard party concept represent a rejection of democratic principles? It certainly involved an abrogation of simple majority rule. The Canadian political theorist C.B. Macpherson explains the dilemma facing revolutionaries who wish to transform society democratically:

> What makes a period revolutionary is a more or less widespread belief that the existing system of power, the existing system of power relations between people, is somehow thwarting their humanity. . . . If you believe . . . that the very structure of society, the dominant power relations in it, have made people less than fully human, have warped them into inability to realize or even to see their full human potentiality, what are you to do? How can the debasing society be changed by those who have themselves been debased by it? . . . The debased people are, by definition, incapable of reforming themselves *en masse*.[3]

Lenin's solution was, of course, that the vanguard party would lead the people to realize their own true interests, interests they might not recognize themselves. How different this is from the liberal view, which defines people's interest as the people themselves see them! Macpherson poses the question, "Can a vanguard state properly be called a democratic state?" His answer underscores the ambiguity of the term *democracy:*

> If democracy is taken in its narrow sense as meaning simply a system of choosing and authorizing governments, then a vanguard state cannot be called democratic. A vanguard state may be a government *for* the people, but it is not government *by* the people, or even by the choice of the people.[4]

But in a broader sense, Macpherson points out, "Democracy has very generally been taken to mean something more than a system of government. Democracy in this broader sense has always contained an ideal of human equality, . . . such an equality as could only be fully realized in a society where no class was able to dominate or live at the expense of others."[5] In this sense, then, a vanguard party may be a legitimate instrument for achieving an otherwise unrealizable goal of democracy.

Repressive political conditions in Russia certainly required a tightly knit organization that generally had to work underground. As Lenin himself suggests in *What Is To Be Done?*:

> "Broad democracy" in party organization, amidst the gloom of autocracy and the domination of the gendarmes, is nothing more than a *useless and harmful toy*. . . . It is a harmful toy, because any attempt to practice the "broad principles of democracy" will simply facilitate the work of the police in making big raids; it will perpetuate the prevailing primitiveness, divert the thoughts of the practical workers from the serious and imperative task of training themselves to become professional revolutionists to that of drawing up detailed "paper" rules for election systems.[6]

To prevent tsarist agents from infiltrating the party and thus exposing party activists to arrest or exile, strict controls had to be maintained over intraparty organization. These repressive conditions were a major impetus for the development of the party's internal political procedure, the principle of "democratic centralism." Based on this principle, party cells at the base level did not have contact with one another but were linked through a hierarchical structure. In this way, if one cell were compromised, its members would not be able to betray their colleagues in other cells. The basic principle of democratic centralism, which guided the party's internal political structure, was freedom of discussion until a decision was taken; following that, strict discipline and unity were required in carrying out the action. Discussion initially took place in all party cells, with the views of lower bodies being transmitted through elected delegates to higher organs in the party hierarchy. Finally, the Central Committee or Party Congress made the decision, which was to be strictly adhered to by all party members.

Elections of party leaders were held within the same hierarchical structure. Elected delegates from party cells (which might be formed in factories, soldiers' contingents, or universities) represented the cell at the next highest party organ in the hierarchy. This organ (perhaps a district or city committee) likewise elected delegates to the next highest organ in the hierarchy, until finally the composition of the highest elective body, the Central Committee, was determined. Delegates were accountable to their constituencies, but once the Central Committee determined a certain path, the minority must submit to the majority. In this way, the party could act effectively in a highly precarious political environment.

Nonetheless, party organizations were repeatedly decimated by arrest. As Lenin stated in January 1903, "We do not know whether people are alive or not; we are compelled, simply compelled, to consider them almost nonexistent."[7] Lenin himself had been arrested in 1895 and exiled to Siberia for three years in 1897. At the time of the collapse of the tsarist government in February, 1917, he was carrying out his revolutionary activities from a base in Switzerland. He had to be secretly conveyed back into the country in the spring of 1917. Under these conditions, it is perhaps understandable that the party should take such extraordinary measures to protect the anonynmity of the revolutionary cells.

In his famous piece, *State and Revolution,* written in 1917 before the Bolshevik Revolution, Lenin presents his understanding of the relationship between democracy and socialism:

> Thus, in capitalist society we have a democracy that is curtailed, wretched, false; a democracy only for the rich, for the minority. The dictatorship of the proletariat, the period of transition to communism, will for the first time create democracy for the people, for the majority, along with the necessary suppression of the minority — the exploiters. Communism alone is capable of giving really complete democracy, and the more complete it is the more quickly will it become unnecessary and wither away of itself.[8]

Lenin cites the example of the Paris Commune (a popular revolutionary regime that ruled Paris for two months in 1871) to elucidate some of the characteristics of "democratic" proletarian rule: all privileges for officials will be abolished; representatives of the working people will be subject to immediate recall by the people; remuneration of all state officials will be at the level of workmen's wages. Finally, once class enemies had been brought under control, Lenin foresaw the "withering away" of the state (and thus the end of the need for democracy). The special apparatus of control and repression would be unnecessary; human freedom would be complete. The division between mental and manual labor would be overcome, and the principle of "from each according to his ability, to each according to his needs" would prevail. Clearly Lenin's vision for communist society was "for the people" and contained an ideal of human equality, as Macpherson suggests, even if it does not correspond to the Western concept of liberal democracy or to a narrower definition of rule "by the people." But could Lenin's vision become reality, or would it be undermined by the very means he proposed to realize it?

The Revolution and its Dilemmas

There were actually two revolutions in 1917: The first toppled the tsarist regime, and the second put the Bolsheviks in power. In February, the tsarist regime was overthrown, and the Provisional Government, a coalition of bourgeois and socialist forces (the Bolsheviks did not participate), took control. Soon "dual power" emerged: Alongside the provisional government, workers' and soldiers' soviets (councils) represented the working elements of the population more directly. The soviets maintained practical control over food distribution, maintenance of order, railroads, the army, and communications. Initially, the Mensheviks and Social Revolutionaries were more heavily represented in the soviets than the Bolsheviks, but by October the Bolsheviks were able to strengthen their position. The Provisional Government hesitated in addressing the major issues that had moved the masses to rebellion. Despite widespread disillusionment with the faltering war effort, the government was not prepared to withdraw (which would, in fact, have meant surrender to Germany), nor was the government willing to address the land issue at once. Rather, the leaders of the Provisional Government planned to wait until late in 1917, when the problem could be thoroughly investigatged and elections to the Constituent Assembly could be held, before making any major policy decision regarding redistribution of land. The elected Constituent Assembly, they felt, would be a more appropriate body to address this controversial question.

Meanwhile, soldiers were deserting and returning to their villages. Peasants were beginning to seize control of large landed estates. When Lenin arrived by train in Petrograd (previously St. Petersburg, now Leningrad) in April of 1917, he recognized the revolutionary potential of the situation. After heated debate, he persuaded his Bolshevik colleagues (with the exception of G.E. Zinoviev and L.B. Kamenev) that the time was ripe to grasp power. The Bolshevik slogan "Land, Bread, Peace" addressed the major issues troubling the population. On October 25, 1917 (November 7th by the new calendar adopted by the revolutionary regime in February, 1917), the revolutionary forces stormed the winter palace in Petrograd, overthrowing the Provisional Government and replacing it with a government of soviets headed by the Bolsheviks. Although power was secured quickly in the capital and in Moscow, four years of civil war would pass before the Bolsheviks were able to subdue major areas of the countryside.

The Bolsheviks gave immediate recognition to the peasants' demands for land. In November, 1917, they went ahead with the elections to the Constituent Assembly but, to their disappointment, won only 136 seats as compared to 237 for the Social Revolutionaries, who were better known and respected in the rural areas, even though they balked at immediate resolution of the land question. The Bolsheviks responded in quick order by disbanding the Assembly following a one-day meeting in January, 1918; they believed that the peasants were ill-informed about the actual land policies of the two parties and therefore were not able to make a choice in their true interests.

The reasons for the Bolsheviks' initial success are clear. The Provisional Government inadequately filled the vacuum left by the tsar; the Bolsheviks, but most especially Lenin, saw the people ripe for revolt and were prepared to act quickly, basing themselves in the workers' and soldiers' soviets. The Bolsheviks' program ("Land, Bread, Peace") expressed the sentiments of the population better than that of the Provisional Government or any of the other socialist parties. These factors probably did more together to ensure the Bolshevik victory than did the tight organizational structure of the party.

Problems of Rulership

Following the 1917 revolutions, a new government was formed under the leadership of the Bolshevik organization (renamed the Russian Communist Party [Bolsheviks] in 1918 and the Communist Party of the Soviet Union in 1952). On December 30, 1922, four constituent republics (the Russian, the Transcaucasian, the Ukrainian, and the Belorussian) formally joined to constitute the Union of Soviet Socialist Republics, henceforth referred to as the Soviet Union. Following 1922, additional constituent republics were added to the Union.

Once in power, the Bolsheviks were quick to learn that it is easier to criticize than to rule. They soon felt compelled to take extraordinary measures to assure the survival of the regime. The initial challenge was an extended civil war for control of the countryside and outlying regions. The Civil War (1918–21) had negative repercussions for the new Soviet state: Many of the most loyal and committed activists, especially from the working class, were killed, thus weakening even further the party's base in the population; the *Cheka,* the internal security arm of the regime, was strengthened to control harmful political tendencies; and the power of the elected local councils, the soviets, was greatly restricted in an effort to retain central control over the war effort.

The party faced other difficulties once it achieved power. Making good on its promise of "peace" meant virtual surrender to the Germans. After heated debate within the party leadership, the Soviet regime finally accepted the unfavorable terms of the Brest-Litovsk Treaty. As a result, Germany took, among other things, large sections of land in the Ukraine, the Baltic states, and Belorussia. Only the defeat of Germany by Russia's former allies, namely, the United States, Britain, and France, reversed some of these concessions. However, these countries were hardly pleased with internal developments in Russia. Not only did the revolution mean expropriation of foreign holdings and Russia's withdrawal from the war effort, it also represented the first successful challenge to the capitalist order. As a result, the former allies sent material aid and troops to oppose the new Bolshevik government in the civil war period. Notwithstanding some humanitarian (famine) aid offered in 1921–22, the Soviet Union did not benefit from Western assistance or investment. However, the most severe blow was the failure of the German workers' revolution in 1918. The entire premise of Lenin's strategy had been proven faulty: The struggling new Soviet state found no socialist revolution in Western Europe to aid it. The new leaders had to find ways to address Russia's economic backwardness without outside assistance. Furthermore, they found no previous models of socialist construction; Marx and Engels themselves had had little to say about the process of building a socialist society. The Bolshevik leaders were forced to undertake their vast, bold experiment with no real historical or theoretical precedents.

Controlling the Opposition

It is hard to overstate how precarious was the situation facing the fledgling Soviet government in the early 1920s. Its survival was by no means assured. The party had only a narrow base in the population, and the tenuousness of its power made the Bolshevik leaders increasingly intolerant of dissent. They first dismantled the Constituent Assembly, as noted above. Gradually, restrictions were placed on other socialist parties, until by 1921, they were effectively banned. Then came limits on intraparty democracy itself.

At the Tenth Party Congress, in March, 1921, a conflict over the demands of the so-called Workers' Opposition led to acceptance of the antifactionalism rule. The Workers' Opposition, under the leadership of the prominent Bolshevik figures A. Kollantai and A.G. Shliapnikov, demanded more autonomy for trade unions and a greater role for the unions in representing workers' interests in industrial management. Furthermore, the Workers' Opposition wanted Communist Party members to be bound by the decisions of higher trade union organs, rather than vice versa, which was the prevailing pattern. After extensive debate in 1920 and 1921, the ideas of the Workers' Opposition were firmly condemned by the party's Central Committee as a deviation from Marxism. Under Lenin's guidance, the trade unions were instructed to emphasize their educational role in bringing the workers to support party initiatives in the economy; they were given no independent role in economic administration, although they were intended to safeguard certain workers' rights in the factory. The resolution of the conflict reflected Lenin's belief that the workers needed no special protection since the party itself was acting in their interests.

More significant than the defeat of the opposition plank was the imposition of the antifactionalism rule. It forbade groups from meeting to develop platforms in advance of party meetings, on the grounds that this could lead to the growth of divisive factions, solidify lines of conflict in the party, and interfere with party discipline; theoretically, however, *individual* Communist Party members could still raise problems or make proposals at the party meeting itself, in line with the precepts of democratic centralism. The Central Committee was authorized to penalize members for factionalism, and penalties included expulsion from the Central Committee itself on a two-thirds vote of all members and alternates.

Adoption of the antifactionalism rule by the Tenth Party Congress followed shortly upon the Kronstadt Rebellion of March, 1921, an unsuccessful uprising of sailors at a naval base near Petrograd. The sailors demanded democratization of the soviets and criticized their domination by the Bolsheviks. The party leadership no doubt felt particularly vulnerable at this time. However, in the years following Lenin's death in 1924, the antifactionalism rule was applied even more rigidly, to control any form of opposition within the party. Aspiring leaders stigmatized their opponents for engaging in factionalism, but in so doing, they gradually undermined a basic premise of democratic centralism itself: that minority viewpoints should be permitted up to the point where a decision was taken. In the mid to late 1920s, as Josef Stalin consolidated his support in the party bureaucracy, he was able to defeat his opponents by charging them with factional activity. By 1929, open dissension within the party was almost eliminated. Major figures who might offer an alternative view, including Leon Trotsky, Nikolai Bukharin, Grigorii Zinoviev, and Lev Kamenev, had all been expelled from the highest party organs. Trotsky had been forced into exile. None of them had felt confident enough of Soviet power to appeal for mass support when they came under attack. Apparently each believed that the survival of Communist party rule was of greater importance than the preeminence of his individual viewpoint. In 1924, Trotsky himself expressed this view: "My party — right or wrong . . . I know one cannot be right against the party . . . for history has not created other ways for the realization of what is right."[9]

The Peasant Problem and Industrialization

The peasantry posed both economic and political problems for the Bolsheviks, as Lenin himself emphasized the importance of an alliance with the peasantry. Indeed, in 1917, recognition of the peasants' desire for control of land represented a political compromise for the Bolsheviks, whose long-term goal was a socialized economy. Once the Civil War was under way, economic demands led the Bolsheviks to introduce the policy of War Communism, which sought to ensure the supply of materials necessary for the war effort. In the industrial sphere, this involved direct state control of the larger productive facilities; in the agricultural sector, the peasants were allowed to maintain control over the land, but grain was forcibly requisitioned to supply the army and cities. This policy effectively negated many of the benefits the peasants had won in the revolution and caused increased tension between the rural population and the regime.

By 1921, the leadership recognized that concessions would be necessary if the alliance with the peasantry were to be maintained. The New Economic Policy (NEP), initiated at the Tenth Party Congress in March, 1921, created greater incentives for the peasantry by abolishing forced requisitioning of grain and replacing it with a tax in kind. Once the tax was paid, peasants could dispose of their surplus as they saw fit, by raising food for their own consumption or by selling it in the free market or to state agencies. In other sectors of the economy, private enterprise and trade were also revived; the state, however, retained control of large-scale industry.

In some regards the NEP represented backtracking from the policies of War Communism. First, it strengthened private property and a market economy, which contradicted the Bolsheviks' long-term goal of socialization of the economy. Second, it limited the state's ability to extract capital from the rural sector to fund rapid industrialization, which the Bolsheviks saw as necessary. The growth of industry would strengthen the Soviet state in dealing with external challenges. It would also be an important step in the construction of socialism, by developing a large working class, which would be the political base of socialist society. Industrialization, however, required capital (money to invest in building factories and machinery, and to pay wages). Where was this capital to come from? Foreign investors were unwilling to cooperate. The small industrial sector could hardly generate enough capital for its own rapid expansion. This left the agricultural sector. If adequate grain could be produced for export, then the industrialization drive could be funded. Further, if the regime were able extract foodstuffs from the countryside at low prices, the cost of maintaining the industrial work force would be reduced. Mandatory requisitioning of grain was the easiest way to achieve these ends, but by 1921, the leadership concluded that the political costs of continuing the War Communism policy were too high. They feared that the peasants' resentment of the forced requisitioning of grain would continue to grow and ultimately undermine the very goals the regime was trying to pursue.

The New Economic Policy, then, was a political compromise. The peasantry was allowed a greater measure of independence in production, so long as taxes were paid. The government would then buy additional grain at established prices. At the same time, a relatively free market was allowed to reign in the countryside, giving rise to the ignominious NEP-men who engaged in speculation to make a profit. By the mid-1920s, the economy had been restored to its prewar level of production and doubts were surfacing in the party over whether the NEP should be altered. Some elements were impatient with the slow pace of industrialization; others were concerned that the present course might allow the growth of a new rural capitalist class as the *kulaks,* "rich peasants," were allowed to accumulate wealth. A major debate developed in the party over economic policy.

In the mid-1920s, the strongest supporter of the NEP was Nikolai Bukharin, who seemed at the time to be expressing the views of Stalin as well. Bukharin argued that the peasants would lose the incentive to work towards making their farms more productive if further restrictions were placed on them:

> The prosperous upper-stratum of the peasantry and the middle peasant who also aspires to become prosperous are at present afraid to accumulate. There is a situation where the peasant is afraid to install an iron roof for fear of being declared a *kulak;* if he buys a machine, then he does it in such a way that the Communists will not notice. Higher technique becomes conspiratorial.

He concluded, "We must say to the whole peasantry, to all its strata: enrich yourselves, accumulate, develop your economy."[10] Bukharin believed that if allowed to flourish, the peasantry would come to accept the new socialist order, and that present agrarian policy could serve as an adequate framework for industrialization.

Another group of Bolsheviks, including first Trotsky, and then Zinoviev and Kamenev, accepted the basic framework of the NEP but felt that too many concessions had been made to the peasantry. Rapid industrialization was of paramount importance, requiring some alterations in present policy. Expressing the sentiment of this so-called Left opposition in the party, Trotsky's ally, E.A. Preobrazhensky, put forth his theory of primitive socialist accumulation. In short, it was necessary to pursue policies that could more effectively extract from the non-socialized agricultural sector a surplus, which could then be used to finance industrialization. To achieve this, prices for agricultural commodities should be lowered, taxes on the peasantry should be increased, and the government should have a monopoly of banking and foreign trade. Trotsky believed that poor peasants should, however, be helped and given incentives to join rural cooperatives. In this way, the socialist sector would be strengthened as the poor peasants benefited from government assistance. These measures would also inhibit the growth of an exploitive capitalist class in the countryside. Meanwhile, rich peasants should be taxed more heavily. In any case, unless industry was developed more quickly, the peasantry would lose its incentive to work, since there would be few goods for the peasants to purchase with their income.

By late 1924, Trotsky was being sharply criticized by other party leaders: He was vilified for lack of faith in the peasantry, for his earlier concept of permanent revolution, and for his failure to believe in the possibilities of building socialism in one country. These were mere pretexts to undermine Trotsky's standing in the party. Although Kamenev and Zinoviev were to voice criticisms of NEP similar to Trotsky's, their strong dislike for him led them to demand his expulsion from the party. At this time, however, Stalin opposed this extreme measure. Instead, Trotsky was removed as head of the army and condemned by the Central Committee in January, 1925. Soon Zinoviev found his base of power in the party threatened by Stalin's growing ambitions; in 1926, he and Kamenev joined other dissident elements to form a united opposition to Stalin's growing power, but it was already too late. In August of 1927, Stalin's support was strong enough to expel Trotsky and Zinoviev from the Central Committee. By November 14, they were expelled from the party, and in January, 1928, Trotsky was exiled from the Soviet Union. In 1940, he was assassinated in Mexico (presumably by Stalinist agents).

Bukharin cooperated with Stalin in removing the so-called Left opposition (Trotsky, Zinoviev, Kamenev) and, by so doing, helped legitimize methods that would later lead to his own removal from the leadership. In 1928, the country faced a major grain procurement crisis: The peasants refused to sell their grain to the government. This seemed to trigger Stalin's reversal in position. He began to emphasize the need for a change that would speed industrialization and more effectively mobilize the agricultural surplus to that end. In late 1929, a policy of rapid collectivization of agriculture was instituted. Though the process was allegedly voluntary, the peasants were actually forced to give up their land, tools, and livestock, and join government-established collectives or state farms. In November, 1929, Bukharin, the most prominent figure in the so-called Right opposition, was expelled from the Politburo, by then the top policy-making body in the party.

By 1929, virtually all internal opposition within the party had been eliminated and Stalin's power was secure. Stalin's rivals did not realize soon enough that Lenin's emphasis on party discipline could be twisted to suppress all debate in the party. Furthermore, Stalin's rivals had been reluctant to appeal to the broad masses of the population for support, fearing that this might mobilize popular sentiment against Communist Party rule itself. Although the Left opposition had held some demonstrations in factories in 1926, they later admitted that, in doing so, they had violated party discipline. It seems most Bolshevik leaders accepted Trotsky's conviction of "my party — right or wrong."

Leadership Succession and Bureaucratization

The struggles over economic policy were closely linked to the struggle for the top leadership position. Lenin's premature death in 1924 (at the age of fifty-four) resulted in competition at the top, which served to reinforce the difficulties facing the regime in consolidating its rule.

In 1919, the party formed several executive bodies, which were to administer party policy between Central Committee meetings. One of these was the Politburo, which gradually emerged as the leading policy-making organ of the party. Likewise in 1919 the party Secretariat was formed; it was initially intended to fulfill largely secretarial functions, that is, keeping records and doing paperwork for the party. A third body, the Orgburo, was formed to handle organizational matters. In 1922, Stalin, who was the only member of the Politburo to also sit on the Orgburo, was chosen as head of the Secretariat. Over time, the Secretariat took on much greater importance than was orginally anticipated; it was a key factor in Stalin's personal consolidation of power and eventually headed the party's extensive administrative bureaucracy.[11]

The Secretariat was staffed with full-time, paid party workers, who along with other full-time paid party workers came to be known as the *apparatchiki*. They were often in a better position to command influence than the elected delegates to party committees who might hold jobs elsewhere. The *apparatchiki* had greater access to information and more time to devote to party work. At each level in the party organization (in larger cells or primary party organizations, city levels, district levels, etc.), party secretaries were elected to fulfill functions similar to those of the Secretariat at the central level. These individuals became the most powerful party figures at the local and regional levels.

As head of the Secretariat, Stalin was able to wield increasing influence over appointments at lower levels in the party. Because democratic centralist tenets mandated strict party discipline in supporting decisions made by the Central Committee, it was necessary to maintain some central overview of policies being pursued by subordinate party committees. If party leaders at lower levels in the hierarchy were deviating from established central policy, measures had to be taken to reexert party discipline by transferring local officials to other work or replacing them. Despite formal election procedures, the party center (primarily through the Secretariat) began to direct the selection of candidates for party office, and during the 1920s, election procedures became more and more formalistic. A pattern developed that Western Sovietologists have subsequently dubbed a "circular flow of power": The central party Secretariat was able to influence election of local party officials and delegates from lower party organs, ultimately playing a large role in determining the composition of the Central Committee itself; the Central Committee, whose members were beholden to the Secretariat for their positions, in turn lent support to the Secretariat and its head (Stalin); and the Secretariat in turn continued to strengthen its control over selection of officials at lower party levels. It was a self-perpetuating system, a type of massive political machine that assured the head of the Secretariat support throughout the party structure. As early as 1923, over 50 percent of the delegates to the party Congress were *apparatchiki,* full-time party officials. By 1924, at the Thirteenth Party Congress, this figure had risen to 65.3 percent. Critics within the party claimed that the apparatus of the Secretariat was gaining control over the election procedures. At the same time, debate within the party over economic policy provided a pretext for Stalin's hard line against any remaining political challengers. By 1929, the Central Committee was packed with individuals who were beneficiaries of Stalin's goodwill. The lack of emphasis on procedural guarantees for democratic decision making (such as an independent judiciary, rights for organized opposition, separation of powers, limits on the tenure of top leaders) was taking its toll.

The Transition to Stalinism

The year 1929 was a turning point in Soviet history. The initial goals of the revolution were in danger: the worker-peasant alliance was weak; the soviets were powerless; intra-party debate was greatly restricted; and a bureaucratic apparatus was growing in the party. But in 1929 itself, Stalin introduced radical changes which further undermined socialist democracy and popular control. Stalin embarked upon a Third Revolution (the first two being the revolutions of 1917), allegedly to remove class enemies but, in practice, directed in an arbitrary manner even against loyal Bolsheviks. While Stalin justified the policies of the 1930s as necessary to advance socialism, their effect was to further compromise many of the initial revolutionary goals, such as social equality, power to the soviets, creative fulfillment of the individual, and "withering away" of the state. Instead, Stalin set the course for rapid industrialization and the aggrandizement of his own personal power. While the industrialization campaign may have seemed necessary to provide the economic foundation for socialism, the methods used to achieve economic advances made realization of the other goals more difficult. Personal dictatorship, arbitrary arrests and political executions, forced collectivization of agriculture, and a moribund Communist Party organization were hallmarks of the Stalinist period. Soviet society in the 1930s was hardly congruent with the image of socialist society found in the writings of Marx and Engels. What could explain this radical turn of events which seemed so at odds with the purposes of the 1917 revolution?

Notes

1. M.E. Falkus, *The Industrialization of Russia, 1700–1914* (London: Macmillan, 1972) pp. 72, 83.
2. V.I. Lenin, *What Is To Be Done?* (New York: International Publishers, 1929), pp. 32–33.
3. C.B. Macpherson, *The Real World of Democracy* (New York: Oxford University Press, 1972), pp. 18–19.
4. Macpherson, *Real World,* p. 20.
5. Macpherson, *Real World,* p. 22.
6. Lenin, *What Is To Be Done?*, p. 130.
7. V.I. Lenin, quoted in Marcel Liebman, *Leninism under Lenin* (London: Merlin Press, 1975), p. 28.
8. V.I. Lenin, "State and Revolution," in *Essential Works of Marxism,* ed. Arthur P. Mendel (New York: Bantam Books, 1961), p. 172.
9. Leon Trotsky, quoted in Leonard Schapiro, *Communist Party of the Soviet Union,* 2d ed. (New York: Vintage Books, 1971), p. 288.
10. N.I. Bukharin, quoted in Stephen F. Cohen, *Bukharin and the Bolshevik Revolution: A Political Biography, 1888–1928* (New York: Vintage Books, 1975), pp. 176–77.
11. This and the discussion that follows draw heavily on the analysis in Jerry Hough and Merle Fainsod, *How the Soviet Union Is Governed* (Cambridge: Harvard University Press, 1979), pp. 124–33.

27

The Rise and Fall of Stalinism

The Stalinist period subjected Soviet society to major political, economic, and social upheavals that betrayed many of the initial Bolshevik goals. In some ways Stalin's Third Revolution also restored some dominant themes of the tsarist period: personal dictatorship, a strong state structure, and appeals to Russian nationalism. From 1929 to 1953, one man, Josef Stalin, dominated the Soviet Union; by 1953 every semblance of Soviet democracy had been destroyed. Although the groundwork for Stalinism was laid in an earlier time, these developments were not inevitable: Other outcomes were both conceivable and possible.

Following Stalin's death in 1953, the Soviet leadership faced the problem of dealing with his legacy. Should the terror, violent purges, and supremacy of the secret police continue? Should power again be placed in the hands of one individual? Should existing economic policies be maintained? The new leaders sought to alter some features of Stalin's rule, while retaining others. Stalin's immediate successor, Nikita Khrushchev, even attempted to revive some of Lenin's original ideals. Over time, however, the post-Stalinist leadership gradually put into place a conservative bureaucratic structure, which responded cautiously to new situations. This process of de-Stalinization was to be the next major transition in Soviet politics. It ushered in contemporary structures of power, which now face major challenges.

Stalinism and Revolution From Above

The Basic Features

The Third Revolution was not the product of a popular initiative from below, but resulted from decisions by Stalin and his political deputies at the top. It was, then, a revolution from above, imposed on an often resistant population. All sectors of Soviet society felt the effects of Stalin's rise to power. But from 1929 to 1934, the most dramatic changes were economic, and they had the most impact in the countryside. The decision to pursue the forced collectivization of agriculture brought immediate results. Near the end of 1928, only an estimated 195,000 peasant families were members of collective or state farms. By June, 1929, this number had increased some fivefold and, by the beginning of March, 1930, was over 14 million. (See Table 27.1.) This was hardly due to a spontaneous mass movement, as the Central Committee claimed in November 1929, but resulted from a process of coercion and intimidation, enforced by arrests and deportations (to Siberia and the Far East). Stalin justified the policy as necessary to eliminate the *kulaks,* "rich peasants," a group that allegedly was threatening to become an entrenched and exploitative class in the countryside. *Kulak* was an ambiguous term in itself, since these peasants were not that distinct from their less fortunate neighbors. Further, the *kulaks* were not the only targets of the collectivization campaign; less affluent peasants (the so-called middle and poor peasants) were also forced to give up control of their land and livestock to join the collective and state farms. To resist was to risk being labeled a *kulak* or class enemy oneself, subject to the same reprisals of arrest or deportation. Official

Table 27.1 Collectivization

	1930	1931	1932	1933	1934	1935	1936
Percentage of peasant households collectivized	23.6	52.7	61.5	64.4	71.4	83.2	89.6
Percentages of crop area collectivized	33.6	67.8	77.6	83.1	87.4	94.1	—

SOURCE *Sotsialisticheskoe stroitel'stvo SSSR* (1936), p. 278. State farm area and households included.

Stalinist dogma justified the campaign with revolutionary rhetoric: Far from being eliminated, class conflict was intensifying, and this required drastic action from the party.

Historical evidence indicates that social inequality in the countryside was hardly as extreme as Stalin implied. The historian Moshe Lewin estimates that in the 1920s, most peasants classified by the regime as *kulaks* had only modest resources, perhaps three or four cows and one paid worker. Some engaged in occasional speculation by holding grain to sell at a propitious moment, but peasants of this type were a small minority — 4 percent of peasant households, according to various estimates.[1] The majority of the peasantry generally did not hire laborers regularly or hire out their own labor. These middle peasants (a broad and vaguely defined category) were more important in terms of grain production. Along with the poor peasants (those who often had to hire out their own labor), they also suffered severe repercussions from the Stalinist collectivization campaign. By July, 1938, over 90 percent of the peasantry was brought into the sphere of the collective and state farms.

Industry was also affected by Stalinization. The state took over almost all industrial operations and introduced central economic planning in the form of five-year economic plans, which have guided Soviet economic production since. The First Five-Year Plan (1929–33) set out unrealistic production targets for both agriculture and industry. The result was neglect of low-priority sectors, such as agriculture and consumer goods production, and emphasis on heavy industry, including machine building, hydroelectric dams, and steel mills. Often, actual production bore little relation to plan indicators, so that the plan itself was little more than a spur to achieve the highest output possible. "Shock methods" were intense campaigns to increase output in key sectors. The Stakhanovite movement was an effort to increase labor productivity by emulating the miner, Aleksei Stakhanov, who exceeded his work norm by fourteen times; during the Stakhanovite movement model workers who produced the most in the shortest time received state honors. These campaigns did succeed in boosting productivity and output. The result was a very rapid increase in industrial output, estimated by A. Gerschenkron at around 14 to 16 percent annually in the period from 1928 to 1938.[2] In this regard, the Stalinist economic strategy had positive payoffs in moving the Soviet Union quickly towards becoming a highly industrialized society. Industrial production lacked balance, however, and was often of mediocre quality; further, benefits to the working class were limited. Many had, indeed, experienced a sort of upward social mobility as they were able to move from subsistence agriculture to steady industrial jobs in urban areas, but the supply of consumer goods increased little, housing was short, and wage levels low. The benefits of socialist construction would have to wait until the economic foundation was stronger.

The political sphere was also revolutionized in the 1930s. In the early 1930s, those most affected by Stalinization were the peasants. Once collectivization had been essentially achieved in the mid-1930s, Stalin turned his attention to other sectors of the population as well. The party, as a viable political institution, was decimated. Open opposition was impossible and the secret police, answerable to Stalin himself through the Minister of Internal Affairs, replaced the party as the most powerful institution in Soviet society. Stalin engineered competition and duplication of duties between various party and state institutions in order to make them all virtually ineffective. No party congress was convened between March, 1939, and October, 1952.

A series of purges (in Russian, *chistka,* "cleansing") swept all levels of society in the mid to late 1930s. They hit central and provincial party officials, military officers, and intellectuals (writers, academics, engineers) with particular impact. All of the individuals mentioned by Lenin as possible successors, with the exception of Stalin himself, were targeted. Nikita Khrushchev, a beneficiary of the purges, notes in his memoirs that Stalin's closest advisors were uncertain of their fate when called to a meeting with him. Seventy percent of Central Committee members died during the purges, as did many high-ranking military officers. It was often unclear why an individual was victimized. Charges of treason, for example, were often clearly trumped up, and the victim might finally confess only under psychological pressure, torture, or threats against family.

Overall, an estimated 5 percent of the Soviet population was arrested at one point or another. Some of the victims were executed; others were condemned to labor camps or prisons. Some were exiled to Siberia, forced to relocate, denied access to education, or removed from their posts. Because the purges seemed to be arbitrary, reflecting Stalin's paranoia or perverse political reasoning, they can best be described as terror. Presumably, the purges were a means of controlling opposition and maintaining the viability of the political system in the face of unprecedented societal upheavals.

The beneficiaries of the purges were those who experienced upward social mobility by filling the spots vacated by the victims. A whole new generation came into the top party posts, changing the complexion of the party elite. These were the very individuals who would fill the major leadership positions after Stalin's death. All were implicated in the purges in some way, even if only by their silence and compliance to Stalin's wishes. At lower levels in the party as well, thousands of sons (and some daughters) of peasants and workers replaced former party officials. The new *apparatchiki* were beholden to Stalin for their positions; this helped assure their political loyalty. The revolutionary leaders who had guided the party through 1917 and the difficult years that followed were replaced by leaders of a different social class, no longer from the intelligentsia but from working-class and peasant origins. Individuals from these groups also rose to respectable positions as engineers, managers, administrators, and the like. Vera Dunham calls this group the Soviet middle class and believes that these people were the real support for the Stalinist system as it emerged after World War II.[3]

Soviet culture also changed. In the 1920s, experimentation in art, literature, education, and family life had been widespread. In the 1930s, there was a return to traditional values. New laws reinforced the nuclear family, making divorce more difficult and abortion illegal. Stalin appealed to Russian patriotism; this was even more marked in the 1940s when World War II became known as the Great Patriotic War, evoking images of Russian nationalism, rather than socialist internationalism. Education emphasized technical skills, and wage differentiation increased. While the rhetoric was revolutionary, the style of politics harkened back to the days of the tsar. There was to be no withering away of the state in the foreseeable future; rather, the state must be strengthened to further socialist construction. As in tsarist times, social classes were made dependent on state power and strong central control was glorified. Economic development was state-led, and the figure of Stalin dominated the political scene. Although the Stalinist state preached atheism, it saw itself, like the tsarist state, as the guardian of correct dogma.

By 1938, the "revolutions from above" were over and were supplanted by what Seweryn Bialer calls "mature Stalinism." During World War II, the main concern was national self-defense, which inspired an appeal to traditional patriotic sentiments. From 1945 to 1953, many features of the Stalinism of the 1930s remained intact; the reliance on terror, party purges, the weakness of the party, and the lack of clear jurisdictions among political institutions. Many veterans of World War II who had spent time in German prison camps or who were deemed to have had too much exposure to Western European life were imprisoned on their return to the Soviet Union, out of fear that they might be conduits for subversive foreign ideas. In the late 1940s and early 1950s, an "anticosmopolitan" campaign victimized Soviet Jews (many were arrested, some were shot), stigmatizing them as disloyal to the Soviet Union. Nonetheless, major social transformations, such as collectivization, did not occur at this time; rather, as Bialer writes, "the key goal of the regime was the reproduction of the existing relations."[4] Not until after Stalin's death in 1953 were patterns of governance questioned.

Why Stalinism?

It is important to explore carefully the origins of Stalinism so as not to apply unwarranted conclusions to other contexts in which communist parties take power. Why did the Soviet system take such a radical turn in the late 1920s? What were the origins of Stalinism? How was the agricultural collectivization campaign related to the terroristic purges of the mid to late 1930s? Does a Leninist revolution necessarily result in Stalinist-type terror? We will attempt to find the answers to these questions by examining the origins of Stalinism.

Economic Backwardness. One group of scholars sees the roots of Stalinism in the attempt to bring socialism to an economically backward country: Economic necessity demanded the brutal collectivization of agriculture, and this in turn engendered the need for Stalin to find scapegoats to divert attention from the debacle. James R. Millar, a critic of this view, which he calls "The Standard Story," summarizes the argument as follows:

> For the purposes of military defense against a possible renewed intervention by the West and for the purposes of establishing socialism in the Soviet Union, it was necessary for the economy to industrialize and modernize rapidly. The means proposed [by Preobrazhensky] to do it — that is, taxing in one form or another the 80 to 85 percent of the population who were peasants — was said to be not feasible, for the peasantry would withdraw from the market and, doing so, would sabotage the possibility of rapid industrialization. . . . Stalin then is said to have thought of something Preobrazhensky had not — coercion. He thought of forcing the peasants into the collective farm and thereby depriving them of discretion over the level of sowings and over the share of marketing. The state was therefore able to ensure rapid industrialization at the expense of the peasantry.[5]

In other words, collectivization was the only effective means of assuring that enough surplus could be squeezed from the agricultural sector to fund the industrialization drive. Once the rural economy was brought under state control, grain and other produce could be extracted easily and cheaply. Presumably, mechanization would proceed more quickly and the benefits of scale would also improve productivity. The state could mobilize labor more effectively and would gain increased political control over the work force as an added benefit. According to this theory, the political purges of the mid to late 1930s were required to divert attention from the real problem (a disastrous and unpopular agrarian policy) to imagined traitors; at the same time, fear would restrain open opposition.

Despite the strength of this argument, one must question whether forcible collectivization of agriculture was the only way to extract enough surplus from the countryside to support industrialization. This is far from self-evident. Many leading Bolsheviks themselves (including both the Right and Left oppositions) *rejected* Stalin's coercive measures and proposed alternatives, even if by 1929 they could no longer do so publicly. Both Bukharin and Preobrazhensky supported a continuance of the New Economic Policy, but they emphasized different goals. Bukharin proposed continued concessions to the peasantry, which would involve a slower pace of industrialization and some greater stratification of income in the countryside; with some controls, however, this need not have implied the emergence of a new rural bourgeois class. As we have seen, the *kulaks,* while relatively well-off compared to some of their neighbors, were hardly wealthy capitalists. Preobrazhensky proposed turning the terms of trade against the peasant, which might have been a feasible method to allow the state to buy agricultural produce at low cost if prices had been lowered on *all* agricultural goods. As it happened, prices for grain were kept low relative to livestock prices, and the peasants withheld their grain to feed the livestock. (In retrospect, the Bolsheviks were not likely to be shrewd in managing market prices, given their training and antimarket inclinations.) The fact that intelligent leaders in Stalin's time offered these proposals indicates that there were realistic alternatives to forced collectivization. Unfortunately, we cannot replay history to test these ideas.

Stalin's agrarian policy was hardly a booming success. It had immense economic, as well as human, costs. Many peasants resisted turning their livestock over to the collective and state farms; they slaughtered them instead, which caused severe and long-lasting damage to Soviet agriculture. In the early 1930s, famine ravished the countryside, especially in the Ukraine and Northern Caucasus region, resulting in a loss of lives (and also of labor power) estimated in the millions. The famine was caused in large part by the disorganization that ensued from the rapid collectivization campaign and from state efforts to extract excessive amounts of grain. Apparently in the 1930s, the state was able to obtain more grain from the countryside to sell abroad than it had in the 1920s. (See Table 27.2 and 27.3.) However, it is not clear that production increased overall; some of this grain was available precisely because the

Table 27.2 State Grain Procurements

(MILLIONS OF TONS)					
1928	1929	1930	1931	1932	1933
10.8	16.1	22.1	22.8	18.5	22.6

SOURCE Malafeev, *Istoriia tsenoobrazovaniia v SSSR* (Moscow, 1964), pp. 175, 177.

Table 27.3 Grain Exports

(MILLIONS OF TONS)					
1927–28	1929	1930	1931	1932	1933
.029	0.18	4.76	5.06	1.73	1.69

SOURCE Soviet trade returns.

livestock slaughtered by the defiant peasantry no longer required it as feed. Millar argues that the agricultural sector did *not* make a significant contribution to industrialization from 1928 to 1932; rather, resources flowed from the industrial sector to agriculture, since peasants could charge high prices for goods produced on private plots and the state needed to provide tractors to replace livestock.[6] If the agricultural sector did not, in fact, fund the industrialization drive, what did? In part, the state was more effective at mobilizing labor, especially integrating women into the work force and shifting labor from the countryside to the city.

Had the state been more adept at using positive incentives (market or otherwise) to encourage the production and sale of the commodities it required, perhaps industrialization could have been spurred without the drastic economic and human costs of the collectivization campaign. The pace of industrialization might have been slower, but the distance between the regime and the agrarian population might have been smaller. Then, in turn, the dramatic political repression of the mid to late 1930s might not have seemed necessary to bolster the regime's stability. Undoubtedly economic backwardness produced strains for the leadership, particularly in the face of international isolation, but it did not *mandate* the extreme measures embraced by Stalin in both the economic and the political spheres.

Leninism and Stalinism. A second group of scholars puts forth a controversial thesis that emphasizes the continuity between Leninism and Stalinism, implying that any government based on Leninism is bound to be one of violence and excess. This theory focuses on the vanguard party concept and the centralized party structure. Once the party leaders perceived themselves as the vessels of "correct" theory, it was easy to defend the elimination of those who held "false," or "counterrevolutionary," viewpoints and to justify control in molding consciousness. Furthermore, according to this view, the centralized party structure could suppress minority viewpoints by demanding adherence to party decisions. The antifactionalism principle and demands for party discipline enabled Stalin to cement his own position at the head of a powerful bureaucratic hierarchy.

Lenin himself had frequently used harsh methods to deal with his opponents, and during the Civil War period, the party oppressed even socialist critics of the regime. One commentator emphasizes the opportunism of Lenin:

> Lenin was thus emphatic in his view that the end justifies any means, and that the means can find no other justification than that it serves the end. And the end, for him, was never constituted by good intentions; it could only be good results. It is not the motive behind the use of means, but success in reaching the objective that justifies the application of any means. . . . But, if success depends on ruthlessness and unscrupulousness, the Leninist must not be squeamish.[7]

In short, Lenin was dogmatic in his goals but pragmatic in his methods, tolerating opposition when it could not yet be crushed but not hesitating a moment when the means became available. This view of Leninism would be fully compatible with Stalin's own brutality in realizing his objectives.

In other ways, the direct link between Stalinism and Leninism is questionable. Stalin may have made use of certain Leninist precepts and ideas to justify his policies, but Lenin's doctrine was hardly congruent with Stalin's policy of forced collectivization of agriculture. Lenin had supported the New Economic Policy and had always emphasized an *alliance* with the peasantry. Bukharin's reasoned defense of the NEP was firmly rooted in the Leninist commitment to the peasant-worker alliance. Despite some resemblance to the economic policy of the Left opposition (i.e., in favoring more rapid industrialization and greater controls on the *kulaks*), Stalin's forced collectivization policy was far more coercive than the system of incentives, taxes, and price policy advocated by Trotsky and Preobrazhensky. Mainstream Bolshevik thought, therefore, did not necessarily lead to the economic strategy embraced by Stalin in 1929.

The measures taken against party opponents under Lenin's leadership were also less radical than Stalin's purges and executions; likewise, Lenin was not always able to impose his will on the party. When Kamenev and Zinoviev broke party discipline by making public their disagreement with the Bolsheviks' decision to grasp state power in 1917, Lenin *did* advocate their expulsion from the top party organs (although certainly not their execution, as Stalin might have done for a similar violation in the 1930s), but the Central Committee did not concur. When the Workers' Opposition, which demanded a greater role for trade unions, was censured in 1921, its two most prominent leaders, Aleksandra Kollantai and Aleksandr Shliapnikov, were allowed to remain in the Central Committee. Thus, Lenin's tolerance for dissent was far greater than Stalin's in the 1930s.

It is, of course, impossible to know what Lenin would have done had he lived longer, but there are ample indications that Lenin saw extreme methods as justified only under the most extreme conditions. Stalin certainly saw conditions in the 1930s as extreme enough to justify his excesses, but was the Soviet regime *in fact* as vulnerable then as it had been during the Civil War period and in the early 1920s? The answer to this question is almost certainly no. In the years following the revolution, an actual civil war gripped the country, foreign and domestic opposition threatened to topple the government, and the country was in economic shambles. By the time of Stalin's Third Revolution in 1929, Communist Party rule was secure, prewar levels of economic production had been regained, and the Soviet Union was not under military attack. Although Communist Party rule was much more precarious in Lenin's time, he did not resort to Stalinist-type terror. Although some political executions did occur, the victims were generally real opponents of Bolshevik power rather than imagined enemies, and the scale did not approach that of the Stalinist purges.

History has shown that other parties based on Lenin's philosophy have applied his doctrine in diverse ways. Tito's brand of Leninism, developed in the 1950s in Yugoslavia, eschewed collectivization and provided the foundation for market socialism and workers' self-management. In China, Mao's version of Leninism relied primarily on the peasantry rather than the working class for political support and engendered a dramatic antibureaucratic campaign during the Cultural Revolution in the late 1960s. Some Western scholars have drawn parallels between Mao's Cultural Revolution and Stalin's purges, as both were instruments to enforce political conformity. However, the Cultural Revolution relied primarily on reeducation and "thought reform" to achieve conformity; violence was used less extensively than during Stalin's purges. Mao also mobilized mass support for his attack on the entrenched bureaucracy, whereas Stalin utilized an elite secret police to carry out attacks on society at large. Leninism, then, has no single heir; its interpretation and application vary depending on unique cultural, economic, and international pressures confronting the leadership of a particular country. For example, in both Yugoslavia and China, the Communist Party was much more firmly rooted in the peasant population when it took power than it was in Russia. Neither country suffered international isolation upon taking power; the Soviet Union provided aid in the early years. Finally, both Tito and Mao lived to see their revolutions consolidated; in the Soviet Union, Lenin's early death produced a power struggle in the party before the party's power was secure. To draw a direct linkage between Leninism and Stalinism overlooks the particular circumstances and pressures that allowed Stalin to emphasize only certain elements of Leninist thought, at the expense of some of the more participatory, democratic strains.

Cultural Continuity. A third theory explaining the rise of Stalinism points to its cultural roots. Many elements of Stalinism are reminiscent of traditional Russian patterns of rulership. The previous theory links Stalinism to revolutionary Leninism; the cultural explanation emphasizes the continuity from tsarism to Stalinism. The cultural theory asks, for example, if collectivization was merely a new form of serfdom (some peasants called it the second serfdom) and the purges another way of asserting the dominance of the state over a potentially powerful social stratum (the intelligentsia). Strong state authority had long-standing precedents in Russian history. Perhaps the active private market and cultural renaissance of the 1920s, rather than Stalinism, represented the more dramatic break with traditional political culture. Certainly, the renewed appeal to nationalism in the 1930s and 1940s resembled the official patriotism of the tsarist period. Stalin also revived many national heroes of the prerevolutionary period.

However, in other ways, Stalinism did represent a truly revolutionary break from traditional patterns: Atheism replaced Orthodoxy as the official state religion; the *mir,* which had survived the 1920s fairly intact, was finally destroyed; traditional social authorities (the family, the *mir,* and the church) in the countryside were replaced by a new breed of party bureaucrats; and industrial and technical values replaced superstition and religious beliefs. Although Stalinism resembled tsarist rule, the form of political control was much more extreme. The terror of the mid to late 1930s had no corollary in the tsarist period.

Stalin's Personality. A fourth group of scholars emphasizes the key role of Stalin himself in shaping Soviet history. The Marxist Soviet dissident Roy Medvedev is a strong advocate of this approach. Official post-Stalinist interpretations from Moscow also place the blame on Stalin as an individual, clearing the party and Marxism of responsibility for the purges and political violence of the 1930s. In the opinion of most Marxists, however, this explanation is inadequate because it attributes too great an influence to a single individual, overlooking the underlying social and economic dynamics that allowed Stalin to exercise power.

Some scholars have suggested psychological reasons for Stalin's behavior. Ethnically, Stalin was a Georgian, not a Russian, and he may have felt a need to compensate by embracing extreme Russian nationalism. In addition, he had little exposure to Western culture or ideas. Stalin may also have had a strong psychological need to prove himself a true revolutionary in the Leninist tradition; by carrying out the Third Revolution in 1929, his revolutionary credentials were demonstrated. Perhaps Stalin simply suffered from clinical paranoia. The definitive psychobiography of Stalin may never be written, due to the difficulty of unearthing the intimate detail required for this type of analysis.

Unquestionably, however, Stalin's personality traits contributed to the extreme methods he used. Had another person taken over the leadership post in 1924, Soviet history probably would have taken a somewhat different turn. Roy Medvedev writes, "It was an historical accident that Stalin, the embodiment of the worst elements of the Russian revolutionary movement, came to power after Lenin, the embodiment of all that was best."[8] Any explanation that emphasizes Stalin's personality, however, begs the question of *why* such a paranoid and dangerous man was able to rise to power. As Medvedev admits, that such a man could become leader reflects the conditions in which he sought power and the mentality or ability of those around him. Therefore, we must return to an examination of the cultural, economic, and political environment in which Stalin was able to make his bid for power.

"The Force of Circumstances." None of the above theories, taken alone, is fully adequate to explain the rise of Stalinism — single-cause explanations rarely are. No doubt all of the above factors, as well as some others, contributed to Stalin's ascendance. Circumstances worked together to produce a situation conducive to Stalin's rule: Lenin's early death; the failure of the party to dismantle the secret police (*Cheka*) established during the Civil War; the economic problems that developed in the late 1920s; and the presence of a shrewd politician (Stalin) who

could take advantage of these circumstances. In addition, the Bolshevik leaders were unable to practice the politics of compromise and bargaining; their skills, perceptions, and responses were profoundly influenced by the repressive cultural and political environment of tsarism. In many ways, the Leninist party structure had to mirror this environment in order to survive: Hierarchy, secrecy, and discipline were required to prevent subversion by tsarist agents. Even exposure to Western European ideas and politics could not make up for the lack of a democratic, participatory tradition at home.

The Soviet experience does not represent a prototype for every socialist experiment. The outcome of a Marxist revolution, and even of a Leninist revolution, might be quite different under other circumstances. But then, such revolutions have not occurred in countries with strong liberal-democratic traditions, so we cannot know what the outcome would be. Perhaps a Leninist party would not be able to achieve power in such an environment.

The Legacy of Stalinism

Stalinism had far-reaching effects on Soviet society that are still felt today. Despite the efforts of Stalin's successor, Nikita Khrushchev, to de-Stalinize Soviet society, many of its fundamental organizational, psychological, and economic features still reflect that era. Presumably the effects of Stalinism may be somewhat mitigated with time, as a new generation educated in the post-Stalinist period comes to power. However, this is certain to be a slow process.

Economically, the Stalinist strategy left the Soviet Union weak in the agricultural and consumer goods sectors. The highly ambitious plans of the 1930s left adequate resources only for the most pressing tasks, which meant the development of heavy industry. Investment in agriculture was low, and effective management methods were virtually ignored. Stalin's support for T. D. Lysenko, an agronomist who suggested that living organisms (in this case, plants) could adapt to environmental change during the course of their lifetimes, damaged agricultural production in the Soviet Union for years thereafter. Lysenko's theory sanctioned inappropriate planting decisions, with disastrous consequences for agricultural output.

The chaos produced by rapid collectivization and the continued resistance of the peasantry forced Stalin to accept the existence of private agricultural plots as early as 1933. By the mid-1930s, each peasant was allowed to cultivate about one-quarter to one-half a hectare (up to about an acre) of land and raise a small number of livestock.[9] Production on private plots proved to be more efficient than on the collective and state farms. Even today, the Soviet leadership is struggling for the appropriate balance between individual initiative and central planning in the agricultural sector. The private plot remains an essential source of fresh produce for the Soviet consumer, producing 64 percent of potatoes, 37 percent of fruit, and 31 percent of meat in 1980.[10]

In recent years Soviet authorities also have had to address Stalin's neglect of consumer goods production. In the 1930s and after World War II, housing was in short supply and consumer services (restaurants, laundries, recreational facilities) were grossly inadequate in the burgeoning urban centers. Individual consumer items, including meat and fresh produce, clothing, and household goods, were often unavailable or of such low quality as to be of little use. From the late 1950s to the present, an increasing level of investment had to be devoted to production of consumer items, which has placed strains on other investment sectors. Only through careful management of consumer expectations has the Soviet leadership thus far been able to handle this legacy of the Stalinist period.

The Stalinist period has left its political mark as well. Stalin's successors were the survivors of the purges, filling the posts vacated by Stalin's victims. Their apprenticeship in the 1930s shaped their attitudes, and they have only gradually modified the secretive, closed style of politics that characterized the Stalinist period. Since Stalin's death, more information on policy debates (at least in less-sensitive areas) has been made public and greater institutional stability has developed, but the actual functioning of top state and party bodies (such as the Politburo, Central Committee, and Council of Ministers) is still shrouded in mystery. High officials are rarely criticized in public, and when they retire or are demoted, reasons are seldom publicized. With the exception of rumor, Soviet citizens learn nothing of the personalities, family life, or personal interests of their leaders. Finally, the circular flow of power remains an important influence on political promotion. Patronage, in which successful party leaders promote loyal clients with whom they have past connections, accounts for many personnel changes within the party structure. This dynamic is currently being supplemented by open conflicts over policy issues, but the legacy of the Stalinist system of power still has a powerful impact.

Stalinism bred a culture of fear and paranoia. Even those too young to have experienced this atmosphere absorbed it from recollections of their parents. The proverbial knock on the door at midnight no longer occurs unexpectedly; those accused of unacceptable political behavior are first given warning by the authorities. But an aura of distrust remains: Citizens are cautious in revealing their true sentiments to all but the closest family or friends, and public demeanor may not reflect genuine sentiments. The citizen may have a private language for use with trusted friends and a different language for use in public.

Much has changed since 1953; however, the profound collective experience of Stalinism is not easily superseded, particularly when an entrenched state and party bureaucracy has an interest in maintaining existing power relationships. Some Soviet emigrés argue that there has been little change since the Stalinist period, and Western commentaries often portray the Soviet system today as similar to the Soviet Union of the 1930s. These assessments appear extreme and one-sided, however. A major transition *did* occur with the death of Stalin, but the roots of the new still lie in the old. Just as the prerevolutionary tsarist era helped shape the politics of the 1920s and 1930s, so Stalinism has influenced economics, culture, and politics since the 1950s.

De-Stalinization: Transition To The Modern State

Stalin died on March 5, 1953. His long reign had made him nearly a secular god: His death came as a shock to the Soviet population and presented major challenges for the remaining leaders. No clear procedures for a change of leadership had been established, and in some thirty-six years of Soviet rule, party leaders had faced this problem only once before. Should Stalin's policies and style of politics be continued? Even Stalin's closest comrades had been subject to insecurity in their positions. Should such an unpredictable system be allowed to remain, or should some attempt be made to introduce greater regularity? If changes did occur, how could they be explained to the Soviet people? If the party reduced its reliance on political repression, wouldn't some greater accommodation with the population also have to occur?

The immediate contenders for the leadership post included: Laventri Beria, head of the security apparatus (NKVD, or People's Commissar of Internal Affairs) since 1938; G. M. Malenkov, Stalin's right-hand man, member of the party Secretariat, and deputy head of the Council of Ministers; and possibly V. M. Molotov, an old Bolshevik who had served as Stalin's foreign affairs deputy and prime minister for some time in the 1930s and 1940s. All three, along with seven others (including Nikita Khrushchev, who seemed a less likely successor in 1953) were members of the Presidium, as the Politburo was known between 1953 and 1966. Shortly after Stalin's death, most of the remaining leaders agreed that the secret police should be brought under the political control of the state and party. Soon Beria and his deputies in the security apparatus were arrested and executed, presumably to prevent use of the secret police to win power. As Alec Nove writes, "The executions of these executioners proved to be the last *political* executions to date."[11] (Executions for criminal offenses and for spying did, however, occur after this time.)

In 1953, Malenkov appeared as the leading candidate; however, he soon lost his post on the party Secretariat. This left Khrushchev as the only Presidium member who also sat on the Secretariat. Malenkov's base of support was primarily in the state bureaucracy, which administered the massive economic bureaucracy established under Stalin's rule, while Khrushchev's support lay mainly in the party structures. Unlike most other members of the Presidium, Khrushchev had spent his entire career in the party apparatus and had considerable experience working in the Ukraine. The party had been drastically weakened as a political institution during the Stalinist period, but the state bureaucratic organs had grown with the increasingly complex economy. It was not immediately clear, therefore, that Khrushchev's stronger political base in the party (and his position as First Secretary in the Secretariat) would be of the same advantage to him as it had been to Stalin during the first succession conflict following Lenin's death.

Malenkov and Khrushchev had not only different constituencies but also diverse policy positions as well. Malenkov emerged as a champion of the consumer industries: During his ascendancy in 1953 and 1954, he strengthened these sectors both in the Soviet Union and in the Soviet-dominated countries of Eastern Europe. Khrushchev, on the other hand, not only expressed a particular interest in agriculture but also supported the continued emphasis on heavy industry and received crucial support from the military. Though Malenkov's position might have been favored among the population at large, the most powerful interests in the bureaucracy were more likely to be supportive of Khrushchev's continued commitment to heavy industrial development. Ironically, once Khrushchev's position as top leader was secured, he proceeded to strengthen the consumer sectors and make substantial improvements in social welfare (e.g., pensions, maternity leave, minimum wages, abolition of tuition fees).

Although party structures were weakened under Stalin, they retained a strong basis of legitimacy, due to the key role the party had played in the revolution and its central position in Leninist theory. Khrushchev made skillful use of his position within the party apparatus and was able to build up support within the party's Central Committee. On this basis, he consolidated his position as the leading figure in the Soviet Union. In 1956, he took a bold step in ensuring his ascendancy: At the Twentieth Congress of the Communist Party of the Soviet Union (CSPU), he made his now-famous Secret Speech, which was addressed only to delegates at the Congress and later published abroad. (It has never been publicly disseminated in the Soviet Union.) He attacked Stalin's "cult of the personality," meaning Stalin's personal usurpation of power and the irregular methods he had used in dealing with his opponents within the party. Khrushchev criticized Stalin for undermining party organs and suggested that Stalin's errors could be rectified only by returning to a Leninist path of firm reliance on party authority. However, Khrushchev praised Stalin's leadership during the war and the economic strategy pursued in the 1930s, including collectivization of agriculture. In this way, he affirmed the fundamental direction of past Soviet policy.

Khrushchev achieved several political purposes with his speech. First, he reassured the party delegates that should *he* be leader, the arbitrary and arrogant abuse of power would cease. Although Khrushchev himself had not been an innocent bystander, he implicated Malenkov and his allies as instruments of Stalin's misguided policies. Khrushchev sought to turn the tide of party opinion against them and, at the same time, reaffirm party dominance over the state bureaucracy in which Malenkov had his political support. In 1957, Malenkov, Molotov, and others challenged Khrushchev's leadership through a vote of the party Presidium. Khrushchev quickly and skillfully convened a special meeting of the Central Committee, to whom the Presidium is theoretically responsible, to condemn the effort to depose him. His opponents were then dubbed the anti-party group because of their alleged attempt to undermine established party procedures for their own advantage. Following this defeat, Malenkov and his allies were demoted to insignificant positions.

Having consolidated his position, Khrushchev embarked on a policy program that was often innovative, but sometimes contradictory and controversial. Western scholars disagree over whether fluctuations in policy were due to successful political opposition to Khrushchev's initiatives or whether his approach was an inherently erratic one. In any case, Khrushchev did succeed in placing a higher priority on agriculture and reorganized Soviet institutions, in part to cement his own political support and in part to give agricultural policy a higher profile. In 1957, before the showdown with the anti-party group, Khrushchev proposed replacing the powerful economic ministries, which were responsible for various branches of the economy (e.g., agriculture, metallurgy, and light industry), by the *sovnarkhozy,* "regional economic councils." Khrushchev's support in the ministries was relatively weak, and this reform served to strengthen party organs, which were organized on a regional basis, where Khrushchev had his strongest political backing. Khrushchev's reorganization attempt was ultimately unsuccessful from an economic viewpoint because regional autarky and poor coordination among the *sovnarkhozy* simply replaced the previous problems that had resulted from the central power of the branch economic ministries. Over the next several years, the *sovnarkhozy* had to be made progressively larger to improve coordination. Once Khrushchev was removed from the top post in 1964, this reform was immediately reversed by his successors and the old economic ministries were restored.

In 1962, Khrushchev instituted yet another reorganization scheme, dividing the regional party organs into two sections: one in charge of industry and the other in charge of agriculture. In this way, agricultural interests would have their own institutional base and, presumably, would be in a stronger position. However, this change was not a shrewd political choice. The old secretaries of the previously united regional party organs lost their posts, and Khrushchev undermined his own base of support among the party *apparatchiki,* many of whom sat on the Central Committee. In addition, Khrushchev's part in the Sino-Soviet split and the Cuban missile crisis did little to improve his image among the party elites. The breakdown in friendly relations with communist China, marked by the withdrawal of Soviet technical assistance from China in 1960, reflected long-standing tensions between the two countries, rooted in geopolitical competition and Chinese resentment of Soviet dominance within the socialist bloc. While Khrushchev was not himself responsible for these conflicts, the fact that they culminated in an open split during his rule undermined his reputation as an effective leader of the socialist bloc. During the Cuban missile crisis of 1961, Khrushchev was forced to reverse his plan to station short-range nuclear missiles in Cuba, under threats of retaliation from the United States. Khrushchev's humiliating capitulation to American strength again made him appear weak and imprudent to his colleagues in the Soviet leadership. In a striking move in 1964, the Central Committee voted to remove Khrushchev from his post as First Secretary. Such an assertion of power by a major party institution over the party leader would have been unthinkable in the Stalinist period. As we shall see in our examination of Soviet institutions in Chapter 29, self-assertion by the Central Committee is still a rare occurrence.

Once removed from power, Khrushchev disappeared from the political scene. Fallen leaders were executed in the Stalinist period, but Khrushchev, like Malenkov, was demoted, not eliminated. Khrushchev retired to his *dacha,* "country cottage," where he lived until his death in 1971. In 1970, Khrushchev's memoirs (generally considered to be authentic) were smuggled out of the Soviet Union and published in the West.[12]

The brief period of Khrushchev's dominance left an important mark on Soviet politics, even though some of his specific policy directions were reversed in 1965. During Khrushchev's rule, Stalinist methods were openly repudiated and some Leninist ideals were revived. Khrushchev was in a sense a populist. He strongly favored increased, though controlled, popular participation: He allowed experts to participate in policy deliberations and to express diverse opinions in the media. The first years of the Khrushchev era are generally referred to as the Thaw because of the loosening of controls on literature. Khrushchev approved the publication of Aleksandr Solzhenitsyn's critical novelette *One Day in the Life of Ivan Denisovich* in the Soviet literary journal *Novyi mir,* "New World," in 1962. However, he soon returned to a somewhat harder line toward artistic experimentation.

The New Program of the CPSU, adopted in 1961 under Khrushchev's leadership, affirmed humanistic and participatory themes. The Soviet Union was declared a "state of the whole people," in which antagonistic class contradictions had been eliminated; the dictatorship of the proletariat was over. The program proclaimed social harmony rather than attacking class enemies; it even forecast the withering away of the state (but not of the party), to which both Marx and Lenin had alluded. Khrushchev also advocated educational policies (not all of which were implemented), making night study more available and requiring vocational experience in conjunction with university education. Social inequalities were reduced, and limits were to be placed on tenure in party posts. Though many of Khrushchev's ideas were too idealistic to be realized during his short term of office, their very expression injected a new spirit into Soviet political discourse.

The Khrushchev period was the first step towards normalcy and predictability in Soviet politics. If Khrushchev's own policies were often erratic and unrealistic, his successors were far more conservative and consistent. This may have been in part a reaction to the upheaval of the previous eras and in part simply a maturing of the Soviet political system. The Soviet Union of the 1960s was no longer a revolutionary society: The revolutionary leaders had largely passed away, and the main task was to maintain the existing patterns of power.

NOTES

1. M. Lewin, *Russian Peasants and Soviet Power* (London: George Allen and Unwin, 1968), pp. 72–78.
2. A. Gerschenkron, cited in David Lane, *State and Politics in the USSR* (Oxford: Basil Blackwell, 1985), pp. 69–70.

3. Vera Dunham, *In Stalin's Time: Middleclass Values in Soviet Fiction* (Cambridge: Cambridge University Press, 1976), chap. 1.
4. Seweryn Bialer, *Stalin's Successors: Leadership, Stability, and Change in the Soviet Union* (Cambridge: Cambridge University Press, 1980), p. 10.
5. James R. Millar and Alec Nove, "A Debate on Collectivization: Was Stalin Really Necessary?" *Problems of Communism* (July/August 1976), p. 51.
6. Millar and Nove, "A Debate," pp. 53–55.
7. Alfred G. Meyer, *Leninism* (New York: Praeger, 1972), p. 87.
8. Roy Medvedev, *Let History Judge: The Origins and Consequences of Stalinism* (New York: Vintage Books, 1973), p. 362.
9. Alec Nove, *An Economic History of the USSR* (Harmondsworth, England: Penguin Books, 1982), p. 242.
10. David Lane, *Soviet Economy and Society* (Oxford: Basil Blackwell, 1985) p. 169.
11. Alec Nove, *Stalinism and After* (London: George Allen and Unwin, 1975), p. 123.
12. N. Khrushchev, *Khrushchev Remembers* (New York: Little, Brown and Co., 1970).

28

Bureaucratic Conservatism and the Post-Stalinist Settlement

Upon Khrushchev's removal as First Secretary of the party, it soon became apparent that Khrushchev's former allies Aleksei Kosygin and Leonid Brezhnev would share power. Gradually Brezhnev was able to assert his dominance as the "first among equals"; however, he was never to gain the personal power enjoyed by Stalin. Since purges of top party ranks had lost their legitimacy as an instrument of control, the new leadership had to find other methods of accommodating both the elite and the population at large.

The new leadership presumably learned several lessons from Khrushchev's experience. First, Khrushchev's ascendancy had reestablished the key position of the party and made clear that support from the heavy industrial and military sectors was important for any aspiring leader. In 1964, one of the factors that had made Khrushchev vulnerable was the neutral position of the military towards him. Second, Khrushchev had legitimized agriculture as a major policy concern, which Brezhnev continued to promote, although with somewhat different methods than Khrushchev. Bureaucratic interests supporting assertive agricultural policy had developed by 1964. Third, a key factor in Khrushchev's downfall was that he had alienated too many elite groups. If pressed, the Central Committee *could* override the General Secretary (called the First Secretary during the Khrushchev era); therefore, it was important that the General Secretary anticipate potential opposition before it materialized. Twice during Khrushchev's leadership, the Central Committee had successfully asserted itself: first in 1957, in supporting Khrushchev against the anti-Party group of the Presidium (now renamed the Politburo); and again, in 1964, in deposing him. However passive a role the Central Committee may seem to have played after 1965, its potential had been demonstrated. Presumably, the new leadership was more cautious, anticipating the reaction of broader segments of Soviet society to its policies.

The Post-Stalinist Settlement

While it would be inappropriate to speak of a postwar settlement in the Soviet Union comparable to the pattern in Western Europe, we can speak of the emergence of a post-Stalinist settlement during the Brezhnev years. Vera Dunham has argued that in the late 1940s, Stalin himself forged a kind of "tacit concordat," or unspoken agreement, with what she calls the Soviet middle class, referring to "solid citizens in positions and style below the top officials and cultural elite, yet above the world of plain clerks and factory workers, of farm laborers and sales girls."[1] This group, many of whom were beneficiaries of Stalin's policies in the 1930s, exchanged political complacency for material gain and a comfortable private life. Dunham suggests that Stalin's power was rooted not in the intellectuals or common working people but in this new and growing social stratum. In the Brezhnev years, the concordat was extended to encompass broader elements of the population, including state and party officialdom, the intelligentsia, and the less-affluent sectors of society.

The late 1960s and early 1970s were a period of relative affluence, a quiet after the storms of Stalinism and de-Stalinization. Economic growth, while moderate compared to the 1930s, was used to a much greater extent to provide the population with a more comfortable lifestyle. As Dunham has suggested, the post-Stalinist leadership under Brezhnev seemed ready and able to extend the concordat to Soviet society at large. What was the nature of this expanding social contract?

The Tacit Social Contract

The political elite (i.e., the highest state and party officials) has had a greater degree of autonomy in the Soviet Union than in Western Europe. The Bolshevik party has always placed great emphasis on the unity of the leadership and has hesitated to expose divisions in its ranks for fear of mobilizing popular discontent. Thus, the first element of Brezhnev's social contract involved accommodating the political elite itself. Both Stalin and Khrushchev had subjected top officials to unpredictability and uncertainty about their positions in the government and about the government's policies — Stalin through the purges, and Khrushchev through repeated bureaucratic upheavals. In contrast, the Brezhnev leadership embarked on a policy of stability. He made few personnel changes, which gained for him the political loyalty of the elite. Some incumbents were demoted, but more importantly, Brezhnev allies were promoted as a result of the expansion of party and state organs. In 1966, the Politburo had eleven full voting members; by 1981, that number was fourteen. Finally, death or retirement allowed additional promotions. In this way, Brezhnev was able to consolidate his own position, making use of the "circular flow of power," without alienating the party/state elites. Brezhnev's social contract with the elite involved a commitment to stability, regularity, and consultation. While Brezhnev was clearly the "first among equals" on the Politburo, it is unlikely that he could have made any major decision without consulting with other members, particularly the small influential inner core, which included Nikolai Podgorny (until 1977), Aleksei Kosygin (until 1980), Mikhail Suslov (until his death in 1982), and Andrei Gromyko. Collective leadership had become a reality, even if Brezhnev's leading position was reinforced when he added the post of president (also chairman of the Presidium of the Supreme Soviet) in 1980 to his role as General Secretary of the party.

Another dimension to the social contract rested in the social and economic policies of the Brezhnev team. While there were few radical initiatives following 1965, the leadership did make an effort to respond to the rising expectations of a more educated citizenry. In the first place, the new leadership continued the increased emphasis on production of consumer goods. By the early 1970s, a considerable improvement had occurred in the Soviet diet, with the addition of more meat and dairy products. At the same time, durable consumer goods, like TVs, washing machines, and refrigerators became accessible to more Soviet families. (See Table 28.1.) An effort was made to substantially increase housing construction, although shortages remained. (Between 1965 and 1982, per capita [useful] living space increased from 9.7 to 13.2 square meters in urban areas.)[2] The proportion of the state budget devoted to consumer goods production increased, as did investment in agriculture. Further, the economic reform program instituted in 1965 (but largely abandoned by the early 1970s) sought to improve product quality.

Table 28.1 Provision of Urban and Rural Population with Various Goods (end of year)

	(ITEMS PER 1,000 PERSONS)			
	1970	1975	1980	1983
Clocks	1,193	1,319	1,523	1,540
TVs.	143	215	249	287
Cameras	77	77	91	99
Refrigerators and freezers	89	178	252	270
Bicycles and mopeds	145	156	144	164
Sewing machines	161	178	190	190
Washing machines	141	189	205	205
Tape recorders	21	46	73	96
Radio sets	199	230	250	280

SOURCE Tsentral'noe statisticheskoe upravlenie SSSR (Central Statistical Administration of the USSR), *Narodnoe khoziaistvo SSSR 1983: statisticheskii ezhegodnik* (The Economy of the USSR in 1983: Statistical Yearbook) (Moscow: Iz. "Finansy i statistika," 1984), p. 442.

Social policies were directed toward the least affluent in society. The Soviet regime continued to assure security of employment and low inflation rates on necessities of life (housing, basic food items, transportation, education, and health care) while raising prices of luxury goods (furs, alcohol, cars). Wage differentials between educated white-collar sectors, on the one hand, and the peasantry and working class, on the other, declined. The peasants who worked on collective farms gained pension coverage, a guaranteed wage level, and an internal passport, which gave them more geographical and social mobility. While schools and social services in rural areas remained inferior and possibilities for social advancement more limited, the advantages of city over country were somewhat reduced.

For the intelligentsia, the regime offered increased opportunities for political participation by involving experts in policy debates; increasing debate in scholarly journals; and frequent calling upon economists, legal scholars, and other experts to provide advice on issues of economic and social policy. The prestigious Academy of Sciences, which has numerous research institutes throughout the country, was given increased autonomy, making a recurrence of the Lysenko fiasco unlikely. While some

Table 28.2 Influence of Social Origin upon Respondent's Social Position at Commencement of Labor Activity

	SOCIAL POSITION OF RESPONDENT (IN %)				
SOCIAL POSITION OF RESPONDENT'S FATHER	Worker	Intelli-gentsia	Non-Specialist Employee	Collective Farmer	TOTAL
Worker	72.7	15.4	9.4	1.5	100.0
Intelligentsia	43.5	45.0	8.8	2.7	100.0
Nonspecialist employee	56.8	22.1	16.0	5.1	100.0
Collective farmer	55.0	12.4	7.3	15.3	100.0

SOURCE N. A. Aitov, "The Dynamics of Social Mobility in the USSR," trans. in *Soviet Sociology*, vol. XIV: 1–3 (1985/86), p. 257. Based on a Soviet Survey conducted in Magnitogorsk in 1976.

members of the intelligentsia complained of inadequate material incentives (because of the regime's more egalitarian wage and social policies), incentives for working within the system were reinforced by increased recognition and access to information.

The Soviet regime continued to exercise strict control over dissidents (e.g., the crackdown on the Helsinki Watch Group, which monitored human rights violations, in the late 1970s). Further, contact with the West was discouraged: Travel to Western countries remained restricted mainly to scholars, state/party functionaries, athletes, or artists. While tourist travel to the Soviet Union from the West became commonplace, Soviet citizens were (and still are) discouraged from having sustained contact with Western visitors. In this way, the regime hoped to stem rising expectations that would be difficult to satisfy. At the same time, the official media continued to disseminate information emphasizing unemployment, inflation, and crime in the West.

The tacit social contract of the Brezhnev era had both positive and negative features. Methods of control, however, were more predictable and less violent than in the Stalinist period. More and more citizens had grown up under Soviet rule and were accustomed to life under the system, and older population groups could compare their present situation favorably with the past. Lacking a democratic tradition, the Soviet people had few alternatives with which to compare Soviet politics. The Brezhnev leadership was apparently quite successful in finding a formula for stability, and possibly even legitimacy.

Incremental Reform

Once Khrushchev's economic reforms and reorganizations were reversed in 1965, basic economic and political institutions were changed only incrementally during the Brezhnev era. The ministerial structure that existed before 1957 was reinstated, the regional economic councils were abolished, and party organs were again reunified at the regional level. In 1965, under Kosygin's guidance, a moderate economic reform was instituted to improve productivity and quality without compromising the basic authority of the central party bodies. However, even this limited reform placed contradictory demands on enterprise managers. Entrenched interests opposed a more comprehensive and far-reaching approach. By the early 1970s these problems resulted in the virtual dismantling of the Kosygin reform. Since then, other moderate attempts to alter the economic structure have been made.

Policy change was cautious and gradual in other areas as well. Increased investment and ambitious programs of land reclamation and irrigation reflected a commitment to improve agricultural production, but the collective and state farm structure was not altered, and the rights of the peasantry to cultivate their private plots were also maintained. Improvements in pension programs and other social benefits for the collective farm workers helped lift the lowest socioeconomic strata. These and other reforms produced no major systemic change but were efforts to smooth out the rough spots in policy performance without antagonizing important elements of the Soviet political elite. Thus, despite the existence of central economic planning, which might have allowed a periodic and thorough reassessment and redirection of priorities, only moderate changes in policy were made during this period. The style of politics was bureaucratic and the content conservative.

Oligarchic Pluralism

The Brezhnev regime allowed experts and bureaucratic interest groups more opportunities for input into decision making. One U.S. scholar has suggested that Soviet politics may be moving in the direction of "institutional pluralism,"[3] which differs from pluralism as we know it in the West in that only certain types of interests receive a hearing from policymakers, primarily interests of large institutional bodies (e.g., economic ministries, prestigious scientific bodies, and regional organs). According to this view, Soviet politics is increasingly characterized by politics of the possible, carried out through bargaining, negotiation, and compromise. Leaders consult with those who have the most at stake in a particular policy area.

Though Western scholars sometimes speak of interest groups in Soviet politics,[4] these groups are informal and are not visible entities. Their existence can be inferred by observing opposing opinions in the Soviet media: Several individuals (e.g., scholars, party officials, or state bureaucrats) express a similar viewpoint and seek to persuade the political authorities. For example, those advocating higher investment in agriculture may form one such interest group, and proponents of more stringent pollution control might form another. Individuals expressing common viewpoints are not joined in an autonomous lobbying organization, such as the National Farmers' Association or Sierra Club, however. Nor do proponents of similar policies hold public meetings to work out political demands or strategies: Such activities would not be permitted. Some Western scholars, therefore, consider it inappropriate to view Soviet politics in terms of interest-group conflict, because here the term *group* has such a different meaning from its common Western usage. These are more potential groups than real groups; there are no mass political lobbies, only conflicting views among the elite. Soviet theoreticians also reject any notion that Soviet politics can be explained in terms of interest-group conflict, although they do increasingly admit that there may be differing interests and viewpoints in Soviet society.

Some Western scholars have suggested that the Soviet political process is more corporatist than pluralist.[5] That is, officially sanctioned organizations provide a link between the state and the population, and it is only through these organizations that the interests and views of the various constituencies may have an impact on policymaking. Because these are state- or party-run organizations, ordinary citizens are still very limited in their ability to exert autonomous political pressure. Passive communication of one's viewpoint, by not buying a certain product or by coming to work late or drunk, may be alternative modes of political protest, since there are no channels of direct political protest.

However one views the process of political conflict in the Soviet Union, it is clear that during the Brezhnev era, open political debate about most domestic policy concerns did expand. As Jerry Hough has written:

> In the post-Krushchev era there have been few party policies and few aspects of Soviet policy that have been immune from attack if the attack

> is carefully phrased. There has been almost no proposal for incremental changes in party policy that has not been published in some form or another. Even on foreign policy and nationalities policy, where actual advocacy of policy change is permitted only in the most veiled terms, scholars have been able to debate the facts of the situation and thereby imply contrasting views of the policy that is required.[6]

Because effective participation in policy deliberation is limited to the elite (including scholars), it seems appropriate to call this pattern oligarchic pluralism.

Many Western scholars feel that the range of permissible debate will continue to expand, as issues facing the leadership become more complex and require greater input from experts. Other scholars emphasize that input from specialists can be turned off as easily as it is turned on, that experts are, in effect, "on tap, not on top."[7] On the other hand, the political elite may not be able to restrict the range of political input without alienating large sectors of the Soviet intelligentsia, as well as some bureaucratic interests. This need not imply, however, that the broad masses of the population will be allowed to organize themselves into true citizen lobbies.

Figure 28.1 Average Annual Percent Rate of Overall Soviet Economic Growth

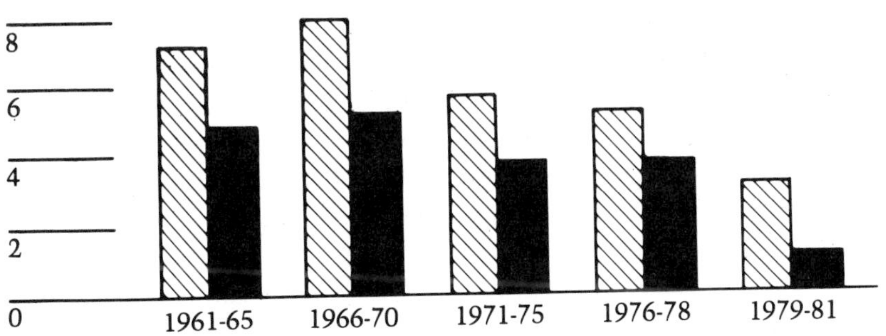

SOURCE M. Elizabeth Denton, "Soviet Perceptions of Economic Prospects," U.S. Congress, Joint Economic Committee, *Soviet Economy in the 1980s: Problems and Prospects,* Part I (Washington, DC: U.S. Government Printing Office, 1983), p. 35.

Figure 28.2 Average Annual Percent Rate of Growth in Per Capita Consumer Welfare

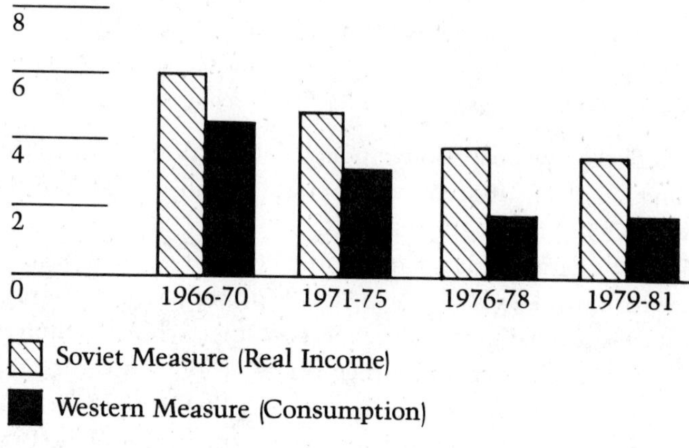

SOURCE See Figure 28.1.

The Decline of the Post-Stalinist Settlement?

The Brezhnev team's implicit social contract was effective at maintaining political stability for some years, but it may not be adequate for the late 1980s and 1990s. By the late 1970s, a series of interconnected problems reached dramatic proportions, just as the aging Brezhnev team seemed to have lost even the minimal dynamism it once had. At the root was a faltering economy: Growth rates, which had been between 6 and 7 percent annually in the 1950s, dipped below 3 percent by the last half of the 1970s and fell even lower in the 1980s. Slower growth meant greater difficulty in satisfying consumer expectations. (See Figures 28.1 and 28.2.) Competition among various sectors of the economy (military, agricultural, industrial, consumer) and among various geographical regions also increased.

While Soviet growth rates may appear healthy compared to the performance of some Western economies, the lower per capita income of the Soviet Union means that a higher level of growth is needed to meet Western levels of affluence. (See Table 28.3.) An equal percentage increase also involves a smaller real increase per capita. The arms race has also placed great pressure on the Soviet economy: To maintain parity with the United States, the Soviets must devote a considerably larger proportion of their gross national product (GNP) to the military sector, because the Soviet GNP is smaller than the U.S. GNP. Western estimates for Soviet expenditures range from 10 to 20 percent of GNP, compared to 7.2% percent for the United States in 1982.[8] The real cost is even greater, because the highest quality materials and personnel are diverted to the Soviet military from other sectors of the economy.

Other factors also complicated economic policy by the late 1970s. Exploitation of natural resources was becoming more expensive, deterioration of the environment was increasing, and demographic patterns

Table 28.3 Retail Prices of Goods and Services in Units of Work-Time, March, 1982 (Weekly Basket of Consumer Goods for Four Persons at Soviet Level of Consumption in March, 1982, Expressed as Work-Time Units)

		(MINUTES OF WORK-TIME)				
ITEM	KILOGRAMS	WASHINGTON	MUNICH	PARIS	LONDON	MOSCOW
Flour	1.0	5	9	6	6	28
Bread	7.0	112	189	126	175	119
Noodles	2.0	28	32	22	28	68
Beef	1.0	69	150	119	115	123
Pork	1.5	63	150	108	117	176
Minced Beef	1.0	37	70	80	63	123
Sausages	1.0	33	75	75	51	160
Cod	1.0	61	45	118	72	47
Sugar	3.3	30	33	30	36	191
Butter	0.5	28	26	24	25	111
Margarine	2.0	46	34	36	64	222
Milk (liters)	12.0	72	84	96	108	264
Cheese	2.0	200	130	118	130	370
Eggs, cheapest (units)	18.0	14	22	23	29	99
Potatoes	9.0	63	36	36	27	63
Cabbage	3.0	27	21	27	30	36
Carrots	1.0	11	10	7	13	19
Tomatoes	1.0	23	28	25	32	62
Apples	1.0	10	15	15	23	92
Tea	.1	10	10	17	5	53
Beer	3.0	33	24	21	54	48
Gin/Vodka (liters)	1.0	87	106	153	187	646
Cigarettes (units)	120	54	96	48	150	90

(Continued)

Table 28.3 (Continued)

ITEM	KILOGRAMS	WASHINGTON	MUNICH	PARIS	LONDON	MOSCOW
			(HOURS OF WORK-TIME)			
Weekly basket, as above		18.6	23.3	22.2	25.7	53.5
Monthly basket, as above		74.2	93.2	88.8	102.8	214.0
Monthly rent		51.0	24.0	39.0	28.0	12.0
Total of monthly basket and rent		125.2	117.2	127.8	130.8	226.0
TV, black and white		38	49	44	35	299
TV, color		65	143	106	132	701
			(MONTHS OF WORK-TIME)			
Small car		5	6	8	11	53
Large car		8	9	12	18	88

SOURCE Keith Bush, "Retail Prices in Moscow and Four Western Cities in March 1982," *Radio Liberty Research Supplement,* June 4, 1982, p. 7.

suggested serious future imbalances in the distribution of labor. In addition, the massive investment in agriculture was producing only minimal improvement, so grain had to be imported from abroad, and food shortages continued. As economic problems have mounted, the legitimacy of the system has probably declined. By the early 1980s, corruption pervaded all levels of the Soviet party/state, generating cynicism and low morale in the population. Slower expansion of the economy meant decreased chances for upward social mobility: Young people had to lower their aspirations, and many took jobs below their skill levels. High levels of alcoholism contributed to a decrease in life expectancy for Soviet men, and an increase in infant mortality signaled a crisis in the health care system. By the late 1970s, social discontent of various types had spawned an active dissident movement, which the regime began to attack with new vigor in 1979.

These social and economic problems converged with a major change in leadership in the early 1980s. The old generation of leaders who had risen in the 1930s were passing away, leaving behind a complex and difficult situation for their successors. To understand the pressures confronting the Soviet system, we must first examine the transition affecting the Soviet leaders themselves.

The Changing of the Guard

The new appointments Brezhnev made at the top level were primarily men of his own generation; thus, the average age of voting Politburo members increased over time, reaching sixty-nine in 1981. At lower levels of the party, there was more turnover and, therefore, younger leadership (e.g., the average age of first secretaries of regional party committees was fifty-seven in 1980), though in virtually every sector of political life, the governing elite was older during the Brezhnev years than during previous regimes.[9] Brezhnev's concern with the stability of cadres was presumably a reaction to the unpredictability of the Stalin and Khrushchev eras. While this may have been a viable way of maintaining the loyalty of the existing elite, it produced a certain stagnation in policy innovation in the later Brezhnev years. Brezhnev's preoccupation with foreign policy questions reinforced the tendency toward immobilization on domestic issues from the late 1970s. The stability of cadres also created a serious block to upward mobility for younger politicians: While some of the younger men and women might rise to posts at the regional level, it was much more difficult to achieve a leading position at the central level. The reluctance of the older generation to give up the reins of power to younger individuals was evidenced by the appointment to the position of party General Secretary of Iurii Andropov (following Brezhnev's death in November, 1982) and, later, of Konstantin Chernenko (following Andropov's death in Feburary, 1984). Andropov was sixty-eight and Chernenko seventy-two when appointed to the post. Once the older generation began to pass away, in the early to mid-1980s (by 1986, eight of the fourteen members of the 1981 Politburo had died or had retired at an advanced age), there was bound to be a rapid shift in the composition of the top elite. This transition had to be handled very carefully.

The men (and a few women) who are taking over the posts vacated by the Brezhnev generation differ in various ways from their predecessors. First, they were socialized in a different era. Leaders from the Brezhnev generation were the beneficiaries of the Stalinist purges and had their first political experience in that environment. Mikhail Gorbachev, elected General Secretary following Chernenko's death in March, 1985, is a representative of the new generation. Born in 1931, he did not join the party until 1952 and thus did not embark upon his political career until shortly before the death of Stalin. Western experts have speculated that this different socialization experience may have some impact on attitudes. Some speculate that the so-called post-Stalinist generation will be more used to the politics of compromise and bargaining; they feel their position to be more secure both at home and in the international sphere, more concerned with pragmatic solutions than with ideological formulas, and more open in political style. However, the implications of generational change will only become clear over the next several years. Change may come as a result of not only this new generation and the younger age of the leadership but also due to the ascendancy of new demands emanating from Soviet society and increasing pressure on the leadership to resolve urgent policy problems.

Economic Problems

In many regards, the economic achievements of the Soviet Union are impressive: a rapid growth of industrial capacity; a marked rise in the standard of living; job security; relative price stability for basic goods; provision of basic education to all and free higher education to many; elimination of some of the worst forms of economic and social inequality; and technological excellence in such areas as nuclear fusion, space technology, and military equipment. Nonetheless, Western analysts and Soviet leaders seem to agree that the economy is the most urgent problem in the Soviet Union. The planning methods that served the country well as it moved from relative backwardness to its present status as an industrial giant are increasingly inadequate to meet the demands of a technologically advanced and interdependent economy. Simple quantitative gains are no longer enough: Innovation, quality, technological improvement, and superior efficiency are now required.

The fundamental economic problem seems intransigent. How can the incentive structure be changed to encourage higher productivity, efficiency, innovation, and quality without radical decentralization of economic power or a competitive market structure? Wouldn't real decentralization encourage ethnic self-assertion at the local level, possibly destabilizing the Soviet system? If a competitive market were accepted, wouldn't essential elements of the Soviet social contract — the guarantee of employment and low inflation — be undermined? So far, the successful formula has not been found. If consumer expectations continue to rise and citizens demand better quality output, then this economic dilemma may become a political crisis for the Soviet leadership. Why has the Soviet economy been so ineffective in responding to citizen demands, and why has economic performance faltered in recent years? To answer these questions, we must first examine the system of economic planning as it existed in the Brezhnev era.

The Planning System. The Soviet economic system is highly centralized, not only due to the predominance of state control and ownership, but also because of the nature of the economic planning system itself. Gosplan, the State Planning Committee, is responsible for working out the one-year and five-year economic plans as well as overseeing their broad implementation. The one-year plans are operational, in that they involve the issuance of specific instructions as to what should be produced, by whom, and in what quantities, and they have the force of law. Gosplan must rely on the large branch ministries that oversee the various sectors of the economy (e.g., machine building, light industry, grain products) and other state committees (e.g., the Committee on Prices) in carrying out this function. Below the economic ministries are the industrial associations, which integrate several enterprises involved in producing a similar product type and often have research and development sections to further technical innovation in the field. At the bottom of the hierarchy are the enterprises themselves, which vary greatly in size. The ministries and larger enterprises or associations in key branches of the economy (e.g., the energy sector, military-related areas, the chemical industry) are powerful institutional actors in the Soviet system. Most workers are employed directly by the enterprise. In the agricultural sphere, the *sovkhoz,* "state farm," is the equivalent of the industrial enterprise. Some agricultural workers, however, are employed by *kolkhozy,* "collective farms," which, theoretically, are not owned by the state but are collectively run and owned (except for the land) by the peasants themselves. In practice, however, production on both state and collective farms is under the guidance of the central plan; only the small, private plots are outside the planning system. To assist in formulating the one- and five-year plans, the enterprises provide information regarding their productive capabilities through the hierarchy to Gosplan. On this basis, the final plan is drafted, and the instructions are transmitted back to the associations and enterprises.

Planning is based primarily on a system of input-output techniques and material balances. The central organs determine output goals, suppliers and buyers, prices, and the balance between wages and consumer goods. In other words, the enterprise does not respond to market forces, such as changing demand or market-price levels, as do firms in the West. Rather, the enterprise is obliged to try to fulfill the goals set out by the central planning organs. For a large economy, such as that of the Soviet Union, planning is, therefore, a very complicated task. If Factory X is to produce a specified number of agricultural vehicles (tractors, trucks, and so forth), it must receive the appropriate inputs, such as tires, transmissions, and metal, from its designated suppliers. The tire factory, in turn, must also receive the necessary amount of rubber and metal. If, for example, the tires delivered to the agricultural machinery factory are the wrong size, then the tractors cannot be produced and the state farms will not be able to meet their output goals. Any bottleneck in the process or any miscalculation by the planning organs can cause a chain reaction that reverberates throughout the economy. Gosplan itself works out the balance of production for over 2,000 products (only a small proportion of the numerous types of output); further instructions must be handled by the ministries and associations, or through direct contacts between suppliers and buyers. The entire process is a giant puzzle in which a change in one set of directions necessitates recalculation of numerous others.

To make the problem even more difficult, planning in the Soviet Union is *taut:* To assure that each enterprise works to maximum capacity, the authorities allow little slack in the plan. But when central planners obligate enterprises to produce at, or even beyond, realistic capacity, bottlenecks are all the more likely, as some enterprises fail to meet the plan and, therefore, cannot supply their customers. The result is a sellers' market: Pervasive shortages of desired goods compel buyers (both the average consumer and the enterprise in need of raw materials) to accept inferior goods, or get nothing at all. On the other hand, Soviet authorities must fear that abandoning taut planning would bring even larger gaps in production. In practice, enterprises may try to manufacture parts needed to produce goods demanded by the plan in order to reduce their dependence on unreliable suppliers; this in turn makes it even more difficult for top planning bodies to retain an overview of productive capacities.

Legal, Semilegal, and Illegal Markets. Prices fulfill an entirely different function in the Soviet system than in the West. Fluctuations in prices do not signal messages about supply and demand as they do in a regulated market economy. Rather, they are primarily instruments to measure enterprise performance and to regulate exchange of commodities in the economy. The enterprises produce according to the plan, not according to the manager's reading of demand. In the West, products in high demand and short supply will command high prices, luring other producers into the field, but in the Soviet Union most prices are centrally established and subject to almost no short-term fluctuations, though they may be reexamined periodically by the Committee on Prices and readjusted to meet changing circumstances. Authorities justify this approach on the grounds that production decisions should be based on socially established goals, not on the anarchy of market fluctuations. For the enterprise manager, prices provide a measure of how efficiently the factory is fulfilling its plans. Prices are used for accounting purposes; if the enterprise is producing as it should, costs and expenditures should balance or show a profit. If the books show a profit due to efficient management, only a certain amount accrues to the enterprise bonus funds; the rest returns to the state, but the manager can be assured that he or she will be rewarded for the good job done by special bonuses, public praise, or even career advancement. Under the Soviet Union's one-person management system, the manager is not responsible to collective or representative bodies (such as workers' councils or boards of directors) in carrying out his or her duties, but to the party and the plan.

There are a few areas where market principles are permitted to operate in modified form in the Soviet economy, however. The consumer may pick and choose from available goods, and here prices may affect the consumer's choice. Consumer preferences, however, may or may not be fulfilled. Although planners have encouraged enterprises to pay more attention to public demands in recent years, the light industrial enterprises producing consumer goods are often at the end of the supply line and thus often lack the materials they need. The labor market is also subject to some principles of supply and demand. Wage levels are generally set at the center, but since Soviet workers can usually choose their own employer, enterprises must sometimes juggle job classifications or central planners must adapt wage levels in certain occupations to achieve the desired distribution; for example, wage levels in Siberia are higher than for the same job in Moscow. Finally, market principles operate in free peasant markets, where produce from private peasant plots can be legally sold and prices can fluctuate to reflect supply and demand.

In other cases, market principles function in a semilegal or illegal manner. Because enterprises often cannot get the materials they actually need to fulfill the plan, the *tolchaki,* "unofficial agents," seek sources of supply outside the plan. The result is an unofficial market, which is neither sanctioned nor suppressed by the authorities, who recognize that without this semilegal trade, bottlenecks would become overwhelming. Similarly, *shabashniki,* "unofficial work brigades," are sometimes hired to complete rural construction projects more quickly and efficiently (and at much higher pay) than state enterprises. The authorities allow the *shabashniki* to operate in the gray area between legality and illegality because they serve a useful economic function. On a smaller scale, the store clerk may put aside a rarely available chandelier for a special customer and receive a "tip" for the effort, effectively raising the price of the valued commodity. These activities are illegal but sometimes tolerated, since they serve as an outlet for consumer frustrations. Other illegal trade, which the authorities try to control, occurs on the underground black market, that is, surreptitiously through informal contacts out of public view. Items traded on the black market include Western commodities, goods stolen from the state at the workplace, and items produced in illegal underground factories operated for private profit. Prices on the black market escape central control, but here the authorities are not as willing to look the other way. Although blue jeans and other Western commodities bought from tourists may command a high price on the black market, exchange in Western goods is especially discouraged since it affects the balance of trade and reinforces a fascination with the West. However, until the official production system can satisfy consumer expectations, the leadership will be hard pressed to eliminate such illegal activities.

Deficiencies in Planning. Several attempts have been made, most notably the 1965 Kosygin reforms and additional reform efforts since, to alter the criteria for evaluating enterprises so as to place more emphasis on quality of output, productivity of labor, technical innovation, and satisfaction of the buyer's specific needs (i.e., in supplying the right size and specifications of tires to the tractor factory or the proper mix of shoe sizes and styles to the retail outlet). In practice, however, it is extremely difficult to work out a set of criteria that achieves all of these objectives at the same time. Therefore success in fulfilling the plan is still primarily judged by fairly crude quantitative measures. The case of the factory that produces oversized screws to meet its weight quota is not far from the truth; small screws may be needed, but it is cheaper and easier for the screw enterprise to meet its output goal (measured in tons) by producing a much smaller number of large screws. The problem multiplies when the factory buying these screws has few powerful connections (such as an enterprise producing consumer appliances or spare parts). Although a sewing machine factory, for example, can presumably refuse to accept the huge screws, if no other supplier is readily available that enterprise may take them to keep in stock for later use. This catch-as-catch-can environment undermines efforts by planners to evaluate enterprises on the basis of the quantity of goods actually accepted by the customer.

This is only one of many problems in trying to operate a centralized planning system. Enterprises often hoard raw materials, hide their reserves, and buy or sell on the unofficial market to obtain the materials they really need. By hoarding, they prepare themselves for a rainy day. Even if the sewing machine enterprise cannot possibly use the huge screws, it may be able to barter them unofficially for something useful at a future date. By hiding productive reserves, the enterprise protects itself from the unrealistic quotas that are endemic to taut planning. This tendency to underestimate productive capacity in turn encourages planners to overestimate enterprise capabilities, since they realize that hidden reserves do exist. And computer technology offers no panacea to planners: If central planners are misfed data from lower levels, no amount of computer sophistication will produce a realistic plan.

Levels of productivity are also generally lower in the Soviet Union than in Western economies at comparable levels of economic development. All resources, including labor, are increasingly in short supply. Workers are hard to fire, and thus are difficult to discipline and drive to higher levels of output. Natural resources are often underutilized: Free use of land is usually granted to enterprises; and charges for use of water and some mineral deposits have only recently been implemented in order to reduce waste of these valuable resources. Mining enterprises are too often oriented toward a single goal. For example, a coal-mining enterprise will use any method to extract coal at a low cost but may discard valuable minerals that could, at some expense, be retrieved for profitable use elsewhere. This type of waste is ever more costly as easily accessible deposits are depleted. Future growth depends on more efficient use of existing capabilities, since new sources of labor, capital, and cheap raw materials are largely exhausted.

Ethnicity and Economics. One of the major social problems confronting the Soviet leadership involves management of the Soviet Union's ethnically diverse population. While we will examine this issue in greater depth in Chapter 30, here we will briefly introduce the manner in which ethnic diversity complicates Soviet economic planning. As in other European countries, there is a certain trade-off between pursuing economic policies that will further regional (and thus ethnic) equality, on the one hand, and policies that will assure the most efficient use of investment capital, on the other hand. Historically, the Soviet regime has sought to reduce, though not eliminate, regional inequality. The most backward regions in Central Asia are considerably better off than previously, but they still lag behind the European part of the country in terms of industrialization and standard of living. In the later Brezhnev years, the leaders apparently decided that national economic goals had to take priority over further efforts at regional equalization. This may seem sensible, given the resource constraints confronting the Soviet Union, but it also may heighten ethnic tensions.

Demographic patterns among the various ethnic groups introduce a new, even more troubling, aspect to future economic planning. At present the most economically developed sections of the Soviet Union, the European areas, generally suffer from a labor shortage. This is aggravated by low birth rates among the Russians, other closely related Slavic peoples (Ukrainians, Belorussians), and the Baltic peoples. The Muslim population groups of Central Asia and Kazakhstan, on the other hand, are reproducing at a much higher rate (see Chapter 30); here the economic infrastructure is not adequate to optimally employ the growing population. Not only does the Russian majority face the prospect of becoming less than 50 percent of the population, but the demographic shift also brings with it the possibility of serious economic dislocations. Valuable labor resources are not located where they are needed, and ethnic tension might result from poor policy choices.

The leadership faces several policy options, all of which have definite costs. More industrial and agricultural investment could be directed to Central Asia and Kazakhstan to take advantage of the labor surplus. However, the area is low in water resources. To solve this problem, a major diversion of several Siberian rivers from North to South has been proposed and debated for several years now. This would be a costly and ecologically risky affair; further, it would divert resources from other essential projects, such as the exploitation of the rich natural resource potential of Siberia. (At the Twenty-Seventh Party Congress in 1986 it appeared that the project had been dropped.) Another option would be to attempt to relocate central Asian labor to the European part of the country or to Siberia, where it is needed. However, these population groups have been reluctant to move, partially because of their strong ties to their traditional communities. The Soviet leadership seems unwilling to engage in forced relocation, and efforts to develop incentive structures to encourage voluntary population movement have thus far had little success. Even if successful, this option might open a Pandora's box of ethnic and racial integration issues.

Demographic shifts are closely linked to other economic problems, for they starkly pose the question of rational resource investment (in this case, labor). Rising costs for energy and natural resource exploitation also complicate issues of regional investment policy. As the more easily accessible deposits of coal and natural gas are being depleted or are becoming too expensive to extract in the European part of the country, Siberian resources present the most economical option for filling raw material and energy needs (along with nuclear energy). The difficulties involved in attracting labor to these intemperate climates are aggravated by the poor social, consumer, and housing facilities. Central Asians, accustomed to warm climates and plentiful supplies of produce, are unlikely to be lured even by the higher salaries offered in Siberia. The movement of Europeans to Siberia would worsen even further the labor shortages in the developed areas of the country.

The Soviet leaders have little slack in the labor supply with which to fill these gaps. While a larger proportion of the Soviet population works in the agricultural sector than in most Western industrialized countries, many of the more productive young men and women have already been lured away to the industrial sector, leaving a disproportionate number of elderly, unskilled women in agricultural work. In addition, women have already been recruited into the labor force in large numbers in the urbanized European sections of the country. Therefore, industrial labor shortages continue to concern economic planners.

These socioeconomic problems are interconnected: Poor economic performance aggravates social problems and spurs consumer discontent; this discontent in turn lowers citizen motivation and spawns resistance to state policy. In the face of these complex problems, will the new leadership be able to forge a new social contract that will ensure continued stability and regime legitimacy? Can planners accurately estimate consumer demand if they refuse to accept some sort of market reform? Will the regime become more responsive to popular interests? Does the Soviet system truly face another major transition, and if so, how will the leaders respond? In subsequent chapters we will seek to answer these questions, as we examine the basic economic and political institutions of the Sovet Union.

Notes

1. Vera Dunham, *In Stalin's Time: Middleclass Values in Soviet Fiction* (Cambridge: Cambridge University Press, 1976), p. 5.
2. Gregory D. Andrusz, *Housing and Urban Development in the USSR* (London: Macmillan, in association with the Centre for Russian and East European Studies, University of Birmingham, 1982), pp. 286–87.
3. Jerry Hough, *The Soviet Union and Social Science Theory* (Cambridge: Harvard University Press, 1977), chap. 1.
4. H. Gordon Skilling and Franklyn Griffiths, eds., *Interest Groups in Soviet Politics* (Princeton: Princeton University Press, 1971).
5. Valerie Bunce and John M. Echols III, "Soviet Politics in the Brezhnev Era: 'Pluralism' or 'Corporatism'?" in *Soviet Politics in the Brezhnev Era,* ed. Donald Kelley (New York: Praeger, 1980).
6. Jerry Hough and Merle Fainsod, *How the Soviet Union Is Governed* (Cambridge: Harvard University Press, 1979), p. 289.
7. Thane Gustafson, *Reform in Soviet Politics* (Cambridge: Cambridge University Press, 1981), p. 158.
8. Cited in David Lane, *Soviet Economy and Society* (Oxford: Basil Blackwell, 1985), p. 56.
9. Jerry Hough, *Soviet Leadership in Transition* (Washington, DC: The Brookings Institution, 1980), p. 61.

29

State and Party Institutions

Principles of Soviet Government

Soviet political institutions often have different functions and powers from their apparent counterparts in liberal democracies. Even more than in Western politics, their actual powers may diverge greatly from descriptions in the constitution. And we have much less opportunity to observe them in practice than we do Western political bodies. Therefore, there is a certain amount of detective work or informed inference involved in trying to understand exactly how the political process works in the Soviet Union. Students of Soviet politics can often find themselves baffled by this lack of information and by the uniqueness of Soviet institutional arrangements.

The foundations for Soviet political institutions were laid down in the 1920s and 1930s. However, over time, the large bureaucratic institutions have taken on some operational features characteristic of bureaucracies in other advanced states. One U.S. expert has dubbed the Soviet Union "USSR Incorporated," highlighting the similarities between the processes of Soviet politics and the operation of large bureaucratic organizations in the United States.[1]

A Single-Party System

There is only one political party in the Soviet Union. By the early 1920s, all alternative parties had been repressed, and none has been allowed to emerge since. (In some Eastern European countries, for example in Czechoslovakia, Bulgaria, the German Democratic Republic, and Poland, other parties are allowed to exist and are in fact represented in the legislative bodies, but they are carefully controlled by the ruling communist party and have no real political power.)

How one can speak of a political party if it has no political competition? In the Western context, the reality reflects the origin of the word *party,* namely, a part or division. However, political parties not only organize political competion but also serve other functions. The Communist Party of the Soviet Union (CPSU), like political parties elsewhere, seeks to mobilize the population in support of certain goals and, in this way, provides a link between the political authorities and the population; it also articulates a distinct political ideology and tries to create a coherent belief system for its adherents. Like Western parties, the CPSU is an important mechanism for selecting political leaders, through membership recruitment and its own internal promotion structure.

Soviet authorities explain that only one party is necessary because Soviet society is free of class contradictions and, therefore, the CPSU can represent all of the working people of the Soviet Union effectively. This is a questionable point: Surely parties can represent social forces other than classes; and it is debatable whether the Soviet Union has eliminated all class conflict. On the contrary, M. Djilas, a former Yugoslavian party leader, later turned dissident, has suggested that the party itself forms the foundation of power for a new ruling class.[2] Party leaders clearly enjoy economic and social privileges sometimes attributed to a ruling class.

Party/State Governance

One of the most confusing aspects of Soviet political life is the existence of parallel party and state institutions throughout the system. In Western polities, there are both party institutions (local party organizations, party conferences, executive committees, and so forth) and state institutions (the legislative, executive, and judiciary). This may seem reasonable in the Western context, since parties alternate in power and, thus, in control of the state structures. Since only one party exists in the Soviet Union, however, the roles of party and state organs are blurred. In practice, functions and personnel overlap between state and party organs.

As a rule of thumb, one can say that the party provides the basic ideological guidelines and sets the broad parameters of policy, while the state administrative organs are in charge of implementing the policies laid out by the party. Thus one could think of party organs as policy-making organs and state organs as executive organs. As Western experience has demonstrated, however, executive organs often take on a *de facto* policy-making role because of their expertise, their day-to-day involvement in dealing with problems and their organizational resources (including their size). This pattern applies in the Soviet Union as well; therefore, state organs also have some policy-making functions and are an important source of information for the party authorities as they formulate policy.

Soviet state institutions look very much like Western parliamentary structures in terms of formal constitutional powers. The Soviet Constitution provides for a parliament (called the Supreme Soviet), a cabinet (called the Council of Ministers), and a prime minister. As in France and West Germany, there is also a president who formally heads the Soviet state. There are even local councils (the soviets) that exist to represent the population at the city, regional, and republic levels. This structural similarity to Western parliamentary institutions provides a useful guide in understanding the constitutional powers and organizational structure of these state institutions, but it can be misleading if one is seeking to grasp the real power of these bodies. True legislative power lies with the party, not the Supreme Soviet, and there are parallel state and party institutions at most levels that interact in a complex manner.

This duality of institutions (the parallel state and party structures) has its origins in the 1920s. Initially, the Soviet Union was to be a land of *soviet* power. The soviets were not a part of the Bolshevik party but represented the broader mass of workers, soldiers, and peasants. These institutions were to be the basis for workers' power, under the ideological leadership of the Communist Party. But as the soviets were weakened during and after the Civil War, they came to be dominated by local Bolshevik party organs. Their functions as representative and legislative bodies gradually gave way to submission to party dominance. The soviets and other state institutions have been maintained to this day, although they have taken on quite diffferent functions than originally foreseen by the early revolutionary leaders.

Democratic Centralism. We have already discussed democratic centralism — discussing policy questions before a decision is made but enforcing strict discipline thereafter, and electing leaders through a hierarchical delegate system — in the context of early party organization. It remains the organizational principle of party operation and has even been extended to apply to state organs in a modified form. Over time, especially from the late 1920s to the mid-1950s, the centralizing dimension came to predominate over the democratic dimension; now elections are uncontested, and minority opinions, at least on controversial or sensitive issues, may be denied expression even before a decision is made. On the other hand, the range of policy debate on less-sensitive domestic issues has been allowed to expand considerably since the death of Stalin.

Political-Economic Centralism. In the Soviet Union, almost all aspects of the economy are state-owned and state-run (exceptions, discussed in Chapter 28, include the private peasant plots and the unofficial black market). Consequently, it is virtually impossible to draw a distinction between economic and political power in the Soviet Union. The leading state organs are ultimately responsible for supervising the operation of economic enterprises and associations; virtually all adults are employees of the state (or of collective farms, which are also subject to state directives). Political and economic institutions are organized in a centralized, hierarchical manner with lower organs responsible in one way or another to higher bodies in the chain.

Administrative Federalism. The Soviet Union is formally a federal system; that is, the constitution delegates specific powers to regional levels of government while the remaining powers are vested in the central All-Union government. The most important federal units are the fifteen union republics. Within some republics there are additional federal units called autonomous republics, autonomous regions, and national areas.

The federal units are founded on ethnic divisions. The Soviet Union has over one hundred distinct ethnic groups; the largest, the Russian, makes up only slightly over half the population. Each republic is dominated by one ethnic group; for example, the Russian republic is dominated by the Russian population. In order to qualify for union republic status, an ethnic group must reside on an external border of the Soviet Union; other sizeable ethnic groups that are located in the interior of the country may be given status as autonomous republics, autonomous regions, or national areas.

According to the Soviet Constitution, "a Union Republic is a sovereign Soviet socialist state that has united with other Soviet Republics. . ." (Article 76). The constitution grants the union republic independent authority in its territory in all fields not granted to the central All-Union authorities (i.e., the authorities of the Soviet Union as a whole). However, in practice, the powers of the union republics are greatly limited and are largely of an administrative, rather than a policy-making, character. While the union republics do adopt their own constitutions, economic plans, and budgets, and can regulate certain elements of cultural life, these powers are exercised under the strict guidance of the highly centralized CPSU. The limited autonomy of the union republics is exemplified by the fact that their budgets are also part of the central All-Union budget of the Soviet Union. The precepts of democratic centralism restrict the ability of the republic authorities to embark upon bold initiatives or to exercise some of the powers granted to them formally in the constitution such as the right to secede from the union (Article 72). The union republics are given little genuine authority to make policy; they generally implement policies made at the center. Therefore, federalism in the Soviet Union is little more than a formality, since federalism, by definition, involves some actual division of decision-making authority among various levels of government. In this sense one can perhaps speak of "administrative federalism," namely delegation of some administrative authority to the constituent federal units, which have an ambiguous status in exercising their constitutionally-defined powers.

However restricted the power of the union republics and other federal units, federalism has allowed ethnic elites to experience upward political mobility within their own regions. The party's first secretary of the republic is almost always of the dominant ethnic group in the region (although the second secretary is usually a Russian, or at least from a Slavic group, ethnically similar to the Russians). Furthermore, in recent years, the indigenous elites in the union republics have become a lobbying force for regional interests. For example, they may press for greater investment funds for their republics or for greater representation of indigenous elites in state and party posts. On the other hand, the division of the Soviet Union into federal units may have made it easier for the Russian-dominated elites to inhibit the formation of strong identifications among ethnically similar groups, such as the various Islamic peoples of Central Asia, where there are five union republics; thus, identification as an Uzbek, a Kazakh, or a Kirghiz may be stronger than having a common Islamic tradition. Federalism has been an important instrument for management of ethnic conflict in the Soviet Union; at the same time, it may provide the institutional foundation for what one Western scholar has called a "new nationalism" among indigenous ethnic elites.[3]

Collective Interests over Individual Rights. Classical liberalism never gained a strong foothold in Russia, nor did there develop a strong ideological commitment to individual rights such as exists in many Western polities. The interests of society as a whole predominate. This notion is rooted in traditional Russian culture; further, Marxism itself emphasizes the social context of human life.

In the Soviet Union, human rights are viewed primarily in socio-economic terms rather than in terms of civil liberties (e.g., freedom of speech, assembly, the press). The constitution guarantees such social rights as the right to work; to rest and leisure; to health protection; to maintenance in old age, sickness, and disability; to housing; to education, and to cultural benefits. The Soviet Constitution also guarantees citizens civil liberties such as freedom of speech, the press, and assembly (Article 50) and "the right to associate in public organizations that promote their political activity and initiative and satisfaction of their various interests" (Article 51). These and other rights guaranteed in Chapter 7 of the constitution, however, are subject to the provision that "citizens exercise their rights and freedoms as inseparable from the performance of their duties and obligations" (Article 59) and to the condition that exercise of these rights "not be to the detriment of the interests of society or the state, or infringe the rights of other citizens" (Article 39). While most Western polities also place limits on the exercise of such individual political rights when they come into conflict with broader social or national interests, in the Soviet Union the range of actions that is considered threatening to state and social interests is broader than in most Western polities and, therefore, the exercise of these civil liberties is more restricted. This different attitude toward individual rights is also reflected in the legal process. There is less emphasis in the Soviet Union on the observation of procedural guarantees in determining legal culpability and more readiness on the part of the authorities to judge the substance of the case without adhering to strict procedural regulations. Since the death of Stalin, however, concerns of "socialist legality" have increased the application of regularized procedures in nonpolitical cases.

Incrementalism. In principle, the highly centralized, state-run economic system of the Soviet Union should enable rational, goal-oriented planning. In other words, theoretically, planners at the center should be able to take all relevant information into account and, on this basis, develop a blueprint for social and economic development. This is, in fact, what Soviet leaders profess to do, but in practice, at least since the beginning of the Brezhnev era, policy making has taken on an incremental character. Thus, last year's plan provides the basis for this year's plan, with only moderate alterations or reforms. Perhaps incrementalism is bound to afflict any complex and interdependent system. Furthermore, predictability and stability are benefits of such a conservative approach to problem-solving. Finally, entrenched bureaucratic interests everywhere seek to protect their prerogatives and, therefore, are unwilling to accept radical departures in policy.

The Party: Policymaker and Pacesetter

The Basic Structures

The most powerful organ in the Soviet Union is the Politburo, the decision-making center of the Communist Party of the Soviet Union. (See Figure 29.1.) This body considers all important policy issues in both the foreign and domestic spheres. Although the nature of its deliberations are a carefully guarded secret, we do know that this body generally meets once a week. Beginning under Andropov, the leading Soviet newspaper *Pravda,* "Truth," began publishing brief, if somewhat sterile, reports on these weekly meetings, so we now have a clearer idea of the range of issues that the Politburo might consider. For example, recent accounts covered such issues as electrical appliance output, book publishing, West Siberian development, economic plan fulfillment, biotechnology, and housing construction. As this list suggests, economic policy is an important focus of the Politburo's deliberations.

The membership of the Politburo has increased over time. However, due to the death of several members in the early 1980s, following the Twenty-Seventh Party Congress of February/March, 1986, it had only twelve full voting members, compared to fourteen in 1981. The head of the Politburo is the General Secretary of the party, presently Mikhail Gorbachev. The General Secretary is also the highest official on another important party body, the Secretariat. Ethnic Russians have dominated the Politburo, although ethnic minorities are also represented. Generally, in recent years, there has been at least one Ukrainian (in 1986 V.V. Shcherbitskii) and someone from Central Asia or Kazakhstan (in 1986 D.A. Kunaev) on the Politburo. Other individuals of non-Russian background on the Politburo in 1986 included E. Shevardnadze (Georgia), promoted to full membership in July, 1985, and G.A. Aliev (Azerbaidzhan), promoted in 1982. Only once in Soviet history has the Politburo included a woman, Ekaterina Furtseva, who was a member from 1956 to 1961. Since Gorbachev's accession to the top post, younger men have been brought into the Politburo; in 1986, following the Twenty-Seventh Party Congress, the average age of full and candidate (nonvoting) mem-

Figure 29.1 Communist Party Structure*

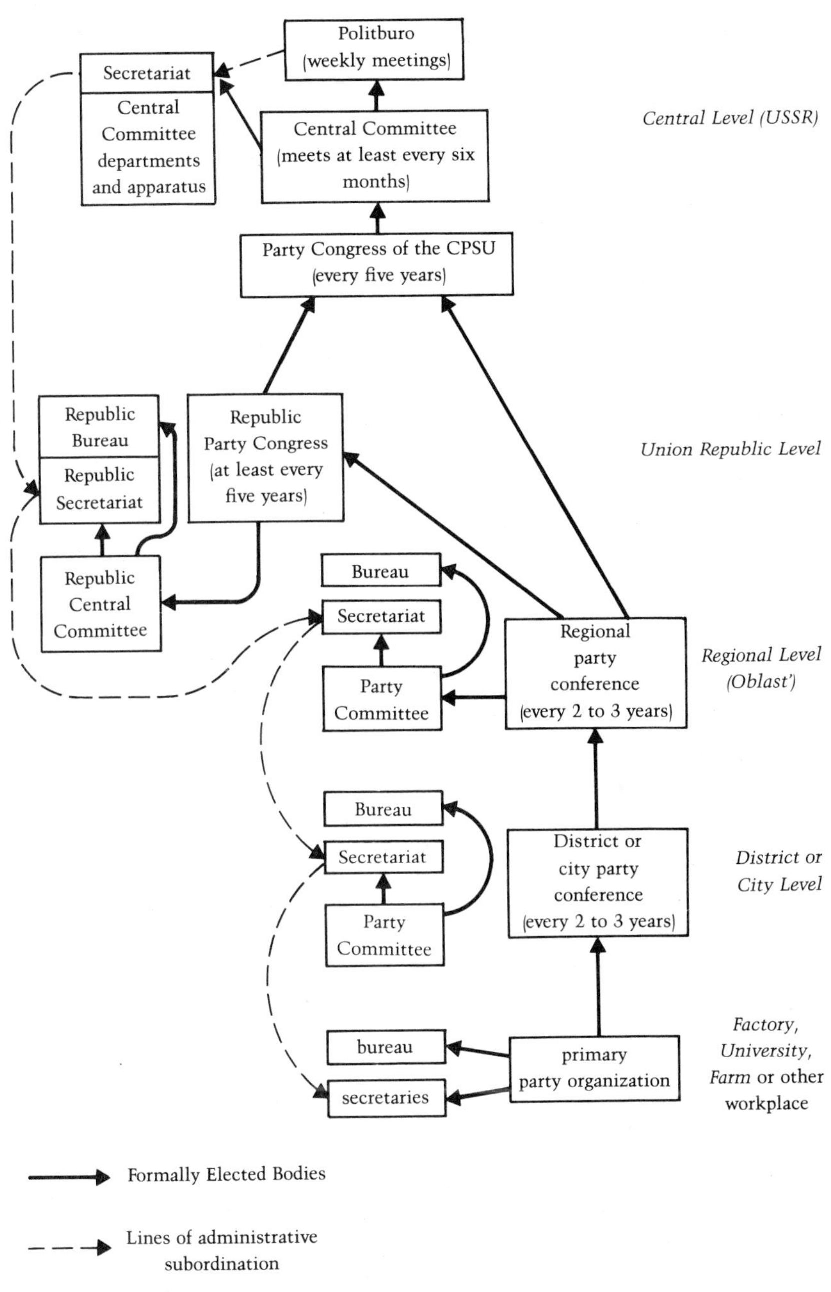

*For clarity of presentation, some administrative levels are omitted (e.g., territories, autonomous republics, etc.).

bers was sixty-three. (However, Gorbachev, at the age of fifty-five, was the youngest full member.)

The Central Committee, another important party organ, formally elects the membership of the Politburo. However, this body is presented with a preselected list of candidates for approval, so in effect the Politburo chooses its own members. Apparently, however, some effort is made to represent major interests among the elite, as reflected in the ethnic composition of the Politburo and the inclusion of the Minister of Foreign Affairs (Eduard Shevardnadze in 1986), Secretariat members, and individuals with experience in both agriculture and industry. From 1973 until D.M. Ustinov's death in December, 1984, the Minister of Defense was also a full voting member; in 1986, his replacement, M.S. Sokolov, was a nonvoting (candidate) member. Under extreme circumstances, as in 1957 when the committee defended Khrushchev from the antiparty group and in 1964 when it deposed him, the Central Committee may in fact play a somewhat independent role in top leadership squabbles; presumably, the Politburo has learned to anticipate possible objections from the Central Committee.

The Central Committee itself is an important political body. Its membership, formally selected by the Party Congress, increased steadily over time until the Twenty-Seventh Party Congress in 1986, when the full voting membership declined from 319 to 307. The Central Committee might be viewed as the Who's Who of Soviet politics, for it includes the most important and powerful political figures. One might think of it as the closest thing to a real parliament, even if legally the Supreme Soviet is the responsible legislative body, according to the Soviet Constitution. Western Sovietologists often study the composition of the Central Committee in order to understand changes in the character of the Soviet elite or to assess the influence of various members of the Politburo. The General Secretary and other important Politburo members may try to assure that their clients (i.e., those with whom they have worked and who have a certain sense of personal loyalty to them) are represented on the Central Committee. During a period of leadership change, such as after the death of Brezhnev, the strength of support a leader has in the Central Committee may have some influence on his or her prospects for selection as the top party leader.

Generally the Central Committee includes individuals from all walks of Soviet political life (see Table 29.1). First party secretaries from the *oblast',* "regional," level are strongly represented, as are other *apparatchiki* (full-time party workers) and officials from central and republic state structures. Although many ethnic minorities are somewhat underrepresented relative to their proportion of the population, apparently some

Table 29.1 Affiliation of Voting Members of the Central Committee of the CPSU, 1966 and 1981

	1966	1981	% CHANGE
Party			
Secretaries of Central Committee	11	10	− 9
Other central officials	4	20	+400
Republic party secretaries	22	21	− 4
Regional/local party secretaries of the Russian Republic	37	66	+ 78
Regional/local party secretaries of other republics	10	20	+ 50
Government institutions			
Presidium USSR Council of Ministers	12	15	+ 25
Ministers and other central government officials	31	62	+100
Premiers and other republic government officials	8	12	+ 33
Regional/local government officials	1	2	+100
Foreign service	13	14	+ 7
Armed forces commanders	12	24	+100
Other organizations			
Officials of 'mass organizations'	5	8	+ 60
Press	1	3	+200
Union and Republic Supreme Soviet officials	8	9	+ 12
Legal officials	1	2	100
Academicians, scientists, technologists	2	2	0
Writers	2	2	0
Industrial executives	5	3	− 40
Industrial workers	3	15	+400
Agricultural executives	1	0	0
Agricultural workers	0	1	0
Retired top officials	3	0	0
Totals	195	319	

SOURCE R.F. Miller and T.H. Rigby, *Twenty-Sixth Congress of the CPSU in Current Political Perspective,* (Canberra: Dept. of Political Science, Research School of Social Sciences, The Australian National University, Occasional Paper No. 16, 1982), p. 77

effort is made to assure ethnic diversity; further, women, manual workers, and collective farm workers are all strongly underrepresented. In recent times, women have made up only about 4 percent of voting Central Committee members, a figure comparable, however, to female representation in many Western legislative bodies.

The Central Committee meets at least twice a year, but sometimes for one or two days only. Little information is available to the public on the content of the meetings — sometimes only the topics discussed and the speakers participating. It appears doubtful that these meetings fulfill any major deliberative function in the party. Except for rare instances noted above, no public dissension emerges from Central Committee meetings; however, these sessions and the interaction that takes place outside of them most likely facilitate communication between the Politburo and the broader elite in the system. Thus, the Central Committee may exert some indirect political influence.

The Central Committee elects not only the Politburo but also the party Secretariat, a small body with only eleven members in 1986. It has, however, taken on a key role in the system, for it heads the party bureaucracy, which at the central level is estimated by political scientist Jerry Hough to include some fifteen hundred officials (*apparatchiki*). The party bureaucracy subordinate to the Secretariat is called the Central Committee apparatus. If one includes full-time party workers at the republic, regional, and local levels, then the apparatus numbers close to, if not over, one hundred thousand individuals.[4]

Each secretary, or member of the Secretariat, supervises one or more departments of the Central Committee apparatus. Each department is in charge of a certain functional area, such as agriculture, culture, propaganda, or science and education. The secretary in charge of personnel matters (Egor Ligachev in 1986) is particularly important. Briefly, the functions fulfilled by the Secretariat and apparatus include: provision of advice to the Politburo on major policy issues; supervision of the state organs; and selection of personnel for important posts throughout the party/state structure. The Politburo must rely on the Secretariat and Central Committee apparatus for information and advice; further, the Secretariat sometimes provides actual drafts of policy for consideration. There is, of course, an overlap in membership between the Politburo and the Secretariat, most notably the General Secretary of the party. In early 1986, other members of the Secretariat also sat on the Politburo (e.g., Egor Ligachev and Lev Zaikov, who were added to the Politburo in April, 1985, and March, 1986, respectively). Also in March, 1986, Aleksandra Biriukova was added to the Secretariat, the first woman to hold high party office since 1961.

Western observers believe that any candidate for the top leadership post in the Soviet Union must be a member of both the Politburo and the Secretariat. Thus, when Andropov, already a Politburo member, was moved from his post as head of the Committee for State Security (KGB) to the Secretariat in May, 1982, shortly before Brezhnev's death in November, 1982, this seemed to indicate that he might be a candidate for the post of General Secretary. Andropov's successor, Konstantin Chernenko, was also a member of both bodies. Likewise, Gorbachev gained a position on the Secretariat in November, 1978, and became a member of the Politburo in October, 1980. He was elected General Secretary in March, 1985, following Chernenko's death.

The Party Congress, which formally elects the Central Committee, convenes every five years and was last held in February/March 1986. The Party Congress is a meeting of about five thousand delegates and has a more ceremonial than deliberative character. Delegates are selected by union republic and regional party conferences, members of which are chosen by lower party bodies, in line with the precepts of democratic centralism. Apparently it is an honor and political plum to be chosen to attend the Party Congress, for it means a trip to Moscow and involvement in a major political event. Selection of delegates is controlled by higher party organs at each stage, reflecting the "circular flow of power" discussed earlier. The Party Congress is presented with a slate of candidates for Central Committee membership, approves the new five-year plan for the economy, and hears reports by various party leaders, including the General Secretary.

Party structures at lower levels (republic, regional, district, and city) roughly parallel those at the top. Primary party organizations are the base organs to which every Communist Party member belongs. Generally, they are located in the workplace or in an educational institution and occasionally in residential areas; larger primary party organizations have a full-time secretary to carry out administrative tasks. The primary party organization is subordinate to the next highest level in the party hierarchy, generally to the city or *raion,* "district," party organs, and elects delegates to the party conference of the city or district organization. The city or district party conference (equivalent to the Party Congress at the center) in turn selects a committee (analogous to the Central Committee at the center), which elects a smaller body, called the bureau, and a secretariat, including a first secretary and deputy secretaries in charge of certain functional areas such as agriculture or culture. In accordance with the principles of democratic centralism, the city or district party conference elects delegates to the conference of the next highest level in the hierarchy (generally the *oblast',* "region"). At each level the basic structure is replicated, although the size of the full-time party staff is progressively larger as one proceeds up the bureaucratic structure.

A particularly important level in this hierarchy is that of the *oblast'*. There are over 120 *oblasti* in the Soviet Union, and the first secretary of the party at this level is a powerful political figure. Jerry Hough has called these individuals "Soviet prefects," since they serve as a crucial administrative link between the center and the region, analogous to the French *préfet*.[5] They are often key figures in bargaining for regional interests with the central party organization, and many of them are members of the Central Committee itself. They may also act as mediators among various conflicting interests at the regional level and in this way learn the important political skills of bargaining and compromise. The position of *oblast'* first secretary is an important stepping-stone for those aspiring to higher party positions. Many of the skills learned at the *oblast'* level may be helpful once a higher post is achieved.

The party is a complex structure organized on a hierarchical basis. While *apparatchiki* may have a common interest in maintaining the authority and strength of the party as an institution, the fact that diverse regional, ethnic, and economic constituencies form the party also means that within the party itself, different groups may lobby for their own particular interests, to benefit a particular region or a particular sector of the economy.

Functions of the Party

One of the most important functions of the top party organs, especially the Politburo, is formulation of policy. One can assume that any major policy proclamation has been considered and approved by that body, even though it may be formally issued as a resolution of the Central Committee, a decree of the Council of Ministers, or a law enacted by the Supreme Soviet. This is not to say that these other institutions have no input into final policy, for the Politburo must rely on other bodies for information and advice. Not only do the Secretariat and the Central Committee apparatus provide such aid, but the Politburo may also turn to the ministries, scholars, or other experts in dealing with specific problems.

The party plays the key role in at least three other areas: personnel selection, oversight, and ideological leadership. Personnel selection is controlled through the *nomenklatura* system. Appointment to offices on the *nomenklatura* list is subject to party approval, which in some cases may be a mere formality, but in others is tantamount to selection by the party. The *nomenklatura* includes not only all important party posts from the local to the central level but also many important state positions in ministries, large enterprises, educational institutions, trade unions, and so forth. The Secretariat at the central level and secretariats at lower levels in the party structure are responsible for overseeing the *nomenklatura* system. Some very important positions are within the *nomenklatura* of the central Secretariat itself, while appointment to local positions may well be in the *nomenklatura* of a secretariat lower in the hierarchy. Since the posts included in the *nomenklatura* system are not made public, Western scholars can only speculate or infer from indirect clues which positions are filled under this system.

Some have suggested that the *nomenklatura* forms the real ruling class in the Soviet Union, for the *nomenklatura* system enables the political elite to act as gatekeeper for its own ranks. The *nomenklatura* may serve a function somewhat similar to inherited wealth in the West. This is not to suggest that the children of the present elite always, or even generally, are selected to fill top posts in the Soviet Union; rather, the elite does have a mechanism by which it can determine who should succeed it.

A second important function of party organs is oversight of activities of the state organizations. In most cases, a particular party body holds a position which is structurally parallel to one or more state institutions and is responsible for seeing that these organs carry out their tasks according to the guidelines set down by the party. For example, most departments of the Central Committee apparatus are responsible for overseeing the activities of a number of state ministries. At lower levels in the structure, the party organizations in enterprises and other institutions see that the basic goals of the party are adhered to. At times this oversight function is not totally effective: The staff of the relevant party organ may be considerably smaller than that of the state organ being supervised; party officials may also lack the expertise necessary to evaluate performance; or party organs may come to share interests with the state organs they are intended to oversee. For example, the Agriculture Department of the party apparatus is to oversee all those ministries and state committees dealing with agricultural affairs. At the same time, it may share an interest in winning increased investment for agriculture and thus be somewhat reluctant to reveal major deficiencies in operations that might weaken the case for preferred treatment. This is somewhat analogous to the relationship that can develop between the regulated and the regulators in Western states. Nonetheless, in other instances, the party organs are able to maintain some distance from the particular interests of the various state bureaucracies and, in this way, introduce a broader-ranging perspective. Even here, it is evident that lower-level party organs cannot always enforce their position without direct intervention and support from the top party bodies.

Another function fulfilled by the party is that of ideological leadership. The party is the source and judge of political orthodoxy: Its program, statutes, and statements provide the guidelines for the entire system of education and propaganda. In the Soviet context, the word *propaganda* does not have the negative connotation it carries in the West, for it is accepted that the party *should* propagate correct political positions among the population. Furthermore, party leaders admit that Soviet ideology does serve particular interests, namely, those of the working people of the Soviet Union. In 1961, under Khrushchev's guidance, the party adopted a new party program that laid out the post-Stalinist interpretation of political reality, but many of its key notions have been superseded or supplemented in the twenty-five years since. A revised party program was adopted at the Twenty-Seventh Party Congress in February/March 1986. This document places particular emphasis on the importance of accelerated socio-economic development in bringing about the transition from socialism to communism. Like the previous party program, the new version affirms the ultimate goal of Soviet policy to be the building of a classless society in which each citizen will freely and fully contribute to the social good.

Why does the CPSU insist on continuing to issue ideological statements that bear little relationship to the actual problems confronting Soviet society? Could not the rhetoric of Marxism-Leninism just as easily be dispensed with, since it is most likely either ignored or viewed with cynicism by large portions of the Soviet population? Do the Soviet leaders themselves believe in their own ideology? These are intriguing questions with no clear answer. The relative isolation of the Soviet population from alternative political viewpoints and ideologies may well make it difficult for citizens to clearly and critically examine Soviet orthodoxy. Observers have commented that official Soviet ideology fulfills much the same function as Fourth of July rhetoric in the United States. Alternatively, a Polish dissident has suggested that the matter is more complex: By appropriating for itself key concepts like equality, socialism, and democracy to describe Soviet society, the regime undermines the ability of the population to develop an alternative conceptualization of these potentially subversive ideas.[6]

Membership and Recruitment

Just under 10 percent of the adult population in the Soviet Union are members of the party. Not all demographic groups are equally represented, so the percentage is much higher in some segments of the population. For example, males with a university education are significantly overrepresented, while females, who make up more than 50 percent of the population, made up only 27.4 percent of party membership as of 1983. (This does, however, represent a steady increase from 19 percent in 1952 and 7.4 percent in 1920.)[7] Manual workers, peasants, and many ethnic minorities are also underrepresented, as indicated in Table 29.2. However, the proportion of manual workers has increased in the last two decades.

Party membership not only provides certain benefits, like improved chances for upward job mobility and, in some cases, access to special stores or facilities, but also involves extra duties. The first of these duties is complete political loyalty to the party line. The party member is to be a model worker and citizen, and to support party positions and decisions. Second, there is a time commitment, for the party member must

Table 29.2 National Composition of the CPSU

	January 1, 1946	January 1, 1973	January 1, 1983	Percent of Soviet population by 1979 census
Russian	67.8	60.9	59.7	52.40
Ukrainian	12.1	16.0	16.0	16.20
Belorussian	2.1	3.5	3.8	3.60
Uzbek	1.1	2.0	2.4	4.75
Kazakh	1.7	1.7	2.0	2.50
Georgian	2.0	1.7	1.7	1.36
Azerbaidzhan	1.0	1.4	1.7	2.09
Lithuanian	0.1	0.7	0.7	1.09
Moldavian	0.1	0.4	0.5	1.13
Latvian	0.1	0.4	0.4	.55
Kirghiz	0.3	0.3	0.4	.73
Tadzhik	0.2	0.4	0.4	1.11
Armenian	1.8	1.5	1.5	1.58
Turkmen	0.2	0.3	0.4	.77
Estonian	0.1	0.3	0.3	.39
Other	9.3	8.5	8.1	9.75

SOURCE "KPSS v tsifrakh," *Partiinaia zhizn'* ("The CPSU in figures," *Party life*), vol. 15 (August, 1983), p. 23.

attend extra meetings, take part in various campaigns to publicize party positions, or help get out the vote on election day. Apart from political socialization and sex discrimination, one explanation for the lower representation of women in the party may be that household and child-care duties deny women the time and energy required to join and rise in the party.

The CPSU attempts to recruit the most promising and able young people for its ranks. Youths between the ages of fifteen and twenty-seven often join the Komsomol, the Communist Youth League, and many proceed from there to party membership. The party tries to attract the most talented individuals to ensure that these people work within the system, rather than against it. This is one way of hindering the development of an alternative technocratic elite that could be a threat to party dominance, and the result of this strategy is a higher level of representation of educated groups (the intelligentsia, especially technical specialists) in the party as compared to workers and peasants. Undoubtedly many recruits join the party primarily out of career ambition rather than political enthusiasm. Others may refuse to join, despite invitations; they may not wish to profess loyalty to an ideology they reject, or they may wish to avoid the demands of party membership.

The State: Administrative and Soviet Structures

Since the 1930s, a huge bureaucratic state structure has developed alongside the party in the Soviet Union. Structurally, the Soviet state organs bear close resemblance to those of Western parliamentary systems, but the functions of these organs differ from those of their formal counterparts in the West. (See Figure 29.2.)

The Soviets

Formally, the legislative organs of Soviet society, the soviets, are directly elected at each level by universal sufferage. Unlike the system in party organs, therefore, selection does not involve a delegate system in which lower bodies elect representatives to higher bodies. Rather, there is a direct popular vote for the Supreme Soviet (the national legislative body) as there is for local soviets. These bodies allegedly represent all of the working people, not just party members. In fact, a substantial portion

Figure 29.2 State Structures of the USSR*

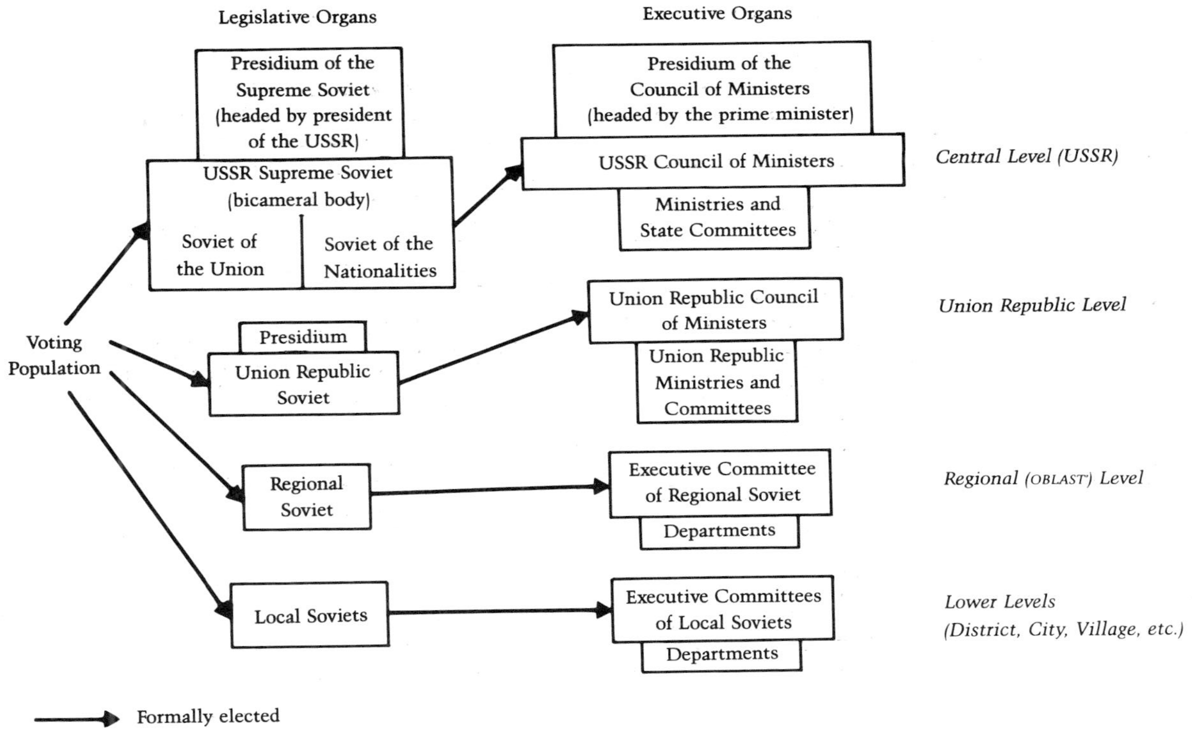

*Levels of government have been simplified for clarity of presentation.

of deputies elected to the soviets are not themselves party members. In 1979, 28.3 percent of Supreme Soviet deputies were not party members, while at the local (city or village) level the figure was somewhat over 50 percent on average.

Elections are not competitive; only one candidate is presented to the electorate. Therefore, the nomination process is crucial. Various public organizations (e.g., trade unions, work collectives, the Komsomol) may make suggestions, but the party has final control over the selection process. Thus, those nonparty candidates who are nominated for office are deemed by the party to be loyal and trustworthy. The citizen is obligated to vote, so that the usual turnout rates are over 99 percent. In the same way, more than 99 percent of the voters approve the name on the ballot, although citizens may cross off the name of the single candidate by entering a special voting booth. Since voters otherwise simply drop their ballots in the box without entering the booth, a voter is advertising his or her dissent by exercising the right to reject the proposed candidate. Nonetheless, in a small number of cases, a majority of the electorate in a district has rejected the candidate offered. When this happens, a new candidate is placed before the electorate.

Demographically, the soviets are much more representative of the population at large than are party bodies such as the Central Committee. For example, in 1984, workers constituted 35.2 percent of the deputies of the Supreme Soviet, whereas only about 4 percent of Central Committee members elected in 1981 were from that group. In the same year, collective farmers constituted 16.1 percent of the Supreme Soviet deputies, but less than 1% of the voting members of the Central Committee. Thus, a large proportion of the population has the occasion to participate in some aspect of soviet life at one point or another. Undoubtedly, one of the real functions of the soviet structure is to involve large numbers of citizens in official political activities and in this way to develop a sense of belonging, even if one's real power or influence is negligible. The soviets also provide formal democratic legitimation for Soviet politics, for it can be claimed that all citizens have the opportunity to participate in the selection of their representatives. While the soviets have little, if any, real political influence (except perhaps at the local level), they may facilitate some communication of popular and regional sentiments to the leadership and of leadership goals to the population. At the local level, the soviets may have some impact on day-to-day activities, related to local recreational facilities, day-care, or housing, for example, although even in this area the executive organs of the local soviets (the soviet executive committee and its various departments and committees) are more important than the elected soviets themselves.

According to the constitution, the Supreme Soviet is the highest legislative body. It is a bicameral institution: The Soviet of the Union has 750 delegates, elected from districts of approximately equal population; and the Soviet of the Nationalities also has 750 members, but these deputies represent the various federal units (that is, union republics, autonomous regions, and so forth). Legislation is apparently always passed without dissent; thus, the deliberative function of meetings of the Supreme Soviet is negligible. The Supreme Soviet meets approximately twice per year, generally for only three or four days each session. More important than these meetings are the legislative commissions that may consider proposed drafts of laws. While these commissions do not initiate legislation or determine amendments on their own, they do allow the airing of diverse viewpoints and generate some proposed revisions that may or may not be integrated into the final draft by state and party leaders. The most active and influential members of these bodies tend to be officials who also hold important posts elsewhere in the system, not the deputies of peasant or working-class background.

Because the Supreme Soviet meets relatively infrequently, and then only briefly, in the interim a smaller body, the Presidium of the Supreme Soviet, acts on its behalf. This means that most legislative enactments are initially approved only by the Presidium, later to be rubber-stamped by the Supreme Soviet itself. The Presidium is formally elected by the Supreme Soviet, but its membership is almost certainly subject to high party approval. The Presidium is headed by the President of the Soviet Union, in 1986 Andrei Gromyko (formerly Minister of Foreign Affairs). Mikhail Gorbachev, as head of the party, might be expected to take on this post once he has consolidated his power (as Leonid Brezhnev did in 1977, when he replaced Nikolai Podgorny in that post). In this capacity, he would represent the Soviet Union as official head of state in his dealings with foreign dignitaries. Currently, Gorbachev either has not chosen or has not been able to do so.

The Executive Organs

The most important state bodies are the Council of Ministers, the ministries, and state committees. According to the Soviet Constitution, the Council of Ministers is "the highest executive and administrative body of state authority in the USSR" (Article 128). It is a large body of over 110 members, formally selected by the Supreme Soviet; membership includes the heads of the various ministries, chairpersons of state committees, and chairpersons of the councils of ministers of the union republics. The chairperson of the Council of Ministers is also prime minister (premier) of the Soviet Union and, thus, head of the government. In September, 1985, Nikolai Ryzhkov, like Gorbachev a member of the post-Stalinist generation, was appointed to this position to replace Brezhnev protégé Nikolai Tikhonov. Ryzhkov also sits on the Politburo, as did Tikhonov before him. Other members of the Council of Ministers, for example, E. Shevardnadzhe (also of the post-Stalinist generation), are Politburo members as well.

Because of the unwieldy size of the Council of Ministers, a smaller body, the Presidium of the Council of Ministers (distinct from the Presidium of the Supreme Soviet discussed above) serves as the working core. While the Council of Ministers itself may meet only once every several weeks, the Presidium undoubtedly convenes more frequently and routinely issues decisions and ordinances, often in conjunction with the party's Central Committee. The Presidium of the Council of Ministers plays a major role in supervising the complex Soviet economy.

Each of the ministries heads a functional branch of the economy, including, for example, the Ministry of Defense, Ministry of the Chemical Industry, Ministry of Transportation Construction, Ministry of Culture, Ministry of the Shipbuilding Industry, Ministry of Light Industry, and so forth. The state committees, on the other hand, have duties cutting across the various functional branches of the economy. The most important is Gosplan, the State Planning Committee, which is responsible for overseeing the drafting and implementation of the five-year and one-year economic plans. Other state committees include the State Committee on Prices, the State Committee on Science and Technology, the State Committee for Material-Technical Supplies, and the State Committee on Wages and Labor. Also attached to the Council of Ministers is the Committee for State Security (KGB).

While state officials are not necessarily party members, in general the higher the post, the greater the likelihood that its occupant will also be a party member. As discussed above, the various ministries are subject to oversight by the Central Committee apparatus of the party; however, the ministries often have much larger staffs than the corresponding departments of the party apparatus, which may make it difficult for the party to exert effective day-to-day oversight of their activities. As in Western polities, the large bureaucracies of the political executive often accrue considerable power through their command of expertise and organizational resources. Therefore, it is difficult to determine what the exact balance of power between the ministries and the party apparatus might be in any given case. While many officials in the ministry structure fall within the *nomenklatura* authority of the party Secretariat, apparently the party often simply confirms candidates who have risen through the ministry structure itself. In other cases, officials may move back and forth between posts in the ministry structure and the party structure, usually working in the same functional area (e.g., agriculture, chemical industry, metallurgy) in both institutions.

Another important state institution, about which little is known, is the Defense Council. This organ most likely is chaired by the General Secretary of the party himself and includes the Minister of Defense, some deputy ministers of defense, the Central Committee secretary responsible for defense matters, and perhaps a few other officials.

The Judiciary

The judiciary does not form an independent branch of the government as it does in some Western states; the notion of separation of powers is not endorsed by Soviet Marxist ideology. Rather, the law is seen as an arm of the political authority to further the process of constructing a socialist society. Since the appointment of judges and procurators is almost certainly part of the *nomenklatura* system, the party can exert some influence over the judiciary in this manner. Judges, who are assisted by two lay (people's) assessors, are formally elected directly by the population at the city or district level (as are the lay assessors) or by the appropriate soviet at higher levels, all under supervision of the party. The highest judicial body, the Supreme Court, is formally responsible to the Supreme Soviet. The Procurator General, also formally appointed by the Supreme Soviet, is responsible for overseeing law enforcement: After conducting an investigation, the procurator prosecutes the cases in the courts. Procurators at lower levels are appointed by the procurator general or the procurators of the union republics.

One should distinguish between the treatment of routine civil cases, routine criminal cases, and political cases (e.g., the trials of political dissidents). While the Soviet system differs in some regards from the U.S. system in civil cases, there is little reason to believe that in the post-Stalinist period, there is direct party intrusion into the administration of justice. In routine criminal cases, direct political intrusion may also be uncommon, but once officially indicted, a suspect is generally convicted; a political decision may also mandate harsh sentences for certain types of criminal charges.

Khrushchev initiated a campaign for "socialist legality," which involved increasing the uniformity of procedures and the codification of civil and criminal law. This has brought considerable predictability into the manner in which routine cases are handled. In some regards, Soviet legal practice resembles continental European patterns. For example, there is no jury trial, the judge is assisted by two lay assessors, and the pretrial investigation takes on more importance than in the United States. Unique aspects of Soviet legal practice center on the educative and deterrent roles attributed to law, as well as on the importance of social rehabilitation and peer involvement. The accused's general character and contribution to society may be considered as relevant evidence, and often coworkers or neighbors may be called to testify on these matters. The comrade courts at the base of the judicial system are in fact run by citizens in the neighborhood or workplace, and consider minor conflicts or infractions. They provide a mechanism of peer pressure to discourage antisocial behavior (such as playing music too loudly, littering the grounds) and can enforce only minimal penalties. Also unique in the Soviet Union is the greater importance assigned to crimes involving state money, such as theft of state property or embezzlement. Such crimes, on occasion, may even warrant the death penalty.

Political cases are another matter. If the defendant is charged with engaging in anti-Soviet propaganda or behavior, it is quite clear that the cards are stacked against him or her at the outset. Public access to these trials is often carefully controlled, as is information about their content. The defendant is limited in the choice of counsel. However, even in this area, greater predictability has been introduced since the early 1970s. Before being arrested, the individual generally is given ample warning by the KGB that his or her behavior is considered unacceptable. In other words, the arbitrary patterns of accusation and arrest characteristic of the Stalinist terror have been replaced by a firm, but fairly predictable, state repression of political dissent.

State-Party Interaction

The average Soviet citizen might well find the distinction between state and party authority pedantic, since the personnel and functions of the two sets of bodies are so intermeshed. For example, resolutions and decrees are regularly issued in the name of both the party Central Committee and the state Council of Ministers. Because of this overlap in activity, it is appropriate to speak of the leading institutions as the party/state.

Nonetheless, the distinction between state and party institutions should be maintained, for two reasons. First, official Soviet theory itself insists on the distinctive character of the two sets of bodies: The party provides ideological leadership, as the vanguard of the working class, while state institutions make policy and carry it out. Even if reality does not always reflect these idological principles, the official view undoubtedly influences the way in which the Soviet leadership understands its own goals. Second, the party, as an institution, does fulfill some roles that are also distinguishing features of the Soviet system: functioning as ideological pacesetter, controlling appointments (*nomenklatura*), and introducing a larger societal perspective in cases of conflict between individual state agencies. In the Soviet press, for example, particular state ministries are often chastised for departmentalism, which refers to the tendency of the particular agency to look at a problem from its own limited institutional perspective without considering the larger social ramifications. An example would be pollution of an important river by a chemical firm: Although discharge into the river would lower costs and improve the economic indicators of the enterprise, it might cause severe damage to other sectors — including the fishing industry, drinking-water supply, recreational facilities, and so forth. Examples of such departmentalism are widespread and probably inevitable as long as the particular branches of the economy are judged by their ability to produce a particular type of output. The party institutions can provide a broader societal perspective, even if particular party organs sometimes may also be advocates for the regions, industries, or branches they oversee. This is not to suggest that the party has no interests of its own — clearly the party *apparatchiki* have an interest in maintaining their own institutional

Theme: Industrial pollution.
Translation: "And our river has its source in this factory."

SOURCE *Krokodil,* no. 5 (February 1984), p. 6. Drawing by Iv. Cherepanova.

strength and the privileges they enjoy — but one should not dismiss entirely the notion that the party does represent, at least potentially, a perspective beyond the narrow concerns of the individual bureaucratic agencies of the state structure.

The Policy Process

Lack of public information makes it difficult to trace the actual policy-making process. Furthermore, there is no uniformity in the policy process from one policy-making area to another. For example, in the foreign policy area, there is little input from lower party or state officials, and public debate is limited. A high-ranking Soviet official who defected to the West in 1978 has suggested that the Politburo rarely, if ever, rejects proposals emanating from the Ministry of Foreign Affairs regarding foreign policy issues.[8] Regarding economic issues, on the other hand, public policy debate is fairly extensive and scholars play a prominent role. Here, particular ministries are likely to be only one of several influences on economic decision making. Public deliberation on sensitive domestic issues, such as ethnic relations, is again minimal or cloaked in esoteric terms understandable only to a select few.

Policy concerning nonsensitive domestic issues is generally initiated by top party officials, though there may be some exceptions (e.g., the widespread concern over ecological damage to Lake Baikal in the early 1960s probably emanated from scientists and journalists first and was then picked up by the party leadership). Of course, party leaders become aware of potential problems through information channels in the party apparatus or ministry structure, but actual placement on the political agenda requires leadership approval. Once an issue has been placed on the policy agenda, the Secretariat or Central Committee apparatus may provide information for discussion to the Politburo, along with supporting proposals and drafts of policy. Broad policy is then determined by the Politburo, with further details worked out in consultation with relevant state bodies, the party apparatus, and experts in the field. Many ministries have their own research institutions, which can provide documentation and scientific substantiation for recommendations. In addition, institutions of the prestigious Academy of Sciences may be consulted or charged with investigating a particular policy problem. This advice may be accepted in full, in part, or rejected altogether.

Once a draft law has been formulated, it may be submitted to a committee of the Supreme Soviet for discussion. Depending on the issue, comments on the draft law by interested citizens may be published in the two major newspapers, *Pravda* and *Izvestiia*. Changes suggested by commissions of the Supreme Soviet or by general public debate may be integrated into the final law, which is then passed unanimously by the Supreme Soviet. Not all policy decisions are enacted as formal legislation, however; some may be issued as decrees of the Presidium of the Supreme Soviet or, more frequently, as resolutions or ordinances promulgated by the Council of Ministers and the Central Committee of the party. The Supreme Soviet itself does not play a role in this form of policy making.

Western critics have devoted considerable attention in recent years to the role of scholars in the policy deliberation process. Some Western experts have concluded that particularly in nonsensitive areas (for example, criminal law and educational policy), Soviet scholars can have substantial impact, perhaps equal to that of scholars in Western polities.[9] Other Western observers are quick to point out that scholars participate in policy debates only when the leadership desires their input and that public discussion can be cut off at any time. Even a cursory reading of the Soviet press, however, does reinforce the impression that scholarly input is a routine part of policy deliberation. A reading of scholarly journals makes this pattern even more evident. Whether scholars actually exert influence is harder to determine, just as it is in Western polities. In the Soviet Union, informal channels of communication between the scholarly community and leadership circles may be even more important than the public debate in the media. But again, the true significance of this type of communication is difficult to assess.

Independent citizen groups comparable to the American Automobile Association, Chamber of Commerce, or National Association for the Advancement of Colored People (NAACP) in the United States simply do not exist in the Soviet Union. If citizens wish to exert influence, they must generally do so indirectly. For example, if women feel that child-care facilities are inadequate, they might express themselves by refusing to bear as many children as the regime prefers. If collective farmers find wages and benefits too low, they can devote less time and effort to their work on the collective farm and more to their private plots. These may be crude mechanisms for communicating political desires, but they have at times proven effective in influencing policymakers.

Local Government

Local government in the Soviet Union consists of the elected soviets and their various executive and administrative organs, which include: the soviet executive committee; various departments concerned with areas such as education, trade, health, or local industry; and standing committees, which involve broader elements of the population in soviet activities. These bodies are subject to dual subordination; they are responsible not only to the local soviet but also to the higher organ in the state bureaucracy responsible for the same functional area. For example, the health department of the local soviet is ultimately answerable to the Ministry of Health, which may create conflicts of interest for these local organs, because local concerns may at times contradict national priorities. Furthermore, these local bodies in the soviet structure are also responsible to local party authorities.

Local soviet structures do provide widespread opportunities for public participation in government. Women, nonparty members, and citizens of working-class or peasant background are more likely to be active at the local level than in national politics. There are, however, severe restrictions on the ability of local organs to effectively influence policy. In addition to budgetary limitations (local budgets are established within the framework of the centralized budgetary structure of the Soviet Union), local organs must often overcome powerful bureaucratic obstacles in trying to improve the provision of local goods and services, assure regional planning, or protect the local environment from industrial pollution. Industrial enterprises located in the area have their own priorities, namely, fulfillment of production plans at minimal cost, and generally will be backed up by the ministry to which they are responsible. These enterprises often have far more political clout than local soviet bodies, partly because national leaders themselves have generally placed a higher priority on achieving production goals than on developing an integrated structure of communal facilities. For example, if a local chemical enterprise is polluting a reservoir in the city, the local soviet may find its own efforts ineffectual in halting the damage; the chemical enterprise has far stronger political support in its ministry than the local soviet has at the top.

Since the death of Stalin, some efforts have been made to reinforce the power of the local soviets in assuring an improved standard of living. Most notably, ownership of housing facilities has been gradually transferred to the municipalities, rather than remaining under the control of the enterprises employing the residents. This change has been part of the effort to upgrade housing conditions in the Soviet Union and has met with some success. Presumably, transferring greater budgetary and administrative authority to the soviets in this area has assured greater attention to housing policy, since, unlike enterprises, the soviets are not tempted to sacrifice housing allocations to achieve higher production goals.

Prospects for Democratization

What are the possibilities for real political reform in the Soviet system to allow more genuine popular involvement in the selection of leaders and in policy making? In Chapter 28, we discussed Western speculation about the development of interest-group politics and institutional pluralism in the Soviet system. It seems clear that since Stalin's death the policy process has opened up; media debate over specific issues is often detailed and substantive; and experts, regional officials, and bureaucratic agencies may have some input. However, direct influence of the population at large has remained limited.

Experiences in Eastern Europe and observations by Soviet dissidents suggest other routes of change. For example, Roy Medvedev, an important Marxist dissident still living in Moscow, sees some support for increased democracy in the party itself.[10] The so-called party democrats, he admits, may be small in number and may be balanced off in political influence by neo-Stalinists in the party, who might favor exertion of even greater political control. Medvedev argues that the party itself would benefit from greater openness in intraparty affairs, and he also supports strengthening the soviets as institutions of popular representation. Medvedev's hope for reform seems, however, to be based primarily in its apparent necessity, rather than in any evidence of widespread support for such change within the party itself.

Before discounting the possibility of reform from within the party, we should take into account the experience of the Eastern European countries. In Hungary in 1956, and in Czechoslovakia in 1968, reform leaders from within the party itself sought to further the democratization of society. Both of these reform movements ended with military intervention by the Soviet Union and its allies. Here we examine the Czechoslovakian case more closely to assess whether or not it might offer a model of democratization for the Soviet Union and other Soviet-bloc polities.

The Prague Spring

Communist Party dominance was not established in the countries of Eastern Europe until after World War II. Czechoslovakia was the only country of the future Soviet-bloc countries of Eastern Europe in which parliamentary democracy survived the period between the two world wars; in all of the other countries (Poland, Bulgaria, Hungary, Rumania,

Yugoslavia, and Germany), representative government succumbed to some form of dictatorship during the interwar period. In Czechoslovakia, despite frequent changes in cabinet and government, the basic democratic infrastructure stood intact until Hitler engulfed the country in the late 1930s. After World War II, the Czechoslovákian experience remained unique. The Yugoslav and Albanian communist parties, which had considerable bases of popular support due to their important role in fighting off the Axis powers, acceded to power without requiring Red Army assistance. They subsequently proved themselves strong enough to establish their own unique forms of Marxist-Leninist rule. On the other hand, the communist parties in Poland, Bulgaria, Hungary, Rumania, and eastern Germany were too weak to take power without help from the Soviet Union's Red Army. The Czechoslovakian party stood somewhere between. In 1946, the Communist Party of Czechoslovakia won more votes in free elections than any other party, about 38 percent, and was thus able to take on a key role in the coalition government formed with two other socialist parties. At the outset it appeared that parliamentary rule might again be reestablished in Czechoslovakia. However, by 1947, international tensions and internal coalition conflicts led to a breakdown of consensus, and the Communist Party seized control of the government. The Soviet Red Army played no direct role in the coup; indeed, thousands of workers meeting in Prague for a workers' and peasants' congress supported the party's actions. This, together with the presence of the Soviet military in surrounding countries, must have made counteraction by the other socialist forces seem futile.

Stalinism and Symbolic De-Stalinization. By 1948, Czechoslovakia was firmly in the orbit of Soviet influence. The Soviet-inspired purges of the late 1940s and early 1950s that took place in all of the bloc countries were particularly brutal in Czechoslovakia, perhaps because Moscow wanted to assure firm control of this potentially powerful party. In each of the bloc countries, the basic features of the Stalinist structure of power were duplicated: The economic strategy emphasized heavy industrial development with neglect of agricultural and consumer interests; the secret police were strengthened; and tight controls were exercised over all aspects of political, economic, and cultural life. Likewise, with the death of Stalin, the process of de-Stalinization carried over into Eastern Europe. However, some of the "little Stalins" who had been installed by the Soviet Union resisted, first, Malenkov's economic de-Stalinization (e.g., increased emphasis on consumer production) and, then, Khrushchev's more political attacks on the Stalinist cult of the personality. The top party leader in Czechoslovakia, Klement Gottwald, died of pneumonia contracted at Stalin's funeral in 1953. After a short period of collective leadership, his successor, Antonin Novotny, was equally resistant to de-Stalinization: Novotny took only symbolic and minor steps to accommodate Khrushchev's de-Stalinization sentiments, and placed the blame for the Stalinist excesses on the former party leader, Rudolf Slansky, who was himself a victim of the purges. Like other "little Stalins," Novotny was reluctant to dismantle the foundations of his own power and perhaps realized that even a small loosening of control could bring upheavals, as were to occur in 1956 in Poland and Hungary.

Crisis. By the early to mid-1960s, the costs of Novotny's resistance to reform were evident. Like the German Democratic Republic (GDR), Czechoslovakia had a relatively industrialized economy. The crude Stalinist methods of planning did not allow the improvements in technology, coordination, and quality that were necessary to fuel continued economic growth. In the early 1960s, the economic growth rates in these two countries began to sag to the point where Czechoslovakia experienced an actual decline in national income from 1962 to 1963. Economic reform, which would involve some decentralization of initiative and emphasize innovation and quality, was required. By the mid-1960s, even the top party leadership realized this and began to allow formulation of reform proposals. Economists, many of whom were themselves Communist Party members, were allowed to articulate their ideas more openly, and some modest beginnings for market-type economic reform ensued in 1965.

With increasing economic problems came discontent with other aspects of official policy. Party intellectuals thought and wrote more critically about the nature of socialist society, turning to Marx's early, more humanistic, writings. Due to the country's advanced economic level, the educated strata in Czechoslovakia formed a relatively large group, and many of these intellectuals had experienced a period of genuine parliamentary democracy between the wars. Many were also members of the party and had some access to leadership circles. The reaction of the regime to the intellectuals' activities was ambivalent, for a kind of scientific and intellectual revival was perhaps necessary if Czechoslovakia's stagnation was to be overcome. However, the situation had become too dangerous, from Novotny's perspective, when at the Fourth Congress of the official Union of Writers in 1967, questions were openly raised about the regime's rejection of Israel in the June, 1967, Arab-Israeli war and about the government's censorship policy. Shortly thereafter, in late October,

1967, student demonstrations in response to poor dormitory conditions elicited a brutal government response, marking a renewal of tension between students and the Novotny government.

An additional issue complicated matters further. The Czechoslovakian population comprises two major ethnic groups, the Czechs (about 65 percent of the population) and the Slovaks (about 29 percent of the population), which are closely related but have distinctive linguistic, economic, and political traditions. Up until 1968, the Czechs dominated the political system and inhabited the more economically prosperous section of the country. The Czech population also had been more strongly influenced in the past by liberal Western European ideas. Slovak discontent increased throughout the 1960s, a major issue being the rehabilitation of the so-called Slovak "bourgeois nationalists," who had been purged in the early 1950s. Slovaks also wanted greater control over their own affairs, which was impossible within the unitary structure of the government and party. Demands for a federal system, and for separate Czech and Slovak sections of the party and other organizations, were also raised.

The Reform Movement. In the face of Novotny's repressive response to the events of 1967, the Central Committee, at its meeting in December, 1967, discussed the idea of reinstituting some form of collective leadership by giving one of the two top posts, first secretary of the party or president of the country, to someone other than Novotny. In January, 1968, Alexander Dubcek, an apparently orthodox and loyal Slovak, was appointed General Secretary of the party. Novotny retained his post as President until March 21, 1968. These personnel changes seemed innocuous and drew no opposition from Moscow.

Under Dubcek's leadership, however, the atmosphere changed. The regime gradually began to tolerate, if not encourage, more open debate about the problems confronting the country. By April, developments took on a momentum of their own. Numerous automonous groups and activities sprung up throughout society; some were received with the party's apparent approval, others with ambivalence. Among the more acceptable groups were K-231, an organization that pressed for further rehabilitation of Stalinist victims, and KAN, an organization of nonparty activists wishing to participate in politics. Gradually censorship was eased, then, for all practical purposes, abolished when the censors refused to carry out their duties. The party recognized the need for a more responsible press law and thus did not crack down. Official organizations, such as the various artists' unions, elected new leaders, and literary-political journals grew in circulation as their content became more provocative.

The most astounding aspect of these developments was the support for the reform from the party itself. Rather than interpreting the movement as a threat to its position, the party leadership sought to play a positive role in the process. While over time the leadership became increasingly concerned that events might get out of control (particularly with the unsanctioned initiation of a new Social Democratic Party that threatened to challenge Communist Party hegemony), the party itself continued to encourage and respond to public opinion, albeit cautiously. Likewise, opinion polls indicated a high level of support and trust for the party's reform leadership. On April 5, 1968, the Central Committee adopted an Action Program, which confirmed the general direction of reform. The Action Program drew broad parameters for change, leaving specifics to be determined at a later point. Among other things, it called for democratization of the party, a new press law excluding preliminary censorship, establishment of a federal constitutional system to assure increased rights for Slovakia, and economic reforms granting greater autonomy to enterprises. While it did not endorse multiparty competition, the program did support a greater role for the official National Front (noncommunist) parties and organizations. It also suggested the need for some form of worker participation in industrial decision making.

The more conservative elements in the party resisted these developments and tried to undermine support by appealing directly to factory workers, who as yet were only marginally involved in the reform activities. But Dubcek and the dominant leadership elements, as well as the Central Committee, accepted and supported the need for change, although fears grew that the situation could become unmanageable. Throughout the spring and summer months, expressions of concern from the Soviet Union and other countries in the Warsaw Treaty Organization (the Soviet Union's military alliance system) grew more urgent, placing additional pressures on the party leadership as it tried to mediate the need for reform with geopolitical realities and the commitment to socialism. In late May, Dubcek announced a special Fourteenth Extraordinary Party Congress to be held in September of 1968 to enable the party to respond more quickly to the changing situation. During the summer months, preparations for the Congress were under way in earnest, including relatively open elections of delegates in local party organizations and development of proposals and reports for discussion.

By June, the situation had become increasingly tense. A group of over sixty individuals, including leading intellectuals, issued a statement called the "Two Thousand Words," indicating that society might have to act without party approval if the party balked in pursuing the reform program. This statement raised the alarm among some party leaders, for it suggested that the party might be losing its control over the situation.

Warnings from the Soviet Union and Warsaw Pact served temporarily to unite the country behind Dubcek, and Dubcek's popularity remained high. No real preparations were made to defend against possible armed intervention by the Soviet Union and its allies, perhaps because Dubcek did not want to trigger intervention by placing in question his proclaimed loyalty to socialism and to the bloc. On August 20–21, just before the scheduled Fourteenth Extraordinary Party Congress, the Warsaw Pact armies stepped in to squelch what came to be known as the Prague Spring. Although unprepared, the country made an impressive show of nonviolent resistance, removing street signs to disorient the invaders and otherwise refusing to cooperate or provide information. Most remarkable was the convening of the Fourteenth Extraordinary Party Congress in a factory in Prague. Elected delegates from throughout the country secretly converged, reaffirmed their support for the Dubcek leadership, and instructed the population to resist the invaders nonviolently. Meanwhile, the party leaders were ferried off to Moscow and forced to accept Moscow's terms of "normalization."

Normalization. Dubcek was left in the leadership post, but only with the understanding that he would reassert control over the country by tightening censorship, restricting autonomous political initiatives, and exercising firm party control over policy. This, of course, placed Dubcek in a difficult position, which he was able to sustain only until mid-April, 1969, when he resigned in the face of Soviet pressure (following upon the famous "ice hockey riots" celebrating Czechoslovakia's victory over the Soviet Union in international hockey competition). The new party leader, Gustav Husak, had himself been imprisoned in 1954 on charges of being a "bourgeois nationalist"; nonetheless, he proceeded to enforce the system of strict political control that remains in force today. Activists in the Prague Spring were arrested, and many intellectuals were forced to take on menial unskilled jobs while remaining at liberty. In 1977, two hundred and forty individuals issued a document publicizing human rights violations in Czechoslovakia, thus forming the dissident group known as Charter 77. This group continues to publicize and protest human rights violations in Czechoslovakia and seeks international support for its cause. In general, however, the country remains depoliticized after the suppression of the Prague Spring; the only real reform that survived was the institution of constitutional federalism and an improvement in the position of the Slovak minority.

Implications of the Prague Spring

The Prague Spring raises the question of whether it is possible to realize both socialist and democratic values within the context of communist party dominance. By allowing intraparty democracy and autonomy to non-party groups, could a new, more humanistic form of socialism, "socialism with a human face," as it is commonly called, emerge? This is precisely what many of the Czech reformers were trying to realize. Even without Soviet interference, the experiment was a difficult one, for once censorship was lifted and autonomous political activity allowed, where were the limits to be drawn? Could it somehow be assured, without recourse to simple repression, that communist party leadership would not be challenged? If it were, and opposition parties were allowed to compete for political power, what would prevent a return to those very features of capitalist society (inequality and exploitative economic relations) that socialism was intended to eliminate? Where should the limits of opposition be set, so as to safeguard socialism but at the same time protect traditional democratic liberties such as freedom of speech, organization, and the press? If other socialist parties were allowed, who would decide what constituted true socialist ideals? Would the party be willing to moderate its vanguard role and allow the citizens themselves to decide what was in their own interest, even if this involved reinstating some elements of a capitalist economy or selecting another party to rule?

Internal democratization also raises the issue of the relationship between economic and political reforms. Many Western observers assume that real democracy requires economic decentralization in the form of some kind of free-market economy. As a respected Polish emigré economist, W. Brus, writes, "A more extensive market means less *economic* power for the state," since enterprise managers would have broader scope for autonomous decision making and the average citizen could make his or her preferences effective through the marketplace. As Brus points out, "In most cases when people in communist countries are able to voice their demand for political pluralization, a market-oriented economic reform is closely associated with or even regarded as an integral part of changes in the polity." But does less economic power for the state really imply a dispersion of political power? Some would argue that it does, since such a system would involve extension of organizational, economic, and information resources to broader sectors of society, giving them greater potential leverage to influence state policy. According to this logic, liberalization of the economy would be an important condition for democratization. Yet this linkage is hardly unambiguous. "Greater economic independence from the state may well have the opposite consequence of promoting both nonpolitical attitudes and the pursuit of strictly private interests, particularly after a string of frustrating political experiences,"[11] Brus declares. Furthermore, introduction of market relations or of some private ownership in production might increase income inequalities and, in this way, make the state responsive only to the economically privileged. (Recall Lenin's view that real democracy requires the *elimination* of private property and of the anarchy of the market.)

What does the Prague Spring tell us about the relationship between economic reform and democratization? Unfortunately, the reform was curtailed before its alluring vision of humanistic socialism could be tested. Many of the reformers did see economic decentralization as a crucial component of the package. Indeed, some of the first reform proposals called for an increasing role for the market in the economy; political pluralism followed. Economists and other intellectuals pushed this economic liberalization, which would allow them greater autonomy in exercising their skills. Factory workers were less certain that such market reforms would serve their interests; such changes implied more pressure for productivity at the workplace, a reduction in job security, and higher prices in the shops. And what would be the state's response to workers' demands for higher wages and improved working conditions? Should strikes be allowed? The Czechoslovakian reformers faced the same problem as Lenin and the Bolsheviks in 1921 — Should one allow the workers to organize themselves and press demands that might threaten the stability of the new order? During the Prague Spring, the reformers were more inclined to say yes to these questions than the Bolsheviks had been in 1921, but the reform was cut off before the issue could really be joined. We will return to this question of the political consequence of economic reform in Chapter 31, when we consider prospects for change in the Soviet Union and examine the experience of Hungary, where a semi-market reform has been in place since 1968.

Could occurrences similar to the Prague Spring emerge in the Soviet Union? Certain unique aspects of Czechoslovakia's history made it a more likely candidate for such a reform movement. The Soviet Union lacks many of the catalysts for change that were present in Czechoslovakia: Russia had no democratic interlude between the wars but, rather, a continuous tradition of autocratic rule; and liberal-democratic ideas have penetrated only a small stratum of the intelligentsia. Furthermore, the more numerous and diverse ethnic groups in the Soviet Union, as compared to Czechoslovakia, would make any step toward decentralization or lifting of censorship more threatening, since it might aggravate ethnic conflicts and encourage demands for local autonomy. Thus, the Prague Spring seems an unlikely model for change in the Soviet Union.

Notes

1. Alfred Meyer, "USSR Incorporated," *Slavic Review,* vol. 20 (October, 1961), pp. 369–76.
2. M. Djilas, *The New Class* (New York, Praeger, 1957).
3. Teresa Rakowska-Harmstone, "The Dialectics of Nationalism in the USSR." *Problems of Communism* (May/June 1974), pp. 300–21.
4. Jerry Hough and Merle Fainsod, *How the Soviet Union Is Governed* (Cambridge: Harvard University Press, 1979), pp. 424, 496.
5. Jerry Hough, *The Soviet Prefects: The Local Party Organs in Industrial Decision-Making* (Cambridge: Harvard University Press, 1969).
6. Michael Szkolny, "Revolution in Poland," *Monthly Review,* vol. 33 (June 1981), pp. 2–4.
7. "KPSS v tsifrakh," *Partinaia zhizn',* vol. 15 (August 1983), p. 24.
8. Arkady N. Shevchenko, *Breaking with Moscow* (New York: Alfred A. Knopf, 1985), p. 187.
9. See, for example: Peter Solomon, *Soviet Criminologists and Criminal Policy* (New York: Columbia University Press, 1978), pp. 151–59.
10. Roy Medvedev, *On Socialist Democracy* (New York: W.W. Norton and Co., 1977).
11. Wlodzmierz Brus, "Political Pluralism and Markets in Communist Systems," in *Pluralism in the USSR: Essays in Honour of H. Gordon Skilling* ed. Susan Gross Solomon (New York: St. Martin's Press, 1983), pp. 122, 126–27.

30

State and Society

Shaping the New Soviet Person

When studying Western polities, we usually assume that the political authorities in these states must respond to forces and pressures from society at large. In examining Soviet society, however, we tend to emphasize the ability of Soviet political authorities to shape and control society. In fact, until the early 1960s, Soviet-type polities were commonly described as totalitarian, reflecting the view that the party/state exercised total control over all aspects of life. Some adherents of this view argued that in Soviet society the distinction between the public and private sectors was undermined as the party imposed a belief system (ideology) and a pervasive system of political socialization that affected even the family and religious spheres. According to this viewpoint, civil society had lost all autonomy through a combination of media control, coercive power, economic monopoly, ideological indoctrination, single-party hegemony, and the personal charisma of the leader. One scholar identified terror itself as the essence of totalitarianism.[1] Proponents of this viewpoint saw great similarities between Naziism and Soviet society under Stalin.

In the last two decades, however, this interpretation of Soviet society has come under increasing attack as Western observers have recognized that political control in the Soviet bloc is far from total. Although the totalitarian explanation might have provided insight into the Stalinist system of power, it did not adequately take into account subsequent changes under Khrushchev and Brezhnev. Even under Stalin's rule, the state never penetrated all aspects of social life as effectively as the totalitarian theorists claimed. On the other hand, centralized control of political socialization is certainly far stronger in the Soviet Union than in most Western polities. Nonetheless, as we shall see below, state control is circumscribed by social forces, and the political authorities often must make concessions or compromises in the face of popular discontent if they are to achieve their goals.

In Chapter 26 we identified some of the sources for the broad scope of state authority in the Soviet Union; in particular, Russian political culture traditionally had strong centralizing and authoritarian characteristics. However, two other factors help to explain the dominance of the state over society in the Soviet Union. First, from the Marxist viewpoint, human beings exist in a social context. There is no abstract human nature; rather, humans are shaped by their relationships to others and to the larger environment in which they live. All people live in specific historical circumstances that influence and form their values and perceptions, attachments, and beliefs, so important aspects of human character are socially conditioned. Thus, from the Marxist viewpoint, individuals are not inherently greedy or competitive; capitalist society rewards and encourages these qualities. For the Marxist, it is possible to conceive of a socialist society in which collective identification is strong, labor is a form of self-fulfillment, and social and individual rights complement and fulfill one another.

Given this view of human nature, building a socialist society must necessarily involve the transformation of the individual. A new consciousness, a new type of human being, must be born. Following the revolution in 1917, the formation of this new type of socialist person became an integral part of the Soviet experiment. This task might prove to be long and arduous, successful only some generations later, but its achievement presumed an aggressive effort on the part of the party/state to eliminate the vestiges of feudal and capitalist consciousness. This included wiping out unscientific and superstitious beliefs (notably religion); discouraging personal greed; instilling an identification with the collective; and propagating sexual, ethnic, and class equality. If both Marx and Lenin foresaw the withering away of state authority once class contradictions were eliminated, both theorists also realized the state's necessary role in the interim period, in part to oversee this transformation of human consciousness.

Perhaps this sounds utopian and idealistic. A more concrete concern, namely, the commitment to rapid economic development, was a second factor that gave the party/state a strong role in the political socialization process. Russia of 1917 was a society pervaded by preindustrial values. Science, technology, and industry were foreign concepts to most of the peasant population, and social authority rested in religious, family, or traditional village figures. If the Soviet leaders were to industrialize the country quickly, these preindustrial values had to be replaced by a new, more rationalistic, technological, and perhaps materialistic mentality. Consequently, hundreds of thousands of people were uprooted and transformed into an efficient industrial labor force. Workers were educated to honor the factory time clock and operate modern machinery. Stalin's attack on the countryside with the agricultural collectivization campaign was just one step in this process, but it was augmented by constant propaganda and educational campaigns. The political leaders wanted to actively mobilize the masses in the industrialization effort.

We have now identified three different reasons for the Soviet state's dominance over society: traditional culture; the revolutionary view of human nature contained in Marxism-Leninism; and the imperative of industrial development. Clearly, if all three elements contributed to the active role of the party/state in shaping citizen attitudes, each might imply the inculcation of a different set of specific values.

The political authorities have supported some elements of traditional Russian culture, such as patriotism, while religious values and preindustrial conceptions of time, causality, and authority have been undermined. An assertive educational campaign that succeeded in virtually eliminating illiteracy in younger age groups as well as much of the adult population by the beginning of World War II was just the first step in moving the Soviet Union toward modernity. In the 1930s, some Marxist ideas also had to be modified, perhaps even sacrificed, in the interests of economic progress. For example, wage differentials between skilled and unskilled workers increased, and, despite rhetoric to the contrary, the commitment to industrialization was in fact overtaking the ultimate Marxist goal of an egalitarian wage structure. Soviet socialization efforts since the 1930s have emphasized the value of hard, honest work, performed for the social good, and the worship of science and technology as sources of human progress.

In other cases, Marxist values interacted with other regime goals. For example, women were integrated into the work force, allegedly as an indication of the regime's commitment to sexual equality. Party theoreticians could claim that women, in gaining some economic independence, were achieving the most important step toward social equality, but the party/state was more likely concerned with expanding the work force than with assuring sexual equality. Women most often had menial jobs, at lower pay levels than men; there was no assertive effort to grant real political influence to women and few attempts, if any, to alter role definitions in the home.

Then, was the Soviet party/state primarily devoted to forming a new *socialist* person to realize the vision of Marx and Lenin or, rather, to produce a better *industrial* worker, committed to the state's economic goals? The answer to this provocative question is a matter of judgment. Clearly, however, economic concerns were forcing a reinterpretation, if not a compromise, of some basic values articulated by Marx and Lenin.

Instruments of Socialization

Today, the Soviet party/state maintains considerable control over all of the major institutional agents of socialization, including the schools, the media, the workplace, and public organizations. Inevitably, however, the regime has much less influence over peer interaction, informal communication, and the family. In these spheres, citizens may express and be exposed to views that differ from those propagated through official channels.

The Media. The media, including television, radio, and the press, are state or party controlled. Printed material is carefully monitored by a complex administrative structure responsible to *Glavlit,* the Chief Administration for the Protection of State Secrets; material that is deemed detrimental to state interests is not permitted to be published. Not only are politically objectionable materials censored, but pornography and other materials of questionable moral quality are also prohibited. The electronic media offer exposure to high-quality cultural events (ballet, symphony), as well as movies (including occasional foreign films), and even rock concerts. Since the Khrushchev era, the scope of viewpoints allowed publication has expanded, particularly regarding economic and nonsensitive policy issues. The wider the circulation of a publication, however, the more controlled its content is likely to be. Scholars and political elites may have access to Western publications denied the average citizen.

In addition to the official media, an informal (and illegal) underground network called *samizdat,* "self-publication," has developed. Manuscripts that would likely receive official opprobrium are often reproduced by typewriter and carbon paper, and circulated informally in dissident circles. Sometimes these manuscripts are smuggled out of the country and published in the West; however, the author is subject to prosecution, as unauthorized publication abroad is considered a crime.

Since specific guidelines are not made public (although censorship manuals apparently exist to guide the censors themselves), writers must perceive indirect cues regarding the range of expression considered permissible at any given time. Often quite critical viewpoints can be articulated in allegorical or metaphoric form, especially in literature. Thus the Russian tradition of using the *belles lettres* as an indirect forum for political commentary has continued into the Soviet period. Of course, for the Western reader, the political intent may be difficult to interpret.

Education. Curricula in the schools are centrally established. While students are expected to master the fundamentals of Marxism-Leninism, there is an even greater emphasis placed on basic scientific knowledge and practical technical training. The post-Khrushchev leadership has committed itself to providing education through the tenth grade for all children, although diverse options are available to the pupil after the eighth grade: Some will attend two more years of general secondary school in preparation for higher education; others will attend polytechnical institutions or trade schools, which may lead to a trade or, in some cases, to higher education.

The school curricula emphasize not only Marxist-Leninist theory (historical and dialectical materialism, party history, and so forth) and scientific and technical fields, but also general moral upbringing. Children are taught the value of work, devotion to the social good, honesty, and other values that closely resemble the Protestant ethic. The Soviet child is motivated through collective competition, in which groups of children compete against one another, encouraging peer pressure to assure both high performance and conformity.

In principle, the Soviet educational system operates on the basis of a meritocracy. Competitive examinations are an important factor in gaining admission to a university. As in the West, children of the intelligentsia do have certain advantages, such as stimulation and encouragement at home, as well as the readiness and ability of the parents to hire tutors to prepare their children for exams. In addition, informal "connections" may be determinant in gaining admission to the university in some cases. University education is free, and many students receive government grants to help cover living expenses. In exchange, the state may assign the individual to a specific post for two years after graduation.

Public Organizations. The schools are aided in their socialization role by public organizations. For children, the most important of these are the youth organizations: the Octobrists (ages seven to ten); the Pioneers (ages ten to fourteen); and the Komsomol (the Communist Youth League, ages fifteen to twenty-seven). While virtually all children participate in the Octobrists and Pioneers, some young people resist Komsomol membership. Active participation in the Komsomol is an important stepping-stone to party membership, although members are not assured admission to the party. These extracurricular organizations introduce young people to communist values and encourage them to actively engage in public activities, such as summer work projects. For adults, other organizations fulfill similar functions. Citizens can pursue special interests by joining state-sponsored groups such as the Society for Nature Protection, societies for the preservation of national monuments, and sports clubs. These organizations serve to mobilize popular support for the government's efforts in the relevant areas. While these are not independent lobbying organizations of the Western variety, they may at times voice support for particular interests, such as wildlife protection.

Professional and trade union organizations are also state-controlled. While union membership is not compulsory, benefits such as access to union vacation and sports facilities make it advantageous enough that some 98 percent of the work force, including managerial personnel, join trade unions. Trade unions also administer health benefits and housing. Strikes are in practice forbidden, although they are occasionally reported in *samizdat* sources. The trade union system is not based on the adversarial, bargaining relationship common in the West. Rather, as determined already in the early 1920s during the conflict over the Workers' Opposition, industrial unions further fulfillment of economic policy and protect certain workers' rights, such as job security, provision of social-welfare benefits, and bonuses. Workers can be laid off only with union approval. The right to employment is considered basic in the Soviet system, so firings are relatively uncommon, even though low labor productivity may be one of the economic costs of the policy.

Professionals, most notably in the cultural field, have their own organizations, including unions for writers, artists, architects, composers, and cinematographers. One must be a member to receive support grants, commissions for work, or official sponsorship in exhibits. An artist or writer whose work exceeds permissible bounds may be expelled from the union, and thus forced to make a living through unofficial channels, or be charged as a social parasite. These professional organizations serve not only as an administrative mechanism to support artists who work within the system, but also as a powerful means to assure political conformity. Members of the intelligentsia who, for political reasons, have been denied access to normal employment are often sustained by informal, temporary jobs, such as private tutoring or translating assignments commissioned by sympathetic colleagues in official institutions.

The Workplace. The workplace forms a primary point of social activity for the worker, since through it and the associated trade unions are organized many spare-time activities, public education campaigns, day-care, housing facilities, and voluntary work efforts (including *subbotniki,* in which workers are asked to freely commit a Saturday to supplement normal work hours). Particularly productive workers receive honors, and their pictures are displayed on public billboards, in a tone-downed version of the Stakhanovite campaigns of the 1930s. Workers are, however, free to change their workplace, a real as well as a theoretical possibility, since there are labor shortages in many fields. Job mobility is somewhat inhibited, however, by the difficulty in finding satisfactory housing and the restrictions placed on internal movement to particularly desirable areas like Moscow. One must have a permit to move to Moscow, as the regime tries, though rather unsuccessfully, to control the growth of this urban conglomerate. In contrast, enterprises offer higher wages and other material incentives to workers who are willing to do a stint in Siberia, where intensive exploitation of rich natural-resource deposits requires a growing work force. In general, levels of labor mobility in the Soviet Union are high enough to cause political leaders concern. Nonetheless, the regime has not resorted to coercive measures to restrict freedom of movement.

The Family. We have focused on instruments of socialization dominated by the party/state. The family presents a somewhat different picture because it is less vulnerable to political influence. Further, since the 1930s, the Soviet regime has supported the nuclear family and has made little effort to subject it to direct political control. In some urban areas, over 75 percent of young children under age seven attend day-care facilities in order to free young women to participate in the work force. The additional income is often needed to support the family, and 80 percent of women between fifteen and fifty-five years of age work outside the home.[2] But there has been no systematic attempt to remove children from the home environment at a young age in order to reinforce the state's control over political socialization. If anything, day-care facilities have expanded at a slower rate than the growth of demand for them, and it seems likely that the primary motivation for the regime's support for day-care is economic, rather than political. As in most industrialized societies, varying work and educational commitments draw members of the nuclear family apart, but the Soviet family does retain an independence and isolation from direct political intrusion and is therefore a potential breeding ground for alternative viewpoints. Unlike during the Stalinist period, betrayal of one's viewpoints to the authorities by spouse or children is now uncommon and not assertively encouraged by the regime. Today family members can confide in one another as they do in close and trusted friends. This official acceptance of the integrity of the nuclear family may simply reflect the increasingly conservative values of the party/state as it has consolidated its power in the past several decades. Perhaps the leaders themselves value the oasis from politics provided by family life, for details of their private lives receive virtually no public attention. Divorce rates in the Soviet Union, though lower than in the United States, are increasing to a level comparable to Western European nations. This is a cause for worry for the regime, since it threatens to weaken the traditional social fabric, as well as lower the birthrate, which is already considered inadequate for labor needs in urban European regions of the country.

The official retirement age is fifty-five for women (sixty for men), and many young families rely on grandmothers to look after children during working hours. Thus children are exposed to values of an earlier era, especially since levels of religious devotion are higher among the older generation. Although relatively few grandparents of today remember the prerevolutionary period, they undoubtedly have a clear recollection of World War II and help to transmit to the younger generation an awareness of the costs of military struggle.

Religious Institutions. The official Soviet policy toward religion is stated in Article 52 of the constitution: "Citizens of the USSR are guaranteed freedom of conscience, that is, the right to profess or not to profess any religion, and to conduct religious worship or atheistic propaganda . . ." One should note that this clause guarantees the right to *propagate* atheism, but only the right to *profess* religious belief. In other words, citizens are not allowed to evangelize about their religious convictions, only to worship for themselves. Atheistic values are taught in the schools and through public organizations. Church attendance is allowed, although over the years it has declined, as is the case in most industrial societies. The practice of religion is threatening to the regime because it offers an alternative to the Marxist-Leninist worldview and thus may encourage indifference or resistance to official propaganda. In addition, there is the danger that the church may serve as an institutional support for opposition, much as the Catholic church did for the Solidarity trade union in Poland in 1980–81. For these reasons, the state attempts to maintain organizational dominance over religious institutions and is relatively successful in the case of the Orthodox church, due to its tradition of accommodation with the political authorities. In exchange for the right to operate a limited number of churches and monasteries (many others have been turned into impressive and well-maintained museums and cultural monuments), the Orthodox church offers basic support for the regime. Evangelical Protestant groups are harder for the state to control, partly because these groups view public propagation of beliefs as an essential element of religious conviction. The officially recognized Baptist church, the All-Union Council of Evangelical Christians/Baptists, has generally accepted the political restrictions placed on evangelism. However, *samizdat* publications report harassment and arrest of adherents of *unofficial* Baptist groups who have attempted to disseminate their doctrine on the streets, set up alternative schools, or otherwise propagate their beliefs. Active Christians may also suffer discrimination in admission to higher educational institutions or in career advancement, although the extent of this type of discrimination is undocumented. Despite government efforts, religious adherence survives in the Soviet Union.

Social Forces

Although the political authorities have sought to gain control over autonomous social forces, society does have an independent existence in the Soviet Union, presenting the leaders with new dilemmas and demands. While organization of political discontent is difficult, social groups can, to some extent, pursue their interests through established institutions, or they can seek out unofficial outlets to express their demands (such as *samizdat* or use of international pressure) and engage in passive resistance (noncooperation).

Ethnic Diversity

Probably the most difficult and potentially disruptive social challenge confronting the Soviet leadership is the ethnic diversity of its population. As noted above, there are over one hundred different ethnic groups in the Soviet Union, twenty-three of which have populations of one million or more. (See Table 30.1.) The dominant group, the Russians, made up about 52.4 percent of the population in 1979, when the last census was taken. The next largest group, the Ukrainians (about 16 percent), is ethnically similar to the Russians, also of Slavic background, although with a distinct language, culture, and history. The Russian-dominated leadership has sometimes placed trusted Ukrainians and other Slavs (such as the Belorussians) in key political posts in regions populated by ethnic groups which are culturally less similar to the Russians. Nonetheless, particularly in the western Ukraine, a desire for greater autonomy as well as resentment of Russian dominance is often expressed in unofficial *samizdat* writings.

Other European groups include the Baltic peoples of Latvia, Lithuania, and Estonia, making up 0.55 percent, 0.1 percent, and 0.39 percent of the population, respectively. These areas were integrated into the Soviet Union only after World War II and at that time already enjoyed a standard of living and level of industrialization comparable to or exceeding that of Russia. These peoples have a strong sense of national identity and are relatively resistant to pressures from the regime to assimilate to the dominant culture. The Estonian language is enough like Finnish to allow access to Western news broadcasts through the Finnish media. The Lithuanians are largely of Roman Catholic heritage and have had close historical links with Poland, which may be troublesome for the authorities, because it provides a potential link between ethnic and religious discontent and may offer fertile ground for transference of Polish unrest to the Soviet Union. Like the Baltic peoples, the Georgians (of the Caucasus region) and the Moldavians (on the Romanian border) both have a strong sense of national identity (although the Georgians were integrated into the Russian empire in 1801).

There are several Islamic population groups in the Soviet Union, making up about 16.5 percent of the Soviet population in 1979 (as compared to 11.6 percent in 1959). Their proportion is growing at a considerably higher rate than the European, urban population. The Islamic peoples inhabit Azerbaidzhan (in the Caucasus) and the five union republics of Central Asia (including Kazakhstan). The Soviet government has had the greatest difficulty in assimilating these groups because of their cultural, linguistic, and religious distinctiveness, and their strong ties to the traditional Islamic family and community. Yet their inclusion in the Soviet mosaic is important due to the strategic significance of these territories and as a demonstration of the Soviet Union's ability to forge a multiethnic state.

Soviet authorities have used several strategies to reduce the risk of ethnic unrest. A policy of disproportionately high investment in the more

Table 30.1 National Groups of Over One Million in the Soviet Union in 1959, 1970, and 1979

	NUMBER OF PERSONS OF GIVEN NATIONALITY (IN THOUSANDS)			PERCENTAGE INCREASE OR DECREASE	
	1959	1970	1979	1959–70	1970–79
Total population of the USSR	208,827	241,720	262,085[a]	15.8	8.4
*Russians	114,114	129,015	137,397	13.1	6.5
*Ukrainians	37,253	40,753	42,347	9.4	3.9
*Uzbeks	6,015	9,195	12,456	52.9	35.5
*Belorussians	7,913	9,052	9,463	14.4	4.5
*Kazakhs	3,622	5,299	6,556	46.3	23.7
**Tatars	4,968	5,931	6,317	19.4	6.5
*Azerbaidzhani	2,940	4,380	5,477	49.0	25.0
*Armenians	2,787	3,559	4,151	27.7	16.6
*Georgians	2,692	3,245	3,571	20.5	10.0
*Moldavians	2,214	2,698	2,968	21.9	10.0
*Tadjiks	1,397	2,136	2,898	52.9	35.7
*Lithuanians	2,326	2,665	2,851	14.6	7.0
*Turkmen	1,002	1,525	2,028	52.2	33.0
Germans	1,620	1,846	1,936	14.0	4.9
*Kirghiz	969	1,452	1,906	49.8	31.3
***Jews	2,263	2,151	1,811	− 5.2	−15.8
**Chuvash	1,470	1,694	1,751	15.2	3.4
**Peoples of Dagestan	844	1,365	1,657	44.6	21.4
*Latvians	1,400	1,430	1,439	2.1	0.6
**Bashkirs	989	1,240	1,371	25.4	10.6
**Mordvins	1,285	1,263	1,192	− 1.7	− 5.6
Poles	1,380	1,167	1,151	−15.4	− 1.4
*Estonians	989	1,007	1,020	1.8	1.3

a. This figure excludes the approximately 351,000 persons, including foreigners, residing temporarily in the Soviet Union at the time of the census.

*National groups with union republic status

**National groups with autonomous republic status

***National groups with autonomous region status

SOURCE Ann Sheehy, "The National Composition of the Population of the USSR According to the Census of 1979," *Radio Liberty Research Bulletin,* no. 123/80 (March 27, 1980), pp. 10–11.

Table 30.2 Share of Nationalities of Union Republic Status in Total Population of the Soviet Union in 1959, 1970, and 1979 (percentage)

	1959	1970	1979
SLAVIC GROUPS			
Russians	54.6	53.4	52.4
Ukrainians	17.8	16.9	16.2
Belorussians	3.8	3.7	3.6
	76.2	74.0	72.2
CENTRAL ASIAN GROUPS			
Uzbeks	2.88	3.80	4.75
Kazakhs	1.73	2.19	2.50
Tadjiks	0.67	0.88	1.11
Turkmen	0.48	0.63	0.77
Kirghiz	0.46	0.60	0.73
	6.22	8.10	9.86
CAUCASUS GROUPS			
Azerbaidzhani	1.41	1.81	2.09
Armenians	1.33	1.47	1.58
Georgians	1.29	1.34	1.36
	4.03	4.62	5.03
BALTIC GROUPS			
Lithuanians	1.11	1.10	1.09
Latvians	0.67	0.59	0.55
Estonians	0.47	0.42	0.39
	2.25	2.11	2.03
Moldavians	1.06	1.12	1.13

SOURCE Ann Sheehy, "The National Composition of the Population of the USSR According to the Census of 1979," *Radio Liberty Research Bulletin*, no. 123/80 (March 27, 1980), p. 14.

backward regions of the country is connected to the Marxist belief that industrialization, urbanization, and economic equality will reduce ethnic consciousness by forging a deeper awareness of common class interests. Although this investment has not been adequate to bring these areas up to the same standard of living and level of industrialization as the European sections of the country, the standard of living in Soviet Central Asia is almost certainly well above that of neighboring Iran, Pakistan, and Afghanistan (even before the Soviet invasion in 1979). Economic advancement has not necessarily assured acquiescence, however; higher levels of education and affluence can generate higher expectations and demands. As discussed in Chapter 29, Central Asian elites themselves have become proponents of regional economic interests. Furthermore, demographic and cultural patterns in Central Asia pose an additional challenge to policymakers, as discussed in Chapter 28.

The Soviet leadership has also dealt with ethnic diversity through cultural policy. The Leninist formula, "national in form, socialist in content," has meant encouragement of traditional ethnic folk arts, music, and dress, and discouragement of nationalistic, separatist, or religious sentiments. "Assymetrical bilingualism," or what some call Russification, involves efforts to encourage ethnic minorities to learn Russian as a second language. Very few ethnic Russians (only 3.5 percent in 1979), however, learn the language of another Soviet population group (excluding German); Russians prefer to take up Western languages like French, English, or German. Nonetheless, minority languages survive: Media broadcasts and book publishing continue in all the major languages (especially those of the union republics); and primary and secondary education is generally carried out in the indigenous language in the union republics, with Russian a required part of the curriculum. However, Russian is the common language in the Soviet Union, necessary for upward social mobility.

The smaller ethnic groups without union republic status do see their linguistic traditions threatened. While the majority of non-Russians still regard the language of their own ethnic group as their first language, the number claiming knowledge of Russian as a second language has increased steadily. (See Table 30.3.) According to the 1979 census, 62.1 percent of non-Russians (82 percent of the total Soviet population) claim Russian as their first or second language. Some groups have been more resistant to Russification than others, most notably the Estonians and the Georgians. According to the official Soviet census of 1979, knowledge of Russian as a second language declined among those claiming Estonian as their first language from 29 percent in 1970 to 24.2 percent in 1979, though some of the respondents may have been unwilling to admit to knowledge of Russian. On the other hand, knowledge of Russian among Uzbeks (in Central Asia) reportedly increased from 14.5 percent in 1970 to 43.9 percent in 1979, a 361 percent gain. Here the figures may be inflated as census takers try to satisfy the hopes and expectations of their superiors.

Table 30.3 Percentage of Members of Non-Russian Nationalities of Union Republic Status Claiming a Good Knowledge of Russian as a Second Language in 1970 and 1979

	PERCENTAGE OF TOTAL		PERCENT INCREASE OR DECREASE	NUMBER OF PERSONS (IN THOUSANDS)	
	1970	1979	1970–1979	1970	1979[a]
SLAVIC GROUPS					
Ukrainians	36.3	49.8	+42.6	14,790	21,089
Belorussians	49.0	57.0	+21.7	4,432	5,394
CENTRAL ASIAN GROUPS					
Uzbeks	14.5	49.3	+361.4	1,331	6,141
Kazakhs	41.8	52.3	+ 54.7	2,216	3,429
Tadjiks	15.4	29.6	+160.8	329	858
Turkmen	15.4	25.4	+119.1	235	515
Kirgiz	19.1	29.4	+102.2	277	560
CAUCASUS GROUPS					
Azerbaidzhani	16.6	29.5	+122.9	725	1,616
Armenians	30.1	38.6	+ 49.4	1,072	1,602
Georgians	21.3	26.7	+ 37.4	691	953
BALTIC STATES GROUPS					
Lithuanians	35.9	52.1	+55.3	956	1,485
Latvians	45.2	56.7	+26.3	646	816
Estonians	29.0	24.2	−15.4	292	247
Moldavians	36.1	47.4	+44.3	975	1,407

[a] The figures in this column have been calculated on the basis of the percentages in column 2.
SOURCE Ann Sheehy, "Language Affiliation Data from the Census of 1979." *Radio Liberty Research Bulletin* no. 130/80 (April 2, 1980), p. 13.

In Chapter 29, we discussed the importance of federalism in addressing ethnic diversity in the Soviet Union. The federal structure was retained in the 1977 constitution, despite some speculation that it might be altered. The Soviet authorities have come to accept that ethnic identification and diversity are permanent features of Soviet life, and they have managed this diversity quite successfully as compared with many

Western polities. Nonetheless, some Western scholars foresee ethnic conflict as a continuing threat, particularly if central authority is weakened by other domestic or international crises.

The Jewish Problem. One ethnic group that has posed a particular dilemma for the Soviet leadership in recent years is the Jews, who are geographically dispersed throughout the Soviet Union, rather than concentrated in one administrative or federal unit. As a group, the Jews are highly urbanized and are linguistically and culturally assimilated; few practice their religion actively. Nonetheless, individuals of Jewish descent carry evidence of their heritage in internal passports stamped "Jewish."

In the 1930s, the proportion of Jews in the party, in the most prestigious occupations, and in higher education, was substantially higher than their proportion in the population as a whole. As John Armstrong has pointed out, the regime needed the skills of this group, which were scarce in the years following the revolution.[3] Now that the economy has stabilized, Jews face obstacles to educational and career advancement, for there are ample qualified candidates for privileged posts among ethnic Russians and other Slavic groups, as general educational levels have risen. Jews are no longer needed for their specific skills, and the regime has made an effort to eliminate the over-representation of Jews in privileged posts, a sort of reverse affirmative action. Nonetheless, based on their proportion of the total Soviet population, Jews are still relatively over-represented among professional groups, such as doctors, lawyers, and artists, although admission to these professions for Jews is now restricted.

Anti-Semitic sentiments have traditionally been fairly strong among the Russian population. This residual prejudice against the Jews undoubtedly makes current policy a popular one. Many Western critics charge that Jews in the Soviet Union are actively and consistently discriminated against and that the regime itself is actually pursuing an anti-Semitic course. Soviet authorities deny being anti-Semitic but admit that they oppose Zionism. (Zionism is a Jewish nationalist movement that, prior to 1948, worked for the establishment of a Jewish State in the Holy Land, and, since that time, has supported the continued existence of the state of Israel.) In practice, however, the distinction between anti-Zionism and anti-Semitism is difficult to draw. The meaning of Zionism is open to interpretation, making it easy to stigmatize Jews as Zionists. Further, Soviet opposition to Israel has probably been intensified by the large number of Soviet Jews requesting the right to emigrate to Israel and by close ties between the Soviet Union and Arab states like Syria and Iraq.

Under international pressure, the Soviet authorities did allow over 240,000 Jews to emigrate between 1970 and 1980, but since 1980, with the deterioration in superpower relations, the Soviets have again restricted the issuance of exit permits (from a high of about 51,000 in 1979, to under 1,000 in 1984).[4] Jews (along with some Soviet citizens of German extraction) have been among the few Soviet citizens allowed to emigrate even to this extent, which may increase popular resentment against Jews even further. The regime apparently fears that other ethnic minorities will also demand emigration rights. Jews as a group may be perceived as more politically suspect than other groups because of the international support they enjoy, which may well intensify the regime's tendency to restrict their access to high positions. Furthermore, the regime dislikes committing educational resources to a group with a high level of emigration.

Religious Activism

Religious dissent is closely linked to ethnicity in the Soviet Union, for frequently the religion of an ethnic minority is a key element of its cultural identity. This is particularly true for the Islamic groups, the Catholics of Lithuania, and some Jews. Levels of religious adherence are hard to estimate, given political pressures against advertising one's faith. Russian Orthodox services are attended primarily by older people (over fifty), women, and rural people. Nonetheless, Christel Lane has determined that in the 1970s a significant proportion of the Russian population still considered itself to be Orthodox believers. Among Baptists, young believers are more common; membership in legal and illegal Baptist congregations is hard to estimate, but according to Lane's research, it may well be over one million, which would make this the third-largest group of Baptists worldwide.[5] The Soviet press occasionally reports on underground Islamic activities and "home mosques" that provide a less visible form of religious community in Central Asia. Interest in Islam is reinforced by contacts between Soviet and Middle Eastern Muslims through official exchanges, the Afghan invasion, radio broadcasts from across the border, and underground printed materials.

Reasons for continued, though declining, religious adherence are many, but Soviet sources themselves suggest that personal support from official organizations is often inadequate and the religious community fills the gap. Religious observance may also be an indirect means to express political discontent or may serve as a link to traditional ethnic communities. Perhaps dissatisfaction with the worldliness and hypocrisy of contemporary Soviet ideology may explain the appeal. Overall, however, the trend toward declining religious adherence, especially among educated urbanites, resembles patterns in other industrial societies.

Incipient Feminism

Although feminism as such is a weak social force in the Soviet Union, some Soviet women are becoming more conscious of their disadvantaged position. In 1979, an unofficial underground feminist group in Leningrad began producing a magazine of poetry, short stories, and essays (*An Almanac: Women and Russia*) to address issues of concern to Soviet women. This publication and one produced shortly thereafter (*Maria*), which linked women's concerns to Orthodox Christian ideas, were banned and their founders subjected to harassment, arrest, and in some cases exile from the Soviet Union. These feminist dissidents drew particular attention not only to women's role in the family and sex-role definitions[6] but also to many of the social inequalities confronting Soviet women.

While Soviet women have achieved virtual equality in educational opportunity, they continue to occupy lower-status and lower-paid jobs. Although, in 1975, 75 percent of Soviet physicians were female, Soviet doctors do not enjoy the status and remuneration of their Western counterparts. In occupations like teaching and medicine, where women outnumber men, higher administrative and scientific posts are more often filled by men. (In 1979–80, only 53 percent of chief physicians were women; further, while 80 percent of Soviet teachers were female, only 32 percent of directors of secondary schools were women.[7] See Table 30.4.) On the other hand, Soviet women are much more likely than their Western counterparts to fill posts in such traditionally male fields as economics and engineering.

In the home, sex roles have changed little since the revolution. Women have primary responsibility for child care and housework, duties that are more time-consuming in the Soviet Union due to long lines and shortages at food outlets; the lack of labor-saving devices, such as dishwashers and automatic washing machines; and inadequate services, such as laundries and carry-out restaurants. Soviet studies indicate that women spend more than twice as much time as men on housework and a third less time on self-education and cultural pursuits.[8] The Soviet press frequently devotes attention to this problem, but the regime has responded only slowly in offering concrete solutions. There seems to be disagreement in the Soviet Union over the appropriate role for women in the home and in social and economic life. Some recent articles provide a disparaging portrayal of the assertive woman, calling for a return to more

Table 30.4 Proportion of Women in High-Level Positions in Selected Fields and Institutions (percentages)

ENTERPRISE MANAGEMENT	1959	1970
Enterprise directors (including state farms)	12	13
Heads of production-technical departments, sectors, groups, offices	20	24
SCHOLARLY RESEARCH AND TEACHING	1970	1979
Academician, corresponding member, professor	9.9	10.7
Senior research associate	25.1	22.5
Junior research associate and assistant	49.8	47.7
Scientific personnel	38.8	40.0
candidate in science	27.0	28.0
doctorate in science	13.0	14.0
EDUCATION	1960/61	1979/80
Directors of secondary schools	20	32
Directors of primary schools	69	80
Teachers	70	80
MEDICINE	1959	1975
Chief physicians	54	53
Physicians	79	74
Midwives and *fel'dshers* (medical assistants)	84	83
Nurses and pharmacists	99	99
COMMUNIST PARTY	1976	1981
Politburo	0	0
Central Committee: full members	2.8	2.5
candidates	4.3	6.0
Urban and district party secretaries	4 (1973)	n.a.
Party membership	24	25

SOURCE Gail Warshofsky Lapidus, "Introduction: Women, Work, and Family: New Soviet Perspectives," in *Women, Work, and Family in the Soviet Union,* ed. Gail Warshofsky Lapidus (Armont, NY: M.E. Sharpe, Inc., 1982), pp. xxii, xxiii.

feminine values, while others emphasize the need for role redefinitions in the home.

What kind of political power do women have in the Soviet Union? Women's lobbying groups are not allowed, so there are few possibilities for direct influence. A woman can, however, have indirect influence by resisting regime efforts to increase the birthrate among the European, especially Russian, population. By failing to cooperate, women may, intentionally or inadvertently, place pressure on the authorities to provide child-care and consumer facilities to ease their burdens. However, oral contraceptives are scarce, and women have turned to abortion as a means of birth control. Reportedly, about 10 percent of women in Moscow have had five abortions or more.[9] It seems strange that the regime, in its effort to increase the birthrate, has made no serious attempt to restrict access to this procedure since it was legalized in 1955.

Workers' Discontent

Evidence of worker discontent is largely inferential, although occasional strikes have been reported through unofficial channels (e.g., among port workers in Riga in 1976, at a rubber goods factory in Kaunas in 1977, at the Togliatti automobile plant in 1980). Although workers tend to be less visibly active than intellectuals in dissident circles, in the late 1970s worker involvement increased markedly.[10] In the Soviet Union, the working class has a relatively weak tradition of independent trade union organization (unlike Eastern European countries like the German Democratic Republic, Poland, and Czechoslovakia). Efforts in 1977–78 to form an independent trade union in Moscow and elsewhere met with severe repression.

Lacking political outlets, workers express their alienation in indirect forms. Levels of labor productivity in Soviet firms tend to be consistently lower than in most Western countries, perhaps in part because the government's commitment to job security allows the manager to exert less effective pressure on workers to increase productivity. Low productivity and high levels of alcoholism and absenteeism might be interpreted as an indirect expression of job discontent. (Alcohol abuse is, however, also a long-standing element of Russian culture that affects all strata of Soviet society.) The regime has responded to these labor problems with discipline campaigns, particularly since Andropov's short period of rule, beginning in November, 1982. The party/state has also attempted to improve worker incentives and supplies of consumer goods to raise motivation levels. For example, the brigade system makes groups of workers collectively responsible for a certain portion of the production process. Individual wage levels then reflect the brigade council's assessment of contribution, bringing peer pressure to bear. In another experiment called the Shchekino method, initiated in the late 1960s in Tula, managers were allowed to release or transfer unneeded labor resources and to increase the wages of the remaining work force accordingly so long as specified output levels were achieved and plan requirements fulfilled. Both experiments have met resistance from some managers, who feel under increased pressure to raise productivity with fewer labor resources. Efforts to initiate genuine worker involvement in production decisions have been avoided, as this would effectively change the balance of power within the enterprise and generate a whole new set of demands on the part of the working class.

Consumerism

In the last two to three decades, consumer expectations have grown, though seemingly not in unmanageable proportions. As indicated in Table 28.1, ownership of consumer durables has risen, with some fluctuations over time, as the regime has increased the priority of this economic sector. However, consumer goods are often of poor quality, and spare parts are difficult, if not impossible, to find. As Timothy Colton suggests, "An individual might be philosophical about not owning a washing machine; when the machine he does own cannot be repaired or stands idle for lack of detergent, he is apt to be less forgiving. . ."[11]

Difficulties in finding desirable or high-quality goods have contributed to an almost institutionalized system of corruption throughout Soviet society, from the top elite to the average clerk or truck driver. Arkady Shevchenko, a high Soviet official who defected in 1978, reports that top officials commonly use state materials and labor to build private dachas or renovate their apartments.[12] The media also report on numerous instances of lower-level corruption, such as truck drivers who sell state-owned gasoline at high prices, or employees who steal choice goods and materials from state shops or enterprises. Clerks in stores may hold particularly valued items for customers willing to pay an extra tip. In addition a black market exists for certain goods, particularly Western commodities that are impossible to buy in official outlets. Ironically, the very shortage of material amenities may contribute to a higher degree of materialism, since one must be always conscious of how to meet one's material needs. Under Andropov, the Soviet authorities initiated a crackdown on many forms of corruption, but the problem has proven difficult to deal with, because these unofficial channels of distribution do compensate for inadequacies in official structures and provide an outlet for consumer frustration. On the other hand, civil morality is undoubtedly undermined. Contacts become as important as wage levels, making it difficult for the authorities to motivate productive activity simply through differential pay scales.

Environmental Activism

As in other industrialized countries, the Soviet Union suffers from increasing levels of environmental pollution and depletion of valuable natural resources. Since the mid-1960s, environmental protection has become a major concern of scientists, writers, and economists. The initial trigger was the threatened pollution of Lake Baikal in Siberia by a factory designed to produce a special type of rayon cord for use in tires. Journalists and scientists drew attention to the danger, and the state took action to reduce the detrimental effects on the lake. Awareness of similar problems in most major rivers and lakes, as well as of high levels of air pollution in industrial centers, has focused further attention on the environment. In this policy area, the main pressure has come from experts on whom, to a large extent, the government must rely in assessing the dangers. However, the serious nuclear accident at the Chernobyl nuclear power plant north of Kiev in the Ukraine in April, 1986, undoubtedly has brought greater awareness of the environmental hazards of nuclear energy, and may stimulate increased mobilization of larger segments of the population in support of environmental protection in general. Despite some increased legal and budgetary commitment since 1970, the investments necessary to control pollution have not been forthcoming. Planners fear that devoting available resources to environmental protection will slow down the economic growth rate by diverting investment from more productive sectors.

The Dissident Movement

The Soviet regime has not had to face a unified opposition movement, because the various dissident groups represent such diverse interests and perspectives. A dissident can be defined as a person who must go outside the permissible channels of expression to articulate his or her demands. Major instruments of dissent are *samizdat* publications, contacts with foreign journalists to stimulate international pressure, and informal meetings held in the homes of activists, as well as less-frequent public demonstrations, including hunger strikes, display of placards, and graffiti.

In 1976, a group of dissidents formed the Helsinki Watch Group in Moscow with the goal of publicizing violations of human rights, rights that the Soviet Union had agreed to honor in signing the Helsinki Accords (the Final Act of the Conference on Security and Cooperation in Europe) in 1975. The Helsinki Watch Group had the potential to serve as a catalyst for diverse elements in the dissident community, since its self-defined mandate included protection of religious freedom, cultural self-expression, the right to emigration, and legal rights for the accused. This group soon developed branches in several cities in the Soviet Union and did in fact briefly become a clearinghouse for information about suppression of dissent as well as a conduit for information to the West.

In the late 1970s, the organizers of the group were arrested (including Iurii Orlov, a former Communist Party member, physicist, and head of the Helsinki Watch Group; Anatoly Shcharansky, especially involved with Jewish emigration rights; and Aleksandr Ginzburg, head of the Aid Fund for Political Prisoners and their Families, which was established in 1974 from the royalties of Aleksandr Solzhenitsyn's three-volume work, *The Gulag Archipelago*). Apparently the regime found the Helsinki Watch Group disturbing both because of the group's international connections and its potential as a unifying force among the various dissident elements.

It is more difficult for the state to deal with very prominent critics like the famous physicist Andrei Sakharov and novelist Aleksandr Solzhenitsyn. Solzhenitsyn was forced to emigrate from the Soviet Union, which reduced his domestic influence; it is difficult for a writer to operate successfully outside his or her own cultural and linguistic milieu. Sakharov's internal exile to the town of Gor'kii since January, 1980, has been less effective, since the exile itself has served to make Sakharov an international *cause célèbre*. (The Soviet authorities allowed Sakharov's wife, Elena Bonner, to travel to the West for medical treatment in 1985, presumably as a gesture of goodwill preceding the summit between Gorbachev and Reagan.) Nonetheless, by firm use of political repression, the regime has been able to prevent the diverse dissident elements in the Soviet Union from forming a viable and effective opposition movement.

Eastern European Examples

While Soviet authorities have been able to prevent major outbursts of public discontent, some Eastern European countries have experienced significant upheavals under communist party rule. The most notable examples were the strikes and protests accompanying de-Stalinization in Hungary and Poland in 1956, the Prague Spring of 1968 (see Chapter 29), and the rise of the Solidarity trade union movement in Poland in 1980–81. Social configurations different from those in the Soviet Union have made some Eastern European polities more susceptible to disruption. Even where the authorities have been able to maintain firm political control, as in the German Democratic Republic (henceforth East Germany), semiautonomous social forces have at times posed challenges that have compelled the authorities to allow scope for independent social action. We will now examine two recent, but quite different, instances of social discontent.

The Polish Renewal

On August 14, 1980, the workers at the Lenin Shipyard in the coastal city of Gdansk went out on strike in reaction to the firing of Anna Walentynowicz, a crane driver active in organizing a free trade union. Earlier in the summer the regime had instituted price increases, which had sparked other work stoppages and protests throughout Poland. Unlike earlier outbreaks of strikes in December of 1970 and June of 1976, the Gdansk workers in 1980 would not be satisfied simply with rollbacks of the price increases or cosmetic changes in the regime. Rather, they formulated a broad-based set of social, economic, and political demands, including, most importantly, the right to form an independent trade union to represent their interests in negotiations with the government. In addition, the workers pressed for limits on censorship; selection of personnel on the basis of qualifications, not patronage; and improvements in maternity leave, pensions, child-care facilities, ration cards, health services, and housing.

The outcome of the 1980 drama is now history: The workers were able to force the government to the negotiating table; the government agreed to recognize Solidarity, the independent trade union formed by the Gdansk workers; and in exchange, the union acknowledged the party's leading role in society. The movement quickly spread to other Polish cities and soon workers in Szczecin were making similar demands. The Solidarity union came to include some 9.4 million members from a total industrial work force of around 12.5 million. An estimated one-third of the membership of the Polish United Workers' Party or PUWP (the Polish communist party), generally of the rank-and-file, joined up, many resigning their party affiliation.

From August, 1980, to the imposition of martial law on December 13, 1981, both Solidarity and the regime faced moments of crisis, as each tried to make as few concessions as possible. First, the party balked at implementing the Gdansk agreement; and in late September, 1980, a Warsaw court rejected the first application for registration of the independent trade union. In November, after weeks of tension, the registration crisis was resolved by an agreement to append to the new trade union statutes a statement recognizing the party's leading role in society. But other impasses ensued: In March, 1981, a police attack on a gathering of Rural Solidarity (the union formed for independent peasants in December, 1980) at Bydgoszcz produced a four-hour general strike on March 27, 1981, and threats of additional strikes. A compromise agreement fashioned between Solidarity leader Lech Walesa and government officials elicited dissension within Solidarity's own ranks as to the appropriateness of calling off the planned strike.

Unlike the Czechoslovakian Communist Party in 1968, the leadership of the Polish communist party resisted concessions and was unwilling to fundamentally change the system. Despite a massive personnel change in top party bodies, the Party Congress of July, 1981, brought no clear shift in direction, although new party statutes did affirm free election procedures and secret balloting in party elections. In September, 1981, the Solidarity union held its first national conference, which produced more radical results, such as calling upon Eastern European comrades to follow in their footsteps by organizing similar unions. While plans to squelch the movement had undoubtedly been afoot for some time, this may have been the final straw. Preparations made for the imposition of military rule were realized in December, 1981, although without direct Soviet intervention.

The Polish Renewal, as it is often called, was a truly unique event in Eastern European history. It was spurred by a broad-based social protest movement, which included not only workers and intellectuals but also Catholic church officials and the peasantry. The Solidarity movement bridged the gap between neo-Marxist and Catholic intellectuals, and brought together workers and intellectuals. Workers, who had generally been more concerned with economic demands, took up the defense of imprisoned intellectuals and extended their interests to a broad range of social and political issues. Intellectuals, often more concerned with issues of self-expression or enhanced influence of specialists, translated their understanding of social rights into support for the workers' union. Cooperation between workers and intellectuals was one result of the government's repression of earlier workers' strikes which occurred in Poland in 1976, also following price increases. After the strikes in June 1976, some intellectuals formed KOR (the Committee for the Defense of Workers' Rights) to help arrested workers. In 1977, this group changed its name to KOR-KSS (KSS, the Committee for Social Self-Defense), reflecting an even broader mandate. The workers were ready to accept this aid from the intellectuals, who acted as advisers to Solidarity in 1980–81. Both groups apparently understood that earlier confrontations with the state had had limited success in part because the opposition did not have a broad enough social base.

In Poland most peasants operate on a private basis, since collectivization of agriculture was largely abandoned in 1956 and never reinstated (as it was in other Soviet bloc countries in Eastern Europe). In 1980 the Polish peasantry pressed for more state support for private agriculture and higher prices for agricultural produce. These concerns seemingly contradicted the workers' demands for lower food prices; nonetheless, both groups united in identifying as the source of their problems the ill-guided and self-serving central policies. The Catholic church, a symbol of national identification and unity, provided institutional and spiritual support for the movement. The church had its own interests to protect and at times exerted a moderating influence on the movement so as not to threaten concessions gained from the state (the right to build new churches, educate priests, and broadcast Masses). But, on the other hand, it offered a powerful source of unity and purpose for the movement and maintained a realistic awareness of the threat to Polish sovereignty should Solidarity overstep the bounds of Soviet tolerance.

The Polish Renewal can be interpreted as an assertion of civil society against the party/state: Society was organizing itself on an autonomous basis to seize back some of the space the political authorities had usurped. The workers were not placated simply by a change in leadership (such as had occurred in 1956 and 1970 after workers' unrest) or by isolated policy concessions. If the winning of such concessions in earlier confrontations had demonstrated that protest could be effective, then past experience also taught that such changes could be as easily rescinded as they were offered. Each time, the gains had been gradually undermined by the regime. In 1980, the workers sought institutional guarantees through an independent social organization rather than through the party. Appropriately, the hero of the moment was not a new reformist party leader but a worker himself, the Gdansk electrician Lech Walesa. Over time, as pressures and the complexity of the situation increased, the Solidarity movement itself became torn over the appropriate strategy, but the basic commitment to social self-expression was unchallenged.

We can identify some of the specific factors that led to the outbreak of protest in Poland. Why did such a movement emerge there? In chapter 29, we concluded that the Prague Spring was unlikely to provide a model for reform in the Soviet Union; however, could something similar to the Polish Renewal occur in the Soviet Union?

National Self-Assertion. The communist party has always had a weak social base in Poland, partly due to its close association with Soviet interests even before it came to power after World War II. Further, the Polish and Russian nations have been historical rivals. Poland had been an important European power in the sixteenth century, but between 1795 and 1918, was partitioned by Prussia, the Austrian Empire, and Russia, and disappeared from the map as an independent nation. With reunification after World War I, Poland found itself sandwiched between two powerful historical adversaries, Germany and Soviet Russia.

Following World War I, the Polish Communist Party had enclaves of support among the ethnic minorities of eastern Poland and in some industrial regions, but generally was not a major political force. Following a coup d'état in 1926, led by Polish national hero Jozef Pilsudski, the government became increasingly authoritarian. Parliamentary power was undermined, electoral procedures were compromised, and restrictions were placed on the activities of political parties, including the communists. Furthermore, whatever appeal the Polish Communist Party might have had was weakened by the party's support for the Soviet invasion of Poland during 1920. As a member of the Soviet-dominated Communist International (Comintern), the Polish party was obligated to demonstrate communist discipline, in true democratic centralist fashion, by supporting the Comintern (and thus the Soviet) position. The Comintern actually abolished the Polish Communist Party in 1938, because it was allegedly a stronghold of Trotskyists and agents of Pilsudski. Although the party was reconstituted in 1942 and played some role in the anti-Nazi underground, it emerged from World War II with a weak base of popular support.

Once communist rule was imposed with the backing of the Soviet Red Army, the traditional animosity between Poland and Russia translated into popular resentment of Soviet domination through the new Polish communist party, now called the Polish United Workers' Party (PUWP). Thus, strong national sentiments have, from the outset, made it difficult for the communist party authorities to gain popular legitimacy in Poland. This is in sharp contrast to the Soviet Communist Party, which could appeal to patriotic sentiments, as in World War II, and could also claim to have lifted Russia to superpower status. In addition, the Catholic church in Poland has always defended *Polish* identity in times of foreign domination and so has served a very different function from the accommodating Russian Orthodox church. As we have seen, the Polish Catholic church also provided support for the Solidarity movement, and popular sentiments were especially aroused by the Pope's visit to Poland in June, 1979.

Economic Crisis. A second factor contributing to the Polish Renewal was the gross mismanagement of the economy. The Polish authorities have never been able to pursue an effective course of economic reform, despite several false starts. There are a few possible reasons for this failure. First, the middle-level bureaucracy in Poland is generally conservative and may have presented opposition to reform measures. Also, the agricultural sector is weak, as the predominantly private farms have received little government help in achieving extensive mechanization. Poor agricultural performance would make the initial stages of any broad ranging economic reform more destabilizing, since embarking on such a reform would necessitate price increases on food to bring them in line with supply and demand. In addition, the working class itself has resisted any changes that might involve price increases or decreased job security. Finally, Wladyslaw Gomulka, who led the party from 1956 to 1970, did not exhibit a personal commitment to economic reform. By the time a significant reform was attempted in 1969–70, the economy was in such dire straits that it was difficult to gain popular acceptance of the measures needed to make the reform effective (such as decreased subsidies on basic goods and wage restraints).

An economic reform program, formulated in 1969 and 1970, included plans for temporary wage freezes and layoffs, in order to spur productivity and bring wage levels and costs in line with real levels of productivity. In 1970, the regime instituted price increases on meat to compensate for bad harvests and import reductions. The workers, feeling they would now bear the cost of government mismanagement, went on strike; this forced the government to rescind the price hikes and abandon the reform. Party leader Gomulka was removed and replaced by Edward Gierek.

In the face of rising consumer demands and poor economic performance, Gierek's team embarked on a bold, but ultimately foolhardy, economic plan. Precisely at this moment Western banks were glutted with international oil money and anxious to lend it out at favorable interest rates. Poland took this opportunity to borrow huge sums of money, in the hope that it could finance both the import of desirable Western consumer goods to placate the population and the development of new industry. These new factories could then produce output for export, which would pay off Poland's foreign debt. However elegant on paper, the implementation of Gierek's blueprint faltered. By 1975, Poland's foreign debt had soared to $6.3 billion; by 1977, to $12 billion; and by 1980, to over $20 billion. The economic downturn in the West undermined the international demand for Polish goods; meanwhile, interest rates jumped, so that Poland had to expend a large proportion of its foreign income simply to pay the interest on its burgeoning debt.

These international developments were aggravated by domestic factors. Because the Polish authorities had not accompanied their radical investment program with real economic reform, resources were poorly invested, projects lay unfinished, capital wasted. Furthermore, consumer expectations had risen dramatically in the brief period of engineered prosperity between 1971 and 1975. Rather than placating consumer appetites, Gierek had succeeded in whetting them even further. By 1974, goods were again in short supply as imports were cut. Wages had risen since 1970, so money accumulated in citizens' bank accounts, but there was little of quality to purchase with the increased income. When further entrenchment measures became necessary in 1975 and 1976 (particularly the price rises in 1976), the working class again responded with an outburst of strikes. Price increases were again rescinded, but imports were also cut back. Following 1976, working-class discontent was further fueled by widespread awareness of government corruption. The elites were diverting resources to build luxurious country villas. Indeed, by this time corruption pervaded the entire system; according to a popular joke, the worst punishment imaginable was to lose one's contacts, for it was becoming increasingly difficult to get anything of value through open and formal channels. Workers saw little relation between reward and work, and changes in leadership such as in 1956 and 1970 were hardly likely to alter things. The 1980 strikes reflected the true proportions of the economic crisis: The government did not have the popular trust necessary to gain acceptance of the required sacrifices to put the economy back on track.

Other Eastern European countries have also faced economic downturns. Only in Hungary has the government pursued a fairly consistent and meaningful economic reform program. Other Eastern European nations, especially East Germany, Hungary, and Rumania, have significant foreign debts. Poland, however, is unique in that an already volatile political situation was aggravated by a government policy that spurred highly unrealistic consumer expectations. The Soviet authorities, by contrast, have managed consumer expectations relatively well, in part because Soviet citizens have less contact with Western levels of prosperity. Polish travel policy was relatively liberal in the 1970s, so many Polish citizens traveled to the West and millions visited the more prosperous Eastern European countries, East Germany and Hungary, often to purchase consumer goods not available at home.

Leeway for Dissent. The Polish dissident movement was also given considerable leeway in the 1970s, perhaps in exchange for Western economic cooperation. Efforts similar to those of KOR (the Committee for the Defense of Workers' Rights), such as distribution of the underground newspaper *Robotnik,* "The Worker," in Polish factories, likely would have been quickly suppressed in the Soviet Union, East Germany, or Czechoslovakia. An underground university (known as the flying university) also survived in Poland. This relative liberalism toward opposition intellectuals in the 1970s allowed the development of underground networks that provided a ready-made infrastructure for the Solidarity movement in 1980–81. In the Soviet Union, dissent in general and efforts to organize independent trade unions in particular have been dealt with more quickly and harshly. The East-West detente of the 1970s allowed greater access to Western ideas and influences in Poland, facilitating to some extent the success of the Polish opposition.

In summary, the conditions that produced the Solidarity movement in Poland are unlikely to be duplicated in the Soviet Union. The Soviet party can more successfully appeal to Russian patriotism. Soviet leaders have also undoubtedly learned from the Polish experience that radical economic initiatives, sudden price increases, and high levels of corruption must be avoided. The discipline campaigns initiated under Andropov, following the Polish upheaval, may have been an attempt to improve public morale by attacking corruption at all levels and by reestablishing some links between work and reward. Further, there is no Soviet equivalent of the Polish Catholic church, and Soviet authorities are much more prone to crack down on dissent in its earliest stages. Finally, Western democratic ideas and the notion of an autonomous civil society have shallow roots in the Soviet Union.

If a Soviet version of Solidarity is unlikely to prosper, some other Eastern European countries might provide more fertile ground. Western influence is stronger in East Germany, Hungary, and Czechoslovakia than it is in the Soviet Union; other countries, most notably Rumania, are suffering severe economic dislocations and have seen workers' strikes in recent years. But none of these countries share the unique configuration of historical, religious, and economic traits that contributed to the rise of Solidarity. More likely, perhaps, is a future upheaval in Poland itself, for the 1980–81 episode may be just one more step in the sequence of experiences that has tutored the rebellious Polish working class and society since 1956.

Peace and Environmental Activism in East Germany

Following the postwar division of Germany, the eastern sector fell firmly within the Soviet orbit of influence. The close association of the new

German Democratic Republic (GDR), also known as East Germany, with the Soviet Union produced severe strains for the new communist leaders. Unlike the Federal Republic of Germany (FRG), or West Germany, East Germany did not receive economic support from its senior partner but was forced to aid the war-torn Soviet Union through reparation payments and the forcible transfer of industrial resources. Meanwhile, West Germany's "economic miracle" made it a powerful magnet for East Germany's middle class. Thousands of East German young people emigrated to West Germany through Berlin, a divided city in the midst of East Germany: East Berlin is the capital of East Germany, and West Berlin maintains close economic, political, and cultural ties to West Germany. In 1961 the East German authorities stopped the wave of emigration by closing the border between East and West Berlin with the Berlin Wall, a closely guarded barrier between the two parts of the city.

Some Western observers dubbed East Germany "the country that shouldn't be," a sentiment probably echoed by many East German citizens who yearned for a united and prosperous Germany. It is not surprising, then, that East German authorities sought support from their Soviet comrades, while imposing an orthodox and controlled regime at home. East Germany has proven itself to be one of the more controlled polities in Eastern Europe: Censorship is tight; emigration controls are strict; and contacts between East German citizens and the West are strongly discouraged. Nonetheless, since the early 1980s, East German young people have organized independent initiatives to draw attention to environmental and peace issues. While these initiatives in no way compare to the broad-based social movement that developed in Poland in 1980–81, they are perhaps equally intriguing because of the pivotal international position of East Germany and the otherwise orthodox nature of the regime.

Environmental Deterioration. Environmental activism in East Germany developed in reaction to real and visible ecological deterioration. Pollution levels in many East German industrial centers are high, particularly due to widespread combustion of the high-sulfur brown coal that is plentiful in the country. Acid rain is also a severe problem, and forest damage near the border with Czechoslovakia is perhaps the worst in Europe. Because of its foreign debt and rising energy costs, East German authorities feel compelled to reduce imports by relying on this energy source, despite the damage from pollution. Public information on pollution levels in East Germany, however, is highly restricted; the regime apparently considers this a sensitive issue. Nevertheless, some types of pollution are evident even to the layperson, so despite regime efforts, public awareness of the problem has grown. Furthermore, East German citizens have virtually free access to West German radio and TV broadcasts; East German authorities gave up the hopeless task of jamming the signals some time ago. Through these broadcasts, East German citizens learn about West German environmental and peace movements and receive information about their society that is not aired in their own media.

The Peace Movement. The peace issue is equally salient. Both Germanies would likely be in the line of fire in any type of East-West military confrontation, conventional or nuclear. The highly visible controversy regarding the stationing of cruise and Pershing missiles in West Germany by the North Atlantic Treaty Organization (NATO) in the early 1980s was again accessible to East German citizens through the West German media. With the announcement, in 1983, that the Warsaw Treaty Organization would also station nuclear weapons in East Germany, the issue was brought even closer to home. In the early 1960s, the seeds of an unofficial peace movement were already sprouting among the so-called *Bausoldaten,* "construction soldiers." (In 1963, when universal male conscription was introduced in East Germany, the authorities did allow conscientious objectors to take up military service without arms, as *Bausoldaten.* The option was not widely publicized, and the choice generally had detrimental effects on future educational opportunities and career progress for these objectors.) Small numbers of *Bausoldaten,* most motivated by religious conviction, began to organize discussion and support groups within East Germany's Evangelical (Lutheran) church once their service was completed.

By the early 1980s, scattered peace forums, workshops, discussions, seminars, and fasts took place throughout East Germany under the auspices of the church. Spokespersons criticized the militarization of East German society and suggested joint East-West responsibility for the arms race. In 1981, the church disseminated badges replicating the *Swords into Ploughshares* emblem that appears on the Soviet-sponsored monument in front of the United Nations building in New York. Ironically, East German authorities interpreted the donning of the badge as a symbolic affront to official peace policy and harassed the young people wearing it. Meanwhile, the Evangelical church has continued to provide a shelter for numerous peace and environmental activities: A yearly "peace decade" involves ten days of discussion, exhibits, and workshops; young people receive counseling about the construction soldier option; and church authorities press for a cutback in the military training that has become widespread in all East German schools and communities since the late 1970s. To dramatize environmental issues, young people have organized bicycle demonstrations to polluted regions, have circulated information on pollution levels, and have sponsored tree-planting campaigns. Following the Chernobel accident in 1986, church activists petitioned the authorities to halt nuclear power development in East Germany.

The Official Response. East German authorities have made some efforts to control these initiatives, particularly when these activists take to the streets or forge contacts with Western counterparts. In early 1984, East German authorities allowed thousands of its citizens to emigrate to West Germany; included in this number were church activists, some of whom did not wish to emigrate but preferred to continue their work inside East Germany itself. Why, however, has the regime not put further clamps on these semiautonomous church-based activities? The Evangelical church is given much greater leeway to organize spare-time activities for its parishioners than are churches in the Soviet Union. Notices of weekend retreats and other church activities frequently appear on church bulletin boards. In the Soviet Union, such activities would hardly be allowed public advertisement, even if they could be organized surreptitiously.

One explanation for the more lenient approach of East German authorities toward church activities rests in the diplomatic isolation of the country until the early 1970s. Until 1972, East Germany was largely excluded from the international community. West Germany refused to recognize East Germany as a legitimate state and refused to maintain diplomatic relations with countries with diplomatic ties to East Germany (the Soviet Union was excluded from the stricture). Between 1970 and 1972, as detente warmed up, a series of agreements were concluded, most importantly, the 1972 Treaty on Basic Relations between West Germany and East Germany. With this agreement, the two Germanies officially recognized each other's existence and opened up fairly normal relations in a whole range of economic, cultural, and political arenas.

Nonetheless, East Germany's long-time diplomatic isolation had forced it to seek other routes of international recognition, one of which was sports: East Germany distinguished itself through its athletes, achieving a certain unofficial international standing. Likewise, the authorities were able to receive representation in nondiplomatic channels through organizations like the churches. The Evangelical church fulfilled a positive function for the authorities simply through its presence in international meetings. By 1978, church and state had reached an arrangement in which the church was allowed a certain latitude in its activities in exchange for its willingness to operate within, rather than against, socialism. By the late 1970s, it would have been difficult for the authorities to clamp down on unofficial peace activities carried out under the umbrella of the church: In the propaganda battle between East and West over the arms race, repression of a genuine East German peace movement would have undermined East German authorities' claim to be the true champions of peace.

The church also serves as an outlet for the potentially rebellious youth of the country. The authorities may recognize that so long as the frustrations and questionings of youth are contained within the church, they are less likely to result in open rebellion. The church may provide an oasis of honesty and dialogue that helps to reconcile young people to the controls imposed on them elsewhere in East German society. The church injects a strong moral component into the environmental and peace discussions. Young people are encouraged by church leaders to work within the system rather than seeking emigration; these leaders preach an ethic of personal responsibility and question the materialistic mentality of the West that contributes to environmental deterioration, messages that may help to direct disaffection into less disruptive channels.

East Germany is unique in the Soviet bloc because of its special relationship with West Germany. The authorities cannot easily appeal to national feeling, since they preside over a divided country, and the least affluent part at that. The communist leaders hope to weaken any sense of common German identity with West Germany, as this might evoke support for the reunification of Germany under conditions unfavorable to the East German elite. The general strategy of the regime has been to control dissent and restrict foreign contacts, but as developments described above suggest, the leadership apparently has felt compelled to cede control in limited areas. Could similar initiatives survive in the Soviet Union? There is a small independent peace movement in the Soviet Union, but it has been subject to greater repression than in East Germany and has been unable to develop a comparable momentum.

The Soviet Union: A New Socialist Culture?

The Soviet party/state has not transformed Soviet society into the type of socialist utopia envisaged by Marx or Lenin. The new socialist person still remains to be born. There are still important social divisions among the population, and the regime's own emphasis on increasing material output has encouraged materialism. The results of a recent study of Jewish emigrés from the Soviet Union suggest that "the modern Soviet system has tended to reinforce traditional clientelistic orientations toward the structures of government;"[13] that is, to strengthen reliance on personal contacts rather than on organized political action to get what one wants. Soviet citizens have a low sense of political efficacy regarding the policy-making process but more often make use of contacts or even bribes to get what they want on an individual basis. For example, a student refused admission to university most often would resort to extralegal methods rather than working through legally established procedures of appeal. Thus, the citizen is neither simply a passive subject nor an involuntary participant in official activities; on the other hand, this approach is hardly an example of socialist collectivism as Marx or Lenin had hoped. Rather, according to Di Franceisco and Gitelman, various forms of covert activity often enable the citizen to affect the impact, if not the formulation, of government policies:

> Much of the Soviet population would probably be more interested in increasing levels of performance by the present system than in fundamental systemic change. Until such time as either of these comes about, the citizen is left to grapple as best he can with those small questions of daily life that he and those who administer the system must solve together.[14]

If the Soviet authorities have not yet created a socialist culture, they have thus far been successful in controlling social discontent. While many Western European and North American countries have experienced increased ethnic tension in the last two decades (e.g., racial tension in the United States; Quebec nationalism in Canada; Scottish, Irish, and Welsh nationalism in Britain; Basque unrest in Spain), expressions of ethnic self-assertion in the Soviet Union have not challenged the fundamental stability of the polity. Furthermore, unlike in some Eastern European countries, in the Soviet Union social class conflict has remained muted, consumer expectations seem under reasonable control, and intellectual dissidents have been effectively isolated. To some extent this success has been a function of simple repression, but as Seweryn Bialer points out, there are also positive reasons for regime support, including: the creditable performance of the regime in improving the standard of living of all major groups and regions, particularly in comparison with the Soviet and Russian past; an improved network of social-welfare measures, particularly for the peasantry and less-privileged groups; maintenance of relatively stable prices for basic goods; provision of continued opportunities for upward social mobility; and the increased international status of the Soviet Union. Furthermore, many professionals have been effectively coopted into the system; that is, the regime has won their cooperation by offering them social status, material benefits, and other privileges (such as access to Western publications and foreign travel). At the same time, the mass of the population remains relatively indifferent to larger political issues, but many citizens may have a sense of "belonging," due to their high levels of participation in routine political activities.[15]

In assessing Soviet performance and prospects for future stability, one must always keep in mind that expectations and perceptions in the Soviet Union may be quite different than in the West. Nonetheless, as we will discuss in the next chapter, new stresses are confronting the Soviet leadership, and the Soviet polity may be at another crucial juncture, just as it was in 1929 and following Stalin's death. In the late Brezhnev era, Soviet leadership initiatives had lost dynamism and a series of unresolved problems remained for the new leaders. Even if disaffected women, workers, peasants, intellectuals, ethnic minorities, and youth cannot openly organize political alternatives, they can attempt to compel a response to their concerns through various indirect and unofficial methods. Likewise, the authorities seem more and more aware that continued stability depends upon improving the responsiveness and performance of the system.

NOTES

1. Hannah Arendt, *The Origins of Totalitarianism,* a new edition with added prefaces (New York: Harcourt Brace Jovanovich, 1973), p. 464.
2. David Lane, *Soviet Economy and Society* (Oxford: Basil Blackwell, 1985), pp. 132–33.
3. John Armstrong, "Mobilized and Proletarian Diasporas," *American Political Science Review,* vol. 70 (1976), p. 403.
4. John L. Scherer, "A Note on Soviet Jewish Emigration 1971–1984," *Soviet Jewish Affairs,* vol. 15, no. 2 (1985), p. 42.
5. Christel Lane, *Christian Religion in the Soviet Union: A Sociological Study* (Albany: State University of New York Press, 1978), pp. 46, 140.
6. See: Tatyana Mamonova and Sarah Matlitsky, eds., *Women and Russia: Feminist Writings from the Soviet Union* (Boston: Beacon Press, 1984).
7. Gail Warshofsky Lapidus, "Introduction: Women, Work, and Family: New Soviet Perspectives," in *Women, Work, and Family in the Soviet Union,* ed. Gail Warshofsky Lapidus (Armont, NY: M.E. Sharpe, Inc., 1982), p. xxii.

8. E. V. Gruzdeva and E. S. Chertikhina, "Soviet Women: Problems of Work and Daily Life," in *Rabochii klass i sovremennyi mir,* no. 6 (1982), translated in *Soviet Sociology,* vol. xiv, 1–3 (1985/86), p. 163.
9. D. Lane, *Soviet Economy and Society,* p. 119.
10. Frederick C. Barghoorn, "Regime-Dissenter Relations after Khrushchev: Some Observations," in *Pluralism in the Soviet Union: Essays in Honour of H. Gordon Skilling,* ed. Susan Gross Solomon (New York: St. Martin's Press, 1982), pp. 139–47.
11. Timothy J. Colton, *The Dilemma of Reform in the Soviet Union* (New York: Council on Foreign Relations, 1984), p. 26.
12. Arkady Shevchenko, *Breaking With Moscow* (New York: Alfred A. Knopf, 1985), p. 148.
13. Wayne Di Franceisco and Zvi Gitelman, "Soviet Political Culture and 'Covert Participation' in Policy Implementation," *American Political Science Review,* vol. 78 (September 1984), p. 619.
14. Di Franceisco and Gitelman, "Soviet Political Culture," p. 619.
15. Seweryn Bialer, *Stalin's Successors: Leadership, Stability, and Change in the Soviet Union* (Cambridge: Cambridge University Press, 1980), chap. 8.

Soviet Politics in Transition

Some Western commentators have been predicting an imminent crisis in the Soviet system for years now; contrary to these expectations, the Soviet leaders have continued to muddle through with few fundamental changes. Is the situation any different now? Is the Soviet polity undergoing yet another major transition such as occurred in 1929 and after the death of Stalin? Do the changes being instituted by the new generation of leaders represent a genuinely new approach? Or do they involve only a continuation of the "treadmill of reform,"[1] as one analyst describes the efforts of the Brezhnev era? By examining the short period since Mikhail Gorbachev's ascension to party leadership in March, 1985, we can perhaps begin to discern some clues to help us answer these questions.

The Gorbachev Team

Each major leader has ushered in a unique era in Soviet politics, so that we generally divide Soviet history in terms of the Stalin era, the Khrushchev era, and the Brezhnev era. As societies become more complex, the ability of any single individual to shape the politics of his or her time in power becomes more limited, for the leader is constrained by more powerful social forces: larger, interdependent institutional structures; a more highly educated population; and the limited capability of any individual to master the necessary knowledge and expertise to maintain the required overview. Furthermore, the unwritten rules of the game have changed in the Soviet Union so that individual dictatorship of the Stalinist variety is no longer acceptable to the elite itself. Nonetheless, the leader's approach as well as the type of men and women that he gathers around him lend a distinctive flavor and direction to Soviet politics.

One factor is, of course, the age of the new leaders. For example, the average age of full Politburo members has declined from sixty-nine in 1981 to sixty-four in early 1986. (See Tables 31.1 and 31.2.) Although younger politicians are not necessarily any more liberal or even more dynamic than their elders, it seems likely that these younger leaders will be more assertive in addressing problems, if only as a reaction to the relative lethargy of the late 1970s and their own blocked career mobility during that time.

As discussed in Chapter 28, the post-Stalinist leadership is not only younger but also of a different generational cohort. These men and women grew up under different circumstances; thus, the formative experiences that shaped their habits and expectations were quite different from those of their predecessors, who rose under the umbrella of the Stalinist purges of the 1930s. One could expect them to have more regular career patterns, less disrupted by World War II; therefore, they are more likely to have pursued university education full-time upon completion of secondary school, unlike their predecessors, who often attended night school or went to work before continuing their education. While most are trained as engineers, agronomists, or in other technical fields, some, like Gorbachev himself, also have less-technical specializations, such as law. (Gorbachev has studied agronomy in addition to law; Lenin, incidentally, was also trained in law.) In other ways the new generation seems to resemble the preceding one. The surest route to the top party body is still through party work, where both Brezhnev and Gorbachev began their careers at an early age. Unlike Brezhnev, however, Gorbachev spent his career, before coming to Moscow, in only one region, Stavropol', a largely agricultural area in the southern part of the Russian republic. Thus he was not able to develop as broad a range of career connections, individuals whom he might carry with him on his *khvost,* "tail" as the Russians say, during his rise to the position of party leader. Likewise, the new generation of leaders is likely to be increasingly specialized in career background, having worked mainly in one region, functional area, or branch of the economy, whereas the Brezhnev team consisted of generalists with diverse career experiences before reaching the top.

Table 31.1 The CPSU Politburo in 1981 following the Twenty-Sixth Party Congress

FULL MEMBERS	OTHER POSTS HELD AT THAT TIME	AGE (MARCH 10, 1981)	DATE OF REMOVAL OR DEATH
Iurii V. Andropov	Chair, Comm. for State Security (KGB)	66	Died in office February, 1984
Leonid I. Brezhnev	General Secretary, CPSU; Chair, Presidium of Supreme Soviet; President of the USSR	74	Died in office November, 1982
Konstantin U. Chernenko	Secretariat of CPSU Central Comm.	69	Died in office March, 1985
Mikhail S. Gorbachev	Secretariat of CPSU Central Comm.	50	
Viktor V. Grishin	Head, Moscow Party Comm.; Member, Presidium of Supreme Soviet	66	Removed from office January, 1986
Andrei A. Gromyko	Minister of Foreign Affairs	71	
Andrei P. Kirilenko	Secretariat of CPSU Central Comm.	74	Retired in November, 1982
Dinmukhamed A. Kunaev	Head, Kazakh party org.	69	
Arvid Ia. Pel'she	Chair, Party Control Comm.	82	Died in office May, 1983
Grigorii V. Romanov	Head, Leningrad party org.	58	Removed from office July, 1985
Vladimir V. Shcherbitskii	Head, Ukrainian party org.	63	
Mikhail A. Suslov	Secretariat of CPSU Central Comm.	78	Died in office January, 1982
Nikolai A. Tikhonov	Prime Minister; Chair, Council of Ministers	75	Retired in September, 1985
Dmitrii F. Ustinov	Minister of Defense	72	Died in office December, 1984

Table 31.2 The CPSU Politburo in 1986 Following the Twenty-Seventh Party Congress

MEMBERSHIP	OTHER POSITIONS HELD AT THAT TIME	ELECTED AS FULL MEMBER	AGE (MARCH 10, 1986)
Geidar A. Aliev	First Deputy Prime Minister of Council of Ministers	November, 1982	62
Viktor M. Chebrikov	Chair, Comm. for State Security (KGB)	April, 1985	63*
Mikhail S. Gorbachev	General Secretary of the CPSU	October, 1980	55
Andrei A. Gromyko	Chair, Presidium of Supreme Soviet; President of the USSR	April, 1973	76
Dinmukhamed A. Kunaev	Head, Kazakh party org.	April, 1971	74
Egor K. Ligachev	Secretariat of CPSU Central Comm.	April, 1985	65
Nikolai I. Ryzhkov	Prime Minister of USSR; Chair, Council of Ministers	April, 1985	56
Vladimir V. Shcherbitskii	Head, Ukrainian party org.	April, 1971	68
Eduard A. Shevardnadze	Minister of Foreign Affairs	July, 1985	58
Mikhail S. Solomentsev	Chair, Party Control Commission	December, 1983	72
Vitalii I. Vorotnikov	Chair, Council of Ministers of the Russian Republic	December, 1983	60
Lev N. Zaikov	Secretariat of CPSU Central Comm.	March, 1986	62

*Chebrikov was born in 1923, but his exact date of birth is not available.

As Timothy Colton has pointed out, all of this may mean that the traditional machine politics, which allowed the General Secretary to firm up his position by installing his clients in subordinate posts, may be less effective than previously.[2] Concrete policy conflicts and positions may form an ever more important basis for political coalitions. However, we often do not know the actual policy preferences of aspiring or existing leaders, so we must try to derive this information from subtle clues in public speeches. Nonetheless, if we examine the individuals who have been promoted to the Politburo and other high posts since Gorbachev's own rise, we notice that most have less extensive career connections with him, as compared to many of Brezhnev's deputies and allies, who worked with Brezhnev while he was studying engineering and beginning his political career in Dnepropetrovsk and Moldavia. On the other hand, Gorbachev's appointees probably share with him a similar approach to problems or a similar political style. For example, Egor Ligachev and Nikolai Ryzhkov, who became members of the Politburo in April, 1985, are likely to be sympathetic to Gorbachev's proclivities in economic policy. (Ryzhkov was also appointed prime minister, replacing Tikhonov, in early 1986). Other appointees may have been protégés of Andropov (e.g., new KGB head and Politburo member Viktor Chebrikov) to whom, in part, Gorbachev apparently owed his fast rise to the top. Still others, for example, Viktor Nikonov, now in charge of agricultural affairs in the party Secretariat, may be linked to Gorbachev both by policy preferences and past career connections. A large number of Gorbachev's new appointees are former first party secretaries at the provincial level, a post Gorbachev himself held for many years in the Stavropol' territory.

Of course, we cannot be certain that Gorbachev will be able to maintain a grip on power for as long a period as Brezhnev did. It bears remembering that in 1954, a year after Stalin's death, G. Malenkov seemed the likely long-term successor to Stalin; Khrushchev himself was deposed after only some eight years on top. Life-long tenure as General Secretary certainly is not assured. Nonetheless, all signs at present indicate that Gorbachev has good prospects to hold the post for some time. Should he seem to falter into major policy blunders, either in the domestic or foreign policy arenas, this could of course also trigger a reshuffling at the top. In addition, Gorbachev must be cautious in turning numerous top posts over to individuals of his own post-Stalinist generation, for a widespread and sudden shift in personnel could also trigger rivalries and instability at the top. On the other hand, shifting personnel too slowly could fuel the existing frustration of those individuals whose careers were blocked at the middle levels of the party throughout the Brezhnev period.

Gorbachev has thus far shown himself to be a shrewd politician in consolidating his power. As of March, 1986, he had succeeded in making a remarkable number of new appointments in both the state and party structures. Two of his presumed rivals, Grigorii V. Romanov, former Leningrad party chief and Secretariat member, and Viktor V. Grishin, former head of the Moscow party organization, were removed from the Politburo by that time. Meanwhile Andrei Gromyko's appointment as President of the Soviet Union allowed Gorbachev to take on an increasing role in foreign policy formulation and administration, an area Gromyko previously had dominated due to his long and distinguished tenure as Minister of Foreign Affairs before becoming President. Due to Gromyko's age (seventy-six in 1986), he would not be expected to occupy this post for an extended period of time, thus leaving open the prospect that Gorbachev himself might take it over upon Gromyko's retirement or death. The new foreign minister, Eduard Shevardnadze, well known for his role in an important anticorruption campaign in the Georgian republic but relatively inexperienced in the foreign policy area, appears to share Gorbachev's more dynamic approach and may turn out to be a useful deputy, rather than a rival, in the foreign policy area.

Gorbachev has quickly made numerous other personnel changes in both state and party positions. Before the opening of the Twenty-Seventh Party Congress in February, 1986, these changes included a new prime minister, over thirty heads of ministries and state committees (including Gosplan), several new deputy prime ministers, four full members of the Politburo (in addition to three new candidate members), two new members of the party Secretariat, four heads of union republic party organizations, ten of the twenty-four department heads in the Central Committee apparatus, and almost a third of the regional *oblast'* "regional" party chiefs. At the party congress itself, a massive turnover of Central Committee membership occurred; 119 (almost 39 percent) of the 307 full members of that body had newly achieved full voting membership. (Only 22 of these had previously been candidate, or nonvoting, members.) Five of the eleven members of the party Secretariat were newly appointed at the end of the Congress, and the Politburo itself acquired one new member with full voting status and two with nonvoting candidate status. Among the new appointees to the Secretariat were Anatoly F. Dobrynin, former ambassador to the United States, and Aleksandra P. Biriukova, a fifty-seven-year-old labor union official, also the first female to achieve high party office in over two decades. In his early months in office, Gorbachev accompanied these personnel shifts with sharp attacks on bureaucratic ineptitude and corruption. At the Twenty-Seventh Party Congress, Gorbachev even made indirect criticisms of former party leader Leonid Brezhnev for running a stagnant bureaucratic government.

In terms of political style, Westerners who have had contact with Gorbachev describe him as pragmatic and business-like. This is perhaps not surprising, since post-Stalinist education has placed a higher premium on empirical training, rather than on tested ideological formulas. Furthermore, after a certain period of policy stagnation in the late 1970s and early 1980s, these new leaders must be impatient to attempt their own practical solutions to obvious policy problems. Gorbachev also seems more at ease with Westerners than his predecessors. He does not recall first-hand the inferiority and insecurity of the Soviet Union's international position in the 1920s and 1930s as his predecessors did.

Careful examination of Gorbachev's speeches suggests a deep concern with the Soviet Union's economic problems. He publicly acknowledges the need for substantial reform, including decentralization of authority, rethinking of the economic incentive system, and continuing emphasis on social discipline and anticorruption initiated during Andropov's short term. Since early 1984, the Soviet press also contains renewed expressions of interest in the New Economic Policy (NEP) of the 1920s and the Eastern European reform efforts. Most Western observers agree that if other goals, like a strong defense or a rising standard of living, are to be realized, economic reform must be addressed. Such reform prospects would also have implications for the implicit social contract the previous leadership forged with the elite and the population at large.

Contemporary Politics: The Search for a New Accord?

Change is rarely without risk; it also can threaten entrenched interests that benefit from the status quo. For both of these reasons, a genuine program of economic, political, or social reform may be hard to carry out in the Soviet Union, even if it does command support from Gorbachev and his allies. Let us examine some of the problems that might arise from any attempt to alter the tacit social accord worked out in the Brezhnev era.

First, as discussed in Chapter 28, an important part of the Brezhnev policy involved stability of personnel. Gorbachev has clearly decided that this must change, as evidenced by the personnel upheavals that have already occurred. But as noted above, managing these changes is a delicate affair, for rapid turnover at the top could spur rivalries and mobilize opposition. Gorbachev himself has identified the state ministries as a particularly strong bastion of bureaucratic inertia, and he has not hesitated to demote many of the old ministry officials. Furthermore, in November, 1985, five ministries dealing with agriculture were actually abolished and replaced by a new State Agro-Industrial Committee, all as part of the effort to streamline the state bureaucracy and achieve an integrated agricultural policy. Such a reorganization, of course, disrupts stable career patterns and breeds uncertainty.

This all seems at least somewhat reminiscent of Khrushchev's organizational upheavals, one of the contributing causes of his downfall. Gorbachev, as a young man, may have admired Khrushchev's vigor; in fact, he scheduled the opening of the Twenty-Seventh Party Congress for February 25, 1986, just thirty years to the day after the opening of the Twentieth Party Congress, which heralded the beginning of Khrushchev's bold de-Stalinization campaign. However, to avoid Khrushchev's fate, Gorbachev may wish to tread more cautiously as he embarks upon major personnel and organizational shifts. More likely than Gorbachev's own early demise, however, is the blockage by entrenched bureaucratic interests of any dramatic reform initiatives.

Declining economic growth rates have eroded another element of Brezhnev's tacit social contract, namely, the steady rise in the standard of living, improvement of social-welfare measures, and wage equalization to help the lower ranks of the work force. The new leadership realizes that continued social harmony depends on improvement in the quality of life for the average citizen. This involves not only increased production of a wide variety of high-quality consumer goods but also a rise in agricultural output (to improve the Soviet diet), better and more housing, high-quality health care, and expanded public services (e.g., day-care, laundries, restaurants, public transport). Without such improvements, worker motivation is likely to remain low and social ills, such as alcoholism, black market activities, petty theft, and absenteeism, are likely to grow. A better quality of life, in turn, depends on a viable economic reform policy. The Soviet leadership confronts here a sort of vicious circle: Economic improvement demands cooperation from the population, which is hard to win if persistent shortages are the reward for effort at the workplace.

Emphasis on consumer goods production faces other obstacles. The Soviet economy is sorely in need of technical modernization: The country is far behind the West in terms of computer technology, sophisticated electronic equipment, and communications. These tools are necessary not only to improve the efficiency of production and international competitiveness of Soviet goods but also to aid the economic planning process itself. However, funds directed toward technical upgrading may not have immediate payoffs for the consumer. Furthermore, exploitation of natural resources and energy sources is becoming more expensive, making it more difficult to divert capital from these areas to the consumer goods sector. Finally, an exhorbitant level of agricultural investment (up to about 27 percent of the capital investment budget in the late Brezhnev years), still did not bring results adequate to upgrade the Soviet diet to desired levels, and further increases in this area would be too costly. The leadership recognizes that resolution of these conflicts depends on the intensification of production, namely, getting more from less. Labor, capital, machinery, and natural resources must be used more efficiently so that output can be increased without raising costs. Successful intensification in turn depends on a revamping of the incentive system to motivate managers and workers. Inefficient factories must be answerable for their waste of valuable materials and labor; unproductive workers must not reap the same benefits as the industrious.

Making the economy more efficient and productive will most likely necessitate measures that threaten other elements of the implicit social contract. For example, increased wage differentials, necessary to generate high-quality work, will undermine the Brezhnev-era commitment to increased social equality. If inefficient enterprises are forced to close down or lay off excess labor, then unemployment might grow. If prices are to communicate the real demand for a product, then suppressed inflation will surface. Finally, workers and managers alike will be under pressure to perform to their optimum and to take the initiative in order to improve production. Would the Soviet worker consider these new pressures an acceptable price to pay for the *promise* of a better supply of consumer goods and services? Won't the old-style managers prefer tried-and-true methods of bureaucratic wrangling to these new demands for efficiency and quality? Furthermore, won't they face replacement by younger, technically trained managers? These types of questions demonstrate the difficulty of forging a new social contract: Demands on the population and the elite alike would change, while the payoff would lie in an uncertain future. And yet, without such changes, it is unlikely that the new Soviet leadership will be able simultaneously to improve consumer goods output, upgrade technology, provide adequate sources of raw materials to fuel growth, *and* compete militarily with the West.

Finally, diverse social problems not only reflect the erosion of the Brezhnev social contract but also present obstacles to its renewal. Such tensions are evidenced by a general decline in civic morality, manifested as rising corruption, crime, and alcoholism; a growing cynicism toward official ideology; the continued existence of a significant dissident movement despite government repression; and a declining commitment to fulfilling one's work obligations. Talent is dissipated or lost as young people join the ranks of the disillusioned, apathetic, or dissident. The active engagement of the population, especially of youth and the gifted, is a prerequisite for real revitalization. Yet declining opportunities for upward social mobility have accompanied the economic and political stagnation of the last several years. Admission to higher education is consequently more competitive; the Soviet media often portray young people as motivated more by Adidas, Sony, and Western blue jeans than by a desire for self-betterment, and juvenile delinquency is also a growing problem. Many of the most creative efforts in society are diverted to the semilegal or black markets or to dissident activities; harnessing these energies to support regime goals is yet another challenge for the new leaders. Gorbachev's own vigorous image may help to instill a sense that the country is on the move again, under a governing team that understands the frustrations of the average citizen. The new General Secretary is a much more impressive figure than any of his recent predecessors (with the possible exception of Iurii Andropov, who held power too short a time to make a lasting mark). He has even walked city streets and visited factory floors to help revive public morale by renewing direct contact with the population. But will this dynamic new tone of politics be enough to inspire popular energies? This seems highly questionable.

Some social discontent may be amenable to repressive control through harassment, arrest, and other sanctions, but growing disaffection among any substantial subgroup in the population might hamper leadership efforts to stimulate the economy and could even produce disruptive outbursts of protest. Most urgent is continued accommodation with the working class, a renewed concordat with those elements of the intelligentsia who possess important technical and scientific skills, and recommitment of the country's youth to the system, perhaps similar to the revitalization of Gorbachev's own generation in the early Khrushchev years.

In light of these difficulties, it is perhaps not surprising that thus far Gorbachev's rhetoric has been sharper than his actions. Gorbachev's first steps have been perhaps the simplest to accomplish: crackdowns on corruption, discipline campaigns, and personnel changes.

New Policy Directions

It is still too early to assess the significance of policy changes undertaken by the Gorbachev regime. Even once passed as laws, ordinances, or resolutions, leadership initiatives still face obstacles to effective implementation. Nonetheless, it seems clear that the Gorbachev team recognizes the imperatives for wide-ranging reform. What are some of the early policies being pursued by the new leadership?

Reestablishment of Social Order

Like his predecessor and patron, Iurii Andropov, Gorbachev has continued to stress social discipline and to attack corruption at all levels in society. Several ministers and regional party leaders have been removed from office after public chastisement for mismanagement, graft, or nepotism. Meanwhile, the average Soviet worker has also often met with reprimands for absenteeism, late arrival at work, drunkenness, or petty theft. In May, 1985, the Central Committee endorsed aggressive measures to fight alcoholism; at the Party Congress in February/March 1986, consumption of alcoholic beverages was prohibited, and it was reportedly difficult for delegates to find a drink. This is also a component of the social discipline campaign, for alcohol abuse has been blamed not only for poor work performance but also in large part for the decline in male life expectancy from 66 years in the mid-1960s to an estimated 61.9 years by the mid-1980s.[3]

Efforts to reinforce social discipline probably should not be seen as a reversion to Stalinist methods. Western observers have reported a prevailing sense among Soviet citizens of an *otsutstvie poriadka,* "lack of order," which causes "deep disquiet" among all sectors of society.[4] Pervasive corruption destroys any real link between honest effort and reward; this not only makes it difficult to motivate productive labor but also undermines popular belief in the fairness of the system. In this sense, the campaign for social discipline is in the interest of the population as a whole, as well as an essential accompaniment to meaningful economic reform. The Polish experience of 1980–81 may well have taught the Soviet leadership the dangers involved in letting this type of social chaos go unattended. The credibility and effectiveness of Gorbachev's discipline measures may depend on the extent to which the Soviet public perceives them to apply equally to all social strata, including the top elite; the extensive publicity given to punishment of high level officials for illegal acts may be intended to achieve this end.

Ideological Renewal?

At the Twenty-Seventh Congress of the CPSU in February/March 1986, the party adopted a new program and revised party statutes. Although revision of the party's program had been placed on the political agenda in 1981 at the Twenty-Sixth Party Congress while Brezhnev was still alive and work on the revised document was undoubtedly well under way when Gorbachev took office in 1985, he almost certainly scrutinized and approved the proposed changes. Furthermore, his public comments give an indication of the importance he attributes to various sections of the new program.

The revised party program offers little ideological innovation. In reporting on the document, Gorbachev himself pointed "first of all, to

Theme: Alcoholism
"He doesn't stand on his feet, but his hands are golden."

SOURCE *Krokodil,* no. 2 (January 1984), p. 12. Drawing by E. Shabel'nika.

the continuity of the basic theoretical and political aims of the CPSU." Like his predecessors, Gorbachev made repeated references to Lenin's views in explaining the revisions. In the same speech Gorbachev pinpointed his understanding of the key notion in the new program: "Using the acceleration of the country's social and economic development to achieve a qualitatively new state of Soviet society — this is the formula that expresses the essence of the Party's present course. . . . the Party proceeds from the decisive role of the economy in the development of society."[5] As these statements indicate, *political* development takes a backseat to economic and social change. While the party document refers to advances in Soviet democracy and increased public involvement in administration and decision making, these goals have secondary status: This emphasis on socioeconomic change as the key to progress is fully in accord with past Soviet orthodoxy.

While it is not possible here to summarize all of the important ideas in the new party program, we can identify some key points. First, the "gradual transition to communism" is reaffirmed. The most important programmatic goal of the CPSU involves achievement of a classless, "highly organized society of free, socially conscious working people. . . ." Second, in the economy, primary importance is attributed to a "new technical reconstruction," increased scientific-technical progress, and higher labor productivity. Mention is made of broadening the economic autonomy of industrial associations and enterprises, but the principles of social ownership and centralized planning are maintained.[6] In other words, the program does not challenge fundamental economic structures or alter the party's traditional focus on scientific-technical advancement as the motor of social progress.

If there has been little formal change in the party's ideology, the tone of public discourse has been modified. Gorbachev's speeches generally are not so heavily laden with ideological cliches and lifeless, worn phraseology; at times he even improvises or injects humor. Gorbachev may simply have a freer personal style, or he may be more flexible in adapting ideological formulas to real-life situations. He has also called for greater public openness. Preceding the Party Congress, letters printed in *Pravda* attacked privileges enjoyed by high officials, a formerly taboo subject. At the Congress itself, the newly appointed head of the Moscow party organizaton, Boris N. El'tsin, blamed the previously untouchable Central Committee for overlooking corruption in high places.[7] Although Western leaders criticized the Soviet leadership for failing to disclose details about radiation dangers to other countries in a timely manner after the Chernobyl nuclear accident in April, 1986, information about the effects of the accident presented to the Soviet public in the following weeks was unprecedented in Soviet history. An earlier nuclear accident that had occurred in the southern Urals in the Soviet Union in 1957, which presumably involved an explosion at a storage site for weapons-related nuclear wastes, was never acknowledged in the Soviet media.

The Quality of Life

Present party policy affirms its primary commitment "to steadily raise the people's material and cultural living standard and to create conditions for the all-round development of the individual."[8] Yet early pronouncements leave it unclear whether any genuinely new approaches will be forthcoming. For example, the July, 1985, meeting of the Supreme Soviet devoted extensive attention to the deficiencies in environmental policy but initiated no important policy departures. In September, 1985, Gorbachev restated his support for the ambitious Food Program announced in 1982. New measures to achieve its goals center around the organizational changes in the agricultural bureaucracy previously discussed in this chapter, and greater scope for the "collective contract" or brigade system, discussed in Chapter 30. This general continuity in agricultural policy is not surprising, since Gorbachev was in charge of overseeing agricultural affairs in the party Secretariat at the time the Food Program was adopted.

In October, 1985, a "Comprehensive Program for the Development of Consumer Goods Production and the Service Sphere in 1986–2000" was enunciated. This document set optimistic goals for such broad-ranging areas as housing construction, household goods production, passenger transport, tourist and excursion services, legal services, and repair services. However no new methods were announced to achieve these targets. Gorbachev's speech at the Twenty-Seventh Party Congress did allude to some economic reforms that might spur consumer goods and food production, for example, linking prices to levels of consumer demand and giving collective and state farms greater leeway in marketing excess produce. There has also been some talk of allowing limited private enterprise in the service sector. This general support for economic reform, however, must still be translated into effective policy.

Political scientist Jerry Hough has suggested that Gorbachev may be less committed to improving the position of the Soviet consumer than the previous leadership. As Hough points out, Gorbachev "has not been talking about agricultural reform or about lines in the shops, but about technology, technology, technology."[9] In other words, investment priorities could shift away from the consumer sector toward overcoming the Soviet Union's lag in high technology. Much depends on whether Gorbachev institutes a broad-ranging reform of economic structures and planning, for if he does, the Soviet citizen as a consumer would almost certainly benefit in the long run.

Economic Reform

Economic reform is the most important issue on Gorbachev's policy agenda; the direction of economic policy will have a significant impact on almost every facet of Soviet life. While Gorbachev clearly supports some type of reform, it is not clear exactly what this will involve. Does he intend to engage in the kind of piecemeal changes typical of past policy, or is he prepared to endorse more radical measures involving greater scope for market forces, such as were adopted in Hungary in 1968 and more recently in China? We know neither Gorbachev's own preferences nor whether he would be capable of mustering enough support to push them through if he tried.

In examining reform prospects in the Soviet Union, we should distinguish between two distinct approaches. The first, incremental administrative reform, has been the road followed thus far by the Soviet Union and by most of its Eastern European allies. This approach retains the existing parameters of central planning but tampers with the incentive system for economic enterprises. The second approach, a modified application of market principles, has been applied in only one Soviet bloc country, Hungary. The New Economic Mechanism, initiated in Hungary in 1968, has as its principle "as much market as possible, as much planning as necessary." While the Soviets thus far have not emulated the experiment, they also have not hindered its continuation. Furthermore, some of Gorbachev's general references to enterprise autonomy, market forces, flexible prices, and financial incentives suggest possible support for a Hungarian-type approach. Some Soviet economists, most notably A. Aganbegian and Tatiana Zaslavskaia, have been supporting such radical departures in both unofficial channels and the official media.[10] Presumably their ideas have some resonance in high circles.

Administrative Reform. The basic hallmark of administrative reform is the maintenence of a controlled price system, which in turn implies central political control over what should be produced. Without challenging this fundamental precept, past efforts (such as the Kosygin reforms of 1965) have been made to rationalize the incentive system and streamline planning procedures, so as to encourage higher quality output that meets societal demands. In Chapter 28, we noted some of the difficulties involved in constructing a consistent and effective set of measures that also facilitate an accurate information flow to planners. Consequently, this type of reform has produced only minimal improvement in economic performance.

So far the Gorbachev team has not gone beyond tinkering with the existing planning system. In July, 1983, Andropov introduced an experiment in several ministries, which allowed enterprises and associations to retain part of their profits for special development and bonus funds.

The intent was to stimulate greater productivity, since the enterprise would benefit directly from improved efficiency. Considerable fanfare has surrounded this experiment, and it has been expanded to include additional branches of the economy. Some Western observers doubt whether it will bring major long-term improvement, since allocation of materials is still centrally controlled in the economy as a whole. Thus, participating enterprises will likely have difficulties using any profits they retain to acquire materials they need to expand their plant. Furthermore, if enterprises prove themselves capable of better performance, central planning bodies might simply raise mandatory plan targets; this in turn would destroy the incentive for further improvement. U.S. economist Marshall Goldman explains aptly the difficulty with such partial reform efforts:

> To reform gradually, the Soviets would have to find ways to integrate the central planning process and the market, each of which leads to different and sometimes contradictory allocation results. In effect, they would have to deal with an economy heading in two different directions at once. A story still being told in Moscow about the effort made to improve Moscow's traffic illustrates the fear of a collision. "The British have an efficient system; let's switch traffic to the left side of the road," argued one Moscow authority. A wiser head warned that the switch might be too confusing if made at once. Instead, he proposed that only trucks and taxis with the most experienced drivers move to the left during the first stage of the experiment. Passenger automobiles would continue on the right side of the road for another six months, so they could prepare themselves at which time they would move to the left.[11]

Most of the incremental administrative reforms adopted in Soviet bloc countries have evoked analogous conflicts.

In addition to alterations in the incentive structure, authorities have relied on what we might call technological fixes, including the importation of foreign technology and use of computers to process information and to develop input-output models. We have already noted problems with computer technology, given the pervasiveness of poor information available to planners. Furthermore, we wonder whether the Soviet authorities would be willing to accept the political risks involved in widespread use of computers; the new information network might also make it easier for dissident elements to tap official information sources and disseminate materials of their own. Gorbachev's apparent support for increased computer education in the schools suggests that he may be willing to take these risks, but at present the level of computer technology remains low.

Reliance on imported technology poses other problems. It places a heavier burden on export capacities to maintain an acceptable balance of trade. Because the Soviet Union has abundant supplies of natural gas, oil, and other raw materials, it has not incurred a large foreign debt to the West, as have its poorly endowed Eastern European allies. Recent declines in oil output, however, have lowered Soviet energy exports. Furthermore, in the long run, the Soviet Union cannot solve its own economic difficulties through reliance on foreign trade; extensive imports of desirable high-quality consumer goods might well create economic pressures and unmanageable expectations similar to those that came to plague Poland in the mid-1970s. Massive importation of foreign technology for the production process would be excessively expensive and might prove useless if the technical know-how to use and repair it were deficient.

If the combination of incremental administrative reform and technological fixes has not proved adequate, does this mean that the Soviet Union must turn to some sort of market principles to solve its economic problems? While this approach may not be a *necessity*, there certainly is pressure on the authorities to look to other reform models, including those tried by Eastern European allies, most notably the semi-market reform embarked upon by Hungary in 1968.

Market Reform: The Hungarian Example. Hungary has produced the most comprehensive and long-lasting economic reform carried out in any of the Soviet bloc countries. The Hungarian reform, however, was motivated not only by the economic downturn of the 1960s but also by the unique political circumstances that followed the Soviet invasion of Hungary in 1956. The invasion squelched an abortive revolution in Hungary that resulted from the reversal of economic and political reforms introduced in the first phase of de-Stalinization under Malenkov's New Course. Imre Nagy, the Hungarian reform leader installed under Malenkov's leadership, was removed from office in 1955 and the position of Hungary's "little Stalin," Matyas Rakosi, was again reinforced. Renewed controls in the economy, cultural life, and political sphere produced widespread alienation among both the intelligentsia and the working class. The revolution, which erupted in October 1956, involved strikes, the formation of mass-based workers' councils, and continued criticisms of government policy by the intelligentsia. Under popular pressure, Nagy was restored to his post as premier; on November 1, 1956, he declared Hungarian neutrality as well as Hungary's withdrawal from the Warsaw Treaty Organization. Non-communist parties were assured a role in the government and free elections were placed on the agenda. Soviet intervention ended the upheaval and reconfirmed Hungary's integration into the Soviet bloc as well as the dominance of a reconstituted communist party (renamed the Hungarian Socialist Workers' Party) in Hungary itself. Once the Hungarian revolution was suppressed, the communist party, under its new leader, Janos Kadar, was very unpopular, for it was seen as the Soviet Union's instrument for the repression of Hungary's genuine aspirations for national self-expression and democracy. Once Kadar had brought the most active instigators of the 1956 revolution under control, he confronted the problem of how to reconcile his party to society.

Unlike Gustav Husak, who later presided over normalization in Czechoslovakia after the 1968 invasion by the Warsaw Pact forces, Kadar did not rely primarily on political repression and control but sought an active Alliance Policy to reestablish positive linkages between the population and the party. In 1962, Kadar expressed the recurring theme of the Alliance Policy: "Whereas the Rakosiites used to say that those who are not with us are against us, we say that those who are not against us are with us." At the Eighth Party Congress in November of that year, Kadar reiterated the point: "The party invites those members of society which previously did not sympathize with [the party] and even opposed its objectives to join in helping to build socialism."[12] Kadar hoped to reconcile not only the working class but also white-collar groups and the intelligentsia to the existing order.

The New Economic Mechanism (NEM), embarked upon in 1968 and still in place today, is an important component of the Alliance Policy. The leadership recognized that if economic performance were not improved so as to assure a higher standard of living for the population, then popular alienation might continue to grow and take on an increasingly politicized form. One Western journalist has described Kadarization as "the theory that people who have washing machines and cars and a limited freedom of expression don't need or want political participation."[13] A major goal of the NEM was to assure the citizens a reliable supply of reasonably good consumer goods. The traditional Soviet-type centralized planning system, as discussed in Chapter 28, is ill-adapted to achieve this goal. In the 1960s, the Hungarian leaders wanted to avoid the severe slow-down in economic growth rates that plagued the more advanced East German and Czechoslovakian economies by improving economic efficiency before a crisis point was reached (such as occurred later in Poland). Furthermore, as a resource-poor country, Hungary is heavily dependent on foreign trade. If quality and efficiency were to be stimulated, Hungary could no longer rely as heavily on trade with its

Eastern European allies, since these countries were willing to accept low-quality goods to maintain the bilateral trade balances mandated by centralized planning. The NEM was intended to make Hungary competitive in the broader world market and to facilitate interaction with Western markets in order to stimulate more efficient, high-quality production.

The NEM combines elements of a free-market system with elements of central planning. Most enterprises are no longer told what to produce, in what quantities, and to whom to sell; they are given considerably more autonomy in decision making. State farms are also allowed to make their own planting decisions and market their produce. Since many prices are allowed to fluctuate to reflect changing supply and demand, enterprises can assess demand for a product through market signals rather than by responding to directives from higher state organs. The central authorities, on the other hand, are involved primarily in establishing global goals and in fashioning financial measures to stimulate the enterprises to adopt these goals as their own (somewhat along the lines of indicative planning in France). Operative, day-to-day planning is generally left to the enterprises.

Most enterprises are still state-owned, but at the same time, some greater scope is given to small-scale private enterprise, the so-called second economy. Not only are private agricultural plots allowed, as in the Soviet Union, but consumer services, such as repairs, professional services, housing construction, and small-scale production of consumer goods, may also be provided outside the state sector. Individuals with the requisite skills may moonlight after completing a day's work at a state job and in this way bring in extra money. Thus, consumer demands are satisfied, while the key industries are still subject to state ownership and centralized guidance. A popular Hungarian joke portrays the relationship between the two sectors as follows:

> An aunt visiting Hungary from the West asked her nephew, "Why does everyone have two jobs here?" "Well," he replies, "in the second one people earn the money they don't get in the first one." "But surely that's very tiring," she responds. "Not at all, they rest in their main jobs," exclaims the nephew.[14]

As this joke illustrates, the reform generated problems of its own, to which we must now turn.

First, the market does not operate as freely as envisaged by some of the reformers; rather, certain constraints are maintained to forestall potentially undesirable social effects. For example, some 70 percent of prices are subject to regulation, whether in the form of maximum levels, ranges of permissible flunctuation, or actual central control. In this way, undesirable inflation is reduced. At the same time, however, messages about supply and demand are interfered with and real opportunity costs (i.e., the cost of using limited resources to produce one product rather than another) are not reflected in prices. Periodically the leadership has felt the need to remedy this circumstance by adjusting subsidized consumer prices upward; although survey data is not available, observers report that these measures are unpopular.

Inefficient enterprises are often allowed to survive, rather than go bankrupt as they might in a Western regulated-market economy. Closing inefficient enterprises in Hungary would possibly lead to major layoffs and social dislocations. The present low rate of unemployment is most likely a function of inefficient use of labor, for the regime is wary of tampering with the traditional socialist guarantee of job security. As in other Soviet bloc countries, workers are hard to fire. But in allowing inefficiency to go unpenalized, the authorities reduce the incentive to improve. Productivity remains lower than in the West, making Hungarian goods less competitive in international markets. Combined with increasingly unfavorable terms of international trade, this has left Hungary with a substantial debt to Western countries. Other factors also reduce enterprise accountability. For example, in practice, enterprises can garner investment funds through political contacts with influential ministry officials, rather than relying on enterprise profits. In many cases, appointment of managers on the basis of patronage, not merit, has been retained to prevent discontent among loyal bureaucrats who do not possess the technical skills to operate in a competitive economic environment. Finally, because trade with other Soviet-bloc countries is negotiated by central trade authorities who seek to maintain bilateral trade balances, some enterprises are simply instructed to produce certain goods to meet these obligations. These enterprises are, in effect, both guaranteed markets and shielded from competitive pressures.

The Conundrum of Reform. The Hungarian case demonstrates elegantly how difficult it is to have the best of all worlds. While a Soviet-type economic structure has clear deficiencies, introduction of a competitive market may also involve unacceptable social costs. Thus, the Hungarian authorities have limited the operation of the market in order to restrict inroads into certain established priorities, such as job security, price stability, and some measure of egalitarianism. The Soviet authorities, as they consider their options, must keep these constraints in mind. In Yugoslavia, a more extreme form of market socialism has been accompanied by all the woes of faltering capitalist economies, namely, high unemployment, inflation, economic cycles, and blatant consumerism. On the other hand, in both Hungary and Yugoslavia, the supply and quality of consumer goods is far superior to the Soviet Union, and this contributes significantly to regime legitimacy (or at least citizen passivity).

It is debatable whether Hungarian economic performance has justified the reform, for growth rates, debt levels, and other measures of economic performance do not clearly distinguish Hungary from a country, such as East Germany, that has maintained an orthodox Soviet-type economic structure. The Hungarian economy has performed especially well only in the agricultural sector. (Tables 31.3 and 31.4 show selected economic indicators of Eastern European countries.)

From Moscow's vantage point, the potential dangers of a market-type reform may outweigh the benefits. In the Soviet Union, ethnic diversity makes decentralization of economic decision making more dangerous politically than it is in Hungary. For if Marx was correct, political power ultimately derives from economic power, making control over the latter the key political commodity. Observing the Czechoslovakian reform movement of the 1960s, Soviet authorities undoubtedly feared that decreased political control might result from a wider distribution of economic power. Furthermore, the Soviet Union does not face the social and political alienation that stimulated Kadar to seek a new type of social

Table 31.3 Annual Rates of Growth of GNP per Capita of Eastern European Countries 1965–85 (Constant prices, percent)

	BULGARIA	CZECHOSLOVAKIA	GDR	HUNGARY	POLAND	ROMANIA	EASTERN EUROPE
1965–70	4.0	3.2	3.2	2.7	3.0	3.2	3.2
1970–75	3.9	2.7	3.8	3.0	5.7	5.2	4.2
1975–80	0.9	1.5	2.5	1.9	0.0	2.9	1.4
1980–85	0.9	1.4	1.8	1.3	0.3	1.5	1.1
1980	−3.3	1.8	2.1	0.9	−3.3	−2.2	−0.8
1981	2.3	−0.6	2.0	0.7	−6.2	−0.4	−1.4
1982	2.8	1.7	−0.2	3.7	−1.9	2.1	0.5
1983	−2.0	1.2	1.7	−0.9	4.0	−0.3	1.4
1984	2.7	2.4	3.4	2.9	2.5	4.2	2.9
1985	−1.0	1.4	2.6	−0.8	0.8	1.3	1.0

SOURCE Thad Alton et al., "Research Project on National Income in East Central Europe, Occasional Paper No. 90, 1986," L. W. International Financial Research, Inc. (New York, 1986).

Table 31.4 Per Capita Growth of Agricultural Output* (Average annual rates) in percent

	1970–1975	1975–1980	1981
Bulgaria	1.1	1.1	5.3
Czechoslovakia	2.5	1.2	−1.1
East Germany	3.8	1.6	1.5
Hungary	4.4	2.9	−2.5
Poland	3.2	−0.6	−8.0
Romania	4.5	1.7	−5.2

SOURCE Gregor Lazarcik, "Comparative Growth of Agricultural Output, Inputs, and Productivity in Eastern Europe, 1965–1982," in U.S. Congress, Joint Economic Committee, *East European Economies: Slow Growth in the 1980's,* vol. 1, "Economic Performance and Policy" (Washington, D.C.: U.S. Government Printing Office, 198), p. 399.

*Includes crops and animal products

contract in his Alliance Policy (and the associated NEM). All of this overlooks perhaps the most important obstacle to a market-type reform in the Soviet Union, namely, the power of the huge bureaucratic institutions, especially the ministries and some central organs, which would stand to lose power with a real devolution of economic decision making. The key role of party officials as mediators in the implementation of the plan would also likely decline. Even the enterprise managers themselves might see a market-type reform as more threatening than empowering, for it would demand new skills and greater economic acuity.

Does all of this mean that Gorbachev will not attempt a Hungarian-style reform? One should be wary of Western assumptions that market reform represents the only reasonable path for the Soviet Union; this road is fraught with political and economic dangers, which may prove too great to risk. The Soviet leadership may well flirt with some elements of a semi-market reform but ultimately balk at the costs and revert to the type of administrative measures so typical of past experience. Would such moderate changes be effective enough to forestall a major systemic crisis? Past Soviet history suggests that they might, despite dire predictions emanating from the West.

Soviet Foreign Policy

The Soviet Union has without doubt achieved superpower status, a likely source of pride and unity between the population and the elite. But unlike the omnipotent adversaries so often portrayed in the Western media, the new Soviet leaders undoubtedly see many threats to their position. Preoccupied with domestic economic problems, the new Gorbachev team may well hope for a renewal of international detente, rather than confrontation and competition.

First, the arms race undoubtedly places a heavy economic burden on the Soviet Union, simply in terms of investment and high-quality inputs that must be diverted from other sectors of the economy. In the United States, the arms industry may be an essential source of employment in certain areas of the country, and large firms may seek defense contracts as a source of additional profit, but in the Soviet Union, continued high military expenditures mainly benefit bureaucratic interests associated with the Soviet military-industrial complex. Granted, these groups form a powerful lobby in the Soviet system, since most of the heavy industrial ministries (metallurgy, the chemical industry, the energy sectors) have some linkages with military production. On the other hand, in the Soviet system there is nothing that makes high military expenditures beneficial to significant sectors of the population. Furthermore, many elements of the Soviet political elite would reap personal benefits from improved detente with the West, in the form of increased contacts and travel to Western countries. There are many reasons to believe Gorbachev when he emphasizes the need for a reduction in the arms race; at the same time, there is no reason to believe that the Soviets would embark upon arms limitations if they felt this represented any threat to their superpower status or national security.

National security is a very real concern for the Soviet leadership. It is worth remembering that the Soviet Union is virtually surrounded by unfriendly nations or bases of her major adversary. Even though Eastern Europe forms a kind of buffer zone with nations of the NATO alliance, Soviet authorities must wonder how reliable the ordinary Polish or Czech, or even East German, comrade would be in a confrontation with Western Europe. To the south and southwest, U.S. bases in Turkey and the Khomeini Islamic regime in Iran hardly present reassuring frontiers. Despite the recent rapprochement with China, even the average Soviet citizen may retain a lingering distrust of the Chinese. The detente between the United States and the People's Republic of China following the death of Mao must appear threatening indeed.

Soviet inroads in the Third World may appear impressive as viewed from Washington, since U.S. policymakers now number Cuba, Nicaragua, Angola, Mozambique, Ethiopia, Afghanistan, Libya, Vietnam, and other countries among real or potential Soviet client states, all recruited since 1960. From the Soviet perspective, however, Third World influence has been disturbingly tenuous. The loss of Egypt as a valuable ally in the early 1970s exemplifies the problem. Other Third World countries recognize that the economic benefits available from the capitalist countries far exceed what the Soviet Union has to offer. Furthermore, the Soviet experience does not offer an attractive model for Third World revolutionaries or socialist regimes; the Soviet revolution is remote (both in time and in terms of its class base) from the challenges facing the largely peasant-based movements in the Third World.

The Soviet's inability to operate with a free hand even in Eastern Europe became surprisingly evident during the Polish crisis of 1980–81. While the Soviet Union would have rallied its allies in the Warsaw Treaty organization to intervene militarily as a last resort, as in Czechoslovakia in 1968, its wariness in using this option demonstrates the constraints the Soviets face. Mired in an extended conflict in Afghanistan and cognizant of the Polish national spirit, the Soviets must have recognized the limits to their power in dealing with the Polish crisis. Should similar crises ever emerge in two or more bloc countries simultaneously, the Soviet leaders might face a threat to communist party hegemony in Eastern Europe; discontent could spread even further and the Soviet Union might not be able to bring the situation under control without making major concessions to opposition groups.

Gorbachev's Approach. Gorbachev's smoother political style with Western leaders and his considerable political savvy in dealing with Western public opinion do not address these fundamental challenges in the foreign policy area. As in the domestic sphere, the new leadership may have to go beyond style to substantial reevaluation if national security is to serve rather than detract from domestic stability.

In November, 1985, Gorbachev met with President Reagan in the first superpower summit meeting since 1979. The concrete results were minimal: agreement in principle to seek accelerated arms control negotiations and to hold talks on a number of other issues, such as chemical weaponry, risk reduction, and regional disputes; resumption of cultural exchanges; and an oblique reference to human rights. Following the summit, the Soviet Union put forth new arms control proposals, most notably a comprehensive plan calling for elimination of all U.S. and Soviet missiles from Europe. The Soviets were apparently willing to accept existing French and British strategic forces. They also conceded that lack of agreement on issues raised by Reagan's Strategic Defense Initiative would not foreclose the possibility of agreement on issues related to intermediate-range missiles. (SDI, popularly called "Star Wars," would rely on highly advanced technologies to provide a defensive shield against nuclear attack.) Nonetheless, when Reagan and Gorbachev met again in October, 1986, in Reykjavik, Iceland, negotiations that promised to bring mutual reduction in nuclear arms faltered due to disagreement over the appropriate limits on testing elements of SDI. Were Soviet concessions on arms reduction at Reykjavik primarily a public relations move designed to split the Western alliance by shifting the blame for the failed negotiations to Reagan's SDI? Or did they represent a genuine effort to reach an arms control agreement? In any case, the Soviets seemed daunted by the prospect of having to match American technology in developing their own defensive shield just when domestic economic problems demanded attention.

Meanwhile, in the human rights area, as noted in Chapter 30, the Soviet leadership allowed Andrei Sakharov's wife, Elena Bonner, to travel to the West for medical treatment shortly before the November summit. In February, 1986, prominent Soviet dissident Anatoly Shcharansky was released, as part of a spy exchange carried out on the border between East and West Berlin. (Before being sentenced to prison and labor camp in 1978, Shcharansky had been the leading spokesperson for Jewish emigration rights.) In October, 1986, Iurii Orlov, former head of the Helsinki Watch Group, was freed as part of a larger exchange between the U.S. and the Soviet Union; the arrangements also involved the release of Nicholas Daniloff, an American journalist whom the Soviets had accused of espionage. These very public gestures to accommodate Western public opinion have not been accompanied by any real reduction of pressure on the dissident movement at home, and as of mid-1986 restrictions on Jewish emigration have not been loosened, despite rumors of a possible change in policy.

Reflections on Change in the Soviet Union

There are internal contradictions that provide a dynamic of change for the Soviet system, even if these are not fully evident to us now. On the economic level, the leadership's desire to maintain firm control may contradict the necessity to improve economic efficiency; high levels of popular education also generate greater citizen demands; and scientific progress brings with it the growth of an articulate intelligentsia, which may desire not only to interpret the world but to change it as well. The working class, even if it has not attained workers' power, has enjoyed certain social benefits, which are hard to rescind in the face of economic stringency and needed reform. The federal system, which in the past helped to make ethnic diversity more manageable by preventing ethnic coalition, may now form a basis for renewed national self-assertion. All of these contradictions produce complicated stresses with no easy resolution.

Like all entrenched groups, the Soviet party/state elite is wary of radical change, for fear that established prerogatives and privileges will be threatened. The Soviet elite has become a preeminently conservative force, stifled by huge institutional structures and self-imposed limits on ideological innovation. One can hardly expect creative responses out of this milieu. Even if Soviet political structures do allow upward social mobility (Gorbachev himself rose from a peasant family), present leaders act as gatekeepers to the inner circles of power and thus exercise careful control over those who enter. Soviet recruitment structures may be highly effective at co-opting the talented but less effective at allowing that talent to blossom. And yet overriding historical concerns with national security and internal stability may make present patterns of power more compatible with broad cultural expectations than they would be in the West or even in countries of Eastern Europe. It is perhaps the congruity between broad cultural patterns and political relationships that underlies the viability of any structure of power; thus, measures to shelter and shield the Soviet population from outside influences may indeed be an important foundation of regime stability. At the same time, elements of the elite itself may yearn for greater exposure to Western ideas.

The Soviet Union's unique cultural heritage and turbulent history make realization of Western-style liberal democracy unlikely. Experiments in Eastern European countries, like Hungary in 1956, Czechoslovakia in 1968, and Poland in 1980–81, thwarted as they were by outside pressures, seemed more promising, yet they demonstrate the difficulties involved in combining strong state control of the economy with genuine popular initiative. In every case we have examined, popular pressure for political reform has included demands for some economic decentralization as well. The challenge is to discover a new model to disperse economic power without at the same time reinstating the inequities of capitalist economies. This question confronts socialists in the East and West alike and has, as yet, no satisfactory answer.

Ultimately, of course, only the future will reveal the dynamic of change in Soviet politics. What seems certain, however, is that political convergence with the West is unlikely. The Soviet Union may indeed face a major transition in the near future as past patterns prove inadequate to deal with future problems, but the Soviet future will be uniquely its own.

Notes

1. Gertrude E. Schroeder, "The Soviet Economy on a Treadmill of 'Reforms,' " in *Soviet Economy in the 1980s: Problems and Prospects,* ed. United States Congress, Joint Economic Committee (Washington, DC: U.S. Government Printing Office, 1979), p. 312.
2. Timothy J. Colton, *The Dilemma of Reform in the Soviet System* (New York: Council on Foreign Relations, Inc., 1984), pp. 43–45.
3. See: David E. Powell, "The Emerging Health Crisis in the Soviet Union," *Current History,* vol. 84, no. 504 (October 1985), pp. 325–26.
4. Peter Reddaway, "Waiting for Gorbachev," *The New York Review of Books* vol. 32, no. 15 (October 10, 1985), p. 5.
5. "Report by M.S. Gorbachev, General Secretary of the CPSU Central Committee," *Pravda,* October 16, 1985, pp. 1–2, translated in *Current Digest of the Soviet Press,* vol. 37, no. 42 (November 13, 1985) pp. 3, 4.
6. "Programma Kommunisticheskoi Partii Sovetskogo Soiuza. Novaia redaktsiia. Priniata XXVII. s"ezdom KPSS" (Program of the Communist Party of the Soviet Union. New edition. Adopted at the Twenty-Seventh Congress of the CPSU), *Partinaia zhizn',* nos. 6–7 (March/April, 1986), pp. 108, 111, 114–116.
7. "Speech by Comrade B.N. El'tsin, First Secretary of the Moscow Party Committee," *Pravda,* February 27, 1986, translated in *Current Digest of the Soviet Press,* vol. 38, no. 9 (April 2, 1986), pp. 4–5.
8. See, for example: "Comprehensive Program for the Development of Consumer Goods Production and the Service Sphere in 1986–2000," *Pravda,* October 9, 1985, p. 1, translated in *Current Digest of the Soviet Press,* vol. 37, no. 41 (November 6, 1985), p. 18.
9. Jerry F. Hough, "Gorbachev's Strategy," *Foreign Affairs,* (Fall 1985), p. 40.
10. See, for example: Tatiana Zaslavskaia, "Paper to a Moscow Seminar," *Russia,* no. 9 (1984), pp. 27–42.
11. Marshall I. Goldman, "Gorbachev and Economic Reform," *Foreign Affairs* (Fall 1985), p. 64.
12. Quoted in Bennett Kovrig, *Communism in Hungary: From Kun to Kadar* (Stanford: Hoover Institution Press, Stanford University, 1979), p. 350.
13. William Shawcross, *Crime and Compromise: Janos Kadar and the Politics of Hungary Since the Revolution,* (London: Weidenfelt and Nicolson, 1974), p. 277.
14. Shawcross, *Crime and Compromise,* p. 182.

Bibliography

Historical Background

Cohen, Stephen F. *Rethinking the Soviet Experience: Politics and History Since 1917.* New York: Oxford University Press, 1985.

Fainsod, Merle. *Smolensk under Soviet Rule.* Cambridge: Harvard University Press, 1958.

Liebman, Marcel. *Leninism under Lenin.* London: Merlin Press, 1975.

Medvedev, Roy. *Let History Judge: The Origins and Consequences of Stalinism.* New York: Vintage Books, 1973.

Pipes, Richard. *Russia under the Old Regime.* London: Widenfeld & Nicolson, 1974.

Szamuely, Tibor. *The Russian Tradition.* Edited by Robert Conquest. London: Secker and Warburg, 1974.

Tucker, Robert C. *Stalinism: Essays in Historical Interpretation.* New York: W.W. Norton and Co., Inc., 1977.

Post-Stalinist Politics

Barghoorn, Frederick C., and Thomas F. Remington. *Politics in the USSR.* 3d ed. Boston: Little, Brown and Co., 1985.

Bialer, Seweryn. *Stalin's Successors: Leadership, Stability, and Change in the Soviet Union.* Cambridge: Cambridge University Press, 1980.

Brown, Archie, "Gorbachev." *Problems of Communism,* vol. 34 (May/June, 1985), pp. 1–23.

Hough, Jerry, and Merle Fainsod. *How the Soviet Union is Governed.* Cambridge: Harvard University Press, 1979.

Lane, David. *State and Politics in the USSR.* Oxford: Basil Blackwell, 1985.

Linden, Carl. *Khrushchev and the Soviet Leadership 1957–1964.* Baltimore: Johns Hopkins Press, 1966.

Soviet State and Society

Alexeyeva, Ludmilla. *Soviet Dissent: Contemporary Movements for National, Religious, and Human Rights.* Translated by Carol Pearce and John Glad. Middletown, CT: Wesleyan University Press, 1985.

Allworth, Edward. *Ethnic Russia in the USSR: The Dilemma of Dominance.* Oxford: Pergamon Press, 1980.

Bennigsen, Alexandre A., and S. Enders Wimbush. *Muslim National Communism in the Soviet Union: A Revolutionary Strategy for the Colonial World*. Chicago: University of Chicago Press, 1979.

Brown, Archie, ed. *Political Culture and Communist Studies*. Armonk, NY: M.E. Sharpe, 1985.

Lane, Christel. *Christian Religion in the Soviet Union: A Sociological Study*. Albany, NY: State University of New York Press, 1978.

Mamanova, Tatyana, and Sarah Matlitsky. *Women and Russia: Feminist Writings from the Soviet Union*. Boston: Beacon Press, 1984.

Matthews, Mervyn. *Education in the Soviet Union: Policies and Institutions since Stalin*. London: George Allen and Unwin, 1982.

Pond, Elizabeth. *From the Yaroslavsky Station: Russian Perceived*. Rev. ed. New York: Universe Books, 1984.

Rakowska-Harmstone, Teresa. "Ethnic Politics in the USSR." *Problems of Communism,* vol. 23 (May/June, 1974), pp. 1–22.

The Soviet Economy

Bornstein, Morris, ed. *The Soviet Economy: Continuity and Change*. Boulder, CO: Westview Press, 1981.

Lane, David. *Soviet Economy and Society*. Oxford: Basil Blackwell, 1985.

Lewin, Moshe. *Political Undercurrents in Soviet Economic Debates: From Bukharin to the Modern Reformers*. Princeton: Princeton University Press, 1974.

Nove, Alec. *The Soviet Economic System*. 2d ed. London: George Allen and Unwin, 1980.

Soviet Foreign Policy and the Military

Colton, Timothy J. *Commissars, Commanders and Civilian Authority: The Structure of Soviet Military Politics*. Cambridge: Harvard University Press, 1979.

Gong, Gerritt W., Angela E. Stent, and Rebecca V. Strode. *Areas of Challenge for Soviet Foreign Policy in the 1980s*. Bloomington: Indiana University Press, 1984.

Holloway, David. *The Soviet Union and the Arms Race*. New Haven, CT: Yale University Press, 1983.

Ulam, Adam. *Expansion and Coexistence: The History of Soviet Foreign Policy 1917–1973*. 2d ed. New York: Praeger, 1974.

East European Politics

Garton Ash, Timothy. *The Polish Revolution: Solidarity*. New York: Scribner, 1984.

Kovrig, Bennett. *Communism in Hungary: From Kun to Kadar*. Stanford: Hoover Institution Press, 1979.

Krisch, Henry. *The German Democratic Republic: The Search for Identity*. Boulder, CO: Westview Press, 1985.

Rakowska-Harmstone, Teresa, ed. *Communism in Eastern Europe*. 2d ed. Bloomington: Indiana University Press, 1984.

Sandford, John. *Sword and the Ploughshare: Autonomous Peace Initiatives in East Germany*. London: Merlin Press, 1985.

Skilling, H. Gordon. *Czechoslovakia's Interrupted Revolution*. Princeton: Princeton University Press, 1976.

Index

4 5 6 7 8 9

65275
European politics
in transition
JN
5
.E95
1987